The Nietzsche Reader

BLACKWELL READERS

In a number of disciplines, across a number of decades, and in a number of languages, writers and texts have emerged which require the attention of students and scholars around the world. United only by a concern with radical ideas, Blackwell Readers collect and introduce the works of pre-eminent theorists. Often translating works for the first time (Levinas, Irigaray, Lyotard, Blanchot, Kristeva), or presenting material previously inaccessible (C. L. R. James, Fanon, Elias), each volume in the series introduces and represents work which is now fundamental to study in the humanities and social sciences.

The Nietzsche Reader

Edited by
Keith Ansell Pearson
and
Duncan Large

Blackwell
Publishing

© 2006 by Blackwell Publishing Ltd

BLACKWELL PUBLISHING
350 Main Street, Malden, MA 02148-5020, USA
9600 Garsington Road, Oxford OX4 2DQ, UK
550 Swanston Street, Carlton, Victoria 3053, Australia

The right of Keith Ansell Pearson and Duncan Large to be identified as the Authors of the Editorial Material in this Work has been asserted in accordance with the UK Copyright, Designs, and Patents Act 1988.

First published 2006 by Blackwell Publishing Ltd

17   2018

Library of Congress Cataloging-in-Publication Data

Nietzsche, Friedrich Wilhelm 1844-1900.
  (Selections. English. 2006)
  The Nietzsche Reader / edited by Keith Ansell-Pearson and Duncan Large.
    p. cm. – (Blackwell Readers)
  Includes bibliographical references (p.   ) and index.
  ISBN 978–0–631–22653–6 (hardcover : alk. paper)
  ISBN 978–0–631–22654–3 (pbk : alk. paper)
  1. Philosophy. I. Ansell-Pearson, Keith, 1960- . II. Large, Duncan.
III. Title. IV. Series.
B3312.E5A57 2006
193–dc22

                                                      2005034572

A catalogue record for this title is available from the British Library.

Set in 10.5/12.5pt Bembo
by Graphicraft Limited, Hong Kong
Printed and bound in the Singapore
by C.O.S. Printers Pte Ltd

The publisher's policy is to use permanent paper from mills that operate a sustainable forestry policy, and which has been manufactured from pulp processed using acid-free and elementary chlorine-free practices. Furthermore, the publisher ensures that the text paper and cover board used have met acceptable environmental accreditation standards.

For further information on
Blackwell Publishing, visit our website:
www.blackwellpublishing.com

Contents

Part V   The Later Writings   **293**

To the memory of R. J. Hollingdale (1930–2001)

Preface

In the decades following the end of World War II Nietzsche has been wedded to a variety of intellectual causes ranging from existentialism to postmodernism. *The Nietzsche Reader* does not seek to promote a particular Nietzsche or to saddle him with all-too-timely philosophical agendas. Instead, it presents him in the guise of the original and singular philosopher he is, as well as the great stylist and thinker of clarity, precision, and profundity he also is. This is the Nietzsche that his many readers inside and outside the academy come to treasure as their philosophical friend and educator. Texts such as *The Gay Science, Beyond Good and Evil*, and *Twilight of the Idols* are admired by such readers as unique texts that can be appreciated at one and the same time as both works of philosophy and works of literature. For many, Nietzsche is a radical and provocative critic of modernity, a liberator of humankind from the reign of superstition and the cult of idols, whose promotion of noble ideals offers a damning indictment of the vacuity of our contemporary systems of education and culture. He is appreciated and esteemed as a questioner and experimenter of rare integrity and honesty. For others his legacy remains tainted by the association of his ideas with fascist thought and practice, and many who encounter him fail to see that beyond the anti-democratic rhetoric there lies one of the great spirits of emancipation of modern times and a thinker who provides doctrines for all and none. Nietzsche has been the site of such contestations since his work first began to attract widespread attention shortly after his descent into madness.

In putting this *Reader* together the editors have been acutely aware of the dangers of offering a selection from Nietzsche's writings. The principal dangers that need to be avoided, so far as is possible, are those of stripping his ideas and thought-experiments of their various contexts, including their philosophical and polemical contexts, and ignoring the mode of their presentation. Nietzsche conceived himself as engaged in 'experiments' of thinking, but these experiments are inseparably bound up with intricate movements, and at times dramatizations, of thought, involving the articulation of questions and the staging of problems. In putting together this *Reader* we have attempted to take cognizance of this and it has informed the selections we have made.

The Nietzsche Reader offers a comprehensive introduction to his writings in English, containing a wide selection from all phases of Nietzsche's intellectual development. It has been designed, in large part, for pedagogical purposes. It includes: a selection of very early writings, including an early set of critical reflections on Schopenhauer's system; some key sections from Nietzsche's first published book, *The Birth of Tragedy*; a seminal essay from the early 1870s, 'On Truth and Lies in a Nonmoral Sense';

several sections from *Philosophy in the Tragic Age of the Greeks*; selections from two of his *Untimely Meditations*; and a generous selection from all the major texts of Nietzsche's middle and later periods, from *Human, All Too Human* (volume 1) to *Twilight of the Idols* and *The Anti-Christ*. In some cases it has been possible to include some especially key parts of Nietzsche's texts in their near-entirety, such as, for example, part I of *Beyond Good and Evil*, the Second Essay of *On the Genealogy of Morality*, and important parts of *Twilight of the Idols*. The reader will find in this volume many of the key moments in Nietzsche's writing, including his articulation of the duality of the Dionysian and the Apollonian, his demand for historical philosophizing, his dramatization of the death of God, his conception of a gay science, his published outlines of the doctrine of the will to power, his presentation of the doctrine of eternal recurrence (both in draft form and in published form), his thoughts on European nihilism, his arguments on the slave revolt in morality and the origin of bad conscience, and so on. In addition, the selection includes many of the key passages where Nietzsche articulates his thoughts on truth and knowledge, on appearance and the thing-in-itself, on art, and on science. We have favored a chronological selection over a thematic or conceptual one so as to give the reader a more adequate sense of Nietzsche's development as a writer and philosopher. We have endeavored not to select from the texts in the mode of plundering soldiers; rather, we have thought carefully which sections and aphorisms to include so as to give the reader a reliable and instructive introduction to Nietzsche. The aim has been to show something of his qualities as a writer and something of his major philosophical preoccupations. The book has been divided into six parts, and each part begins with a short introduction that highlights particularly significant ideas in the selections that follow. In addition, the main introduction offers an outline of Nietzsche's life and some general comments on his style(s) of writing and the nature of his philosophical project. There is an extensive bibliography at the end, which lists the principal German editions of Nietzsche's works, most of the currently available English translations, and a large selection of important secondary texts.

This *Reader* offers, ultimately, only a small selection of Nietzsche's writings and has been put together with due acceptance of the necessary constraints of space and limited entitlement to permissions. It does not offer itself as any adequate substitute for a reading and knowledge of the complete texts. We very much hope, however, that it will serve well the pedagogical purposes it has been designed for. *The Nietzsche Reader* differs from R. J. Hollingdale's *A Nietzsche Reader* in favoring a chronological over a thematic approach. In addition, it contains extensive and, we hope, instructive editorial material that reflects the tremendous advances that have been made in recent years in the area of Nietzsche studies. No selection has been made from the text known as *The Will to Power*: a new edition of excerpts from Nietzsche's late notebooks edited by Rüdiger Bittner was published by Cambridge University Press as this *Reader* was nearing its completion, and that text offers readers a more reliable encounter with Nietzsche's unpublished notebooks from the 1880s than the existing edition by Kaufmann and Hollingdale that simply copied the German edition prepared by Nietzsche's sister, Elisabeth Förster-Nietzsche. *The Nietzsche Reader* does, however, feature new translations of pieces from the *Nachlass*, including Nietzsche's first outline of his doctrine of eternal recurrence from 1881 and his notebook of 1887 on European nihilism.

The notes that appear in the extracts are based on those provided by the translators and editors of the English translations from which the selections have been made. We

have provided additional notes where this seemed appropriate; where we have modified translations of some key terms this is also noted.

The editors are grateful to Jeff Dean for inviting them to edit *The Nietzsche Reader*
and to Nirit Simon and Danielle Descoteaux, also at Blackwell Publishing, for the
assistance they have lent this project.

Keith Ansell Pearson
Duncan Large

Acknowledgments

The editors and publisher gratefully acknowledge the permission granted to reproduce the copyright material in this book (chapter details in small capitals relate to this
volume):

Cambridge University Press: for selections from *Daybreak: Thoughts on the Prejudices
of Morality* (CHAPTER 14), translated by R. J. Hollingdale (1982), and selections from
Nietzsche: On the Genealogy of Morality (CHAPTER 21), including the additional essays
"The Greek State" (CHAPTER 7) and "Homer on Competition" (CHAPTER 8, published
as "Homer's Contest"), trans. Carol Diethe (1994; 2nd rev. edn 2006).

Hackett Publishing: for selections from *Selected Letters of Friedrich Nietzsche* (CHAPTER
26), translated and edited by Christopher Middleton (Indianapolis: Hackett, 1996),
pp. 292–4 (April 10, 1888), pp. 229–300 (June 21, 1888), pp. 314–15 (October 18,
1888), pp. 346–8 (January 6, 1889). Reprinted by permission of Hackett Publishing
Company, Inc. All rights reserved.

Humanity Books: for "On Truth and Lies in a Nonmoral Sense" (CHAPTER 10),
translated by Daniel Breazeale, in Breazeale (ed.), *Philosophy and Truth: Selections from
Nietzsche's Notebooks of the Early 1870s* (Amherst, NY: Humanity Books, 1999),
pp. 79–91. © 1979 by Daniel Breazeale. Reprinted by permission of the publisher.

Journal of Nietzsche Studies: for inclusion of the essays "My Life" (CHAPTER 3),
translated by R. J. Hollingdale, issue 3 (Spring 1992), pp. 5–9, and "On Moods"
(CHAPTER 4), translated by Graham Parkes, issue 2 (Autumn 1991), pp. 5–10.

Oxford University Press: for selections from *The Birth of Tragedy* (CHAPTER 6). ©
Douglas Smith 2000. Reprinted from Friedrich Nietzsche, *The Birth of Tragedy*, translated
with an introduction and notes by Douglas Smith (Oxford World's Classics, 2000) by
permission of Oxford University Press. For selections from *Beyond Good and Evil: Prelude*

to a Philosophy of the Future (CHAPTER 18). Translation © Marion Faber. Reprinted from Friedrich Nietzsche, *Beyond Good and Evil*, translated and edited by Marion Faber (Oxford World's Classics, 1998) by permission of Oxford University Press. For selections from *Twilight of the Idols; or, How to Philosophize with a Hammer* (CHAPTER 23). © Duncan Large 1998. Reprinted from Friedrich Nietzsche, *Twilight of the Idols*, translated with an introduction and notes by Duncan Large (Oxford World's Classics, 1998) by permission of Oxford University Press.

Penguin: for selections from *The Anti-Christ: Curse on Christianity* (CHAPTER 24), 1968; *Ecce Homo: How One Becomes What One Is* (CHAPTER 25), 1992; and *Thus Spoke Zarathustra: A Book for Everyone and No One* (CHAPTER 17), 1961, all translated by R. J. Hollingdale. © by R. J. Hollingdale. Reprinted by permission of Penguin Books Ltd.

Philosophy Today: for inclusion of the essays "Fate and History" (CHAPTER 1) and "Freedom of Will and Fate" (CHAPTER 2), translated by George J. Stack (Summer 1993), pp. 154–8.

Random House: for selections from *The Case of Wagner: A Musicians' Problem* (CHAPTER 22) © 1967 by Random House, Inc., and *The Gay Science* (CHAPTERS 15 AND 19) © 1974 by Random House, Inc., both translated by Walter Kaufmann and reprinted by permission of Random House, Inc.

Regnery Publishing: for selections from *Philosophy in the Tragic Age of the Greeks* (CHAPTER 9), translated by Marianne Cowan (1962). © 1962. All rights reserved. Reprinted by special permission of Regnery Publishing, Inc.

Stanford University Press: for selections from *Unfashionable Observations* (vol. 2 in *The Complete Works of Friedrich Nietzsche*), translated by Richard T. Gray (Palo Alto, CA: Stanford University Press, 1995). © 1995 by the Board of Trustees of the Leland Stanford Jr. University. With the permission of Stanford University Press, www.sup.org. Under the title *Unzeitgemässe Betrachtungen*, Nietzsche collected four essays published separately between 1873 and 1876: "David Strauss the Confessor and the Writer," "On the Utility and Liability of History for Life" (CHAPTER 11), "Schopenhauer as Educator" (CHAPTER 12), and "Richard Wagner in Bayreuth."

University of Nebraska Press: for selections from *Human, All Too Human: A Book for Free Spirits*, volume I (CHAPTER 13). Reprinted from *Human, All Too Human: A Book for Free Spirits* by Friedrich Nietzsche, translated by Marion Faber, with Stephen Lehmann, by permission of the University of Nebraska Press. © 1984, 1986 by the University of Nebraska Press.

Walter de Gruyter: for inclusion of the essay "On Schopenhauer" (CHAPTER 5), translated by Claudia Crawford and first published in Crawford, *The Beginnings of Nietzsche's Theory of Language* (Berlin and New York: de Gruyter, 1988), pp. 226–32; and for permission to use a facsimile of two pages from the original Nietzsche notebook published as *Werke: Kritische Gesamtausgabe*, vol. IX/3 (2001): *Notizheft N VII 3*, pp. 13–24, and translated for this volume as "European Nihilism" (CHAPTER 20).

Every effort has been made to trace copyright holders and to obtain their permission for the use of copyright material. The publisher apologizes for any errors or omissions in the above list and would be grateful if notified of any corrections that should be incorporated in future reprints or editions of this book.

Abbreviations

Works by Nietzsche

AC	*The Anti-Christ*
BGE	*Beyond Good and Evil*
BT	*The Birth of Tragedy*
CW	*The Case of Wagner*
D	*Daybreak*
EH	*Ecce Homo*
GM	*On the Genealogy of Morality*
GS	*The Gay Science*
HH	*Human, All Too Human*
KSA	*Sämtliche Werke: Kritische Studienausgabe*
KSB	*Sämtliche Briefe: Kritische Studienausgabe*
PTG	*Philosophy in the Tragic Age of the Greeks*
SE	*Schopenhauer as Educator*
TI	*Twilight of the Idols*
UM	*Untimely Meditations*
WP	*The Will to Power*
WS	*The Wanderer and his Shadow*
Z	*Thus Spoke Zarathustra*

Works by Schopenhauer

WWR	*The World as Will and Representation*

General Introduction

With some justification Friedrich Nietzsche can be described as the most brilliant, most challenging, and most demanding philosopher of the modern period. In the opening years of the twenty-first century he continues to be a major reference point in our intellectual culture: along with Karl Marx and Sigmund Freud he is widely taken to be a "modern master of suspicion."[1] The influence of his ideas on twentieth-century artists, novelists, poets, and essayists was arguably greater than that of any other modern intellectual figure. The work of some of the most important writers of the modern period, such as Georges Bataille, Gottfried Benn, Maurice Blanchot, Albert Camus, André Gide, Ernst Jünger, Franz Kafka, Pierre Klossowski, D. H. Lawrence, Thomas Mann, Robert Musil, and Rainer Maria Rilke, to name but a few, bears ample testimony to his influence. His influence on post-war intellectual figures and currents has been no less extensive, with Jean-Paul Sartre's atheistic existentialism, Martin

---

1   This description was first coined by Paul Ricoeur, who suggested that Marx, Nietzsche, and Freud could be said to constitute a "school of suspicion," about which he noted a number of important things. First, each one of them takes up the problem of Descartes's doubt – the doubt as to having certain knowledge of self and world – and carries it to the heart of the "Cartesian stronghold." They do this by seeking to expose the illusions of consciousness and demoting its significance in the total economy of life. Second, this does not mean that they are simply to be construed as masters of ultra-skepticism; rather, they are three "great destroy-ers." However, this "destruction" is to be understood in the sense it has in Heidegger's *Being and Time* (1927), where it is a moment of every new transformation. Third, and following on from this insight, all three clear the way for a new reign of "truth" not only by means of a destructive critique but also by having recourse to an art of interpretation: "to seek meaning is no longer to spell out the consciousness of meaning, but to *decipher its expressions*." Consciousness is not what it thinks it is and each thinker opens up this problem in a distinc-tive way. Fourth, although all three expose the illusions of consciousness they do not simply stop there, they also "aim at extending it." In the case of Nietzsche, Ricoeur writes: "What Nietzsche wants is the increase of man's power, the restoration of his force; but the meaning of the will to power must be recaptured by meditating on the ciphers 'superman,' 'eternal return,' and 'Dionysus,' without which the power in question would be but worldly violence." For Ricoeur the task of assimilating "the positive meaning of the enterprises of these three thinkers" remains to be carried out. See Paul Ricoeur, *Freud and Philosophy: An Essay on Interpretation*, trans. Denis Savage (New Haven and London: Yale University Press, 1970), pp. 32–6.

Heidegger's thinking on the history of Being as a history of nihilism, Theodor Adorno's critique of identity thinking, Michel Foucault's genealogies of power and truth, Jacques Derrida's deconstruction, and Gilles Deleuze's novel empiricism all bearing its stamp. In addition, aspects of his thought have had an influence on major philosophical figures in both North America and Great Britain, including Stanley Cavell, Richard Rorty, and Bernard Williams. There are many who continue to lament his rise to prominence and regard his widespread influence as pernicious. If philosophy is defined as an activity of thought committed to modes of sustained argumentation, then Nietzsche's penchant for sophistry and rhetoric is enough for many to dispute his entitlement to being a philosopher. However, Nietzsche is far from being the enemy of reason that he is often made out to be (appeals to reason can be found throughout his writings), and his peculiar styles of writing were not designed to work against the tasks of critical thought. Today he is the subject of a vast array of philosophical treatments, having been adopted by philosophers both of so-called "analytical" persuasions and so-called "continental" ones. Philosophical appreciation of Nietzsche has perhaps never been in a healthier state. Today there are lively debates over every aspect of his thinking, and sophisticated academic studies of his ideas are published on a regular basis.

For some, Nietzsche is a great liberator from the illusions of metaphysics; for others, he belongs to a small but select band of anti-philosophers whose destruction of metaphysics has proved premature.[2] It is not clear that we have yet come to terms with his questions in the sense of taking full measure of them. For Nietzsche, traditional metaphysics may well have come to an end, but questions concerning the "meaning" (*Sinn*) of human existence after the death of God have yet to be adequately developed. This is something he invites us to consider in one of his most powerful and complex pieces of writing, the Third Essay of his *On the Genealogy of Morality*. It is also in this essay that he writes of the curious appearance of the philosopher on the earth, forced to assume "an ascetic mask and set of clothes" in order to make himself possible, and Nietzsche poses the question whether the philosopher who has thrown off the monk's habit is, in fact, "really" possible on earth even today, in our age of enlightenment (*GM* III. 10). Far from being an anti-philosopher, Nietzsche himself believed that the modern age called for a new practice of philosophy, and he devoted a great deal of his intellectual labors to outlining the form such a practice might take (for example, the exercise of philosophical legislation and the determination of questions of value). The tasks required of the new philosophers and free spirits of the modern age include the need for a new philosophical cheerfulness (the practice of "the gay science"), thinking beyond good and evil, calling into question the will to truth, and the need for a new selection and breeding of the human animal so as to ensure the production of the higher human type.

---

2   The French philosopher Maurice Merleau-Ponty argued that the kind of negation of metaphysics that we find in Nietzsche (and Marx) cannot take the place of philosophy. He sought to show that the rise of "non-philosophy" which is part of the legacy of these two major modern intellectual figures brings with it a new obscurity. See Merleau-Ponty's essay "Philosophy as Interrogation," in Merleau-Ponty, *In Praise of Philosophy and Other Essays*, trans. John Wild and James M. Edie (Evanston: North-western University Press, 1963), pp. 167–81, especially pp. 168–70.

There have been two main barriers standing in the way of a serious philosophical engagement with Nietzsche's texts and their posthumous fate: first, the fact that his thought was taken up by the Nazis in the 1930s and, second, the widespread view, common for a long time amongst readers, that his thought is not really philosophy but an over-excited poetry made up of aphorisms, aperçus, and fragments which reveal a highly inconsistent mind. It is not only the labeling of Nietzsche as a proto-Nazi that has served to put off many readers. Other strategies are put into play to avoid dealing with him, and here mention should perhaps be made of his madness. As Gilles Deleuze pointed out (in an effort to write intelligently on this subject), madness is never a source of inspiration in Nietzsche's work. Philosophy for Nietzsche does not proceed from suffering or anguish even if the philosopher is someone who suffers in excess. Notions of health and sickness, and an attention to the differing moods and tempi of life, certainly abound in Nietzsche's writings. He wrote against the idea of there being such a thing as normal health and insisted that there were innumerable *healths* of the body, in which what is healthy depends on the individual's goal and horizon, on their energies and impulses, and "above all on the ideals and phantasms" of their soul (GS 120). Nietzsche proposes that medicine should give up on ideas such as a normal diet and the normal course of an illness. Moreover, illness is not just an event that affects the body and the brain from outside; rather, illness contains a perspective on health and vice versa. Nietzsche located within the "will to health" a prejudice, even cowardice, speaking of it as a "subtle barbarism and backwardness." He chose instead to write about and to esteem the "great health" which recognizes that health is not a constant or a transcendent state of the body. Genuine knowledge and self-knowledge about matters of body and soul can only be attained through living a "dangerous health" (GS 382) which allows for the evolution of different and shifting perspectives on health. There is no doubt, however, as Deleuze notes, that Nietzsche's life did end badly, "for the mad Nietzsche is precisely the Nietzsche which lost this mobility, this art of displacement, when he could no longer *in his health* make of sickness a point of view on health."[3] At this point, when Nietzsche's art fails him, and his masks are conflated into that of a buffoon under the influence of an organic process, the illness from which he suffered becomes inseparable from the end of his oeuvre.[4]

The abuse to which Nietzsche's ideas were subjected during the Nazi period was exposed and taken to task by the translator and commentator Walter Kaufmann, in his study of 1950.[5] This study alone prepared the way for a fresh and serious encounter with Nietzsche's ideas in the Anglo-American world which has lasted up to the present day, influencing a whole generation of scholars and commentators,

---

3   Gilles Deleuze, *Pure Immanence: Essays on a Life*, trans. Anne Boyman (New York: Zone Books, 2001), p. 59.

4   One of the finest accounts of the question of madness as it concerns Nietzsche's case is to be found in Pierre Klossowski's *Nietzsche and the Vicious Circle*, trans. Daniel W. Smith (London: Athlone Press, 1997); see especially the chapter "The Euphoria of Turin," pp. 208–53.

5   Walter Kaufmann, *Nietzsche: Philosopher, Psychologist, Antichrist*, 4th edn (Princeton: Princeton University Press, 1974).

especially those working in North America. It is not that there were no probing philosophical encounters with Nietzsche prior to the 1950s – three in particular are worthy of mention and still merit the attention of the student of Nietzsche, those by Georg Simmel (first published in 1907), Karl Löwith (first published in 1935),[6] and Karl Jaspers (also first published in 1935) – but it is fair to say that for the most part Nietzsche was read as a literary figure and philosophical dilettante. In the 1960s two very different readings were published, the titles of which are highly significant: Gilles Deleuze's *Nietzsche and Philosophy*, published in France in 1962 and translated into English in 1983, and Arthur C. Danto's *Nietzsche as Philosopher* (1965). The titles were meant to be provocative: Deleuze was keen to promote Nietzsche as a radical empiricist and pluralist, while Danto subjected Nietzsche's ideas to the requirements of an analytical reading. Mention should also be made of Martin Heidegger's *Nietzsche*, based on lectures delivered in the mid-1930s to the early 1940s but published in two volumes in Germany in 1961. Heidegger's lectures were given during the time he was a member of the Nazi party, but they also include a confrontation with the interpretation of Nietzsche promoted by prominent Nazi philosophers such as Alfred Baeumler. Heidegger laid special emphasis on the importance of learning how to read Nietzsche and adequately encounter his principal doctrines such as the will to power, eternal recurrence of the same, the Overman, perspectivism, and nihilism. While the overall effect is to subordinate Nietzsche to Heidegger's own project of thinking the history of Being, in which Nietzsche assumes the role of the last metaphysician of the West (in Heidegger's genuinely thought-provoking designation), his reading contains numerous insights into many core aspects of Nietzsche's thinking and is essential reading for any serious student of him.

Nietzsche now exerts an influence on work being done in all the major branches of philosophical inquiry. Some readers of Nietzsche choose to lament his assimilation into academic philosophy since it undoubtedly domesticates the challenges his mode of philosophizing was seeking to present to habitual and conventional ways of thinking. However, in our view, if Nietzsche's ideas are now the subject of sustained critical inquiry and judgment this is a good thing; it is evidence that the reception of his texts is taking place in an intellectually mature manner. A critical reception of his work within the academy does not mean that more creative appropriations of Nietzsche are no longer possible and can no longer flourish. With respect to the need to provide an assessment of Nietzsche, we should pay heed to the words of one of his most able readers:

> Lucid thought, delirium and the conspiracy form an indissoluble whole in Nietzsche – an indissolubility that would become the criterion for discerning what is of consequence or not. This does not mean, since it involved delirium, Nietzsche's thought was "pathological"; rather, because his thought was lucid to the extreme, it took on the appearance of a delirious interpretation – and also required the entire experimental initiative of the modern world. It is modernity that must now be charged with determining whether this initiative has failed or succeeded.[7]

---

6   An interesting history surrounds Löwith's book. For insight into it, see Bernd Magnus's foreword to the book's English translation (1997).

7   Klossowski, *Nietzsche and the Vicious Circle*, p. xvi.

Nietzsche's Life

Friedrich Wilhelm Nietzsche was born on October 15, 1844 in Röcken, a tiny village near Lützen in Saxony. His father was a Lutheran pastor and was to die only five years after Nietzsche's birth as a result of softening of the brain. The experience of death, of its brute eruption into life and the violent separations it effects, took place early in Nietzsche's life, and the deaths of both his father and his brother Joseph (who was to die before he reached the age of 2) continued to deeply affect Nietzsche throughout the course of his adolescent life and even into maturity. David Krell's text *The Good European* reveals that on the occasion of a court settlement against one of his publishers in the mid-1880s Nietzsche, after paying off his debts to bookstores, bought an engraved tombstone for his father. It was thirty-six years since Carl Ludwig Nietzsche had died.[8]

On the death of his father Nietzsche's family, which included his mother, his sister Elisabeth, and two unmarried aunts, relocated to Naumburg. Nietzsche began learning to play the piano and composed his first philosophical essay, "On the Origin of Evil." In 1858 he entered Pforta school in the Saale valley and was a student at this famous boarding-school for six years. During this formative period of his youth he developed a love of various writers and poets, including Friedrich Hölderlin and Lord Byron. It was also during this period that he composed his first essay in classical philology, and isolated pieces of philosophical reflection, such as "Fate and History" (included in this volume). On his fifteenth birthday Nietzsche declared that he had been "seized" and taken over by an "inordinate desire for knowledge and universal enlightenment." In an autobiographical fragment dated 1868/9 he reveals that it was only in the final stages of his education at Pforta that he abandoned his artistic plans to be a musician and moved into the field of classical philology. He was motivated by a desire to have a counterweight to his changeable and restless inclinations. The science of philology on which he chose to focus his labors was one he could pursue with "cool impartiality, with cold logic, with regular work, without its results touching me at all deeply" (Nietzsche's mature approach to the matter of knowledge could not be more different!).[9] When he got to university Nietzsche realized that although he had been "well taught" at school he was also "badly educated"; he could think for himself but did not have the skills to express himself, and he had "learned nothing of the educative influence of women."[10]

In October 1864 Nietzsche began life as an undergraduate at Bonn University, studying theology and classical philology. He attended the lectures of the classicist Friedrich Ritschl, who was later to play an influential role in securing Nietzsche a professorship at Basel. In his first year of university life he underwent the rite of passage offered by a duel and began his journey of alienation from his mother and sister by refusing to take communion. In 1865 he moved university to study just classical philology,

---

8   David Farrell Krell and Donald L. Bates, *The Good European: Nietzsche's Work Sites in Word and Image* (Chicago and London: University of Chicago Press, 1997), p. 15.

9   See *Selected Letters of Friedrich Nietzsche*, ed. and trans. Christopher Middleton (Chicago and London: University of Chicago Press, 1969; repr. Indianapolis: Hackett, 1996), p. 47.

10   Ibid., p. 48.

following his teacher Ritschl to Leipzig. He speaks of his move from Bonn to Leipzig in a letter to his sister Elisabeth dated June 11, 1865, where he states that if a person wishes to achieve peace of mind and happiness then they should acquire faith, but if they want to be a disciple of truth, which can be "frightening and ugly," then they need to search.[11] In his second year of university he discovered Schopenhauer, who suited his melancholic disposition, and in 1866 he found a veritable "treasure-chest" of riches in Friedrich Albert Lange's magisterial study *History of Materialism*. In 1867 he was awarded a prize by Leipzig University for his study of Diogenes Laertius, and he spent the third year of his university studies in military service. During this year he had a serious riding accident; to deal with the intense pain caused by the injury to his sternum he took morphine and had a number of drug-induced hallucinations. He began to experience a disaffection with the study of philology and a more profound one with German cuisine and culture that was to endure throughout his lifetime and intensify in his later years.

In early 1869 Nietzsche was appointed to Basel University as Extraordinary Professor of Classical Philology (he was to apply for the Chair in Philosophy a few years later when it became vacant, but was not successful). He assumed the role and duties of a professor at the age of 24 without completing his dissertation or postgraduate thesis. In May of this year he made his first visit to Richard Wagner and his mistress (later wife) Cosima at Tribschen on Lake Lucerne (he had first met the composer the previous year), and he gave his inaugural lecture, on "Homer's Personality." He also began his acquaintance with the cultural historian Jacob Burckhardt, a colleague in Basel. Cosima regarded Nietzsche as a cultured and pleasant individual, while Richard Wagner tried to get Nietzsche to give up his commitment to a vegetarian diet (Nietzsche speaks of his conversion by Wagner in *Ecce Homo*). Between 1869 and 1872 Nietzsche would make over 20 visits to Tribschen.

In 1870 and 1871 Nietzsche lectured on topics, such as Socrates and tragedy and the "Dionysian world-view," that would form the basis of his first book, *The Birth of Tragedy*. He had the intimation that he was about to give birth to a "centaur" with art, philosophy, and scholarship all growing together inside him. In the Franco-Prussian War Nietzsche served for a few weeks as a medical orderly, but was invalided out when he contracted dysentery and diphtheria himself; on his return to Basel he began to suffer from insomnia, and he was to suffer from serious bouts of ill health and migraine attacks throughout the rest of his life. He wrote most of *The Birth of Tragedy* while on convalescent leave from his university, in 1871, and it was published at the beginning of 1872. Nietzsche's first book is influenced by Schopenhauer's philosophy of music, and proposes that it is only as an "aesthetic phenomenon" that existence and the world can be justified. Nietzsche was later, in 1886, to write an incisive and revealing "self-criticism" of the book in which he considered it to be "badly written," "image-mad and image-confused," as well as "sentimental" and "saccharine to the point of effeminacy." Upon its publication Nietzsche's book met with vehement rejection by the philological community, and after being rejected by his mentor, Ritschl, Nietzsche had to admit that he had fallen from grace and was now ostracized from the guild of philologists. His friendship with Wagner continued to deepen, however, and he lectured on the future of educational institutions and on "Homer's Contest." In a letter to Wagner

11 Selected Letters, p. 7.

he noted that not a single student of philology had enrolled in his courses at the university for the winter semester 1872/3. In 1873 Nietzsche undertook a study of a work by Afrikan Spir entitled *Denken und Wirklichkeit* (*Thought and Reality*) and worked on various projects, such as "Philosophy in the Tragic Age of the Greeks," the essay "On Truth and Lies in a Non-Moral Sense," and his *Untimely Meditations*. Nietzsche planned 13 of these but only four actually materialized, and he regarded the whole exercise of writing them as a way of extracting everything he saw as negative in himself. In 1875 he was to make the acquaintance of Heinrich Köselitz, who adopted the pseudonym of Peter Gast upon becoming a composer and who was to become Nietzsche's assistant, editing and copying his texts; in 1876 Nietzsche struck up an important friendship with Paul Rée, author of *Psychological Observations*. Although his fourth *Untimely Meditation*, on Wagner in Bayreuth, had recently been published, it is in this year that Nietzsche publicly began to distance himself from the Wagner cause and articulate the serious doubts he had held for some time about Wagner as an artist.

The year 1878 proved to be a decisive one in Nietzsche's life: he published the first volume of *Human, All Too Human*, which is remarkably different in tone and outlook from his previous published work. Wagner was repulsed by Nietzsche's new philosophical outlook, and even Nietzsche's closest friends wondered how it was possible for someone to discard their soul and don a completely different one in its place. In *The Birth of Tragedy* Nietzsche had attacked theoretical optimism and the Socratic faith in knowledge, as well as all forms of realism and naturalism in art (where the emphasis is on environmental and biological determinism and on the exclusion of any dimension beyond the factual and the material). Now he was inviting his readers to value "little, unpretentious truths," to celebrate the science of physics for its "modest" and "insignificant" explanations, and to lose faith in all inspiration and in any knowledge acquired by miraculous means. In early 1879 deteriorating health forced Nietzsche to resign from his position at Basel University, which granted him an annual pension. In the course of the next ten years Nietzsche became a veritable European traveler and tourist, with periods of residence in Venice, Genoa, St. Moritz and Sils-Maria, Rome, Sorrento, Nice (where he was to witness an earthquake in 1887), and Turin.

In the summer of 1881 Nietzsche made his first trip to Sils-Maria in the Upper Engadine, which was to become his regular summer residence. It was at this time that he had the experience and inspiration of eternal recurrence, "6,000 feet beyond man and time," as he was later to express it in *Ecce Homo*. In a letter to Gast from Sils-Maria dated August 14, Nietzsche spoke of leading an extremely perilous life and of being "one of those machines which can explode."[12] The intensity of his feelings, he confided, made him shudder and laugh, weeping not sentimental tears but tears of joy (Nietzsche would now oscillate between states of euphoria and depression). In the summer of 1881 he also discovered a precursor in Spinoza, to whom he was brought, he said, through the guidance of instinct. The affinity he felt with Spinoza, as he perceived it, was one of a shared set of doctrines (he mentions the denial of free will, of purposes, of a moral world order, and of evil), and the fundamental tendency to make knowledge the most powerful passion. *Daybreak* was published in July 1881 and *The Gay Science* followed in 1882. It is in these texts that Nietzsche practices his "cheerful" and transfigurative "philosophy of the morning" and conceives of life experimentally

12 Ibid., p. 178.

as a means to knowledge. It is in a famous section of the latter work that he has a madman declare that "God is dead. And we have killed him" (GS 125). In one section of the book Nietzsche suggests replacing churches with botanical gardens in our busy towns and cities as places of reflection where the godless can go to give expression to the sublimity of their thoughts and see themselves translated into stones and plants (GS 280). The original text of 1882 closes with three sections on the dying Socrates, on eternal recurrence (presented as the "greatest weight" and as a daimonic thought that will either crush or change us as we are), and on "the tragedy begins," with an appeal to the redeeming figure of Zarathustra. The year 1882 was eventful for Nietzsche: he visited a casino in Monaco with his friend Rée, who lost a large sum of money; he acquired a typewriter; and he met Lou Salomé and proposed to her, unsuccessfully, twice. In the early part of 1883 he began work on *Thus Spoke Zarathustra* and was badly affected by the death of Wagner. Nietzsche would hold alternating views on *Zarathustra*, having serious doubts about it yet regarding it as an epochal work. During all this time Nietzsche's relationship with his sister had been extremely tense, and in 1884 he spoke of her anti-Semitism as the cause of a "radical break." She married Bernhard Förster in May 1885 and they moved to Paraguay in 1886, founding a German colony there.

In 1886 Nietzsche worked on and published *Beyond Good and Evil*, which bore the subtitle "prelude to a philosophy of the future."[13] By now he had also begun writing a major work that was to consist of four books and had the working title "Will to Power: Attempt at a Revaluation of All Values." He was never to bring this planned *magnum opus* to fruition, but something of its nature can be found in the texts *Twilight of the Idols* (published in 1889) and *The Anti-Christ* (published in 1895 and regarded by Nietzsche as the first book of the transvaluation of all values). It is also in 1886 that he composed a set of new prefaces for second editions of most of his back catalog of published texts, and many scholars regard these prefaces as among the finest pieces of philosophical self-reflection Nietzsche ever wrote. In 1887 a new edition of *The Gay Science* was published with an added fifth book which began with a discourse entitled "The Meaning of Our Cheerfulness" and in which Nietzsche elaborated upon the significance of the death of God as a "monstrous event" that heralded a new dawn in which all the daring of the lover of knowledge could once again be permitted. He also read Dostoevsky, began to compose notes on "European nihilism," and published *On the Genealogy of Morality* with its three striking inquiries into the spirit of *ressentiment*, the origins of the bad conscience, and the meaning of the ascetic ideal. He wrote to the renowned French historian Hippolyte Taine, presenting himself as a hermit and sending two of his books (*Daybreak* and *The Gay Science*). Nietzsche regarded it as a "comic fact" that he was beginning to have a subterranean influence among a diverse array of radical parties and circles. He also revealed that at the age of 43 he felt as alone as when he was a child. He spoke of his solitude in terms of a condemned destiny, in which the "unusual and difficult task" that commanded him to continue

---

13 Nietzsche had been experimenting with the idea of a "philosophy of the future" as early as 1872 in his "Philosophers' Book" (*Philosophenbuch*), no doubt inspired by Wagner's conception of his art as a "music of the future" (*Zukunftsmusik*), which in turn emulated Ludwig Feuerbach's *Principles of the Philosophy of the Future* (1843).

living also commanded him to avoid people and to be free of all normal human bonds. In a letter written in December of 1887 to the Danish critic Georg Brandes, the first person ever to lecture on his work, Nietzsche responded favorably to his description of his thinking as an "aristocratic radicalism."

In 1888 Nietzsche spent what turned out to be his last summer in Sils-Maria. Earlier in the year he had written to his friend Franz Overbeck that the world should expect no more "beautiful things" from him just as one should not expect a suffering and starving animal to attack its prey with grace. He confessed to being devoid of a "refreshing and healing human love" and spoke of his "absurd isolation," which made the residues of a connection with people only something that wounded him. In another letter from the early part of this year he spoke of himself as a "sick animal" and *la bête philosophe*. He was becoming fully aware that the philosopher who embarks on a relentless struggle against everything that human beings have hitherto revered will be met with a hostile public reception, one that will condemn him to an icy isolation with his books being judged by the language of pathology and psychiatry. He resolved to set time aside to tackle the "psychological problem" of Kierkegaard, and developed a liking for the city of Turin (recommended to him by Gast). He was in the city in April and May of this year and returned in September, staying there up to the point of his mental collapse in January 1889. In it he found not a modern metropolis but, he wrote, a "princely residence of the seventeenth century" and an "aristocratic calm" with no "petty suburbs" and a unity of commanding taste. He especially liked the beautiful cafés, the lovely sidewalks, the organization of trams and buses, and the fact that the streets were clean. It was also cheap. *The Case of Wagner* was published, and though it received some vitriolic reviews it was welcomed enthusiastically by August Strindberg. While in Turin in May Nietzsche came across a French translation (carried out in India) of Manu's book of laws, which he thought supplemented his views on religion in a "most remarkable way." In a letter to Carl Fuchs written in Sils in July, Nietzsche says that it is neither necessary nor desirable to argue in his favor, and suggests instead that a more intelligent attitude towards him would be to adopt the pose one would in the presence of a foreign and alien plant, namely, one of curiosity and ironic resistance. Nietzsche began work on *Ecce Homo: How One Becomes What One Is* on his birthday, October 15. The text was designed as a way of testing the risks that could be taken with "German ideas of freedom of speech," Nietzsche said in a letter to Gast, in which he would talk about himself and his writings with "all possible psychological cunning and gay detachment." The last thing he wanted, he confided, was to be treated as some kind of prophet, and he hoped it would prevent readers from confusing him with what he was not. He also wrote to various people, including Fuchs and his sister, saying that his health had never been better. He drafted various letters, including one to his sister in which he informs her that he is compelled to part with her for ever, and one to Kaiser Wilhelm II. In December *Ecce Homo* was sent to the publishers and Nietzsche was observed by his landlady chanting and dancing naked in his room.

On the morning of January 3, 1889, as Nietzsche was taking a stroll through the piazza Carlo Alberto in Turin, he witnessed a carriage driver beating a horse. He threw his arms around the horse's neck and then collapsed to the ground, losing consciousness. In the course of the next few days he composed a series of dramatic and disturbing letters. He wrote to Gast announcing that the world had become transfigured.

To Brandes, his champion in Copenhagen, he wrote that now he had discovered him the great difficulty was how to lose him. To Cosima Wagner he wrote, famously, "Ariadne, I love you"; to Overbeck that he was having all anti-Semites shot; and to Burckhardt that he was all the names in history. Burckhardt showed the letter he had received to Overbeck, who then traveled to Turin and brought Nietzsche back to Basel. The diagnosis was "progressive paralysis." Nietzsche spent a year in a psychiatric clinic in Jena; in 1890 his mother took him to Naumburg, and, upon her death in 1897, his sister Elisabeth brought Nietzsche to the Villa Silberblick in Weimar and inaugurated the Nietzsche cult. Nietzsche died in Weimar on August 25, 1900.

Reading Nietzsche

A collection of this kind is primarily intended to give the reader a detailed insight into the range and evolution of Nietzsche's philosophical ideas, but at the same time it also provides an opportunity to survey the range and evolution of his means of expressing them. Nietzsche is often referred to as an "aphoristic" writer, but on the evidence of this collection such a description falls far short of capturing the sheer variety of forms and styles he adopted. How else, then, might we characterize the formal features of Nietzsche's writing? The underlying organization of this *Reader* follows the generally accepted tripartite division of Nietzsche's career into "early" (pre-1878), "middle" (1878–82) and "late" (1883–8) periods based on phases in the development of his ideas, and to a certain extent such a tripartite division holds for his stylistic development, too. More specifically, such a division recognizes that, stylistically as well as philosophically (and the coincidence of the two is entirely *uncoincidental*), *Human, All Too Human* and *Thus Spoke Zarathustra* mark the two great breakthroughs in his career.

In the period up to 1878 (which in fact includes the juvenilia and early published works up to and including the fourth *Untimely Meditation* in 1876), the standard form Nietzsche adopted for his writings – in accordance with his professional training as an academic classicist – was the essay or pamphlet. In the "middle period" he explored not only a new kind of philosophy, drawing inspiration from the psychological observations of French Enlightenment thinkers, but a new means of expressing it, which was equally inspired by the aphoristic works of the French *moralistes*.[14] The break with this period was marked by the rhapsodic philosophical poem *Thus Spoke Zarathustra*, which was stylistically *sui generis*, but thereafter Nietzsche moved freely between the more "essayistic" and more "aphoristic" modes of before, according to the nature of his material. After completing *Zarathustra* in 1885 he recognized that the "free spirit period" had not yet run its course, after all, so his next two substantial works – *Beyond Good and Evil* and the extra Book V added to the second edition of *The Gay Science* – were

---

14 *The Wanderer and his Shadow* lists six of the most important – Montaigne, La Rochefoucauld, La Bruyère, Fontenelle, Vauvenargues, and Chamfort (*WS* 214) – to which must be added Pascal, "the most instructive of all sacrifices to Christianity" (*EH* II. 3). On Nietzsche's French inspiration in this period and beyond, see the classic study by W. D. Williams, *Nietzsche and the French: A Study of the Influence of Nietzsche's French Reading on his Thought and Writing* (Oxford: Blackwell, 1952), and more recently Brendan Donnellan, *Nietzsche and the French Moralists* (Bonn: Bouvier, 1982).

both conceived as thematic and stylistic continuations of the middle-period works.[15] On the other hand, the more polemical works of sustained advocacy that follow – *On the Genealogy of Morality* (explicitly subtitled "A Polemic"), *The Case of Wagner*, and *The Anti-Christ* – return to the more "essayistic" style of the first period.

Even a more nuanced schematization such as the above still fails to do justice to Nietzsche's formal repertoire, though, and in two different respects: on the one hand it underestimates the stylistic versatility of his writings, especially in the last period, and on the other, paradoxically, it also underestimates their stylistic continuities. In *Ecce Homo* Nietzsche claims for himself "the most manifold art of style any man has ever had at his disposal" (*EH* III. 4), and a work such as *Twilight of the Idols* – a dazzlingly varied stylistic *tour de force* – goes some way towards bearing out the claim. *Ecce Homo* itself, Nietzsche's late autobiography, is another work that belongs in a category of its own, with a stylistic breadth encompassing lengthy quotations from *Zarathustra* and an extensive chapter devoted to book reviews (that is, reviews of Nietzsche's own earlier books). His two last works, though, both emphasize the thematic and formal continuities in his career: in order to demonstrate to the readership of *The Case of Wagner* that such anti-Wagnerian polemic is no flash in the pan, *Nietzsche contra Wagner* gathers together anti-Wagnerian excerpts from all of Nietzsche's writings since *Human, All Too Human*, while his very last book – on which he was found still attempting to work after his mental collapse in January 1889 – is a slim volume of poetry from the period of *Thus Spoke Zarathustra*, *Dithyrambs of Dionysus*, which reminds us that no categorization of Nietzsche's styles would be complete without the poems, or small groups of poems, which he would routinely sprinkle around his earlier (supposedly more "prosaic") works, too – from "Among Friends: An Epilogue" at the end of Book I of *Human, All Too Human*, to "From High Mountains: Aftersong" appended to *Beyond Good and Evil*, and the two substantial collections added to the second edition of *The Gay Science* ("Joke, Cunning and Revenge" and "Songs of Prince Vogelfrei").[16]

Perhaps the most distinctive feature of Nietzsche's style, however, and the true common denominator which links both the more "essayistic" and the more "aphoristic" works, is not the occasional flash of poetry but what amounts to the essential building block of his prose style, namely the (numbered) paragraph. The Nietzschean paragraph is an extraordinarily supple unit, ranging in length from a bare line to several pages. The number of genuine aphorisms in his works is relatively small; instead, most of what are called Nietzsche's "aphorisms" are more substantial paragraphs (imitating the classical period), which exhibit a unified train of thought frequently encapsulated in a paragraph heading indicating the subject-matter, and it is from these building blocks that the other, larger structures are built in more or less extended sequences. A thinker

---

15   In the case of *The Gay Science* Book V this continuity is overt; the book that eventually became *Beyond Good and Evil*, on the other hand, was initially conceived as a continuation of *Human, All Too Human*, then as a continuation of *Daybreak*, and indeed includes a section entitled "The Free Spirit." See Laurence Lampert, *Nietzsche's Task: An Interpretation of "Beyond Good and Evil"* (New Haven and London: Yale University Press, 2001), p. 5f.

16   On Nietzsche's poetry, see Philip Grundlehner, *The Poetry of Friedrich Nietzsche* (New York and Oxford: Oxford University Press, 1986).

for whom "The will to system is a lack of integrity" (*TI* I. 26) is inevitably going to balk at constructing the kind of conceptual edifice in which his philosophical pre-decessors so often delighted,[17] and Nietzsche at times deliberately disperses groups of thematically related paragraphs, but on the other hand he is also capable of linking such paragraphs together into an extended sequence with a single thematic unity stretch-ing for a whole "essayistic" book, as in *The Anti-Christ*, and contemporary criticism is beginning at last to give adequate recognition to the surprising degree of structural coherence shown by even his more fragmentary works.[18]

Unfortunately Nietzsche's English (and other) translators have routinely seen fit to divide up his longer paragraphs in order to emphasize their points of articulation; where this had occurred with the passages included here we have restored Nietzsche's ori-ginal paragraphing. Another feature of his style which has been easily obscured by trans-lations and other later editions of his works (and here our *Reader* is no different) is that he himself refrained from using footnotes. Across the whole of his (voluminous) published output Nietzsche uses only four notes in total – one at the end of the First Essay of *On the Genealogy of Morality* (*GM* I. 17, included here), and three in *The Case of Wagner* (*CW* 9, Postscript 1 and Epilogue).[19] Significantly, then, when he had a chance to revise his published works for second editions in the mid-1880s he wrote new contextualizing prefaces but left the texts themselves untouched; moreover, in the first place his texts are remarkably innocent of references, even in the early years when he was still trying to establish himself as a university professor. Throughout his career, then, his style is very different from standard academic writing, from that of the "philosophical workers" he describes so condescendingly in *Beyond Good and Evil* (*BGE* 211): in the words of Ulrich von Wilamowitz-Möllendorff, Nietzsche's noto-rious early antagonist who published a pamphlet attacking *The Birth of Tragedy* for its professional shortcomings, "Mr Nietzsche by no means presents himself as a scholarly researcher."[20] Nietzsche's own critiques of scholarly myopia and asceticism are scath-ing; above all, he wants to distinguish himself from the tradition of German academic philosophy that preceded him, which he finds lifeless and, ultimately, simply boring. In turn he is highly conscious of what he calls, in a letter to his friend Paul Deussen,

17 Not that that has prevented commentators from seeking to derive an esoteric Nietzschean system. See especially John Richardson, *Nietzsche's System* (New York and Oxford: Oxford University Press, 1996). For Nietzsche's most systematic critique of systematizing, see the essay "On Truth and Lies" and the analysis of it by Sarah Kofman in *Nietzsche and Metaphor*, trans. Duncan Large (London: Athlone Press; Stanford: Stanford University Press, 1993), especially pp. 59–80 ("Metaphorical Architectures").

18 For a superb example of such an approach, see Lampert, *Nietzsche's Task*.

19 Kaufmann is thus mistaken when he describes the *CW* notes as "the only footnotes Nietzsche himself included in any of his books." See "A Note On This Edition" in *"The Birth of Tragedy" and "The Case of Wagner."*

20 Ulrich von Wilamowitz-Möllendorff, "Future Philology! A Reply to Friedrich Nietzsche's 'Birth of Tragedy'," trans. Gertrude Postl, *New Nietzsche Studies*, 4/1–2 (Summer–Fall 2000), pp. 1–32 (p. 3). Nietzsche himself would of course object to the book in his later (1886) "Attempt at a Self-Criticism" from quite the opposite direction – finding it an "impossible book" because it was too much like what had gone before: "It should have *sung*, this 'new soul' – rather than spoken!" (*BT*, "Attempt," 3).

his "whole *philosophical heterodoxy*":[21] he does not simply present his reader with problems concerning truth and knowledge, but he dramatizes them through a series of parables, thought-experiments, imagined conversations, and the like. His aim is always to energize and enliven philosophical style through an admixture of aphoristic and poetic – broadly speaking, "literary" – forms.

The specificity of Nietzsche's style, then – what J. P. Stern terms his "middle mode of discourse"[22] – lies in the fact that it occupies the ground midway between what one might call philosophy and poetry "proper." Perhaps the most appropriate way of describing Nietzsche's style is with reference to its multifarious "impropriety," for its lack of scholarly niceties is but the least of its provocations. Nietzsche's favorite lyric poet was Heinrich Heine, whom he praises in *Ecce Homo* for possessing "that divine malice [*Bosheit*] without which I cannot imagine perfection" (*EH* II. 4), and this transgressive "wickedness" is of course a quality he himself assiduously cultivates. His stylistic ideal, as he puts it on the title page of *The Case of Wagner* (parodying Horace), is the paradoxical one of "ridendo dicere *severum*" ("saying what is *somber* through what is laughable"), and these two modes, the somber and the sunny, are mischievously intertwined in his philosophy, without the reader necessarily being sure which one is uppermost at any one time. Nietzsche is the masked philosopher *par excellence* – "Everything deep loves a mask," he writes in *Beyond Good and Evil* (*BGE* 40) – which means that his work is an unsettling provocation not just for his philosophical antagonists but for his readers, too, especially when his breadth of allusion and lack of references, the love of impropriety and paradox, are combined with an ideal of concision spelt out in *Twilight*: "my ambition is to say in ten sentences what everyone else says in a book – what everyone else does *not* say in a book . . ." (*TI* IX. 51). The texture of Nietzsche's work, then, is often very dense: he is under no illusions that he is straightforward to read, and indeed deliberately erects barriers to understanding him. As he puts it in *Ecce Homo*: "My triumph is precisely the opposite of Schopenhauer's – I say '*non legor, non* legar'" (*EH* III. 1 – "I am not read, I *will* not be read"), and when he conjures up "a perfect reader" later in the same chapter, he envisages "a monster of courage and curiosity, also something supple, cunning, cautious, a born adventurer and discoverer" (*EH* III. 3). He lays down a challenge to his readers, and sets them – us – a pedagogical, hermeneutic task, that of learning to read him well, before we can begin to appreciate the philosophical tasks he invites us to undertake.

Nietzsche's Tasks

One of the pre-eminent intellectual figures of the post-war period, Michel Foucault, contested the idea that there is such a thing as a single or core Nietzscheanism (a view endorsed by Bernard Williams). Foucault suggested that the right question to ask is "What serious use can Nietzsche be put to?" However, while it is the case that there is no single or core Nietzscheanism, he did bequeath to us moderns a set of novel philosophical tasks, and seeking to comprehend these tasks and secure the measure of

21   See Letter to Paul Deussen, September 14, 1888, in *Selected Letters of Friedrich Nietzsche*, pp. 310–11.
22   J. P. Stern, *A Study of Nietzsche* (Cambridge and New York: Cambridge University Press, 1979), p. 199.

them is one of the best ways of introducing Nietzsche to the new reader. These projects and tasks include "historical philosophizing," "the gay science," thinking "beyond good and evil," a "genealogy of morality" (entailing a critique of moral values), the self-overcoming of the will to truth, and a new conception of the "tragic." What unites these projects is Nietzsche's strongly held view that metaphysics has come to an end and reached a crisis-point. By metaphysics he means something quite specific, namely, belief in something unconditioned, i.e. something which would be true, absolutely and unconditionally, outside of all temporal and perspectival conditions. In addition to this belief in a "true" world that stands outside time, history, and nature, metaphysics also refers for Nietzsche to the positing of supernatural and imaginary causes, forces, and entities, to a preoccupation with the otherworldly, to an ascetic denial of human impulses and drives that comes close to a pathological hatred of the human, and to a quest to encounter the "thing-in-itself" (another term for the "true" world).

"Real" and "apparent" worlds

At the center of Nietzsche's work is an attack on modes of thought, such as Platonism and Christianity, which posit a dualism between a "true" world and a merely "apparent" one. In such modes of thinking the "true" world is held to be outside the order of time, change, multiplicity, and becoming – it is a world of "being" – while the world of change, becoming, and evolution is held to be a false world, a world of error and mere semblance. In section 1 of "'Reason' in Philosophy" in *Twilight* he argues that the peculiar idiosyncrasy of philosophers in general is their lack of historical sense and their hatred of the idea of becoming, what he calls their "Egypticism." Philosophers dehistoricize things and in the process mummify the concepts they are using to comprehend things. What has not been adequately dealt with are processes of life – such as death, change, procreation, growth – so that whatever truly has "being" is held not to become and what becomes is held to be nothing real and without being. In section 4 of this part of the book he notes how in metaphysics the most general and emptiest concepts – the absolute, the good, the true, the perfect – are posited as the highest and richest concepts. These concepts must be posited as miraculous causes of themselves and be free of the "contamination" of growth and evolution. The thinnest and emptiest of all these concepts is that of "God." In section 5 Nietzsche argues that metaphysicians have been led astray by the language of reason. Language emerged at the time of the most rudimentary form of psychology and scientific knowledge, and within its emergence there can be identified a "crude fetishism" that makes us think in certain ways that have now become habitual, such as positing the will as a cause of things and of actions, and positing a unified "I" as the center of our being in the world (the "I" as substance), and so on. In short, words and concepts have developed in a way that has led us to forget their empirical grounding and to the extent that we are led to think that they arise spontaneously out of some independent faculty of reason which has no connection with anything empirical, historical, and evolutionary.

Nietzsche locates the seduction of the concept of "Being" at work even in the most progressive forms of thought such as the naturalism and materialism of the Greek atomists. He concludes this section on "'Reason' in Philosophy" with his famous statement that we cannot get rid of God because we cannot get rid of grammar. Our metaphysics – and, in part, our science – lead us to think in certain ways and modes owing to the conceptual fetishism concealed in language and the forgetting of this reification within our history and evolution. In the final section Nietzsche advances four positive theses. First, the reasons why metaphysicians have designated the empirical world as something merely apparent actually serve to show that it is the only reality that there is, and any other reality is simply unprovable. Second, what is called the "real world" has been constructed through a series of negative deductions from the features of the actual world. This is a point Nietzsche makes as early as 1868 in his critique of Schopenhauer – it means that the real world is simply an idealized projection of a true world, one that is held to be outside time, change, becoming, and evolution. Third, attempts to invent stories about another world are literally "senseless" and can serve only to denigrate the empirical world, casting suspicion on life and on its most essential conditions (growth, change, death, etc.). Fourth, all attempts to divide the world into real and apparent dimensions are a symptom of declining and decadent modes of life. Nietzsche concludes by speaking of the artist: what the artist deifies as "appearance" (*Schein*) is reality but reality "selected, strengthened, and corrected."[23] The "tragic" artist – tragic because of the recognition that there is only appearance and this must be willed in all its forms, even the form of illusion – is not a pessimist, since this artist "says *yes* to all that is questionable and even terrible; he is *Dionysian*. . . ."

23   The word *Schein* is rich in ambiguity and Nietzsche makes extensive use of this richness in his writings. It means semblance, deception, illusion, apparentness, and it can also refer to the "being" of that which appears or shines (from the verb *scheinen*, to shine or to glisten). In *BGE* 34 Nietzsche argues that "life" is only possible "on the basis of perspectivist assessments and apparentnesses [*Scheinbarkeiten*]." He adds, however, that the nature and extent of this perspectivism is neither given nor fixed, and stresses that there are "degrees of apparentness [*Scheinbarkeit*] . . . lighter and darker shadows and hues of appearance [*Scheins* . . .]"). In a note from August–September 1885 entitled "Against Appearance [*Erscheinung*]" he writes that he does "not set '*Schein*' in opposition to 'reality'" but rather, on the contrary, takes "*Schein* as the reality that resists transformation into an imaginary 'truth-world'." He then adds that a "determinative name for this world would be 'will to power', namely, characterized from inside and not from its ungraspable, flowing Proteus-nature" (*KSA* 11:654). For insight into Nietzsche's use of *Schein*, see Michel Haar, *Nietzsche and Metaphysics*, trans. Michael Gendre (Albany: State University of New York Press, 1996), pp. 52–67; Heidegger, *Nietzsche*, ed. David Farrell Krell, trans. David Farrell Krell et al., 4 vols (San Francisco and London: Harper & Row, 1979–87), vol. 1, pp. 211–20; and especially the superb analysis in Karl Heinz Bohrer, *Suddenness: On the Moment of Aesthetic Appearance*, trans. Ruth Crowley (New York: Columbia University Press, 1994), ch. 6, pp. 113–48. A series of original insights into *Schein* can be found in various writings of Walter Benjamin (1892–1940). See, for example, "On Semblance" (which name-checks Nietzsche) and "Goethe's Elective Affinities" (which reads Goethe's novel in terms of notions of beautiful semblance and the Dionysian shock of the sublime), in Walter Benjamin, *Selected Writings, Volume 1 (1913–26)*, ed. Marcus Bullock and Michael W. Jennings (Cambridge, MA: Harvard University Press, 1996), pp. 223–6, 297–361 (esp. pp. 349–51), and "The Significance of Beautiful Semblance," in *Selected Writings, Volume 3 (1935–8)*, ed. Howard Eiland and Michael W. Jennings (Cambridge, MA: Harvard University Press, 2002), pp. 137–8.

This positive estimation of art, on account of its displaying "the good will to appearance" (*Schein*), is one that runs throughout Nietzsche's writings (see, for example, *GS* 107, *GM* III. 25).

"Historical philosophizing"

It is with the publication of *Human, All Too Human* in 1878 that Nietzsche first began to outline an approach to philosophical questioning that would inform all his subsequent work. It is what he called "historical philosophizing." The position Nietzsche adopts on philosophical questions and topics in the opening of *Human, All Too Human* finds an echo in the first section of *Beyond Good and Evil* entitled "On the Prejudices of Philosophers." In the opening section of *Human, All Too Human* he focuses on the question of how something can originate in its opposite, and sets up a contrast between "metaphysical philosophy" and "historical philosophy." The former answers the question by appealing to a miraculous source to explain the origin of something held to be of a higher value. The latter, by contrast – which Nietzsche insists can no longer be separated from the natural sciences and which he names as the youngest of all philosophical methods – seeks to show that there are no opposites but that all things arise from and are implicated in a process of sublimation (*Sublimirung*), hence his call for a "chemistry of concepts and sensations." This historical mode of philosophizing gives rise to a number of provocative ideas that have proved seminal in modern thought: that there are no "unalterable facts of mankind," that everything that exists is subject to "becoming," that our faculty of cognition, far from being the transcendental source or originator of our knowledge of the world (the reference is to Kant), has itself become, and that a society's order of rank concerning what it holds to be good and evil actions is constantly changing (*HH* 2. 107). We do not require certainties with regard to the "first and last things" in order to live a "full and excellent human life" (*WS* 16). Nietzsche proposes that a fundamental rupture be effected with regard to customary habits of thinking. Concerning the first and last or ultimate things – What is the purpose of man? What is his fate after death? How can man be reconciled with God? – it should not be felt necessary to develop knowledge against faith; rather, we should practice an *indifference* towards faith and supposed knowledge in the domains of metaphysics, morality, and religion. One of the reasons why Nietzsche takes issue with "philosophical dogmatists" of all persuasions – be they idealists or materialists or realists, he says – is that they seek to force us into taking decisions "in domains where neither faith nor knowledge is needed" (*WS* 16). The "greatest lovers of knowledge" will thus practice knowledge in a different way and remain steadfastly and gaily indifferent to the first and last things.

In *Beyond Good and Evil* Nietzsche teaches the responsibilities of the "dangerous Perhaps" and argues that it is necessary now to wait "for a new category of philosophers" to arrive (*BGE* 2). These "coming" philosophers will be ones who do not accept at face value the belief of the "metaphysicians" in the "opposition of values." The taste and inclination of these philosophers will be very different from that which has hitherto guided philosophical inquiry. They will ask some new questions – Might truth arise out of error? Might altruism be a form of egoism? Might the pure contemplation of the wise man arise out of covetous desire? – and so on. In the opening part of this book Nietzsche attacks what he regards as a large number of philosophical reifications and mystifications. For example, he argues that logical thinking is informed by value judgments that are "physiological demands for the preservation of a particular kind of life" (*BGE* 3); that the world is continually "falsified" through our schemas of thought (such as number) (*BGE* 4); that our thinking is fundamentally informed by a multiplicity of warring instincts (*BGE* 6); that questions of truth and knowledge have to be situated and assessed in the context of an appreciation of "the perspectival optics of life" (*BGE* 11); that the primary desire of a living being is to discharge and release its strength (life is "will to power") and thus the drive to self-preservation, often conceived by philosophers as the fundamental drive of life, needs to be regarded as "only one of its indirect and most frequent *consequences*" (*BGE* 13); that many concepts deployed in philosophy – free will, for example – are of the order of a "cloddish simplicity" (*BGE* 21); and, finally, that questions of psychology must be pursued in a completely free manner, that is, free of moral prejudices and fears, and, furthermore, rendered subordinate to what he calls "the morphology and *evolutionary theory of the will to power*" (*BGE* 23).

"The death of God"

Informing Nietzsche's views on the demise of metaphysics is the statement that "God is dead." This statement is presented in the final book of Nietzsche's "free spirit" trilogy, *The Gay Science*. Book III of this text opens with the declaration of God's death (*GS* 108); this death is then put in dramatic form several sections later (*GS* 125), and its "meaning" receives a further clarification at the opening of Book V, which Nietzsche added in 1887 (*GS* 343). He is not the first philosopher to speak of the death of God (the expression can be found in Hegel). Furthermore, this death is a fundamental feature of Christianity itself; indeed, it could be said that the Christian religion is built upon the death of God. It is not simply that Christ, as the Son of God, died on the cross for our sins, but that God himself died on it, too.[24] Ever since,

---

24   Hegel understands the death of God in these terms in his *Philosophy of Religion*, which has a section entitled "The Death of Christ and the Transition to Spiritual Presence." He cites from a Lutheran hymn of 1641 which contains the phrase "God himself is dead." For Hegel this expresses "an awareness that the human, the finite, the fragile, the weak, the negative are themselves a moment of the divine, that they are within God himself [. . .] This involves the highest idea of spirit." On the one hand, Hegel says, there is the death of Christ which "means principally that Christ was the God-man, the God who at the same time had human nature, even unto death. It is the lot of human finitude to die." On the other hand, a further determination is brought into play, which is that "*God has died, God is dead*," and which is "the most frightful of all thoughts" since it means that "everything eternal and true *is not*, that negation is found in God." See *The Hegel Reader*, ed. Stephen Houlgate (Oxford: Blackwell, 1998), p. 497f. An attempt to contrast Hegel and Nietzsche on the death of God can be found in Deleuze's *Nietzsche and Philosophy*, trans. Hugh Tomlinson (London: Athlone Press; New York: Columbia University Press, 1983), especially pp. 152–9. Deleuze argues that Nietzsche's conception of the death of God differs from Hegel's in that it is not offered as a "speculative" proposition but rather as a dramatic one, by which Deleuze means that it is "pluralist, typological, differential." Everything depends, he says, on the kind of forces that seize on this death

a Christian-moral culture and civilization has been mourning the death of God and bound to him in terms of an infinite debt. With the death of God, then, Nietzsche is giving this death a new form and meaning. For him the death has the status of an "event." The humanity that emerges in the wake of this death, and that now has to give it a sense and a meaning, and to do so as a task, will be very different to the humanity that preceded it. For Nietzsche there is a sense in which we have to become equal to the event, hence his emphasis on new tasks and on a new philosophy conceived as a "philosophy of the future." The most demanding task he sets is that which he names the "self-overcoming" of "the will to truth" (*GS* 344; *GM* III. 27).

The death of God can be interpreted in two senses: it can mean the death of the "symbolic God," that is, the death of the very specific and particular God of Christianity that has held European humanity in bondage for two millennia. It can also mean the death of the God of theologians, philosophers, and some scientists, that is, the "God" that serves as a guarantor of order, structure, and purpose in the universe. We think it is clear that for Nietzsche God is now dead for us in both of these senses. There are a number of passages in his work that show this, and an important passage for gaining an insight into this issue is *GS* 109, a long section which comes immediately after the very short section where Nietzsche has the death of God first announced. It is significant because in it he makes clear that there are "shadows" of God that continue to emit a curious light and must now be vanquished. There are a number of things we now need to "beware of," he tells us: for example, thinking of the universe as either a living being or a machine, thinking that there are "laws of nature" when there are only necessities, thinking that death is opposed to life, thinking that there are enduring substances, and recognizing that "matter" is as much a fiction as God, and so on. Nietzsche argues, in short, that we now face a situation of difficulty because we realize that none of our aesthetic and moral judgments apply to the universe. Hence his call at the end of this section for these shadows of God to stop "darkening" the human mind – a situation which can only come about, he thinks, if we carry out a specific task, one that he calls the "de-deification of nature."

Nietzsche does not offer pronouncements on the death of God by deliberating on the value and validity of various proofs and disproofs of God's existence (see *D* 95). For him the key point to grasp is that it is *belief* in God that has now become *unbelievable*. He explicitly approaches the issue in these terms at the opening of Book V of *The Gay Science* (*GS* 343). For Nietzsche it is not necessary for atheists to engage

and give it a sense. He writes: "Nietzsche, in contrast, to his predecessors, does not believe in this death. He does not bet on this cross. That is to say: he does not make this death an event possessing its meaning in itself. The death of God has as many meanings as there are forces capable of seizing Christ and making him die" (p. 156). This contrasts with Hegel's view that the death has an essential and single meaning (the becoming of spirit, the reconciliation of finite and infinite, the unity of God and the individual, and so on). The contrast between Hegel and Nietzsche on the death of God is also made in instructive terms by Karl Löwith in his important text, *Nietzsche's Philosophy of the Eternal Recurrence of the Same*, trans. J. Harvey Lomax (Berkeley, Los Angeles, and London: University of California Press, 1997), p. 36ff.

in counter-proofs of God's existence. The new philosophical approach operates in a very different manner, deploying methods and insights from the various sciences to show how belief in God arose, the place of this belief in the context of a specific historical culture, and so on. A number of things have contributed to making the belief in the Christian God simply unbelievable, including advances in knowledge in the natural sciences, the cultivation of scientific methods, including the philological methods of reading and interpretation, and the development of the intellectual or scientific conscience, or what Nietzsche calls the desire for intellectual purity and cleanliness (see *GM* III. 27 and *GS* 2). This is also a conscience that has developed through a process of sublimation out of the "confessional punctiliousness of Christian conscience" itself (*GM* III. 27).

Nietzsche responds to the event of the death of God in a number of ways. He clearly wishes to see taking place the cultivation of a new spiritual maturity that will enable us to deal adequately with the new situation we find ourselves in and make it possible for us not to be overcome by disillusionment and despair. He calls on us to "purify" our valuations and opinions in an effort to live post-metaphysically – free of the meta-physics of morality and the morality of metaphysics – in short, to become "over-human" (*GS* 335). He seeks to ward off a simple-minded philosophy of destruction (see *HH* 34). Of course, Nietzsche will advocate a certain philosophy of negation and destruction himself in his later work (from *Beyond Good and Evil* onwards), but for him everything turns on what informs acts and activities of destruction, that is, whether our desire to destroy, which is essential to the task of creating, stems from a spirit of resentment and revenge or whether it springs from an overflowing health and desire for new modes of living. It is in these terms that he conceived his Zarathustra-type as a figure that says "No" and does "No" to everything that has hitherto been greeted with a "Yes" but remains the opposite of a spirit of denial (*EH* III, "Z," 6). Nietzsche mentions the need in a post-metaphysical age for the "requisite temperament," namely, a "cheerful soul" (*HH* 34): this appeal to cheerfulness runs throughout his writings almost from first to last and can be said to constitute the distinctive mood of his thinking. In section 343 of *The Gay Science* he makes it clear that the death of God concerns the Christian one, and he seeks to unfold the sense of his cheerfulness and indicate how it is to be understood: it is intimately connected to his desire to practice "the gay science." In his notebooks of the 1880s the two projects of "the gay science" and thinking "beyond good and evil" become entwined and subsumed within the more general and wider project of preparing the ground for a "philosophy of the future." Clues to what Nietzsche had in mind with his practice of the "gay science" can be found, among other places, in sections 324 and 327 of *The Gay Science* and in the Preface to the *Genealogy* (section 7).

In section 125 of *The Gay Science* Nietzsche makes it clear, through the intoxicated questioning of the madman, that it is we humans who have killed God. We have unchained the earth from its sun in order to release infinity from the judgment of God. Only when God dies can eternity appear in the concrete, transient world. In the discourse on the seven seals in *Zarathustra*, the title character says that he sits with pleasure on the broken churches "like grass and red poppy." As Eugen Fink has noted, these words do not express an unrestrained hatred of God but disclose the essential insight of Nietzsche's atheistic ontology, which conceives the world in terms of chance, chaos, and the innocence of becoming:

The eternal Gods must die so that finite man can understand his finitude as eternity and as eternal recurrence. Human and cosmic infinity cannot tolerate a separate divine infinity. The desire for the world kills God.[25]

"Gay science"

Science is crucially important to Nietzsche's project, but it is not a question for him of philosophical thinking and questioning being completely subsumed within its ambit. From an early point in his intellectual development Nietzsche read widely in the natural sciences, including new work in the fields of biology, physiology, geology, and physics, and he drew heavily on this work in the articulation of his own philosophical doctrines. A recurring theme in his work is the importance of a correct appreciation of scientific methods. In section 635 of *Human All Too Human*, for example (not included in this volume), he argues that such methods are as important as any other result of inquiry: simply knowing scientific facts is not enough; one must also practice the scientific spirit which teaches "an instinctive mistrust of wrong ways of thinking" and the necessity of "the most extreme circumspection." Nietzsche picks up on this again in section 59 of *The Anti-Christ*, where he criticizes Christianity for ruining the ancient world which had put into place the prerequisites of an "erudite culture," including scientific methods, natural science and the "sense for facts," and the "incomparable" art of reading well, without which there can be no cultural tradition and uniform science. However, Nietzsche does not hold that scientific methods on their own can promote knowledge (*D* 432). There is need for a further level of experimentation, and this is the task of philosophy.

Nietzsche sought to combat what he saw as the timid reduction of philosophy to the "theory of knowledge" (*BGE* 204). He sought to draw attention to what he saw as the debasement of the concept of philosophy at the hands of certain "*Engländer*" – he names Hobbes, Hume, Locke, Carlyle, Darwin, John Stuart Mill, Herbert Spencer (*BGE* 252–3). He speaks of philosophy as entailing "spiritual perception" or vision of "real depth" (*BGE* 252), and argues that true and genuine philosophers are "commanders and lawgivers" (*BGE* 211). Moreover, the philosopher is "*necessarily* a man of tomorrow and the day after tomorrow" who exists in conflict with his "today" and must, therefore, assume the guise of an *untimely* one (*BGE* 212). Furthermore, science has its own prejudice, on which Nietzsche comments in section 373 of *The Gay Science*. Here he takes to task what he calls the "faith" of "materialistic natural scientists," which rests on the supposition that the world can find an equivalence and measure in human thought and valuations, such as a "'world of truth'." He mainly has in mind a mechanistic interpretation of the world, one that "permits counting, calculating, weighing, seeing, and touching," and he argues that such an interpretation amounts to "a crudity and naiveté" and might be "one of the *most stupid* of all possible interpretations of the world" as it would be "one of the poorest in meaning": "an essentially mechanical world would be an essentially *meaningless* [*sinnlose*] world." Nietzsche has to be read carefully when he makes this criticism. There are places in his writings where he

25 Eugen Fink, *Nietzsche's Philosophy*, trans. Goetz Richter (London and New York: Continuum, 2003), p. 100.

recognizes the achievement of scientific mechanism; it wins an important victory over the teleological view of the world that would see final or ultimate purposes everywhere. The new science becomes stupid, however, when it seeks to take over and dominate all questions that can be asked of existence. He is keen to protect what he calls the "*rich ambiguity*" of existence, and calls attention to "ambiguity" a "dictate of good taste, [. . .] the taste of reverence for everything that lies beyond your horizon."

Perhaps Nietzsche's most important and demanding engagement with science takes place in his treatment of the ascetic ideal in the Third Essay of the *Genealogy* (see especially sections 23–7). With God now dead Nietzsche thinks that all the "daring of the lover of knowledge" is permitted once again. This love of knowledge is clearly not philosophy in its traditional sense (*philo-sophia* or the love of wisdom), but neither is it simply scientific knowledge, precisely because a necessary part of the present task is to question science itself, especially the extent to which science continues to rest on a metaphysical faith, notably its belief in the unconditional and absolute value of truth (*GS* 344; *GM* III. 23–5). Because science itself rests on a moral foundation, it cannot spearhead the fundamental task now facing us, which is what Nietzsche defines as the "self-overcoming" of morality and of the will to truth (*GM* III. 27 – just how science can be said to rest on a "moral" foundation is explained in *GS* 344). Science "never creates values" but rather places itself in the service of a value-creating power, from which it acquires its belief in itself (*GM* III. 25).

Nietzsche appreciates that his claim that science is linked to the ascetic ideal will sound strange to our ears. Nevertheless, he maintains that science is "a *hiding-place*" for all kinds of ill-humor, "nagging worms," and "bad conscience" (*GM* III. 23).[26] By "science" here he does not simply mean natural science but the modern practice of knowledge in general which would include, for example, the historical sciences. But as his references to astronomy make clear, he does not exclude the natural and physical sciences from his claim, either. From section 24 of the Third Essay it is apparent that his appeal to "us knowers," in whom he places hope for opponents of ascetic ideals, has an ambiguous sense to it (the text of the *Genealogy* opens, in fact, by speaking immediately of these "knowers" who are said to be "unknown" to themselves). On the one hand it names "us moderns" as "idealists of knowledge" in whom the intellectual conscience has taken root; on the other hand, it is the ideal of a genuinely free spirit that has emancipated itself from the "metaphysical" valuation of truth and thus gone beyond the "idealism" of knowledge. It is clear that Nietzsche holds this emancipation to be part of a process that is under way but has not yet been attained, and the intellectual effort of his work is to contribute towards its actualization. It is no small task, but a vitally important one, to work out precisely what Nietzsche means by our present valuation of truth remaining a "metaphysical" one and just what the "critique" of the will to truth entails.

26   For some especially perspicacious insights into Nietzsche on science see Klossowski, *Nietzsche and the Vicious Circle*, p. 138ff. See also Maurice Blanchot, *The Infinite Conversation*, trans. Susan Hanson (Minneapolis and London: University of Minnesota Press, 1993), p. 145ff.

"The will to truth"

Nietzsche's views on truth present the reader with numerous paradoxes and a series of genuinely difficult and complex challenges. Is he proposing that in order to overcome the will to truth and science's overestimation of the value of truth we should abandon truth and give up on this will? It is prudent to pay close and careful attention to his exact words in the key sections that make up his argument in the final part of the Third Essay of the *Genealogy* (*GM* III. 23–8). Nietzsche asks us to bring – "tentatively" – the will to truth into question. He calls for a "critique" of the will to truth, and we must hear this word in its Kantian sense of setting limits and boundaries in which the scope and range, the value and validity, of something – in this case the will to truth – is to be determined. For Nietzsche critique will not, in contrast to Kant's position, be determined by the needs of faith, but rather by the needs and desires of a new and higher humanity which emerges in the wake of the death of God (Nietzsche does not know whether such a humanity is possible; he is merely posing the question and establishing a goal and task). Neither modern science nor atheism is sufficient in itself for this task of critique to be properly carried out; nor can either be adequate to the task of giving a new sense or direction to human existence and to the earth.

Nietzsche is often taken to be a thinker unconcerned with truth, but this applies only with respect to a metaphysical conception of truth (that is, one that would place truth outside the world and its perspectival conditions and without regard for evolutionary and anthropological factors). He repeatedly insists on the anthropological character of our forms of knowing: we cannot suppose that our forms of knowledge and categories of thought give us truths that are valid outside of our existential domain; "truth" does have a sense and significance, but only as part of a human economy of living. He is best read as a thinker who seeks to ask new and experimental questions of truth. The testing of existential truths lies at the heart of his own experimental philosophy and its free-spiritedness (Nietzsche repeatedly speaks of "his truths" as truths that he has won), and it is essential to his wrestling with the fate of knowledge after the death of God, where life itself is now a "means to knowledge" (*GS* 327). Why is truth now such a problem for us, according to Nietzsche? And why does he speak of a crisis of the will to truth? (*GM* III. 27; see also *BGE*, Preface, and sections 1 and 2). His argument, in part, is that the discoveries of modern science and the insights of modern inquiries of knowledge have demonstrated the extent to which humankind has evolved by occupying the place and site of untruth (*GS* 121; *BGE* 4, 11). The fundamental errors of humanity – the error or imprecision of the judgment that there are identical things, enduring and unconditioned substances, a free will, and so on – have been shown by modern science, such as evolutionary theory, to be errors that have their basis in *organic life* (*HH* 18). These errors are deeply rooted in our evolutionary history and physiological constitution; our reliance on error cannot, therefore, be easily overcome. On a deeper level, however, Nietzsche is concerned that humanity may perish as a result of the blind will to truth which, in his terms, is fundamentally "ascetic." It is for this reason that the will to truth requires a "critique." For Nietzsche questions of truth need to be situated in the context of a consideration of the economy of life as a whole, and for him this is the task of the new philosophers and free spirits. An essential part of what it means to think "beyond good and evil" consists in the philosopher placing himself or herself in a critical space that resists "familiar values in a dangerous way" (*BGE* 4), and this involves resisting conventional and normal ways of valuing truth. However, this should not be taken to mean that truth is not important to Nietzsche. The opposite is, in fact, the case: his conception of the "passion of knowledge" contains an essential *passion* for truth. Nietzsche knows that truth challenges us – this is its specific *raison d'être* – and the issue he wants us to focus our attention on is that of truth's *incorporation*, which he conceives as a great experiment.

Nietzsche is, in effect, attempting a reform of truth and proposing an education in what he calls the "abyss" of the scientific conscience (*GM* III. 23). Questions of truth are to be situated in the context of a thinking of life, of nature, of history and culture, of impulses and drives. He wonders whether anyone has yet been sufficiently truthful in speaking about truthfulness (*BGE* 77). For Nietzsche the real question concerns the extent to which truth can "endure incorporation. That is the question; that is the experiment" (*GS* 110). Can we live with truth and dwell in the space of truth? If we can, to what extent? Can there be a diet of knowledge? In his early writings we find Nietzsche arguing that although science can probe the processes of nature it can never "command" human beings: "Science knows nothing of taste, love, pleasure, displeasure, exaltation, or exhaustion. Man must in some way *interpret*, and thereby evaluate, what he lives through and experiences."[27] The mature Nietzsche comes to the view that science must now inform what constitutes the matter of interpretation and evaluation (for example, the physiology of the body, the chemistry of concepts and sensations, and so on). However, the disciplines of interpretation and evaluation also require an education in a superior empiricism that knows how to discriminate between noble and base ways of thinking and is able to determine the question of value. Nietzsche writes: "*All* sciences must, from now on, prepare the way for the future work of the philosopher: this work being understood to mean that the philosopher has to solve the *problem of values* and that he has to decide on the *hierarchy of values*" (*GM* I. 17, "Note").

The gay science is intended by Nietzsche to mark a new stage in the history of our becoming-human, in which humankind has become mature enough to ask of the world and of itself the most challenging and demanding questions. It seeks to show us that the intellect does not have to be a "clumsy, gloomy, creaking machine" (*GS* 327). The specific "gravity" of this new gay science stems from the fact that there now takes place a return of the fundamental questions, but staged and encountered in new-found conditions and circumstances: How do we now live? And what do we love? This supposes we are still capable of life and love and that we desire to live and to love.

We would like to close by citing Nietzsche's own demanding words:

> All great problems demand *great love*, and of that only strong, round, secure spirits who have a firm grasp on themselves are capable. It makes the most telling difference whether a thinker has a personal relationship to his problems and finds in them his destiny, his distress, and his greatest happiness, or an "impersonal" one, meaning that he can do no better than touch them and grasp them with the antennae of cold, curious thought. (*GS* 345)

---

27 Nietzsche, "The Struggle Between Science and Wisdom" (1875), in *Philosophy and Truth: Selections from Nietzsche's Notebooks of the Early 1870s*, ed. and trans. Daniel Breazeale (Atlantic Highlands, NJ: Humanities Press, 1979), p. 141.

A Chronology of Friedrich Nietzsche

1844   Friedrich Wilhelm Nietzsche born in Röcken (Saxony) on October 15, son of Karl Ludwig and Franziska Nietzsche. His father and both grandfathers are Protestant clergymen.

1846   Birth of sister Elisabeth.

1849   Birth of brother Joseph; death of father.

1850   Death of brother; family moves to Naumburg.

1858–64 Attends renowned boys' boarding-school Pforta, where he excels in classics. Begins to suffer from migraine attacks which will plague him for the rest of his career.

1864   Enters Bonn University to study theology and classical philology.

1865   Follows classics professor Ritschl to Leipzig University, where he drops theology and continues with studies in classical philology. Discovers Schopenhauer's philosophy and becomes a passionate admirer.

1867   Begins publishing career with essay on Theognis; continues publishing philological articles and book reviews till 1873.

1867–8   Military service in Naumburg, until invalided out after a riding accident.

1868   Back in Leipzig, meets Richard Wagner for the first time and quickly becomes a devotee. Increasing disaffection with philology: plans to escape to Paris to study chemistry.

1869   On Ritschl's recommendation, appointed Extraordinary (Associate) Professor of Classical Philology at Basel University. Awarded doctorate without examination; renounces Prussian citizenship. Begins a series of idyllic visits to the Wagners at Tribschen, on Lake Lucerne. Develops admiration for Jacob Burckhardt, his new colleague in Basel.

1870   Promoted to full professor. Participates in Franco-Prussian War as volunteer medical orderly, but contracts dysentery and diphtheria at the front within a fortnight.

1871   Granted semester's sick leave from Basel and works intensively on *The Birth of Tragedy*. Germany unified; founding of the Reich.

1872   Publishes *The Birth of Tragedy from the Spirit of Music*, which earns him the condemnation of professional colleagues. Lectures "On the Future of our Educational Institutions"; attends laying of foundation stone for Bayreuth Festival Theatre.

1873   Publishes first *Untimely Meditation: David Strauss the Confessor and the Writer*.

1874   Publishes second and third *Untimely Meditations: On the Utility and Liability of History for Life* and *Schopenhauer as Educator*. Relationship with Wagner begins to sour.

1875   Meets musician Heinrich Köselitz (Peter Gast), who idolizes him.

1876   Publishes fourth and last *Untimely Meditation: Richard Wagner in Bayreuth*. Attends first Bayreuth Festival but leaves early and subsequently breaks with Wagner. Further illness; granted full year's sick leave from the university.

1877   French translation of *Richard Wagner in Bayreuth* published, the only translation to appear during his mentally active lifetime.

1878   Publishes *Human, All Too Human: A Book for Free Spirits*, which confirms the break with Wagner.

1879   Publishes supplement to *Human, All Too Human, Assorted Opinions and Maxims*. Finally retires from teaching on a pension; first visits the Engadine, summering in St. Moritz.

1880   Publishes *The Wanderer and his Shadow*. First stays in Venice and Genoa.

1881   Publishes *Daybreak: Thoughts on the Prejudices of Morality*. First stay in Sils-Maria.

1882   Publishes *The Gay Science*. Infatuation with Lou Andreas-Salomé, who spurns his marriage proposals.

1883   Publishes *Thus Spoke Zarathustra: A Book for Everyone and No One*, Parts I and II (separately). Death of Wagner. Spends the summer in Sils and the winter in Nice, his pattern for the next five years. Increasingly consumed by writing.

1884   Publishes *Thus Spoke Zarathustra*, Part III.

1885   *Thus Spoke Zarathustra*, Part IV, printed but circulated to only a handful of friends. Begins in earnest to amass notes for *The Will to Power*.

1886   Publishes *Beyond Good and Evil: Prelude to a Philosophy of the Future*. Change of publisher results in new expanded editions of *The Birth of Tragedy* and *Human, All Too Human* (now with a second volume comprising the *Assorted Opinions and Maxims* and *The Wanderer and his Shadow*).

1887   Publishes *On the Genealogy of Morality: A Polemic*. New expanded editions of *Daybreak* and *The Gay Science*.

1888   Begins to receive public recognition: Georg Brandes lectures on his work in Copenhagen. Discovers Turin, where he writes *The Case of Wagner: A Musicians' Problem*. Abandons *The Will to Power*, then completes in quick succession: *Twilight of the Idols; or, How to Philosophize with a Hammer* (first published 1889), *The Anti-Christ: Curse on Christianity* (first published 1895), *Ecce Homo: How One Becomes What One Is* (first published 1908), *Nietzsche contra Wagner: Documents of a Psychologist* (first published 1895), and *Dithyrambs of Dionysus* (first published 1892).

1889   Suffers mental breakdown in Turin (January 3) and is eventually committed to an asylum in Jena. *Twilight of the Idols* published January 24, the first of his new books to appear after his collapse.

1890   Discharged into the care of his mother in Naumburg.

1894   Elisabeth founds Nietzsche Archive in Naumburg (moving it to Weimar two years later).

1897   Mother dies; Elisabeth moves her brother to Weimar.

1900   Friedrich Nietzsche dies in Weimar on August 25.

Part I
Beginnings

Introduction

This section features four short pieces of writing from Nietzsche's youth and an early, unfinished essay on Schopenhauer. The first two pieces afford an insight into Nietzsche's earliest attempt to express his reflections in philosophical form. They were written in March and April of 1862 and presented to the small literary club "Germania" which Nietzsche had founded in this year with a few friends. Although they are pieces of juvenilia they do anticipate themes we associate with Nietzsche's mature philosophy. At the time of their composition Nietzsche has ceased to be a believing Christian and the waning of his faith leads him not only to have doubts about the tenability of religion as such but also to question the extent to which those who find themselves shipwrecked on the sea of doubt can go on to discover new lands. Pulling things down is easy, but rebuilding and creating new things is something else and proves much more difficult. In our quest for new existential modes of living and social forms we are perpetually working against deeply rooted prejudices and the force of custom and ingrained habits. In our desire for the dissolution of society and in our intimation that humankind may have been living under a deception we may be simply feeding our own arrogance and asserting an unearned and unproven superiority. Nietzsche is grappling with questions that will come to typify his work in the 1870s and 1880s: How do we learn to live in time? What should be our relation to history and the past? What is the place of man in the course of things? His questioning in these early pieces bears the imprint of Ralph Waldo Emerson, whose essays had been translated into German in 1858 under the title *Versuche*. Emerson had written two essays on "History" and "Fate," and Nietzsche's early *Versuch* amalgamates the two.[1]

The essay on freedom of the will and fate offers a glimpse into Nietzsche's early efforts to negotiate a position between the extremes of absolute free will and complete determinism. He argues that both a false spirituality and a false naturalness are to be avoided. The essay reveals that a preoccupation with individuation and individuality is present from the very beginnings of his philosophical reflections. The essay entitled "On Moods" from 1864, written in Naumburg during a school vacation, finds Nietzsche affirming a condition of uncertainty, of continually changing views and moods: "strife" or "conflict" (*Kampf*) is declared to be "the perpetual food of the soul," and "spirit" (*Geist*) wishes to advance to ever greater heights and dive into ever greater depths. "My Life" is an autobiographical sketch dating from September 1863: it was

---

1 Emerson's essays can be found in *The Portable Emerson*, ed. Carl Bode and Malcolm Cowley (Harmondsworth: Penguin, 1981), pp. 115–38 and 346–75 respectively.

first discovered in 1936 and published in a special edition by the Nietzsche Archive in Weimar on the recommendation of Heidegger. Nietzsche's first attempt at auto-biography dates from 1858, and the idea of transforming a life into a book intrigued Nietzsche throughout his youth. His aim was to approach the key moments and events of his life as a naturalist would, namely, in terms of their climatic zones (temperate or tropical) and historical characters, all of which would disclose a life of potential and promise. As Rüdiger Safranski has noted, Nietzsche saw his life as a testing ground for his thinking, and the essay form itself was for him a mode of living.[2]

The final piece in this opening selection is an incomplete essay on Schopenhauer written in 1868. It shows that Nietzsche's reception of Schopenhauer is an astutely critical one from the outset, and recognition of this suggests that the view that Nietzsche's early period can be characterized as straightforwardly Schopenhauerian is in need of some revision. The criticisms Nietzsche makes in this piece center on the coherence of Schopenhauer's division of the world into representation and will.

Nietzsche's thought developed under the influence of certain strands of neo-Kantianism.[3] In 1867–8 he outlined a plan for a dissertation on the topic of the organic since Kant.[4] Several scholars have examined the importance of neo-Kantian texts for our appreciation of his philosophical education and development, such as his early readings of Lange's *History of Materialism* and of Spir's *Thought and Reality*.[5] Nietzsche continued to read texts in this area well into the 1880s.[6] One of the most important issues that emerges from Kant, and which lay at the center of neo-Kantian debates, is the

2   See Rüdiger Safranski, *Nietzsche: A Philosophical Biography*, trans. Shelley Frisch (New York: Norton, 2001), p. 28.

3   A number of sensible remarks on the importance of appreciating Nietzsche's neo-Kantian context are made by Michael Steven Green in *Nietzsche and the Transcendental Tradition* (Urbana and Chicago: University of Illinois Press, 2002), pp. 36–57. See also the information contained in Greg Whitlock's commentary to his translation of Nietzsche's lectures on *The Pre-Platonic Philosophers* (Urbana and Chicago: University of Illinois Press, 2001). For insight into the different currents of neo-Kantianism see Herbert Schnädelbach, *Philosophy in Germany 1831–1933*, trans. Eric Matthews (Cambridge: Cambridge University Press, 1984), pp. 105–7. The most important study of Nietzsche's relation to Kant is R. Kevin Hill's recent book *Nietzsche's Critiques: The Kantian Foundations of his Thought* (Oxford: Clarendon Press; New York: Oxford University Press, 2003).

4   It was decided against including this piece in the *Reader* owing to its highly sketchy character. An English translation of it can be found in Claudia Crawford, *The Beginnings of Nietzsche's Theory of Language* (Berlin and New York: de Gruyter, 1988), pp. 238–53. Two highly instructive readings can be found in Elaine P. Miller, *The Vegetative Soul: From Philosophy of Nature to Subjectivity in the Feminine* (Albany: State University of New York Press, 2002), ch. 6, and in Alberto Toscano, "The Method of Nature, the Crisis of Critique," *Pli: The Warwick Journal of Philosophy*, 11 (2001), pp. 36–62. See also Hill, *Nietzsche's Critiques*.

5   See, respectively, George J. Stack, *Lange and Nietzsche* (Berlin and New York: de Gruyter, 1983), and Green, *Nietzsche and the Transcendental Tradition*.

6   One example is a text by Gustav Bunge (a professor of physiology at Nietzsche's old University of Basel) entitled *Vitalismus und Mechanismus* (*Vitalism and Mechanism*), which was published in 1886 and from which Nietzsche made notes as part of his own researches in the area of biophilosophy.

nature and status of the distinction between "appearance" and "thing-in-itself." This is also a crucial element in Schopenhauer's philosophy. Schopenhauer does what Kant sought to tell us we cannot do: he names the thing-in-itself and develops the doctrine of the will to life.

In his *Critique of Pure Reason* (1781/7) Kant set out to show the extent to which our knowledge of the world is determined by ourselves, that is, by our own mental faculties or powers. This is primarily what Kant means by the word "transcendental" (not to be confused with the transcendent). He names "transcendental" the knowledge of objects that refers to *a priori* representations, that is, prior to experience. Kant's critique aims to show that while our knowledge must have reference to experience this does not mean that it simply arises out of experience (as in typical empiricism). While in the order of time we have no knowledge that is antecedent to experience, this does not mean that experience is without *a priori* subjective principles. For example, the proposition that every change or alteration has a cause is not one that can be derived from experience, simply because it is the basis of the possibility of any experience (as are the propositions that there are objects outside of me in space and that my thoughts succeed one in another in a sequential order of time – these are forms of intuition that are independent of any actual experience). For an empiricist like Hume our belief that the effect always follows the cause is arrived at from a repeated association of events and based on a custom of connecting representations. It is, in effect, the result of a psychological habituation of the mind. For Kant, by contrast, without a proper transcendental support human knowledge would lack the features of universality and necessity, and our experience of the world would be reduced to something arbitrary. The necessity of knowledge would be merely "subjective" in a psychological sense and could have no claim to (subjective) objectivity. Kant thus seeks knowledge that is synthetic and *a priori*.

Kant restricts this knowledge to the realm of appearances. We can know the world with certainty only in terms of how it is structured and given form by our *a priori* modes of intuition (space and time) and cognition (the categories of the understanding). This means that the traditional aspirations of metaphysics cannot be met, simply because they rest on the belief that it is possible for us to transcend the sensory conditions of our nature and so arrive at a knowledge of the nature of things themselves. This point introduces us to what is without doubt one of the most important legacies of the Kantian critique, one that was to have a major influence on Schopenhauer and other mentors of Nietzsche such as Lange.[7] If our modes and forms of knowledge give us the world only in the aspect of its appearance, then this suggests that it is meaningful to speak of the world as it might be independently of how we intuit and cognize it. Kant's position is to insist that while the "thing-in-itself" is "indeed real *per se*" we cannot know it. We do not know any object as it might be in itself but only as an object of a sensible intuition (as an appearance). Still, Kant insists that while we cannot know objects as things-in-themselves "we must yet be in a position

7 Nietzsche speaks of his reading of Lange's book and what he found of special importance in it, in a letter to his friend Carl von Gersdorff written at the end of August 1866, describing Lange as "an extremely enlightened Kantian and natural scientist." See *Selected Letters of Friedrich Nietzsche*, ed. and trans. Christopher Middleton (Chicago and London: University of Chicago Press, 1969; repr. Indianapolis: Hackett, 1996), pp. 18–19.

at least to *think* them as things in themselves, otherwise we should be landed in the absurd conclusion that there can be appearance without anything that appears."[8]

Kant divides the realm of appearance (*Erscheinung*) into the "matter" of sensation and the "form" of representation. For Kant the matter of sensation requires the ordering of form to give us transcendental conditions of experience, but this form cannot itself be derived from sensation (it is thus an *a priori* form of intuition such as space and time). This ordering of form needs to be further articulated in terms of the *a priori* categories of the understanding, giving us appearances that have become synthesized and which we can then call "phenomena." Kant presents the issue in this way in order to separate appearance (*Erscheinung*) from mere "illusion" (*Schein* – this is the word that figures in varied and complicated ways in Nietzsche's texts). Kant, then, has done a number of things with appearances: he has sought to distinguish them from arbitrary sense impressions and the field of illusion; and he has argued that while we can have knowledge only of appearances this does not mean that our knowledge is simply drawn from appearances. It is the job of the faculty of the understanding to organize appearances in space and time according to *a priori* categories, the origin of which does not reside in the realm of appearances but which have no meaning if they are applied outside this realm. However, because Kant posits a relation between appearances and the object as well as between appearances and the subject (which he must do to avoid the subjective idealism of a figure such as Berkeley, in which the distinction between appearance and illusion collapses), the whole issue of the object in itself is

---

8   Kant, *Critique of Pure Reason*, trans. Norman Kemp Smith (London: Macmillan 1978), preface to the second edition B xxvii. Kant's argument involves a set of subtle but important distinctions between the thing-in-itself, the transcendental object, and the noumenon. If appearances are only representations and not things-in-themselves, then the object of such appearances cannot be intuited by us since it is non-empirical. This is what Kant calls the "transcendental object = x" (A 109). Objects exist, then, in two manners: as appearances or representations which we can intuit immediately and as "transcendental," lying beyond our intuition. Here Kant thinks he is simply following his prefatory argument about the notion of the thing-in-itself necessarily following from the insight that we know with certainty only the world in the aspect of its appearance. But he is also led to this notion of the transcendental object on account of his commitment to there being a genuine objective reality (he is keen to distinguish the position of his transcendental idealism from that of Berkeley's "dogmatic idealism," as Kant called it, and in the second edition of the text he added a new section on the "refutation of idealism"). By the "noumenon" Kant means a thing or an object considered as an object independent of our sensible intuition. He insists that the noumenon can only be understood in a negative sense. If we developed a positive meaning for it this would mean things could be rendered accessible through the superior (nonhuman or extrahuman) faculty of intellectual intuition. But we have no such faculty for Kant since all our intuition is of the sensible or sensory kind. This explains why he holds that the employment of the categories of the understanding can extend no further than to objects of experience. The concept of a noumenon is a merely limiting concept which serves the function of curbing the pretensions of our sensibly conditioned intellect. "It is no arbitrary invention," Kant insists, and it is "bound up with the limitation of sensibility" (B 309).

raised. In short, we can know the world only through representation, which serves to give it a subjective determination but without reducing it to a dream or hallucination (an illusion); and yet we have to admit the world considered independently of our representation of it is an in-itself that is completely unknowable.

In the Preface to the second edition of his great work *The World as Will and Representation* (*WWR*) (1844), Schopenhauer argues that the person who has not mastered Kant's philosophy remains in a state of philosophical innocence, in the grasp of a childlike realism (the view that our knowledge actually corresponds to and captures the world as it is in itself). He begins by declaring that the world is a "representation" (*Vorstellung*) and that this is a truth valid for all living and knowing beings. It is in man, however, that it is brought into reflective and abstract consciousness. What this means is that we do not know a sun and an earth but only an *eye that sees a sun* and a *hand that feels an earth*. In other words, all we ever encounter in our knowledge is our own representation of the world that primarily and fundamentally assumes the character of forms, notably space, time, and causality. Schopenhauer also construes these forms as particular modes of the principle of sufficient reason (PSR), which explains why something is what it is at a specific time and place, the causal laws it is subject to and of which it is the expression. Schopenhauer acknowledges that this account of knowledge presupposes the division of the world into subject and object. This is to posit a subject of perception for which the whole world exists only in relation to it. Time and space are thus conditioned by the subject and exist only for the subject. This subject, moreover, is only ever the knower and not the known, and so it does not lie within the realm of forms but is presupposed by them. Schopenhauer also wishes to claim that there is another dimension of the world, the world as will, and this is the thing-in-itself outside space, time, and causality. He devotes the first part of volume 1 of *The World as Will and Representation* (1819) to an inquiry into the world as representation, and the second part to an inquiry into the world as will. Like Kant, Schopenhauer, too, is sensitive to the problem of "illusion" that is generated by the transcendental philosophy, and he follows Kant in arguing for both "empirical reality" and "transcendental ideality." The perceived world, which takes place through the forms of space and time, "is absolutely what it appears to be; it appears wholly and without reserve as representation" (section 5). On the other hand, the "actual world" (a world of causality) is thoroughly conditioned by the understanding. Moreover, because we cannot conceive of an object without a subject, it is impossible to follow the dogmatist and allow for the reality of an external world that would be completely independent. Thus, "the whole world of objects is and remains representation," and it is on account of this that we speak of the world enjoying for the subject a "transcendental ideality." Schopenhauer insists: "But it is not on that account falsehood or illusion" (section 5).[9]

---

9 Schopenhauer goes on in this section to discuss "the question of the reality of the external world" from "yet another origin," namely that of dreams, and he considers the idea that the whole of life may be nothing more than a dream in which the difference between phantasms and real objects would no longer be sustainable. The details of his position cannot be examined here, but see Nietzsche, *GS* 54, for a similar consideration. See also *BT* 1 and 4 (in the latter section Nietzsche speaks of the dream as the "appearance of appearance," *der Schein des Scheins*), and the opening argument of the essay "On Truth and Lies in a Nonmoral Sense."

It is in book 2 of *The World as Will and Representation* that Schopenhauer's argument undergoes a quite dramatic shift and the text loses its anchorage in Kant's transcendental idealism. He is now preoccupied with a set of new problems which center on the following issue: the knowledge given to us by mathematics and the natural sciences is only a knowledge of the world as representation (as it appears to the subject) and, as such, it is knowledge of the world in its quantitative and external aspects. For example, mathematics states with great accuracy the "how-many" and the "how-large" of things relative to one another, while natural science, in its two principal divisions, gives us a description of forms and shapes (morphology) and an account of changes through a knowledge of cause and effect (aetiology). What is not revealed in these forms of knowledge, however, is "the slightest information about the inner nature" of any of the phenomena under investigation (section 17). All that science can know, Schopenhauer insists, are laws of nature, which give us knowledge of things in terms of their stability, constancy, reliability, and so on; that is, knowledge of things in terms of their conditions and appearances at a definite time and in a definite place. There is something which lies beyond the aetiological inquiry, namely the "natural force," or the "inner nature" of a thing (be it a stone, a body, or the movement of an animal). In pursuing this line of inquiry Schopenhauer is assuming that the world of representation requires that there is another secret dimension hidden from our forms of knowledge and which must ultimately be referred to as that which is sub-representational. What is the significance of our representations? What are they representations "of"? Is the world as representation all that there is? If this is the case, Schopenhauer argues, it must pass by us like some empty dream or ghostly vision unworthy of any truly serious consideration.

Schopenhauer insists that we cannot access the world that is beyond representation from without. If we proceed in this way we will only ever encounter our own images and shadows. It is at this stage in the unfolding of his argument that he makes an appeal to the body and to immediate data: not to the body as an object among objects and as representation, but to the body as something affective in which the subject encounters itself as a desiring individual, or a being of *will*. The action of a body is nothing other than an act of "will" objectified or translated into perception. This is the case, Schopenhauer argues, for both voluntary and involuntary movements of the body. One of the reasons why we experience ourselves as cut off from the world as will, in this case bodily will, is because of the nature of our representational cognition. It is only when we reflect that we artificially separate willing and acting: "in reality they are one" (section 18). Moreover, because I exist as a being in time I know my will not as the whole or unity but only in terms of its individual acts. In certain key respects, then, I am cut off from the real ground of my being – which turns out to be "groundless" – because of my existence as a representational subject. It is our bodies that individuate us. Thus, every individual knows itself immediately as a thing-in-itself insofar as it appears as its own body. Ultimately, however, this individual will we feel within ourselves whenever we act, move, desire, etc. is a manifestation of a more primordial will that is the true unitary and indivisible substance of everything that comes into existence and passes away. We may think that knowledge must always be bound to individuality but it is this limitation that actually creates the need for philosophy in which we go beyond the merely individual and the particular and explore the universal and the eternal.

Why does Schopenhauer come to argue that the will is groundless? He draws a distinction between the motives of our willing, which are to be understood in terms of specific grounds and reasons, such as that I will "at this time" and "in this place," and the whole inner nature of willing in general which cannot be explained in terms of a law of motivation. This is to posit a distinction between a person's empirical character and their "intelligible" character. Schopenhauer argues that the character of each individual "corresponds" to a particular act of the will's objectification. It is this "act" which constitutes their intelligible character, while their empirical character is their manifest phenomenon. The latter is determined entirely by the former, which is the groundless will as thing-in-itself. In the course of an actual lifetime all the empirical character does is to "furnish a copy" of the intelligible one and it cannot deviate from the demand of its inmost nature (*WWR* 2, section 28). This is the case with respect to only what is essential about the character of any individual. For example, it is not essential whether a particular individual plays for nuts or for crowns, only that they cheat or play honestly. The former is the subject of accidental external influences, but the intelligible character determines the latter. So time, place, and circumstances inform the empirical character that any individual will shall take, but they cannot explain why a person has this will or why they will what they will. This is groundless because it resides outside of the province of the principle of sufficient reason. All individual action through motive is merely the phenomenal appearance of a groundless will. While physiology and mechanics can ably explain the empirical character of a body's actions and movements, then, there is something that they can never explain, namely, why there is movement and desire in the first place. Thus, the whole existence of the body and the sum total of its function are the objectifications of a will which cannot be simply "known." This constitutes the "permanent substratum" of an actual, individuated body. Schopenhauer goes so far as to claim that the different parts of the body merely correspond to the demands and desires of the will which manifests and expresses itself: "Teeth, gullet, and intestinal canal are objectified hunger; the genitals are objectified sexual impulse," and so on (section 20). That which is whole is that which will also be found in every one of its parts, a "blindly acting force of nature" or the will as thing-in-itself. Because we are creatures of forms of reflection we can only ever mis-recognize the true ground of our being – the groundless will acting within us.

There is a problem, however, in probing further than what is given to us in the domain of representation. If we take seriously the proposition that there is another aspect to the world to that which we perceive and conceive as subjects of representation, how are we to know anything of it since, by definition, it must be something wholly other and different? The task is to determine whether Schopenhauer has hit upon a genuine philosophical problem or has simply created a false problem. It is not, for him, a problem science can address, simply because materialism, which he holds to be the proper mode of science, cannot get beyond representation and gain access to the inmost nature of things. In "stupidly denying vital force," mechanistic materialism reduces life to an arithmetical problem. Science reduces the "what" of something, understood as the manner of its existence and true essence, to the "how"; but this "how" can only be on the level of appearance and thinkable in accordance with the PSR. Thus, what is left out of the picture is what the "how" is an appearance *of*, which cannot be explained in terms of the PSR. Schopenhauer is insistent that it is

possible through philosophy to make the transition from our representational conception of the will (the will that is guided by knowledge and has motives) to a completely different understanding of the will that is known "absolutely and immediately."
This is not the will simply as force but rather force subsumed under an unfamiliar
conception of the will and accessible to us through our own body. This will, therefore,
is not being thought under the operations of the representational intellect or consciousness. But what is to say it is not being thought merely negatively in terms of the mere
absence of those qualities we attribute to representation? This was Nietzsche's concern about Schopenhauer's metaphysics, and he expresses it as early as 1868.

Nietzsche believes that Schopenhauer articulates his theory of the will almost entirely
in terms of a series of abstract negations. The will is everything which does not belong
to representation (what belongs to representation are time, space, causality, plurality, etc.).
Nietzsche considers the "will" to be a clumsily coined and all-too-encompassing word.
He does not argue that a philosopher has no right to pursue the "dangerous Kantian
path" of the thing-in-itself, but draws attention to the fact that what Schopenhauer
puts in the place of the Kantian x, namely the will, is articulated in terms of a poetic
intuition, and the logical proofs that are offered in support of the theory fail to convince. Nietzsche argues that the world does not allow itself to be so easily fastened
into a system like Schopenhauer's, but also that Schopenhauer's recognition that the
most difficult problem of philosophy remained unsolved is correct. This is the question "concerning the borders of individuation."

Nietzsche further argues that Schopenhauer's pursuit of a philosophy of the will
assumes a "dictatorial tone," asserting a number of negative characteristics of the thing-
in-itself which lie outside the realm of knowledge. As Nietzsche notes, something that
can never be an object is nevertheless held to be a being that needs to be thought of
objectively. Schopenhauer seeks to ground his philosophy of the will not in terms of
some suprahuman intuition but by appealing to the affections and perceptions of our
own willing. But he fails to appreciate the contradictions this generates for his philosophy: this perception is a human perception and thus belongs to the phenomenal
realm of subject and object. Schopenhauer is positing a will that, as soon as it is spoken
of and thought about, must become an object for a subject. Nietzsche makes the point
even more strongly, arguing that the three principal predicates of the will conceived
as the thing-in-itself – unity, eternity or timelessness, and freedom (existing without cause) – are all inextricably bound up with our organization and it is, therefore,
highly doubtful if they have any meaning outside of the sphere of human cognition.
The criticisms of Schopenhauer that Nietzsche makes in this early piece inform much
of his subsequent thinking on the ontological predicament that Kant's philosophy had
opened up, and they find an echo in his later reflections on the duality of "real"
and "apparent" worlds which voice the suspicion that what is posited as the "real"
world is but the apparent world once again.

It is not simply Schopenhauer's metaphysics of the will and knowledge that
Nietzsche will take to task in his writings but also his ethics and aesthetics. In the
remaining two parts of *The World as Will and Representation* Schopenhauer goes on to
show how pure knowledge can exist as a "clear mirror of the world" in the form of
art, and teaches how it is possible to attain salvation from the world in the form
of a self-elimination of the will. The essential feature of the will, reflected in its
objectification in particular individuals, is that it is always striving but can never attain

satisfaction or find tranquility. "Eternal becoming, endless flux," Schopenhauer writes, "belong to the revelation of the essential nature of the will" (section 29). Happiness is really a form of pain, merely a temporary cessation of desire, and thus something always negative and never positive (it does not last and it cannot last). Moreover, each individual being strives to assert its own existence over other things, and thus the world is marked by conflict as a kind of permanent Hobbesian state of nature (the war of all against all). Schopenhauer's pessimism, his ethics and theories of art and the state, all follow from his metaphysics of the will. Nietzsche criticizes Schopenhauer for his pessimism and resignationism and develops a very different thinking of art.[10] In section 99 of *The Gay Science* he provides a succinct statement of his mature objections to Schopenhauer's thinking.

In spite of the fact that Nietzsche came to distance himself from Schopenhauer on so many key issues, the latter's thinking on life and representation continued to exert an influence on him. This can be seen in the manner in which he articulates the doctrine of the will to power in section 36 of *Beyond Good and Evil*, in terms of a "pre-form of life." Although the will to power is very different in character from the will to life, it remains the case for Nietzsche, following Schopenhauer, that the world cannot be made reducible entirely to the level of representation. This should not be taken to mean that the will to power is simply Nietzsche's name for the thing-in-itself or a simple substitution of what Schopenhauer called the will to life (Nietzsche posits a plurality of *wills* to power, there is no unitary will, and so on). Throughout his writings Nietzsche continues to position himself with regard to the Kantian legacy, and the reader will encounter a set of diverse and provocative thoughts on issues of life and representation, appearance, and the thing-in-itself running throughout his writings from beginning to end.

10   In *GS* 37 Nietzsche says that Schopenhauer was a pessimist as a "good European" and not simply as a German. In *BGE* 186, however, he questions – albeit in a witty fashion – whether Schopenhauer *really* was a pessimist.

1

Fate and History: Thoughts (1862)

Easter Vacation 1862

If we could look upon Christian doctrines and church-history in a free and impartial way, we would have to express several views that oppose those that are generally accepted. But confined as we are from our earliest days under the yoke of custom and prejudice and inhibited in the natural development of our spirit, determined in the formation of our temperament by the impressions of our childhood, we believe ourselves compelled to view it virtually as a transgression if we adopt a freer standpoint from which to make a judgment on religion and Christianity that is impartial and appropriate to our time.

Such an attempt is not the work of a few weeks, but of a lifetime.

How could one destroy the authority of two millennia and the security of the most perceptive men of all time as a consequence of youthful pondering? How could one dismiss all the sorrows and blessings of a religious development so deeply influential on world history by means of fantasies and immature ideas?

It is entirely impertinent to want to solve philosophical problems over which a conflict of opinion has waged for many millennia; to contest views that, according to the faith of ingenious men, first raised man to the level of true man; to unify natural science with philosophy without even knowing the fundamentals of either; or, finally, to construct a system of reality out of natural science and history even though the unity of world history and its most elementary foundations have not yet been revealed to the spirit.

It is folly and doom for undeveloped heads to venture out into the sea of doubt without compass and guide: most will be driven off course by storms; only very few discover new lands.

Out in the middle of the immense ocean of ideas one often longs to return to firm land. How often has the longing for natural science and history crept over me in the course of my fruitless speculations!

History and natural science, the wonderful legacies of our past, the harbingers of our future: They alone are the secure foundation upon which we can build the tower of our speculation.

How often has our entire previous philosophy seemed to me a tower of Babel. The goal of all great aspirations is to attain heaven, and "the kingdom of heaven on earth" means almost the same thing.

An endless confusion of thought in the people is the bleak result. There will be great revolutions once the masses finally realize that the totality of Christianity is grounded in presuppositions; the existence of God, immortality, Biblical authority, inspiration, and other doctrines will always remain problems. I have attempted to deny everything: Oh, pulling down is easy; but rebuilding! And pulling down seems easier than it is. We are determined in our innermost being by the impressions of our childhood, the influence of our parents, our educations. These deeply rooted prejudices are not so easily removed by reasoning or mere will. The power of habit, the need to strive for higher ideals, the break with all that is established, the dissolution of all forms of society, the question whether mankind hasn't been deceived for two thousand years by a phantom, the sense of one's arrogance and rashness: all struggle against one another in an uncertain strife until, finally, painful experiences and mournful events lead our heart back again to the old childhood beliefs. However, observing the impression that such doubts make on the mind must surely be a contribution to one's own cultural history. It is otherwise unthinkable that something should remain as a result of all this speculation, a result that cannot always be knowledge, but perhaps only a belief that may occasionally stimulate or oppress a moral feeling.

Just as custom appears as a consequence of an era, a people, a direction of spirit, so morality is the result of a universal development of mankind. It is the sum of all truths of our world. Perhaps it means no more in the infinite world than the consequence of our own spiritual direction. Perhaps a universal truth develops out of the results of truth in individual worlds!

We hardly know whether mankind itself is only a stage, a phase in the universal, in becoming; whether it is not merely a voluntary appearance of God. Is man not perhaps the development of stone through the medium of plant or animal? Could it be that perfection is already attained here, that herein lies history? Has this eternal becoming no end? What are the mainsprings that drive this great clockwork? They are hidden. But they are the same in the great clock we call history. Events are its face. From hour to hour the hand moves ahead; at twelve o'clock its course begins anew: a new world-period dawns.

And could one not call immanent humanity each mainspring? (Then both views would be reconciled.) Or do higher considerations guide the whole? Is man only the means, or is he the end?

Ends exist only for us. For us there is change. For us there are epochs and periods. How could we see higher planes? We only see how from a single source, from humanity itself, from ideas formed out of external impressions. We see how these acquire life and form, how they become a common good for all, conscience, a sense of duty. We see how the eternal productive drive shapes them, as raw material, into new ideas. We see how, through struggle, they intermix and how out of this combination new forms emerge. A struggling and undulating of the most diverse currents, ebbing and flowing, all to the eternal ocean.

Everything revolves around one another in monstrous, ever expanding circles. Man is one of the innermost circles. If man wants to estimate the oscillations of the outer circles, he must completely abstract from his own and from the nearest wider circle on to far-reaching ones. To find the common center of all oscillations, the infinitely small circle, is the task of natural science. Because man looks for the center in and for himself, we now know what a unique meaning history and natural science must have for us.

However, as man is carried away into the circle of world history, a contest is generated between the individual will and the general will. Here lies every important, unending problem: the question of justifying the individual to the people, the people to mankind, and of mankind to the world. And here, too, is the fundamental relationship of *fate* and *history*.

The highest comprehension of universal history is impossible for man. But great historians become like the great philosopher-prophets: both abstract from the inner circles to the outer ones. However, the place of fate has not yet been secured. We must cast our eye on human life in order to understand its justification both in regard to the individual and the collective.

What determines our happiness in life? Do we have to thank events whose whirlpool carries us away? Or is not our temperament, as it were, the coloration of events? Do we not encounter everything in the mirror of our personality? And do not events provide, as it were, only the key of our history while the strength or weakness with which it affects us depends merely on our temperament? Ask gifted doctors, Emerson says,[1] how much temperament decides, and what, in general, it does not decide?

But our temperament is nothing other than our mind, upon which the impressions of our relationships and experiences have been stamped. What is it that pulls the soul of so many men of power down to the commonplace, thereby hindering a higher flight of ideas? A fatalistic structure of skull and spine; the condition and nature of their parents; the triviality of their relationships; the commonness of their environment; even the monotony of their homeland. We have been influenced. And we lack the strength to react against this influence or even to recognize that we have been influenced. It is a painful feeling to have given up one's independence through an unconscious acceptance of external impressions, stifling the capacity of the soul through force of habit, and enduring the planting of the seeds of abberations within the soul and against the will.

On a larger scale we find this repeated in the history of peoples. Many people affected by the same events have been influenced by them in the most diverse ways.

It is narrow-minded, therefore, to want to force the whole of mankind into some specific form of state or society, into stereotypes, as it were. All socialist and communist conceptions lead to this error. Mankind is never the same twice. If it became possible completely to demolish the entire past through a strong will, we would immediately be transported into the realm of autonomous gods, and world history would suddenly be for us nothing but a dreamy self-deception: the curtain falls, and man finds himself like a child playing with worlds, like a child who awakens at the glow of dawn and, laughing, wipes the terrible dreams from his brow.

Free will appears as unfettered, deliberate; it is boundlessly free, wandering, the spirit. But fate is a necessity: unless we believe that world history is a dream-error, the unspeakable sorrows of mankind fantasies, and that we ourselves are but the toys of our fantasies. Fate is the boundless force of opposition against free will. Free will without fate is just as unthinkable as spirit without reality, good without evil. Only antithesis creates the quality.

---

1   For the importance of Nietzsche's reading of the American philosopher Ralph Waldo Emerson (1803–82) to these early essays, see the introduction to Part I.

Fate always prescribes the principle: "Events are determined by events." If this were the only true principle, man would be the plaything of dark, effective forces, not responsible for his mistakes, completely free from moral distinctions, a necessary link in a chain. And it would benefit him not to see through his condition, if he didn't convulsively twitch in the chains that bind him, if he didn't try, with mad desire, to disarrange the world and its mechanism.

Perhaps, in similar fashion, as spirit is only the smallest infinitesimal substance, the good is only the most subtle evolution of evil, so, perhaps, free will is nothing but the highest potency of fate. World history is, then, the history of matter, if one takes the meaning of these words in the broadest sense. For it is necessary that there be yet higher principles into which all distinctions flow together in a great unity, in which all development is in stages: everything flowing into a monstrous ocean wherein once again all the levers of development of the world unite, consolidate, all-one. –

2

Freedom of Will and Fate
(1862)

Freedom of will, in itself nothing but freedom of thought, is also circumscribed in a similar way as is freedom of thought. Thoughts cannot go beyond the boundary of the circle of ideas. But the circle of ideas is based upon mastered intuitions that can, with amplification, grow and become stronger without going beyond the limits determined by the brain. Likewise, freedom of will is capable of enhancement within the limits of the same farthest point. It is another matter to put the will to work. The capacity for this is dispensed to us in a fatalistic way.

Because fate appears to man in the mirror of his own personality, individual freedom of will and individual fate are well-matched opponents. We find that people believing in fate are distinguished by force and strength of will; whereas men and women who, according to an inverted comprehension of Christian tenets, let things happen (since "God will make everything turn out right") allow themselves, in a degrading manner, to be presided over by circumstances. In general, "Surrender to the will of God" and "humility" are often only a cloak for the timid cowardice to confront destiny with decisiveness.

But if fate, as a limit-determination, still seems more powerful than free will, there are two things we should not forget: first, that fate is only an abstract concept, a force without matter; that for the individual there is only an individual fate; that fate is nothing else but a chain of events; that man, as soon as he acts, creates his own events, determines his own fate; that, in general, events, insofar as they affect him, are, consciously or unconsciously, brought about by himself and must suit him. The activity of man, however, does not first begin with birth. But already with the embryo and perhaps – who can be certain here – already with his parents and forefathers. All of you who believe in the immortality of the soul, unless you are willing to allow the development of the mortal out of something immortal or are willing to grant that the soul flies about in thin air until it is at last lodged in a body, must also believe in the pre-existence of the soul. The Hindu says: Fate is nothing but the acts we have committed in a prior state of our being.

How can you refute the claim that one has not already acted with consciousness for eternity? Out of the wholly undeveloped consciousness of the child? Can we not otherwise insist that our actions always stand in relation to our consciousness? As Emmerson [*sic*] says:

Thought is always compatible
With the thing that is apparent as its expression.[1]

Can a tone, in general, touch us if there is no corresponding string in us? Or, expressed differently, can we receive an impression in our brain if our brain is not already endowed with a receptivity for that purpose?

Likewise, free will is only an abstraction indicating the capacity to act consciously; whereas by fate we understand the principle that we are under the sway of unconscious acts. Action in and for itself always presses, at the same time, an activity of the soul, a tendency of the will, an object that we do not yet need to keep an eye on. In conscious action we allow ourselves to be ruled as much or as little by impressions as by the unconscious. One often says about a successful act: I've hit upon this by accident. By no means need this always be true. The activity of the soul continues undiminished even if we do not observe it with the mind's eye.

We often, in a similar way, think that if we shut our eyes in broad daylight, the sun no longer shines. But its effects on us, the liveliness of its light, its gentle warmth, never stop even if we no longer perceive it directly.

Therefore, if the concept of unconscious action is not merely taken as a submission to earlier impressions, then the strict distinction between fate and free will disappears and both concepts fuse with the idea of individuality.

The more things move away from the inorganic, and the more the structure extends, the more pronounced individuality becomes and the more manifold its qualities. Spontaneous, inner power and external impressions – its levers of development –, what are they other than freedom of will and fate?

In freedom of will lies, for the individual, the principle of emancipation, the separation from the whole, absolute limitlessness. But fate places man once more in an organic relation to the total development and requires him, insofar as it seeks to dominate him, to a free counteractive development. Absolute freedom of will, absent fate, would make man into a god; the fatalistic principle would make him an automaton.

---

1   The opening of Emerson's essay "Fate" (in *The Conduct of Life*, 1860), in the German translation by E. S. von Mühlberg (*Die Führung des Lebens*, 1862).

3

My Life
(1863)

How can we produce a picture of the life and character of a person we have come to know? In the same way, generally speaking, as we produce a picture of a place we once saw. We have to recall its physiognomical characteristics: the nature and shape of its mountains, its plant and animal life, the azure of its sky, all this taken together determines the impression we receive. But it is not precisely that which first meets the eye – the mountain ranges, the forms of cliffs and rocks – which in itself gives a place its physiognomical character: in different zones of the earth, however, they may attract or repel when taken as a whole, similar species of rock, the same forms of inorganic nature, step forth in accordance with the same laws. It is different with the inorganic [error for organic]. Especially in the plant world do there lie the subtlest clues for the comparative study of nature.

Something similar applies if we seek to survey a human life and to appreciate it correctly. We ought not to be guided by chance events, the gifts of fortune, the changing external eventualities which arise from conflicting external circumstances, when, like mountain peaks, they leap first to the eye. It is precisely those little events and inner occurrences we believe we have to neglect which in their totality reveal the individual character most clearly, they grow organically out of the nature of the man, while the former appear only in inorganic connection with him.

After this introduction it seems as though I intended to write a book about my life. Never. I wish only to indicate how I want the following sketches from my life to be understood: namely, in the way a gifted naturalist recognises, in his collections of plants and stones ordered according to the zone of the earth from which they came the history and character of each of them, while the ignorant child finds in them only stones and plants to play with, and the man who seeks only what is useful in things looks down on them as something purposeless and unserviceable as food or clothing.

As a plant I was born close to the churchyard, as a man in a parsonage.

And does this explain this schoolmasterly tone? Possibly, but I am not apologising for it on that account. But what better can an introduction to a life do than teach if the life itself does not teach? And these following brief biographical notes can neither teach nor entertain; they are polished stones; in reality these stones are nicely clothed in moss and earth.

Along the highway that runs from Weissenfels through Lützen to Leipzig there lies the village of Röcken. It is enclosed all around with plantations of willows and single-standing poplars and elm trees, so that from a distance only the projecting chimneys and the ancient church tower can be seen peeping through the green treetops. Within the village there extend several largish ponds separated from one another only by narrow strips of land; bright verdure and gnarled willows all around. Somewhat higher up there lies the personage and the church, the former surrounded by gardens and plantations of trees. Close by is the edge of the cemetery, full of sunken gravestones and crosses. The parsonage itself is shaded by three finely formed, wide-branched acacias.

Here I was born on 15th October 1844, and received, as was appropriate to my birthday, the names Friedrich Wilhelm.[1] The earliest event which happened to me as I awakened to consciousness was the illness of my father. It was a softening of the brain. His increasing suffering, his growing blindness, his wasted figure, my mother's tears, the physician's anxious demeanour, finally the incautious remarks of the people of the village, led me to fear that misfortune threatened. And this misfortune in fact appeared. My father died. I was not yet four years old.

A few months later I lost my only brother, a lively and gifted child who, suddenly attacked by cramps, was in a very short time dead.

Thus we had to leave our home; on the evening of the last day I was still playing with several other children, and then had to bid farewell to them, as I did to all the places I loved. I could not sleep; I tossed and turned on my bed, and towards midnight I got up. Several laden carts were standing in the yard, which was illumined by the feeble light of a lantern. As soon as morning dawned the horses were harnessed; through the morning mist we drove off to Naumburg, the goal of our journey. Here, at first intimidated, afterwards somewhat livelier, but always with the dignity of a thorough little philistine, I began to become acquainted with life and with books. Here I also learned to love nature in its fair mountains and its river valleys, halls and castles, and mankind in my friends and relations.

The time for me to attend the Gymnasium arrived, and with it new interests and endeavours. In particular my inclination for music began to show itself at this time, despite the fact that the earliest instruction I received in it was wholly calculated to destroy it at its roots. For my first teacher was a precentor infected with all the amiable failings of a precentor, and in addition those of a *precentor emeritus*.

With becoming tardiness and regularity I finally attained the fourth form. It was certainly time for one to emerge from the home circle and finally to break free from the endlessly impractical courses one was accustomed to follow. I contained the wisdom of several lexicons, every possible inclination awoke in me, I wrote poems and tragedies, blood-curdling and unbelievably boring, tormented myself with the composition of complete orchestral scores, and had grown so obsessed with the idea of appropriating universal knowledge and universal capability that I was in danger of becoming a real muddle-head and fantasist.

It was thus beneficial in many ways as a boarder at Landesschule Pforta to devote oneself for six years to a greater concentration of one's forces and to directing them to firm goals.

1 Appropriate because October 15 was also the birthday of Friedrich Wilhelm IV, the reigning king of Prussia.

I do not yet have these six years behind me; but I can nonetheless already regard the products of this time as completed, for I feel their effects in everything I now undertake.

Thus I can look back with gratitude upon almost everything, whether it be joy or sorrow, that has happened to me, and events have up to now led me along like a child.

Perhaps it is time to seize the reins of events oneself and step out into life.

And thus man outgrows everything that once embraced him; he has no need to burst the fetters, for, if a god should command it, they fall away of themselves; and where is the ring that finally encloses him? Is it the world? Is it God? –

F. W. Nietzsche,
written on 18th September 1863

4

On Moods

(1864)

Let the reader imagine me sitting at home, wrapped in a dressing gown, on the evening of the first day of Easter. A fine rain is falling outside, and I am alone in the room. I stare for a long time at the blank sheet of paper lying in front of me, pen in hand, vexed by the confused crowd of things, events, and thoughts all demanding to be written down. Some of them are tempestuous in their demands, being young still and effervescent like new wine; but in opposition to these many an old, ripened, clarified thought arises, like an old master who surveys the strivings of the youthful world with an equivocal eye. Let us say it openly: our temperament is conditioned by the conflict between these old and new worlds, and the current situation of the conflict is what we call 'mood' or also, with some disdain, 'temper'.

Like a good diplomat I rise above the quarreling parties and describe the state of the commonwealth with the impartiality of a man who every day attends inadvertently the sessions of all the parties, applying in practice the very principle that he mocks and scorns from the rostrum.

Let us admit it: I am writing about moods, insofar as I am right now *in* a certain mood; and it is fortunate that I am just in the mood for describing moods.

Today I played Liszt's *Consolations* many times over, and now I feel how its tones have penetrated my being and continue, spiritualized, to resonate within me. I recently underwent a painful experience that had to do with a parting or a not-parting, and now I notice how this feeling and those tones have fused together, and I see that the music would not have appealed to me had I not just had this experience. So the soul strives to attract what is like it, and the current mass of feelings squeezes like a lemon the new events that impinge upon the heart, but always in such a way that only a part of what is new fuses with what is old, and a residue is left over which is not yet able to find anything related to it in the household of the soul, and thus lodges here alone, quite often to the displeasure of the older residents with whom it often comes into conflict. But look! Here comes a friend, there a book is opening, a girl passes by. Listen! Music! Already new guests are streaming in from all sides into the house that stands open to all, and the one who was just now standing alone finds many noble relatives.

It is quite marvellous: it is not that the guests come because they want to, nor that the guests come as they are; but rather those guests come who must, and indeed only those who must come. Anything the soul *cannot* reflect simply does not touch it; but since it does not lie within the power of the will to make the soul reflect or not, the soul is touched only by what it wants. And that seems absurd to many people: for they recall how there are many sensations that they resist. But what is it that ultimately determines the will? Or how often the will sleeps and only the drives and desires are awake! But one of the strongest desires of the soul is a certain curiosity, a taste for the unusual, which explains why we often allow ourselves moods that are unpleasant.

But it is not only through the will that the soul assimilates things: the soul is composed of the same or similar stuff as experiences, and thus it is that an event which finds no sympathetic resonance can lie so heavily on the soul as a burdensome mood, and can eventually assume such a preponderance that it compresses and constricts the other contents of the soul.

Moods thus arise either from inner conflicts or else from external pressure on the inner world. Here there is a civil war between two enemy camps, there an oppression of the populace by a particular class, a small minority.

Often, when I eavesdrop on my own thoughts and feelings and silently attend to myself, it is as if I heard the hum and buzzing of those wild factions, as if there were a rushing through the air as when a thought or an eagle flies to the sun.

Conflict is the constant nourishment of the soul, and the soul knows how to extract from it much that is sweet and fine. The soul destroys and thereby gives birth to new things, it fights energetically and yet gently draws the opponent over to its own side for an intimate union. And the most marvellous thing is that it never pays attention to the exterior – names, persons, places, fine words, handwriting are all relatively unimportant – but it treasures what lies within the covering.

That which is perhaps now your whole happiness or your entire sorrow may soon turn out to be only the garment of a yet deeper feeling, and will thus disappear when the greater thing comes. And thus our moods deepen themselves continually: no one of them is quite the same as the next, but each is unfathomably young and the birth of the moment.

I think of many a thing that I used to love; names and persons changed, and I don't want to claim that in actuality their natures would have become ever more beautiful and profound. What is true, though, is that each one of these similar moods signifies a step forward for me, and that for the spirit it is intolerable to go through the same stages again that it has already gone through: it wants to keep on extending itself into the depths and heights.

Dear moods, I salute you, marvellous variations of a tempestuous soul, as manifold as nature itself, but more magnificent than nature, since you eternally transcend yourselves and strive eternally upwards, whereas the plant still exhales the same fragrance it did on the day of creation. I no longer love as I loved some weeks ago; I am no longer this moment in the mood I was in as I began to write.

First I tried it in music, but it didn't work: the heart stormed on, and the music remained dead. Then I tried in verse: no, rhyme failed to capture it, at least not calm and measured rhythms. Away with the paper: take a new sheet, and now pen quickly scribble, ink – quick – here!

Mild summer evening, twilight streaked with pallor. Children's voices in the lanes, in the distance noise and music. A fair: people are dancing, colourful lanterns blaze, wild animals growl; here a shot rings out, there a rattle of drums, steady and insistent.

Inside the room it is darker. I light a lamp, but the eye of the day looks inquisitively through the half-drawn curtains. It would like to see farther, right into the middle of this heart which – hotter than the light, duskier than the evening, more animated than the voices in the distance – reverberates deep within, like a huge bell sounded in a storm.

And I implore a thunderstorm; does the tolling of the bell not attract the lightning? Now, you approaching thunderstorm, clarify, purify, blow fragrances of rain into my dull nature; welcome, at last, welcome!

There! You first bolt of lightning, there you flash, right into my heart; and from it arises something like a long, pale column of mist. Do you know it, the dark, treacherous one? My eye is already brighter, and I stretch my hand out after it, as if to curse. The thunder growls, and a voice rang out: 'Be cleansed!'

Heavy sultriness; my heart swells. Nothing moves. There – a light breath, on the ground the grass trembles – welcome, rain, soother, my saviour! Here it is desert, empty, dead: plant anew!

There! A second bolt! Dazzling and two-edged, right into my heart! And a voice rang out: 'Hope!'

A gentle fragrance rises from the ground, a wind comes up, and the storm follows, howling in pursuit of its prey. It drives broken-off blossoms before it, as the rain swims joyfully after.

Right through the middle of my heart. Storm and rain! Thunder and lightning! Right through the middle! And a voice rang out: 'Become new!'

5

On Schopenhauer
(1868)

An attempt to explain the world by an accepted factor.

The thing in itself becomes one of its possible forms.

The attempt fails.

Schopenhauer did not consider it an attempt.

His thing in itself was opened up by him.

That he did not see this failure can be explained, in that he did not want to feel the dark contradictoriness in the region where individuality ceases to be.

He did not trust his judgment.

Places.

The dark drive brought about through a representation mechanism reveals itself as world. This drive is not included under the *principium individuationis*.[1]

I

The title page of *The World as Will and Representation* already discloses to us what Schopenhauer claims to have performed for mankind through this work.

The most longed after question of all metaphysicians as Goethe said it, the "if not" – was daringly answered by him with Yes: and so that the new knowledge be noticed far and wide like a temple inscription, he wrote the redeeming formula for the oldest and most important riddle of the world as a title on the brow of his book, The World as Will and Representation.

The so-called solution then:

In order to comfortably get ahold of in what the redeeming and explanatory elements of this formula are to be found, it is recommended that they be transposed partly into images:

The groundless, unknowing will reveals itself, through a representation mechanism, as world.

When we subtract from this sentence, what passed to Schopenhauer as the legacy of the great Kant, a legacy which he always, in his grand manner, regarded with the most proper respect: there remains the one word "will" along with its predicates. It

1 Latin: principle of individuation. See Schopenhauer's *magnum opus*, *Die Welt als Wille und Vorstellung* (*The World as Will and Representation*, 1819/44), vol. 1: 2. 23 and 4. 68.

is a clumsily coined, very encompassing word, when with it such an important thought, going well beyond Kant, is to be labelled differently. A thought so important that its discoverer could say of it that he considered it to be that "which has been sought for a very long time under the name of philosophy, and that whose discovery is for this very reason regarded by those versed in history as just as impossible as the discovery of the philosophers' stone."

In light of this, we remember that to Kant as well, a no less questionable discovery appeared as a great, as the greatest, most fruitful deed of his life, achieved by means of the old-fashioned table of categories, even though with the important difference that with the conclusion of "the most difficult thing that could be undertaken on behalf of metaphysics", Kant admired himself as a force of nature powerfully bursting forth and received consecration to appear "as reformer of philosophy",[2] in contrast to which Schopenhauer at all times thanks the inspired thoughtfulness and power of clarity of his intellect for his supposed find.

The errors of great men are worth honoring because they are more fruitful than the truths of small men.

If we now turn to the above quoted sentence, to dissect and probe the essence of the Schopenhauerian system, no thought remains farther from us than to attack Schopenhauer himself, to triumphantly parade before his eyes the individual pieces of his proofs and, at the end, to raise the question how in the world a man can reach such a level of pretension with a system so full of holes.

II

In fact it is not to be denied, that the clause which we offered above as the essence of the Schopenhauerian system, can be attacked very successfully from four sides.

1. The first, and most general – aimed at Schopenhauer only in so far as he did not here, where it was necessary, go beyond Kant – aims at the concept of the thing in itself and sees in it, to speak with Überweg,[3] "only a hidden category".

2. Although one should give Schopenhauer the right to follow that dangerous Kantian path, yet that which he puts in place of the Kantian x, the will, is only born with the help of a poetic intuition, while the attempted logical proofs cannot satisfy either Schopenhauer or us. (See *Die Welt als Wille und Vorstellung* (*WWV*), pp. 125, 131; *WWR* 1, pp. 103, 109.)[4]

2   Quotation from Friedrich Albert Lange's *Geschichte des Materialismus* (*History of Materialism*, 1866).

3   Friedrich Überweg (1826–71), author of the three-volume *Grundriss der Geschichte der Philosophie von Thales bis auf die Gegenwart* (*History of Philosophy in Outline, from Thales to the Present*, 1867).

4   Nietzsche cites *Die Welt als Wille und Vorstellung* in the third edition of 1859 (abbreviated *WWV*); additional references by the translator are to the English translation in two volumes (*The World as Will and Representation*, abbreviated *WWR*) by E. F. J. Payne (New York: Dover, 1969). An alternative translation of this essay by Christopher Janaway, featuring additional notes, can be found as appendix I to his edited volume *Willing and Nothingness: Schopenhauer as Nietzsche's Educator* (Oxford: Clarendon Press, 1998), pp. 258–65.

3. Thirdly, we are compelled to guard against the predicates which Schopenhauer ascribes to his will, which for something simply unthinkable sound much too certain and all stem from the contradiction to the world of representation: while between the thing in itself and its appearance not even the concept of this opposition has any meaning.

4. Nevertheless one could posit, to the credit of Schopenhauer, against all three objections a possibility of threefold power: There may be a thing in itself, however, only in the sense that in the subject area of transcendence all is possible which at some-time was hatched in a philosopher's brain. This possible thing in itself can be the will: a possibility, which because it arises out of the joining of two possibilities, is nothing more than the negative power of the first possibility, in other words, already a good step toward the other pole, which signifies impossibility. We heighten this concept of an always decreasing possibility once again, in that we admit the predicates of the will, which Schopenhauer took to belong to it: just because an opposition is unprov-able between thing in itself and appearance but can still be thought. Against such a knot of possibilities every ethical thought could explain itself: but even against this ethical pretext one could still object that the thinker who stands before the riddle of the world, has no other means than to guess in the hope that a moment of height-ened awareness will place the word upon his lips. A word which offers the key to that text lying before all eyes still unread, which we call world. Whether this world is will? – Here is the point at which we must make our fourth attack. The Schopenhauerian warp and weft gets tangled in his hands: in the smallest part as a result of a certain tactical clumsiness of its author, but mostly because the world does not let itself be so easily fastened into the system as Schopenhauer had hoped in the first inspiration of discovery. In his old age he complained that the most difficult problem of philosophy had not been solved in his own. He meant the question concerning the borders of individuation.

III

Further, a certain species of that contradiction with which the Schopenhauerian sys-tem is perforated, will occupy us on occasion; a species of extremely important and hardly avoidable contradictions, which to a certain extent while still resting under their mother's heart arm themselves and, scarcely born, do their first deed by killing her. They concern themselves collectively with the borders of individuation and have their $\pi\rho\tilde{\omega}\tau o\nu\ \psi(\epsilon\tilde{\upsilon}\delta o\varsigma)$[5] in the point considered under 3. above. "The will as thing in itself" said Schopenhauer (*WWV* 1, p. 134), "is quite different from its phenomenon, and is entirely free from all the forms of the phenomenon into which it first passes when it appears, and which therefore concern only its objectivity, and are foreign to the will itself. Even the most universal form of all representation, that of object for subject, does not concern it, still less the forms that are subordinate to this and collectively have their common expression in the principle of sufficient reason. As we know, time and space belong to this principle, and consequently plurality as well, which exists and has become possible only through them. In this last respect I shall call time and space the *principium individuationis*, an expression borrowed from the old scholasticism" (*WWR* 1, p. 112). In this description, which we meet in countless variations in

---

5   Greek: *proton ps(eudos)*, false first premise.

Schopenhauer's writings, what surprises is its dictatorial tone, which asserts a number of *negative* characteristics of the thing in itself which lies completely outside the sphere of knowledge, and which does not remain in accord with the assertion that it is not subject to the most universal form of knowledge, namely, to be object for a subject. Schopenhauer expresses this himself: *WWV* 1, p. 131: "this thing in itself (. . .), which as such is never object, since all object is its mere appearance or phenomenon, and not it itself, *is to be thought of objectively*, then we must *borrow its name and concept* from an object, from something in some way objectively given, and therefore from one of its phenomena" (*WWR* 1, p. 110). Schopenhauer demands that something, which can never be an object, nevertheless should be thought of objectively: a path which can only lead to an apparent objectivity, in so far as a completely dark and ungraspable x is draped with predicates, as with colorful clothes, which are taken from the world of phenomena, a world foreign to it. The demand follows, that we take the draped clothes, namely the predicates for the thing in itself: for that is what the sentence means: "if it is to be thought objectively, it must borrow its name and concept from an object." The concept "the thing in itself" is then removed, "because it should be so", and another is secretly pressed into our hands.

The borrowed name and concept is the will, "because it is the clearest and most developed appearance of the thing in itself, which is most directly illuminated by knowledge." But that does not concern us here: more important for us is that all the predicates of the will are also borrowed from the world of appearance. True, Schopenhauer makes here and there the attempt to describe the sense of these predicates as completely ungraspable and transcendent, for example, *WWV* 2, p. 368: "The unity of that will . . . in which we have recognized the inner being of the phenomenal world, is a metaphysical unity. Consequently, knowledge of it is transcendent; that is to say, it does not rest on the functions of our intellect, and is therefore not to be really grasped with them" (*WWR* 2, p. 323). Compare *WWV* 1, p. 134, 132, *WWR* 1, pp. 110–12. On the basis of the whole Schopenhauerian system, in particular because of the first description of it in the first book of *WWV* we persuade ourselves, however, that where he wishes, he allows himself the human and completely non-transcendental use of unity of the will, and really only then goes back to that transcendence where the holes in the system present themselves as obvious to him. It is then with this "unity" as it is with the "will", they are predicates of things in themselves taken from the world of appearance under which the actual essence, that transcendental evaporates. What is valid even of the three predicates of unity, eternity (that means timelessness), freedom (that means causelessness), is valid for the thing in itself: they are all indivisibly knotted together with our organization, so that it is completely doubtful whether they have any meaning outside of the human sphere of knowledge. That they should belong to the thing in itself, while their opposites dominate the world of appearances, that neither Kant nor Schopenhauer will prove for us, yes, not even make plausible for us, the latter because his thing in itself, the will, with those three predicates, cannot get along and manage, rather it is continually required to borrow from the world of appearance, that is, to transfer the concepts of multiplicity, temporality, and causality to itself.

In contrast he is fully correct when he says that (*WWV* 1, p. 118) "from outside one can never come close to the essence of things: no matter how one searches one wins only images and names" (*WWR* 1, p. 99).

IV

The will appears; how could it appear? Or to ask it another way: where does the representation mechanism come from through which the will appears? Schopenhauer answers with a curious turn of expression, in that he indicates the intellect as the μηχανή[6] of the will: *WWV* 2, p. 315: "The growth of the development of the brain has come about by the ever increasing and more complicated need of the corresponding appearances of the will" (*WWR* 2, p. 279). "Knowledge and the conscious ego are at basis tertiary, in that they presuppose the organism, but the organism presupposes the will" (*WWV* 2, p. 314; *WWR* 2, p. 278). Schopenhauer posits then a hierarchical progression of representations of the will with ever increasing needs of existence: in order to satisfy these, nature uses a matching progression of tools among which the intellect, from its first dawning feelings to its extreme clarity, has a place. From such a point of view a world of appearance is placed before the world of appearance: if we wish to hold fast to the Schopenhauerian *termini* concerning the thing in itself. Even before the appearance of intellect we see the *principium individuationis*, the law of causality in full effect. The will grasps life in haste and searches everywhere for ways to appear; it begins modestly with the lowest steps and rises to a certain extent from the ranks. In this region of the Schopenhauerian system everything is already dissolved in words and images: from the primal determination of things in themselves, almost all, except the memory is lost. And where memory takes root, it serves only to place the completed contradiction in full light of day. Par. II. p. 150[7] "That all life on earth did not exist in any consciousness at all, either in their own because they had none or in the consciousness of another because no such consciousness existed . . . that is, they did not exist at all; but then what does their having existed signify? At bottom, it is merely *hypothetical*, namely, *if* a consciousness had existed in those primeval times, then such events would have appeared in it; thus far does the *regressus* of phenomena lead us. And so it lay in the very nature of the thing in itself to manifest itself in such events." (PP 2: 140). They are, as Schopenhauer says on the same page, only "translations into the language of our observing intellect."

But, if we ask after these prudent considerations, how was it once possible that the intellect arose? The existence of the last step before the appearance of the intellect is certainly as hypothetical as that of earlier ones, that means it was not in existence because consciousness was not in existence. With the next step, consciousness is supposed to appear, that means out of a non-existing world the flower of knowledge is to suddenly and directly break forth. This is also to have happened in a sphere of timelessness and spacelessness without the mediation of causality: what stems out of such an otherworldly world, however, must itself – after Schopenhauer's reasoning – be thing in itself: either the intellect must rest as a new predicate eternally joined with the thing in itself; or there can be no intellect because at no time could an intellect have become.

But one exists: it follows that it could not be a tool of the world of appearance, as Schopenhauer would have it, but rather thing in itself, that is, will.

6   Greek: *mechane*, instrument.
7   The reference is to Schopenhauer's *Parerga und Paralipomena* (*Parerga and Paralipomena*, 1851) in the second edition of 1862, trans. E. F. J. Payne in two volumes (Oxford: Clarendon Press, 1974).

The Schopenhauerian thing in itself would therefore become simultaneously the *principium individuationis* and basis of necessitation: in other words: the present world. Schopenhauer wanted to find an equation for the x: and it revealed itself out of his calculation that it = x, that means that he did not find it.

5. Ideas

6. Character

7. Teleology and its opposite

8.

One should take note with what caution Schopenhauer avoided the question of the origin of intellect: as soon as we come into the region of this question and secretly hope, that it will now come, he hides himself to some extent behind clouds: although it is apparent that the intellect in the Schopenhauerian sense already presupposes a world caught in the *principium individuationis* and the laws of causality. Once, as far as I can see, this admission lay upon his tongue: but he swallows it again in such a curious manner, that we need to look at it closer. *WWV* 2, p. 310. "Now if in the objective comprehension of the intellect we go back as far as we can, we shall find that the necessity or need of *knowledge in general* arises from the plurality and *separate* existence of beings, from individuation. For let us imagine that there exists only a *single* being, then such a being needs no knowledge, because there would not then exist anything different from that being itself, – anything whose existence such a being would therefore have to take up into itself only indirectly through knowledge, in other words, nothing foreign that could be apprehended as object. On the other hand, with the plurality of beings, every individual finds itself in a state of isolation from all the rest, and from this arises the necessity for knowledge. The nervous system, by means of which the animal individual first of all becomes conscious of itself, is bounded by a skin; yet in the brain raised to intellect, it crosses this boundary by means of its form of knowledge, causality, and in this way perception arises for it as a consciousness of *other* things, as a picture or image of beings in space and time, which change in accordance with causality." (*WWR* 2, p. 274).

Part II
Early Writings

Introduction

The Birth of Tragedy is Nietzsche's first published book and appeared at the beginning of 1872, when he was 27 years old and had been Professor of Classical Philology at the University of Basel for three years. In its first edition its full title was *The Birth of Tragedy from the Spirit of Music*. A second edition containing slight textual amendments was printed in 1874 and eventually appeared in 1878. In 1886, however, the two earlier editions were reissued with a new title page, as *The Birth of Tragedy; Or, Hellenism and Pessimism*.[1] The original full title of the work bears testimony to Nietzsche's initial investment in the philosophy of Schopenhauer and the art of Wagner, in both cases to the "spirit of music" that informs their work. The second subtitle Nietzsche gave to the work in 1886 reflects his mature position, when he had fundamentally changed his appreciation of both.

As Douglas Smith has noted in the introduction to his translation of the text (from which our selection has been made), Nietzsche is conducting what is essentially a double argument in it. On the one hand we find a controversial argument about the origin and decline of Greek tragedy; on the other, we encounter an impassioned tract arguing in favor of a regeneration of contemporary German culture in the wake of the Franco-Prussian War. What links the two arguments together is the role Nietzsche ascribes to music: Greek tragedy is born of music, and Nietzsche places his hopes for cultural renewal in Wagnerian music-drama. In his book of 1870 on Beethoven, written to commemorate the centenary of the composer's birth and during the time he was developing an intimate rapport with Nietzsche and his ideas, Wagner argues that music can be understood only through the category of the sublime. In his text, Wagner celebrates music because it gives us more than the beautiful and more than *Schein* or appearance (the domain of the plastic arts), that is, more than the merely pleasing which flatters our senses. For Wagner music excites in us the highest ecstasies and proceeds, he says, "without all manner of return": with music we do not return to ourselves but go beyond and out of ourselves, so gaining a consciousness of our boundlessness. In *The World as Will and Representation* Schopenhauer argues that music is a unique art because of its non-representational nature: music can bypass the superficial and apparent world (a world of representation) and provide us with access to the world

---

1   For full details on the publication histories of all Nietzsche's works, see William H. Schaberg, *The Nietzsche Canon: A Publication History and Bibliography* (Chicago and London: University of Chicago Press, 1995).

in its essence, the world as will. These arguments are at work in Nietzsche's first published book. As the unmediated language of the will, music, for Nietzsche, provides immediate insight into the Dionysian "truth" of existence. The tragic cannot be deduced from the aesthetic category of appearance and the beautiful, but only, Nietzsche argues, on the basis of the "spirit of music." Only through this spirit do we encounter the joy experienced in the destruction of the individual. The Dionysian "truth" of eternal life, also conceived by Nietzsche in terms of "the eternally creative original mother," shows itself in individual examples of annihilation. The eternal joy of existence can only be sought not *in* phenomena (*Erscheinungen*) but *behind* them. At the same time, however, Nietzsche wishes to argue and show us that the original unity needs "the pleasurable appearance [*Schein*], for its continual redemption" (*BT* 4).

The argument of the book opens with Nietzsche defining two competing but also complementary impulses in Greek culture, the duality of the Apollonian and the Dionysian. The first takes its name from Apollo, the god of light (*der Scheinende*, the shining one), dream, and prophecy, while the second takes its name from Dionysus, the god of intoxication and rapture (*Rausch*). While Apollo is associated with visible form, comprehensible knowledge, and moderation, Dionysus is linked with formless flux, mystical intuition, and excess. Furthermore, while the Apollonian world is one of distinct individuals, the Dionysian world is one where these separate individual identities have been dissolved and human beings find themselves reconciled with the elemental energies of nature. Through Dionysian rapture we become part of a single, living being with whose joy in eternal creation we are fused. In artistic terms, Apollo is the god of the plastic or representational arts (painting and sculpture) and has a strong association with architecture, while Dionysus is the god of the non-representational art of music, which is without physical form. One of the innovative aspects of Nietzsche's argument in the book is the way in which it contests the idealized image of the Greeks which had been handed down and which depicted ancient Greek culture as one of serenity and calm grandeur. Nietzsche seeks to show that the calm Apollonian surface of Greek art and culture is the product of a long and complex wrestling with the tragic insights afforded by the Dionysian state. In Nietzsche's argument the monumental achievement of the Attic tragedy of the fifth century B.C., contained in the work of tragedians like Aeschylus and Sophocles, amounts to a fusion of the Apollonian and the Dionysian. Nietzsche's book is a search for an adequate knowledge of the union between the two artistic powers (a union he calls a "mystery") and of the origin (*Ursprung*) of Greek tragedy. Among other things, the search leads him to an examination of the main tendencies of Greek poetry (Homer, Archilochus, and Pindar) and of the tragic chorus. Here Nietzsche accepts the prevailing Aristotelian view that tragedy has its origins in the chorus, and he also accepts the argument (found in Schiller, for example) that the chorus serves as a barrier between the real, empirical world and the tragic action taking place on stage. But he dissents markedly from the view that the chorus is a representation of the spectators on stage; rather, Nietzsche sees the chorus as representative of the Dionysian state and its insight that life remains indestructible and pleasurable in the face of the suffering, anguish, and death that characterize our existence as discrete individuals.

The selection featured here is designed to capture something of the essential movements at work in Nietzsche's text: the duality of Dionysus and Apollo, the quest for an adequate comprehension of this union and the origin of tragedy, the argument on the decline of tragedy at the hands of Euripides and Socrates, the critique of Alexandrian culture, the argument on the spirit of music and on the rebirth of tragedy, and the reworking of Schopenhauer's metaphysics. In section 18 of *The Birth of Tragedy* Nietzsche speaks of the courage of Kant and Schopenhauer in overcoming the optimism concealed within modern culture, namely, the belief that thought, using the thread of causality, can penetrate into the deepest abysses of being. Kant's critique has succeeded in showing the relativity of knowledge, halting science in its quest for the unconditioned and casting a healthy doubt on its claims to universal validity. A key question to reflect upon, however, concerns the extent to which Nietzsche's duality simply replicates Schopenhauer's division of the world into "will" and "representation," which in turn refers back to Kant's distinction between "thing-in-itself" and "appearance."

Schopenhauer borrowed the expression *principium individuationis* from scholastic thinking and used it to denote the phenomenal world of time and space as that which gives us a plurality of coexistent and successive things (*WWR* vol. 1, section 23). By contrast, the will is the thing-in-itself and outside the order of time and space. Because it also lies outside the province of the principle of sufficient reason, the will is equally groundless and can be said to be primordially "one" (not simply one as either an object or a concept). In their coming to be and perishing individuals exist only as phenomena of the will (conceived as a "blind, irresistible urge"). Schopenhauer views the expression of the will in phenomena in Platonic terms: "the will is indivisible and wholly present in every phenomenon, although the degrees of its objectification [. . .] are very different" (section 28). Schopenhauer goes on to talk of the crystal, the plant, the animal, and man as examples of objectified will. Each species of life and every original force of inorganic nature has an empirical character, but this character is nothing more than the phenomenon (manifestation) of an underlying intelligible character, namely, an indivisible will that is outside time.

Nietzsche's argument in *The Birth of Tragedy* relies heavily on the terms of Schopenhauer's metaphysics but it does not simply replicate them. Apollo is conceived as the "transfiguring genius" of the *principium individuationis*, through whom "redemption in appearance" (*Schein*) can be attained (*BT* 16). Dionysus, by contrast, stands for the bursting apart of the spell of this *principium* that provides the path to the innermost being of things. Nietzsche finds something "sublime" in the way the pleasure to be had from the "beauty of appearance" can be experienced through the Apollonian (*BT* 1). A different kind of sublime is opened up, however, through the Dionysian and the breakdown of cognitive forms it inaugurates (it is the sublime of "horror"). The play between the two opposing forces gives rise in Nietzsche's text to a series of tensions between the one and the multiple, the sub-phenomenal and the phenomenal (the intelligible and the empirical), the desire for eternal life and the heroic trials of individuals. But Nietzsche gives equal weight to the two forces or powers, and he does not follow Schopenhauer in simply arguing for a mystical suppression of the will; rather, in the text we find Nietzsche attempting a justification of the plane of appearance (*Schein*) itself. Moreover, as David B. Allison has noted, Nietzsche's account of the performance of musical mood and dissonance means that the Dionysian state of disindividuation cannot be thought in terms of some noumenal reality, for if it was such a reality it could never be rendered accessible to human experience. If the Dionysian was simply noumenal we would confront a world-will closed in on itself, a world in itself that we could only distort by subjecting it to the order of appearance. As he puts it, music for Nietzsche expresses the infinitely polymorphous character of a dynamic world that is capable of every tension, stress, intensity, pulsion, and so on – and this dynamic world *is* accessible to human experience.[2]

In looking back on the book from the perspective of 1886 Nietzsche locates a "strange voice" at work in the text, the voice of a disciple of a still "unknown god"[3] concealed under the hood of the scholar, the dialectical ill humor of the German, and the bad manners of the Wagnerian. At work in it is a "spirit of memory," one that is bursting forth with questions, experiences, concealed things, and question marks. It is a work which "stammers" its attempt to comprehend the Greeks through the question "what is Dionysian?" It is in terms of this deeply enigmatic issue that Nietzsche will read his first book in his later self-criticism and in his late autobiographical text, *Ecce Homo*. For the later Nietzsche the task is one of articulating a pessimism of strength and of locating the origin of tragedy in overflowing health and fullness of life, within which the affliction of life is not viewed as a mere curse but as a promise. *The Birth of Tragedy* is a book which tries to express by means of Kantian and Schopenhauerian formulas a set of strange and new valuations that are at odds with the spirit and taste of these thinkers (the "strange voice" at work in the text is not a Schopenhauerian one). Tragedy, for Nietzsche, concerns affirmation and not resignation, it inspires an affirmation of the pains of growth rather than simply reproducing the sufferings of individuation (this is the "spirit of music" Nietzsche wishes us to hear in *BT* 16). As he puts it in his self-criticism, and as a question designed to challenge psychiatry, are there such things as healthy neuroses? His greatest regret about the book was not so much that he obscured its premonitions about the Dionysian with Schopenhauerian formulations, but rather that he "spoiled" the grandiose Greek problem by introducing entirely "modern things" (notably German music, German culture, and German spirit).

In *The Birth of Tragedy* Nietzsche presents the Dionysian and the Apollonian as "tendencies," "drives," but also as artistic "energies" and "impulses" that burst forth from nature itself. A whole series of complex questions present themselves around Nietzsche's first book: What is the relation between art and nature? What exactly is the status of the "artist's metaphysics" propounded in the book? How exactly are we to "hear" the statement that it is only as an aesthetic phenomenon that the world and existence can be justified to eternity (*BT* 5)? What is the sense of the "aesthetic" here? What is the status of the "justification"? And, finally, to whom are the world and existence justified in this way? Today, *The Birth of Tragedy* is appreciated as one of the most important attempts within European modernism to acknowledge the so-called destructive forces and energies of life and subject them to philosophical work. In this respect it anticipates Freud's focus on the play between Eros and Thanatos explored in such works as *Beyond the Pleasure Principle* (1919) and *Civilization and its Discontents* (1930). *The Birth of Tragedy* is a text that has always had its supporters and detractors, with some commentators locating in it a dangerous irrationalism and aestheticism (Jürgen Habermas in his *Philosophical Discourse of Modernity*, for example), and others approaching it as a work of the cultural avant-garde that challenges an identity-bound

---

2   David B. Allison, *Reading the New Nietzsche* (Lanham and Oxford: Rowman & Littlefield, 2001), p. 47f.
3   The notion of an "unknown god" is from Acts 17: 23.

perception of ourselves and encourages the release of more fluid energies (Peter Sloterdijk in his *Thinker on Stage: Nietzsche's Materialism*, for example).[4]

Nietzsche himself would not remain content with his initial staging of the problem of individuation in his first book, and a different thinking of individuation, as well as different configurations of art, of science, and of philosophy, begin to emerge in his work from 1878 onwards. For example, in texts such as *The Gay Science* (1882) and *Thus Spoke Zarathustra* (1883–5) it is clear that, for Nietzsche, to exist as an individual is no longer to suffer from a state of metaphysical affliction; rather, we suffer from our finitude and from time – but what enchains us can also free and heal us. Nietzsche remained attached to the Dionysian as a fundamental philosophy of life, though. The Dionysian mysteries symbolize for Nietzsche the primacy of a *life-drive*, one that he would link with his own doctrines such as the eternal return or recurrence.[5] In the much later text *Twilight of the Idols*, for example, he presents the Dionysian as a "faith" in which "the most profound instinct of life," namely, the instinct for its future and eternity, is felt in a religious manner. In the Dionysian mysteries and in the psychological state of the Dionysian the Hellene secures for himself "the eternal return of life" in which the future is consecrated in the past and there is a triumphant "yea-saying" to life over and above death and change. At the heart of the mysteries is a sanctification of pain, simply because the "eternal joy of creation" cannot exist without "the 'torment of the woman in labor'." For Nietzsche everything that "vouchsafes the future," including development and growth, presupposes pain. This is why, he tells us, "for the Greeks the *sexual* symbol was the venerable symbol in itself [. . .]. Every particular about the act of procreation, of pregnancy, of birth evoked the loftiest and solemnest of feelings" (*TI* X. 4).

This section of our selection also features two pieces that are coterminous with *The Birth of Tragedy*: *The Greek State*, which Nietzsche originally intended to be included as a chapter in his first book, and *Homer's Contest*.[6] These two pieces formed part of a handwritten manuscript entitled "Five Prefaces to Five Unwritten Books" which Nietzsche gave to Cosima Wagner as a birthday present in December 1872.[7] The essay on the Greek state is of interest because it shows that there was a political dimension to Nietzsche's conception of the Greeks, while the essay on Homer shows the special importance he attached to the Greek conception of an *agonistic* education. The essay begins with Nietzsche drawing attention to the necessary role played by the "inhuman"

4   See, respectively, Jürgen Habermas, *The Philosophical Discourse of Modernity: Twelve Lectures*, trans. Frederick Lawrence (Cambridge: Polity; Cambridge, MA: MIT Press, 1987), and Peter Sloterdijk, *Thinker on Stage: Nietzsche's Materialism*, trans. Jamie Owen Daniel (Minneapolis: University of Minnesota Press, 1989).

5   In *TI* X. 4 Nietzsche writes "eternal return" (*ewige Wiederkehr*), while in the following section he writes "eternal recurrence" (*ewige Wiederkunft*). For insight into Nietzsche's thinking on return and recurrence see, among others, studies by Karl Löwith and Joan Stambaugh.

6   We have changed the translation from "Homer on Competition" back to its more familiar "Homer's Contest" (*Wettkampf*).

7   The other three pieces are: "On the Pathos of Truth," "On the Future of our Educational Institutions," and "The Relation of Schopenhauerian Philosophy to German Culture."

capacities in our becoming-human, something he continues to appeal to in his later thinking of culture, morals, and the economy of life viewed "beyond good and evil."

For most of 1872 Nietzsche was preoccupied with his study of pre-Platonic philosophy (he had first given a lecture course on this topic in the winter semester of 1869–70 and repeated it in revised form in the summer semesters of 1872, 1873, and 1876). Nietzsche's "book" *Philosophy in the Tragic Age of the Greeks* is an unfinished text composed in the spring of 1873 and based upon the texts of his lectures. A fair copy of this draft was made by a student of his in 1874, to which Nietzsche made some minor corrections in 1879. However, it was never published in Nietzsche's lifetime.[8] From it we have included the opening section and further sections treating Anaximander (ca. 610–ca. 546 B.C.) (*PTG* 4) and Heraclitus (ca. 540–ca. 480 B.C.) (*PTG* 5–7). Nietzsche's attention is focused on the significance of Heraclitus' denial of being and teaching on "becoming," which concerns the "impermanence of everything actual." For Nietzsche, Heraclitus possessed the power to think in terms of intuition and outside the reification of concepts and logical combinations. Heraclitus "sees" time in the way Kant and Schopenhauer spoke of it, without definite content and independently of all experience (an *a priori* form of intuition or time as a pure, empty form). What Heraclitus sees is a complicated process of becoming in which things separate and oppositions seek to reunite. This is an insight, says Nietzsche, which Heraclitus transforms into something "sublime." He then links up this teaching on becoming with another key doctrine of Heraclitus, namely the idea that all is strife and endless contest. Thus, the Greek idea of the *agon* that informs their conception of the individual and of the state ultimately rests on a cosmology. In section 6 Nietzsche addresses himself to some of the deepest puzzles surrounding Heraclitus' intuitions and teachings. For example, how should we read and make sense of the claim that "the one *is* the many"? Should we read it as the claim that the one expresses itself in the many, that there is indeed a "one"? Or that only the many exists and that there is no "one"? Consideration of this issue leads Nietzsche into an exploration of the true meaning of Heraclitus' vision and riddle of the world in terms of an innocent and beautiful game, a game of "the aeon," which is a game of eternal creation and destruction (compare also section 24 of *BT* on this theme). In the section on *The Birth of Tragedy* in *Ecce Homo* Nietzsche articulates his "Dionysian philosophy" in terms of Heraclitus' teachings; it entails the affirmation of transitoriness, of destruction, of antithesis and war, the affirmation of becoming and the "radical rejection" of the concept of being. He even states that the doctrine of eternal recurrence – conceived as the "endlessly repeated circular course [*Kreislauf*] of all things" – could possibly already have been taught by Heraclitus.

We also feature in this section the essay "On Truth and Lies in a Nonmoral Sense" which Nietzsche composed in 1873 but refrained from publishing. The essay emerged out of the material he was amassing on the pre-Platonic philosophers and his plan for a book on philosophy and philosophers (the *Philosophenbuch*). Much later, in the opening section to the Preface he wrote in 1886 for the second edition of volume 2 of *Human, All Too Human*, Nietzsche says that at the time he composed this essay he

---

8   The text of the lecture series Nietzsche gave at Basel between 1872 and 1876 has recently been translated into English. See Nietzsche, *The Pre-Platonic Philosophers*, trans. Greg Whitlock (Urbana and Chicago: University of Illinois Press, 2001).

was "deep in the midst of moral skepticism and destructive analysis," and writing as one who no longer believed in anything. The opening paragraph of the 1873 essay is marked by this tone of skepticism, destruction, and intensified pessimism. In this essay Nietzsche seeks to draw attention to the conceited nature of human knowing and to deflate its pretensions: there have been eternities when the human intellect did not exist and we can envisage eternities in the future when it will once again no longer exist. A critical task facing the reader of Nietzsche is that of determining which insights he will retain from this early essay for the tasks of his later thinking and which he will jettison. We see in it an anticipation of his calling into question of the "will to truth" in his mature work: here he speaks of the "drive for truth" and takes to task humanity's overestimation of the value of knowing. The intensified pessimism at work in the essay is connected with his insight into the extent to which human life is immersed in illusions and dream images, in which the human intellect "glides over the surface of things" and sees only the form of things. Moreover, the investigator of truth seeks "only the metamorphosis of the world into man." In statements such as these we find Nietzsche essentially working out the sense of disappointment he thought would emerge in the wake of the turning effected by Kant's Copernican Revolution, which teaches us that we know only a world we have made for ourselves. What is novel about Nietzsche's account in this essay is how he applies this turn to questions of language and metaphor. Although he articulates a distrust of the word "appearance" (*Erscheinung*) and speaks of the thing-in-itself as something incomprehensible to language-creators and -users, something that is not worth striving for, his own thinking on questions of truth and knowledge in this essay is governed by the metaphysical dualisms he has inherited from Kant and Schopenhauer. The whole mood of Nietzsche's thinking would undergo a fundamental shift in his texts of the middle and late periods (see "Reason in Philosophy" and "How the 'Real World' Finally Became a Fable" in *Twilight of the Idols* for a succinct, and enigmatic, articulation of his mature thinking on "appearance" [*Schein*]). There are undoubtedly deep continuities in Nietzsche's thinking: here, for example, one can interpret his wide-ranging thinking on metaphor as an attack on the conceptual mummification that he exposes in "Reason in Philosophy" in *Twilight*. There are also, however, subtle but decisive shifts in his thinking. There is no evidence that in 1873 Nietzsche has yet learned the essential lessons of "the gay science." And one of the key lessons of *Thus Spoke Zarathustra* is that we need to unlearn the universe (it is too large a problem and cannot be digested).

In the essay "On Truth and Lies" Nietzsche (as a philologically minded psychologist) contends that the drive toward the formation of metaphors is the fundamental human drive. His attention is focused on the human ability to "volatilize perceptual metaphors in a schema" and thus to be able to think in terms of concepts and not simply images. In his *Critique of Pure Reason* Kant refers to schematization as an art that lies concealed in the depths of the human soul. In this essay Nietzsche says that it is this "art" that distinguishes man from the animals. Schemata are procedures that enable the subsumption of objects under concepts. They are not images as such, but rather what allows for the generation of images. As Kant points out, an image of a triangle or a dog could never be adequate to the concept of these things, and while a series of five dots may serve as an image of the number five, this presupposes the schema of number which is nothing other than the successive addition of homogeneous units. Schemata, Nietzsche says, enable the human animal to construct a "pyramidal order" of things (thinking in terms of castes, degrees, laws, boundaries, etc.). In this "conceptual crap game" "truth" means nothing more than using every die in the conventionally desig-nated manner and thinking in accordance with the constructed order of things. Man is a forgetful animal and forgets the extent to which he is "an *artistically creating* sub-ject." This takes place, for example, when we forget that our perceptual metaphors are just that, metaphors, and we erroneously think that they give us things in them-selves (the error of realism). Nietzsche then reflects on the relation between concept and intuition, between the need for conceptual order and the desire for creative destruc-tion and between the rational human and the human of intuition. The principal move-ment of thought at play in the essay seems to be from "perceptual contents" to "conceptual schemas" and then to "intuition." One might say that for Nietzsche intuitions have a *vital* character in that they serve to keep us attuned to the dynamics of life (the need for growth, change, transformation) and enable us to overcome the ossification, petrification, and reification introduced into life by concepts and metaphors. It is not that the human being of intuition lives without concepts and metaphors, but rather that he or she "speaks only in forbidden metaphors and in unheard-of combinations of concepts." In the final paragraph of the essay Nietzsche contrasts the intuitive human being with the human who is guided only by concepts and abstractions and with the stoical person, and we get a glimpse (it is only a foreshadowing) of the spirit of cheer-fulness that characterizes the later practitioner of gay science.

As we have noted, Nietzsche speaks in this essay of the thing-in-itself as inaccess-ible to conceptual and metaphorical language, and states that it is not anything worth striving for. "Things" are conceivable to us only in terms of "sums of relations," so we can never access something (an "in-itself") that would be independent of rela-tionality and conditionality (what the later Nietzsche calls an essential "perspectivism"). Nietzsche examines language in this essay on the basis of the belief that there is a difference between nature and our representation of it. Nature, he notes, is not acquainted with concepts, forms, or species, while the contrast we make between individual and species is anthropomorphic "and does not originate in the essence of things." In making this point Nietzsche accepts the Kantian stricture: we cannot claim that this contrast does not correspond to the essence of things since both this and its opposite are quite indemonstrable.

We have made selections from two of Nietzsche's *Untimely Meditations*. The first selection is from the second essay, on the practice of historical inquiry (*Historie*), and includes the opening three sections in full and part of the final section; the second is from the third essay, on Schopenhauer as Nietzsche's educator, containing the first and fifth sections in full. In the meditation or observation on history, published in early 1874, Nietzsche argues that we serve history to the extent that we make it serve "life," and he distinguishes between three essential types of history: the antiquarian, which seeks to preserve the past; the monumental, which seeks to emulate the past; and the critical, which seeks to emancipate the present from the past. To each of these types of history there corresponds a particular attitude which Nietzsche designates as the historical, the suprahistorical, and the unhistorical respectively. He argues in favor of a combination of the suprahistorical and the unhistorical, which involves a search for useful precedents in the past and a forgetting placed in the service of creative action in the present, for the sake of a time to come. The essay on history and life also contains an intriguing encounter with time which comes to play such a prominent role in Nietzsche's thinking in the 1880s, notably time's pastness, named here, as in the extraordinary discourse "On Redemption" in *Zarathustra*, the "*it was*" (*es war*). Nietzsche would not work out a solution to this problem until the period of *Zarathustra*, in which he offers a teaching on time that seeks to show how it is possible to cultivate a new relation to the past and to time's pastness.

In his reflections on the *Untimely Meditations* in *Ecce Homo*, Nietzsche says that his aim in composing them was to pursue "the problem of education," to develop a "new concept of self-discipline" and to do so as "a way to greatness" (which is one of Nietzsche's questions in *Beyond Good and Evil*, section 212: "is greatness possible?"). In *Schopenhauer as Educator* he explores questions of nature, culture, and education without ever discussing the details of Schopenhauer's philosophy. The third of Nietzsche's four *Untimely Meditations* was written in the summer of 1874 and published on his thirtieth birthday. He had realized for some time that his philosophy was moving in a quite different direction to Schopenhauer's. Nevertheless, in this essay he chose to honor him as his educator, or rather, as a thinker who showed him how to become his own educator. Nietzsche's essay seeks an affirmation of the materiality and mortality of individual existence. This is an existence, however, that has to be situated in the context of a comprehension of culture and its tasks of liberation in relation to a highly complex and variegated nature (said to be at once motherly and merciful, and cruel and merciless). As section 5 makes clear, Nietzsche's deepest reflections on this whole question are informed by a recognition that we live in fear of the strange power, spectral and virtual, of time, including the time of memory: "There are spirits all around us, every moment of our life wants to say something to us, but we refuse to listen to these spirit-voices. We are afraid that when we are alone and quiet something will be whispered into our ear, and so we hate quietness and deafen ourselves with sociability" (*SE* 5). It is for this reason that we need educators, especially asocial ones who know how to hear and see, who sometimes hear and see too much. It is not merely the liberation of the individual that Nietzsche seeks but the creation of a new kind of community of free-spirited individuals. Thus, while the issue of solitude is thematized in the *Meditation*, the cultural task for Nietzsche is that of creating new existential and social modes of living. The same dialectic will inform and structure the development of Zarathustra as a free spirit and an educator of the future.

6

The Birth of Tragedy from the Spirit of Music

(1872)

1

We will have achieved much for the discipline of aesthetics when we have arrived not only at the logical insight but also at the immediate certainty of the view that the continuing development of art is tied to the duality of the *Apollonian* and the *Dionysian*: just as procreation depends on the duality of the sexes, which are engaged in a continual struggle interrupted only by temporary periods of reconciliation. These names are borrowed from the Greeks who revealed the profound secret doctrines of their view of art to the discerning mind precisely not in concepts but rather in the insistently clear forms of their pantheon. To both of their artistic deities, Apollo and Dionysus,[1] is linked our knowledge that in the Greek world there existed a tremendous opposition, in terms of origin and goals, between the Apollonian art of the sculptor and the imageless Dionysian art of music: these two very different drives run in parallel with one another, for the most part diverging openly with one another and continually stimulating each other to ever new and more powerful births, in order to perpetuate in themselves the struggle of that opposition only apparently bridged by the shared name of 'art'; until finally, through a metaphysical miracle of the Hellenic 'will',[2] they appear coupled with one another and through this coupling at last give birth to a work of art which is as Dionysian as it is Apollonian – Attic tragedy.

1   Apollo, god of light, prophecy, and medicine whose attributes are the lyre and the bow, is associated with the discipline and beauty of form and individual identity, and is traditionally the patron of the art of music. Nietzsche insists on his close links with sculpture and architecture. Dionysus, the son of Zeus and Semele, daughter of Cadmus, king of Thebes, is traditionally the god of wine and tragedy. His worship was associated with intoxication and loss of identity, sometimes leading to sexual excess and violence, and he is frequently represented in animal form as half-goat. According to myth, only women were permitted to participate in the celebration of Dionysian rites.
2   Nietzsche presupposes the existence of an underlying "will" which expresses itself through the Apollonian and Dionysian drives.

In order to acquaint ourselves more closely with both of these drives, let us think of them first of all as the opposed artistic worlds of *dream* and *intoxication*; the opposition between these physiological phenomena corresponds to that between the Apollonian and the Dionysian. According to Lucretius,[3] it was in dreams that the magnificent forms of the gods first appeared before the souls of men, it was in dreams that the great sculptor first beheld the delightful anatomy of superhuman beings, and the Hellenic poet, if questioned about the secret of poetic creation, would likewise have referred to dreams and given a similar explanation to that of Hans Sachs in *The Mastersingers*:

> My friend, it is the task of the poet
> To note dreams and interpret.
> The truest delusion of man seems,
> Believe me, revealed to him in dreams:
> All the art of poetry and versification
> Is nothing but the true dream-interpretation.[4]

The beautiful appearance[5] of the worlds of dream, in whose creation every man is a consummate artist, is the precondition of all plastic art, even, as we shall see, of an important half of poetry. We take pleasure in the direct understanding of form, all shapes speak to us, there is nothing indifferent or superfluous. And yet even in the most intense life of this dream-reality, the sense of its status as *appearance* still shimmers through: this at least is my experience, for whose frequency, even normality, I could adduce much evidence, including the sayings of the poets. The philosophical man even senses that under this reality in which we live and exist, there lies hidden a second and completely different reality, and that this surface reality is therefore also an appearance. Schopenhauer designates precisely the gift of occasionally seeing men and all things as mere phantoms or dream-images as the distinctive characteristic of the capacity for philosophy.[6] So the artistically sensitive man responds to the reality of the dream in the same way as the philosopher responds to the reality of existence; he pays close attention and derives pleasure from it: for out of these images he interprets life for himself, in these events he trains himself for life. He experiences not only the agreeable and friendly images with that universal understanding: but also the serious, the gloomy, the sad, the dark aspects of life, the sudden inhibitions, the teasing of

---

3   See Lucretius, *De rerum natura* (*On the Nature of Things*), V. 1169–82.
4   Quotation from Richard Wagner's opera *Die Meistersinger von Nürnberg* (*The Mastersingers of Nuremberg*, 1868), III. ii.
5   In German: *Schein*. Throughout this text, the translator has adopted the practice of translating *Schein* as "appearance" and *Erscheinung* as "phenomenal appearance" and "phenomenon"/"phenomena." For insight into the significance of the distinction between the two German terms, see the main introduction to the present volume, note 23. In the *Kritik der reinen Vernunft* (*Critique of Pure Reason*, 1781/87), Kant uses the German *Erscheinung* and the Latin "phenomenon"/"phenomena" to denote the field of appearances (objects considered as objects of possible experience). In Kant the term "appearance" refers to that which precedes the logical use of the understanding (A 20), while "phenomena" are appearances insofar as they are thought as objects in accordance with the categories of the understanding (A 248–50).
6   See *WWR*, vol. 1, 1. 5.

chance, the fearful expectations. In short the whole 'divine comedy' of life, including the Inferno,[7] passes before him, not only as a game of shadows – since he participates in the life and suffering of these scenes – yet also not without that fleeting sense of their status as appearance. And perhaps many will remember, as I do, calling out to themselves in encouragement amid the dangers and terrors of the dream, not without success: 'This is a dream! I want to dream on!' I have likewise heard of people who were able to extend the causal sequence of one and the same dream over three consecutive nights and more: facts which clearly prove that our innermost being, the substratum common to us all, experiences the dream with profound pleasure and joyful necessity.

The Greeks have likewise expressed this joyful necessity of the dream experience in their Apollo: Apollo, as the god of all plastic energies, is at the same time the god of prophecy. He, who according to the etymological root of his name is the 'one who appears shining', the deity of light, is also master of the beautiful appearance of the inner world of the imagination. The higher truth, the perfection of these states in contrast to the only partial comprehensibility of everyday reality, the deep consciousness of nature as it heals and helps in sleep and dream is at the same time the symbolic analogue of the capacity for prophecy and of the arts as a whole, which make life possible and worth living. But our image of Apollo must include that delicate and indispensable line which the dream image may not overstep if it is not to have pathological effects, otherwise appearance would deceive us as clumsy reality: that measured restraint, that freedom from the wilder impulses, that calm wisdom of the image-creating god. His eye must 'shine like the sun',[8] in accordance with his origins; even when it rages and looks displeased, it remains consecrated by the beauty of appearance. And so what Schopenhauer says about man caught in the veil of Maya[9] might apply to Apollo in an excentric sense – *World as Will and Representation*, I: 'As a sailor sits in a small boat in a boundless raging sea, surrounded on all sides by heaving mountainous waves, trusting to his frail vessel; so does the individual man sit calmly in the middle of a world of torment, trusting to the *principium individuationis*.'[10] In fact, it might be said of Apollo that in him the unshaken trust in that *principium* and the calm repose of the man caught up in it has found its most sublime expression, and Apollo might even be described as the magnificent divine image of the *principium individuationis*, through whose gestures and looks all the pleasure and wisdom and beauty of 'appearance' speak to us.

In the same passage, Schopenhauer has depicted the tremendous *horror* which grips man when he suddenly loses his way among the cognitive forms of the phenomenal world,[11] as the principle of reason[12] in any of its forms appears to break down. When

---

7   Allusion to Dante's *La divina commedia* (*The Divine Comedy*, 1311–21), with its three-part depiction of the afterlife: "Inferno," "Purgatorio," and "Paradiso."

8   Allusion to Goethe's aphorism collection "Zahme Xenien" ('Tame Xenia'), III: "If the eye were not sunlike, it could never gaze on the sun."

9   On the veil of Maya as the deceptive world of human perception, see *WWR*, vol. 1, 1. 3.

10   *WWR*, vol. 1, 4. 63.

11   In German: *Erkenntnissformen der Erscheinung*.

12   Reference to the "principle of sufficient reason," formulated by Leibniz and the subject of Schopenhauer's doctoral dissertation *Über die vierfache Wurzel des Satzes vom zureichenden Grunde* (*On the Fourfold Root of the Principle of Sufficient Reason*, 1813), trans. E. F. J. Payne (La Salle, IL: Open Court, 1974).

we add to this horror the blissful rapture which rises up from the innermost depths of man, even of nature, as a result of the very same collapse of the *principium individuationis*, we steal a glimpse into the essence of the *Dionysian*, with which we will become best acquainted through the analogy of *intoxication*. Either under the influence of the narcotic drink of which all original men and peoples sing in hymns, or in the approach of spring which forcefully and pleasurably courses through the whole of nature, those Dionysian impulses awaken, which in their heightened forms cause the subjective to dwindle to complete self-oblivion. In mediaeval Germany, too, increasingly large throngs of singing and dancing people surged from place to place under the influence of the same Dionysian force: in these St John's and St Vitus's dancers we recognize again the Bacchic choruses of the Greeks, with their prehistory in Asia Minor, stretching all the way back to Babylon and the orgiastic Sacaea.[13] There are men who from lack of experience or from stupidity turn away in contempt and pity from such phenomena as they would from 'folk diseases' with a greater sense of their own good health: but these poor men do not suspect how cadaverous and ghostly their 'health' looks, compared to the glowing life of Dionysian enthusiasts which roars past them.

Under the spell of the Dionysian it is not only the bond between man and man which is re-established: nature in its estranged, hostile, or subjugated forms also celebrates its reconciliation with its prodigal son,[14] man. The earth voluntarily gives up its spoils while the predators of cliffs and desert approach meekly. The chariot of Dionysus overflows with flowers and wreaths: beneath its yoke tread the panther and the tiger. If one were to allow one's imagination free rein in transforming Beethoven's 'Hymn to Joy' into a painting, particularly the moment when the multitudes kneel down awestruck in the dust: then one might come close to an idea of the Dionysian. Now the slave is a free man, now all the inflexible and hostile divisions which necessity, caprice, or 'impudent fashion'[15] have established between men collapse. Now, with the gospel of world-harmony, each man feels himself not only reunified, reconciled, reincorporated, and merged with his neighbour, but genuinely one, as if the veil of Maya had been rent and only its shreds still fluttered in front of the mysterious original Unity.[16] In song and dance man expresses himself as a member of a higher communal nature: he has forgotten how to walk and speak and is well on the way to dancing himself aloft into the heights. His gestures communicate an entranced state. Just as now the animals speak and the earth gives forth milk and honey,[17] so something supernatural sounds forth from him: he feels himself as god, now he himself strides forth as enraptured and uplifted as he saw the gods stride forth in dreams. Man is no longer an artist, he has become a work of art: the artistic force of the whole of nature, to the most intense blissful satisfaction of the original Unity, reveals itself here in the

13 The Bacchic choruses were worshipers of Dionysus (also known as Bacchus). The Sacaea were originally a Babylonian festival where the transgression of social and sexual boundaries was permitted. From Babylon, the Sacaea spread throughout Asia Minor.
14 Reference to the New Testament parable. See Luke 15: 11–32.
15 Quotation from Beethoven's reworking of Schiller's poem "An die Freude" ("Ode to Joy," 1786/1803), used as the text for the choral conclusion to his Ninth Symphony (1824).
16 In German: *das Ur-Eine*.
17 Formulation in the Bible. See e.g. Exodus 3: 8.

shudder of intoxication. Here the noblest clay, the most expensive marble, man, is kneaded and hewn, and the chisel-blows of the Dionysian artist of worlds are accompanied by the sound of the Eleusinian Mysteries[18] calling: 'Do you fall to your knees, multitudes? World, do you sense the creator?' –[19]

2

Until now we have considered the Apollonian and its opposite, the Dionysian, as artistic powers, which burst forth from nature itself, *without the mediation of the human artist*, and in which their artistic drives at first satisfy themselves directly: first as the image-world of the dream, whose perfection is wholly unconnected to the intellectual level of artistic education of the individual, and then as intoxicated reality, which again pays no heed to the individual, and even seeks to annihilate the individual and to redeem him through a mystical feeling of unity. In relation to these direct artistic states of nature, every artist is an 'imitator', that is, either Apollonian dream-artist or Dionysian artist of intoxication, or finally – as for example in Greek tragedy – simultaneously artist of dream and intoxication: such as we have to imagine him as he stands alone to one side of the infatuated choruses before sinking to his knees in Dionysian drunkenness and mystical self-abandonment and as, through the effect of the Apollonian dream, his own state, that is, his unity with the innermost ground of the world, is revealed to him *in an allegorical dream-image*.

Having established these general preconditions and comparisons, let us now approach the *Greeks* in order to learn the degree and extent to which those *artistic drives of nature* have developed in them: this will then enable us to understand and appreciate more deeply the relation of the Greek artist to his archetypes, or, to use the Aristotelian term, 'the imitation of nature'.[20] In spite of all the dream literature recounting their countless dream anecdotes, we can only speculate as to the *dreams* of the Greeks, but with some confidence none the less: given the incredibly precise and sure plastic capacity of their eye, with its vivid and honest pleasure in colour, we must, to the shame of all succeeding generations, presuppose also for their dreams a causality and logic of lines and outlines, colours and groups, a sequence of scenes resembling one of their finest reliefs, whose perfection would justify, were a comparison possible, our describing the dreaming Greeks as Homers and Homer as a dreaming Greek: in a more profound sense than that in which the modern man in speaking of his dreams dares to compare himself to Shakespeare.

On the other hand, we have no need to speculate with regard to the huge chasm which separates the *Dionysian Greeks* from the Dionysian barbarian. In all corners of the ancient world – to leave the modern one to one side here – from Rome to Babylon, we can prove the existence of Dionysian festivities, whose type is at best related to the Greek type as the bearded satyr,[21] to whom the goat lent its name and attributes,

---

18   The secret religious rites celebrated by initiates at Eleusis in honor of Demeter, goddess of corn. Elements of the rites were associated with the worship of Dionysus.
19   Quotation from Schiller's "Ode to Joy."
20   Reference to the notion of mimesis in Aristotle's *Poetics*.
21   The satyr is a figure from Greek mythology – half-man, half-goat – characterized by a wild sexuality and associated with the celebration of Dionysian cults.

is to Dionysus himself. Almost everywhere the centre of these festivities lay in an effusive transgression of the sexual order, whose waves swept away all family life and its venerable principles; none other than the wildest beasts of nature were unleashed here to the point of creating an abominable mixture of sensuality and cruelty which has always appeared to me as the true 'witches' brew'.[22] Against the feverish impulses of these festivities, knowledge of which reached them across land and sea, the Greeks were, it seems, for a while completely sheltered and shielded by the figure of Apollo who stood tall and proud among them and who with the Medusa's head warded off this grotesque barbaric Dionysian force, the most dangerous power it had to encounter. That majestic repudiation of Apollo has immortalized itself in Doric art.[23] This resistance became more questionable and even impossible as, from the deepest roots of the Hellenic character itself, similar drives finally broke through: now the influence of the Delphic god[24] was limited to avoiding annihilation by disarming the powerful adversary through a well-timed reconciliation. This reconciliation is the most important moment in the history of Greek religion: wherever one looks, one sees the revolutions wrought by this event. It was the reconciliation of two adversaries, clearly defining the boundaries to be respected from now on and instituting periodic exchanges of tokens of esteem; at bottom the chasm which separated them remained unbridged. If, however, we see how the Dionysian power revealed itself under the pressure of that peace settlement, then we recognize in the Dionysian orgies of the Greeks, in contrast to those Babylonian Sacaea and their regression of man to the tiger and the ape, the meaning of festivities of world redemption and days of transfiguration. Here nature first attains its artistic exultation, here the tearing asunder of the *principium individuationis* first becomes an artistic phenomenon. That horrific witches' brew of sensuality and cruelty was powerless here: only the peculiar mixture and duality of the emotions on the part of the Dionysian enthusiasts recalls it – as cures recall lethal poisons – the phenomenon that pain arouses pleasure, that exultation tears cries of agony from the breast. Out of the most intense joy the scream of terror or the yearning lament for an irreplaceable loss sounds forth. In those Greek festivities a sentimental[25] trait of nature breaks through, so to speak, as if it has reason to lament its dismemberment into

22   Allusion to Goethe's *Faust I* (1808), the "Witches' Kitchen" scene.

23   The Dorians were a tribe which settled in northern Greece in the thirteenth and twelfth centuries B.C., establishing political and cultural centers in Argos, Corinth, and Sparta. Their politics were based on an aggressive independence founded in a military caste, while their art was characterized by clarity and simplicity. Doric architecture inspired the Romantic classicism of German architects such as Karl Friedrich Schinkel (1781–1841). Such emulation formed part of a more widespread nineteenth-century tendency to assert ethnic and political parallels between the Dorians and the Prussians as twin representatives of a pure and warlike Aryan race. The beginnings of this process can be traced in the classicist Karl Otfried Müller's *Die Dorier* (*The Dorians*, 1824).

24   Epithet for Apollo, the god of prophecy and thus the patron of the oracle at Delphi.

25   Term borrowed from Schiller's aesthetic treatise *Über naive und sentimentalische Dichtung* (*On Naive and Sentimental Poetry*, 1795–6), where "naïve" refers to ancient and spontaneous culture, and "sentimental" to a modern, self-conscious culture.

individuals. The song and gestures of such ambivalent enthusiasts were something new and unheard-of in the Homeric Greek world: and Dionysian *music* in particular awakened its fear and horror. If music was apparently already known as an Apollonian art, this was strictly speaking only as the wave-like beat of rhythm, whose plastic force was developed for the representation of Apollonian states. The music of Apollo was Doric architecture rendered in sound,[26] but in the merely suggestive notes characteristic of the cithara.[27] Carefully kept at a distance is precisely that element which defines the character of Dionysian music and so of music itself, the shattering force of sound, the unified flow of melody and the utterly incomparable world of harmony. In the Dionysian dithyramb,[28] all the symbolic faculties of man are stimulated to the highest pitch of intensity; something never before experienced struggles towards expression, the annihilation of the veil of Maya, unity as the spirit of the species, even of nature. Now the world of nature is to be expressed in symbols; a new world of symbols is necessary, a symbolism of the body for once, not just the symbolism of the mouth, but the full gestures of dance, the rhythmic movement of all the limbs. Then the other symbolic forces will develop, particularly those of music, suddenly impetuous in rhythm, dynamism, and harmony. In order to grasp this complete unleashing of all symbolic forces, man must already have reached that height of self-abandonment which seeks to express itself symbolically through those forces: so the dithyrambic servant of Dionysus will only be understood by those like him! With what astonishment the Apollonian Greek must have regarded him! With an astonishment which was all the greater for being accompanied by the horror that all this was really not so unfamiliar to him after all, even that his Apollonian consciousness did no more than cast a veil over this Dionysian world before him.

3

In order to understand this, we must as it were dismantle stone by stone the elaborate edifice of *Apollonian culture* until we can see the foundations upon which it is built. Here we see first the magnificent figures of the *Olympian* pantheon which stand on the gables of this building and whose deeds adorn its friezes in brilliant reliefs visible from a great distance. If Apollo too stands among them as one deity among others without claiming a preeminent place, we should not allow ourselves to be led astray by this. The same drive which took on concrete form in Apollo has given birth to the whole Olympian world, and in this sense Apollo may serve for us as its father. From what great need did such a brilliant company of Olympian beings spring?

26   Allusion to Goethe's description of architecture as "frozen music" ("erstarrte Musik") in the *Gespräche mit Eckermann* (*Conversations with Eckermann*), March 23, 1829. The phrase derives from Schelling's *Philosophie der Kunst* (*Philosophy of Art*, 1809).
27   Ancient Greek stringed instrument.
28   The dithyramb was the ancient Greek hymn to Dionysus, whose use was extended to other gods from the sixth century B.C. Towards the end of the fifth century B.C. the new dithyramb appeared, characterized by a looser structure and more independent musical accompaniment. The form was imitated by Goethe, Schiller, Hölderlin, and Nietzsche himself: see *Dithyrambs of Dionysus*, bilingual edition, trans. R. J. Hollingdale, 2nd edn (London: Anvil Press, 2001).

Whoever approaches these Olympians with another religion at heart, in search of moral elevation, even saintliness, disembodied spirituality, glances of compassion and love, will soon be obliged to turn his back on them. There is nothing here to remind us of asceticism, spirituality, and duty: everything here speaks to us of a sumptuous, even triumphant, existence, an existence in which everything is deified, regardless of whether it is good or evil. And so the spectator might stand full of consternation before this fantastic exuberance of life, wondering what magic potion these arrogant men took in order to have enjoyed life in such a way that wherever they look, Helen, the ideal image of their own existence 'hovering in sweet sensuality',[29] smiles back at them, laughing. But to this spectator who has already turned to leave we must shout: Do not leave just yet, but listen first to what Greek folk wisdom says about this same life, which stretches out before you here with such inexplicable serenity. According to an ancient legend, King Midas had long hunted the forest for the wise *Silenus*, the companion of Dionysus, without catching him. When Silenus finally fell into his hands, the king asked him what is the very best and most preferable of all things for man. The stiff and motion-less daemon refused to speak; until, forced by the king, he finally burst into shrill laughter and uttered the following words: 'Miserable ephemeral race, children of chance and toil, why do you force me to tell you what it is best for you not to hear? The very best of all things is completely beyond your reach: not to have been born, not to *be*, to be *nothing*. But the second best thing for you is – to meet an early death.'

How is the Olympian pantheon related to this folk wisdom? As the delightful vision of the tortured martyr is to his torments.

Now the Olympian magic mountain opens itself up to us as it were and shows us its roots. The Greek knew and felt the terrors and horrors of existence: in order to be able to live at all, he had to use the brilliant Olympians, born of dream, as a screen. That great mistrust of the Titanic powers of nature,[30] those ruthless Moira[31] ruling over all knowledge, that vulture of the great friend of man, Prometheus,[32] that fearful

---

29 Allusion to Goethe's *Faust I*, l. 2603f.: "Having taken this potion, / You will soon see Helen in every woman."

30 According to the Greek poet Hesiod, the Titans are the second generation of the gods who emerged from the original chaos. The first generation, Uranus and Gaia, give birth to six sons and six daughters. This second generation of Titans, under the leadership of the youngest son, Chronos, overthrow their parents, only to be overthrown in turn by the third generation of Olympians led by Chronos' son Zeus.

31 In Greek mythology the three Fates (Clotho, Lachesis, Atropos), who determine the dura-tion and happiness of human life. While Clotho spins the thread of life, Lachesis draws it off the spindle and Atropos cuts it.

32 In Greek mythology the Titan Prometheus defies the authority of Zeus by stealing fire and giving it to man. For this he is punished by being bound to a cliff face where an eagle picks out his liver daily. He is eventually saved through the self-sacrifice of Chiron, who agrees to give up his immortality in exchange for Prometheus' freedom. The myth fascinated artists by its embodiment of libidinal and political revolution, and it recurs frequently in Romantic art and literature. The title page of the first edition of *BT* had a design that depicted Prometheus freeing himself from his bondage. In writing the book, Nietzsche casts himself in the mythic role of a liberated rather than imprisoned rebel against an unjust order.

fate of the wise Oedipus,[33] that curse on the house of the Atrides which drove Orestes[34] to matricide, in short that whole philosophy of the forest god,[35] together with its mythical examples, on which the melancholy Etruscans[36] foundered, was continually overcome anew, in any case veiled and removed from view by the Greeks through that artistic *middle world* of the Olympians. In order to be able to live, the Greeks were obliged to create these gods, out of the deepest necessity: a process which we should probably imagine in the following way – through the Apollonian drive towards beauty, the Olympians' divine reign of joy developed in a slow series of transitions from the original Titans' divine reign of terror: as roses burst forth from the thorn-bush. How else could that people, so sensitive in its emotions, so impetuous in its desires, so uniquely equipped for *suffering*, have tolerated existence, if the very same existence had not been shown to it surrounded by a higher glory in its gods. The same drive which calls art into life as the completion and perfection of existence which seduces the living into living on, also brought into being the Olympian world in which the Hellenic 'will' holds up before itself a transfiguring mirror. So the gods justify the life of men by living it themselves – the only adequate theodicy! Existence under the bright sunlight of such gods will be felt to be in itself worth striving for, and the real *pain* of the Homeric men relates to their taking leave of it, above all in the near future: so that now it could be said of them in a reversal of the wisdom of Silenus that 'the very worst thing of all would be to meet an early death, the second worst to die at all'. Once lament sounds forth, it is heard again for the premature death of Achilles,[37] for the continual passing of mankind, like leaves in the wind, for the decline of the age of heroes. It is not unworthy of the greatest heroes to yearn to live on, even as a day labourer.[38] So impetuously does the 'will' in its Apollonian form desire this existence, so at one does the Homeric man feel with it, that even lament becomes its hymn of praise.

It must be said here that this harmony which more modern men view with such yearning, this unity of man with nature, whose designation by the artistic term 'naïve' was popularized by Schiller,[39] is a by no means simple, self-evident, as it were unavoidable state, which is *necessarily* to be found at the gate of all cultures, as paradise for mankind: only an age which sought to imagine Rousseau's *Émile*[40] as an artist

33 Allusion to the myth of Oedipus, the king of Thebes who inadvertently kills his father Laius and marries his mother Jocasta. His story formed the basis of Sophocles' tragedies *Oedipus the King* and *Oedipus at Colonus*.
34 Allusion to the myth of the Atrides on which Aeschylus based his Oresteian trilogy of tragedies (*Agamemnon*, *The Libation-Bearers*, *The Eumenides*).
35 Dionysus.
36 Ancient inhabitants of Etruria in western Italy.
37 Greek hero of Homer's *Iliad*, son of Peleus and Thetis, killed by Paris during the Trojan War.
38 Allusion to Homer's *Odyssey*, XI. 489–91.
39 See note 25 above.
40 The educational treatise in novel form *Émile, ou De l'éducation* (*Émile; or, On Education*, 1762) proposes a form of natural education designed to forestall the corrupting effects of civilization and to preserve Émile as a child of nature.

and imagined that it had found in Homer such an artistic Émile, brought up in the heart of nature, could believe this. Wherever we encounter the 'naïve' in art, we must recognize the greatest effect of Apollonian culture: which must always first overthrow a realm of Titans, slay monsters, and triumph over a horrific depth of contemplation of the world and the most sensitive capacity for suffering by resorting to powerful misleading delusions and pleasurable illusions. But how seldom is that naïve state, that complete embrace by the beauty of appearance achieved! How inexpressibly sublime *Homer* is, therefore, who as a single individual relates to that Apollonian folk culture as the single dream-artist to the dream-capacity of the people and of nature itself. Homeric 'naïveté' is only to be understood as the complete triumph of the Apollonian illusion: this is such an illusion as nature so often uses to realize her intentions. The true goal is concealed by a hallucinatory image: we stretch out our hands towards the latter and nature achieves the former by deceiving us. In the Greeks, 'will' wanted to contemplate itself, in the transfiguration of the genius and the world of art; in order to glorify itself, its creatures had to feel themselves worthy of glorification, they had to see themselves again in a higher sphere, without this perfect world of contempla- tion acting as an imperative or a reproach. This is the sphere of beauty, in which they saw their mirror-images, the Olympians. With this mirroring of beauty, the Hellenic 'will' struggled against the artistically correlative talent for suffering and for the wisdom of suffering: and as a monument to its triumph Homer stands before us, the naïve artist.

4

The dream analogy goes some way towards explaining this naïve artist. Let us imagine the dreamer, as in the middle of the illusion of the dream-world and without disturb- ing it he shouts to himself: 'This is a dream, I want to dream on.' If we must deduce from this a deep inner joy in contemplating the dream, or if, on the other hand, in order to be able to dream with this inner joy in looking at all, we must first forget the present with its horrific urgency, then, under the guidance of Apollo the inter- preter of dreams, we may interpret all these phenomena in the following way. Although of the two halves of life, the waking half and the dreaming half, the first appears to us incomparably preferable, more important, more worthy, more worth living, even as the only half which is really lived, I would still like, however paradox- ical it may seem, to assert precisely the opposite evaluation of the dream on behalf of the secret ground of our essence, whose phenomenal appearance[41] we are. For the more I become aware of those omnipotent artistic drives in nature and in them of a fervent yearning for appearance,[42] for redemption through appearance, the more I feel myself compelled to make the metaphysical assumption that that which truly exists and the original Unity, with its eternal suffering and contradiction, needs at the same time the delightful vision, the pleasurable appearance, for its continual redemption: the very appearance which we, completely enmeshed in it and consisting of it, are forced to experience as that which does not truly exist, to experience then as a

---

41   In German: *Erscheinung.*
42   In German: *Schein.*

continual becoming in time, space, and causality, to experience in other words as empirical reality. So if for once we look away from our own 'reality' for a moment, if we grasp our empirical existence, like that of the world as a whole, as a concept produced at each moment by the original Unity, then the dream must seem to us now as the *appearance of appearance*[43] and therefore as an even higher satisfaction of the original desire for appearance. It is for this same reason that the innermost core of nature takes that indescribable pleasure in the naïve artist and the naïve work of art, which is likewise only the 'appearance of appearance'. In an allegorical painting, *Raphael*,[44] himself one of those immortal naïves, has represented this relegation of appearance to the status of appearance, the original process of the naïve artist and also of Apollonian culture. In his *Transfiguration*,[45] the lower half with the possessed boy, his despairing bearers, and the helplessly fearful disciples, shows us the reflection of the eternal original suffering, of the sole ground of the world: 'appearance' here is the reflection of the eternal contradiction, of the father of things. Now out of this appearance rises like the scent of ambrosia[46] a new vision-like world of appearance, which remains invisible to those who are caught in the first world of appearance – a brilliant hovering in purest bliss and painless contemplation through beaming wide-open eyes. Here we have before our eyes, rendered in the highest symbolism of art, that Apollonian world of beauty and its substratum, the horrific wisdom of Silenus, and we understand intuitively their reciprocal necessity. But Apollo appears to us again as the apotheosis of the *principium individuationis*, in which the eternally achieved goal of the original Unity, its redemption through appearance, is alone completed: he shows us with sublime gestures how the whole world of torment is necessary in order to force the individual to produce the redeeming vision and then to sit in calm contemplation of it as his small boat is tossed by the surrounding sea.

This apotheosis of individuation, if we think of it as at all imperative and prescriptive, knows only *one* law, the individual, that is, respect for the limits of the individual, *moderation* in the Hellenic sense. Apollo, as an ethical deity, demands of his disciples moderation and in order to maintain it, self-knowledge. And so in parallel with the aesthetic necessity of beauty runs the imperative of the 'know thyself'[47] and the 'nothing to excess!',[48] while arrogance and lack of moderation are regarded as the really hostile daemons of the non-Apollonian sphere, and hence as characteristics of the age before Apollo, of the age of the Titans, and of the world beyond the Apollonian, that is, the world of the barbarians. It was because of his Titanic love for men that Prometheus had to be torn apart by vultures, it was because of his arrogant wisdom, which solved

---

43   In German: *der Schein des Scheins*.
44   Raffaello Sanzio (1483–1520), Italian painter and architect.
45   Raphael's last painting, now in the Vatican Museum. Although Nietzsche had not seen the painting at this stage, it is highly praised by his Basel colleague Jacob Burckhardt in his *Cicerone* (1855).
46   The food of the gods.
47   The inscription on the Temple of Apollo at Delphi.
48   This maxim is variously ascribed to the Spartan politician Chilon (ca. 550 B.C.), the Athenian statesman Solon (640–560 B.C.), Socrates (470–399 B.C.) and Pythagoras (570–480 B.C.).

the riddle of the Sphinx,[49] that Oedipus had to plunge into a bewildering spiral of atrocities: in such a way did the Delphic god interpret the Greek past.

The effect aroused by the *Dionysian* also seemed 'Titanic' and 'barbaric' to the Apollonian Greek: while he was at the same time unable to conceal from himself the fact that he was inwardly related to those fallen Titans and heroes. Indeed, he was obliged to sense something even greater than this: his whole existence, with all its beauty and moderation, rested on a hidden substratum of suffering and knowledge, which was once again revealed to him by the Dionysian. And look! Apollo was unable to live without Dionysus! The 'Titanic' and the 'barbaric' were ultimately as much a necessity as the Apollonian! And let us now imagine how the ecstatic sound of the Dionysian celebration rang in an ever more seductive and spellbinding way through this artificially dammed-up world built on appearance and moderation, how in these spells the whole *excess* of nature in pleasure, pain, and knowledge resounded to the point of a piercing scream: let us imagine what meaning the ghostly harp music and psalm-singing of the Apollonian artist could have when compared to this daemonic song of the people! The muses of the art of 'appearance'[50] paled before an art which in its intoxication spoke the truth, in which the wisdom of Silenus cried out woe! woe! to the Olympians in their serenity. The individual, with all his limits and moderation, sank here into the self-oblivion of the Dionysian state and forgot the Apollonian principles. *Excess* revealed itself as the truth, and the contradiction, the bliss born of pain spoke out from the heart of nature. And so, wherever the Dionysian broke through, the Apollonian was cancelled, absorbed, and annihilated. But it is equally certain that in the place where the first assault was successfully resisted, the reputation and majesty of the Delphic god expressed itself in more inflexible and more threatening forms than ever before. Indeed, I can only explain the *Doric* state and Doric art as the extension of the Apollonian war camp: only in a continual struggle against the Titanic-barbarian essence of the Dionysian could such a defiantly stubborn and heavily fortified art, such a warlike and severe education, such a cruel and ruthless state, survive for any length of time.

So far, I have been elaborating the remark made at the beginning of this essay: how the Dionysian and the Apollonian have dominated the essence of the Hellenic in an ongoing sequence of new births in a relationship of reciprocal stimulation and intensification: how under the influence of the Apollonian drive to beauty the Homeric world developed out of the 'bronze' age[51] with its struggles between the Titans and its severe folk philosophy, how this 'naïve' magnificence was again swallowed up by the encroaching flood of the Dionysian, and how in face of this new power the

---

49   The Sphinx, a winged lioness with human head, persecutes the people of Thebes on behalf of the goddess Hera by killing anyone who cannot solve her riddle, which asks for the name of the being which first walks on four, then on two, and finally on three legs. The answer (human beings: as babies they crawl on all fours, as adults they walk upright, and in old age they walk with the aid of a stick) is provided by Oedipus, who, having rid Thebes of the Sphinx, returns to the city in triumph, inadvertently to marry his mother Jocasta, the widowed queen.

50   In German: "*Scheins.*"

51   Hesiod distinguishes between three periods of history in declining order: the Golden, the Silver and the Bronze.

Apollonian elevated itself to the inflexible majesty of Doric art and the Doric world-view. If in this way the more ancient history of the Hellenic world falls into four great artistic periods[52] in the course of the struggle between these two hostile principles, then we are forced at this point to ask further questions about the last phase of this development and growth, unless the latest period, that of Doric art, is to stand as the culmination and intended goal of those artistic drives: and here the sublime and highly praised work of art of *Attic tragedy* and the dramatic dithyramb[53] offers itself to our eyes as the common goal of both drives, whose secret marriage, following a long struggle, has glorified itself in such a child – at once Antigone and Cassandra.[54]

5

We are now approaching the real goal of our enquiry, which is directed towards know-ledge of the Dionysian–Apollonian genius and its work of art, or towards some sense of the mystery of that union. At this point we ask first where that new seed which later developed into tragedy and the dramatic dithyramb first attracted attention in the Hellenic world. On this matter the ancient world itself gives us an answer in visual form, when it places *Homer and Archilochus*[55] side by side on sculptures, intaglios, and so on as the original fathers and torchbearers of Greek poetry, sure in the feeling that only these two completely and equally original natures merited consideration, these two from whom a torrent of fire streams forth into the whole of the later Greek world. Homer, the old self-absorbed dreamer, the type of the Apollonian naïve artist, gazes in astonishment at the passionate head of Archilochus, the warlike servant of the muses as he is pursued wildly through existence: and modern aesthetics[56] could only add by way of interpretation that this was the moment when the 'objective' artist first

---

52   Nietzsche distinguishes here between four periods of Greek art, characterized respect-ively by myth ("Bronze" or "Titanic"), epic ("Homeric"), lyric poetry ("Dionysian"), and sculp-ture ("Doric").

53   According to Aristotle (*Poetics*, 1449a), tragedy grew out of the dithyramb.

54   Antigone is the daughter of Oedipus and Jocasta. After the death of Oedipus, his brother Creon becomes king of Thebes. The city is then attacked by Polynices, the brother of Antigone, who is killed in the fighting. When, against the orders of Creon, Antigone insists on burying her brother according to religious custom, Creon orders that she should be walled up in a cave, where she hangs herself. Aeschylus, Sophocles, and Euripides all based tragedies on the story. Cassandra is a Trojan prophetess, doomed never to be believed. Her gift of prophecy is cursed by Apollo when she refuses his sexual advances. During the Trojan War, Cassandra is raped by Ajax and enslaved by Agamemnon. Upon her arrival in Greece, she is murdered by Agamemnon's wife, Clytemnestra. For Nietzsche, Antigone's sense of religious ritual associates her with the Apollonian, while Cassandra's refusal of Apollo's advances and her foresight of disaster ally her with the Dionysian.

55   Greek lyric poet (ca. 680–640 B.C.), author of short poems characterized by the relation of personal experience and expression of intense feeling.

56   Allusion to Hegel's *Vorlesungen über die Ästhetik* (*Aesthetics*, 1835), which distinguishes between the objective art of the epic poet and the subjective art of the lyric poet.

confronts his 'subjective' counterpart. This interpretation is of little help to us, because we know the subjective artist only as a bad artist and demand above all in art the defeat of the subjective, redemption from the 'I' and the silencing of each individual will and craving, indeed we cannot conceive of the slightest possibility of truly artistic creation without objectivity, without pure disinterested contemplation.[57] For this reason our aesthetic must first solve the problem of how the 'lyric poet' is possible as an artist: he who according to the experience of all ages always says 'I' and sings out before us the whole chromatic scale of his passions and desires. In comparison with Homer, it is precisely this Archilochus who terrifies us, with the scream of his hatred and scorn, with the drunken outburst of his desires: is he, the first artist to be called subjective, not therefore none other than the true non-artist? But in that case what explains the reverence shown to this poet by even the Delphic oracle itself, the hearth of 'objective' art, in a number of remarkable pronouncements?

Schiller shed light on the process of the composition of his poetry in a psychological observation which did not give him pause although he was at a loss as to how to explain it; for he admitted that in the preparatory state which precedes the act of writing poetry he did not have before him and within him a series of images and causally organized thoughts, but rather a *musical mood* ('In my case, the feeling lacks a definite and clear object to begin with; this only takes shape later. A certain musical and emotional mood develops and for me the poetic idea only follows subsequently'[58]). If we now include the most important phenomenon of the whole of ancient lyric poetry, the unity, even identity of the *lyric poet* and the *musician*, which was universally taken for granted − in comparison with which our more modern lyric poetry appears like the headless image of a god − then we can now, on the basis of the aesthetic metaphysics presented earlier, explain the lyric poet in the following way. He has in the first place as a Dionysian artist become entirely fused with the original Unity, with its pain and contradiction, and produced the copy of this original Unity in the form of music, assuming, that is, that it is correct to identify music as a repetition and cast of the world; but now this music becomes visible to him again, as in an *allegorical dream-image*, under the influence of the Apollonian dream. That reflection of original suffering in music, devoid of image and concept, with its redemption in appearance, now produces a second mirror-image, as a single allegory or example. The artist has already surrendered his subjectivity in the Dionysian process: the image which now shows him his unity with the heart of the world is a dream-scene which gives concrete form to the original contradiction and pain, along with the original pleasure in appearance. So the 'I' of the lyric poet sounds forth from the abyss of being: his 'subjectivity' in the sense of the more modern aestheticians is a delusion. When Archilochus, the first of the Greek lyric poets, simultaneously declares his raging love and contempt to the daughters of Lycambes,[59] it is not his passion which dances before

---

57   Allusion to a notion found in Kant's and Schopenhauer's thinking on the aesthetic. For Kant, see *Kritik der Urteilskraft* (*Critique of Judgment*, 1790), 2. For Schopenhauer, see *WWR*, vol. 1, 3. 34.

58   Letter from Schiller to Goethe, March 18, 1796.

59   When Lycambes reneges on his promise to give his daughter Neobule in marriage to Archilochus, the poet avenges himself by writing defamatory verses about Neobule and her sisters, who all commit suicide as a result.

us in orgiastic frenzy: we see Dionysus and the Maenads, we see the intoxicated enthusiast Archilochus sunk in sleep – sleep as Euripides describes it in the *Bacchae*,[60] sleep
in high alpine meadows, in the midday sun –: and now Apollo draws near and touches
him with the laurel.[61] The sleeping poet, enchanted by Dionysian music, now begins
as it were to spray sparkling images around him, lyrical poems which at the height of
their development are called tragedies and dramatic dithyrambs.

The sculptor, and also the related figure of the epic poet, is absorbed in the pure
contemplation of images. Bereft of images, the Dionysian musician is himself wholly
and exclusively original pain and original echo of that pain. The lyrical genius feels
a new world of images and allegories grow forth from that state of mystical self-
abandonment and unity, a world which is completely different in colouring, causality,
and tempo from that of the sculptor and epic poet. While the epic poet lives in these
images a life of comfort and joy otherwise impossible and never tires of contemplating them lovingly in their minutest details, while he regards even the fury of the raging Achilles as nothing more than an image, whose raging expression he enjoys with
that dreamer's pleasure in appearance – so that he is protected by this mirror of appearance from unification and fusion with its forms – the images of the lyric poet are on
the other hand nothing other than himself, are as it were only different objectivations
of himself, which is why he may as the moving centre of that world say 'I': only this
'self'[62] is not the same as that of the empirically real waking man, but rather the only
I which truly exists, the eternal I, resting on the ground of things, the I by means of
whose copies the lyrical genius sees through to the very ground of things. Let us now
imagine how among these copies he regards *himself* as non-genius, that is, as 'subject',
the whole throng of subjective passions and impulses of the will directed towards a
definite object which appears real to him; and if it now appears as if the lyrical genius
and the non-genius associated with him were one and the same and as if the former
spoke of its own accord the little word 'I', then this apparent state of affairs will no
longer lead us astray, as it has certainly led astray those who have designated the lyric
poet as the subjective poet. In truth, Archilochus, who loves and hates and is consumed by burning passion, is only a vision of the genius which has long since ceased
to be Archilochus but become instead the world-genius which expresses in symbolic
form its original pain through that allegory of Archilochus the man, while Archilochus

60   Euripides' *Bacchae* is part of a trilogy comprising also *Alcmaeon in Corinth* and *Iphigenia
at Aulis*. The *Bacchae* relates the conflict between Dionysus and Pentheus, king of Thebes. In
retaliation for the refusal of the people of Thebes to recognize him as a god, Dionysus drives
the women of the city mad and forces them to celebrate his rites on Mount Cithaeron. Against
the advice of his grandfather Cadmus and the seer Tiresias, Pentheus rejects the new religion
and imprisons Dionysus, who then destroys the king's palace by causing an earthquake. Under
the influence of Dionysus, Pentheus disguises himself as a woman to observe the rites but is
discovered and torn apart by the celebrants, with his mother Agave bearing his severed head
into the city. The play ends with the banishment of the family of Cadmus from Thebes.
61   Laurel is an attribute of Apollo, who carries a laurel branch in memory of the nymph
Daphne, whom he transformed into a laurel tree when she refused his advances.
62   In German: *Ichheit*.

the man, who subjectively wills and desires, can never at any time be a poet. But it is not at all necessary for the lyric poet to see before him only the phenomenon of Archilochus the man as the reflection of eternal being; and tragedy proves how far removed the vision-world of the lyric poet can be from that least distant of phenomena.

Schopenhauer, who did not conceal from himself the difficulty which the lyric poet posed for the philosophical view of art, believed that he had found a way out of the impasse, one along which I cannot follow him. Yet it was into his hands alone that the means were given to deal decisively with this difficulty, in the form of his profound metaphysics of music: and here I believe I have accomplished this task in his spirit and in his honour. It was in the following terms, however, that he characterized the particular essence of song (World as Will and Representation, I): 'It is the subject of the will, that is, his own particular willing which fills the consciousness of the singer, often in the form of an unburdened, satisfied willing (joy) but probably even more often in the form of an inhibited willing (sorrow), always as affect, passion, agitated emotional state. But alongside this state, through looking at his natural surroundings, the singer at the same time becomes conscious of himself as the subject of pure knowledge devoid of will, whose unshakeable spiritual calm then comes into conflict with the pressure of the increasingly restricted, increasingly needy willing: the feeling of this contrast, of this alternation is really what is expressed in the whole of the song and what constitutes the lyrical state itself. In this state, pure knowledge as it were approaches us in order to redeem us from willing and its pressure: we follow, yet only momentarily: willing, the memory of our personal goals, tears us away again and again from calm contemplation; but equally the next beautiful surroundings in which pure knowledge devoid of will presents itself to us entice us away again from willing. For that reason, in the song and lyrical mood, willing (the personal interest in goals) and the pure contemplation of the available surroundings are blended together in a wonderful mixture: relations between both are sought and imagined; subjective mood, the affection of will communicates its colour to the contemplated surroundings and vice versa in a reflexive movement: the genuine song is the imprint of the mixed and divided feelings of this emotional state.'[63]

Who could fail to notice in this depiction the fact that lyric poetry is characterized as an incompletely achieved art, an art which as it were reaches its goal only seldom and sporadically, even as a half-art, whose *essence* should consist in the miraculous blending together of willing and pure contemplation, that is of the unaesthetic and the aesthetic state? We assert rather that the whole opposition between subjective and objective, which even Schopenhauer still used as a yardstick to classify the arts, is completely irrelevant to aesthetics, since there the subject, the willing individual who promotes his own ends, can only be conceived as the enemy and not as the origin of art. But in so far as the subject is an artist, he has already been redeemed from his individual will and become as it were a medium, through which the only subject which truly exists celebrates its redemption in appearance. For this above all must be clear to us, as a cause of both humiliation *and* exultation, that the whole comedy of art is not in any way performed for our benefit, for our improvement and edification, and that we are to an even lesser extent the real creators of that world of art: but we may assume that we are already images and artistic projections for the true creator of that world and have our greatest dignity in our meaning as works of art – for only as an *aesthetic phenomenon*[64] are existence and the world *justified* to eternity: – while admittedly our consciousness of this meaning of ours scarcely differs from that which warriors in a painting have of the battle depicted on the canvas. Consequently, our whole knowledge of art is at bottom completely illusory, because we are not as knowing beings at one and identical with that essence, which as sole creator and spectator of that comedy of art prepares for itself an eternal pleasure. Only in so far as the genius in the act of artistic creation fuses with that original artist of the world does he know something about the eternal essence of art: for in that state he miraculously resembles the uncanny image of the fairy-tale, which can turn its eyes inside out and contemplate itself; now he is simultaneously subject and object, simultaneously poet, actor and spectator.

[. . .]

7

We must now avail ourselves of all the principles of art discussed so far in order to find our way in the labyrinth, for there is no other way to describe it, of the *origin of Greek tragedy*. I do not think I am speaking nonsense if I say that the problem of this origin has not yet even been seriously posed, let alone solved, no matter how many times before the torn and fluttering shreds of the ancient tradition have been sewn together and then torn asunder. This tradition[65] tells us decisively that *tragedy emerged from the tragic chorus* and was originally only the chorus and nothing but the chorus: which obliges us to look into the heart of the tragic chorus as the real original drama, without somehow satisfying ourselves with the current artistic clichés – that the chorus represents the ideal spectator or represents the princely area of the stage to the people. The latter explanation, which sounds sublime to many politicians – as if the immutable moral law of the democratic Athenians were represented in the people's chorus, which is always in the right in its dealings with the passionate excesses and extravagances of the kings – might well be suggested by a word of Aristotle's:[66] none the less, it has no influence whatsoever on the original formation of tragedy, since those purely religious origins exclude the whole opposition of people and prince and indeed any political-social sphere whatsoever; but with reference to the classical form of the chorus known to us from Aeschylus and Sophocles we might also regard it as blasphemy to speak of a presentiment of a 'constitutional representation of the people', a blasphemy from which others have not shrunk. The ancient state constitutions had no knowledge of constitutional representation of the people *in praxi*[67] and hopefully did not even have so much as a 'presentiment' of it in their tragedy.

   Much more famous than this political explanation of the chorus is A. W. Schlegel's thought which advises us to regard the chorus to a certain extent as the epitome and

64   In German: *aesthetisches Phänomen*.
65   Allusion to Aristotle's *Poetics*, 1449a.
66   In his *Politics* (1284b), Aristotle compares the practice of ostracism in Athenian society to the constitution of the tragic chorus.
67   Latin: in practice.

essence of the audience, as the 'ideal spectator'.[68] This opinion, when compared with that historical tradition which tells us that tragedy was nothing but the chorus, reveals itself for what it is, a crude, unscientific, yet brilliant assertion, whose brilliance derives exclusively from its concentrated form of expression, from the truly German prejudice in favour of everything going by the name of 'ideal', and from our momentary astonishment. We are indeed astonished once we compare the theatre public which we know so well with the chorus and ask ourselves if it would be at all possible to idealize this public into something analogous to the tragic chorus. We silently deny this and are no less surprised by the audacity of Schlegel's assertion than by the completely different nature of the Greek public. For we had always believed that the true spectator, whoever he might be, must always remain aware of the fact that he has before him a work of art and not an empirical reality: while the Greek tragic chorus is compelled to recognize incarnations of real existence in the figures of the stage. The chorus of Oceanides really believes that it sees the Titan Prometheus[69] before it and considers itself as real as the god of the stage. And we are asked to believe that this should be the highest and purest kind of spectator, one which like the Oceanides would consider Prometheus as physically present and real? And so it would be the sign of the ideal spectator that he would run onto the stage and free the god from his torture? We had believed in an aesthetic public and considered the individual spectator the better equipped the more he could regard the work of art as art, that is, aesthetically; and now Schlegel's expression suggests to us that the completely ideal spectator lets the world of the stage work its effect on him not at all in an aesthetic but in an embodied and empirical way. Oh these Greeks! we sighed; they overturn our aesthetics. But being used to that, we repeated Schlegel's aphorism every time the chorus came up in discussion.

But here the tradition, which is quite categorical, bears witness against Schlegel: the chorus in itself, without a stage, the primitive form of tragedy, is not consistent with the chorus of the ideal spectator. What sort of artistic genre would it be which was derived from the concept of the spectator, and which was represented in its true form by the 'spectator in himself'? The spectator without a play is a nonsensical concept. We fear that the birth of tragedy can be explained neither by reverence for the moral intelligence of the masses nor by the concept of the spectator without a play, and consider such shallow points of view incapable of even skimming the surface of this deep problem.

Schiller had already divulged an infinitely more valuable insight into the meaning of the chorus in the famous foreword to *The Bride of Messina*,[70] where he viewed the

---

68   August Wilhelm Schlegel (1767–1845), German poet, translator, critic, literary historian, Orientalist, and translator of Shakespeare into German, who, along with his brother Friedrich, became a central figure in the Jena circle of Romantic thinkers and writers. In the fifth of his lectures *Über dramatische Kunst und Literatur* (*On Dramatic Art and Literature*, 1808), he describes the chorus as an "idealized spectator."
69   Allusion to Aeschylus' tragedy *Prometheus Bound* (ca. 458 B.C.), where the chorus consists of Oceanides, the daughters of the Titan Oceanus, who come to console and comfort Prometheus during his punishment for stealing fire from the gods and giving it to humans.
70   Reference to Schiller's text *Über den Gebrauch des Chors in der Tragödie* (*On the Use of the Chorus in Tragedy*), published as the foreword to his play *Die Braut von Messina* (*The Bride of Messina*, 1803).

chorus as a living wall which tragedy built around itself in order to shut out the real world and to protect its ideal ground and poetic freedom.

Using this as his main weapon, Schiller engages in a struggle against the commonly held concept of the natural, against the illusion commonly demanded of dramatic poetry. According to Schiller, even if in the theatre the daylight is merely artificial, the architecture merely symbolic and the metrical language of an ideal character, the naturalist error still dominates overall: for Schiller, it is not enough that the very thing which constitutes the essence of all poetry be merely tolerated as a poetic licence. The introduction of the chorus is, for Schiller, the decisive step through which war with naturalism in art is openly and honestly declared. – It seems to me that this is the kind of point of view which our arrogant and condescending age dismisses with the catchword 'pseudo-idealism.'[71] I fear that with our contemporary reverence for the natural and the real we have arrived at the opposite pole of all idealism, that is, in the region of the wax museum. There too there is a kind of art, as in certain contemporary popular novels: only spare us the torture of asking us to believe that this art has overcome the 'pseudo-idealism' of Schiller and Goethe.

Admittedly, the ground upon which the Greek satyr chorus, the chorus of the original tragedy, used to tread, is, following Schiller's correct insight, an 'ideal' ground, a ground elevated high above the real paths trodden by mortals. For this chorus, the Greek has erected the scaffolding of an invented *state of nature* and placed upon it invented *creatures of nature*. Tragedy has grown up on this foundation and has of course from the very beginning dispensed with an embarrassing counterfeiting of reality. And yet this is not a world arbitrarily imagined into existence between heaven and earth; but rather a world of equal reality and credibility to that which Olympus and its inhabitants possessed for the Hellenic believer. The satyr as Dionysian chorist lives in a reality admitted by faith, under the sanction of myth and religion. The fact that tragedy begins with him, that the Dionysian wisdom of tragedy speaks through him is a phenomenon which disconcerts us as much as the original emergence of tragedy from the chorus. Perhaps we might gain a starting point for reflection if I make the assertion that the satyr, the invented creature of nature, has the same relationship to the man of culture as Dionysian music has to civilization. Richard Wagner said of the latter that it would be cancelled and absorbed by music as lamplight is by daylight.[72] The Greek man of culture, I believe, felt himself cancelled and absorbed in a similar way by the chorus of satyrs: and this is the most immediate effect of Dionysian tragedy, that state and society, indeed the whole chasm separating man from man, gives way to an overpowering feeling of unity which leads back to the heart of nature. The metaphysical consolation – with which, as I have already suggested here, all true tragedy leaves us – that life at the bottom of things, in spite of the passing of phenomena, remains indestructibly powerful and pleasurable, this consolation appears in embodied clarity in the chorus of satyrs, of creatures of nature who live on as it were ineradicably behind all civilization and remain eternally the same in spite of the passing of generations and of the history of peoples.

71   Polemical term criticizing an art which seeks to embody timeless ideals in the manner of Goethe and Schiller during their Weimar period. It implies a position in favor of realist and naturalistic art, based on the imitation of contemporary reality.
72   Quotation from Wagner's essay *Beethoven* (1870).

The profound Hellene, who is uniquely equipped for the most delicate and intense suffering, who has directed his acute gaze down into the middle of that fearful swirling compulsive process of annihilation which goes by the name of world history as well as into the cruelty of nature, and is in danger of longing for a Buddhist negation of the will, finds consolation in this chorus. Rescued by art, he is rescued, for its own purposes, by – life.

The ecstasy of the Dionysian state, with its annihilation of the usual limits and borders of existence, contains for its duration a *lethargic* element in which all past personal experience is submerged. And so this chasm of oblivion separates the world of everyday reality from that of Dionysian reality. However, as soon as that everyday reality returns to consciousness, it is experienced for what it is with disgust: an ascetic mood which negates the will is the fruit of those conditions. In this sense the Dionysian man is similar to Hamlet: both have at one time cast a true glance into the essence of things, they have acquired *knowledge*, and action is repugnant to them; for their action can change nothing in the eternal essence of things, they feel that it is laughable or shameful that they are expected to repair a world which is out of joint.[73] Knowledge kills action, to action belongs the veil of illusion – that is the lesson of Hamlet, not that cheap wisdom of Hans the Dreamer,[74] who fails to act because he reflects too much, as a result as it were of an excess of possibilities; not reflection, no! – but true knowledge, insight into the horrific truth, outweighs any motive leading to action, in Hamlet as well as in the Dionysian man. Now no consolation is accepted, the longing goes beyond the world after death, goes beyond even the gods, now existence, together with its glittering reflection in the gods or in an immortal other world, is negated. Conscious of the truth once glimpsed, man now sees all around him only the horrific or the absurd aspects of existence, now he understands the symbolic aspect of Ophelia's fate,[75] now he recognizes the wisdom of the forest god Silenus: it disgusts him.

Here, at this point of extreme danger for the will, *art* draws near as the enchantress who comes to rescue and heal; only she can reshape that disgust at the thought of the horrific or absurd aspects of life into notions with which it is possible to live: these are the *sublime*, the artistic taming of the horrific, and the *comic*,[76] the artistic discharge of disgust at the absurd. The satyr chorus of the dithyramb is the rescuing deed of Greek art; those feelings previously described exhaust themselves in the middle world of these companions of Dionysus.

[. . .]

73   See Shakespeare, *Hamlet*, I. v. 188.
74   A double allusion: first to Hamlet's soliloquy at II. ii. 563–6, where he speaks of himself as "like a John-a-dreams" (rendered as "Hans der Träumer" in the standard German translation); second, to the monologue of Hans Sachs in Wagner's *Meistersinger*, III. i.
75   In *Hamlet*, Ophelia is the daughter of Polonius; she goes insane and drowns herself when Hamlet rejects her and kills her father.
76   The opposition of the sublime and the comic is developed by Romantic aesthetics, superseding the prior distinction, made by Edmund Burke and Kant, between the finite and reassuring category of the beautiful and the infinite and terrifying sublime. See, for example, Jean Paul's *Vorschule der Ästhetik* (*School for Aesthetics*, 1804/13).

12

[. . .] let us pause here for a moment to remind ourselves of the impression of duality and incommensurability at the heart of Aeschylean tragedy as we have previously described it. Let us think how disconcerted we felt by the *chorus* and the *tragic hero* of that tragedy, both of which were as difficult to reconcile with our habits as with the tradition – until we rediscovered that duality itself as the origin and essence of Greek tragedy, as the expression of two interwoven artistic drives, *the Apollonian and the Dionysian.*

To excise that original and all-powerful Dionysian element from tragedy and to rebuild tragedy purely on the basis of an un-Dionysian art, morality, and world-view – that is the Euripidean tendency which now reveals itself to us in radiant clarity.

At the end of his life, Euripides himself posed the question of the value and meaning of this tendency to his contemporaries most emphatically in the form of a myth. Is the Dionysian entitled to exist at all? Should it not be forcibly eradicated from Hellenic soil? Certainly, the poet tells us, if only that were possible: but the god Dionysus is too powerful: his most intelligent opponent – such as Pentheus in the *Bacchae* – is unsuspectingly caught in his spell and subsequently plunges to his doom under its influence. The judgement of the two old men Cadmus and Tiresias also seems to be the judgement of the aged poet: that the thought of the cleverest individuals cannot overthrow those old folk traditions, the eternally self-perpetuating veneration of Dionysus, and indeed that it is proper to show at least a cautious diplomatic interest in such miraculous forces: which still allows the possibility that the god might take offence at such a lukewarm interest and finally transform the diplomat – like Cadmus in this instance – into a dragon. This is said by a poet who with heroic strength resisted Dionysus throughout a long life – in order finally to conclude his career with a glorification of his opponent and a suicide, like someone who throws himself from a tower to escape the horrific dizziness of unbearable vertigo. The tragedy in question is a protest against the impossibility of implementing his tendency; ah, but it had already been implemented! The miraculous had happened: by the time the poet retracted, his tendency had already triumphed. Dionysus had already been driven from the tragic stage, and by a daemonic power which spoke through Euripides. Even Euripides was in a certain sense only a mask: the deity which talked through him was neither Dionysus nor Apollo but a newly born daemon called *Socrates.*[77] This is the new opposition: the Dionysian and the Socratic, and the work of art of Greek tragedy foundered on it. In spite of Euripides' efforts to console us with his retraction, he fails: the most magnificent temple lies in ruins; of what use to us is the lament of the man who destroyed it and his admission that it had been the most beautiful of all temples? And even if Euripides has been punished by being transformed into a dragon by the artistic arbiters of all ages – whom might this pitiful compensation satisfy?

Let us now approach that *Socratic* tendency, with which Euripides fought and conquered Aeschylean tragedy.

---

77 *Daemon* is the Greek term for a divine being without a specific form, a protective or persecuting spirit. In Plato's *Apology* (31d), Socrates in his defense talks of his daemonium, a spirit which often advised him against, but never in favor of, a specific course of action.

What could have been the goal – this is the question which we must now ask ourselves – of the Euripidean intention, in the most ideal form in which it was implemented, to found drama exclusively on the un-Dionysian? What form of drama remained if it were not to be born from the womb of music, in that mysterious Dionysian twilight? Only the *dramatized epic*: in whose Apollonian artistic domain the *tragic* effect is admittedly unattainable. It is not a matter here of the content of the events represented; indeed I would like to argue that Goethe in his projected *Nausicaa*[78] would have found it impossible to make the suicide of that idyllic being – which was to constitute the fifth act – tragically moving; so tremendous is the power of the epic-Apollonian that it conjures away from before our very eyes the most horrific things through that pleasure in appearance and in redemption through appearance. The poet of the dramatized epic is as unable to fuse completely with his images as the epic rhapsode: he remains for ever calm and unmoved, a wide-eyed contemplation, which sees images *before* itself. The actor in his dramatic epic remains at the profoundest level for ever a rhapsode; the consecration of the inner dreaming settles over all his actions so that he is never completely an actor.

How then does the Euripidean play relate to this ideal of Apollonian drama? As the young rhapsode of Plato's *Ion* relates to the solemn rhapsode of an earlier age, describing his being in the following terms: 'When I say something sad, my eyes fill with tears: but if what I say is terrifying and horrific, then my hair stands on end and my heart pounds with fear.'[79] Here we no longer see that epic loss of the self in appearance, the cool absence of emotion of the true actor, who, particularly at the moment of his most intense activity, is completely appearance and pleasure in appearance. Euripides is the actor whose heart pounds and hair stands on end; as Socratic thinker, he elaborates his plan, as passionate actor he executes it. Neither in the planning nor in the execution is he a pure artist. Thus Euripidean drama is a thing at once cool and on fire, as likely to freeze as to burn; it is impossible for it to attain the Apollonian effect of epic, while on the other hand it has freed itself as much as possible from the Dionysian elements and now, in order to be able to have any effect at all, it needs new stimulants, which now no longer lie within the sphere of the two single artistic drives, the Apollonian and the Dionysian. These new stimulants are cool paradoxical *thoughts* – instead of Apollonian visions – and fiery *emotions* – in the place of Dionysian raptures – and they really are highly realistic imitations of thoughts and emotions devoid of any trace of the ether of art.

So, now that we have acknowledged that Euripides failed utterly to provide an exclusively Apollonian basis for drama, and that its un-Dionysian tendency developed rather into a naturalistic and unartistic aberration, we may approach the essence of *aesthetic Socratism*, whose highest law runs approximately as follows: 'In order to be beautiful, everything must be intelligible'; as a counterpart to the Socratic principle 'Knowledge is virtue'.[80] With this doctrine in hand, Euripides measured all the

78   Goethe planned to write a tragedy based on the story of Nausicaa as related in Homer's *Odyssey*. The plot was to turn on the tragic fate of Nausicaa, the daughter of the Phaeacian king Alcinous, who drowns herself after being rejected by Odysseus. Goethe abandoned the project after completing a fragment of the first act in 1787.
79   Plato, *Ion*, 535c.
80   Cf. Plato, *Protagoras*, 361a–c.

individual elements of drama and rectified them accordingly: language, characters, the dramatic structure, the music of the chorus. What we are so often accustomed to considering in comparison to Sophoclean tragedy as poetic shortcoming and regression on Euripides' part is to a large extent the product of that penetrating critical process, of that audacious intelligence. May the Euripidean *prologue*[81] serve as an example for the productivity of that rationalistic method. Nothing could be further from the technique of our own stage than the prologue in Euripidean drama. That a single character should emerge at the beginning of the play, say who he is, what precedes the action, what has happened up until now, indeed what will happen in the course of the play, would be condemned by a modern dramatist as a wilful and unpardonable renunciation of the effect of suspense. One knows what will happen; who will want to wait until it really happens? – since in this case there exists nothing of the exciting relationship between a prophetic dream and what happens subsequently in reality. Euripides did not think like that at all. The effect of tragedy was never based on epic suspense, on the stimulating uncertainty of what will happen now and afterwards: but rather on those great rhetorical-lyrical scenes in which the passion and the dialectic of the protagonists swelled up into a broad and powerful torrent. Everything served to enhance not plot but pathos:[82] and whatever did not serve to enhance pathos was regarded as reprehensible. But what disturbs the pleasurable devotion to these scenes most for the spectator is a missing link, a gap in the weave of the story so far; as long as the spectator is still obliged to work out what such and such a character represents, or the presuppositions of such and such a conflict of inclinations and intentions, full absorption in the suffering and actions of the main characters, in the breathless sympathy of compassion and fear[83] remains impossible. Aeschylean–Sophoclean tragedy used the most ingenious artistic means to give the spectator, as if by chance, all the strands necessary for understanding in the opening scenes: a process in which the noble artistry of masking formal *necessity* and letting it appear as accident proves itself. All the same, however, Euripides believed that he detected during those opening scenes a peculiar anxiety on the part of the spectator to solve the problem of the story so far, so that the poetic beauties and the pathos of the exposition were lost on him. So in Euripides' plays the prologue preceded even the exposition and was placed in the mouth of a character who could be trusted: often a deity had to guarantee so to speak the plot of the tragedy to the public and allay any doubt as to the reality of the myth: in a similar way to that in which Descartes[84] was only able to prove the reality of the empirical world through an appeal to God's truthfulness and his inability to lie. Euripides needed this same divine truthfulness once again at the end of his drama in order to assure the public of the future of his heroes: this is the task of the notorious *deus ex machina*.[85] Between the epic prologue and epilogue lies the dramatic-lyrical present, the 'drama' proper.

---

81   While earlier tragedians began with the entrance of the chorus, Euripides added a prologue delivered by a single actor to explain the plot and characters of the drama to follow.
82   According to Aristotle's definition, traditional tragedy was driven by action and plot rather than by character and psychology (*Poetics*, 1449b).
83   Allusion to Aristotle's discussion of the function of tragedy as catharsis, a sympathetic discharge of the emotions of fear and pity (*Poetics*, 1449b).
84   René Descartes (1596–1650), French philosopher and mathematician.
85   Latin: god from the machine (i.e. providential interposition or divine intervention).

Euripides as a poet is therefore above all the echo of his conscious insights; and it is precisely this which gives him such a memorable place in the history of Greek art. Looking back on his critical and creative production he must often have felt that it was his duty to give dramatic life to the beginning of Anaxagoras' text: 'In the beginning all things were mixed together; then came understanding and created order.'[86] And if Anaxagoras with his *nous*[87] appeared among the philosophers like the first sober man among a crowd of mere drunks, then Euripides too might have used a similar image to understand his relation to the other tragic poets. As long as the sole ordering and governing principle of all things, the *nous*, was excluded from artistic creation, then everything remained mixed together in a chaotic primal soup; this is the judgement Euripides had to make, as the first 'sober man' he had to condemn the 'drunken' poets in this way. What Sophocles said of Aeschylus, that he acted justly, albeit unconsciously, was certainly not said in the spirit of Euripides: who would at most have allowed that Aeschylus created something unjust *because* he created unconsciously. Even the divine Plato speaks almost always only ironically of the creative capacity of the poet, in so far as it is not conscious insight, and equates it with the gift of the soothsayer and interpreter of dreams;[88] as if the poet is only capable of composing poetry when unconscious and abandoned by reason. Euripides undertook the task, which Plato had also undertaken, to show to the world the reverse of the 'unreasonable' poet; his basic aesthetic principle 'in order to be beautiful, everything must be conscious' is, as I said, the counterpart to the Socratic 'in order to be good, everything must be conscious'. Accordingly, Euripides may stand for us as the poet of aesthetic Socratism. Socrates however was that *second spectator* who failed to understand and so to respect the earlier tragedy; in alliance with him, Euripides dared to be the herald of a new artistic creation. If it destroyed the earlier tragedy, then aesthetic Socratism is the lethal principle: but in so far as the struggle was directed against the Dionysus of the older art, we recognize in Socrates the opponent of Dionysus, the new Orpheus[89] who rises up against Dionysus and, although destined to be torn apart by the Maenads of the Athenian court, still puts the more powerful god to flight: Dionysus, who, as when he fled from Lycurgus[90] king of the Edoni, sought refuge in the depths of the sea, namely in the mystical tides of a secret cult which was gradually spreading over the whole world.

---

86   Saying attributed to Anaxagoras (ca. 500–425 B.C.) by Diogenes Laertius in *Lives and Opinions of Eminent Philosophers*, II. 6.

87   Term used by Anaxagoras in two different senses: first, human knowledge of being, and second, the creator of the universe.

88   See Plato, *Ion*, 533e–534d; *Phaedrus*, 244a–245a; *Laws*, 719c.

89   Orpheus, the son of a Muse and a gifted musician, teaches that man is a guilty and polluted being. He is dismembered by Maenads after attempting to displace the cult of Dionysus, and his severed head is cast into the river Hebrus, which carries it singing to the island of Lesbos, where it is buried. Nietzsche identifies Socrates with Orpheus as an opponent of Dionysus.

90   In the course of an attempt to invade Thrace, Dionysus' army is captured by Lycurgus, king of the Edoni. Dionysus himself escapes by diving into the sea and taking refuge in the cave of the goddess Thetis. In revenge, the Dionysian cults later overrun Thrace.

13

[. . .]

That miraculous phenomenon which is described as the 'daemonium of Socrates' offers us a key to the essence of Socrates. In certain circumstances, when his great powers of reason began to waver, a divine voice made itself heard and gave him a sure indication. This voice, when it comes, always *dissuades*. In this completely abnormal nature, instinctive wisdom only shows itself sporadically in order to oppose and *obstruct* conscious knowledge. While in all productive people it is precisely instinct which is the creative-affirmative force and it is consciousness which criticizes and dissuades, in Socrates, however, instinct becomes the critic and consciousness the creator – a true monstrosity *per defectum!*[91] Actually, we have before us here a monstrous *defectus* of that mystic disposition, so that Socrates might be characterized as the very type of the *non-mystic*, in whom the logical nature has through uncontrolled growth developed itself to excess in the same way as instinctive wisdom has in the mystic. On the other hand, however, the logical drive which emerged in Socrates was utterly forbidden to turn against itself; in this boundless torrent it demonstrated a power of nature such as we encounter to our horrified surprise only in the greatest instinctive forces. Anyone who has received even the slightest hint of the divine naïveté and certainty of the Socratic way of life from Plato's writings will also feel how this huge driving wheel of logical Socratism is in motion *behind* Socrates as it were and how, in order to contemplate it, we must see through Socrates himself as if he were only a shadow. But that he himself had a sense of this relationship is expressed in the dignified seriousness with which he everywhere asserted his divine calling, continuing to protest it even before his judges. It was at bottom as impossible to refute him on this point as it was to approve his instinct-dissolving influence. In this insoluble conflict, once he had been summoned before the forum of the Greek state, only one form of sentence was imperative – exile; as something completely enigmatic, unclassifiable, inexplicable, he might have been dispatched over the border, and no posterity could have rightfully accused the Athenians of a shameful deed. But that a sentence of death rather than one of exile only was passed seems to have been brought about by Socrates himself, with complete clarity and without the natural horror in the face of death: according to Plato's account, he approached death with the calm with which he left the symposium[92] in the early dawn as the last of the revellers; while behind him on the benches and on the floor his fellow carousers remained behind asleep, dreaming of Socrates, the true eroticist. *The dying Socrates* became the new ideal, never seen before, of the noble Greek youth: above all the typical Hellenic youth, Plato, threw himself down before this image with all the fervent devotion of his enthusiast's soul.[93]

14

Let us now imagine the single great Cyclops's eye of Socrates turned towards tragedy, that eye which never glowed with the sweet madness of artistic enthusiasm – let us

---

91 Latin: from weakness or infirmity.
92 See Plato, *Symposium*, 223c–d.
93 On the dying Socrates see also *GS* 341 and *TI* II. 1.

imagine how this eye was denied the pleasure of looking into the Dionysian abyss –
what must it have really seen in the 'sublime and much praised' tragic art, as Plato[94]
calls it? Something utterly unreasonable, where causes appear to lack effects and effects
appear to lack causes; and moreover the whole so colourful and diverse that it could
only repel a balanced constitution, while it might dangerously inflame touchy and sensitive souls. We know what single genre of poetry Socrates understood, the *Aesopian
fable*:[95] and this certainly occurred with that same smiling accommodation with which
the good old honest Gellert sings the praises of poetry in the fable of the bee and
the hen:

> You see from me how useful it can be
> To use an image to tell the truth
> To someone who is not very bright.[96]

But to Socrates tragic art did not even appear to tell 'the truth': quite apart from
the fact that it addresses the man who 'is not very bright', rather than the philosopher: two reasons for avoiding it. Like Plato, he counted it among the flattering arts,
which portray the pleasing rather than the useful[97] and therefore demanded of his disciples abstinence and strict segregation from such unphilosophical stimulants; with such
success that the youthful tragic poet Plato[98] first burnt his poetry in order that he might
become a pupil of Socrates. And even where unconquerable constitutions fought against
the Socratic maxims, their power, together with the force of his tremendous character,
was still great enough to force poetry itself into new and unprecedented positions.

An example of this is Plato, whom we have just mentioned: in his condemnation
of tragedy and of art as a whole, he certainly did not lag behind the naïve cynicism
of his master, and yet he was obliged by full artistic necessity to create an art-form
essentially related to the existing art-forms which he had rejected. The main reproach
which Plato addressed to the older art – that it is the imitation of an apparent image,
and so belongs to an even lower sphere than the empirical world – certainly could
not be directed against the new work of art: and so we see Plato's efforts to go beyond
reality and to represent the idea which lies at the basis of that pseudo-reality. But in
this way Plato the thinker arrived by a circuitous route at the place which had always
been his home as an artist and from where Sophocles and the whole of the earlier
art mounted their solemn protest against such a reproach. If tragedy had absorbed all

---

94   Plato, *Gorgias*, 502b.
95   Aesop was the most famous Greek composer of fables, short narratives with a moral in
which animals play the part of humans. While awaiting execution, Socrates rewrote some of
Aesop's fables in verse (Plato, *Phaedo*, 61b).
96   Quotation from *Die Biene und die Henne* (*The Bee and the Hen*, 1744) by Christian Fürchtegott
Gellert (1715–69), a German writer specializing in dramatic comedy and verse fables.
97   Allusion to the *Ars poetica* of the Roman poet Horace (65–8 B.C.), according to which
the dual function of art is to please and to provide useful moral instruction.
98   According to Diogenes Laertius, Plato wrote poetry and tragedies before meeting
Socrates, but burnt his work when Socrates advised against having it performed in a theatre
contest (*Eminent Philosophers*, III. 5).

earlier artistic genres, so the same might be said in an eccentric sense of the Platonic dialogue, which, created from a mixture of all available styles and forms, is suspended between narrative, lyric, and drama, between prose and poetry, and so broke the strict older law of the unity of linguistic form; this was taken much further in the writings of the *Cynics*,[99] who with the greatest stylistic diversity, in the oscillation between prosaic and metric forms, realized the literary image of the 'raving Socrates' whom they represented in life. The Platonic dialogue was the raft as it were on which the earlier poetry rescued itself and all its children from shipwreck: huddled together in a confined space and fearfully subservient to the single helmsman Socrates, they now sailed into a new world which never tired of the fantastic image passing before it. Plato really gave to all posterity the model for a new art-form, the *novel*: which may be characterized as the infinitely intensified Aesopian fable, in which poetry lives in a hierarchical relation to dialectical philosophy similar to that in which for centuries this same philosophy lived with theology: namely as *ancilla*.[100] This was the new posi-tion into which poetry was forced by Plato under the pressure of the daemonic Socrates.

At this point, art is overgrown by *philosophical thought* and forced to cling closely to the trunk of dialectic. The *Apollonian* tendency has disguised itself in logical schematism: just as we were obliged to perceive something similar in Euripides, accompanied by a translation of the *Dionysian* into naturalistic emotion. Socrates, the dialectical hero in the Platonic drama, reminds us of the related nature of the Euripidean hero, who must defend his actions by argument and counter-argument and in the process so often risks forfeiting our tragic compassion: for who could fail to recognize the *optimistic* element in the essence of the dialectic, which celebrates exultantly in each conclusion and needs the cool radiance of consciousness in order to breathe: the optimistic ele-ment which, once it has penetrated tragedy, gradually overgrows its Dionysian regions and must necessarily drive it to self-annihilation – to the lethal plunge into bourgeois drama.[101] Let us consider the consequences of the Socratic principles: 'Knowledge is virtue; sin is the result of ignorance; the virtuous man is the happy man': in these three basic forms of optimism lies the death of tragedy. For now the virtuous hero must be a dialectician, now there must be a necessary visible link between virtue and knowledge, belief and morality, now Aeschylus' solution of transcendental justice is degraded to the shallow and impudent principle of 'poetic justice' with its usual *deus ex machina*.

How does the *chorus* and above all the whole musical-Dionysian substratum appear when faced with this new Socratic-optimistic stage-world? As something accidental, as an in all probability dispensable memory of the origin of tragedy; while we, how-ever, have seen that the chorus can only be understood as the *cause* of tragedy and of

99   Group of philosophers who followed the teaching of Diogenes of Sinope (ca. 400–ca. 325 B.C.), characterized by a rejection of social convention and a mordant view of those who remain governed by it. The term is derived from the Greek word for dog (*kyon*), which the Greeks considered the most shameless of animals.

100   Latin: maidservant.

101   A type of eighteenth-century German drama which enacted social and ideological conflicts between the middle class and the aristocracy or within the bourgeoisie itself, as represented, for example, by Lessing's *Emilia Galotti* (1772) or Schiller's *Kabale und Liebe* (*Intrigue and Love*, 1783).

the tragic itself. This embarrassment with respect to the chorus is already evident in Sophocles – an important sign that the Dionysian ground of tragedy is already beginning to crumble in his work. Sophocles no longer dares to entrust to the chorus the main share of the effect, but restricts its domain to such an extent that it now appears almost co-ordinated with the actors, just as if it were lifted out of the orchestra onto the stage: in the process, of course, its essence is completely destroyed, even if Aristotle approves precisely this definition of the chorus.[102] This displacement of the chorus, which Sophocles in any case recommended through his practice and according to tradition even in a treatise, is the first step towards the *annihilation* of the chorus, whose phases follow one another with frightening rapidity in Euripides, Agathon,[103] and the New Comedy. The optimistic dialectic drives *music* out of tragedy with the whip of its syllogisms: that is, it destroys the essence of tragedy, which can only be interpreted as a manifestation and transformation into images of Dionysian states, as visible symbolization of music, as the dream-world of a Dionysian intoxication.

If as a result we must assume the existence of an effective anti-Dionysian tendency even prior to Socrates, in whom it merely achieved unprecedented greatness of expression, then we must not shrink from the question of the direction in which a phenomenon such as Socrates points: a phenomenon which we, in the face of the Platonic dialogues, are not yet in a position to understand as an exclusively negative dissolving power. And while the most immediate effect of the Socratic drive was undoubtedly to bring about a disintegration of the Dionysian tragedy, a profound experience undergone by Socrates himself forces us to ask whether the relationship between Socratism and art is *necessarily* only an antipodal one and whether the birth of an 'artistic Socrates' is actually a contradiction in terms.

For, with respect to art, that despotic logician experienced sporadically the feeling of a gap, a void, a half reproach, perhaps of a neglected duty. As he told his friends in prison, there often came to him the same recurring dream phenomenon, which always said the same thing: 'Socrates, make music!'[104] Up to his last days, he comforted himself with the thought that his philosophizing was the highest art of the muses and did not really believe that a deity wished to remind him of that 'common popular music'. Finally, in prison, in order completely to unburden his conscience, he even agreed to make the music for which he had so little respect. And in this frame of mind, he composed a *proemium*[105] to Apollo and rewrote some Aesopian fables in verse. It was something resembling a daemonic warning voice which forced him to undertake these exercises, it was his Apollonian insight that he, like a barbarian king, was failing to understand a noble image of a god and was, through his failure to understand, in danger of sinning against its deity. This mention of the Socratic dream-phenomenon is the only sign of an apprehension on his part about the limits of the logical nature: he must have asked himself the following question – perhaps whatever is not intelligible

102   In the *Poetics* (1455b), Aristotle states that the chorus should be integrated into the action of the stage.
103   Athenian dramatist (ca. 448–ca. 405 B.C.), who began to invent his own characters and plots rather than rely on myth.
104   Plato, *Phaedo*, 60e.
105   In rhetoric, the introduction to the subject of a speech. In poetry, introductions which preceded recitals by rhapsodes.

to me is not necessarily immediately unintelligent? Perhaps there is a domain of wisdom which excludes the logician? Perhaps art is even a necessary correlative of and supplement to science?

15

In the spirit of these last suggestive questions, it must now be said how the influence of Socrates has extended down through posterity to this very moment and indeed stretches out into the future in its entirety, like a shadow which grows in the evening sun, as the same influence again and again necessitates the re-creation anew of *art* – of art in the already metaphysical, broadest, and deepest sense – and how its own infinity guarantees the infinity of art also.

Before this could be recognized, before the innermost dependence of all art on the Greeks from Homer to Socrates had been convincingly demonstrated, we were obliged to undergo the same experience with these Greeks as the Athenians were obliged to do with Socrates. Almost every period and stage of cultural development has at one time or another with profound moroseness sought to free itself from the Greeks, because in comparison with the latter everything which has been achieved on one's own account, everything which appeared completely original and was admired with proper honesty suddenly seemed to pale and flag, shrivelling to a failed copy, even to a caricature. And so there broke out again and again that heart-felt wrath against that presumptuous little people which had the audacity to characterize everything non-indigenous as 'barbaric': who are these people, one wonders, who, with only an ephemeral historical brilliance, only ridiculously limited institutions, only a dubious moral competence to show for themselves and who are even marked by ugly vices, yet lay claim to the dignity and exceptional status among peoples which is accorded to the genius among the masses? Unfortunately, one was not sufficiently fortunate to find the cup of hemlock[106] which could do away with such a being: for all the poison which envy, slander, and wrath produced was not enough to annihilate that self-sufficient splendour. And one feels ashamed and fearful before the Greeks; unless one respects truth in all things and so also dares to admit to oneself that the Greeks as charioteers hold the reins of our and every other culture in their hands, but that almost always the chariot and horses are too slight and frail to live up to the glory of their drivers, who then consider it a jest to spur such a team into the abyss: while they themselves jump to safety with a leap of Achilles.[107]

In order to show the dignity which such a position of leadership held for Socrates, one need only recognize in him the type of an unprecedented form of existence, the type of the *theoretical man*, whose meaning and goal it is our next task to investigate. Like the artist, the theoretical man takes an infinite pleasure in that which exists, a pleasure which likewise protects him from the practical ethic of pessimism with its eyes of Lynceus[108] which glow only in the dark. For if in the course of all unveiling

---

106   Allusion to the execution of Socrates by poison.

107   Allusion to Achilles' renowned ability to leap across great distances: see Homer, *Iliad*, XXI. 303–5.

108   Lynceus, one of the Argonauts, possessed the gift of seeing great distances and even of seeing through the earth.

of the truth the delighted gaze of the artist remains perpetually fixed on the truth which has been unveiled but remains even now a veil, the theoretical man derives delight and satisfaction rather from the discarded veil and finds his greatest pleasure in a happy process of unveiling which always succeeds through its own efforts. There would be no science, if science were concerned exclusively with that *single* naked goddess[109] and with nothing else. For then her disciples would have to feel like those men who wanted to dig a tunnel right through the earth: each individual realizes that the greatest lifelong effort will merely scratch the surface of the vast depths and that before his very eyes his own work will be undone by the efforts of the next man digging alongside, so that a third man appears to do well when he chooses on his own initiative a new site for his tunnelling attempts. If at this point someone persuasively demonstrates that the goal of the Antipodes cannot be reached in this direct way, who will want to continue working in the old depths, unless he has in the mean time settled for the satisfaction of discovering precious stones or the laws of nature? For this reason, Lessing, the most honest theoretical man, dared to express the idea that he was more concerned with the search for truth than with truth itself: in the process, the fundamental secret of science was exposed, to the astonishment, even annoyance of the scientists. Now admittedly this isolated insight, as an excess of honesty, if not of arrogance, is accompanied by a profound *delusion*, which first came into the world in the person of Socrates – the unshakeable belief that, by following the guiding thread of causality, thought reaches into the deepest abysses of being and is capable not only of knowing but also even of *correcting* being. This sublime metaphysical madness accompanies science as an instinct and leads it again and again to its limits, where it must transform itself into *art: which is the real goal of this mechanism.*

By the torchlight of this thought, let us now take a look at Socrates: he appears to us now as the first man who was able not only to live according to that instinct of science, but – what is more significant by far – also to die according to it: and so the image of the *dying Socrates*, the man elevated above the fear of death through knowledge and reasoning, is the heraldic shield hung above the entrance gate to science in order to remind everyone of its purpose, namely to make existence appear intelligible and so justified: and, if reasons prove insufficient, even *myth* must finally serve this end, myth which I have just characterized even as the necessary consequence, indeed as the intended goal of science.

Once one imagines how after Socrates, the mystagogue of science, one school of philosophy succeeded another, wave after wave, how the craving for knowledge attained a never suspected universality in the widest domain of the educated world, established itself as the real task for those with higher abilities, and steered science onto the high seas, from which it has never since been driven completely, how through this universality a shared net of thought was first cast over the whole globe, holding out the prospect of discovering the law-governed nature of the whole solar system; once one imagines all this, including the astonishingly high pyramids of present knowledge, one is obliged to see in Socrates the single point around which so-called world-history turns and twists. For if one were to imagine the whole incalculable sum of energy which has been consumed by this world tendency, employed *not* in the service of knowledge but instead to the practical, that is, egoistic ends of individuals and peoples, then

109   Literally, truth. Cf. Nietzsche's Preface to *Beyond Good and Evil.*

the instinctive pleasure in life would probably have been so weakened in widespread struggles of annihilation and ongoing emigrations that, with suicide having become habitual, the individual would perhaps feel driven to strangle his parents and friends by the last vestige of a sense of duty towards them, like the inhabitants of the Fiji islands: a practical pessimism which could produce a horrific ethic of genocide from compassion – a pessimism which moreover exists and has existed everywhere in the world, where art in some form or other, particularly as religion and science, has not appeared as a remedy and defence against that miasma.

In contrast to this practical pessimism, Socrates is the archetype of the theoretical optimist who in his belief in the fathomability of the nature of things ascribes to knowledge and insight the strength of a panacea and understands error as evil in itself. To fathom those reasons and to separate true knowledge from appearance and error seemed to the Socratic man to be the noblest, even the sole truly human vocation: just as, from Socrates on, that mechanism of concepts, judgements, and conclusions was valued above all other capacities as the highest activity and the most astonishing gift of nature. Even the most sublime moral deeds, the impulses of compassion, of sacrifice, of heroism, and that oceanic calm of the soul which is so difficult to achieve and which the Apollonian Greek calls *sophrosyne*,[110] were deduced from the dialectic of knowledge and accordingly designated as teachable by Socrates and his like-minded successors down to the present. Anyone who has personally experienced the pleasure of Socratic knowledge and feels how it seeks through ever widening circles to encompass the whole world of phenomena, will feel no more intense spur to existence than the desire to complete the conquest and to draw the net impenetrably tight. To someone so disposed, the Platonic Socrates then appears as the teacher of a completely new form of 'Greek serenity' and blissful existence, which seeks to discharge itself in actions and will find this discharge mostly in maieutic[111] and educational influences on noble youths for the purpose of the final production of genius.

But now science, spurred on by its powerful delusion, hurtles inexorably towards its limits where the optimism hidden in the essence of logic founders. For the periphery of the circle of science has an infinite number of points and while there is no telling yet how the circle could ever be fully surveyed, the noble and gifted man, before he has reached the middle of his life, still inevitably encounters such peripheral limit points and finds himself staring into an impenetrable darkness. If he at that moment sees to his horror how in these limits logic coils around itself and finally bites its own tail[112] – then the new form of knowledge breaks through, *tragic knowledge*, which in order to be tolerated, needs art as a protection and remedy.

110   Greek: equanimity, self-control.
111   Literally, inducing or encouraging childbirth. Socrates used the metaphor of midwifery or maieutics to describe his pedagogical method: see Plato, *Theaetetus*, 149a–151d.
112   The ancient motif of a serpent biting its own tail, known as Ouroboros, appears on gemstones and in other visual representations. It is often interpreted as representing time or eternity, and although it has no such resonance here, it recurs in Nietzsche's *Thus Spoke Zarathustra* in the form of Zarathustra's emblematic pair of animals – the eagle with a serpent wrapped around its neck.

If we look with eyes strengthened and refreshed by the sight of the Greeks at the highest spheres of that world which surges around us, then we perceive how the craving of an insatiable optimistic knowledge, which appears in an exemplary form in Socrates, is transformed into tragic resignation and need for art; while admittedly this same craving in its lower stages must express itself as hostile to art and must have a particular inner aversion to Dionysian-tragic art, as illustrated earlier for example in the struggle of Socratism against Aeschylean tragedy.

At this point, we knock with stirred emotions at the gates of the present and the future: will this 'transformation' lead to ever new configurations of genius and precisely of *Socrates as maker of music*? Will the net of art which is cast over existence, whether under the name of religion or science, be woven ever more tightly and delicately or is it destined to be torn to shreds in the swirling restlessness and barbaric turmoil which now calls itself the 'present'? – Anxious yet not disconsolate, we stand to one side for a moment, as contemplative bystanders to whom it has been granted to witness these great struggles and transitions. Oh! it is the magic of these struggles that whoever observes them must also enter into the fray!

16

By way of the historical example set out here we have sought to clarify how tragedy dies with the disappearance of the spirit of music as surely as it can only be born from that same spirit. In order to mitigate the unusual nature of this assertion and to demonstrate the origin of this knowledge, we must now cast an unprejudiced eye on the analogous phenomena of the present; we must plunge right into the middle of those struggles which, as I said, are being waged in the highest spheres of our contemporary world between knowledge with its insatiable optimism and the tragic need for art. In the process, I want to leave to one side all the other opposing drives which are always working against art and against tragedy in particular and which are at present expanding with such certainty of victory that, of the theatrical arts for example, only farce and ballet blossom and flourish with any lavishness, and their fragrance perhaps smells not so sweet to some. I want to speak only of the most *illustrious opponent* of the tragic worldview, and by that I mean science, which is optimistic in its deepest essence, with its ancestor Socrates to the forefront. And presently I shall name the powers which seem to me to guarantee *a rebirth of tragedy* – and other blissful hopes for the German character!

Before we plunge into the middle of these struggles, let us shield ourselves in the armour of the knowledge which we have acquired so far. In contrast to all those who conscientiously seek to deduce the arts from a single principle as the necessary source of life for every work of art, my gaze remains fixed on those two artistic deities of the Greeks, Apollo and Dionysus, and recognizes in them the living and clearly visible representatives of *two* worlds of art which differ in their deepest essence and their highest goals. Apollo stands before me as the transfiguring genius of the *principium individuationis*, through which alone true redemption in appearance can be attained, while under the mystical cry of exultation of Dionysus the spell of individuation is burst apart and the path to the Mothers of Being,[113] to the innermost core of things, lies

---

113   Reference to Goethe, *Faust II* (1832), ll. 6173–6306. The essence of existence is here identified with a feminine and maternal principle.

open. The revelation of this tremendous opposition which stretches like a yawning abyss between the Apollonian plastic arts and the Dionysian art of music has been granted to only one of the great thinkers to the extent that, even without this clue to the Hellenic symbolism of the deities, he recognized that music possessed a character and origin different from all other arts, because music, unlike all the other arts, is not a copy of the phenomenon but an unmediated copy of the will itself, and so represents *the metaphysical in relation to the whole physical world* and the thing in itself in relation to the phenomenal world (Schopenhauer, *The World as Will and Representation*, I). On this most important insight of aesthetics, which, in a more serious sense, represents the beginning of all aesthetics, Richard Wagner stamped his seal of approval, strengthening its eternal truth, when in his *Beethoven* he asserts that music is to be judged according to aesthetic principles completely different from those of the plastic arts and absolutely not according to the category of beauty: although a mistaken aesthetic, along with a misguided and degenerate art has on the basis of that concept of beauty which is valid in the world of the visual arts become accustomed to demand of art in general a similar effect to that produced by works of plastic art, namely the stimulation of *pleasure in beautiful forms*. Having recognized that tremendous opposition, I felt a strong need to approach the essence of Greek tragedy and in it the most profound revelation of Hellenic genius: for only now did I believe myself in possession of the magic necessary for my soul to envisage vividly the original problem of tragedy, beyond the phraseology of our habitual aesthetic: and in the process I was granted such a disconcertingly peculiar insight into the Hellenic essence that it necessarily seemed to me as if our classical-Hellenic science which conducts itself with such pride has so far done little more than revel in shadow games and superficialities.

We might perhaps touch on this original problem by way of the following question: what aesthetic effect is produced when those intrinsically separate artistic powers of the Apollonian and the Dionysian come together actively? Or to put it more succinctly: how is music related to image and concept? – Schopenhauer, whom Richard Wagner praised for his unsurpassable clarity and transparency of exposition on precisely this point, expresses himself most exhaustively on this matter in the following passage which I shall reproduce here in full. *The World as Will and Representation*, I:[114] 'As a result of all this, we can regard the phenomenal world,[115] or nature, and music as two different expressions of the same thing, which is therefore itself the sole mediating element in the analogy between the two, and knowledge of which is required in order to see the analogy. Music is accordingly, when viewed as the expression of the world, a universal language to the highest degree, which even has roughly the same relationship to the universality of concepts as concepts have to individual things. Its universality is, however, far removed from that empty universality of abstraction, and of a completely different kind, linked with a clear and thorough definition. In this respect, it resembles the geometric figures and numbers which as the universal forms of all possible objects of experience may be applied to all a priori, and yet are not abstract but visible and thoroughly defined. All possible strivings, impulses, and expressions of the will, all those processes which take place within the heart of man, which reason comprehends under the broad negative concept of feeling, are to be expressed through the infinite number

114   *WWR*, vol. 1, 3. 52.
115   In German: *die erscheinende Welt*.

of possible melodies, but always in the universality of mere form, without content, always only according to the in-itself, not according to the phenomenon, but according to its innermost soul as it were, without the body. This intimate relationship between music and the true essence of all things can also explain how when appropriate music accompanies any scene, action, event, or surroundings, it seems to reveal to us its most secret meaning and emerges as the most accurate and clearest commentary upon it: to such an extent that he who devotes himself entirely to the impression of a symphony feels as if he is watching within himself all the possible events of life and the world move past in procession: and yet he cannot, when he stops to reflect, demonstrate any similarity between that play of melody and the things which hovered before him. For music, as we have said, differs from all the other arts in that it is not a copy of the phenomenon or, more accurately, of the adequate objectivity of the will, but an unmediated copy of the will itself and so represents the metaphysical in relation to the whole physical world and the thing in itself in relation to the whole phenomenal world. Accordingly, one could just as well call the world embodied music as embodied will: so, on this basis, it is possible to explain why music allows every picture, indeed every scene of real life and the world to stand out with greater meaning; all the more so, admittedly, the more analogous its melody is to the inner spirit of the given phenomenon. This is why it is possible to subordinate to music a poem as song, a visual representation as pantomime, or both as opera. Such individual images of human life, subordinated to the universal language of music, are never bound to it nor do they correspond to it with complete necessity; rather they stand in relation to it as a random example to an universal concept: they represent in the certainty of reality that which music expresses in the universality of pure form. For the melodies are, as it were, like all universal concepts, an *abstractum* of reality. This reality, then, the world of individual things, supplies the visible, the particular and individual, the individual case, both to the universality of concepts and to the universality of melodies, these two universalities being united but also in a certain respect opposed; while the concepts contain only the forms which are abstracted in the first place from the visible world, the outer shell of things as it were once it has been removed, and so are completely genuine *abstracta*, music on the other hand gives the innermost core which preceded all assumption of form, or the heart of things. This relationship may be perfectly well expressed in the language of the Scholastics by saying that: the concepts are the *universalia post rem*, but music gives the *universalia ante rem*, and the real world the *universalia in re*.[116] – But that a relationship between a composition and a visible representation is at all possible rests, as we have said, on the fact that both are no more than different, albeit completely different, expressions of the same inner essence of the world. When now in a particular case such a relationship really exists, when the composer has been able to express the impulses of the will which constitute the core of an event in the universal language of music, then the melody of the song, the music of the opera becomes expressive. The analogy between these two found by the composer must have proceeded from the unmediated knowledge of the essence of the world, without the conscious intervention of reason, and must not be a conscious and deliberate imitation mediated by concepts, otherwise music does not express the inner essence,

---

116   Latin: universals after the thing; universals before the thing; universals in the thing.

the will itself, but only offers an unsatisfactory imitation of its phenomenal appearance,[117] like all truly imitative music.'

So, following Schopenhauer's doctrine, we understand music as the unmediated language of will and feel our imagination stimulated to give shape to that invisible and yet so vivid world of spirits which speaks to us, and to embody it in an analogous example. On the other hand, under the influence of a music which provides a true correspondence, image and concept reach a heightened significance. So Dionysian art usually exercises two types of influence on the Apollonian capacity for art: music stimulates the *allegorical contemplation* of Dionysian universality, and music allows the emergence of the allegorical image *in its most significant form*. From these facts, intelligible in themselves and accessible to any more perceptive observer, I deduce the capacity of music to give birth to *myth*, which is the most significant example, and precisely the *tragic* myth: the myth which speaks of Dionysian knowledge in allegories. With respect to the phenomenon of the lyric poet, I have shown how in the lyric poet music struggles to reveal its essence in Apollonian images: if we now imagine that music in its most heightened form must also seek to reach its greatest transformation into images, then we must consider it capable of finding symbolic expression for its real Dionysian wisdom; and where else should we look for this expression if not in tragedy and above all in the concept of the *tragic*?

The tragic cannot be honestly deduced from the essence of art as it is commonly understood in terms of the single category of appearance[118] and beauty; it is only on the basis of the spirit of music that we can understand the joy experienced in the annihilation of the individual. For it is only in the individual examples of such an annihilation that the eternal phenomenon[119] of Dionysian art is made clear to us, the Dionysian art which gives expression to the will in its omnipotence as it were behind the *principium individuationis*, the eternal life beyond all phenomena[120] and in spite of all annihilation. The metaphysical joy in the tragic is a translation of the instinctively unconscious Dionysian wisdom into the language of images: the hero, the greatest phenomenon of the will, is negated for our pleasure, because he remains only phenomenon and the eternal life of the will remains untouched by his annihilation. 'We believe in eternal life', such is the cry of tragedy; while music is the unmediated idea of this life. The art of the sculptor has a completely different goal: here Apollo overcomes the suffering of the individual through radiant glorification of the *eternity of the phenomenon*,[121] here beauty triumphs over the suffering which is inherent to life, pain is in a certain sense effaced from the features of nature by a lie. In Dionysian art and in its tragic symbolism, this same nature speaks to us in its true undistorted voice: 'Be as I am! Beneath the incessantly changing phenomena,[122] I am the eternally creative original mother, eternally compelling people to exist, eternally finding satisfaction in this changing world of phenomena!'

[. . .]

117   In German: *Erscheinung*.
118   In German: *Scheines*.
119   In German: *Phänomen*.
120   In German: *Erscheinung*.
121   In German: *Ewigkeit der Erscheinung*.
122   In German: *Erscheinungen*.

18

It is an eternal phenomenon: the craving will always find a way to maintain its creatures in life and to compel them to live on by spreading an illusion over things. One man is held fast by the Socratic delight in knowledge and the delusion that it can help him to heal the eternal wound of life, another is entangled in the seductive veil of artistic beauty which hovers before his eyes, yet another enthralled by the metaphysical consolation that under the whirl of phenomena eternal life flows on indestructible, not to mention the more common and almost more powerful illusions which the will holds ready at any moment. Those three stages of illusion are reserved exclusively for the more nobly constituted natures who feel the burden and weight of existence with profound displeasure and who must be deluded into forgetting this displeasure through a selection of stimulants. From these stimulants arises everything which we call culture: according to the proportions of the mixture we have a predominantly *Socratic* or *artistic* or *tragic* culture; or if I may avail myself of historical examples: either an Alexandrian or a Hellenic or an Indian (Brahmanic) culture.

The whole of our modern world is caught in the net of Alexandrian culture and takes as its ideal the *theoretical man* who is equipped with the highest powers of knowledge, works in the service of science, and whose archetype and progenitor is Socrates. All our means of education have originally had this ideal in view, every other form of existence has to struggle laboriously upwards alongside it, as tolerated but not intended forms of existence. In an almost terrifying sense the educated man has long been found here only in the form of the scholar; even our poetic arts have had to develop from scholarly imitations and in the main effect of rhyme we recognize still the emergence of our poetic forms out of artificial experiments with a non-indigenous, genuinely scholarly language. How unintelligible must *Faust*, the in himself intelligible modern man of culture, have appeared to a true Greek, the Faust who storms dissatisfied through all faculties, who is devoted to magic and the Devil because of his drive for knowledge, the Faust whom we have only to compare with Socrates to recognize that the modern man begins to sense the limits of that Socratic delight in knowledge and in the middle of that wide and desolate expanse of the sea of knowledge longs for land. When Goethe said to Eckermann with reference to Napoleon: 'Yes, my good man, there is such a thing as a productiveness of deeds',[123] he reminds us in a gracefully naïve way that the nontheoretical man is for the modern man something incredible and astonishing, so that the wisdom of a Goethe is required to find such a disturbing form of existence intelligible and even pardonable.

And at this point we should not conceal from ourselves what lies hidden in the womb of this Socratic culture! An optimism which deludedly believes itself without limits! Now we should not be afraid if the fruits of this optimism ripen, if the society which is steeped in such a culture down to its lowest depths gradually starts to tremble with the surge of rampant desires, if the belief in the happiness on earth for all, if the belief in the possibility of such a universal culture of knowledge, gradually turns into the threatening demand for such an Alexandrian happiness on earth, in the conjuring up of a Euripidean *deus ex machina*! Let us take note: Alexandrian culture needs a slave-class in order to be able to sustain its existence over any length of time, but in

123 Goethe, *Conversations with Eckermann*, March 11, 1828.

its optimistic view of existence, it denies the necessity of such a class and therefore, when the effect of its beautiful words of seduction and reassurance about the 'dignity of man' and the 'dignity of labour' is exhausted, it gradually drifts towards its end in horrific annihilation. There is nothing more fearful than a barbaric slave-class which has learnt to regard its existence as an injustice and is preparing to take revenge not just for itself but for all generations. In the face of such threatening storms, who dares to call calmly on our pale and exhausted religions, whose very foundations have even degenerated into religions for scholars? This is so to such an extent that myth, the necessary presupposition of every religion, is already everywhere paralysed and even this religious domain has succumbed to the domination of that optimistic spirit which we have just characterized as the seed of our society's annihilation.

While the disaster slumbering in the womb of theoretical culture gradually begins to frighten modern man, and he searches in agitation among the treasure of his experiences for means to avert the danger without himself really believing in these means, while he therefore begins to sense the consequences of his predicament, great men of versatility have meanwhile been able with incredible level-headedness to use the tools of science itself in order to lay bare the limits and relative nature of knowledge itself and so to deny decisively the claim of science to universal validity and universal goals. In the process, the delusion which presumed to fathom the innermost essence of things with the aid of causality was for the first time recognized for what it was. The great audacity and wisdom of *Kant* and *Schopenhauer* succeeded in winning the most difficult victory, the victory over the optimism which lies hidden in the essence of logic, the optimism which is also the substratum of our culture. While this optimism, founded firmly on the *aeternae veritates*,[124] had believed that all the enigmas of the world could be known and fathomed, and had treated space, time, and causality as utterly absolute laws of the most universal validity, Kant revealed how all these only really served to elevate the mere phenomenon, the work of Maya, to the status of the single and highest reality and to put it in the place of the innermost and true essence of things, thereby making real knowledge of the latter impossible, that is, according to an expression of Schopenhauer's, lulling the dreamer into a deeper sleep (*The World as Will and Representation*, I).[125] With this knowledge a culture is introduced which I dare to describe as tragic, a culture whose most important characteristic is that wisdom replaces science as the highest goal, wisdom which, undeceived by the seductive distractions of the sciences, turns a calm gaze towards the whole image of the world and seeks to grasp as its own the eternal suffering found there with a sympathetic feeling of love. Let us imagine a future generation with this fearless gaze, with this heroic predisposition towards the tremendous, let us imagine the bold stride of these dragon-slayers, the proud audacity with which they turn their back on all the weakling doctrines of optimism, in order to 'live resolutely'[126] as completely as possible: would it not be necessary for the tragic man of this culture in the process of his self-education in seriousness and terror to desire a new art, the art of metaphysical consolation, to desire tragedy as his own Helen and to cry out with Faust:

124   Latin: eternal truths.
125   See *WWR*, vol. 1: "Appendix: Critique of the Kantian Philosophy," 2.
126   Quotation from Goethe's poem "Generalbeichte" ("General Confession," 1802).

> And should I not, most yearning power,
> Bring this most unique form to life?[127]

But now that Socratic culture only manages to hold on to the sceptre of its infallibility with trembling hands, having been shaken from two sides – once out of fear of its own consequences, which it at last begins to sense, and then again as it begins to doubt its former naïve trust in and conviction of the eternal validity of its foundations – it is a sad spectacle to behold as the dance of its thought continually plunges longingly towards new forms in order to embrace them, only then suddenly to recoil with a shudder, like Mephistopheles with the seductive Lamiae.[128] This is indeed the characteristic sign of that 'break' of which everyone customarily speaks as constituting the original suffering of modern culture, that the theoretical man, horrified and dissatisfied by the consequences of his predicament, no longer dares to entrust himself to the fearful icy current of existence, but instead runs anxiously up and down the river bank. He no longer wants anything whole, with its share of the natural horror of things. To such an extent has he been softened by the optimistic view of things. Moreover, he feels how a culture which is constructed on the principle of science must meet its end when it begins to become *illogical*, that is to flee from its own consequences. Our art reveals this universal distress: it is in vain that one relies on all the great productive periods and natures for models to imitate, it is in vain that one assembles the whole of 'world literature'[129] around modern man in order to console him and surrounds him with the artistic styles and artists of all times, so that he might, like Adam with the animals, give them a name:[130] he still remains eternally hungry, the weak and joyless 'critic', the Alexandrian man, who is basically a wretched librarian and proof-reader blinded by book dust and printer's errors.

19

[. . .]

Let us recall then how Kant and Schopenhauer made it possible for the spirit of *German philosophy*, which flows from the same sources, to annihilate the complacent delight in existence taken by the scientific Socratic system, through the demonstration of the latter's limits, and how this demonstration introduced an infinitely more profound and serious consideration of ethical questions and art, which we might describe as the *Dionysian wisdom* grasped in concepts. In what direction does the *mysterium*[131] of this unity between German music and German philosophy point if not towards a new form of existence, whose content we can only surmise on the basis of Hellenic analogies? For us who stand on the watershed between two different forms of existence, the Hellenic precedent possesses the incalculable value of bearing the stamp of all these transitions and struggles in a classical-didactic form: only we by analogy are living through the great periods of the Hellenic character in *reverse* as it were and now for example

---

127 Quotation from Goethe's *Faust II*, ll. 7438–9.
128 Allusion to Goethe's *Faust II*, ll. 7697–7810. The Lamiae are vampire-like women.
129 Term coined by Goethe in his *Conversations with Eckermann*, January 31, 1827.
130 Cf. Genesis 2: 20.
131 Latin: mystery.

appear to be moving backwards from the Alexandrian age into the age of tragedy. In the process we feel as if the birth of a tragic age represents for the German spirit a return to itself, a blissful rediscovery of the self, after a long period during which the previously helpless barbaric form of this spirit had been suppressed by tremendous encroaching powers and forced into a feudal subservience to outside form. Now at last this spirit may, upon its return home to the original source of its character, dare to stride boldly and freely before all peoples, cut loose from the apron strings of a Romanic civilization: if only that spirit understands how to learn untiringly from a people, the Greeks, whose pupils enjoy high praise and rare distinction merely for their ability to learn from such teachers. And when did we need these very greatest of teachers more than now, as we experience the *rebirth of tragedy* and are in danger of neither knowing where it comes from nor being able to interpret where it is going?

[. . .]

21

Slipping back from these exhortatory tones into the mood which befits the contemplative man, I repeat that only from the Greeks can we learn what such a sudden miracle-like awakening of tragedy means for the innermost foundation of the life of a people. It is the people of the tragic mysteries which fights the battles against the Persians: and in turn the people which fought these wars needs tragedy as a necessary healing draft. Who would have suspected precisely in this people, after several generations during which its innermost being was stimulated by the strongest convulsions of the Dionysian daemon, that such a regular powerful effusion of the simplest political feeling, of the most natural home-instincts, of the original manly pleasure in struggle should continue to exist? Yet, if on the one hand, in any significant expansion of Dionysian agitation, one can always sense how the Dionysian loosening of the chains of the individual manifests itself first of all in a reduction of the political instincts, to the point of indifference or even hostility, then just as certainly on the other hand Apollo the genius of the *principium individuationis* is also the builder of states, and the affirmation of the individual personality is indispensable to the existence of the state and the sense of home. From the orgy there leads only one path for a people, the path to Indian Buddhism, which, in order for its longing for nothingness to be tolerated, needs those rare ecstatic states with their elevation above space, time, and the individual, as these states in turn require a philosophy which teaches how to overcome the indescribable displeasure of the intervening states through the force of an idea. A people which takes as its point of departure the absolute validity of the political instincts will just as necessarily end up following a path of extreme secularization, whose greatest but also most terrifying expression is the Roman *imperium*.

Situated between India and Rome and forced to make a seductive choice, the Greeks managed to invent with classical purity an additional third form, admittedly not one they used personally for long, but for that very reason they achieved immortality. For that the favourites of the gods die young holds true in all things, but it is just as certain that they then enjoy eternal life with the gods. One should not ask of the noblest thing of all that it have the toughness and durability of leather; stout perseverance, as is typical for example of the Roman national drive, is in all probablity not one of the necessary predicates of perfection. But when we ask which remedy enabled the

Greeks in their period of greatness, at the time of the extraordinary strength of their Dionysian and political drives, to avoid exhausting themselves either in ecstatic brooding or in a consuming pursuit of global power and prestige, and to achieve rather that glorious mixture resembling a noble wine, which both inflames and induces contemplation on the part of the drinker, then we must remember the tremendous power of *tragedy* which stimulates, purifies, and discharges the whole life of the people; whose highest value we only sense when it draws near us, as in the case of the Greeks, as the epitome of all prophylactic healing powers, as the mediator which holds sway over the strongest and in themselves most disastrous characteristics of the people.

Tragedy absorbs the most intense musical orgy into itself, so that it truly brings music to perfection, for the Greeks as for us. But then it juxtaposes to music tragic myth and the tragic hero, who, like a mighty Titan, relieves us of the burden of the whole Dionysian world by taking it on his shoulders. On the other hand, through this same tragic myth, in the person of the tragic hero, tragedy can also offer redemption from the craven impulse for this existence and with an admonishing gesture remind us of another being and of a higher joy, for which with a sense of foreboding the struggling hero prepares himself through his destruction rather than through his triumphs. Tragedy inserts between the universal validity of its music and the listener who is receptive to the Dionysian a sublime allegory, myth, and gives the spectator the impression that music is merely the highest means of representing and bringing to life the plastic world of myth. Trusting to this noble illusion, tragedy may now move its limbs to the dithyrambic dance and surrender itself without a thought to an orgiastic feeling of freedom, in which it is allowed to flourish as music in itself, thanks alone to this illusion. Myth protects us from music, while on the other hand myth alone gives music its highest freedom. For that reason, music in return lends tragic myth a penetrating and persuasive metaphysical significance which word and image could never achieve without that unique help. In particular, it is precisely here that the tragic spectator experiences a certain presentiment of a higher joy, the highest joy[132] which lies at the end of the path through destruction and negation, so that it appears to him as if the innermost abyss of things speaks to him audibly.

If in these preceding sentences I have been able to give no more than a provisional expression to this difficult idea, one which will be understood by only a few, then especially at this point I must continue to exhort my friends to further effort and ask them to use a single example of our common experience to prepare themselves for a universal principle. In this example, I will refrain from referring to those men who use the images of what takes place on stage, the words and emotions of the characters, to help them to approach the feeling of music; for none of these men speak music as their mother-tongue and in spite of the help they acquire proceed no further than the entrance-hall of the perception of music, without ever being permitted to touch its innermost shrines; some of these men, such as Gervinus,[133] do not even get as far as the entrance-hall. But I address myself exclusively to those who, directly related to music, born of its maternal womb as it were, relate to things almost exclusively through

132   Allusion to the closing lines of Wagner's opera *Tristan und Isolde* (1865), Isolde's "Liebestod" (III. iii).
133   Georg Gottfried Gervinus (1805–71), German literary historian and author of a two-volume study of Shakespeare.

unconscious musical relations. To these genuine musicians I direct the question of whether they can imagine someone capable of experiencing the third act of *Tristan and Isolde* purely as a vast symphonic movement, with no help from word and image, without expiring under the convulsive beating of the wings of the entire soul? Imagine a man, who as here has laid his ear as it were on the heart chamber of the world-will, who feels the mad desire for existence flow outwards into all the veins of the world in the form of a thundering torrent or of the gentlest spraying brook, should such a man not suddenly shatter into pieces? How could such a man, enclosed in the miserable glass shell of human individuality, endure the echo of countless cries of pleasure and woe from the 'wide space of the night of the worlds',[134] without inexorably fleeing to his original home in this pastoral roundel of metaphysics? But if such a work could still be perceived as a whole, without negating individual existence, is such a creation possible, without smashing its creator to pieces? Where do we find the solution to such a contradiction?

Here the tragic myth and the tragic hero interpose themselves between out highest musical stimulation and this music, basically as mere allegories of the most universal facts of which music alone can speak directly. If we experienced feelings as pure Dionysian beings, however, myth would now, as allegory, come to a standstill beside us, completely ineffective and ignored, and fail to distract us for a moment from listening to the echo of the *universalia ante rem*.[135] Yet here the *Apollonian* power breaks out, directed towards the restoration of the almost shattered individual, with the curative balm of a blissful illusion: suddenly we believe that we still see nothing more than Tristan standing motionless, asking himself in muffled tones: 'The old melody; why does it wake me?'[136] And what appeared to us earlier as a hollow sigh from the centre of being now only wants to say how 'desolate and empty is the sea'.[137] And where we wrongly imagined our breathless extinction, in the racked convulsions of all our feelings, and imagined ourselves with little to tie us to this existence, we now see and hear the hero, mortally wounded and yet not dying, with his desperate cry: 'Longing! Longing! To die longing and through longing not to die!'[138] And if earlier, after such an excess and surplus of consuming torments, the jubilation of the horn cuts us to the heart almost as the highest torment, so the exultant Kurwenal[139] now stands between us and this 'jubilation in itself', turned towards the ship which carries Isolde. In spite of the violence with which compassion affects us internally, its sympathetic suffering[140] rescues us in a certain sense from the original suffering of the world, just as the allegorical image of myth rescues us from the direct contemplation of the highest world idea, just as thought and word rescue us from the unbridled outpouring of the unconscious will. That magnificent Apollonian illusion makes it appear as if even the realm

---

134   Slightly altered quotation from Wagner's *Tristan und Isolde*, III. i, "in the wide realm of the night of the worlds."
135   See note 116 above.
136   Quotation from *Tristan und Isolde*, III. i.
137   Ibid.
138   Ibid.
139   Character in *Tristan und Isolde*.
140   In German: *Mitleiden*.

of music confronts us as a plastic world, as if Tristan and Isolde's fate had been formed and moulded in it too, as in the most tender and expressive material.

So the Apollonian tears us away from the Dionysian universality and allows us to delight in individuals; it chains the arousal of our compassion to these individuals, and through them it satisfies the sense of beauty which craves great and sublime forms; it leads a procession of images of life past us and stimulates us to grasp in thought the core of life contained in them. With the tremendous proliferation of the image, the concept, the ethical doctrine, the arousal of sympathy, the Apollonian principle tears man up out of his orgiastic self-annihilation and deceives him about the universality of the Dionysian process by deluding him that he sees one single image of the world, Tristan and Isolde for example, and that, *through music*, he should merely *see* it better and more inwardly. What can the healing magic of Apollo not achieve, when it can even arouse in us the illusion that the Dionysian is really in the service of the Apollonian and that it is really capable of heightening the latter's effects, and indeed even that music is essentially a representational art with an Apollonian content?

In that pre-established harmony which reigns between the perfect drama and its music, theatre reaches a very high degree of vividness, otherwise unattainable for verbal drama. In the independently moving melodic lines, all the living forms of the stage resolve themselves before us into the simplified clarity of the curved line, and the juxtaposition of these lines rings out to us in the alternation of harmonies which sympathizes in the most delicate way with the movement of the action on stage: through these harmonies, the relations of things become directly available to our senses in a concrete and not at all abstract manner, as we likewise recognize that it is only through these relations that the essence of character and of melodic line reveals itself clearly. And while music thus forces us to see more widely and more inwardly than other-wise and to spread out the action of the stage before us like a delicate web, the world of the stage is for our spiritualized inward-looking eye infinitely expanded and illu-minated from within. What could the poet offer by way of comparison, the poet who strives to achieve that inward expansion of the visible world of the stage and its inward illumination with a much less perfect mechanism, by indirect means, through word and concept? Although the musical tragedy itself admittedly includes the word, it can still at the same time juxtapose the underworld and the birth-place of the word and clarify its development for us from the inside.

But one could with equal certainty say of the process just described that it is merely a magnificent appearance, namely that Apollonian *illusion* which was mentioned before, whose effect seeks to unburden us of the Dionysian compulsion and excess. Indeed, at bottom, the relation between music and drama is precisely the opposite: music is the real idea of the world, drama is only the reflection of this idea, its iso-lated shadow image. That identity between the melodic line and the living form, between harmony and the character relations of that form is true in an opposite sense to that in which it might appear to us as we contemplate musical tragedy. However much we agitate, animate, and illuminate this form from within with the greatest visibility, it still remains a mere phenomenon, from which there is no bridge leading to the true reality, to the heart of the world. But music speaks from this heart; and no matter how many phenomena of that kind may accompany the same music, they would never exhaust its essence, but rather always remain only its externalized copies. With respect to the difficult relation between music and drama, nothing is to be explained and everything to be confused by the popular and completely false opposition between soul and body; but the unphilosophical crudity of that opposition seems to have become precisely for our aestheticians a well-known article of faith – for who knows what reasons – while they have learnt nothing about the opposition between the phenomenon and the thing in itself, or, for likewise unknown reasons, refuse to learn anything about it.

If our analysis has yielded the result that the Apollonian element in tragedy has through its illusion triumphed completely over the original Dionysian element of music and subordinated it to its aims, namely, the highest clarification of the drama, then it would be necessary to add a very important qualification: at the most essential point that Apollonian illusion is broken through and annihilated. Drama, which with the aid of music unfolds before us all its movements and forms in such inwardly illuminated clarity – as if the fabric is being woven on the loom before our very eyes as the shuttle moves back and forth – achieves an overall effect which lies *beyond all Apollonian artistic effects*. In the overall effect of tragedy, the Dionysian again achieves predominance: tragedy concludes with a sound which could never ring forth from the realm of Apollonian art. And in the process the Apollonian illusion shows itself for what it is, the veiling for the duration of the tragedy of a real Dionysian effect. Yet this Dionysian effect is so powerful that it ultimately forces the Apollonian drama itself into a sphere where it begins to speak with Dionysian wisdom, negating itself and its Apollonian visibility. So the difficult relation between the Apollonian and the Dionysian in tragedy should really be symbolized through a fraternal bond between both deities: Dionysus speaks the language of Apollo, and Apollo finally speaks the language of Dionysus, and so the highest goal of tragedy and of art itself is achieved.

[. . .]

24

Among the peculiar artistic effects of the musical tragedy we had to emphasize an Apollonian *illusion*, through which we were supposed to be rescued from direct unity with Dionysian music, while our musical agitation could discharge itself in an Apollonian domain and on a visible middle-world interposed between the two. In the process, we thought we had observed how it was precisely through this discharge that the middle-world of stage action, drama itself, became visible and intelligible from the inside out to an extent unattainable in all other Apollonian art: so that here, where Apollonian art was as it were swept up elated into the heights by the spirit of music, we had to recognize the greatest intensification of its powers and thus see in that fraternal bond between Apollo and Dionysus the pinnacle of the Apollonian as well as the Dionysian aims of art.

Admittedly, the Apollonian projected image did not achieve the peculiar effect of the weaker degrees of Apollonian art through inner illumination by means of music; what the epic or the sculpted stone infused with soul can do – force the contemplating eye to that calm delight in the world of the *individuatio* – that could not be achieved here, in spite of a greater infusion of soul and clarity. As we watched the drama, our penetrating gaze entered the turbulent inner world of motives – and yet it seemed to us as if this were only an allegorical image which was passing before us, whose most profound meaning we almost believed we had guessed, and which we wished to pull back like a curtain, in order to catch sight of the original image behind. The most radiant clarity of the image was not enough for us: for this appeared to conceal as much as it revealed; and while its allegorical revelation seemed to invite the tearing of the veil and the disclosure of the secret background, at the same time the total visibility of that radiance held the eye in its spell and prevented it from penetrating more deeply.

Anyone who has not undergone this experience of having to see and at the same time to long for something beyond seeing, will have difficulty imagining how definitely and clearly these two processes are felt to exist in parallel in the contemplation of the tragic myth: while the truly aesthetic spectators will confirm for me that among the peculiar effects of tragedy this existence of two processes in parallel is the most remarkable. If one now translates this phenomenon of the aesthetic spectator into an analogous process in the tragic artist, one will have understood the genesis of the *tragic myth*. The tragic artist shares with the Apollonian sphere of art the full pleasure in appearance and in seeing, and at the same time he negates this pleasure and takes an even higher satisfaction in the annihilation of the visible world of appearance. The content of the tragic myth is in the first place an epic event involving the glorification of the struggling hero: but what explains the in itself enigmatic trait of the hero's fateful suffering, the most painful triumphs, the most tormented conflicts of motive, in brief the illustration of the wisdom of Silenus, or, aesthetically expressed, of ugliness and disharmony, what explains that all this is represented again and again in such countless forms, and with such predilection in precisely the most sumptuous and youthful age of a people, if it is not the source of a very great pleasure?

To say that in life things really do turn out so tragically would be the least satisfactory explanation of the emergence of an art form, if art is not merely an imitation of the reality of nature, but rather a metaphysical supplement to the reality of nature, set alongside it for the purpose of overcoming it. The tragic myth, in so far as it belongs to art at all, also participates fully in art's metaphysical intention to transfigure: but what does it transfigure, when it presents the world of phenomena in the image of the suffering hero? Least of all the 'reality' of this world of phenomena, for it says to us: 'Look here! Take a close look! This is your life! This is the hour hand on the clock of your existence!'

And myth showed us this life in order to transfigure it? But if this is not the case, then wherein lies the aesthetic pleasure, with which we let those images pass before us? I ask about aesthetic pleasure but know very well that many of these images can produce, at the same time moreover, a moral delight, for instance in the form of compassion or of a moral triumph. But as for those who would wish to deduce the effect of the tragic exclusively from these moral sources, as has admittedly for all too long usually been the case in aesthetics, let them at least not believe that they have in the process accomplished something for art: art which above all must demand purity in its domain. To explain the tragic myth, the first requirement is none other than to seek the pleasure peculiar to it in the purely aesthetic sphere, without reaching over into the domain of compassion, fear, of the moral-sublime. How can ugliness and disharmony, the content of the tragic myth, stimulate an aesthetic pleasure?

At this point it now becomes necessary for us to launch ourselves with a bold leap into the metaphysics of art, repeating the earlier principle that existence and the world appear justified only as an aesthetic phenomenon: in this sense the tragic myth has to convince us that even ugliness and disharmony is an artistic game which the will plays with itself in the eternal abundance of its joy. But this original and not easily understood phenomenon of Dionysian art may be grasped in intelligible and unmediated form in the miraculous meaning of *musical dissonance*: music alone, when placed alongside the world, can give an idea of what is to be understood by the justification of the world as an aesthetic phenomenon. The pleasure produced by the tragic myth shares the same home as the pleasurable sensation of dissonance in music. The Dionysian, with its original joy perceived even in pain, is the shared maternal womb of music and of tragic myth.

Is it not the case that the difficult problem of the tragic effect has not in the mean time been made essentially easier by our enlisting the aid of the musical relation of dissonance? But let us now understand what it means to want to see tragedy and at the same time to long for something beyond seeing: a condition which we would, with respect to the artistic use of dissonance, equally have to characterize as wanting to hear and at the same time longing for something beyond hearing. That striving towards the infinite, the beating of the wings of longing, which accompanies the highest joy[141] in clearly perceived reality, recall that we must recognize in both states a Dionysian phenomenon, which reveals to us again and again the playful construction and destruction of the individual world as the overflow of an original joy, in a similar way to that in which Heraclitus the Obscure compares the world-forming force to a child at play, arranging and scattering stones here and there, building and then trampling sand-hills.

[. . .]

25

Music and tragic myth are equal expressions of the Dionysian capacity of a people and are inseparable from one another. Both stem originally from an artistic domain which lies beyond the Apollonian; both transfigure a region in whose chords of joy both dissonance and the terrible world-image fade away seductively; both play with the thorn of displeasure, trusting to their extremely powerful magic arts; and through this play, both justify the existence of even the 'worst world'. Here the Dionysian shows itself, in comparison with the Apollonian, as the eternal and original power of art, which calls the whole world of phenomena into existence: in whose midst a new transfiguring appearance becomes necessary in order to keep alive the busy world of individuation. If we could imagine dissonance in human form – and what is man but that? – then this dissonance, in order to be able to live, would need a magnificent illusion to cast a veil of beauty over its own essence. This is the true artistic intention of Apollo: whose name summarizes all those countless illusions of beautiful appearance, which in each moment make existence worth living and compel us to live on to experience the next moment.

In the process, only precisely as much of that foundation of all existence, of the Dionysian substratum of the world, may enter into the consciousness of the human individual as can be overcome again by the Apollonian power of transfiguration, so that both of these artistic drives are compelled to develop their forces in strict proportion

141   In German: *höchste Lust* (again). See note 132 above.

to one another, according to the law of eternal justice. Where the Dionysian powers rise up so impetuously, as we are now experiencing them, there Apollo must already have descended to us veiled in a cloud; Apollo, whose most sumptuous effects of beauty will probably be seen by the next generation.

But that this effect is necessary should be sensed intuitively and most surely by everyone, who has once, even in dream, felt himself transported back into an ancient Hellenic existence: strolling beneath lofty Ionian colonnades, gazing up towards a horizon defined by pure and noble lines, accompanied by reflections of his transfigured form in the shining marble at his side, surrounded by men who move with solemn stride or delicate gait, speaking a language of harmonious sounds and rhythmic gestures – would he not, in the face of this continual stream of beauty, have to raise big hand to Apollo and call out: 'Blessed people of the Hellenes! How great Dionysus must be among you, if the god of Delos[142] considers such magic necessary to cure you of your dithyrambic madness!' – But a venerable old Athenian, observing him with the sublime eye of Aeschylus, might reply to someone so moved: 'Yet say this too, you miraculous stranger: how much must this people have suffered in order to become so beautiful! But now follow me to the tragedy and let us perform a sacrifice in the temple of both deities!'

142   The Aegean island of Delos was, according to myth, the birthplace of Apollo.

7

The Greek State
(1871-2)

We moderns have the advantage over the Greeks with two concepts given as consolation, as it were, to a world which behaves in a thoroughly slave-like manner whilst anxiously avoiding the word 'slave': we speak of the 'dignity of man' and of the 'dignity of work'. We struggle wretchedly to perpetuate a wretched life; this terrible predicament necessitates exhausting work which man – or, more correctly – human intellect, seduced by the 'will', now and again admires as something dignified. But to justify the claim of work to be honoured, existence itself, to which work is simply a painful means, would, above all, have to have somewhat more dignity and value placed on it than appears to have been the case with serious-minded philosophies and religions up till now. What can we find, in the toil and moil of all the millions, other than the drive to exist at any price, the same all-powerful drive which makes stunted plants push their roots into arid rocks!

Only those individuals can emerge from this horrifying struggle for existence who are then immediately preoccupied with the fine illusions of artistic culture, so that they do not arrive at that practical pessimism which nature abhors as truly unnatural. In the modern world which, compared with the Greek, usually creates nothing but freaks and centaurs, and in which the individual man is flamboyantly pieced together like the fantastic creature at the beginning of Horace's *Ars Poetica*, the craving of the struggle for existence and of the need for art often manifests itself in one and the same person: an unnatural combination which gave rise to the need to excuse and consecrate the first craving before the dictates of art. For that reason, people believe in the 'dignity of man' and the 'dignity of work'.

The Greeks have no need for conceptual hallucinations like this, they voice their opinion that work is a disgrace with shocking openness – and a more concealed, less frequently expressed wisdom, which was nevertheless alive everywhere, added that the human being was also a disgraceful and pathetic non-entity and 'shadow of a dream'.[1] Work is a disgrace because existence has no inherent value: even when this very existence glitters with the seductive jewels of artistic illusions and then really does seem to have an inherent value, the pronouncement that work is a disgrace is still valid – simply because we do not feel it is possible for man, fighting for sheer survival, to be

---

1 Pindar, *Pythian Odes*, VIII. 95.

an *artist*. Nowadays it is not the man in need of art, but the slave who determines general views: in which capacity he naturally has to label all his circumstances with deceptive names in order to be able to live. Such phantoms as the dignity of man, the dignity of work, are the feeble products of a slavery that hides from itself. These are ill-fated times when the slave needs such ideas and is stirred up to think about himself and beyond himself! Ill-fated seducers who have destroyed the slave's state of innocence with the fruit of the tree of knowledge! Now he must console himself from one day to the next with transparent lies the like of which anyone with deeper insight would recognize in the alleged 'equal rights for all' or the 'fundamental rights of man', of man as such, or in the dignity of work. He must be prevented at any cost from realizing what stage or level must be attained before 'dignity' can even be mentioned, which is actually the point where the individual completely transcends himself and no longer has to procreate and work in the service of the continuation of his individual life.

And even at this level of 'work', a feeling similar to shame occasionally overcomes the Greeks. Plutarch says somewhere,[2] with ancient Greek instinct, that no youth of noble birth would want to be a Phidias himself when he saw the Zeus in Pisa or a Polycletus when he saw the Hera in Argos: and would have just as little desire to be Anacreon, Philetas or Archilochus, however much he delighted in their poetry. Artistic creativity, for the Greek, falls into the same category of undignified work as any philistine craft. However, when the compelling force of artistic inspiration unfolds in him, he *has* to create and bow to the necessity of work. And as a father admires his child's beauty and talent whilst thinking of the act which created the child with embarrassed reluctance, the Greek did the same. His pleased astonishment at beauty did not blind him to its genesis – which, like all genesis in nature, seemed to him a powerful necessity, a thrusting towards existence. That same feeling which sees the process of procreation as something shameful, to be hidden, although through it man serves a higher purpose than his individual preservation: that same feeling also veiled the creation of the great works of art, although they inaugurate a higher form of existence, just as that other act inaugurates a new generation. Shame, therefore, seems to be felt where man is just a tool of infinitely greater manifestations of will than he considers himself to be, in his isolated form as individual.

We now have the general concept with which to categorize the feelings the Greeks had in relation to work and slavery. Both were looked on by them as a necessary disgrace which aroused the feeling of *shame*, at the same time disgrace and necessity. In this feeling of shame there lurks the unconscious recognition that these conditions are *required* for the actual goal. In that *necessity* lies the horrifying, predatory aspect of the Sphinx of nature who, in the glorification of the artistically free life of culture [*Kultur*], so beautifully presents the torso of a young woman. Culture [*Bildung*], which is first and foremost a real hunger for art, rests on one terrible premise: but this reveals itself in the nascent feeling of shame. In order for there to be a broad, deep, fertile soil for the development of art, the overwhelming majority has to be slavishly subjected to life's necessity in the service of the minority, *beyond* the measure that is necessary for the individual. At their expense, through their extra work, that privileged class is to be removed from the struggle for existence, in order to produce and satisfy a new world of necessities.

2 Plutarch, *Parallel Lives*, "Life of Pericles," ch. 2.

Accordingly, we must learn to identify as a cruel-sounding truth the fact that *slavery belongs to the essence of a culture*: a truth, though, which leaves open no doubt about the absolute value of existence. *This truth* is the vulture which gnaws at the liver of the Promethean promoter of culture. The misery of men living a life of toil has to be increased to make the production of the world of art possible for a small number of Olympian men. Here we find the source of that hatred which has been nourished by the Communists and Socialists as well as their paler descendants, the white race of 'Liberals' of every age against the arts, but also against classical antiquity. If culture were really left to the discretion of a people, if inescapable powers, which are law and restraint to the individual, did not rule, then the glorification of spiritual poverty and the iconoclastic destruction of the claims of art would be *more* than the revolt of the oppressed masses against drone-like individuals: it would be the cry of pity tearing down the walls of culture; the urge for justice, for equal sharing of the pain, would swamp all other ideas. Actually, an over-exuberant pity did break down the flood-gates of cultural life for a brief period now and then; a rainbow of pitying love and peace appeared with the first radiance of Christianity, and beneath it, Christianity's most beautiful fruit, the Gospel of St John, was born. But there are also examples of powerful religions fossilizing certain stages of culture over long periods of time, and mowing down, with their merciless sickle, everything that wants to continue to pro-liferate. For we must not forget one thing: the same cruelty which we found at the heart of every culture also lies at the heart of every powerful religion, and in the nature of *power* in general, which is always evil; so we shall understand the matter just as well, if a culture breaks down an all too highly raised bulwark of religious claims with the cry for freedom, or at least justice. Whatever wants to live, or rather must live, in this horrifying constellation of things is quintessentially a reflection of the primeval pain and contradiction and must seem, in our eyes, 'organs made for this world and earth',[3] an insatiable craving for existence and eternal self-contradiction in terms of time, there-fore as *becoming*. Every moment devours the preceding one, every birth is the death of countless beings, procreating, living and murdering are all one. Therefore, we have the right to compare the magnificent culture to a victor dripping with blood, who, in his triumphal procession, drags the vanquished along chained to his carriage as slaves: the latter having been blinded by a charitable power so that, almost crushed by the wheels of the chariot, they still shout, 'dignity of work!', 'dignity of man!' Culture, the voluptu-ous Cleopatra, still continues to throw the most priceless pearls into her golden goblet: these pearls are the tears of pity for the slave and the misery of slavery. The enormous social problems of today are engendered by the excessive sensitivity of modern man, not by true and deep compassion for that misery; and even if it were true that the Greeks were ruined because they kept slaves, the opposite is even more certain, that we will be destroyed because we *fail* to keep slaves: an activity which neither the original Christians nor the Germanic tribes found at all objectionable, let alone reprehensible. What an elevating effect on us is produced by the sight of a medieval serf, whose legal and ethical relationship with his superior was internally sturdy and sensitive, whose narrow existence was profoundly cocooned – how elevating – and how reproachful!

Whoever is unable to think about the configuration of society without melancholy, whoever has learnt to think of it as the continuing, painful birth of those exalted men

3   Goethe, *Faust II*, l. 11906.

of culture in whose service everything else has to consume itself, will no longer be deceived by that false gloss which the moderns have spread over the origin and meaning of the state. For what can the state mean to us, if not the means of setting the previously described process of society in motion and guaranteeing its unobstructed continuation? However strong the sociable urges of the individual might be, only the iron clamp of the state can force huge masses into such a strong cohesion that the chemical separation of society, with its new pyramidal structure, *has* to take place. But what is the source of this sudden power of the state, the aim of which lies far beyond the comprehension and egoism of the individual? How did the slave, the blind mole of culture, *come about*? The Greeks have given us a hint with their instinct for the law of nations which, even at the height of their civilization and humanity, never ceased to shout from lips of iron such phrases as 'the defeated belong to the victor, together with his wife and child, goods and blood. Power gives the first *right*, and there is no right which is not fundamentally presumption, usurpation and violence'.

Here again we see the degree to which nature, in order to bring society about, uses pitiless inflexibility to forge for herself the cruel tool of the state – namely that *conqueror* with the iron hand who is nothing but the objectification of the instinct indicated. The onlooker feels, from the indefinable greatness and power of such conquerors, that they are just the means of an intention which reveals itself through them and yet conceals itself from them. It is as though a magic will emanated from them, so curiously swiftly do weaker powers gravitate to them, so wonderfully do they transform themselves, when that avalanche of violence suddenly swells, and enter into a state of affinity which did not previously exist, enchanted by that creative kernel.

If we now see how, in no time at all, the subjected hardly bother about the dreadful origin of the state, so that basically history informs us less well about the way those sudden, violent, bloody and at least in *one* aspect inexplicable usurpations came about than about any other kind of event: if, on the contrary, hearts swell involuntarily towards the magic of the developing state, with the inkling of an invisibly deep intention, where calculating reason can only see the sum total of forces: if the state is actually viewed enthusiastically as the aim and goal of the sacrifices and duties of the individual: then all this indicates how enormously necessary the state is, without which nature might not succeed in achieving, through society, her salvation in appearance [*Schein*], in the mirror of genius. How much knowledge does not man's instinctive pleasure in the state overcome! One should really assume that a person investigating the emergence of the state would, from then on, seek salvation only at an awe-struck distance from it; and is there a place where we do not see monuments to its development, devastated lands, ruined towns, savage men, consuming hatred of nations! The state, of ignominious birth, a continually flowing source of toil for most people, frequently the ravishing flame of the human race – and yet, a sound which makes us forget ourselves, a battle-cry which has encouraged countless truly heroic acts, perhaps the highest and most revered object for the blind, egoistic mass which wears the surprising expression of greatness on its face only at tremendous moments in the life of the state!

We must, however, construe the Greeks, in relation to the unique zenith of their art, as being *a priori* 'political men *par excellence*'; and actually history knows of no other example of such an awesome release of the political urge, of such a complete sacrifice of all other interests in the service of this instinct towards the state – at best, we could honour the men of the Renaissance in Italy with the same title, by way of comparison and for similar reasons. This urge is so overcharged amongst the Greeks that it continually and repeatedly starts to rage against itself, sinking its teeth into its own flesh. This bloody jealousy of one town for another, one party for another, this murderous greed of those petty wars, the tiger-like triumph over the corpse of the slain enemy, in short, the continual renewal of those Trojan battle-scenes and atrocities which Homer, standing before us as a true Hellene, contemplated with deep *relish* – what does this naïve barbarism of the Greek state indicate, and what will be its excuse at the throne of eternal justice? The state appears before it proudly and calmly: leading the magnificently blossoming woman, Greek society, by the hand. For this Helen, he waged those wars – what grey-bearded judge would condemn this?[4] –

It is through this mysterious connection which we sense here between the state and art, political greed and artistic creation, battlefield and work of art, that, as I said, we understand the state only as the iron clamp producing society by force: whereas without the state, in the natural *bellum omnium contra omnes*,[5] society is completely unable to grow roots in any significant measure and beyond the family sphere. Now, after states have been founded everywhere, that urge of *bellum omnium contra omnes* is concentrated, from time to time, into dreadful clouds of war between nations and, as it were, discharges itself in less frequent but all the stronger bolts of thunder and flashes of lightning. But in the intervals, the concentrated effect of that *bellum*, turned inwards, gives society time to germinate and turn green everywhere, so that it can let the radiant blossoms of genius sprout forth as soon as warmer days come.

With regard to the political Hellenic world, I will not remain silent about those present-day phenomena in which I believe I detect dangerous signs of atrophy in the political sphere, equally worrying for art and society. If there were to be men placed by birth, as it were, outside the instinct for nation and state, who thus have to recognize the state only to the extent to which they conceive it to be in their own interest: then such men would necessarily imagine the state's ultimate aim as being the most undisturbed co-existence possible of great political communities, in which *they*, above all, would be permitted by everyone to pursue their own purposes without restriction. With this idea in their heads, they will promote that policy which offers greatest security to these interests, whilst it is unthinkable that, contrary to their intentions, they should sacrifice themselves to the state purpose, led perhaps by an unconscious instinct, unthinkable because they lack precisely that instinct. All other citizens are in the dark about what nature intends for them with their state instinct, and follow blindly; only those who stand outside this know what *they* want from the state, and what the state ought to grant them. Therefore it is practically inevitable that such men should win great influence over the state, because they may view it as *means*, whilst all the rest, under the power of the unconscious intention of the state, are themselves only means to the state purpose. In order for them to achieve the full effect of their selfish aims through the medium of the state, it is now, above all, essential for the state to be completely freed from those terrible, unpredictable outbreaks of war, so that it can be used rationally; and so, as consciously as possible, they strive for a state of affairs in which war is impossible. To this end, they first have to cut off and weaken the specifically political impulses as much as possible and, by establishing large

4   Homer, *Iliad*, III. 146ff.
5   Latin: war of all against all. Cf. Thomas Hobbes, *Leviathan* (1651), ch. 13.

state bodies of *equal importance* with mutual safeguards, make a successful attack on them, and therefore war in general, extremely unlikely: whilst on the other hand they try to wrest the decision over war and peace away from the individual rulers, so that they can then appeal to the egoism of the masses, or their representatives: to do which they must in turn slowly dissolve the monarchical instincts of the people. They carry out this intention through the widest dissemination of the liberal-optimistic world view, which has its roots in the teachings of the French Enlightenment and Revolution, i.e. in a completely un-Germanic, genuinely Romanistically flat and unmetaphysical philosophy. I cannot help seeing, above all, the effects of the *fear of war* in the dominant movement of nationalities at the present time and in the simultaneous spread of universal suffrage, indeed, I cannot help seeing those truly international, homeless, financial recluses as really those whose fear stands behind these movements, who, with their natural lack of state instinct, have learnt to misuse politics as an instrument of the stock exchange, and state and society as an apparatus for their own enrichment. The only counter-measure to the threatened deflection of the state purpose towards money matters from this quarter is war and war again: in the excitement of which at least so much becomes clear, that the state is not founded on fear of the war-demon, as a protective measure for egoistic individuals, but instead produces from within itself an ethical momentum in the love for fatherland and prince, which indicates a much higher destination. If I point to the use of revolutionary ideas in the service of a self-seeking, stateless money aristocracy as a dangerous characteristic of the contemporary political scene, and if, at the same time, I regard the massive spread of liberal optimism as a result of the fact that the modern money economy has fallen into strange hands, and if I view all social evils, including the inevitable decline of the arts, as either sprouting from that root or enmeshed with it: then you will just have to excuse me if I occasionally sing a pæan to war. His silver bow might sound terrifying; but even if he does swoop in like the night,[6] he is still Apollo, the just god who consecrates and purifies the state. But first, as at the beginning of the *Iliad*, he shoots his arrows at mules and dogs. Then he actually hits people and, everywhere, pyres with corpses blaze. So let it be said that war is as much a necessity for the state as the slave for society: and who can avoid this conclusion if he honestly inquires as to the reasons why Greek artistic perfection has never been achieved again?

Whoever considers war, and its uniformed potential, the *military profession*, in connection with the nature of the state as discussed so far, has to conclude that through war, and in the military profession, we are presented with a type, even perhaps the *archetype of the state*. Here we see as the most general effect of the war tendency, the immediate separation and division of the chaotic masses into *military castes*, from which there arises the construction of a 'war-like society' in the shape of a pyramid on the broadest possible base: a slave-like bottom stratum. The unconscious purpose of the whole movement forces every individual under its yoke, and even among heterogeneous natures produces, as it were, a chemical transformation of their characteristics until they are brought into affinity with that purpose. In the higher castes, it becomes a little clearer what is actually happening with this inner process, namely the creation of the *military genius* – whom we have already met as original founder of the state. In several states, for example in Sparta's Lycurgian constitution, we can clearly make out

6   Homer, *Iliad*, I. 47–52.

the imprint of that original idea of the state, the creation of the military genius. If we now think of the original military state, alive with activity, engaged in its proper 'work', and picture for ourselves the whole technique of war, we cannot avoid correcting our concepts of 'dignity of man', 'dignity of work', absorbed from all around us, by asking whether the concept of dignity is appropriate for work which has, as its purpose, the destruction of the 'dignified' man, or for the man to whom such 'dignified work' is entrusted, or if, in view of the warlike mission of the state, those concepts do not rather cancel each other out as being mutually contradictory. I would have thought the war-like man was a *means* for the military genius and that his work was, again, just a means for the same genius; and that a degree of dignity applies to him, not as absolute man and non-genius but as means of genius – who can even choose his own destruction as a means to the masterpiece which is war, – that dignity, then, *of being acknowledged as worthy to be a means for genius*. But what I have demonstrated here, with a single example, is valid in the most general sense: every man, with his whole activity, is only dignified to the extent that he is a tool of genius, consciously or unconsciously; whereupon we immediately deduce the ethical conclusion that 'man as such', absolute man, possesses neither dignity, nor rights, nor duties: only as a completely determined being, serving unconscious purposes, can man excuse his existence.

Plato's perfect state is, according to these considerations, certainly something even greater than is believed by his warmest-blooded admirers themselves, to say nothing of the superior smirk with which our 'historically'-educated reject such a fruit of antiquity. The actual aim of the state, the Olympian existence and constantly renewed creation and preparation of the genius, compared with whom everything else is just a tool, aid and facilitator, is discovered here through poetic intuition and described vividly. Plato saw beyond the terribly mutilated Herm of contemporary state life, and still saw something divine inside it.[7] He *believed* that one could, perhaps, extract this divine image, and that the angry, barbarically distorted exterior did not belong to the nature of the state: the whole fervour and loftiness of his political passion threw itself onto that belief, that wish – he was burnt up in this fire. The fact that he did not place genius, in its most general sense, at the head of his perfect state, but only the genius of wisdom and knowledge, excluding the inspired artist entirely from his state, was a rigid consequence of the Socratic judgment on art, which Plato, struggling against himself, adopted as his own. This external, almost accidental gap ought not to prevent us from recognizing, in the total concept of the Platonic state, the wonderfully grand hieroglyph of a profound *secret doctrine of the connection between state and genius*, eternally needing to be interpreted: in this preface we have said what we believe we have fathomed of this secret script. –

7   Nietzsche conflates two things here: the incident of the mutilation of the herms (reported in Thucydides, *History of the Peloponnesian War*, VI. 27ff.), and Alcibiades' panegyric on Socrates at the end of Plato's *Symposium* (221^d1–222^a6).

8

Homer's Contest

(1872)

If we speak of *humanity*, it is on the basic assumption that it should be that which *separates* man from nature and is his mark of distinction. But in reality there is no such separation: 'natural' characteristics and those called specifically 'human' have grown together inextricably. Man, in his highest, finest powers, is all nature and carries nature's uncanny dual character in himself. Those capacities of his which are terrible and are viewed as inhuman are perhaps, indeed, the fertile soil from which alone all humanity, in feelings, deeds and works, can grow forth.

Thus the Greeks, the most humane people of ancient time, have a trait of cruelty, of tiger-like pleasure in destruction, in them: a trait which is even clearly visible in Alexander the Great, that grotesquely enlarged reflection of the Hellene, and which, in their whole history, and also their mythology, must strike fear into us when we approach them with the emasculated concept of modern humanity. When Alexander has the feet of the brave defender of Gaza, Batis, pierced, and ties his live body to his chariot in order to drag him around to the scorn of his soldiers: this is a nauseating caricature of Achilles, who abused the corpse of Hector at night by similarly dragging it around; but for us, even Achilles' action has something offensive and horrific about it. Here we look into the abysses of hatred. With the same sensation, we observe the bloody and insatiable mutual laceration of two Greek factions, for example in the Corcyrean revolution.[1] When, in a battle between cities, the victor, according to the *rights* of war, puts the whole male population to the sword and sells all the women and children into slavery, we see, in the sanctioning of such a right, that the Greek regarded a full release of his hatred as a serious necessity; at such moments pent-up, swollen sensation found relief: the tiger charged out, wanton cruelty flickering in its terrible eyes. Why did the Greek sculptor repeatedly have to represent war and battles with endless repetition, human bodies stretched out, their veins taut with hatred or the arrogance of triumph, the wounded doubled up, the dying in agony? Why did the whole Greek world rejoice over the pictures of battle in the *Iliad*? I fear we have not understood these in a sufficiently 'Greek' way, and even that we would shudder if we ever did understand them in a Greek way.

---

1   Cf. Thucydides, *History of the Peloponnesian War*, III. 70–85.

But what lies *behind* the world of Homer, as the womb of everything Hellenic? In the *former*, we are already lifted beyond the purely material fusion by the extraordinary artistic precision, calmness and purity of the lines: its colours, through an artistic deception, seem lighter, gentler and warmer, its people, in this warm, multi-coloured light, seem better and more likeable – but where do we look if we stride backwards into the pre-Homeric world, without Homer's guiding and protecting hand? Only into night and horror, into the products of a fantasy used to ghastly things. What earthly existence is reflected in these repellingly dreadful legends about the origins of the gods: a life ruled over by the *children of the night* alone, by strife, lust, deception, age and death. Let us imagine the air of Hesiod's poems, difficult to breathe as it is, still thicker and darker and without any of the things to alleviate and cleanse it which poured over Hellas from Delphi and numerous seats of the gods: let us mix this thickened Bœotian air with the dark voluptuousness of the Etruscans; such a reality would then *extort* from us a world of myths in which Uranus, Chronos and Zeus and the struggles of the Titans would seem like a relief; in this brooding atmosphere, combat is salvation and deliverance, the cruelty of the victory is the pinnacle of life's jubilation. And just as, in truth, the concept of Greek law developed out of *murder* and atonement for murder, finer culture, too, takes its first victor's wreath from the altar of atonement for murder. The wake of that bloody period stretches deep into Hellenic history. The names of Orpheus, Musaeus and their cults reveal what were the conclusions to which a continual exposure to a world of combat and cruelty led – to nausea at existence, to the view of existence as a punishment to be discharged by serving out one's time, to the belief that existence and indebtedness were identical. But precisely these conclusions are not specifically Hellenic: in them, Greece meets India and the Orient in general. The Hellenic genius had yet another answer ready to the question 'What does a life of combat and victory want?', and gives this answer in the whole breadth of Greek history.

In order to understand it, we must assume that Greek genius acknowledged the existing impulse, terrible as it was, and regarded it as *justified*: whereas in the Orphic version there lay the thought that a life rooted in such an impulse was not worth living. Combat and the pleasure of victory were acknowledged: and nothing severs the Greek world so sharply from ours as the resultant *colouring* of individual ethical concepts, for example *Eris* and *envy*.

When the traveller Pausanias visited the Helicon on his travels through Greece, an ancient copy of the Greeks' first didactic poem, Hesiod's *Works and Days*, was shown to him, inscribed on lead plates and badly damaged by time and weather.[2] But he still saw this much, that in contrast to the usual copies it did *not* carry that little hymn to Zeus at the head, but began straight with the assertion: 'There are *two* Eris-goddesses on earth'.[3] This is one of the most remarkable of Hellenic ideas and deserves to be impressed upon newcomers right at the gate of entry to Hellenic ethics. 'One should praise the one Eris as much as blame the other, if one has any sense; because the two goddesses have quite separate dispositions. One promotes wicked war and feuding, the cruel thing! No mortal likes her, but the yoke of necessity forces man to honour the heavy burden of this Eris according to the decrees of the Immortals. Black Night

2   See Pausanias, *Description of Hellas*, IX. 31. 4.
3   Ibid., l. 11.

gave birth to this one as the older of the two; but Zeus, who reigned on high, placed the other on the roots of the earth and amongst men as a much better one. She drives even the unskilled man to work; and if someone who lacks property sees someone else who is rich, he likewise hurries off to sow and plant and set his house in order; neighbour competes with neighbour for prosperity. This Eris is good for men. Even potters harbour grudges against potters, carpenters against carpenters, beggars envy beggars and minstrels envy minstrels.'[4]

The two last verses, about *odium figulinum*,[5] seem to our scholars incomprehensible in this place. In their judgment, the predicates 'grudge' and 'envy' fit only the nature of the bad Eris; and for this reason they make no bones about declaring the verses not genuine or accidently transposed here. But another ethic, not a Hellenic one, must have inspired them to this: for Aristotle makes no objection to referring these verses to the good Eris.[6] And not just Aristotle, but the whole of Greek antiquity thinks about grudge and envy differently from us and agrees with Hesiod, who first portrays one Eris as wicked, in fact the one who leads men into hostile struggle-to-the-death, and then praises the other Eris as good who, as jealousy, grudge and envy, goads men to action, not, however, the action of a struggle-to-the-death but the action of the *contest*. The Greek is *envious* and does not experience this characteristic as a blemish, but as the effect of a *benevolent* deity: what a gulf of ethical judgment between him and us! Because he is envious, he feels the envious eye of a god resting on him whenever he has an excessive amount of honour, wealth, fame and fortune, and he fears this envy; in this case, the god warns him of the transitoriness of the human lot, he dreads his good fortune and, sacrificing the best part of it, he prostrates himself before divine envy. This idea does not estrange his gods at all from him: on the contrary, their significance is made manifest, which is that man, having a soul which burns with jealousy of every other living thing, *never* has the right to enter into contest with them. In Thamyris' fight with the Muses, Marsyas' with Apollo, in the moving fate of Niobe, there appeared the terrible opposition of the two forces which ought never to fight one another, man and god.

However, the greater and more eminent a Greek man is, the brighter the flame of ambition to erupt from him, consuming everyone who runs with him on the same track. Aristotle once made a list of such hostile contests in the grand style: amongst them is the most striking example of how even a dead man can excite a living man to consuming jealousy.[7] Indeed, that is how Aristotle describes the relationship of the Kolophonian Xenophanes to Homer. We do not understand the full strength of this attack on the national hero of poetry unless we take into account the immense desire to step into the shoes of the overthrown poet himself and inherit his fame, something which is later true of Plato, too. Every great Hellene passes on the torch of contest; every great virtue strikes the spark of a new grandeur. If the young Themistocles could not sleep at the thought of Miltiades' laurels,[8] his early-awakened urge found release

---

4   Hesiod, *Works and Days*, 12–26.
5   Latin: potters' hatred.
6   See Aristotle, *Rhetoric*, 1388ª16, 1381ᵇ16–17; *Nicomachean Ethics*, 1155ª35–ᵇ1.
7   See Aristotle, *Select Fragments*, ed. and trans. W. D. Ross (Oxford: Clarendon Press, 1952),
7   (from Diogenes Laertius, *Lives and Opinions of Eminent Philosophers*, II. 5. 46).
8   Cf. Plutarch, *Parallel Lives*, "Life of Themistocles," ch. 3.

only in the long rivalry with Aristides, when he developed that remarkable, purely instinctive genius for political action which Thucydides describes for us.[9] How very typical is the question and answer, when a notable opponent of Pericles is asked whether he or Pericles is the best wrestler in the city and answers: 'Even if I throw him he will deny having fallen and get away with it, convincing the people who saw him fall.'[10]

If we want to see that feeling revealed in its naïve form, the feeling that competition is vital, if the well-being of the state is to continue, we should think about the original meaning of *ostracism*: as, for example, expressed by the Ephesians at the banning of Hermodor. 'Amongst us, nobody should be the best; but if somebody is, let him be somewhere else, with other people.'[11] For why should nobody be the best? Because with that, the contest would dry up and the permanent basis of life in the Hellenic state would be endangered. Later, ostracism acquires a different relation to the contest: it is used when there is the obvious danger that one of the great contending politicians and party leaders might feel driven, in the heat of battle, to use harmful and destructive means and to conduct dangerous *coups d'etat*. The original function of this strange institution is, however, not as a safety valve but as a stimulant: the pre-eminent individual is removed so that a new contest of powers can be awakened: a thought which is hostile to the 'exclusivity' of genius in the modern sense, but which assumes that there are always *several* geniuses to incite each other to action, just as they keep each other within certain limits, too. That is the kernel of the Hellenic idea of competition: it loathes a monopoly of predominance and fears the dangers of this, it desires, as *protective measure* against genius – a second genius.

Hellenic popular teaching commands that every talent must develop through a struggle: whereas modern educators fear nothing more than the unleashing of so-called ambition. Here, selfishness is feared as 'evil as such' – except by the Jesuits, who think like the ancients in this and probably, for that reason, may be the most effective educators of our times. They seem to believe that selfishness, i.e. the individual, is simply the most powerful *agens*, which obtains its character of 'good' and 'evil' essentially from the aims towards which it strives. But for the ancients, the aim of agonistic education was the well-being of the whole, of state society [*staatlichen Gesellschaft*]. For example, every Athenian was to develop himself, through competition, to the degree to which this self was of most use to Athens and would cause least damage. It was not a boundless and indeterminate ambition like most modern ambition: the youth thought of the good of his native city when he ran a race or threw or sang; he wanted to increase its reputation through his own; it was to the city's gods that he dedicated the wreaths which the umpires placed on his head in honour. From childhood, every Greek felt the burning desire within him to be an instrument of bringing salvation to his city in the contest between cities: in this, his selfishness was lit, as well as curbed and restricted. For that reason, the individuals in antiquity were freer, because their aims were nearer and easier to achieve. Modern man, on the other hand, is crossed everywhere by infinity, like swift-footed Achilles in the parable of Zeno of Elea: infinity impedes him, he cannot even overtake the tortoise.

9   See Thucydides, *History of the Peloponnesian War*, I. 90ff.
10   Plutarch, *Parallel Lives*, "Life of Pericles," ch. 8.
11   Heraclitus (Diels–Kranz edn), fragment 121.

But as the youths to be educated were brought up to compete with one another, their educators in their turn were in rivalry with each other. Full of mistrust and jealousy, the great music masters Pindar and Simonides took their places next to each other; the sophist, the advanced teacher of antiquity, competed with his fellow sophist; even the most general way of teaching, through drama, was only brought to the people in the form of an immense struggle of great musicians and dramatists. How wonderful! 'Even the artist has a grudge against the artist!' And modern man fears nothing so much in an artist as personal belligerence, whilst the Greek knows the artist *only in personal struggle*. Where modern man senses the weakness of a work of art, there the Hellene looks for the source of its greatest strength! What, for example, is of particular artistic importance in Plato's dialogues is mostly the result of a competition with the art of the orators, the sophists, the dramatists of his time, invented for the purpose of his finally being able to say: 'Look: I, too, can do what my great rivals can do; yes, I can do it better than them. No Protagoras has written myths as beautiful as mine, no dramatist has written such a lively and fascinating whole as the *Symposium*, no orator has composed such speeches as I present in the *Gorgias* – and now I reject all of that and condemn all imitative art! Only the contest made me a poet, sophist and orator!' What a problem reveals itself to us when we enquire about the relationship of the contest to the conception of the work of art! –

On the other hand, if we take away the contest from Greek life, we gaze immediately into that pre-Homeric abyss of a gruesome savagery of hatred and pleasure in destruction. Unfortunately, this phenomenon appears quite often when a great figure was suddenly withdrawn from the contest through an immensely glorious deed and was *hors de concours* in his own judgment and that of his fellow citizens. Almost without exception the effect is terrible; and if we usually draw the conclusion from these effects that the Greek was unable to bear fame and fortune: we should, perhaps, say more exactly that he was not able to bear fame without further competition or fortune at the end of the contest. There is no clearer example than the ultimate fate of Miltiades.[12] Placed on a lonely pinnacle and carried far beyond every fellow competitor through his incomparable success at Marathon: he feels a base lust for vengeance awaken in him against a citizen of Para with whom he had a quarrel long ago. To satisfy this lust he misuses his name, the state's money and civic honour, and disgraces himself. Conscious of failure, he resorts to unworthy machinations. He enters into a secret and godless relationship with Timo, priestess of Demeter, and at night enters the sacred temple from which every man was excluded. When he has jumped over the wall and is approaching the shrine of the goddess, he is suddenly overwhelmed by a terrible, panic-stricken dread: almost collapsing and unconscious, he feels himself driven back and, jumping back over the wall, he falls down, paralysed and badly injured. The siege must be lifted, the people's court awaits him, and a disgraceful death stamps its seal on the glorious heroic career to darken it for all posterity. After the battle of Marathon he became the victim of the envy of the gods. And this divine envy flares up when it sees a man without any other competitor, without an opponent, at the lonely height of fame. He only has the gods near him now – and for that reason he has them against him. But these entice him into an act of hubris, and he collapses under it.

12 Cf. Herodotus, *History*, VI. 133–6.

Let us also mention that even the finest Greek states perish in the same way as Miltiades when they, too, through merit and fortune have progressed from the race-course to the temple of Nike. Both Athens, which had destroyed the independence of her allies and severely punished the rebellions of those subjected to her, and Sparta, which, after the battle of Aegospotamoi,[13] made her superior strength felt over Hellas in an even harder and crueller fashion, brought about their own ruin, after the example of Miltiades, through acts of hubris. This proves that without envy, jealousy and competitive ambition, the Hellenic state, like Hellenic man, deteriorates. It becomes evil and cruel, it becomes vengeful and godless, in short, it becomes 'pre-Homeric' – it then only takes a panicky fright to make it fall and smash it. Sparta and Athens surrender to the Persians as Themistocles[14] and Alcibiades[15] did; they betray the Hellenic after they have given up the finest Hellenic principle, the contest: and Alexander, the rough copy and abbreviation of Greek history, now invents the standard-issue Hellene and so-called 'Hellenism'. –

Finished on 29 December 1872

13   Decisive Athenian naval defeat at the hands of the Spartans in 405 B.C. Cf. Xenophon, *Hellenica*, II. 1. 10–32.
14   Cf. Thucydides, *History of the Peloponnesian War*, I. 135ff.
15   Ibid., VIII. 45ff.

9

Philosophy in the Tragic Age of the Greeks
(1873)

1

There are people who are opposed to all philosophy and one does well to listen to them, particularly when they advise the diseased minds of Germans to stay away from metaphysics, instead preaching purification through *physis*[1] as Goethe did, or healing through music, as did Richard Wagner. The physicians of our culture repudiate philosophy. Whoever wishes to justify it must show, therefore, to what ends a healthy culture uses and has used philosophy. Perhaps the sick will then actually gain salutary insight into why philosophy is harmful specifically to them. There are good instances, to be sure, of a type of health which can exist altogether without philosophy, or with but a very moderate, almost playful, exercise of it. The Romans during their best period lived without philosophy. But where could we find an instance of cultural pathology which philosophy restored to health? If philosophy ever manifested itself as helpful, redeeming, or prophylactic, it was in a healthy culture. The sick, it made ever sicker. Wherever a culture was disintegrating, wherever the tension between it and its individual components was slack, philosophy could never re-integrate the individuals back into the group. Wherever an individual was of a mind to stand apart, to draw a circle of self-sufficiency about himself, philosophy was ready to isolate him still further, finally to destroy him through that isolation. Philosophy is dangerous wherever it does not exist in its fullest right, and it is only the health of a culture – and not every culture at that – which accords it such fullest right.

And now let us look around for the highest authority for what we may term cultural health. The Greeks, with their truly healthy culture, have once and for all *justified* philosophy simply by having engaged in it, and engaged in it more fully than any other people. They could not even stop engaging in philosophy at the proper time; even in their skinny old age they retained the hectic postures of ancient suitors, even when all they meant by philosophy was but the pious sophistries and the sacrosanct

---

1   Greek: nature. Derived from the verb *phuo*, to grow, it refers to the nature of anything but with the connotation of growth or potential growth.

hair-splittings of Christian dogmatics. By the fact that they were unable to stop in time, they considerably diminished their merit for barbaric posterity, because this posterity, in the ignorance and unrestraint of its youth, was bound to get caught in those too artfully woven nets and ropes.

On the other hand the Greeks knew precisely how to begin at the proper time, and the lesson of how one must start out in philosophy they demonstrate more plainly than any other people. Not to wait until a period of affliction (as those who derive philosophy from personal moroseness imagine), but to begin in the midst of good fortune, at the peak of mature manhood, as a pursuit springing from the ardent joyousness of courageous and victorious maturity. At such a period of their culture the Greeks engaged in philosophy, and this not only teaches us what philosophy is and does, but also gives us information about the Greeks themselves. For if they had been the sober and precocious technicians and the cheerful sensates that the learned philistines of our day imagine they were, or if they had floated solely in a self-indulgent fog, reverberating with heavy breathings and deep feelings, as the unscholarly fantasts among us like to assume, the well-spring of philosophy should never have seen the light of day in Greece. At most it would have produced a rivulet soon to lose itself in the sands or evaporate in a haze. It never could have become that broad proud stream which we know as Greek philosophy.

It has been pointed out assiduously, to be sure, how much the Greeks were able to find and learn abroad in the Orient, and it is doubtless true that they picked up much there. It is a strange spectacle, however, to see the alleged teachers from the Orient and their Greek disciples exhibited side by side: Zoroaster next to Heraclitus, Hindus next to Eleatics, Egyptians next to Empedocles, or even Anaxagoras amidst the Jews and Pythagoras amidst the Chinese. As to specifics, very little has been discovered by such juxtaposition. As to the general idea, we should not mind it, if only its exponents did not burden us with their conclusion that philosophy was thus merely imported into Greece rather than having grown and developed there in a soil natural and native to it. Or worse, that philosophy being alien to the Greeks, it very likely contributed to their ruin more than to their well-being. Nothing would be sillier than to claim an autochthonous development for the Greeks. On the contrary, they invariably absorbed other living cultures. The very reason they got so far is that they knew how to pick up the spear and throw it onward from the point where others had left it. Their skill in the art of fruitful learning was admirable. We *ought* to be learning from our neighbors precisely as the Greeks learned from theirs, not for the sake of learned pedantry but rather using everything we learn as a foothold which will take us up as high, and higher than our neighbor. The quest for philosophy's beginnings is idle, for everywhere in all beginnings we find only the crude, the unformed, the empty and the ugly. What matters in all things is the higher levels. People who prefer to spend their time on Egyptian or Persian philosophy rather than on Greek, on the grounds that the former are more "original" and in any event older, are just as ill-advised as those who cannot deal with the magnificent, profound mythology of the Greeks until they have reduced it to the physical trivialities of sun, lightning, storm and mist which originally presumably gave rise to it. They are the people, also, who imagine they have found a purer form of religion than that of Greek polytheism when they discover the good old Aryans restricting their worship to the single vault of heaven. Everywhere, the way to the beginnings leads to barbarism. Whoever concerns himself with the

Greeks should be ever mindful that an unrestrained thirst for knowledge for its own sake barbarizes men just as much as a hatred of knowledge. The Greeks themselves, possessed of an inherently insatiable thirst for knowledge, controlled it by their ideal need for and consideration of all the values of life. Whatever they learned, they wanted to live through, immediately. They engaged in philosophy, as in everything else, as civilized human beings, and with highly civilized aims, wherefore, free of any kind of autochthonous conceit, they forebore trying to re-invent the elements of philosophy and science. Rather they instantly tackled the job of so fulfilling, enhancing, elevating and purifying the elements they took over from elsewhere that they became inventors after all, but in a higher sense and a purer sphere. For what they invented was *the archetypes of philosophic thought*. All posterity has not made an essential contribution to them since.

All other cultures are put to shame by the marvellously idealized philosophical company represented by the ancient Greek masters Thales, Anaximander, Heraclitus, Parmenides, Anaxagoras, Empedocles, Democritus and Socrates. These men are monolithic. Their thinking and their character stand in a relationship characterized by strictest necessity. They are devoid of conventionality, for in their day there was no philosophic or academic professionalism. All of them, in magnificent solitude, were the only ones of their time whose lives were devoted to insight alone. They all possessed that virtuous energy of the ancients, herein excelling all men since, which led them to find their own individual form and to develop it through all its metamorphoses to its subtlest and greatest possibilities. For there was no convention to meet them half-way. Thus all of them together form what Schopenhauer in contrast to the republic of scholars has called the republic of creative minds: each giant calling to his brother through the desolate intervals of time.[2] And undisturbed by the wanton noises of the dwarfs that creep past beneath them, their high spirit-converse continues.

Of this high spirit-converse I have resolved to tell the story. At least whatever part of it our modern hardness of hearing can hear and understand – probably a negligible amount. It seems to me that those ancient wise men, from Thales through Socrates, have touched in their conversation all those things, albeit in their most generalized form, which to our minds constitutes typical Hellenism. In their conversation as in their personalities they form the great-featured mold of Greek genius whose ghostly print, whose blurred and less expressive copy, is the whole of Greek history. If we could interpret correctly the sum total of Greek culture, all we would find would be the reflection of the image which shines forth brightly from its greatest luminaries. The very first experience that philosophy had on Greek soil, the sanction of the Seven Sages, is an unmistakable and unforgettable feature of the Hellenic image. Other peoples have saints; the Greeks have sages. It has been rightly said that a people is characterized not as much by its great men as by the way in which it recognizes and honors its great men. In other times and places, the philosopher is a chance wanderer, lonely in a totally hostile environment which he either creeps past or attacks with clenched fist. Among the Greeks alone, he is not an accident. When he appears in the sixth and fifth centuries, among the enormous dangers and temptations of increasing secularization, walking as it were out of the cave of Trophonius[3] straight into the midst

---

2 See Schopenhauer, *Der handschriftliche Nachlass*, 5 vols, ed. Arthur Hübscher (Frankfurt am Main: Waldemar Kramer, 1966–75), vol. 3, p. 188.

3 Boeotian oracular god who led inquirers to the underworld for direct revelations.

of the lavish luxuriance, the pioneer freedom, the wealth and sensuality of the Greek colonies, we may suspect that he comes, a distinguished warning voice, to express the same purpose to which the tragic drama was born during that century, and of which the Orphic mysteries hint in the grotesque hieroglyphics of their rites.[4] The judgment of those philosophers as to life and existence in general means so much more than any modern judgment, for they had life in lavish perfection before their eyes, whereas the feeling of our thinkers is confused by our split desire for freedom, beauty and greatness on the one hand and our drive toward truth on the other, a drive which asks merely "And what is life worth, after all?" The philosopher's mission when he lives in a genuine culture (which is characterized by unity of style) cannot be properly derived from our own circumstances and experiences, for we have no genuine culture. Only a culture such as the Greeks possessed can answer our question as to the task of the philosopher, and only it, I repeat, can justify philosophy at all, because it alone knows and can demonstrate why and how the philosopher is *not* a chance random wanderer, exiled to this place or to that. There is a steely necessity which binds a philosopher to a genuine culture. But what if such a culture does not exist? Then the philosopher is a comet, incalculable and therefore terror-inspiring. When all is well, he shines like a stellar object of the first magnitude in the solar system of culture. That is why the Greeks justify philosophers. Only among them, they are not comets.

[. . .]

4

While the archetype of the philosopher emerges with the image of Thales only as out of shifting mists, the image of his great successor already speaks much more plainly to us. *Anaximander* of Miletus, the first philosophical author of the ancients, writes exactly as one expects a typical philosopher to write when alienating demands have not yet robbed him of his innocence and naiveté. That is to say, in graven stylized letters, sentence after sentence the witness to fresh illumination, each the expression of time spent in sublime meditation. Each single thought and its form is a milestone upon the path to the highest wisdom. Thus, with lapidary impressiveness, Anaximander says upon one occasion, "Where the source of things is, to that place they must also pass away, according to necessity, for they must pay penance and be judged for their injustices, in accordance with the ordinance of time." Enigmatic proclamation of a true pessimist, oracular legend over the boundary stone of Greek philosophy: how shall we interpret you?

The only serious moralist of our century,[5] in *Parerga and Paralipomena* (Vol. II, Chapter 12), charges us with a similar reflection. "The proper measure with which to judge any and all human beings is that they are really creatures who should not exist at all and who are doing penance for their lives by their manifold sufferings and their death. What could we expect of such creatures? Are we not all sinners under sentence of

---

4   See *BT* note 89 above. In the religious movements of Orphism and Pythagoreanism there is to be found a series of phenomena untypical of Greek religion: asceticism, a preoccupation with the afterlife, a rejection of profane society, the notion of a special religious way of life, and doctrines of guilt and salvation.

5   Schopenhauer.

death? We do penance for having been born, first by living and then by dying." A man who can read such a lesson in the physiognomy of our common human lot, who can recognize the basic poor quality of any and all human life in the very fact that not one of us will bear close scrutiny (although our era, infected with the biographical plague, seems to think quite different and statelier thoughts as to the dignity of man), a man who, like Schopenhauer, has heard "upon the heights of India's clear air" the holy word of the moral value of existence – such a man will find it difficult to keep from indulging in a highly anthropomorphic metaphor. He will extract that melancholy doctrine from its application to human life and project it unto the general quality of all existence. It may not be logical, but it certainly is human, to view now, together with Anaximander, all coming-to-be as though it were an illegitimate emancipation from eternal being, a wrong for which destruction is the only penance. Everything that has ever come-to-be again passes away, whether we think of human life or of water or of hot and cold. Wherever definite qualities are perceivable, we can prophesy, upon the basis of enormously extensive experience, the passing away of these qualities. Never, in other words, can a being which possesses definite qualities or consists of such be the origin or first principle of things. That which truly *is*, concludes Anaximander, cannot possess definite characteristics, or it would come-to-be and pass away like all the other things. In order that coming-to-be shall not cease, primal being must be indefinite. The immortality and everlastingness of primal being does not lie in its infinitude or its inexhaustibility, as the commentators of Anaximander generally assume, but in the fact that it is devoid of definite qualities that would lead to its passing. Hence its name, "the indefinite." Thus named, the primal being is superior to that which comes to be, insuring thereby eternity and the unimpeded course of coming-to-be. This ultimate unity of the "indefinite," the womb of all things, can, it is true, be designated by human speech only as a negative, as something to which the existent world of coming-to-be can give no predicate. We may look upon it as the equal of the Kantian thing-in-itself.

Now anyone who can quarrel as to what sort of primal stuff this could have been, whether an intermediate substance between air and water or perhaps between air and fire, has certainly not understood our philosopher at all. This is equally true of those who ask themselves seriously whether Anaximander thought of his primal substance as perhaps a mixture of all existent materials. Instead, we must direct our glance to that lapidary sentence which we cited earlier, to the place where we may learn that Anaximander was no longer dealing with the question of the origin of this world in a purely physical way. Rather, when he saw in the multiplicity of things that have come-to-be a sum of injustices that must be expiated, he grasped with bold fingers the tangle of the profoundest problem in ethics. He was the first Greek to do so. How can anything pass away which has a right to be? Whence that restless, ceaseless coming-into-being and giving birth, whence that grimace of painful disfiguration on the countenance of nature, whence the never-ending dirge in all the realms of existence? From this world of injustice, of insolent apostasy from the primeval one-ness of all things, Anaximander flees into a metaphysical fortress from which he leans out, letting his gaze sweep the horizon. At last, after long pensive silence, he puts a question to all creatures: "What is your existence worth? And if it is worthless, why are you here? Your guilt, I see, causes you to tarry in your existence. With your death, you have to expiate it. Look how your earth is withering, how your seas are diminishing and drying up; the seashell on the mountain top can show you how much has dried up already. Even now, fire is destroying your world; some day it will go up in fumes and smoke. But ever and anew, another such world of ephemerality will construct itself. Who is there that could redeem you from the curse of coming-to-be?"

A man who poses questions such as these, whose thinking in its upward flight kept breaking all empirical ropes, catching, instead, at superlunary ones – such a man very likely does not welcome an ordinary mode of living. We can easily credit the tradition that he walked the earth clad in an especially dignified garment and displayed a truly tragic pride in his gestures and customs of daily living. He lived as he wrote; he spoke as solemnly as he dressed; he lifted his hands and placed his feet as though this existence were a tragic drama into which he had been born to play a hero. In all these things, he was the great model for Empedocles. His fellow-citizens elected him to lead a colony of emigrants. Perhaps they were glad to honor him and get rid of him at the same time. His thought, too, emigrated and founded colonies. In Ephesus and in Elea, people could not rid themselves of it, and if they could not make up their minds to remain where it left them, they also knew that they had been led there by it, and that it was from there they would travel on without it.

Thales demonstrated the need to simplify the realm of the many, to reduce it to the mere unfolding or masking of the *one* and only existent quality, water. Anaximander takes two steps beyond him. For the first, he asks himself: How is the many possible if there is such a thing as the eternal one? And he takes his answer from the self-contradictory, self-consuming and negating character of the many. Its existence becomes for him a moral phenomenon. It is not justified, but expiates itself forever through its passing. But then he sees another question: Why hasn't all that came-to-be passed away long since, since a whole eternity of time has passed? Whence the ever-renewed stream of coming-to-be? And from this question be can save himself only by a mystic possibility: eternal coming-to-be can have its origin only in eternal being; the conditions for the fall from being to coming-to-be in injustice are forever the same; the constellation of things is such that no end can be envisaged for the emergence of individual creatures from the womb of the "indefinite." Here Anaximander stopped, which means he remained in the deep shadows which lie like gigantic ghosts upon the mountains of this world view. The closer men wanted to get to the problem of how the definite could ever fall from the indefinite, the ephemeral from the eternal, the unjust from the just, the deeper grew the night.

5

Straight at that mystic night in which was shrouded Anaximander's problem of becoming, walked *Heraclitus* of Ephesus and illuminated it by a divine stroke of lightning. " 'Becoming' is what I contemplate," he exclaims, "and no one else has watched so attentively this everlasting wavebeat and rhythm of things. And what did I see? Lawful order, unfailing certainties, ever-like orbits of lawfulness, *Erinnyes*[6] sitting in judgment on all transgressions against lawful order, the whole world the spectacle of sovereign justice and of the demonically ever-present natural forces that serve it. Not the

6   Avenging deities but also restorers of order. See Heraclitus (Diels–Kranz edn), fragment 122.

punishment of what has come-to-be did I see, but the justification of that which is coming-into-being. When did hubris, when did apostasy ever reveal itself in inviolable forms, in laws held sacred? Where injustice rules, there are caprice, disorder, lawlessness, contradiction. But where law and Zeus's daughter *Dike*[7] rule alone, as they do in this world, how could there be the sphere of guilt, of penance, of judgment? How could this world be the execution-arena of all that is condemned?"

From such intuition Heraclitus derived two connected negations. Only through comparison with the doctrines of his predecessor can they be illuminated. One, he denied the duality of totally diverse worlds – a position which Anaximander had been compelled to assume. He no longer distinguished a physical world from a metaphysical one, a realm of definite qualities from an undefinable "indefinite." And after this first step, nothing could hold him back from a second, far bolder negation: he altogether denied being. For this one world which he retained – supported by eternal unwritten laws, flowing upward and downward in brazen rhythmic beat – nowhere shows a tarrying, an indestructibility, a bulwark in the stream. Louder than Anaximander, Heraclitus proclaimed: "I see nothing other than becoming. Be not deceived. It is the fault of your myopia, not of the nature of things, if you believe you see land somewhere in the ocean of coming-to-be and passing away. You use names for things as though they rigidly, persistently endured; yet even the stream into which you step a second time is not the one you stepped into before."

Heraclitus' regal possession is his extraordinary power to think intuitively. Toward the other type of thinking, the type that is accomplished in concepts and logical combinations, in other words toward reason, he shows himself cool, insensitive, in fact hostile, and seems to feel pleasure whenever he can contradict it with an intuitively arrived-at truth. He does this in dicta like "Everything forever has its opposite along with it," and in such unabashed fashion that Aristotle accused him of the highest crime before the tribunal of reason: to have sinned against the law of contradiction. But intuitive thinking embraces two things: one, the present many-colored and changing world that crowds in upon its in all our experiences, and two, the conditions which alone make any experience of this world possible: time and space. For they may be perceived intuitively, even without a definite content, independent of all experience, purely in themselves. Now when Heraclitus contemplates time in this fashion, apart from all experience, he finds in it the most instructive monogram of everything that might conceivably come under the head of intuition. As Heraclitus sees time, so does Schopenhauer. He repeatedly said of it that every moment in it exists only insofar as it has just consumed the preceding one, its father, and is then immediately consumed likewise. And that past and future are as perishable as any dream, but that the present is but the dimensionless and durationless borderline between the two. And that space is just like time, and that everything which coexists in space and time has but a relative existence, that each thing exists through and for another like it, which is to say through and for an equally relative one. – This is a truth of the greatest immediate self-evidence for everyone, and one which for this very reason is extremely difficult to reach by way of concept or reason. But whoever finds himself directly looking at it must at once move on to the Heraclitan conclusion and say that the whole nature of reality [*Wirklichkeit*] lies simply in its acts [*Wirken*] and that for it there exists no other

7   Greek: right, law, justice, here personified as a goddess.

sort of being. Schopenhauer elucidates this point also (*World as Will and Representation*, Vol. I, Book 1, §4):

> Only by way of its acts does [reality] fill space and time. Its activity upon the immediate object conditions the intuitive perception in which alone it has existence. The consequence of the activity of any material object upon another is recognized only insofar as the latter now acts differently from what it did before upon the immediate object. Reality consists of nothing other than this. Cause and effect [*Wirkung*] in other words make out the whole nature of materiality: its being is its activity. That is why in German the epitome of all materiality is properly called *Wirklichkeit* [actuality], a word much more apt than *Realität*. That upon which it acts is likewise invariably matter; its whole being and nature consists only in the orderly changes which one of its parts produces in another. *Wirklichkeit* therefore is completely relative, in accordance with a relationship that is valid only within its bounds, exactly as is time, exactly as is space.

The everlasting and exclusive coming-to-be, the impermanence of everything actual, which constantly acts and comes-to-be but never is, as Heraclitus teaches it, is a terrible, paralyzing thought. Its impact on men can most nearly be likened to the sensation during an earthquake when one loses one's familiar confidence in a firmly grounded earth. It takes astonishing strength to transform this reaction into its opposite, into sublimity and the feeling of blessed astonishment. Heraclitus achieved this by means of an observation regarding the actual process of all coming-to-be and passing away. He conceived it under the form of polarity, as being the diverging of a force into two qualitatively different opposed activities that seek to re-unite. Everlastingly, a given quality contends against itself and separates into opposites; everlastingly these opposites seek to re-unite. Ordinary people fancy they see something rigid, complete and permanent; in truth, however, light and dark, bitter and sweet are attached to each other and interlocked at any given moment like wrestlers of whom sometimes the one, sometimes the other is on top. Honey, says Heraclitus, is at the same time bitter and sweet; the world itself is a mixed drink which must constantly be stirred. The strife of the opposites gives birth to all that comes-to-be; the definite qualities which look permanent to us express but the momentary ascendency of one partner. But this by no means signifies the end of the war; the contest endures in all eternity. Everything that happens, happens in accordance with this strife, and it is just in the strife that eternal justice is revealed. It is a wonderful idea, welling up from the purest springs of Hellenism, the idea that strife embodies the everlasting sovereignty of sprict justice, bound to everlasting laws. Only a Greek was capable of finding such an idea to be the fundament of a cosmology; it is Hesiod's good *Eris* transformed into the cosmic principle;[8] it is the contest-idea of the Greek individual and the Greek state, taken from the gymnasium and the palaestra, from the artist's *agon*,[9] from the contest between political parties and between cities – all transformed into universal application so that now the wheels of the cosmos turn on it. Just as the Greek individual fought as though he alone were right and an infinitely sure measure of judicial opinion were determining the trend of victory at any given moment, so the qualities wrestle with

8   Cf. *Homer's Contest*, p. 96f.
9   Greek: conflict, strife.

one another, in accordance with inviolable laws and standards that are immanent in the struggle. The things in whose definiteness and endurance narrow human minds, like animal minds, believe have no real existence. They are but the flash and spark of drawn swords, the quick radiance of victory in the struggle of the opposites.

That struggle which is peculiar to all coming-to-be, that everlasting alternation of victory, is again something also described by Schopenhauer (*World as Will and Representation*, Vol. I, Book 2, §27):

> Forever and ever, persistent matter must change its form. Grasping the clue of causality, mechanical, physical, chemical and organic phenomena greedily push to the fore, snatching matter from one another, for each would reveal its own inherent idea. We can follow this strife throughout the whole of nature. In fact we might say that nature exists but by virtue of it.

The pages that follow this passage give some notable illustrations of such struggle, except that the basic tone of their description is quite different from that which Heraclitus offers, because strife for Schopenhauer is a proof of the internal self-dissociation of the Will to Life, which is seen as a self-consuming, menacing and gloomy drive, a thoroughly frightful and by no means blessed phenomenon. The arena and the object of the struggle is matter, which the natural forces alternately try to snatch from one another, as well as space and time whose union by means of causality is this very matter.

6

While Heraclitus' imagination was eyeing this never-ceasing motion of the cosmos, this "actuality," like a blissful spectator who is watching innumerable pairs of contestants wrestling in joyous combat and refereed by stern judges, a still greater intuition overtook him. He could no longer see the contesting pairs and their referees as separate; the judges themselves seemed to be striving in the contest and the contestants seemed to be judging them. Now, perceiving basically nothing but everlastingly sovereign justice itself, he dared proclaim: "The struggle of the many is pure justice itself! In fact, the one is the many. For what are all those qualities, in essence? Are they the immortal gods? Are they separate beings, acting on and in themselves, from the beginning and without end? And if the world which we see knows only coming-to-be and passing away, but no tarrying, is it possible that those qualities might constitute a different kind of world, a metaphysical one? Not a world of unity, to be sure, such as Anaximander sought beyond the fluttering veils of the many, but a world of eternal substantive multiplicities?" Did Heraclitus take a detour, after all, back into a dual world order, however violently he might deny it, with an Olympus of numerous immortal gods and demons – of *many* realities in other words – and with a human world which sees but the dust cloud of the Olympic battle and the flash of divine spears – a coming-into-being, in other words? Anaximander had fled into the womb of the metaphysical "indefinite" to escape the definite qualities; because they came-to-be and passed away, he had denied them true, nuclear existence. But does it now look as though "becoming" were but the coming-to-be-visible of the struggle between eternal qualities? Should our talk of coming-to-be perhaps be derived from the peculiar weakness of human insight, whereas in the true nature of things there is no coming-to-be at all, but only a synchronicity of many true realities which were not born and will not die?

But these are un-Heraclitan loop-holes and labyrinths. Once again he proclaims, "The one is the many." The many perceivable qualities are neither eternal substances nor fantasms of our senses (Anaxagoras is later to imagine the former, Parmenides the latter); they are neither rigid autocratic being nor fleeting semblance flitting through human minds. The third possibility, the only one for Heraclitus, cannot be guessed by dialectic detective work nor figured out with the help of calculations. For what he here invented is a rarity even in the sphere of mystic incredibilities and unexpected cosmic metaphors. "The world is the *game* Zeus plays," or, expressed more concretely, "of the fire with itself. This is the only sense in which the one is at the same time the many."

In order to elucidate the introduction of fire as a cosmos-creating force, I remind the reader of the way in which Anaximander had developed the theory of water as the primal origin of things. Essentially trusting Thales, and supporting his observations with new evidence, Anaximander yet could not convince himself that there was no further quality-stage before water – beyond water as it were. It seemed to him as though the moist formed itself from warm and cold, and warm and cold, therefore, seemed to be preliminary stages of water, the even more aboriginal qualities. With their departure from the primal essence of the "indefinite," coming-to-be begins. Heraclitus who, as far as being a physicist was concerned, subordinated himself to Anaximander, re-interprets the Anaximandrian warm as warm breath, dry vapor, in other words, as fire. Of this fire he now says what Thales and Anaximander had said of water; that it coursed in countless transformations through the orbits of becoming; above all, in its three major occurrences as warmth, moisture and solidity. For water is transformed into earth on its way down, into fire on its way up, or, as Heraclitus seems to have declared more precisely: from the sea rise only the pure vapors which nourish the heavenly fire of the celestial bodies; from the earth only the dark misty ones, from which moisture draws its nourishment. The pure vapors are the transformation of sea into fire, the impure ones the transformation of earth to water. Thus the two transformation-orbits of fire run forever upward and downward, back and forth, side by side: from fire to water, from thence to earth, from earth back to water, from water to fire. While Heraclitus is Anaximander's disciple as to the main ideas, such as fire being fed by vapors, or water separating into earth and fire, he is independent of Anaximander and in opposition to him in that he excludes cold from the physical process. Anaximander had juxtaposed cold and warm as equal terms, in order to produce moisture from both. Heraclitus of necessity could not allow this, for if everything is fire, then in spite of all its transformations there can be no such thing as an absolute opposite. Hence he probably interpreted what is called "cold" as but a degree of warmth. He certainly could have justified such an interpretation without any difficulty. But far more important than this deviation from Anaximander's doctrine is a further agreement. He believes, like Anaximander, in a periodically repeated end of the world, and in an ever renewed rise of another world out of the all-destroying cosmic fire. The period in which the world hurries toward the conflagration and dissolves into pure fire Heraclitus characterizes, with notable emphasis, as a desire, a want, or lack; the full consumption in fire he calls satiety. It remains for us to ask how he interpreted and what he might have called the newly awakening impulse toward cosmic formation, the new outpouring into the forms of plurality. The Greek proverb "Satiety gives birth to hubris"[10] seems to come to our aid here, and indeed one may ask, for a moment, if Heraclitus did not perhaps derive the return to the many from hubris. We have but to take this thought seriously to see by its illumination how the countenance of Heraclitus is transformed before our eyes. The proud light in his eyes is extinguished, wrinkles of painful renunciation, of impotence, become apparent; we seem to know why later antiquity called him the "weeping philosopher." Is not the entire world process now an act of punishment for hubris? The many the result of evil-doing? The transformation of the pure into the impure the consequence of injustice? Is guilt not now transplanted into the very nucleus of materiality and the world of becoming and of individuals thereby unburdened of responsibility, to be sure, but simultaneously sentenced to carry the consequences of evil forever and anew?

7

That dangerous word "hubris" is indeed the touchstone for every Heraclitan. Here he must show whether he has understood or failed to recognize his master. Do guilt, injustice, contradiction and suffering exist in this world?

They do, proclaims Heraclitus, but only for the limited human mind which sees things apart but not connected, not for the con-tuitive god. For him all contradictions run into harmony, invisible to the common human eye, yet understandable to one who, like Heraclitus, is related to the contemplative god. Before his fire-gaze not a drop of injustice remains in the world poured all around him; even that cardinal impulse that allows pure fire to inhabit such impure forms is mastered by him with a sublime metaphor. In this world only play, play as artists and children engage in it, exhibits coming-to-be and passing away, structuring and destroying, without any moral additive, in forever equal innocence. And as children and artists play, so plays the ever-living fire. It constructs and destroys, all in innocence. Such is the game that the aeon plays with itself. Transforming itself into water and earth, it builds towers of sand like a child at the seashore, piles them up and tramples them down. From time to time it starts the game anew. An instant of satiety – and again it is seized by its need, as the artist is seized by his need to create. Not hubris but the ever self-renewing impulse to play calls new worlds into being. The child throws its toys away from time to time – and starts again, in innocent caprice. But when it does build, it combines and joins and forms its structures regularly, conforming to inner laws.

Only aesthetic man can look thus at the world, a man who has experienced in artists and in the birth of art objects how the struggle of the many can yet carry rules and laws inherent in itself, how the artist stands contemplatively above and at the same time actively within his work, how necessity and random play, oppositional tension and harmony, must pair to create a work of art.

Who could possibly demand from such a philosophy an ethic with its necessary imperatives "thou shalt," or, worse yet, accuse Heraclitus of lacking such! Man is necessity down to his last fibre, and totally "unfree," that is if one means by freedom the

---

10   Greek: overweening pride and arrogance, as distinct from aristocratic pride. It is a kind of pride that leads to disaster, whether by nature or divine agency or both.

foolish demand to be able to change one's *essentia*[11] arbitrarily, like a garment – a demand which every serious philosophy has rejected with the proper scorn. Very few people live consciously by the standards of the logos and the all-encompassing eye of the artist, and their eyes and ears and their intellect in general is a poor witness when "moist slime fills their souls." Why this is, is not asked, just as it is not asked why fire turns into water and earth. Heraclitus after all had no reason why he *had* to prove (as Leibniz did) that this is the best of all possible worlds.[12] It is enough for him that it is the beautiful innocent game of the aeon. Man, generally speaking, is for Heraclitus an irrational creature which is no contradiction of the fact that in all aspects of his nature the law of sovereign reason is fulfilled. He does not occupy an especially favored position in nature, whose loftiest phenomenon is fire, as exemplified by the celestial bodies. By no means is simple-minded man an equally lofty phenomenon. Insofar as he shares, of necessity, in fire, he has a plus of rationality; insofar as he consists of water and earth, his reason is in a bad way. There is no obligation on man to recognize the logos just because he is man. But why does water, why does earth exist? This, for Heraclitus, is a much more serious question than why human beings are so stupid and so wicked. The same immanent lawful order and justice reveals itself in the highest and in the wrongest man. But if we press upon Heraclitus the question why fire is not always fire, why it is sometimes water and sometimes earth, he could only say, "It is a game. Don't take it so pathetically and – above all – don't make morality of it!" Heraclitus only describes the world as it is and takes the same contemplative pleasure in it that an artist does when he looks at his own work in progress. Gloomy, melancholy, tearful, sinister, bilious, pessimistic, generally hateful: only those can find him thus who have good cause to be dissatisfied with his natural history of mankind. But he would consider such people negligible, together with their antipathies and sympathies, their hatreds and their loves, and only condescend to offer advice like "Dogs bark at everyone whom they do not recognize," or "Donkeys prefer straw to gold."

   Such dissatisfied people are also responsible for the numerous complaints about the obscurity of Heraclitus' style. The fact is that hardly anyone has ever written with as lucid and luminous a quality. Very tersely, to be sure, and for that reason obscure for readers who skim and race. How can people imagine that a philosopher would intentionally write obscurely – as they often say of Heraclitus – barring that he has good cause for hiding certain thoughts, or else were rascal enough to hide his thought-lessness behind words. After all, even in matters of ordinary practical life one must, as Schopenhauer says, be most careful to make one's meaning plain in order to prevent misunderstanding, if possible; how could one then permit oneself to express unclearly or enigmatically those most difficult, abstruse, scarcely attainable goals of thinking that it is philosophy's task to express. So far as terseness is concerned, however, Jean Paul has a useful admonition:

> Generally speaking, it is quite right if great things – things of much sense for men of rare sense – are expressed but briefly and (hence) darkly, so that barren minds will declare

---

11   Latin: essence.
12   For Leibniz, "It follows from the supreme perfection of God that in producing the universe he chose the best possible" (*Principles of Nature and Grace, Based on Reason*, 1714).

it to be nonsense, rather than translate it into a nonsense that they can comprehend. For mean, vulgar minds have an ugly facility for seeing in the profoundest and most pregnant utterance only their own everyday opinion.[13]

Nonetheless Heraclitus has not escaped the "barren minds"; already the Stoics reinterpreted him on a shallow level, dragging down his basically aesthetic perception of cosmic play to signify a vulgar consideration for the world's useful ends, especially those which benefit the human race. His physics became, in their hands, a crude optimism with the continual invitation to Tom, Dick and Harry to *plaudite amici*.[14]

13   "Jean Paul" was the pseudonym of Johann Paul Friedrich Richter (1763–1825), German novelist and aesthetician. The quotation is from his *Vorschule der Ästhetik* (*School for Aesthetics*, 1804/13).
14   Latin: applaud, my friends. Suetonius (*Lives of the Caesars*, ch. 99) records that these were among the last words spoken by the Roman emperor Augustus on his deathbed.

10

On Truth and Lies in a Nonmoral Sense

(1873)

1

Once upon a time, in some out of the way corner of that universe which is dispersed into numberless twinkling solar systems, there was a star upon which clever beasts invented knowing. That was the most arrogant and mendacious minute of "world history," but nevertheless, it was only a minute. After nature had drawn a few breaths, the star cooled and congealed, and the clever beasts had to die. – One might invent such a fable, and yet he still would not have adequately illustrated how miserable, how shadowy and transient, how aimless and arbitrary the human intellect looks within nature. There were eternities during which it did not exist. And when it is all over with the human intellect, nothing will have happened. For this intellect has no additional mission which would lead it beyond human life. Rather, it is human, and only its possessor and begetter takes it so solemnly – as though the world's axis turned within it. But if we could communicate with the gnat, we would learn that he likewise flies through the air with the same solemnity, that he feels the flying center of the universe within himself. There is nothing so reprehensible and unimportant in nature that it would not immediately swell up like a balloon at the slightest puff of this power of knowing. And just as every porter wants to have an admirer, so even the proudest of men, the philosopher, supposes that he sees on all sides the eyes of the universe telescopically focused upon his action and thought.

It is remarkable that this was brought about by the intellect, which was certainly allotted to these most unfortunate, delicate, and ephemeral beings merely as a device for detaining them a minute within existence. For without this addition they would have every reason to flee this existence as quickly as Lessing's son.[1] The pride connected with knowing and sensing lies like a blinding fog over the eyes and senses of men, thus deceiving them concerning the value of existence. For this pride contains within itself the most flattering estimation of the value of knowing. Deception is the

---

1   Reference to the offspring of Lessing and Eva König, who died on the day of his birth.

most general effect of such pride, but even its most particular effects contain within themselves something of the same deceitful character.

As a means for the preserving of the individual, the intellect unfolds its principal powers in dissimulation, which is the means by which weaker, less robust individuals preserve themselves – since they have been denied the chance to wage the battle for existence with horns or with the sharp teeth of beasts of prey. This art of dissimulation reaches its peak in man. Deception, flattering, lying, deluding, talking behind the back, putting up a false front, living in borrowed splendor, wearing a mask, hiding behind convention, playing a role for others and for oneself – in short, a continuous fluttering around the *solitary* flame of vanity – is so much the rule and the law among men that there is almost nothing which is less comprehensible than how an honest and pure drive for truth could have arisen among them. They are deeply immersed in illusions and in dream images; their eyes merely glide over the surface of things and see "forms." Their senses nowhere lead to truth; on the contrary, they are content to receive stimuli and, as it were, to engage in a groping game on the backs of things. Moreover, man permits himself to be deceived in his dreams every night of his life. His moral sentiment does not even make an attempt to prevent this, whereas there are supposed to be men who have stopped snoring through sheer will power. What does man actually know about himself? Is he, indeed, ever able to perceive himself completely, as if laid out in a lighted display case? Does nature not conceal most things from him – even concerning his own body – in order to confine and lock him within a proud, deceptive consciousness, aloof from the coils of the bowels, the rapid flow of the blood stream, and the intricate quivering of the fibers! She threw away the key. And woe to that fatal curiosity which might one day have the power to peer out and down through a crack in the chamber of consciousness and then suspect that man is sustained in the indifference of his ignorance by that which is pitiless, greedy, insatiable, and murderous – as if hanging in dreams on the back of a tiger. Given this situation, where in the world could the drive for truth have come from?

Insofar as the individual wants to maintain himself against other individuals, he will under natural circumstances employ the intellect mainly for dissimulation. But at the same time, from boredom and necessity, man wishes to exist socially and with the herd; therefore, he needs to make peace and strives accordingly to banish from his world at least the most flagrant *bellum omnium contra omnes*.[2] This peace treaty brings in its wake something which appears to be the first step toward acquiring that puzzling truth drive: to wit, *that* which shall count as "truth" from now on is established. That is to say, a uniformly valid and binding designation is invented for things, and this legislation of language likewise establishes the first laws of truth. For the contrast between truth and lie arises here for the first time. The liar is a person who uses the valid designations, the words, in order to make something which is unreal appear to be real. He says, for example, "I am rich," when the proper designation for his condition would be "poor." He misuses fixed conventions by means of arbitrary substitutions or even reversals of names. If he does this in a selfish and moreover harmful manner, society will cease to trust him and will thereby exclude him. What men avoid by excluding the liar is not so much being defrauded as it is being harmed by means of fraud. Thus, even at this stage, what they hate is basically not deception itself, but rather the

2   Latin: war of all against all. Cf. *The Greek State* note 5 above.

unpleasant, hated consequences of certain sorts of deception. It is in a similarly restricted sense that man now wants nothing but truth: he desires the pleasant, life-preserving consequences of truth. He is indifferent toward pure knowledge which has no consequences; toward those truths which are possibly harmful and destructive he is even hostilely inclined. And besides, what about these linguistic conventions themselves? Are they perhaps products of knowledge, that is, of the sense of truth? Are designations congruent with things? Is language the adequate expression of all realities?

It is only by means of forgetfulness that man can ever reach the point of fancying himself to possess a "truth" of the grade just indicated. If he will not be satisfied with truth in the form of tautology, that is to say, if he will not be content with empty husks, then he will always exchange truths for illusions. What is a word? It is the copy in sound of a nerve stimulus. But the further inference from the nerve stimulus to a cause outside of us is already the result of a false and unjustifiable application of the principle of sufficient reason. If truth alone had been the deciding factor in the genesis of language, and if the standpoint of certainty had been decisive for designations, then how could we still dare to say "the stone is hard," as if "hard" were something otherwise familiar to us, and not merely a totally subjective stimulation! We separate things according to gender, designating the tree as masculine and the plant as feminine. What arbitrary assignments![3] How far this oversteps the canons of certainty! We speak of a "snake": this designation touches only upon its ability to twist itself and could therefore also fit a worm.[4] What arbitrary differentiations! What one-sided preferences, first for this, then for that property of a thing! The various languages placed side by side show that with words it is never a question of truth, never a question of adequate expression; otherwise, there would not be so many languages. The "thing in itself" (which is precisely what the pure truth, apart from any of its consequences, would be) is likewise something quite incomprehensible to the creator of language and something not in the least worth striving for. This creator only designates the relations of things to men, and for expressing these relations he lays hold of the boldest metaphors. To begin with, a nerve stimulus is transferred into an image:[5] first metaphor. The image, in turn, is imitated in a sound: second metaphor. And each time there is a complete overleaping of one sphere, right into the middle of an entirely new and different one. One can imagine a man who is totally deaf and has never had a sensation of sound and music. Perhaps such a person will gaze with astonishment at Chladni's sound figures;[6] perhaps he will discover their causes in the vibrations of the string and will now swear that he must know what men mean by "sound." It is this way with all of us concerning language: we believe that we know something about the things themselves when we speak of trees, colors, snow, and flowers; and yet we possess nothing but metaphors for things – metaphors which correspond in no way to the original entities. In the same way that the sound appears as a sand figure, so the mysterious X of the thing

---

3   All common nouns in German are assigned a gender: the tree is *der Baum*, the plant is *die Pflanze*.
4   *Schlange*, the German for "snake," is related to the verb *schlingen* (to wind or twist).
5   In German: *Bild*.
6   Ernst Florens Friedrich Chladni (1756–1827), German physicist, was one of the founders of modern scientific acoustics. His "sound figures," sometimes called "Chladni figures" or "sand figures," are patterns made on a sand-covered flat surface by the sonic vibrations produced by a string affixed below the plane.

in itself first appears as a nerve stimulus, then as an image, and finally as a sound. Thus the genesis of language does not proceed logically in any case, and all the material within and with which the man of truth, the scientist, and the philosopher later work and build, if not derived from never-never land,[7] is at least not derived from the essence of things.

In particular, let us further consider the formation of concepts. Every word instantly becomes a concept precisely insofar as it is not supposed to serve as a reminder of the unique and entirely individual original experience to which it owes its origin; but rather, a word becomes a concept insofar as it simultaneously has to fit countless more or less similar cases – which means, purely and simply, cases which are never equal and thus altogether unequal. Every concept arises from the equation of unequal things. Just as it is certain that one leaf is never totally the same as another, so it is certain that the concept "leaf" is formed by arbitrarily discarding these individual differences and by forgetting the distinguishing aspects. This awakens the idea that, in addition to the leaves, there exists in nature the "leaf": the original model according to which all the leaves were perhaps woven, sketched, measured, colored, curled, and painted – but by incompetent hands, so that no specimen has turned out to be a correct, trustworthy, and faithful likeness of the original model. We call a person "honest," and then we ask "why has he behaved so honestly today?" Our usual answer is, "on account of his honesty." Honesty! This in turn means that the leaf is the cause of the leaves. We know nothing whatsoever about an essential quality called "honesty"; but we do know of countless individualized and consequently unequal actions which we equate by omitting the aspects in which they are unequal and which we now designate as "honest" actions. Finally we formulate from them a *qualitas occulta*,[8] which has the name "honesty." We obtain the concept, as we do the form, by overlooking what is individual and actual; whereas nature is acquainted with no forms and no concepts, and likewise with no species, but only with an X which remains inaccessible and undefinable for us. For even our contrast between individual and species is something anthropomorphic and does not originate in the essence of things; although we should not presume to claim that this contrast does not correspond to the essence of things: that would of course be a dogmatic assertion and, as such, would be just as indemonstrable as its opposite.

What then is truth? A movable host of metaphors, metonymies, and anthropomorphisms: in short, a sum of human relations which have been poetically and rhetorically intensified, transferred, and embellished, and which, after long usage, seem to a people to be fixed, canonical, and binding. Truths are illusions which we have forgotten are illusions; they are metaphors that have become worn out and have been drained of sensuous force, coins which have lost their embossing and are now considered as metal and no longer as coins.

We still do not yet know where the drive for truth comes from. For so far we have heard only of the duty which society imposes in order to exist: to be truthful means to employ the usual metaphors. Thus, to express it morally, this is the duty to lie according to a fixed convention, to lie with the herd and in a manner binding upon everyone. Now man of course forgets that this is the way things stand for him. Thus he lies in the manner indicated, unconsciously and in accordance with habits which are centuries old; and precisely *by means of this unconsciousness* and forgetfulness he arrives

7   In German: *Wolkenkukuksheim* (literally, "cloud-cuckoo-land").
8   Latin: occult quality.

at his sense of truth. From the sense that one is obliged to designate one thing as "red," another as "cold," and a third as "mute," there arises a moral impulse in regard to truth. The venerability, reliability, and utility of truth is something which a person demonstrates for himself from the contrast with the liar, whom no one trusts and everyone excludes. As a *"rational"* being, he now places his behavior under the control of abstractions. He will no longer tolerate being carried away by sudden impressions, by intuitions. First he universalizes all these impressions into less colorful, cooler concepts, so that he can entrust the guidance of his life and conduct to them. Everything which distinguishes man from the animals depends upon this ability to volatilize perceptual metaphors in a schema, and thus to dissolve an image into a concept. For something is possible in the realm of these schemata which could never be achieved with the vivid first impressions: the construction of a pyramidal order according to castes and degrees, the creation of a new world of laws, privileges, subordinations, and clearly marked boundaries – a new world, one which now confronts that other vivid world of first impressions as more solid, more universal, better known, and more human than the immediately perceived world, and thus as the regulative and imperative world. Whereas each perceptual metaphor is individual and without equals and is therefore able to elude all classification, the great edifice of concepts displays the rigid regularity of a Roman columbarium[9] and exhales in logic that strength and coolness which is characteristic of mathematics. Anyone who has felt this cool breath [of logic] will hardly believe that even the concept – which is as bony, foursquare, and transposable as a die – is nevertheless merely the *residue of a metaphor*, and that the illusion which is involved in the artistic transference of a nerve stimulus into images is, if not the mother, then the grandmother of every single concept. But in this conceptual crap game "truth" means using every die in the designated manner, counting its spots accurately, fashioning the right categories, and never violating the order of caste and class rank. Just as the Romans and Etruscans cut up the heavens with rigid mathematical lines and confined a god within each of the spaces thereby delimited, as within a *templum*,[10] so every people has a similarly mathematically divided conceptual heaven above themselves and henceforth thinks that truth demands that each conceptual god be sought only within *his own* sphere. Here one may certainly admire man as a mighty genius of construction, who succeeds in piling up an infinitely complicated dome of concepts upon an unstable foundation, and, as it were, on running water. Of course, in order to be supported by such a foundation, his construction must be like one constructed of spiders' webs: delicate enough to be carried along by the waves, strong enough not to be blown apart by every wind. As a genius of construction man raises himself far above the bee in the following way: whereas the bee builds with wax that he gathers from nature, man builds with the far more delicate conceptual material which he first has to manufacture from himself. In this he is greatly to be admired, but not on account of his drive for truth or for pure knowledge of things. When someone hides something behind a bush and looks for it again in the same place and finds it there as well, there is not much to praise in such seeking and finding. Yet this is how matters stand regarding seeking and finding "truth" within the realm of reason.

9   Vault with niches for funeral urns containing the ashes of cremated bodies.
10   Delimited space restricted to a particular purpose, especially a religiously sanctified area.

If I make up the definition of a mammal, and then, after inspecting a camel, declare "look, a mammal," I have indeed brought a truth to light in this way, but it is a truth of limited value. That is to say, it is a thoroughly anthropomorphic truth which contains not a single point which would be "true in itself" or really and universally valid apart from man. At bottom, what the investigator of such truths is seeking is only the metamorphosis of the world into man. He strives to understand the world as something analogous to man, and at best he achieves by his struggles the feeling of assimilation. Similar to the way in which astrologers considered the stars to be in man's service and connected with his happiness and sorrow, such an investigator considers the entire universe in connection with man: the entire universe as the infinitely fractured echo of one original sound – man; the entire universe as the infinitely multiplied copy of one original picture – man. His method is to treat man as the measure of all things, but in doing so he again proceeds from the error of believing that he has these things [which he intends to measure] immediately before him as mere objects. He forgets that the original perceptual metaphors are metaphors and takes them to be the things themselves.

Only by forgetting this primitive world of metaphor can one live with any repose, security, and consistency: only by means of the petrification and coagulation of a mass of images which originally streamed from the primal faculty of human imagination like a fiery liquid, only in the invincible faith that *this* sun, *this* window, *this* table is a truth in itself, in short, only by forgetting that he himself is an *artistically creating* subject, does man live with any repose, security, and consistency. If but for an instant he could escape from the prison walls of this faith, his "self consciousness" would be immediately destroyed. It is even a difficult thing for him to admit to himself that the insect or the bird perceives an entirely different world from the one that man does, and that the question of which of these perceptions of the world is the more correct one is quite meaningless, for this would have to have been decided previously in accordance with the criterion of the *correct perception*, which means, in accordance with a criterion which is *not available*. But in any case it seems to me that "the correct perception" – which would mean "the adequate expression of an object in the subject" – is a contradictory impossibility. For between two absolutely different spheres, as between subject and object, there is no causality, no correctness, and no expression; there is, at most, an *aesthetic* relation: I mean, a suggestive transference, a stammering translation into a completely foreign tongue – for which there is required, in any case, a freely inventive intermediate sphere and mediating force. "Appearance"[11] is a word that contains many temptations, which is why I avoid it as much as possible. For it is not true that the essence of things "appears"[12] in the empirical world. A painter without hands who wished to express in song the picture before his mind would, by means of this substitution of spheres, still reveal more about the essence of things than does the empirical world. Even the relationship of a nerve stimulus to the generated image is not a necessary one. But when the same image has been generated millions of times and has been handed down for many generations and finally appears on the same occasion every time for all mankind, then it acquires at last the same meaning for men it would have if it were the sole necessary image and if the relationship of the original nerve stimulus to the generated image were a strictly causal one. In the same manner, an

11   In German: *Erscheinung.*
12   In German: *erscheint.*

eternally repeated dream would certainly be felt and judged to be reality. But the hardening and congealing of a metaphor guarantees absolutely nothing concerning its necessity and exclusive justification.

Every person who is familiar with such considerations has no doubt felt a deep mistrust of all idealism of this sort: just as often as he has quite clearly convinced himself of the eternal consistency, omnipresence, and infallibility of laws of nature. He has concluded that so far as we can penetrate here – from the telescopic heights to the microscopic depths – everything is secure, complete, infinite, regular, and without any gaps. Science will be able to dig successfully in this shaft forever, and all the things that are discovered will harmonize with and not contradict each other. How little does this resemble a product of the imagination, for if it were such, there should be some place where the illusion and unreality can be divined. Against this, the following must be said: if each of us had a different kind of sense perception – if we could only perceive things now as a bird, now as a worm, now as a plant, or if one of us saw a stimulus as red, another as blue, while a third even heard the same stimulus as a sound – then no one would speak of such a regularity of nature, rather, nature would be grasped only as a creation which is subjective in the highest degree. After all, what is a law of nature as such for us? We are not acquainted with it in itself, but only with its effects, which means in its relation to other laws of nature – which, in turn, are known to us only as sums of relations. Therefore all these relations always refer again to others and are thoroughly incomprehensible to us in their essence. All that we actually know about these laws of nature is what we ourselves bring to them – time and space, and therefore relationships of succession and number. But everything marvelous about the laws of nature, everything that quite astonishes us therein and seems to demand our explanation, everything that might lead us to distrust idealism: all this is completely and solely contained within the mathematical strictness and inviolability of our representations of time and space. But we produce these representations in and from ourselves with same necessity with which the spider spins. If we are forced to comprehend all things only under these forms, then it ceases to be amazing that in all things we actually comprehend nothing but these forms. For they must all bear within themselves the laws of number, and it is precisely number which is most astonishing in things. All that conformity to law, which impresses us so much in the movement of the stars and in chemical processes, coincides at bottom with those properties which we bring to things. Thus it is we who impress ourselves in this way. In conjunction with this, it of course follows that the artistic process of metaphor formation with which every sensation begins in us already presupposes these forms and thus occurs within them. The only way in which the possibility of subsequently constructing a new conceptual edifice from metaphors themselves can be explained is by the firm persistence of these original forms. That is to say, this conceptual edifice is an imitation of temporal, spatial, and numerical relationships in the domain of metaphor.

2

We have seen how it is originally *language* which works on the construction of concepts, a labor taken over in later ages by *science*.[13] Just as the bee simultaneously constructs

---

13   In German: *Wissenschaft*. The word refers to any rigorous and systematic inquiry, and is not restricted to the natural sciences.

cells and fills them with honey, so science works unceasingly on this great columbarium of concepts, the graveyard of perceptions. It is always building new, higher
stories and shoring up, cleaning, and renovating the old cells; above all, it takes pains
to fill up this monstrously towering framework and to arrange therein the entire empirical world, which is to say, the anthropomorphic world. Whereas the man of action
binds his life to reason and its concepts so that he will not be swept away and lost,
the scientific investigator builds his hut right next to the tower of science so that
he will be able to work on it and to find shelter for himself beneath those bulwarks
which presently exist. And he requires shelter, for there are frightful powers which
continuously break in upon him, powers which oppose scientific "truth" with completely different kinds of "truths" which bear on their shields the most varied sorts of
emblems.

The drive toward the formation of metaphors is the fundamental human drive, which
one cannot for a single instant dispense with in thought, for one would thereby dispense with man himself. This drive is not truly vanquished and scarcely subdued by
the fact that a regular and rigid new world is constructed as its prison from its own
ephemeral products, the concepts. It seeks a new realm and another channel for its
activity, and it finds this in *myth* and in *art* generally. This drive continually confuses
the conceptual categories and cells by bringing forward new transferences, metaphors,
and metonymies. It continually manifests an ardent desire to refashion the world which
presents itself to waking man, so that it will be as colorful, irregular, lacking in results
and coherence, charming, and eternally new as the world of dreams. Indeed, it is only
by means of the rigid and regular web of concepts that the waking man clearly sees
that he is awake; and it is precisely because of this that he sometimes thinks that he
must be dreaming when this web of concepts is torn by art. Pascal is right in maintaining that if the same dream came to us every night we would be just as occupied
with it as we are with the things that we see every day. "If a workman were sure to
dream for twelve straight hours every night that he was king," said Pascal, "I believe
that he would be just as happy as a king who dreamt for twelve hours every night that
he was a workman."[14] In fact, because of the way that myth takes it for granted that
miracles are always happening, the waking life of a mythically inspired people – the
ancient Greeks, for instance – more closely resembles a dream than it does the waking world of a scientifically disenchanted thinker. When every tree can suddenly speak
as a nymph, when a god in the shape of a bull can drag away maidens, when even
the goddess Athena herself is suddenly seen in the company of Peisistratus driving
through the market place of Athens with a beautiful team of horses[15] – and this
is what the honest Athenian believed – then, as in a dream, anything is possible
at each moment, and all of nature swarms around man as if it were nothing but a

---

14   Blaise Pascal (1623–62), French prose writer and convert to Jansenism who also made
contributions to mathematics, physics, and religious controversy. Author of *Les Lettres provin-
ciales* (*Provincial Letters*, 1656–7) and the posthumously published *Pensées* (written 1657–8). The
passage quoted here is from *Pensées*, no. 386 (Brunschwicg edn).
15   According to Herodotus (*History*, I. 60), the tyrant Peisistratus adopted the following ruse
to secure his popular acceptance upon his return from exile: he entered Athens in a chariot
accompanied by a woman named Phye who was dressed in the costume of Athena. Thus the
people were supposed to have been convinced that it was the goddess herself who was conducting the tyrant back to the Acropolis.

masquerade of the gods, who were merely amusing themselves by deceiving men in all these shapes.

But man has an invincible inclination to allow himself to be deceived and is, as it were, enchanted with happiness when the rhapsodist tells him epic fables as if they were true, or when the actor in the theater acts more royally than any real king. So long as it is able to deceive without *injuring*, that master of deception, the intellect, is free; it is released from its former slavery and celebrates its Saturnalia.[16] It is never more luxuriant, richer, prouder, more clever and more daring. With creative pleasure it throws metaphors into confusion and displaces the boundary stones of abstractions, so that, for example, it designates the stream as "the moving path which carries man where he would otherwise walk." The intellect has now thrown the token of bondage from itself. At other times it endeavors, with gloomy officiousness, to show the way and to demonstrate the tools to a poor individual who covets existence; it is like a servant who goes in search of booty and prey for his master. But now it has become the master and it dares to wipe from its face the expression of indigence. In comparison with its previous conduct, everything that it now does bears the mark of dissimulation, just as that previous conduct did of distortion. The free intellect copies human life, but it considers this life to be something good and seems to be quite satisfied with it. That immense framework and planking of concepts to which the needy man clings his whole life long in order to preserve himself is nothing but a scaffolding and toy for the most audacious feats of the liberated intellect. And when it smashes this framework to pieces, throws it into confusion, and puts it back together in an ironic fashion, pairing the most alien things and separating the closest, it is demonstrating that it has no need of these makeshifts of indigence and that it will now be guided by intuitions rather than by concepts. There is no regular path which leads from these intuitions into the land of ghostly schemata, the land of abstractions. There exists no word for these intuitions; when man sees them he grows dumb, or else he speaks only in forbidden metaphors and in unheard-of combinations of concepts. He does this so that by shattering and mocking the old conceptual barriers he may at least correspond creatively to the impression of the powerful present intuition.

There are ages in which the rational man and the intuitive man stand side by side, the one in fear of intuition, the other with scorn for abstraction. The latter is just as irrational as the former is inartistic. They both desire to rule over life: the former, by knowing how to meet his principal needs by means of foresight, prudence, and regularity; the latter, by disregarding these needs and, as an "overjoyed hero," counting as real only that life which has been disguised as illusion and beauty. Whenever, as was perhaps the case in ancient Greece, the intuitive man handles his weapons more authoritatively and victoriously than his opponent, then, under favorable circumstances, a culture can take shape and art's mastery over life can be established. All the manifestations of such a life will be accompanied by this dissimulation, this disavowal of indigence, this glitter of metaphorical intuitions, and, in general, this immediacy of deception: neither the house, nor the gait, nor the clothes, nor the clay jugs give evidence of having been invented because of a pressing need. It seems as if they were all

16 Roman religious festival held annually in December in honor of Saturn; the prototype of modern Christmas celebrations. Unusually, the merry-making extended to slaves, who were served by their masters for the day.

intended to express an exalted happiness, an Olympian cloudlessness, and, as it were, a playing with seriousness. The man who is guided by concepts and abstractions only succeeds by such means in warding off misfortune, without ever gaining any happiness for himself from these abstractions. And while he aims for the greatest possible freedom from pain, the intuitive man, standing in the midst of a culture, already reaps from his intuition a harvest of continually inflowing illumination, cheer, and redemption – in addition to obtaining a defense against misfortune. To be sure, he suffers more intensely, *when* he suffers; he even suffers more frequently, since he does not understand how to learn from experience and keeps falling over and over again into the same ditch. He is then just as irrational in sorrow as he is in happiness: he cries aloud and will not be consoled. How differently the stoical man who learns from experience and governs himself by concepts is affected by the same misfortunes! This man, who at other times seeks nothing but sincerity, truth, freedom from deception, and protection against ensnaring surprise attacks, now executes a masterpiece of deception: he executes his masterpiece of deception in misfortune, as the other type of man executes his in times of happiness. He wears no quivering and changeable human face, but, as it were, a mask with dignified, symmetrical features. He does not cry; he does not even alter his voice. When a real storm cloud thunders above him, he wraps himself in his cloak, and with slow steps he walks from beneath it.

11

On the Utility and Liability of History for Life

(1874)

Foreword

"Moreover, I hate everything that only instructs me without increasing or immediately stimulating my own activity."[1] These words of Goethe's, a boldly expressed *ceterum censeo*,[2] provide an appropriate beginning for our observations on the worth and worthlessness of history.[3] My purpose here is to demonstrate why instruction without stimulation, why knowledge that inhibits activity, why history as a costly intellectual superfluity and luxury must, in accordance with Goethe's words, arouse our intense hatred – for the simple reason that we still lack the most basic necessities, and because the superfluous is the enemy of necessity. To be sure, we need history; but our need for it is different from that of the pampered idler in the garden of knowledge – regardless of the noble condescension with which he might look upon our crude and inelegant needs and afflictions. That is, we need it for life and for action, not for the easy withdrawal from life and from action, let alone for whitewashing a selfish life and cowardly, base actions.

1 Letter from Goethe to Schiller, December 19, 1798.
2 Latin: but I am of the opinion. Allusion to the famous sentence with which the elder Cato is purported to have closed every speech before the Roman Senate: "But I am of the opinion that Carthage must be destroyed."
3 In German: *Historie*. This is the word Nietzsche uses throughout the Foreword, along with derived terms such as *historisch*. In the argument of the text he will also deploy the word *Geschichte* and frequently move between the two words. We have given an indication of his usage of the two terms in the notes that follow on section 1. In German *Geschichte* has the meaning of "event" or "happening," being closely connected with *Geschehen* as that which has taken place. It refers primarily to the events that are retold, but has also assumed the meaning of a report of specific events in terms of their unfolding and connections. *Historie* comes from the Latin *historia*, meaning "inquiry." In this second *Untimely Meditation* Nietzsche is taking to task not simply "history" as a chronicling or recording of what has happened and of events, but history in the wider sense of our need and desire to look backwards and recollect, to pursue "inquiry" in this historical sense.

We only wish to serve history to the extent that it serves life, but there is a way of practicing history and a valorization of history in which life atrophies and degenerates: a phenomenon that it will likely be as painful as it is necessary to diagnose in the striking symptoms of our present age.

I have sought to depict a feeling that has often tormented me; I am taking my revenge on it by exposing it to public scrutiny. Perhaps this depiction will cause someone or other to declare that he is also familiar with this feeling, but that I have not experienced it in all its purity and originarity, and that I hence have failed to express it with the confidence and maturity of experience that it requires. A few people may, perhaps, make this assertion, but most will say that it is a wholly perverse, unnatural, repulsive, and downright illicit feeling; indeed, they will say that by feeling it, I have proven myself unworthy of that powerful historical orientation of our age, which, as is well known, has made itself evident for two generations now, particularly among the Germans. However, the very fact that I dare to go public with the natural description of my feeling will tend to promote rather than injure general propriety, since I will thereby give many the opportunity to say flattering things about the aforementioned orientation of our age. But I stand to gain something for myself that is worth even more than propriety – to be publicly instructed and set right about our age.

The observations offered here are also unfashionable[4] because I attempt to understand something in which our age justifiably takes pride – namely, its historical cultivation – as a detriment, an infirmity, a deficiency of the age, and furthermore, because I am even of the opinion that all of us suffer from a debilitating historical fever and that we at the very least need to recognize that we suffer from it. But if Goethe was correct in saying that when we cultivate our virtues we simultaneously cultivate our faults,[5] and if, as everyone knows, a hypertrophied virtue – and the historical sensibility of our time seems to me to be just such a hypertrophied virtue – can cause the demise of a people just as easily as a hypertrophied vice, then perhaps just this once I will be permitted to speak up. By way of exculpation, I should not conceal the fact, first, that I have mainly drawn the occurrences that aroused in me those tormenting feelings from my own experiences and that I have drawn on the experiences of others only by way of comparison, and second, that it is only to the extent that I am a student of more ancient times – above all, of ancient Greece – that I, as a child of our time, have had such unfashionable experiences. But I have to concede this much to myself as someone who by occupation is a classical philologist, for I have no idea what the significance of classical philology would be in our age, if not to have an unfashionable effect – that is, to work against the time and thereby have an effect upon it, hopefully for the benefit of a future time.

I

Observe the herd as it grazes past you: it cannot distinguish yesterday from today, leaps about, eats, sleeps, digests, leaps some more, and carries on like this from morning to night and from day to day, tethered by the short leash of its pleasures and displeasures to the stake of the moment, and thus it is neither melancholy nor bored. It is hard on the human being to observe this, because he boasts about the superiority of his humanity over animals and yet looks enviously upon their happiness – for the one

---

4 In German: *unzeitgemäss*.
5 See Goethe, *Dichtung und Wahrheit* (*Poetry and Truth*), III, ch. 13.

and only thing that he desires is to live like an animal, neither bored nor in pain, and yet he desires this in vain, because he does not desire it in the same way as does the animal. The human being might ask the animal: "Why do you just look at me like that instead of telling me about your happiness?" The animal wanted to answer, "Because I always immediately forget what I wanted to say" – but it had already forgotten this answer and hence said nothing, so that the human being was left to wonder.

But he also wondered about himself and how he was unable to learn to forget and always clung to what was past; no matter how far or how fast he runs, that chain runs with him. It is cause for wonder: the moment, here in a flash, gone in a flash, before it nothing, after it nothing, does, after all, return as a ghost once more and disturbs the peace of a later moment. Over and over a leaf is loosened from the scroll of time, falls out, flutters away – and suddenly flutters back into the human being's lap. Then the human being says "I remember," and he envies the animal that immediately forgets and that sees how every moment actually dies, sinks back into fog and night, and is extinguished forever. Thus the animal lives *unhistorically*,[6] for it disappears entirely into the present, like a number that leaves no remainder; it does not know how to dissemble, conceals nothing, and appears in each and every moment as exactly what it is, and so cannot help but be honest. The human being, by contrast, braces himself against the great and ever-greater burden of the past; it weighs him down or bends him over, hampers his gait as an invisible and obscure load that he can pretend to disown, and that he is only too happy to disown when he is among his fellow human beings in order to arouse their envy. That is why the sight of a grazing herd or, even closer to home, of a child, which, not yet having a past to disown, plays in blissful blindness between the fences of the past and the future, moves him as though it were the vision of a lost paradise. And yet the child's play must be disturbed; all too soon it will be summoned out of its obliviousness. Then it will come to understand the phrase "it was," that watchword that brings the human being strife, suffering, and boredom, so that he is reminded what his existence basically is – a never to be perfected imperfect.[7] When death finally brings him the much longed-for oblivion, it simultaneously also suppresses the present; and with this, existence places its seal on the knowledge that existence itself is nothing but an uninterrupted having-been, something that lives by negating, consuming, and contradicting itself.

If happiness, if striving for new happiness, is in any conceivable sense what binds the living to life and urges them to live on, then perhaps no philosopher is closer to the truth than the cynic, for the happiness of the animal, who is, after all, the consummate cynic, provides living proof of the truth of cynicism. The smallest happiness, if it is uninterruptedly present and makes one happy, is an incomparably greater form of happiness than the greatest happiness that occurs as a mere episode, as a mood, so to speak, as a wild whim, in the midst of sheer joylessness, yearning, and privation. But in the case of the smallest and the greatest happiness, it is always just one thing alone that makes happiness happiness: the ability to forget, or, expressed in a more scholarly fashion, the capacity to feel unhistorically over the entire course of its

6   In German: *unhistorisch*. The translation has been modified to "unhistorical" here and throughout the text.

7   The word Nietzsche uses here, *Imperfectum*, not only evokes the notion of imperfection but also signifies the imperfect tense.

duration. Anyone who cannot forget the past entirely and set himself down on the threshold of the moment, anyone who cannot stand, without dizziness or fear, on one single point like a victory goddess, will never know what happiness is; worse, he will never do anything that makes others happy. Imagine the most extreme example, a human being who does not possess the power to forget, who is damned to see becoming everywhere; such a human being would no longer believe in his own being, would no longer believe in himself, would see everything flow apart in turbulent particles, and would lose himself in this stream of becoming; like the true student of Heraclitus, in the end he would hardly even dare to lift a finger. All action requires forgetting, just as the existence of all organic things requires not only light, but darkness as well. A human being who wanted to experience things in a thoroughly historical manner would be like someone forced to go without sleep, or like an animal supposed to exist solely by rumination and ever repeated rumination. In other words, it is possible to live almost without memory, indeed, to live happily, as the animals show us; but without forgetting, it is utterly impossible to live at all. Or, to express my theme even more simply: *There is a degree of sleeplessness, of rumination, of historical sensibility,*[8] *that injures and ultimately destroys all living things, whether a human being, a people, or a culture.*

In order to determine this degree and thereby establish the limit beyond which the past must be forgotten if it is not to become the grave digger of the present, we would have to know exactly how great the *shaping power*[9] of a human being, a people, a culture is; by shaping power I mean that power to develop its own singular character out of itself, to shape and assimilate what is past and alien, to heal wounds, to replace what has been lost, to recreate broken forms out of itself alone. There are people who possess so little of this power that they bleed to death from a single experience, a single pain, particularly even from a single mild injustice, as from a tiny little cut. On the other hand, there are those who are so little affected by life's most savage and devastating disasters, and even by their own malicious actions, that, while these are still taking place, or at least shortly thereafter, they manage to arrive at a tolerable level of well-being and a kind of clear conscience. The stronger the roots of a human being's innermost nature, the more of the past he will assimilate or forcibly appropriate; and the most powerful, most mighty nature would be characterized by the fact that there would be no limit at which its historical sensibility would have a stifling and harmful effect; it would appropriate and incorporate into itself all that is past, what is its own as well as what is alien, transforming it, as it were, into its own blood. Such a nature knows how to forget whatever does not subdue it; these things no longer exist. Its horizon is closed and complete, and nothing is capable of reminding it that beyond this horizon there are human beings, passions, doctrines, goals. And this is a universal law: every living thing can become healthy, strong, and fruitful only within a defined horizon; if it is incapable of drawing a horizon around itself and too selfish, in turn, to enclose its own perspective within an alien horizon, then it will feebly waste away or hasten to its timely end. Cheerfulness, good conscience, joyous deeds, faith in what is to come – all this depends, both in the instance of the individual as well as in that of a people, on whether there is a line that segregates what is discernible and bright from what is unilluminable and obscure; on whether one knows how to forget things

8   In German: *historischen Sinne.*
9   In German: *die plastische Kraft.*

at the proper time just as well as one knows how to remember at the proper time; on whether one senses with a powerful instinct which occasions should be experienced historically, and which unhistorically. This is the proposition the reader is invited to consider: *the unhistorical and the historical*[10] *are equally necessary for the health of an individual, a people, and a culture.*

Everyone has made at least this one simple observation: a human being's historical knowledge and sensitivity can be very limited, his horizon as narrow as that of the inhabitant of an isolated alpine valley; each of his judgments may contain an injustice, each experience may be marked by the misconception that he is the first to experience it – yet in spite of all these injustices and all these misconceptions, he stands there, vigorously healthy and robust, a joy to look at. At the same time, someone standing close beside him who is far more just and learned grows sick and collapses because the lines of his horizon are restlessly redrawn again and again, because he cannot extricate himself from the much more fragile web of his justice and his truths and find his way back to crude wanting and desiring. By contrast, we saw the animal, which is wholly unhistorical and dwells within a horizon almost no larger than a mere point, yet still lives in a certain kind of happiness, at the very least without boredom and dissimulation. We will therefore have to consider the capacity to live to a certain degree unhistorically to be more significant and more originary, insofar as it lays the foundation upon which something just, healthy, and great, something that is truly human, is able to grow at all. The unhistorical is like an enveloping atmosphere in which alone life is engendered, and it disappears again with the destruction of this atmosphere. It is true: only when the human being, by thinking, reflecting, comparing, analyzing, and synthesizing, limits that unhistorical element, only when a bright, flashing, iridescent light is generated within that enveloping cloud of mist – that is, only by means of the power to utilize the past for life and to reshape past events into history[11] once more – does the human being become a human being; but in an excess of history the human being ceases once again, and without that mantle of the unhistorical he would never have begun and would never have dared to begin. What deeds could a human being possibly accomplish without first entering that misty region of the unhistorical? Or, to put metaphors aside and turn instead to an illustrative example: imagine a man seized and carried away by a vehement passion for a woman or for a great idea; how his world changes! Looking backward he feels he is blind, listening around him he hears what is unfamiliar as a dull, insignificant sound; and those things that he perceives at all he never before perceived in this way; so palpably near, colorful, resonant, illuminated, as though he were apprehending it with all his senses at once. All his valuations are changed and devalued; many things he can no longer value because he can scarcely feel them any more; he asks himself whether all this time he was merely duped by the words and opinions of others; he marvels that his memory turns inexhaustibly round and round in a circle and yet is still to weak and exhausted to make one single leap out of this circle. It is the most unjust condition in the world, narrow, ungrateful to the past, blind to dangers, deaf to warnings; a tiny whirlpool of life in a dead sea of night and oblivion; and yet this condition – unhistorical, antihistorical through and through – is not only the womb of the unjust deed, but of every just

---

10   In German: *das Unhistorische und das Historische.*
11   In German: *Geschichte.* See note 3 above.

deed as well; and no artist will create a picture, no general win a victory, and no people gain its freedom without their having previously desired and striven to accomplish these deeds in just such an unhistorical condition. Just as anyone who acts, in Goethe's words, is always without conscience, so is he also without knowledge:[12] he forgets most things in order to do one thing, he is unjust to whatever lies behind him and recognizes only one right, the right of what is to be. Thus, everyone who acts loves his action infinitely more than it deserves to be loved, and the best deeds occur in such an exuberance of love that, no matter what, they must be unworthy of this love, even if their worth were otherwise incalculably great.

If in many cases any one person were capable of sniffing out and breathing once again this unhistorical atmosphere in which every great historical event is born, then such a person, as a cognitive being, would be able to elevate himself to a *suprahistorical*[13] standpoint, something Niebuhr[14] once depicted as the possible result of historical reflections. "History,"[15] he says, "when understood clearly and fully, is at least useful for one thing: so that we might recognize how even the greatest and loftiest intellects of the human race do not know how fortuitously their eye has taken on its manner of seeing and forcibly demanded that all others see in this same manner; forcibly, because the intensity of their consciousness is exceptionally great. Anyone who has not recognized and understood this fully and in many individual instances will be enslaved by the presence of any powerful intellect that places the loftiest passion into a given form."[16] Such a standpoint could be called suprahistorical because anyone who occupies it could no longer be seduced into continuing to living on and taking part in history,[17] since he would have recognized the single condition of all events:[18] that blindness and injustice dwelling in the soul of those who act. From that point onward he would be cured of taking history[19] overly seriously. For he would have learned, for every human being, for every experience – regardless of whether it occurred among the Greeks or the Turks, or in the first or the nineteenth century – to answer the question: Why and to what purpose do people live? Anyone who asks his acquaintances whether they would like to relive the last ten or twenty years will easily recognize which of them are suited for that suprahistorical standpoint. To be sure, they will all answer "No!," but they will give different reasons for this answer. Some, perhaps, by consoling themselves with the claim "but the next twenty will be better." Of such people David Hume once said derisively:

> And from the dregs of life hope to receive,
> What the first sprightly running could not give.[20]

---

12   See Goethe, *Maximen und Reflexionen* (*Maxims and Reflections*), no. 251.
13   In German: *überhistorischen*.
14   Barthold Georg Niebuhr (1776–1831), Prussian diplomat and historian.
15   In German: *Geschichte*.
16   The source of this quotation from Niebuhr is not known.
17   In German: *Geschichte*.
18   In German: *Geschehens*.
19   In German: *Historie*.
20   Quoted in the original English. The passage is taken from Part X of Hume's *Dialogues Concerning Natural Religion* (1776), where Hume himself is quoting from John Dryden's play *Aureng-Zebe* (IV. i).

We shall call them historical human beings;[21] a glance into the past drives them on toward the future, inflames their courage to go on living, kindles their hope that justice will come, that happiness is waiting just the other side of the mountain they are approaching. These historical human beings believe that the meaning of existence will come ever more to light in the course of a *process*; they look backward only to understand the present by observation of the prior process and to learn to desire the future even more keenly; they have no idea how unhistorically they think and act despite all their history,[22] nor that their concern with history stands in the service, not of pure knowledge, but of life.

But that question, whose first answer we have just heard, can also be answered differently. Of course, once again with a "No!," but for different reasons: with the No of the suprahistorical human being, who does not seek salvation in a process, but for whom instead the world is complete and has arrived at its culmination in every individual moment. What could ten new years possibly teach that the past ten could not!

Suprahistorical human beings[23] have never agreed whether the substance of this doctrine is happiness or resignation, virtue or atonement; but, contrary to all historical modes of viewing the past, they do arrive at unanimity with regard to the statement: the past and the present are one and the same. That is, in all their diversity, they are identical in type, and as the omnipresence of imperishable types they make up a stationary formation of unalterable worth and eternally identical meaning. Just as the hundreds of different languages conform to the same constant types of human needs, so that anyone who understood these needs would be able to learn nothing new from these languages, the suprahistorical thinker illuminates the entire history of peoples and individuals from the inside, clairvoyantly divining the primordial meaning of the different hieroglyphs and gradually even exhaustedly evading this constantly rising flood of written signs: for, given the infinite superabundance of events, how could he possibly avoid being satiated, oversatiated, indeed, even nauseated! Ultimately, perhaps the rashest of these suprahistorical human beings will be prepared to say to his heart, as did Giacomo Leopardi:

> Nothing exists that is worthy
> of your emotions, and the earth deserves no sighs.
> Our being is pain and boredom, and the world
> is excrement – nothing else.
> Calm yourself.[24]

But let us leave the suprahistorical human beings to their nausea and their wisdom: today we instead want to rejoice with all our hearts in our unwisdom and to make things easier for ourselves by playing the roles of those active and progressive people who venerate process. Our evaluation of what is historical might prove to be nothing

---

21   In German: *die historischen Menschen.*
22   In German: *Historie.*
23   In German: *die überhistorischen Menschen.*
24   Nietzsche followed Schopenhauer in his admiration for the work of the Italian poet Leopardi (1798–1837). The lines Nietzsche quotes are taken from the poem "A se stesso" ("To himself").

more than an occidental prejudice, but let us at least move forward and not simply stand still in these prejudices! If we could at least learn how to pursue history better for the purpose of *life*! Then we would gladly concede that suprahistorical human beings possess more wisdom than we do; at least, as long as we are certain of possessing more life, for then, at least, our unwisdom would have more of a future than their wisdom. And so as to banish all doubts about the meaning of this antithesis between life and wisdom, I will come to my own aid by employing a long-standing practice and propound, without further ado, some theses.

A historical phenomenon, when purely and completely understood and reduced to an intellectual phenomenon, is dead for anyone who understands it, for in it he understands the delusion, the injustice, the blind passion, and in general the whole darkened earthly horizon of that phenomenon, and from this simultaneously its historical power.[25] At this point this power becomes powerless for him as someone who understands it, but perhaps it is not yet powerless for him as someone who lives.

History,[26] conceived as a pure science and accorded sovereignty, would be for humanity a kind of conclusion to life and a settling of accounts. But historical cultivation is beneficial and holds out promise for the future only when it follows in the wake of a powerful new torrent of life, for example, an evolving culture; that is, only when it is governed and guided by a superior power, instead of governing and guiding itself.

Insofar as it stands in the service of life, history[27] also stands in the service of an unhistorical power, and because of this subordinate position, it neither could nor should become a pure science on the order of mathematics, for example. But the question about the degree to which life needs the service of history at all is one of the supreme questions and worries that impinges on the health of a human being, a people, or a culture. For at the point of a certain excess of history, life crumbles and degenerates – as does, ultimately, as a result of this degeneration, history itself, as well.

2

That life requires the service of history must be comprehended, however, just as clearly as the proposition that will subsequently be proved – that an excess of history is harmful to life. History pertains to the living person in three respects: it pertains to him as one who acts and strives, as one who preserves and venerates, and as one who suffers and is in need of liberation. These three relations correspond to three kinds of history: insofar as it is permissible to distinguish between a *monumental*, an *antiquarian*, and a *critical* kind of history.

Above all, history pertains to the active and powerful human being, to the person who is involved in a great struggle and who needs exemplars, teachers, and comforters, but is unable to find them among his contemporaries and in the present age. This is how it pertained to Schiller, for, as Goethe observed,[28] our age is so wretched that the poet encounters no useful qualities in the lives of the human beings around him.

---

25   In German: *geschichtliche Macht*.
26   In German: *Geschichte*.
27   In German: *Historie*.
28   See Goethe, *Conversations with Eckermann*, July 21, 1827.

Polybius, for example,[29] was thinking of the person who takes action when he called political history the proper preparation for governing a state and the best teacher, who admonishes us steadfastly to endure the vicissitudes of fortune by reminding us of the misfortunes of others. Anyone who has come to recognize in this the meaning of history cannot help but be annoyed to see curious tourists or meticulous micrologists climbing about on the pyramids of great past ages; where he finds inspiration to emulate and to improve, he does not wish to encounter the idler who, longing for diversion or excitement, saunters about as though among the painted treasures in a gallery. So as not to experience despair and disgust amid these weak and hopeless idlers, amid these excited and fidgety contemporaries, who in fact only appear to be active, the person who takes action must, in order to catch his breath, glance backward and interrupt the progress toward his goal. However, his goal is some kind of happiness – not necessarily his own, but often that of a people or of all of humanity; he shrinks from resignation and uses history as a means to combat it. For the most part, he can hope for no reward other than fame, that is, the expectation of a place of honor in the temple of history, where he can, in turn, serve later generations as a teacher, comforter, and admonisher. For his commandment reads: Whatever was once capable of extending the concept of "the human being" and of giving it a more beautiful substance must be eternally present in order for it perpetually to have this effect. That the great moments in the struggles of individuals form links in one single chain; that they combine to form a mountain range of humankind through the millennia; that for me the highest point of such a long-since-past moment is still alive, bright, and great – this is the fundamental thought in the belief in humanity that expresses itself in the demand for a *monumental* history. Precisely this demand that what is great be eternal sparks the most terrible struggle, however. For every other living thing cries out: "No! The monumental shall not come into being" – this is the watchword of those who oppose it. Dull habit, the trivial and the common, fill every nook and cranny of the world, gather like a dense earthly fog around everything great, throw themselves in the path that greatness must travel to attain immortality so as to obstruct, deceive, smother, and suffocate it. But this path leads through human minds! Through the minds of frightened and short-lived animals who constantly return to the same needs and only with great effort ward off destruction for a short time. For first and foremost they want only one thing: to live at all costs. Who could possibly imagine that they would run the difficult relay race of monumental history that greatness alone can survive! And yet again and again a few awaken who, viewing past greatness and strengthened by their observation of it, feel a sense of rapture, as if human life were a magnificent thing and as if the most beautiful fruit of this bitter plant were the knowledge that in an earlier time some person once passed through this existence with pride and strength, another pensively, a third helpfully and with compassion – all of them leaving behind the single lesson that the most beautiful life is led by those who do not hold existence in high regard. While the common human being clutches to this span of time with such greed and gloomy earnest, those who were on the way to immortality and to monumental history at least knew how to treat it with Olympian laughter, or at least with sublime derision; often they went to their graves with a sense of irony – for what was left of them to bury! Certainly only that which as waste, refuse, vanity, and animality had

29   See Polybius, *Histories*, I. 1. 2.

always oppressed them, something that now would fall into oblivion after long being the object of their contempt. But one thing will live on: the signature of their most authentic being, a work, a deed, a rare inspiration, a creation; it will live on because posterity cannot do without it. In this, its most transfigured form, fame is something more than just the tastiest morsel of our self-love, as Schopenhauer called it;[30] it is the belief in the coherence and continuity of what is great in all ages, it is a protest against the change of generations and against transitoriness.

Of what utility to the contemporary human being, then, is the monumental view of the past, the occupation with the classical and rare accomplishments of earlier times? From it he concludes that the greatness that once existed was at least *possible* at one time, and that it therefore will probably be possible once again; he goes his way with more courage, for the doubt that befalls him in his weaker moments – Is he not, in fact, striving for the impossible? – is now banished. Suppose someone believed that no more than one hundred productive human beings, educated and working in the same spirit, would be needed to put an end to the cultivatedness that has just now become fashionable in Germany; would he not be strengthened by the recognition that the culture of the Renaissance was borne on the shoulders of just such a band of one hundred men?

And yet – so that we might immediately learn something new from the same example – how fluid and tentative, how imprecise that comparison would be! If it is to be effective, how many differences must be overlooked, with what violence the individuality of what is past must be forced into a general form, its sharp edges and its lines broken in favor of this conformity. Basically, in fact, what was possible once could only become possible a second time if the Pythagoreans were correct in believing that when an identical constellation of the heavenly bodies occurs, identical events – down to individual, minute details – must repeat themselves on the earth as well; so that whenever the stars have a particular relation to each other a Stoic will join forces with an Epicurean to murder Caesar,[31] and whenever they are in another configuration Columbus will discover America. Only if the earth always began its drama all over again after the conclusion of the fifth act, only if it were certain that the same entanglement of motives, the same *deus ex machina*,[32] the same catastrophe would recur at fixed intervals, could the powerful human being possibly desire monumental history in its absolute iconic *veracity*, that is, with every fact depicted in all its peculiarity and uniqueness. This is unlikely to happen until astronomers have once again become astrologers. Until then, monumental history will have no need for that absolute veracity: it will continue to approach, generalize, and ultimately identify nonidentical things, it will continue to diminish the differences between motives and causes in order to present, to the detriment of the *causae*, the *effectus* as monumental – that is, as exemplary and worthy of emulation. As a result, since it disregards all causes, one would with little exaggeration be able to call monumental history a collection of "effects in themselves,"

30 See Schopenhauer, "Von Dem, was Einer vorstellt" ("About That which One Imagines"), ch. 4 of "Aphorismen zur Lebensweisheit" ("Aphorisms for Worldly Wisdom"), in *Parerga und Paralipomena* (1851), vol. 1.
31 Allusion to the conspiracy between Gaius Cassius and Marcus Brutus to assassinate Julius Caesar.
32 Latin: god from the machine (cf. *BT* note 85 above).

of events that will have an effect on every age. What is celebrated at popular festivals and at religious or military commemorations is really just such an "effect in itself": this is what disturbs the sleep of the ambitious, what lies like an amulet on the heart of the enterprising – not the true historical *connexus* of causes and effects, which, once fully comprehended, would only prove that the dice game of the future and of chance would never again produce something wholly identical to what it produced in the past.

As long as the soul of historiography[33] lies in the great *stimuli* that a powerful person derives from it; as long as the past must be described as worthy of imitation, as capable of imitation and as possible a second time; it is in danger of becoming somewhat distorted, of being reinterpreted more favorably, and hence of approaching pure fiction. Yes, there are ages that are entirely incapable of distinguishing between a monumental past and a mythical fiction, because they could derive the very same stimuli from the one as from the other. Thus, if the monumental view of the past *prevails* over other modes of viewing it, over the antiquarian and the critical views, then the past itself is *damaged*: entire large parts of it are forgotten, scorned, and washed away as if by a gray, unremitting tide, and only a few individual, embellished facts rise as islands above it. There seems to be something unnatural and wondrous about those rare persons who become visible at all, much like the golden hip by which the disciples of Pythagoras claimed to recognize their master.[34] Monumental history deceives by means of analogies: with seductive similarities it arouses rashness in those who are courageous and fanaticism in those who are inspired; and if one imagines this history in the hands and heads of talented egoists and wicked fanatics, then empires will be destroyed, princes murdered, wars and revolutions incited, and the number of historical "effects in themselves" – that is, of effects without sufficient causes – further increase. So much as a reminder of the damage that monumental history can cause among powerful and active human beings, regardless of whether they are good or evil: just imagine the effect it would have if it were seized and exploited by the powerless and inactive!

Let's take the simplest and most common example. Just picture to yourself the unartistic and insufficiently artistic natures clad and armored in the monumental history of art: against whom will they now turn their weapons! Against their arch-enemies, the strong artistic spirits; in other words, against those who alone are capable of truly learning – that is, learning with an eye to life – from history and of translating what they have learned into a higher form of praxis. Their path is obstructed; their air is darkened when zealous idolaters dance around the shrine at some half-understood monument of a great past, as if they wanted to say: "Look, this is the only true and real art; of what concern to you is art that is just coming into being or has not yet been realized!" Apparently this dancing mob even has the privilege of determining what "good taste" is, for anyone who himself actually creates has always been at a disadvantage to those who merely observe and do not themselves take a hand in creation; just as in all ages the bar-stool politician is more intelligent, just, and reflective than the governing statesman. But if one insists on transposing the custom of popular referendum and majority rule into the realm of art and thereby forcing, as it were, the artist to defend himself before

33   In German: *Geschichtschreibung.*
34   For the story of Pythagoras' golden hip, see Diogenes Laertius, *Lives and Opinions of Eminent Philosophers*, VIII. 11.

a jury of aesthetic do–nothings, then you can bet that he will be condemned; and this not despite the fact that, but precisely *because*, his judges have ceremoniously proclaimed the canon of monumental art – that is, according to our earlier explanation, of the art that in all ages "produced an effect": whereas for the appreciation of all art that is nonmonumental simply because it is contemporary, these judges lack, first, the need, second, the genuine inclination, and third, precisely that authority of history. On the other hand, their instinct tells them that art can be murdered by art: the monumental should by no means come into being again, and to prevent this they deploy the authority of the monumental derived from the past. Thus they are connoisseurs of art because they want to do away with art altogether; thus they masquerade as physicians, while in fact they intend to administer a poison; thus they cultivate their tongue and their taste in order to explain from their position of fastidiousness why they so persistently reject all the nourishing artistic dishes offered them. For they don't want great art to come into being: their strategy is to say: "Look, great art already exists!" In truth, however, they are as little concerned with this great art that already exists as they are with that art that is coming into being; their lives bear witness to this. Monumental history is the costume under which their hatred of all the great and powerful people of their age masquerades as satiated admiration for the great and powerful people of past ages, the costume in which they surreptitiously turn the actual meaning of the monumental view of history into its opposite; whether they are clearly aware of it or not, they act as though their motto were "Let the dead bury the living."

Each of these three types of history is valid only in one soil and in one climate; in any other it develops into the most devastating weed. If the human being who wants to create something great needs the past at all, then he takes control of it by means of monumental history; those, on the other hand, who wish to remain within the realm of the habitual and the time-honored, foster the past in the manner of antiquarian historians; and only those who are oppressed by the affliction of the present and who wish to throw off this burden at all costs sense the need for critical history – that is, for history that judges and condemns. Much harm stems from the thoughtless transplanting of these plants: the critic without affliction, the antiquarian without piety, the connoisseur of greatness unable to create something great are just such plants that, alienated from the natural soil that nurtures them, have degenerated and shot up as weeds.

3

Second, history pertains to the person who preserves and venerates, to him who looks back with loyalty and love on the origins through which he became what he is; by means of this piety he gives thanks, as it were, for his existence. By attending with caring hands to what has subsisted since ancient times, he seeks to preserve for those who will emerge after him the conditions under which he himself has come into being – and by doing so he serves life. For such a soul the possession of ancestral household effects[35] takes on a different meaning, for far from the soul possessing these objects, it is possessed by them. Small, limited, decaying, antiquated things obtain their own dignity and sanctity when the preserving and venerating soul of the antiquarian human being

---

35   Allusion to Goethe's *Faust I*, 1. 408.

takes up residence in them and makes itself a comfortable nest. The history of his city becomes his own history; he understands its wall, its towered gate, its ordinances, and its popular festivals as an illustrated diary of his youth, and he rediscovers himself in all of this, his strength, his diligence, his joy, his judgments, his foolishness, and his ill manners. "It was possible to live here," he says to himself, "because it is possible to live here and will in the future be possible to live here, for we are tough and cannot be broken overnight." With this "we" he looks beyond his own transient, curious, individual existence and senses himself to be the spirit of his house, his lineage, and his city. At times he even greets across the distance of darkening and confusing centuries the soul of his people as his own soul; the ability to empathize with things and divine their greater significance, to detect traces that are almost extinguished, to instinctively read correctly a past frequently overwritten, to quickly understand the palimpsests, indeed, polypsests – these are his gifts and his virtues. It was with these that Goethe stood before Erwin von Steinach's monumental work; the historical veil of clouds that separated them was torn apart in the storm of his emotions: he recognized this German work for the first time, "exerting its effect out of a strong and rugged German soul."[36] It was just such a sensibility and impulse that guided the Italians of the Renaissance and reawakened in their poets the ancient Italian genius to "a marvelous new resounding of the lyre," as Jacob Burckhardt has expressed it.[37] But that antiquarian sense of veneration has its greatest worth when it infuses the modest, rough, even wretched conditions in which a human being or a people live with a simple and stirring sense of joy and satisfaction. Just as Niebuhr, for example, admits with honest frankness that he lived contentedly, without missing art, in moor and meadow among free peasants who had a history. How could history serve life better than by binding even less-favored generations and populations to their native land and native customs, helping them settle in, and preventing them from straying into foreign lands in search of better things for whose possession they then compete in battle? At times what ties individuals, as it were, to these companions and surroundings, to these tiresome habits, to these barren mountain ridges, seems to be obstinacy and imprudence – but it is an imprudence of the healthiest sort, one that benefits the totality. Anyone is aware of this who has ever come to understand the dreadful consequences of the adventurous joy of migration, especially when it takes hold of an entire population, or who has studied up close the conditions of a people that has forfeited loyalty to its own past and has succumbed to restless, cosmopolitan craving for new and ever newer things. The opposite sensation, the contentment the tree feels with its roots, the happiness of knowing that one's existence is not formed arbitrarily and by chance, but that instead it grows as the blossom and the fruit of a past that is its inheritance and that thereby excuses, indeed, justifies its existence – this is what today we are in the habit of calling the true historical sensibility.

36   Reference to Goethe's essay "Von deutscher Baukunst" ("On German Architecture") written in Strasbourg in 1772 and dedicated to the builder of Strasbourg Cathedral, Erwin von Steinach.

37   Quotation from the celebrated work of Nietzsche's colleague at Basel, Jacob Burckhardt's *Die Cultur der Renaissance in Italien* (*The Civilization of the Renaissance in Italy*, 1860). The excerpt is from the section on "Neo-Latin Poetry" in Part III, "The Revival of Antiquity."

Now, to be sure, this is not the condition in which the human being would be most capable of reducing the past to pure knowledge; so that even here we also perceive, as we already perceived in the case of monumental history, that the past itself suffers as long as history serves life and is governed by the impulses of life. To take some freedoms with our metaphor: the tree feels its roots more than it sees them; however, this feeling estimates their size in analogy to the size and strength of the visible limbs. Even if the tree is wrong about this: how wrong must it then be about the surrounding forest, about which it knows and feels anything only to the extent that it hinders or promotes its own growth – but nothing else! The antiquarian sensibility of a human being, of a civic community, of an entire people always has an extremely limited field of vision; most things it does not perceive at all, and the few things it does see, it views too closely and in isolation; it is unable to gauge anything, and as a result it regards everything to be equally important, and consequently the individual thing to be too important. There is no criterion for value and no sense of proportion for the things of the past that would truly do them justice when viewed in relation to each other; instead, their measure and proportions are always taken only in relation to the antiquarian individual or people that looks back on them.

This always brings with it one immediate danger: ultimately, anything ancient and past that enters into this field of vision is simply regarded as venerable, and everything that fails to welcome the ancient with reverence – in other words, whatever is new and in the process of becoming – is met with hostility and rejected. Thus, in the plastic and graphic arts even the Greeks tolerated the hieratic style alongside the free and great style; indeed, later they not only tolerated pointed noses and frosty smiles, but even turned them into a sign of refined taste. When a people's sensibility hardens in this way; when history serves past life to the extent that it not only undermines further life but especially higher life; when the historical sense no longer conserves but rather mummifies it, then beginning at its crown and moving down to its roots, the tree gradually dies an unnatural death – and eventually the roots themselves commonly perish. Antiquarian history degenerates from the moment when the fresh life of the present no longer animates and inspires it. At this point, piety withers, the scholarly habit persists without it and revolves with self-satisfied egotism around its own axis. Then we view the repugnant spectacle of a blind mania to collect, of a restless gathering together of everything that once existed. The human being envelops himself in the smell of mustiness; by this antiquarian behavior he even succeeds in reducing a more significant impulse, a nobler need, to this insatiable curiosity – or more accurately, to an all-encompassing desire for what is old. Often he sinks so low that in the end he is satisfied with any fare and even devours with gusto the dust of bibliographical minutiae.

But even if that degeneration does not occur, if antiquarian history does not lose that foundation in which alone it can take root if it is to serve the well-being of life: there are still enough dangers that remain, should it become too powerful and stifle the other modes for viewing history. For antiquarian history understands only how to *preserve* life, not how to create it; therefore, it always underestimates those things that are in the process of becoming because it has no divining instinct – as, for example, monumental history has. Thus, antiquarian history impedes the powerful resolve for the new, it lames the person of action, who, as person of action, must always offend certain acts of piety. The fact that something has grown old gives rise to the demand that it be immortal; for if we add up all the experiences such an antiquity – an old custom, a religious belief, an inherited political privilege – has accumulated over the course of its existence, calculating the entire sum of piety and veneration that individuals and generations have felt toward it, then it seems presumptuous or even impious to replace such an antiquity with a novelty and to oppose such a numerical accumulation of acts of piety and veneration with the single digit of something that is still in the process of becoming and is contemporary.

With this it becomes clear just how badly the human being often needs, in addition to the monumental and antiquarian modes of viewing the past, a *third* mode, the *critical*; and this once again in the service of life. In order to live, he must possess, and from time to time employ, the strength to shatter and dissolve a past; he accomplishes this by bringing this past before a tribunal, painstakingly interrogating it, and finally condemning it. But every past is worthy of being condemned – for this is simply how it is with human affairs: human violence and weakness have always played a powerful role in them. It is not justice that sits in judgment here; even less so is it mercy that passes judgment: rather, it is life and life alone, that dark, driving, insatiable power that lusts after itself. Its verdict is always merciless, always unjust, because it has never flowed from the pure fountain of knowledge; but in most instances the verdict would be the same, even if spoken by justice itself. "For everything that comes into being is *worthy* of perishing. Thus it would be better if nothing came into being."[38] It takes great strength to be able to live and forget the extent to which living and being unjust are one and the same thing. Even Luther once expressed the opinion that the world came into being only due to an act of forgetfulness on God's part: for if God had thought of "heavy artillery," he would never have created the world. But at times this very life that requires forgetfulness demands the temporary suspension of this forgetfulness; this is when it is supposed to become absolutely clear precisely how unjust the existence of certain things – for example, a privilege, a caste, or a dynasty – really is, and how much these things deserve to be destroyed. This is when its past is viewed critically, when we take a knife to its roots, when we cruelly trample on all forms of piety. It is always a dangerous process, one that is, in fact, dangerous for life itself; and human beings or ages that serve life by passing judgment on and destroying a past are always dangerous and endangered human beings and ages. For since we are, after all, the products of earlier generations, we are also the products of their aberrations, passions, and errors – indeed, of their crimes; it is impossible to free ourselves completely from this chain. If we condemn these aberrations and regard ourselves as free of them, this does not alter the fact that we are descended from them. At best we arrive at an antagonism between our inherited, ancestral nature and our knowledge, or perhaps even at the struggle of a new, stricter discipline against what was long ago inborn and inbred. We cultivate a new habit, a new instinct, a second nature, so that the first nature withers away. This is an attempt to give ourselves *a posteriori*, as it were, a new past from which we would prefer to be descended, as opposed to the past from which we actually descended – this is always dangerous because it is so difficult to set limits on this negating of the past, and because second natures are usually feebler than first natures. Too frequently we stop at knowing what is good without actually doing it, because we also know what is better without being capable of doing it. But here and

38   Goethe, *Faust I*, ll. 1339–41.

there a victory is nonetheless achieved, and for those embroiled in this struggle – for those who make use of critical history in the service of life – there is one noteworthy consolation: the knowledge, namely, that even that first nature was once a second nature, and that every victorious second nature will become a first nature. –

[. . .]

10

[. . .]

With the term "the unhistorical" I designate the art and power to be able to *forget* and to enclose oneself in a limited *horizon*; I term "suprahistorical" those powers that divert one's gaze from what is in the process of becoming to what lends existence the character of something eternal and stable in meaning, to *art* and *religion*. *Science* – for it is science that here would speak of "poisons" – views in this strength, in these powers, antagonistic powers and strengths, for it considers the mere observation of things to be true and correct, that is, to be scientific observation, which everywhere perceives only what has already become something, something historical, and nowhere does it perceive something being, something eternal. Science lives in an internal contradiction with the eternalizing powers of art and religion, just as it hates oblivion, the death of knowledge; it seeks to suspend all the limitations placed on horizons and to catapult the human being into an infinite, unlimited light-wave sea of known becoming.

If only he could live in it! Just as in an earthquake cities collapse and are destroyed and human beings build their houses but fearfully and fleetingly on volcanic ground, so life caves in on itself and becomes feeble and discouraged when the *concept-quake* unleashed by science robs the human being of the foundation for all his security and tranquillity, his belief in what is lasting and eternal. Should life rule over knowledge and science, or should knowledge rule over life? Which of these forces is higher and more decisive? No one will doubt: life is the higher, the ruling force; for any knowledge that destroyed life would simultaneously destroy itself. Knowledge presupposes life; hence it has the same interest in the preservation of life that every creature has in its own continued existence. This is the reason why science needs the supervision and surveillance of a higher power; a *hygiene of life* occupies a place close by the side of science; and one proposition of this hygiene would be: the unhistorical and the suprahistorical are the natural antidotes to the stifling of life by the historical, to the historical sickness. It is likely that we, the historically sick, will also have to suffer from these antidotes. But the fact that we suffer from them provides no evidence that could call the correctness of the chosen therapy into question.

And it is in this that I recognize the mission of that *youth* of which I have spoken, of that first generation of fighters and dragon slayers who will advance a happier, more beautiful cultivation and humanness, without themselves ever having more than a promising inkling of this future happiness and coming beauty. This youth will suffer simultaneously from the illness and the cure, but despite this they believe that they can boast better health and even a more natural nature than the generations that preceded them, the cultivated "men" and "old men" of the present. But it is their mission to shatter the conceptions that this present age has of "health" and "cultivation," and to arouse scorn and hatred against these monstrous conceptual hybrids. And the symptom that will vouch for their greater health will be that this youth will be able to use no concepts, no party slogans from among the verbal and conceptual coins that are currently in circulation, to designate their own being. Rather, their conviction will derive only from a power active within them that struggles, discriminates, and analyzes, and from a feeling for life that is constantly heightened in every good hour. Some may disagree with the claim that his youth will already have cultivation – but what youth would consider this a reproach? We may accuse them of being crude and intemperate – but they are not yet old and wise enough to moderate their demands. But above all, they do not need either to feign or defend a ready-made cultivation, and they enjoy all the consolations and privileges of youth, especially the privilege of courageous, unreflected honesty, and the inspiring consolation of hope.

I know that these hopeful individuals have a concrete understanding of these generalizations and will translate them by means of their own experience into a doctrine that is personally meaningful. In the meantime, others may perceive nothing but covered dishes that could possibly even be empty, until one day they are surprised to see with their own eyes that these dishes are full and that assaults, demands, life drives, and passions that could not remain concealed for very long are packed into and compressed within these same generalizations. Calling the attention of these skeptics to time, which brings everything to light, I will conclude by turning to that society of hopeful individuals, in order to relate to them by means of a parable the course and progress of their cure, their redemption from the historical sickness, and hence their own personal history up to that point at which they will once again be healthy enough to pursue history anew and to make use of the past in the service of life in the sense of the three historical modes described above, namely, the monumental, the antiquarian, and the critical. At that moment they will be less knowledgeable than the "cultivated people" of the present, for they will have forgotten much of what they learned and will even have lost all desire to attend at all to the things that those cultivated persons want to know. Seen from the perspective of these cultivated persons, their distinguishing marks are precisely their "lack of cultivation," their indifference and reserve with regard to many things that are otherwise celebrated, even with regard to many things that are good. But when they have arrived at the conclusion of their cure, they have once again become *human beings* and have ceased to be humanlike aggregates – that's quite an accomplishment! There is still hope. Don't your hearts rejoice at this, you hopeful individuals?

"And how will we arrive at this goal?," you will ask. At the very beginning of your journey to that goal the God of Delphi will call out to you his imperative, "Know thyself." It is a difficult imperative, for this God, as Heraclitus has said, "neither conceals nor reveals, but merely alludes."[39] What does he allude to?

There were centuries in which the Greeks found themselves threatened by a danger similar to the one we face today, the danger, namely, of perishing in a flood of things alien and past, of perishing of "history."[40] They never lived in proud isolation; on the contrary, their "cultivation" was for many years a chaos of foreign – Semitic, Babylonian, Lydian, and Egyptian – forms and concepts, and their religion represented a veritable struggle among the gods of the entire Orient. This is similar to the manner in which today "German cultivation" and religion represent an internally struggling chaos of all foreign lands and all prior history. But despite this, and thanks to that

39   Heraclitus (Diels–Kranz edn), fragment 93.
40   In German: *an der "Historie" zu Grunde zu gehen*.

Apollonian imperative, Hellenic culture did not become an aggregate. The Greeks gradually learned how *to organize this chaos* by concentrating – in accordance with this Delphic doctrine – on themselves, that is, on their genuine needs, and by letting those pseudoneeds die out. They thereby took possession of themselves again; they did not long remain the glutted heirs and epigones of the entire Orient; based on the practical interpretation of Apollo's imperative, they themselves became, after a difficult struggle with themselves, the happiest enrichers and increasers of that inherited treasure; they became the first cultured people, and hence the model for all future cultured peoples.

This is a parable for every individual among us: he must organize the chaos within him by concentrating on his genuine needs. His honesty, his sound and truthful character, must at some point rebel against the constant imitation – imitation of speech and imitation of learning – that he finds everywhere around him. He then will begin to grasp that culture can be something other than the *decoration of life* – that is, at bottom always only mere dissimulation and disguise, for all ornaments have the purpose of concealing what they adorn. In this way the Greek concept of culture – as opposed to the Roman – will be disclosed to him, the concept of culture as a new and improved *physis*,[41] without interior and exterior, without dissimulation and convention, a concept of culture as the harmony of life, thought, appearance, and will. He thus will learn from his own experience that it was the higher power of *moral* nature that made the Greeks' victory over other cultures possible, and that every increase in truthfulness is always a necessary step toward the furthering of *true* cultivation – even though this truthfulness may sometimes do serious harm to that cultivatedness that is held in esteem at the time, even though it may hasten the downfall of an entire decorative culture.

41   Greek: nature. See *PTG* note 1 above.

12

Schopenhauer as Educator
(1874)

1

When a traveler who had seen many lands and nations and several continents was asked what characteristic he discovered to be common to all of humanity, he replied: "They have a tendency toward laziness." To many it will seem that his reply would have been more accurate and valid if he had said: "They are all fearful. They hide behind customs and opinions." At bottom, every human being knows perfectly well that he lives in the world just once, as a *unicum*,[1] and that no coincidence, regardless how strange, will ever for a second time concoct out of this amazingly variegated diversity the unity that he is. He knows this, but he conceals it like a bad conscience. Why? Out of fear of his neighbor who demands convention and who cloaks himself with it. But what is it that forces the individual to fear his neighbor, to think and act like a part of a herd instead of taking pleasure in being himself? Modesty, perhaps, in a few rare instances. In most instances it is convenience, indolence – in short, that tendency toward laziness of which the traveler spoke. He is right: human beings are lazier than they are fearful, and what they fear most are those hardships that unconditional honesty and nakedness would foist upon them. Artists alone despise this lethargic promenading draped in borrowed manners and appropriated opinions, and they expose the hidden secret, everyone's bad conscience, the principle that every human being is a one-of-a-kind miracle. They dare to show us how every human being, down to each movement of his muscles, is himself and himself alone; moreover, they show us that in the strict consistency of his uniqueness he is beautiful and worthy of contemplation, as novel and incredible as every work of nature, and anything but boring. When the great thinker disdains human beings, it is their laziness he disdains, for it is laziness that makes them appear to be mass-produced commodities, to be indifferent, unworthy of human interchange and instruction. The human being who does not want to be a part of the masses need only cease to go easy on himself; let him follow his conscience, which cries out to him: "Be yourself! You are none of those things that you now do, think, and desire."

---

1 Latin: unique being, "one of a kind." Nietzsche here is paraphrasing the Orientalist and political theorist Paul de Lagarde (1827–91).

Every young soul hears this cry night and day and trembles, for when it thinks of its true liberation, it has an inkling of the measure of happiness for which it is destined from eternity. As long as it is shackled by the chains of opinions and fear, nothing can help it attain this happiness. And how bleak and senseless life can become without this liberation! There is no more desolate or repulsive creature in nature than the human being who has evaded his genius and who then casts furtive glances left and right, behind himself, and all about. In the end we can no longer even take hold of a person like this, for he is all exterior without a kernel, a tattered, painted, puffed-up garment, a decked-out ghost that can arouse no fear, and certainly no pity. And if it is correct to say that the lazy person kills time, then we must seriously be concerned that a time that stakes its salvation on public opinions – that is, on private lazinesses – will one day really be killed: by which I mean that it will be stricken from the history of the true liberation of life. Imagine how great the revulsion of future generations will be when dealing with the legacy of a time ruled not by living human beings, but instead by publicly opining pseudo-human beings. This is why for some distant posterity our age will perhaps constitute the darkest and most unknown – because least human – chapter of history. I walk through the new streets of our cities and think how a century from now none of these atrocious houses the generation of public opinionators had built for themselves will be left standing, and how by then even the opinions of these house builders will have collapsed. How hopeful, by contrast, can all those people be who do not feel that they are citizens of this time; for if they were citizens of this time, they too would be helping to kill their time and would perish with it – whereas they actually want to awaken their time to life, so that they themselves can go on living in this life.

But even if the future were to give us no cause for hope – our curious existence in precisely this Now gives us the strongest encouragement to live according to our own standards and laws: the inexplicable fact that we live precisely today and yet had the infinity of time in which to come into being, that we possess nothing but this brief today in which to show why and to what purpose we have come into being precisely at this moment. We are accountable to ourselves for our own existence; consequently, we also want to be the real helmsmen of our existence and keep it from resembling a mindless coincidence. We have to approach existence with a certain boldness and willingness to take risks: especially since in both the worst and the best instances we are bound to lose it. Why cling to this clod of earth, to this trade; why heed what your neighbor says? It is so provincial to bind oneself to views that already a few hundred miles away are no longer binding. Orient and Occident are chalk lines drawn before our eyes in order to mock our timidity. "I want to try to attain freedom," the young soul tells itself; and it is supposed to be hindered in this simply because by chance two nations hate and wage war on each other, or because two continents are separated by an ocean, or because a religion that did not even exist a few thousand years ago is now taught everywhere. "None of this is you yourself," the young soul tells itself. No one can build for you the bridge upon which you alone must cross the stream of life, no one but you alone. To be sure, there are countless paths and bridges and demigods that want to carry you through this stream, but only at the price of your self; you would pawn and lose your self. There is one single path in this world on which no one but you can travel. Where does it lead? Do not ask, just take it.

Who was it who made the statement: "A man never rises higher than when he does not know where his path may lead him"?[2]

But how can we find ourselves again? How can the human being get to know himself? He is a dark and veiled thing; and if the hare has seven skins, the human being can shed seven times seventy skins and still not be able to say: "This is really you, this is no longer outer shell." Besides, it is an agonizing, dangerous undertaking to dig down into yourself in this way, to force your way by the shortest route down the shaft of your own being. How easy it is to do damage to yourself that no doctor can heal. And moreover, why should it be necessary, since everything – our friendships and enmities, our look and our handshake, our memory and what we forget, our books and our handwriting – bears witness to our being. But there is only one way in which this crucial inquiry can be carried out. Let the young soul look back on its life with the question: What have you up to now truly loved, what attracted your soul, what dominated it while simultaneously making it happy? Place this series of revered objects before you, and perhaps their nature and their sequence will reveal to you a law, the fundamental law of your authentic self. Compare these objects, observe how one completes, expands, surpasses, transfigures the others, how they form a stepladder on which until now you have climbed up to yourself; for your true being does not lie deeply hidden within you, but rather immeasurably high above you, or at least above what you commonly take to be your ego. Your true educators and cultivators reveal to you the true primordial sense and basic stuff of your being, something that is thoroughly incapable of being educated and cultivated, but something that in any event is bound, paralyzed, and difficult to gain access to. Your educators can be nothing other than your liberators. And that is the secret of all cultivation: it does not provide artificial limbs, wax noses, or corrective lenses – on the contrary, whatever might provide these things is merely a parody of education. Instead, education is liberation, removal of all weeds, rubble, and vermin that seek to harm the plant's delicate shoots, a radiance of light and warmth, the loving rush of rain falling at night; it is imitation and adoration of nature where nature displays its maternal and merciful disposition; it is perfection of nature when it prevents nature's cruel and merciless onslaughts and turns them to good, when it drapes a veil over the expressions of nature's stepmotherly disposition and sad lack of understanding.

Certainly, there are other ways of finding oneself, of coming to oneself out of the stupor in which we usually float as in a dark cloud, but I know of no better way than to reflect on one's own educators and cultivators. And hence today I want to remember the one teacher and taskmaster of whom I can be proud, *Arthur Schopenhauer* – so that subsequently I will be able to recall others.

[. . .]

5

But I promised, on the basis of my experience, to depict Schopenhauer as *educator*, and hence it is by no means enough for me to paint a picture, and an inadequate one,

---

2   Oliver Cromwell, as quoted by Emerson in "Circles," in *Essays, First Series* (1841). Nietzsche read Emerson's *Essays* in the German trans. by G. Fabricius (Hanover: Meyer, 1858), and marked the quoted passage several times in the copy which was in his personal library.

at that, of that ideal human being who, as his Platonic Idea, as it were, holds sway in and around Schopenhauer. But the most difficult task still remains: to describe how we can derive a new set of duties from this ideal, and how we can get in touch with such an ambitious goal on the basis of regulated activity: in short, to demonstrate that this ideal *educates*. Otherwise we might suppose that it is nothing but an enrapturing, indeed intoxicating, vision that grants us individual moments only to let us down all the more immediately afterward and deliver us over to an even deeper sense of disheartenment. It is also certain that we will *begin* our association with this ideal *in this way*, with these sudden alternations between light and darkness, intoxication and disgust, and that in this respect we are repeating an experience that has been around as long as there have been ideals. However, we should no longer remain standing on the threshold, but proceed quickly past the initial stage. And we must therefore ask, seriously and resolutely: Is it possible to bring that incredibly lofty goal so near to us that it will educate us while drawing us upward? – so that in us those great words of Goethe will not be proved true: "The human being is born into a limited situation; he is capable of understanding simple, near, and definite goals, and he grows accustomed to using the means that are immediately available to him; but as soon as he goes beyond these limits, he knows neither what he wants nor what he ought to do, and it makes no difference whether he is distracted by the multitude of objects or whether he is transported beyond himself by their loftiness and dignity. He is always unhappy when he is forced to strive for something with which he cannot get in touch on the basis of a regulated, self-initiated activity."[3] This objection might appear to have a certain justification when raised against the Schopenhauerian human being: his loftiness and dignity are only able to transport us beyond ourselves, thereby transporting us once again outside any community of active people; the coherence of duties, the stream of life vanish. Perhaps someone may eventually accustom himself despondently to self-division and to living by a double standard, that is, to living in conflict with himself, uncertain both here and there, and hence becoming weaker and less fruitful by the day, whereas someone else principally refuses to act in concert with others and scarcely even notices when others act. The dangers are always great when things are made too difficult for people and when they are unable to *fulfill* any duties: stronger natures can be destroyed by it; weaker natures – the more numerous ones – sink into a contemplative laziness and ultimately even forfeit out of laziness their ability to contemplate.

Now, in reply to such objections I am willing to admit that our work here has barely just begun, and that based on my own experiences I perceive and know only one thing for sure: that starting from that ideal image it is possible to impose upon you and me a chain of fulfillable duties, and that some of us already feel the weight of this chain. However, before I can state without hesitation the formula under which I would like to subsume this new set of duties, the following preliminary observations must be made.

Human beings of greater profundity have always felt compassion with animals precisely because they suffer from life and yet do not possess the strength to turn the sting of suffering against themselves and understand their existence metaphysically; indeed, the sight of senseless suffering arouses profound indignation. That is why at more

---

3   Goethe, from the "Bekenntnisse einer schönen Seele" ("Confessions of a Beautiful Soul"), in *Wilhelm Meisters Lehrjahre* (*Wilhelm Meister's Apprenticeship*, 1795), Book VI.

than one place on this earth the conjecture arose that the souls of guilt-laden human beings were trapped inside the bodies of these animals, and that that suffering whose senselessness at first glance arouses indignation acquires sense and significance as punishment and penance when viewed against the backdrop of eternal justice. It is truly a harsh punishment to live in the manner of an animal, subject to hunger and desires, and yet without arriving at any insight into the nature of this life, and we can conceive of no harsher fate than that of the beast of prey, who is driven through the desert by its gnawing torment, is seldom satisfied, and this only in such a way that this satisfaction turns into agony in the flesh-tearing struggle with other beasts, or from nauseating greediness and oversatiation. To cling so blindly and madly to life, for no higher reward, far from knowing that one is punished or why one is punished in this way, but instead to thirst with the inanity of a horrible desire for precisely this punishment as though it were happiness – that is what it means to be an animal. And if all of nature presses onward toward the human being, then in doing so it makes evident that he is necessary for its salvation from animal existence and that in him, finally, existence holds before itself a mirror in which life no longer appears senseless but appears, rather, in its metaphysical meaningfulness. But consider carefully: where does the animal cease, where does the human being begin! That human being who is nature's sole concern! As long as someone desires life as he desires happiness, he has not elevated his gaze above the horizon of the animal, the only difference being that he desires with more awareness what the animal craves out of blind instinct. But for the greatest part of our lives this is the way it is for all of us: usually we do not transcend animality, we ourselves are those creatures who seem to suffer senselessly.

But there are moments *when we understand this*; then the clouds break and we perceive how we, along with all of nature, are pressing onward toward the human being as toward something that stands high above us. In this sudden brightness we gaze with a shudder around and behind us: here the refined beasts of prey run, and we run in their midst. The tremendous mobility of human beings on the great earthly desert, their founding of cities and states, their waging of wars, their ceaseless gathering and dispersing, their confused mingling, their imitation of one another, their mutual outwitting and trampling underfoot, their cries in distress and their joyous cheers in victory – all this is a continuation of animality, as if human beings were intended to regress and be cheated out of their metaphysical disposition; indeed, as if nature, having yearned and labored for human beings for so long, now recoiled from them in fear and preferred to return to the unconsciousness of instinct. Alas, nature needs knowledge, and it is horrified at the knowledge it actually needs; and so the flame flickers unsteadily, trembling, as it were, out of fear of itself, and seizes upon a thousand things before seizing upon that thing on whose account nature needs knowledge at all. All of us know in individual moments how the most extensive arrangements of our own lives are made only in order to flee from our true task; how we like to hide our heads somewhere, as though our hundred-eyed conscience would not find us there; how we hasten to sell our soul to the state, to moneymaking, to social life, or to scholarship just so that we will no longer possess it; how even in our daily work we slave away without reflection and more ardently than is necessary to make a living because it seems to us more necessary not to stop and reflect. Haste is universal because everyone is fleeing from himself; universal, too, is the timid concealment of this haste, because we want to appear satisfied and deceive the most perceptive observers about our wretchedness; universal, as well, the need for new-sounding word bells with which life can be adorned and lent an air of noisy festivity. Everyone is familiar with the peculiar state in which unpleasant memories suddenly force themselves upon us and we make an effort to drive them out of our heads by means of violent gestures and sounds; but the gestures and sounds of common life indicate that all of us always find ourselves in such a state of fear of memory and of turning inward. What is it that assails us so often, what mosquito is this that refuses to let us sleep? Ghostly things are occurring ground us, every moment of life wants to tell us something, but we do not want to hear this ghostly voice. When we are quiet and alone we are afraid that something will be whispered into our ear, and hence we despise quiet and drug ourselves with sociability.

As I said, now and again we realize all of this and are quite astonished at all this dizzying fear and haste and at the entire dreamlike state of our life, which seems to dread awakening and whose dreams become all the more vivid and restless the closer it comes to this awakening. But we simultaneously feel that we are too weak to endure those moments of deepest communion very long and that we are not those human beings toward which all of nature presses onward for its own salvation. It is already no small achievement that we can at least sometimes manage to lift our heads enough to notice the stream in which we are so deeply submerged. And we do not accomplish even this – this coming to the surface and awakening for a fleeting instant – by means of our own strength. We have to be lifted up, and who are those who lift us up?

They are those true *human beings, those no-longer-animals, the philosophers, artists, and saints*; with their appearance and by means of their appearance, nature, which never leaps, takes its only leap; and it is a leap of joy, for it feels that for the first time it has arrived at its goal, arrived at that place where it realizes that it must unlearn its goals and that it staked too much on the game of living and becoming. With this recognition, nature is transfigured, and a gentle weariness of evening – what human beings call "beauty" – spreads across its face. What it now expresses with these transfigured features is the great *enlightenment* about existence, and the supreme wish that mortals can wish is to participate constantly and with open ears in this enlightenment. When we think about everything Schopenhauer, for example, must have *heard* over the course of his life, then we may in retrospect say to ourselves: "Oh, these deaf ears of mine, this dull head, this flickering reason, this shriveled heart; oh, how I despise all that I call mine! Not to be able to fly, but only to flap one's wings! To be able to look up beyond oneself and not be able to climb up beyond oneself! To know and nearly set foot on the path that leads to the immeasurably unobstructed view of the philosopher, only to come staggering back after a few steps! And if that greatest of all wishes were fulfilled for only one single day, how willingly we would give the rest of life in exchange for it! To climb as high as any thinker ever climbed into the icy purity of the alpine air, to that place where there is no longer any fog or mist and where the fundamental nature of things expresses itself, stark and unbending, but with unavoidable clarity! Just thinking about this the soul becomes lonely and infinite; but if its wish were fulfilled, if its gaze were once to fall precipitously and radiantly on things, like a ray of light, if shame, anxiety, and desire were to die out – what words could possibly describe the soul's state, that new and enigmatic emotion without commotion with which it then, like Schopenhauer's soul, would settle over the huge hieroglyphs of existence, over the petrified doctrine of becoming – not as a night, but rather as a radiant crimson light that streams out over the entire world. And what a fate, on the other hand, to have enough of an inkling of the peculiar definition and blessedness of the philosopher to sense all the definitionlessness and unblessedness of the nonphilosopher, he who desires without hope! To know that one is a fruit on a tree that cannot ripen because there is too much shade, and yet to see close by the sunshine one lacks!"

This would be torment enough to make such a misgifted person envious and malicious – if he were even capable of envy and malice. But in all probability he will ultimately turn his soul in another direction so that it does not consume itself in vain longing, and it is at this point that he will *discover* a new set of duties.

Having said this, I am now in a position to supply an answer to the question posed earlier: whether it is possible to get in touch with the great ideal of the Schopenhauerian human being on the basis of a regulated, self-initiated activity. One thing, above all, is certain: those new duties are not the duties of a solitary individual; on the contrary, through them one is integrated into a powerful community, one that, to be sure, is not held together by external forms and laws, but by a fundamental idea. This is the fundamental idea of *culture*, insofar as it is capable of charging each of us with one single task: *to foster the production of philosophers, artists, and saints within us and around us, and thereby to work toward the perfection of nature.* For just as nature needs philosophers for a metaphysical purpose, so, too, it also needs artists; for the purpose of its own self-enlightenment, so that it might finally be presented with a pure and finished image of what, in the tumultuousness of its own becoming, it never has the opportunity to see clearly – in short, for the purpose of its own self-recognition. It was Goethe who observed, with arrogant profundity, that all of nature's experiments are of value only insofar as the artist eventually divines its stammerings, meets nature halfway, and gives expression to what it actually intends with these experiments. "I have often said," he once exclaimed, "and I will say it over and over again, that the *causa finalis*[4] of worldly and human affairs is dramatic literature. For otherwise this stuff is of absolutely no use."[5] And hence nature ultimately needs the saint, whose ego has entirely melted away and whose life of suffering is no longer – or almost no longer – felt individually, but only as the deepest feeling of equality, communion, and oneness with all living things; the saint, in whom that miracle of transformation occurs that the game of becoming never hits upon, that ultimate and supreme becoming human toward which all of nature presses and drives onward for its own salvation. There can be no doubt that all of us are related and connected to this saint, just as we are related to the philosopher and the artist. There are moments and, as it were, sparks of the brightest, most ardent fire in whose light we no longer understand the word "I"; there, beyond our being something exists that in those moments becomes a here and now, and that is why we long with all our hearts for bridges connecting the here and the there. Of course, in our customary state of mind we can contribute nothing to the production of the redeeming human being, and we therefore *hate* ourselves when we are in this state of mind, a hate that is the root of that pessimism that Schopenhauer had again to teach to our age, but that is as old as the longing for culture itself. Its root, but not its flower; its foundation, but not its roof; the beginning of its course, but not its goal, for at some point we have to learn to hate something else, something more universal, something

4   Latin: final purpose, ultimate aim.
5   See Goethe's letter to Charlotte von Stein, March 3, 1785.

other than our individuality and its wretched limitations, its changeability and tur-moil, in that heightened state in which we will also love something other than what we are now able to love. Only after, in our present or in some future incarnation, we have been taken up into that most sublime order of philosophers, artists, and saints will a new goal be established for our love and our hate. In the meantime, we have our task and our sphere of duties, our hate and our love. For we know what culture is. When applied to the Schopenhauerian human being, it requires that we continually pave the way for and promote the production of this human being by discovering what is hostile to its development and sweeping it aside – in short, that we tirelessly fight against everything that, by preventing us from becoming such Schopenhauerian human beings ourselves, robbed *us* of the supreme fulfillment of our existence. –

Part III
The Middle Period

Introduction

It is customary to divide Nietzsche's corpus of published texts into three distinct periods, with the second period covering the three texts of 1878–82, beginning with *Human, All Too Human*. Indeed, beginning with this text Nietzsche's writing does adopt a quite different tone. Many of the ideas that appear in it had been germinating in his mind since 1875–6. Where the first edition of *The Birth of Tragedy* was dedicated to Wagner (and brought out by Wagner's publisher), taking up the Romantic cause against modern enlightenment and opposing indigenous German culture to superficial French civilization, the first edition of *Human, All Too Human*, published in 1878, is dedicated to Voltaire and takes up the cause of the Enlightenment against revolutionary Romantics (the dedication had the desired effect of causing Wagner great offense). However, it is mistaken to suppose that the move from *The Birth of Tragedy* to *Human, All Too Human* amounts to a straightforward shift in his thinking, from a concern with art and metaphysics to a new privileging of science over both. Of the three texts included in this section, *The Gay Science* represents Nietzsche's most mature philosophical position: here he praises art for teaching us about the "good will to appearance" (*GS* 107; see also *GM* III. 25). Art always has a wider significance for Nietzsche than is commonly accorded to it: he notes in an aphorism from a later text that "there may be much *more* to the concept of 'art' than we usually think" (*BGE* 291). In short, an understanding of art is necessary to a fuller appreciation of the nature and activity of knowing and knowledge, and *The Gay Science* contains many important lessons in how we are to negotiate both the surfaces and the depths of things, the field of appearance and apparentness and the depths sought by scientific knowledge. Nietzsche continues to provide such lessons in *Beyond Good and Evil* (see especially *BGE* 230) and the Third Essay of *On the Genealogy of Morality*.

Nietzsche described the texts that make up his so-called middle period as his "free spirit trilogy." In them we find him seeking to emancipate himself as a thinker and coming to terms with what he regards as the end of metaphysics, an end which now calls into being a new kind of love of knowledge. He always had sympathies with ancient traditions of materialism and naturalism (Democritus and Empedocles, for example). At the same time, however, he recognizes that the tradition of materialism concealed its own metaphysics (Democritus and his atoms, for example)[1] and that, in

---

1   See *TI* III. 5. Nietzsche is attacking what he sees as a Parmenidean bias in Western metaphysics which he locates in Democritus' teaching in which each atom embodies the properties of Being on a small scale (being unitary, indivisible, unchanging, etc.). For

another sense, metaphysics cannot readily be given up since it constitutes an essential part of the treasure of human tradition and culture. In section 251 of *Human, All Too Human* he speaks of our health demanding that the two experiences of science and non-science should lie next to each other, self-contained and without confusion: "Illusions, biases, passions must give heat; with the help of scientific knowledge, the pernicious and dangerous consequences of overheating must be prevented" (see also *HH* 222, where he speaks of the scientific man as a further development of the artistic man). A "great culture," he argues, is one in which individuals have the flexibility to pursue knowledge in a rigorous manner while at the same time appreciating the power and beauty of art, religion, and metaphysics (*HH* 278). A higher culture will give the human being a "double brain, two brain chambers [. . .], one to experience science, and one to experience nonscience" (*HH* 251). Nietzsche's position gives rise to tremendous tensions in his thinking, since it is clear that traditional metaphysics cannot survive the interrogation afforded by the new methods of knowledge and inquiry. The way in which we think the matter of knowledge (epistemology), the question of being (ontology), as well as our entire understanding of moral concepts and sensations, must undergo a radical transformation.

The first volume of *Human, All Too Human* bears the subtitle "a book for free spirits." In his reflections on this text in *Ecce Homo*, Nietzsche says that the expression "free spirit" needs to be heard in terms of a spirit that has *become* free. In other words, a process of self-liberation is involved which includes a victory over "idealism": where we see "ideal things," Nietzsche will see "human, alas all-too-human things." "Human, all too human," then, as the title of the book and the name of a project, amounts to the "memorial" of a crisis and of a rigorous self-discipline in Nietzsche's becoming. From it we include several paragraphs from sections 1 and 2, and samples from sections 4, 5, 8, and 9. They find Nietzsche reflecting on metaphysics and science, on morality, art, and politics, practicing the art of the extended aphorism and the short maxim. The aphoristic mode offered Nietzsche a tremendous liberation since it enabled him to see things from many different angles and to approach topics from several directions at once. The notion of the free spirit informs Nietzsche's understanding of his crisis of the 1870s, most profoundly his break with Wagner and feeling of complete alienation from everything that surrounded him at the first festival in Bayreuth (principally German things, including German virtues) – Nietzsche had to free himself from his *self*. It continues to inform and shape his thinking on metaphysics and on morality in the later texts, including the second chapter of *Beyond Good and Evil*, entitled "The Free Spirit" (in which Nietzsche presents the doctrine of will to power in terms of a conscience of method), and the complex engagement with the democrat presented in section 9 of the First Essay of the *Genealogy*. On one level the free spirit is an uncomplicated notion: it names the seeker of knowledge who has freed himself from tradition and requires no faith (see *HH* 225, where Nietzsche calls the free spirit a "relative concept"). On another level much more is involved in the notion, and the free spirit is not simply the same as the free thinker. In his later writings Nietzsche would

further insight into Nietzsche's critique of atomism, see Alistair Moles, *Nietzsche's Philosophy of Nature and Cosmology* (New York: Lang, 1990), pp. 148–54; see also *GS* 112 and *BGE* 12.

continue to speak of the free spirit in terms of one who can "take leave of all faith and wish for certainty" (*GS* 357), but such a spirit must know what it means to dance "near abysses" and to keep its energy and enthusiasm in bounds (see *AC*, Foreword). A free spirit, then, is a thinker who knows something of the processes of "spirit" itself (digestion, incorporation, assimilation, regulation, and so on).

With *Human, All Too Human* begins Nietzsche's commitment to an examination of the origins of morality, which was now to become a feature of all his work and constitutes one of its most essential tasks. In this text the focus is largely on the origin of moral sensations and on demonstrating the illusory and mythical character of the belief that individuals are free willing centers and originators of actions. Nietzsche endorses as a tenet possessing both frightful and fruitful consequences the insight of his friend Paul Rée that the moral human being is situated no nearer to the metaphysical or intelligible world than the physical man. Nietzsche states that this is an insight that needs to grow hard and sharp with the "hammerblow of historical knowledge" (*HH* 37). It is in *Human, All Too Human* that Nietzsche calls for a mode of "historical philosophizing" as a way of eliminating problems of metaphysics (including the thing-in-itself). In section 9 he allows for the fact that there could be a "metaphysical world," but because we cannot chop off our own head all we can ever say of it is that it has a "differentness" that is inaccessible to us (a critical point Nietzsche had first articulated in his 1868 essay on Schopenhauer and which he also utilizes in his reading of Anaximander's "Indefinite" or *apeiron*, in section 4 of *Philosophy in the Tragic Age of the Greeks* from 1873). Nietzsche also holds that knowledge of a metaphysical world would prove inconsequential to us, "even more inconsequential than the knowledge of the chemical analysis of water must be to the boatman facing a storm." In section 10 he insists that art, religion, and morality do not provide us with access to another dimension of reality simply because we always find ourselves within representation and no intuition can take us further. He suggests that the question how our image of the world might be different to the "disclosed essence of the world" is a matter best left to physiology, and what he calls "the ontogeny of organisms and concepts," to solve. Section 16 makes it clear that Nietzsche is approaching the problem of the thing-in-itself in a specific way. The notion is now considered faulty because it is based on the idea that there are some things (or a big thing like the "Will") which stand outside evolution, that is, as fixed, immutable, devoid of change and development. This section contains a powerful attack on Schopenhauer's metaphysics (see also *GS* 99 and 127; *BGE* 19 and 56; *TI* IX. 21). The section concludes with Nietzsche reflecting on how an "ontogeny of thought" will come to show us that what today we call the world is the result of numerous errors and fantasies and part of the development of organic life. This collection of errors and fantasies also constitutes the treasure of a tradition (the "value" of humanity depends upon it), thus giving rise to a necessary conflict between, on the one hand, our reliance on error and our need for fantasy, and on the other the development of science and of scientific truth (see also *GS* 110).

Section 54 of *The Gay Science* continues this theme with Nietzsche noting that all we could say of any "essence" would be "to name the attributes of its appearance." It is not simply that we cannot adequately think the thing-in-itself, through some act of intellectual intuition, but rather that we cannot easily abandon that which has trained us, namely, our humanity and animality, and we need to learn how to cultivate our inheritance (*GS* 57). The insight that what things are called is much more important than what they are is, Nietzsche confides to us in the following section, one that has given him the greatest trouble (GS 58). What we now call an "essence," and consider to be "effective," is the product of an evolutionary process of different appearances. Thus, we can "destroy" only as creators of new appearances. These appearances are not appearances "of" a thing-in-itself. Nietzsche's later doctrine of the will to power adds a level of complication to this position. In the Second Essay of the *Genealogy*, for example, he speaks of the non-linear history of things in terms of a continuous chain of signs that continually reveals "new interpretations and adaptations," and within which the variable use function of things — from a physiological organ to a legal institution or form of art — is a sign that a will to power has achieved mastery over something less powerful (*GM* II. 12).

Daybreak, not *Human, All Too Human*, is the book with which Nietzsche says he commenced his campaign against morality. It is thus a significant text in the development of his creative evolution as a critic of morality. Nietzsche began composing ideas for the book at the start of 1880 and finished it around the middle of 1881. His campaign needs to be understood and received in a specific sense. He tells us that we should not smell gunpowder in this campaign but rather, and providing we have the necessary subtlety in our nostrils that will enable us to smell them, more pleasant odors. There is, in fact, a "gateway" to this book, Nietzsche reveals in *Ecce Homo*, and over it stands an Indian inscription: "There are so many daybreaks that have not yet dawned." Already at this stage in his development, then, Nietzsche is, in effect, carrying out a revaluation of all values and disclosing the nature of his interest in the question of the origin of moral values: it is a question of a future vitality in which the unegoistic is revalued. Our selection includes Nietzsche's conception of the morality of custom (see also *HH* 96) and his treatment of how we draw false conclusions from utility, which are concepts and problems he takes up again, refines and deepens, in the Second Essay of the *Genealogy*; a long section on Paul as the first Christian, an important section on just what it means to "deny" morality; a section on why Nietzsche thinks we continually misread inner processes and drives; a section on purposes and will; an aphorism on "grand politics" and the "need for the feeling of power"; a long section on the people of Israel; a section on the "impossible class" and the struggle between labor and capital; and, finally, a section on "freedom" from towards the end of the book. Section 119 provides a good example of the manner in which Nietzsche thinks that questions of morality and agency should now be approached. In it he notes that our moral judgments and valuations are in fact "images and fantasies based on a physiological process unknown to us, a kind of language for designating certain nervous stimuli." Our consciousness, therefore, needs to be treated as "a more or less fantastic commentary on an unknown, perhaps unknowable felt text." This "text" is further explored and opened up by Nietzsche in the later works such as *Beyond Good and Evil* and *On the Genealogy of Morality*. Section 560 of *Daybreak*, on liberty or freedom (in German entitled "Was uns frei steht," literally "what remains free for us"), shows how Nietzsche understands freedom. Here he questions the prejudice that our drives exist as "fully developed facts" and the philosophical doctrine of the unchangeability of character which gives support to this view (a doctrine articulated by Schopenhauer, for example). Nietzsche opens up ethical questions of character, freedom, and fate in fertile ways in many of the sections that make up Book IV of *The Gay Science* (see, for example, 276, 290, 304, 335, 341).

This section of our volume includes a generous selection from *The Gay Science*, which was published in four books in 1882 and to which Nietzsche added a fifth book in 1887, featured in our fifth section. As Walter Kaufmann noted in the introduction to his translation of the text, it is one of Nietzsche's most beautiful and important books (an estimation more recently echoed by David B. Allison).[2] An intense degree of self-reflexivity begins to characterize Nietzsche's thinking and he seeks to introduce new experimental modes of thinking with regard to questions of truth and knowledge, to situate these questions in the context of a consideration of life and evolution. As Kaufmann notes, key sections in the book are part of a long train of thought and can only be excised from their embeddedness in the text at a great cost to their meaning. The text begins with a reflection on the "eternal comedy of existence" and ends with a paragraph which announces that the tragedy is about to begin. Nietzsche called the book *Die fröhliche Wissenschaft: "la gaya scienza"* and it is important to "hear" the word "science" (*Wissenschaft*) and not simply "wisdom" in the title (the text has been translated as "The Joyful Wisdom," which is inaccurate but not wholly without legitimacy). By "science," however, Nietzsche is not equating his project with an existing set of practices of knowledge – such as the natural sciences – but giving expression to the full range of capacities of thought that the lover of knowledge must now cultivate.[3] In the wake of the death of God the love of knowledge has to be defined anew. Kaufmann suggested that the "gay" in Nietzsche's title should be heard in the sense of something unconventional, indicating a "knowledge" that defies convention and provides Nietzsche's "immoralism" with a distinctive mood (the desire is to continue to think free of the fears and prejudices of morality). In section 260 of *Beyond Good and Evil* Nietzsche speaks of "love as passion" and notes that this (courtly love) was invented by the "Provençal knight-poets [. . .] inventive people of the *gai saber*" to whom Europe owes so much. Another commentator has defined the gay science in terms of a "philosophical beatitude in which the most lucid and thus the least reassuring knowledge is accompanied by the most euphoric mood." Hence, "Nietzschean gaiety is not a simple psychological affair but implies knowledge in the most intellectual and theoretical sense of the term."[4] The "gay science," then, names a specific kind of philosophical praxis. Its investment is not in disappointment over the death of God and the demise of traditional and conventional metaphysics, and it does not lament the absence of a possible acquaintance with the thing-in-itself. The refrain recurring throughout the

2 See David B. Allison, *Reading the New Nietzsche* (Lanham and Oxford: Rowman & Littlefield, 2001), p. 71.
3 See also Heidegger's remarks on the "gay science" in his *Nietzsche*, ed. David Farrell Krell, trans. David Farrell Krell et al., 4 vols (San Francisco and London: Harper & Row, 1979–87), vol. 2, p. 20f. Heidegger notes that by "science" Nietzsche means something more than merely acquired knowledge: "the word *Wissenschaft* (science) resounds like *Leidenschaft* (passion), namely, the passion of a well-grounded mastery over the things that *confront* us and over own way of *responding* to what confronts us, positing all these things in magnificent and essential goals." He further notes that Nietzsche's cheerfulness comes from a certain superiority, one "that is not dashed by even the hardest and most terrifying matters."
4 Clément Rosset, *Joyful Cruelty: Toward a Philosophy of the Real*, trans. David F. Bell (New York and Oxford: Oxford University Press, 1993), p. 49.

text seems to be that we do not as yet know enough about ourselves and our modes of knowing to speak adequately about knowledge. We have yet to learn how to live with practices of truth and to become ourselves experimental bodies of knowledge. Hence the importance of the fundamental question Nietzsche poses, "to what extent can truth endure incorporation [*Einverleibung*]?" (*GS* 110; see also *GS* 11).[5]

In his Preface to the book's second edition Nietzsche speaks of the gay science as signifying the "saturnalia of a spirit" who has resisted a long and terrible pressure or burden severely, coldly, and without hope but who now is suddenly attacked by hope. In speaking of his recovery Nietzsche is not claiming to have found answers to his questions in the past but rather to have discovered new and original things. The faith of this spirit is in "tomorrow and the day after tomorrow." The free spirit who practices the gay science has given up on the need for some finale to life and for a final state which can only lead to a craving for a beyond, an outside, or an above. Self-liberation consists essentially in liberation from one's own romanticism. The anticipation of the future and the new cannot simply or only be that of the distressed and impotent. Important insights into how Nietzsche configures the reception and adoption of his gay science are to be found in the later sections to Book V of the text. Here we find Nietzsche invoking the "ideal of a spirit" who knows how to play naively with all that has hitherto been called holy, good, and divine – the ideal of "human, superhuman well-being and benevolence," one that will often appear "inhuman" when it confronts all earthly seriousness to date (*GS* 382). In short, Nietzsche is seeking a community of free spirits who will not be oppressed by the weight of the past, including the weightiness contained in the task of unmasking morality and raising the question of its value, but who feel "*very light*" with respect to their will to knowledge (*GS* 380). These spirits will overcome their time within themselves, they will know what it means to de-deify nature without belittling man in the process and adding to the aversion to the human that has arisen as a result of modern discoveries, and they will know the immanent character of their vision and riddle of the more-than-human. Nietzsche stresses that the key question is "how light or heavy we are," which is "the problem of our 'specific gravity'" (*GS* 380).

There is a real intricacy to Nietzsche's conception of gay science, and its precise nature and specific tasks merit being worked through carefully: there is a new seriousness but one that is executed with a spirit of laughter and of comedy; there are serious "overhuman" tasks to be carried out in accordance with a deep will of knowledge that is not based on any hatred of the human or ascetic self-denial; and there are weighty thought-experiments which are not to be adopted and practiced in a manner meant to oppress or to be experienced as oppressive. The "specific gravity" of the free spirits to come is not that of the *spirit of gravity* and its cry that "all is in vain!" The "greatest weight" of eternal recurrence is capable of being experienced as the most divine thought and offers, Nietzsche contends in *Ecce Homo*, the "highest formula of affirmation attainable." One commentator, Paul Loeb, rightly directs our attention to the precise location of section 341 of *The Gay Science*, where the doctrine of recurrence is first formulated in Nietzsche's published work. The section comes after a paragraph on the image of

5 For a detailed analysis of the "incorporation" of truth, see Keith Ansell Pearson, "The Incorporation of Truth: Towards the Overhuman," in id. (ed.), *A Companion to Nietzsche* (Malden, MA and Oxford: Blackwell, 2006).

the dying Socrates, showing that the teaching is directed against Socrates' belief in an afterlife where the soul has been liberated from the body, from time and its endless recurrence.[6] The doctrine is designed to have the truth of a "deathbed revelation." What is revealed is not the promise of eternal life after death but the promise of the time of one's mortal, earthly life needing to find its last and ultimate "eternal confirmation and seal" ("Was that life?" – "Once more then – and again and again!").

Heidegger went so far as to claim that "gay science" is Nietzsche's name for a philosophy that teaches the eternal return of the same as its fundamental doctrine.[7] The teaching of eternal return has been extensively treated in terms of its cosmological, existential, and "ethical" aspects, but commentators do not agree over the precise significance of the thought or on what role it is playing in Nietzsche's thinking. For some it has tremendous transformational effects;[8] for others, it is simply a means to reveal the type of being that one is and has no such effects (our response to the thought, it is claimed, is predetermined). In its formulation in section 341 of *The Gay Science* the thought is designed to provide nothing other and nothing less than a shock to our thinking about existence. In this paragraph the three principal aspects of the thought appear to be in evidence: the disclosure by the demon of our cosmological eternal recurrence, which we can greet with indifference; the quasi-ethical and practical import of the doctrine, "do you wish this again and again?", which is an invitation to become the creator, judge, and avenger of one's own law, and which we cannot be indifferent towards if our desire is to become the one that we are (see GS 335); and the existential test of affirmation, which necessitates becoming well disposed towards ourselves and life so as to want nothing more fervently than the ultimate eternal confirmation and seal afforded by eternal recurrence. In his later writings Nietzsche construed eternal return working primarily in terms of a principle of selection. As a new means of discipline and breeding it would contest the law of gregariousness that he holds has dominated evolution (natural selection) and history (the will to power of the weakest) to date.

We include a selection of translations of some of Nietzsche's initial sketches of the doctrine, including the first complete translation of his very first sketch of the thought. These sketches help provide greater insight into the concerns that informed his articulation of the thought than it is possible to glean from section 341 of *The Gay Science* alone. In the very first sketch Nietzsche wrote, which was for a book in five parts on the return of the same, it is clear that the teaching is addressing us moderns in our singularity: although our piece of human history will eternally repeat itself it is necessary to ignore this insight so as to focus on what is our singular task, namely to "outweigh" the whole past of previous humanity. Nietzsche states that to be equal to our task "indifference" needs to have worked its way deep inside us, and even the misery of a future humanity cannot concern us. The question for us moderns, as knowers who are essentially unknown to ourselves and who have yet to learn whether truth

---

6   See Plato, *Phaedo* 80a–81c, 114a–115d, and Paul S. Loeb, "The Moment of Tragic Death in Nietzsche's Dionysian Doctrine of Eternal Recurrence: An Exegesis of Aphorism 341 in *The Gay Science*," *International Studies in Philosophy*, 30/3 (1998), pp. 131–43.

7   Heidegger, *Nietzsche*, vol. 2, p. 21.

8   See especially Gilles Deleuze, *Nietzsche and Philosophy*, trans. Hugh Tomlinson (London: Athlone Press; New York: Columbia University Press, 1983).

and knowledge can be incorporated, is whether "we still *want to* live: and how!" Another sketch in which Nietzsche presents it as "the thought of thoughts" lends support to Deleuze's reading of the doctrine as fundamentally selective in character. For Deleuze eternal return institutes the creation of the superior forms of everything that exists and produces a becoming-active of forces: whatever has "being," or comes into being, is forced to change its nature when subjected to the eternal return. For Deleuze this means that the "same" can only refer to this reprise of the superior forms and the becoming-active. However, the key insight contained in the doctrine of eternal recurrence appears to be this: within the eternal circulation and recurrence of all things there takes place a set of *singular* becomings and events, and our task as modern human beings is to understand what constitutes our specific singular becoming and event. As Eugen Fink has astutely noted, Nietzsche's "revolution" with respect to time is to conceive of it as eternal by positing transience as permanence and singularity as recurrence: "Recurrence is not supposed to oppose singularity but to eternalize it and to give it concrete and factual existence and an infinite dimension."[9] He further helpfully notes that Nietzsche's metaphors and images, for example those concerning the question of time, must be translated into *thoughts* if we are not to hear in them only an opulent, overloaded, and loquacious voice. Although the reader of Nietzsche has to work very hard to effect this translation, it is well worth the effort.

From the first edition of *The Gay Science*, containing Books I–IV, we include from Book I the opening sections on the eternal comedy of existence and the intellectual conscience, paragraphs dealing with science (7), with consciousness (11), and with appearance (*Schein*; 54); from Book II there are sections on our evolutionary condition (57–8), on woman and art (59–60, 72), a long section on Schopenhauer and his followers (99), and on "our ultimate gratitude to art" (107); from Book III there are paragraphs on the death of God (beginning with the opening section 108 and extending to section 125, one of the most famous sections in Nietzsche's corpus), an important paragraph entitled "Let us beware" that reflects on what is required to effect a complete de-deification of nature (109 – this paragraph needs to be read very carefully since it gives the impression that the task is a wholly negative one but this is far from being the case), a set of sections on the origins of knowledge and of logic, and on cause and effect (110–12), on the changing aspects of moral conscience (117) and on the will (127), and some examples of Nietzsche's art of the short maxim (264–75). From Book IV we include sections on *amor fati* (276–7), on why the thought of life needs to be considered to be more appealing than the thought of death (278), on friendship (279), on living dangerously (283), on the need for a new justice (289), on the higher human beings (301), on "will and wave" that addresses the vital life as one of constant play whose only aim and purpose is this play (310), on the learning involved in love (334), on the voice of conscience and the need for our valuations of life to be purified (335), and the closing paragraphs on life as a woman (339), on the dying Socrates (340), on the "greatest weight" (eternal recurrence; 341), and on "the tragedy begins" (342).

9 Eugen Fink, *Nietzsche's Philosophy*, trans. Goetz Richter (London and New York: Continuum, 2003), p. 91.

13

Human, All Too Human: A Book for Free Spirits, volume 1 (1878)

Section 1: Of First and Last Things

1

Chemistry of concepts and feelings. In almost all respects, philosophical problems today are again formulated as they were two thousand years ago: how can something arise from its opposite – for example, reason from unreason, sensation from the lifeless, logic from the illogical, disinterested contemplation from covetous desire, altruism from egoism, truth from error? Until now, metaphysical philosophy has overcome this difficulty by denying the origin of the one from the other, and by assuming for the more highly valued things some miraculous origin, directly from out of the heart and essence of the "thing in itself." Historical philosophy, on the other hand, the very youngest of all philosophical methods, which can no longer be even conceived of as separate from the natural sciences, has determined in isolated cases (and will probably conclude in all of them) that they are not opposites, only exaggerated to be so by the popular or metaphysical view, and that this opposition is based on an error of reason. As historical philosophy explains it, there exists, strictly considered, neither a selfless act nor a completely disinterested observation: both are merely sublimations. In them the basic element appears to be virtually dispersed and proves to be present only to the most careful observer: All we need, something which can be given us only now, with the various sciences at their present level of achievement, is a *chemistry* of moral, religious, aesthetic ideas and feelings, a chemistry of all those impulses that we ourselves experience in the great and small interactions of culture and society, indeed even in solitude. What if this chemistry might end with the conclusion that, even here, the most glorious colors are extracted from base, even despised substances? Are there many who will want to pursue such investigations? Mankind loves to put the questions of origin and beginnings out of mind: must one not be almost inhuman to feel in himself the opposite inclination?

2

Congenital defect of philosophers. All philosophers suffer from the same defect, in that they start with present-day man and think they can arrive at their goal by analyzing him. Instinctively they let "man" hover before them as an *aeterna veritas*,[1] something unchanging in all turmoil, a secure measure of things. But everything the philosopher asserts about man is basically no more than a statement about man within a *very limited* time span. A lack of historical sense is the congenital defect of all philosophers. Some unwittingly even take the most recent form of man, as it developed under the imprint of certain religions or even certain political events, as the fixed form from which one must proceed. They will not understand that man has evolved, that the faculty of knowledge has also evolved, while some of them even permit themselves to spin the whole world from out of this faculty of knowledge. Now, everything *essential* in human development occurred in primeval times, long before those four thousand years with which we are more or less familiar. Man probably hasn't changed much more in these years. But the philosopher sees "instincts" in present-day man, and assumes that they belong to the unchangeable facts of human nature, that they can, to that extent, provide a key to the understanding of the world in general. This entire teleology is predicated on the ability to speak about man of the last four thousand years as if he were eternal, the natural direction of all things in the world from the beginning. But everything has evolved; there are *no eternal facts*, nor are there any absolute truths. Thus *historical philosophizing* is necessary henceforth, and the virtue of modesty as well.

3

Esteeming humble truths. It is the sign of a higher culture to esteem more highly the little, humble truths, those discovered by a strict method, rather than the gladdening and dazzling errors that originate in metaphysical and artistic ages and men. At first, one has scorn on his lips for humble truths, as if they could offer no match for the others: they stand so modest, simple, sober, even apparently discouraging, while the other truths are so beautiful, splendid, enchanting, or even enrapturing. But truths that are hard won, certain, enduring, and therefore still of consequence for all further knowledge are the higher; to keep to them is manly, and shows bravery, simplicity, restraint. Eventually, not only the individual, but all mankind will be elevated to this manliness, when men finally grow accustomed to the greater esteem for durable, lasting knowledge and have lost all belief in inspiration and a seemingly miraculous communication of truths. The admirers of *forms*, with their standard of beauty and sublimity, will, to be sure, have good reason to mock at first, when esteem for humble truths and the scientific spirit first comes to rule, but only because either their eye has not yet been opened to the charm of the *simplest* form, or because men raised in that spirit have not yet been fully and inwardly permeated by it, so that they continue thoughtlessly to imitate old forms (and poorly, too, like someone who no longer really cares about the matter). Previously, the mind was not obliged to think rigorously; its importance lay in spinning out symbols and forms. That has changed; that importance of symbols has become the sign of lower culture. Just as our very arts are becoming

1   Latin: eternal truth.

ever more intellectual and our senses more spiritual, and as, for example, that which is sensually pleasant to the ear is judged quite differently now than a hundred years ago, so the forms of our life become ever more *spiritual* – to the eye of older times *uglier*, perhaps, but only because it is unable to see how the realm of internal, spiritual beauty is continually deepening and expanding, and to what extent a glance full of intelligence can mean more to all of us now than the most beautiful human body and the most sublime edifice.

[. . .]

6

The scientific spirit[2] *is powerful in the part, not in the whole.* The distinct, *smallest* fields of science are treated purely objectively. On the other hand, the general, great sciences, taken as a whole, pose the question (a very unobjective question, to be sure): what for? to what benefit? Because of this concern about benefit, men treat the sciences less impersonally as a whole than in their parts. Now, in philosophy – the top of the whole scientific pyramid – the question of the benefit of knowledge itself is posed automatically and each philosophy has the unconscious intention of ascribing to knowledge the *greatest* benefit. For this reason, all philosophies have so much high-flying metaphysics and so much wariness of the seemingly insignificant explanations of physics. For the importance of knowledge for life *ought* to appear as great as possible. Here we have the antagonism between individual scientific fields and philosophy. The latter, like art, wishes to render the greatest possible depth and meaning to life and activity. In the sciences, one seeks knowledge and nothing more – whatever the consequences may be. Until now, there has been no philosopher in whose hands philosophy has not become an apology for knowledge. In this way, at least, every one is an optimist, by thinking that knowledge must be accorded the highest usefulness. All philosophers are tyrannized by logic: and logic, by its nature, is optimism.

[. . .]

9

Metaphysical world. It is true, there might be a metaphysical world; one can hardly dispute the absolute possibility of it. We see all things by means of our human head, and cannot chop it off, though it remains to wonder what would be left of the world if indeed it had been cut off. This is a purely scientific problem, and not very suited to cause men worry. But all that has produced metaphysical assumptions and made them *valuable, horrible, pleasurable* to men thus far is passion, error, and self-deception. The very worst methods of knowledge, not the very best, have taught us to believe in them. When one has disclosed these methods to be the foundation of all existing religions and metaphysical systems, one has refuted them. That other possibility still remains, but we cannot begin to do anything with it, let alone allow our happiness, salvation, and life to depend on the spider webs of such a possibility. For there is nothing at all we could state about the metaphysical world except its differentness,[3] a differentness

---

2 In German: *Der Geist der Wissenschaft*. On "Wissenschaft" see *On Truth and Lies* note 13 above.

3 In German: *ein Anderssein* (literally, "a different being").

inaccessible and incomprehensible to us. It would be a thing with negative qualities. No matter how well proven the existence of such a world might be, it would still hold true that the knowledge of it would be the most inconsequential of all knowledge, even more inconsequential than the knowledge of the chemical analysis of water must be to the boatman facing a storm.

10

The harmlessness of metaphysics in the future. As soon as the origins of religion, art, and morality have been described, so that one can explain them fully without resorting to the use of *metaphysical intervention* at the beginning and along the way, then one no longer has as strong an interest in the purely theoretical problem of the "thing in itself" and "appearance."[4] For however the case may be, religion, art, and morality do not enable us to touch the "essence of the world in itself." We are in the realm of representation,[5] no "intuition" can carry us further. With complete calm we will let physiology and the ontogeny of organisms and concepts determine how our image of the world can be so very different from the disclosed essence of the world.

11

Language as an alleged science. The importance of language for the development of culture lies in the fact that, in language, man juxtaposed to the one world another world of his own, a place which he thought so sturdy that from it he could move the rest of the world from its foundations and make himself lord over it. To the extent that he believed over long periods of time in the concepts and names of things as if they were *aeternae veritates,*[6] man has acquired that pride by which he has raised himself above the animals: he really did believe that in language he had knowledge of the world. The shaper of language was not so modest as to think that he was only giving things labels; rather, he imagined that he was expressing the highest knowledge of things with words; and in fact, language is the first stage of scientific effort. Here, too, it is the *belief in found truth* from which the mightiest sources of strength have flowed. Very belatedly (only now) is it dawning on men that in their belief in language they have propagated a monstrous error. Fortunately, it is too late to be able to revoke the development of reason, which rests on that belief. *Logic,* too, rests on assumptions that do not correspond to anything in the real world, e.g., on the assumption of the equality of things, the identity of the same thing at different points of time; but this science arose from the opposite belief (that there were indeed such things in the real world).

---

4   In German: *Erscheinung.*
5   The translation of *Vorstellung* has been modified in all these sections from "idea" to "representation." The principal meaning of the German word is that of "placing before" (*vor-stellen*). The term plays an important role in Kant's *Critique of Pure Reason,* but Nietzsche would have been largely acquainted with it from his knowledge of Schopenhauer's *The World as Will and Representation,* where it refers to a complex process in the brain which produces the consciousness of a picture or image. The word serves to stress the subjective mental state of a subject rather than the nature of the object that is being represented (the sun is the sun that I see, etc.).
6   Latin: eternal truths.

So it is with *mathematics*, which would certainly not have originated if it had been known from the beginning that there is no exactly straight line in nature, no real circle, no absolute measure.

[. . .]

16

Appearance[7] *and the thing-in-itself.* Philosophers tend to confront life and experience (what they call the world of appearance) as they would a painting that has been revealed once and for all, depicting with unchanging constancy the same event. They think they must interpret this event correctly in order to conclude something about the essence which produced the painting, that is, about the thing-in-itself, which always tends to be regarded as the sufficient reason for the world of appearance. Conversely, stricter logicians, after they had rigorously established the concept of the metaphysical as the concept of that which is unconditioned and consequently unconditioning, denied any connection between the unconditioned (the metaphysical world) and the world we are familiar with. So that the thing-in-itself does *not* appear in the world of appearances, and any conclusion about the former on the basis of the latter must be rejected. But both sides overlook the possibility that that painting – that which to us men means life and experience – has gradually *evolved*, indeed is still *evolving*, and therefore should not be considered a fixed quantity, on which basis a conclusion about the creator (the sufficient reason) may be made, or even rejected. Because for thousands of years we have been looking at the world with moral, aesthetic, and religious claims, with blind inclination, passion, or fear, and have indulged ourselves fully in the bad habits of illogical thought, this world has gradually *become* so strangely colorful, frightful, profound, soulful; it has acquired color, but we have been the painters: the human intellect allowed appearance to appear,[8] and projected its mistaken conceptions onto the things. Only late, very late, does the intellect stop to think: and now the world of experience and the thing-in-itself seem so extraordinarily different and separate that it rejects any conclusion about the latter from the former, or else, in an awful, mysterious way, it demands the *abandonment* of our intellect, of our personal will in order to come to the essential by *becoming essential*. On the other hand, other people have gathered together all characteristic traits of our world of appearances (that is, our inherited idea of the world, spun out of intellectual errors) and, *instead of accusing the intellect*, have attacked the essence of things for causing this real, very uncanny character of the world, and have preached salvation from being. The steady and arduous progress of science, which will ultimately celebrate its greatest triumph in an *ontogeny of thought*,[9] will deal decisively with all these views. Its conclusion might perhaps end up with this tenet: That which we now call the world is the result of a number of errors and fantasies, which came about gradually in the overall development of organic beings, fusing with one another, and now handed down to us as a collected treasure of our entire past – a treasure: for the *value* of our humanity rests upon it. From this world of idea strict science can, in fact, release us only to a small extent (something we by no means desire), in that it

7   In German: *Erscheinung.*
8   In German: *die Erscheinung erscheinen.*
9   In German: *Entstehungsgeschichte des Denkens.*

is unable to break significantly the power of ancient habits of feeling. But it can illuminate, quite gradually, step by step, the history of the origin of that world as representation – and lift us, for moments at least, above the whole process. Perhaps we will recognize then that the thing-in-itself deserves a Homeric laugh,[10] in that it *seemed* to be so much, indeed everything, and is actually empty, that is, empty of meaning.

[. . .]

18

Basic questions of metaphysics. Once the ontogeny of thought is written, the following sentence by an excellent logician will be seen in a new light: "The original general law of the knowing subject consists in the inner necessity of knowing each object in itself, in its own being, as an object identical with itself, that is, self-existing and fundamentally always the same and unchangeable, in short, as a substance."[11] This law, too, which is here called "original" also evolved. Some day the gradual origin of this tendency in lower organisms will be shown, how the dull mole's eyes of these organizations at first see everything as identical; how then, when the various stimuli of pleasure and unpleasure become more noticeable, different substances are gradually distinguished, but each one with One attribute, that is, with one single relationship to such an organism. The first stage of logic is judgment, whose essence consists, as the best logicians have determined, in belief. All belief is based on the *feeling of pleasure or pain* in relation to the feeling subject. A new, third feeling as the result of two preceding feelings is judgment in its lowest form. Initially, we organic beings have no interest in a thing, other than in its relationship to us with regard to pleasure and pain. Between those moments in which we become aware of this relationship (i.e., the states of sensation) lie those states of quiet, of non-sensation. Then we find the world and every thing in it without interest; we notice no change in it (just as even now, a person who is intensely interested in something will not notice that someone is passing by him). To a plant, all things are normally quiet, eternal, each thing identical to itself. From the period of low organisms, man has inherited the belief that there are *identical things* (only experience which has been educated by the highest science contradicts this tenet). From the beginning, the first belief of all organic beings may be that the whole rest of the world is One and unmoved. In that first stage of logic, the thought of *causality* is furthest removed. Even now, we believe fundamentally that all feelings and actions are acts of free will; when the feeling individual considers himself, he takes each feeling, each change, to be something *isolated*, that is, something unconditioned, without a context. It rises up out of us, with no connection to anything earlier or later. We are hungry, but do not think initially that the organism wants to be kept alive. Rather, that feeling seems to assert itself *without reason or purpose*; it isolates itself and takes itself to be *arbitrary*. Thus the belief in freedom of the will is an initial error of all organic beings, as old as the existence in them of stirrings of logic. Belief in unconditioned substances and identical things is likewise an old, original error of all that is organic. To the extent that all metaphysics has dealt primarily with substance

10   Cf. *Iliad*, I. 599; *Odyssey*, VII. 326, XX. 346.
11   From Afrikan Spir, *Denken und Wirklichkeit* (*Thought and Reality*, 1873), which Nietzsche read in Basel in the year of its publication.

and freedom of the will, however, one may characterize it as that science which deals with the basic errors of man – but as if they were basic truths.

19

Number. The laws of numbers were invented on the basis of the initially prevailing error that there are various identical things (but actually there is nothing identical) or at least that there are things (but there is no "thing"). The assumption of multiplicity always presumes that there is *something*, which occurs repeatedly. But this is just where error rules; even here, we invent entities, unities, that do not exist. Our feelings of space and time are false, for if they are tested rigorously, they lead to logical contradictions. Whenever we establish something scientifically, we are inevitably always reckoning with some incorrect quantities; but because these quantities are at least *constant* (as is, for example, our feeling of time and space), the results of science do acquire a perfect strictness and certainty in their relationship to each other. One can continue to build upon them – up to that final analysis, where the mistaken basic assumptions, those constant errors, come into contradiction with the results, for example, in atomic theory. There we still feel ourselves forced to assume a "thing" or a material "substratum" that is moved, while the entire scientific procedure has pursued the task of dissolving everything thing-like (material) into movements. Here, too, our feeling distinguishes that which is moving from that which is moved, and we do not come out of this circle, because the belief in things has been tied up with our essential nature from time immemorial. When Kant says "Reason does not create its laws from nature, but dictates them to her,"[12] this is perfectly true in respect to the *concept of nature* which we are obliged to apply to her (Nature = world as representation, that is, as error), but which is the summation of a number of errors of reason. To a world that is *not* our representation, the laws of numbers are completely inapplicable: they are valid only in the human world.

20

A few rungs down. One level of education, itself a very high one, has been reached when man gets beyond superstitious and religious concepts and fears and, for example, no longer believes in the heavenly angels or original sin, and has stopped talking about the soul's salvation. Once he is at this level of liberation, he must still make a last intense effort to overcome metaphysics. *Then*, however, a *retrograde movement* is necessary: he must understand both the historical and the psychological justification in metaphysical ideas. He must recognize how mankind's greatest advancement came from them and how, if one did not take this retrograde step, one would rob himself of mankind's finest accomplishments to date. With regard to philosophical metaphysics, I now see a number of people who have arrived at the negative goal (that all positive metaphysics is an error), but only a few who climb back down a few rungs. For one should look out over the last rung of the ladder, but not want to stand on it. Those who are most enlightened can go only as far as to free themselves of metaphysics and look back on

---

12 Kant, *Prolegomena zu einer jeden künftigen Metaphysik* (*Prolegomena to any Future Metaphysics*, 1783), 36.

it with superiority, while here, as in the hippodrome, it is necessary to take a turn at the end of the track.

21

Presumed triumph of skepticism. Let us accept for the moment the skeptical starting point: assuming there were no other, metaphysical world and that we could not use any metaphysical explanations of the only world known to us, how would we then look upon men and things? One can imagine this; it is useful to do so, even if one were to reject the question of whether Kant and Schopenhauer proved anything metaphysical scientifically. For according to historical probability, it is quite likely that men at some time will become *skeptical* about this whole subject. So one must ask the question: how will human society take shape under the influence of such an attitude? Perhaps the *scientific proof* of any metaphysical world is itself so *difficult* that mankind can no longer keep from distrusting it. And if one is distrustful of metaphysics, then we have, generally speaking, the same consequences as if metaphysics had been directly refuted and one were no longer *permitted* to believe in it. The historical question about mankind's unmetaphysical views remains the same in either case.

[. . .]

25

Private morality, world morality. Since man no longer believes that a God is guiding the destinies of the world as a whole, or that, despite all apparent twists, the path of mankind is leading somewhere glorious, men must set themselves ecumenical goals, embracing the whole earth. The older morality, namely Kant's,[13] demands from the individual those actions that one desires from all men – a nice, naive idea, as if everyone without further ado would know which manner of action would benefit the whole of mankind, that is, which actions were desirable at all. It is a theory like that of free trade, which assumes that a general harmony would *have* to result of itself, according to innate laws of melioration. Perhaps a future survey of the needs of mankind will reveal it to be thoroughly undesirable that all men act identically; rather, in the interest of ecumenical goals, for whole stretches of human time special tasks, perhaps in some circumstances even evil tasks, would have to be set. In any event, if mankind is to keep from destroying itself by such a conscious overall government, we must discover first a *knowledge of the conditions of culture*, a knowledge surpassing all previous knowledge, as a scientific standard for ecumenical goals. This is the enormous task of the great minds of the next century.

26

Reaction as progress. Sometimes there appear rough, violent, and impetuous spirits, who are nevertheless backward; they conjure up once again a past phase of mankind. They serve as proof that the new tendencies which they are opposing are still not strong enough, that something is lacking there; otherwise, those conjurors would be opposed

13   See Kant, *Kritik der praktischen Vernunft* (*Critique of Practical Reason*, 1788), 7: "Always act in such a way that the maxims of your will could function as the basis of a universal law of action."

more effectively. For example, Luther's Reformation proves that in his century all the impulses of freedom of the spirit were still uncertain, delicate, juvenescent. Science could not yet raise her head. Indeed, the whole Renaissance appears like an early spring, which almost gets snowed away. But in our century, too, Schopenhauer's metaphysics proved that the scientific spirit is still not strong enough. Thus, in Schopenhauer's teaching the whole medieval Christian world view and feeling of man could again celebrate a resurrection, despite the defeat, long since achieved, of all Christian dogmas. His teaching is infused with much science, but what rules it is not science but rather the old, well-known "metaphysical need."[14] Certainly one of the greatest and quite inestimable benefits we gain from Schopenhauer is that he forces our feeling for a time back to older, powerful forms of contemplating the world and men, to which other paths could not so readily lead us. History and justice benefit greatly. I believe that without Schopenhauer's aid, no one today could so easily do justice to Christianity and its Asian cousins; to attempt to do so based on the Christianity still existing today is impossible. Only after this great *achievement of justice*, only after we have corrected in such an essential point the historical way of thinking that the Enlightenment brought with it, may we once again carry onward the banner of the Enlightenment, the banner with the three names: Petrarch, Erasmus, Voltaire.[15] Out of reaction, we have taken a step forward.

[. . .]

32

Unfairness necessary. All judgments about the value of life have developed illogically and therefore unfairly. The impurity of the judgment lies first in the way the material is present (that is very incompletely), second, in the way it is assessed, and third, in the fact that every separate part of the material again results, as is absolutely necessary, from impure knowledge. No experience of a man, for example, however close he is to us, can be so complete that we would have a logical right to evaluate him *in toto*. All evaluations are premature, and must be so. Finally, the gauge by which we measure, our own nature, is no unchangeable quantity; we have moods and vacillations; yet we would have to know ourselves to be a fixed gauge if we were to evaluate fairly the relationship of any one thing to ourselves. Perhaps it will follow from all this that one ought not to judge at all; if only one could *live* without evaluating, without having disinclinations and inclinations! For all disinclination depends upon an evaluation, just as does all inclination. Man cannot experience a drive to or away from something without the feeling that he is desiring what is beneficial and avoiding what is harmful, without evaluating knowingly the merit of the goal. We are from the start illogical and therefore unfair beings, *and this we can know*: it is one of the greatest and most insoluble disharmonies of existence.

[. . .]

14   See *WWR*, vol. 2, ch. 17.
15   The Italian poet and scholar Petrarch (1304–74) represents the Renaissance in this triumvirate; the Dutch humanist Erasmus (1466–1536) represents humanism, and the French philosopher Voltaire (1694–1778), the Enlightenment. The first edition of *Human, All Too Human* was published in 1878 to mark the centenary of Voltaire's death, and was dedicated to his memory.

34

Some reassurance. But does not our philosophy then turn into tragedy? Does not truth become an enemy of life, an enemy of what is better? A question seems to weigh down our tongues, and yet not want to be uttered: whether one *is capable* of consciously remaining in untruth, or, if one *had* to do so, whether death would not be preferable? For there is no "ought" anymore. Morality to the extent that it was an "ought" has been destroyed by our way of reflection, every bit as much as religion. Knowledge can allow only pleasure and unpleasure, benefit and harm, as motives. But how will these motives come to terms with the feeling for truth? These motives, too, have to do with errors (to the extent that inclination and disinclination, and their very unfair measurements, essentially determine, as we have said, our pleasure and unpleasure). All human life is sunk deep in untruth; the individual cannot pull it out of this well without growing profoundly annoyed with his entire past, without finding his present motives (like honor) senseless, and without opposing scorn and disdain to the passions that urge one on to the future and to the happiness in it. If this is true, is there only one way of thought left, with despair as a personal end and a philosophy of destruction as a theoretical end? I believe that a man's *temperament* determines the aftereffect of knowledge; although the aftereffect described above is possible in some natures, I could just as well imagine a different one, which would give rise to a life much more simple, more free of affects than the present one. The old motives of intense desire would still be strong at first, due to old, inherited habit, but they would gradually grow weaker under the influence of cleansing knowledge. Finally one would live among men and with oneself as in *nature*, without praise, reproaches, overzealousness, delighting in many things as in a spectacle that one formerly had only to fear. One would be free of appearance and would no longer feel the goading thought that one was not simply nature, or that one was more than nature. Of course, as I said, a good temperament would be necessary – a secure, mild, and basically cheerful soul; such a disposition would not need to be on guard for tricks and sudden explosions, and its expressions would have neither a growling tone nor sullenness – those familiar bothersome traits of old dogs and men who have lain a long time chained up. Rather, a man from whom the ordinary chains of life have fallen in such measure that he continues to live on only to better his knowledge must be able to renounce without envy and chagrin much, indeed almost everything, that other men value. He must be *content* with that free, fearless hovering over men, customs, laws and the traditional evaluations of things, which is for him the most desirable of states. He is glad to communicate his joy in this state, and perhaps he has nothing else *to* communicate, which is, to be sure, one renunciation, one self-denial the more. But if one nevertheless wants more from him, with a benevolent shake of the head he will indicate his brother, the free man of action, and perhaps not conceal a little scorn: for that man's "freedom" is another matter entirely.

Section 2: On the History of Moral Feelings

35

The advantages of psychological observation. That meditating on things human, all too human (or, as the learned phrase goes, "psychological observation") is one of the means by which man can ease life's burden; that by exercising this art, one can secure presence of mind in difficult situations and entertainment amid boring surroundings; indeed, that from the thorniest and unhappiest phases of one's own life one can pluck maxims and feel a bit better thereby: this was believed, known – in earlier centuries. Why has it been forgotten in this century, when many signs point, in Germany at least, if not throughout Europe, to the dearth of psychological observation? Not particularly in novels, short stories, and philosophical meditations, for these are the work of exceptional men; but more in the judging of public events and personalities; most of all we lack the art of psychological dissection and calculation in all classes of society, where one hears a lot of talk about men, but none at all *about man*. Why do people let the richest and most harmless source of entertainment get away from them? Why do they not even read the great masters of the psychological maxim any more? For it is no exaggeration to say that it is hard to find the cultured European who has read La Rochefoucauld[16] and his spiritual and artistic cousins. Even more uncommon is the man who knows them and does not despise them. But even this unusual reader will probably find much less delight in those artists than their form ought to give him; for not even the finest mind is capable of adequate appreciation of the art of the polished maxim if he has not been educated to it, has not been challenged by it himself. Without such practical learning one takes this form of creating and forming to be easier than it is; one is not acute enough in discerning what is successful and attractive. For that reason present-day readers of maxims take a relatively insignificant delight in them, scarcely a mouthful of pleasure; they react like typical viewers of cameos, praising them because they cannot love them, and quick to admire but even quicker to run away.

36

Objection. Or might there be a counterargument to the thesis that psychological observation is one of life's best stimulants, remedies, and palliatives? Might one be so persuaded of the unpleasant consequences of this art as to intentionally divert the student's gaze from it? Indeed, a certain blind faith in the goodness of human nature, an inculcated aversion to dissecting human behavior, a kind of shame with respect to the naked soul, may really be more desirable for a man's overall happiness than the trait of psychological sharpsightedness, which is helpful in isolated instances. And perhaps the belief in goodness, in virtuous men and actions, in an abundance of impersonal goodwill in the world has made men better, in that it has made them less distrustful. If one imitates Plutarch's[17] heroes with enthusiasm and feels an aversion toward tracing skeptically the motives for their actions, then the welfare of human society has benefited (even if the truth of human society has not). Psychological error, and dullness in this area generally, help humanity forward; but knowledge of the truth might gain more from the stimulating power of an hypothesis like the one La Rochefoucauld places at the beginning of the first edition of his *Sentences et maximes*

16   François, duc de la Rochefoucauld (1613–80), French aphorist whose *Sentences et maximes* (*Sentences and Maxims*, 1665) Nietzsche read on a train journey to Sorrento shortly before beginning to write *Human, All Too Human*.
17   The purpose of Plutarch's (A.D. 50–120) *Parallel Lives* was to exemplify private virtue in the careers of great men.

morales: "Ce que le monde nomme vertu n'est d'ordinaire qu'un fantôme formé par nos passions, à qui on donne un nom honnête pour faire impunément ce qu'on veut."[18] La Rochefoucauld and those other French masters of soul searching (whose company a German, the author of *Psychological Observations*, has recently joined)[19] are like accurately aimed arrows, which hit the mark again and again, the black mark of man's nature. Their skill inspires amazement, but the spectator who is guided not by the scientific spirit, but by the humane spirit, will eventually curse an art which seems to implant in the souls of men a predilection for belittling and doubt.

37

Nevertheless. However the argument and counterargument stand, the present condition of one certain, single science has made necessary the awakening of moral observation, and mankind cannot be spared the horrible sight of the psychological operating table, with its knives and forceps. For now that science rules which asks after the origin and history of moral feelings and which tries as it progresses to pose and solve the complicated sociological problems; the old philosophy doesn't even acknowledge such problems and has always used meager excuses to avoid investigating the origin and history of moral feelings. We can survey the consequences very clearly, many examples having proven how the errors of the greatest philosophers usually start from a false explanation of certain human actions and feelings, how an erroneous analysis of so-called selfless behavior, for example, can be the basis for false ethics, for whose sake religion and mythological confusion are then drawn in, and finally how the shadows of these sad spirits also fall upon physics and the entire contemplation of the world. But if it is a fact that the superficiality of psychological observation has laid the most dangerous traps for human judgment and conclusions, and continues to lay them anew, then what we need now is a persistence in work that does not tire of piling stone upon stone, pebble upon pebble; we need a sober courage to do such humble work without shame and to defy any who disdain it. It is true that countless individual remarks about things human and all too human were first detected and stated in those social circles which would make every sort of sacrifice not for scientific knowledge, but for a witty coquetry. And because the scent of that old homeland (a very seductive scent) has attached itself almost inextricably to the whole genre of the moral maxim, the scientific man instinctively shows some suspicion towards this genre and its seriousness. But it suffices to point to the outcome: already it is becoming clear that the most serious results grow up from the ground of psychological observation. Which principle did one of the keenest and coolest thinkers, the author of the book *On the Origin of Moral Feelings*, arrive at through his incisive and piercing analysis of human actions? "The moral man," he says, "stands no nearer to the intelligible (metaphysical) world than does the physical man."[20] Perhaps

18   "That which men call virtue is usually no more than a phantom formed by our passions, to which one gives an honest name in order to do with impunity whatever one wishes."
19   The author referred to is Nietzsche's friend Paul Rée (1849–1901), whose *Psychologische Beobachtungen* (*Psychological Observations*) had appeared in 1875.
20   Paraphrased from Rée, *Der Ursprung der moralischen Empfindungen* (*The Origin of Moral Sensations*, 1877).

at some point in the future this principle, grown hard and sharp by the hammerblow of historical knowledge, can serve as the axe laid to the root of men's "metaphysical need" (whether *more* as a blessing than as a curse for the general welfare, who can say?). In any event, it is a tenet with the most weighty consequences, fruitful and fright-ful at the same time, and seeing into the world with that double vision which all great insights have.

38

How beneficial. Let us table the question, then, of whether psychological observation brings more advantage or harm upon men. What is certain is that it is necessary, for science cannot do without it. Science, however, takes as little consideration of final purposes as does nature; just as nature sometimes brings about the most useful things without having wanted to, so too true science, *which is the imitation of nature in concepts,* will sometimes, nay often, further man's benefit and welfare and achieve what is useful – but likewise *without having wanted to.* Whoever feels too wintry in the breeze of this kind of observation has perhaps too little fire in him. Let him look around meanwhile, and he will perceive diseases which require cold poultices, and men who are so "moulded" out of glowing spirit that they have great trouble in finding an atmosphere cold and biting enough for them anywhere. Moreover, as all overly earnest individuals and peoples have a need for frivolity; as others, who are overly excitable and unstable, occasionally need heavy, oppressive burdens for their health's sake; so should not we – the *more intellectual* men in an age that is visibly being set aflame more and more – reach for all quenching and cooling means available to remain at least as steady, harmless, and moderate as we now are and thus render service to this age at some future time as a mirror and self-reflection of itself?

39

The fable of intelligible freedom. The history of those feelings, by virtue of which we consider a person responsible, the so-called moral feelings, is divided into the follow-ing main phases. At first we call particular acts good or evil without any considera-tion of their motives, but simply on the basis of their beneficial or harmful consequences. Soon, however, we forget the origin of these terms and imagine that the quality "good" or "evil" is inherent in the actions themselves, without considera-tion of their consequences; this is the same error language makes when calling the stone itself hard, the tree itself green – that is, we take the effect to be the cause. Then we assign the goodness or evil to the motives, and regard the acts themselves as morally ambiguous. We go even further and cease to give to the particular motive the predic-ate good or evil, but give it rather to the whole nature of a man; the motive grows out of him as a plant grows out of the earth. So we make man responsible in turn for the effects of his actions, then for his actions, then for his motives and finally for his nature. Ultimately we discover that his nature cannot be responsible either, in that it is itself an inevitable consequence, an outgrowth of the elements and influences of past and present things; that is, man cannot be made responsible for anything, neither for his nature, nor his motives, nor his actions, nor the effects of his actions. And thus we come to understand that the history of moral feelings is the history of an error, an error called "responsibility," which in turn rests on an error called "freedom of the will." Schopenhauer, on the other hand, concluded as follows: because certain actions produce *displeasure* ("sense of guilt"), a responsibility must exist. For there would be *no reason* for this displeasure if not only all human actions occurred out of necessity (as they actually do, according to this philosopher's insight), but if man himself also acquired his entire *nature* out of the same necessity (which Schopenhauer denies). From the fact of man's displeasure, Schopenhauer thinks he can prove that man somehow must have had a freedom, a freedom which did not determine his actions but rather determined his nature: freedom, that is, *to be* this way or the other, not *to act* this way or the other. According to Schopenhauer, *operari* (doing), the sphere of strict causality, necessity, and lack of responsibility, follows from *esse* (being) the sphere of freedom and responsibility. The displeasure man feels seems to refer to *operari* (to this extent it is erroneous), but in truth it refers to *esse*, which is the act of a free will, the primary cause of an individual's existence. Man becomes that which he *wants* to be; his volition precedes his existence. In this case, we are concluding falsely that we can deduce the justification, the rational *admissibility* of this displeasure, from the fact that it exists; and from this false deduction Schopenhauer arrives at his fantastic conclusion of so-called intelligible freedom. But displeasure after the deed need not be rational at all: in fact, it certainly is not rational, for its rests on the erroneous assumption that the deed did *not* have to follow necessarily. Thus, because he thinks he is free (but not because he is free), man feels remorse and the pangs of conscience. Furthermore, this displeasure is a habit that can be given up; many men do not feel it at all, even after the same actions that cause many other men to feel it. Tied to the development of custom and culture, it is a very changeable thing, and present perhaps only within a relatively short period of world history. No one is responsible for his deeds, no one for his nature; to judge is to be unjust. This is also true when the individual judges himself. The tenet is as bright as sunlight, and yet everyone prefers to walk back into the shadow and untruth – for fear of the consequences.

[. . .]

41

The unchangeable character. In the strict sense, it is not true that one's character is unchangeable; rather, this popular tenet means only that during a man's short lifetime the motives affecting him cannot normally cut deeply enough to destroy the imprinted writing of many millennia. If a man eighty thousand years old were conceivable, his character would in fact be absolutely variable, so that out of him little by little an abundance of different individuals would develop. The brevity of human life misleads us to many an erroneous assertion about the qualities of man.

[. . .]

45

Double prehistory[21] *of good and evil.* The concept of good and evil has a double prehistory: namely, first of all, in the soul of the ruling clans and castes. The man who has the power to requite goodness with goodness, evil with evil, and really does practice requital by being grateful and vengeful, is called "good." The man who is unpowerful

21 In German: *Vorgeschichte.*

and cannot requite is taken for bad. As a good man, one belongs to the "good," a community that has a communal feeling, because all the individuals are entwined together by their feeling for requital. As a bad man, one belongs to the "bad," to a mass of abject, powerless men who have no communal feeling. The good men are a caste; the bad men are a multitude, like particles of dust. Good and bad are for a time equivalent to noble and base, master and slave. Conversely, one does not regard the enemy as evil: he can requite. In Homer, both the Trojan and the Greek are good. Not the man who inflicts harm on us, but the man who is contemptible, is bad. In the community of the good, goodness is hereditary; it is impossible for a bad man to grow out of such good soil. Should one of the good men nevertheless do something unworthy of good men, one resorts to excuses; one blames God, for example, saying that he struck the good man with blindness and madness. *Then*, in the souls of oppressed, powerless men, every *other* man is taken for hostile, inconsiderate, exploitative, cruel, sly, whether he be noble or base. Evil is their epithet for man, indeed for every possible living being, even, for example, for a god; "human," "divine" mean the same as "devilish" "evil." Signs of goodness, helpfulness, pity are taken anxiously for malice, the prelude to a terrible outcome, bewilderment, and deception, in short, for refined evil. With such a state of mind in the individual, a community can scarcely come about at all – or at most in the crudest form; so that wherever this concept of good and evil predominates, the downfall of individuals, their clans and races, is near at hand.

Our present morality[22] has grown up on the ground of the *ruling* clans and castes.

[. . .]

57

Morality[23] *as man's dividing himself.* A good author, who really cares about his subject, wishes that someone would come and destroy him by representing the same subject more clearly and by answering every last question contained in it. The girl in love wishes that she might prove the devoted faithfulness of her love through her lover's faithlessness. The soldier wishes that he might fall on the battlefield for his victorious fatherland, for in the victory of his fatherland his greatest desire is also victorious. The mother gives the child what she takes from herself: sleep, the best food, in some instances even her health, her wealth. Are all these really selfless states, however? Are these acts of morality[24] *miracles* because they are, to use Schopenhauer's phrase, "impossible and yet real"? Isn't it clear that, in all these cases, man is loving *something of himself*, a thought, a longing, an offspring, more than *something else of himself,* that he is thus *dividing up* his being and sacrificing one part for the other? Is it something *essentially* different when a pigheaded man says, "I would rather be shot at once than move an inch to get out of that man's way"? The *inclination towards something* (a wish, a drive, a longing) is present in all the above-mentioned cases; to yield to it, with all its consequences, is in any case not "selfless." In morality, man treats himself not as an "individuum," but as a "dividuum."

[. . .]

22 In German: *Sittlichkeit*. See *D* note 2 below.
23 In German: *Moral*.
24 In German: *Moralität*.

92

Origin of justice. Justice (fairness) originates among approximately *equal powers*, as Thucydides (in the horrifying conversation between the Athenian and Melian envoys)[25] rightly understood. When there is no clearly recognizable supreme power and a battle would lead to fruitless and mutual injury, one begins to think of reaching an understanding and negotiating the claims on both sides: the initial character of justice is *barter*. Each satisfies the other in that each gets what he values more than the other. Each man gives the other what he wants, to keep henceforth, and receives in turn that which he wishes. Thus, justice is requital and exchange on the assumption of approximately equal positions of strength. For this reason, revenge belongs initially to the realm of justice: it is an exchange. Likewise gratitude. Justice naturally goes back to the viewpoint of an insightful self-preservation, that is, to the egoism of this consideration: "Why should I uselessly injure myself and perhaps not reach my goal anyway?" So much about the *origin* of justice. Because men, in line with their intellectual habits, have *forgotten* the original purpose of so-called just, fair actions, and particularly because children have been taught for centuries to admire and imitate such actions, it has gradually come to appear that a just action is a selfless one. The high esteem of these actions rests upon this appearance, an esteem which, like all estimations, is also always in a state of growth: for men strive after, imitate, and reproduce with their own sacrifices that which is highly esteemed, and it grows because its worth is increased by the worth of the effort and exertion made by each individual. How slight the morality of the world would seem without forgetfulness! A poet could say that God had stationed forgetfulness as a guardian at the door to the temple of human dignity.

[. . .]

96

Mores and morality.[26] To be moral, correct, ethical means to obey an age-old law or tradition. Whether one submits to it gladly or with difficulty makes no difference; enough that one submits. We call "good" the man who does the moral thing[27] as if by nature, after a long history of inheritance – that is, easily, and gladly, whatever it is (he will, for example, practice revenge when that is considered moral, as in the older Greek culture). He is called good because he is good "for" something. But because, as mores changed, goodwill, pity, and the like were always felt to be "good for" something, useful, it is primarily the man of goodwill, the helpful man, who is called "good." To be evil is to be "not moral" (immoral),[28] to practice bad habits, go against tradition, however reasonable or stupid it may be. To harm one's fellow, however, has been felt

---

25   In *History of the Peloponnesian War* (V. 85–113), Thucydides recounts the surrender of Melos in 416 B.C.

26   In German: *Sitte und sittlich* (correction of translator's note). The first three words Nietzsche uses in this paragraph to speak of the moral are, in German: *Moralisch, sittlich, ethisch.*

27   In German: *das Sittliche.*

28   In German: *"nicht sittlich"* (*unsittlich*).

primarily as injurious in all moral codes of different times, so that when we hear the word "bad" now, we think particularly of voluntary injury to one's fellow. When men determine between moral and immoral, good and evil, the basic opposition is not "egoism" and "selflessness," but rather adherence to a tradition or law, and release from it. The *origin* of the tradition makes no difference, at least concerning good and evil, or an immanent categorical imperative; but is rather above all for the purpose of main-taining a *community*, a people. Every superstitious custom, originating in a coincidence that is interpreted falsely, forces a tradition that it is moral to follow. To release oneself from it is dangerous, even more injurious for the *community* than for the individual (because the divinity punishes the whole community for sacrilege and violation of its rights, and the individual only as a part of that community). Now, each tradition grows more venerable the farther its origin lies in the past, the more it is forgotten; the respect paid to the tradition accumulates from generation to generation; finally the origin becomes sacred and awakens awe; and thus the morality of piety is in any case much older than that morality which requires selfless acts.

[. . .]

106

At the waterfall. When we see a waterfall, we think we see freedom of will and choice in the innumerable turnings, windings, breakings of the waves; but everything is neces-sary; each movement can be calculated mathematically. Thus it is with human actions; if one were omniscient, one would be able to calculate each individual action in advance, each step in the progress of knowledge, each error, each act of malice. To be sure, the acting man is caught in his illusion of volition; if the wheel of the world were to stand still for a moment and an omniscient, calculating mind were there to take advantage of this interruption, he would be able to tell into the farthest future of each being and describe every rut that wheel will roll upon. The acting man's delusion about himself, his assumption that free will exists, is also part of the calculable mechanism.

107

Irresponsibility and innocence.[29] Man's complete lack of responsibility, for his behavior and for his nature, is the bitterest drop which the man of knowledge must swallow, if he had been in the habit of seeing responsibility and duty as humanity's claim to nobil-ity. All his judgments, distinctions, dislikes have thereby become worthless and wrong: the deepest feeling he had offered a victim or a hero was misdirected; he may no longer praise, no longer blame, for it is nonsensical to praise and blame nature and necessity. Just as he loves a good work of art, but does not praise it, because it can do nothing about itself, just as he regards a plant, so he must regard the actions of men and his own actions. He can admire their strength, beauty, abundance, but he may not find any earned merit in them: chemical processes, and the clash of elements, the agony of the sick man who yearns for recovery, these have no more earned merit than do those inner struggles and crises in which a man is torn back and forth by various motives until he finally decides for the most powerful – as is said (in truth until the most power-ful motive decides about us). But all these motives, whatever great names we give

---

29   In German: *Unverantwortlichkeit und Unschuld.*

them, have grown out of the same roots which are thought to hold the evil poisons. Between good and evil actions there is no difference in type; at most, a difference in degree. Good actions are sublimated evil actions; evil actions are good actions become coarse and stupid. The individual's only demand, for self-enjoyment (along with the fear of losing it), is satisfied in all circumstances: man may act as he can, that is, as he must, whether in deeds of vanity, revenge, pleasure, usefulness, malice, cunning, or in deeds of sacrifice, pity, knowledge. His powers of judgment determine where a man will let this demand for self-enjoyment take him. In each society, in each individual, a hierarchy of the good is always present, by which man determines his own actions and judges other people's actions. But this standard is continually in flux; many actions are called evil, and are only stupid, because the degree of intelligence which chose them was very low. Indeed, in a certain sense *all* actions are stupid even now, for the highest degree of human intelligence which can now be attained will surely be surpassed. And then, in hindsight, all *our* behavior and judgments will appear as inadequate and rash as the behavior and judgments of backward savage tribes now seem to us inadequate and rash. To understand all this can cause great pain, but afterwards there is consolation. These pains are birth pangs. The butterfly wants to break through his cocoon; he tears at it, he rends it: then he is blinded and confused by the unknown light, the realm of freedom. Men who are *capable* of that sorrow (how few they will be!) will make the first attempt to see if mankind *can transform itself* from a *moral* into a *wise* mankind. In those individuals, the sun of a new gospel is casting its first ray onto the highest mountaintop of the soul; the fog is condensing more thickly than ever, and the brightest light and cloudiest dusk lie next to each other. Everything is necessity: this is the new knowledge, and this knowledge itself is necessity. Everything is innocence: and knowledge is the way to insight into this innocence. If pleasure, egoism, vanity are *necessary* for the generation of moral phenomena and their greatest flower, the sense for true and just knowledge; if error and confusion of imagination were the only means by which mankind could raise itself gradually to this degree of self-illumination and self-redemption – who could scorn those means? Who could be sad when he perceives the goal to which those paths lead? Everything in the sphere of morality[30] has evolved; changeable, fluctuating, everything is fluid, it is true: but *everything is also streaming onward* – to one goal. Even if the inherited habit of erroneous esteeming, loving, hating continues to govern us, it will grow weaker under the influence of growing knowledge: a new habit, that of understanding, non-loving, non-hating, surveying is gradually being implanted in us on the same ground, and in thousands of years will be powerful enough perhaps to give mankind the strength to produce wise, innocent (conscious of their innocence)[31] men as regularly as it now produces unwise, unfair men, conscious of their guilt[32] – *these men are the necessary first stage, not the opposite of those to come.*

[. . .]

30   In German: *Moral.*
31   In German: *unschuld-bewussten.*
32   In German: *schuldbewussten.*

Section 4: From the Soul of Artists and Writers

178

The incomplete as the effective. As figures in relief sometimes strike the imagination so powerfully because they seem to be on the point of stepping out of the wall and, hindered by something, suddenly come to a stop; so the relieflike, incomplete representation of a thought, or of a whole philosophy, is sometimes more effective than its exhaustive realization. More is left to the effort of the viewer; he is incited to continue developing what comes so intensely lit and shaded into relief before him, to think it through, and to overcome himself the obstacle that hindered until then its complete emergence.

[. . .]

208

The book become almost human. Every writer is surprised anew when a book, as soon as it has separated from him, begins to take on a life of its own. He feels as if one part of an insect had been severed and were going its own way. Perhaps he almost forgets the book; perhaps he rises above the views set down in it; perhaps he no longer understands it and has lost those wings on which he soared when he devised that book. Meanwhile, it goes about finding its readers, kindles life, pleases, horrifies, fathers new works, becomes the soul of others' resolutions and behavior. In short, it lives like a being fitted out with mind and soul − yet it is nevertheless not human. The most fortunate author is one who is able to say as an old man that all he had of life-giving, invigorating, uplifting, enlightening thoughts and feelings still lives on in his writings, and that he himself is only the gray ash, while the fire has been rescued and carried forth everywhere. If one considers, then, that a man's every action, not only his books, in some way becomes the occasion for other actions, decisions, and thoughts; that everything which is happening is inextricably tied to everything which will happen; then one understands the real *immortality*, that of movement: what once has moved is like an insect in amber, enclosed and immortalized in the general intertwining of all that exists.

[. . .]

213

Joy in nonsense. How can men take joy in nonsense? They do so, wherever there is laughter − in fact, one can almost say that wherever there is happiness there is joy in nonsense. It gives us pleasure to turn experience into its opposite, to turn purposefulness into purposelessness, necessity into arbitrariness, in such a way that the process does no harm and is performed simply out of high spirits. For it frees us momentarily from the forces of necessity, purposefulness, and experience, in which we usually see our merciless masters. We can laugh and play when the expected (which usually frightens us and makes us tense) is discharged without doing harm. It is the slaves' joy at the Saturnalia.

[. . .]

222

What remains of art. It is true that with certain metaphysical assumptions, art has a much greater value – if it is believed, for example, that one's character is unchangeable and that the essence of the world is continually expressed in all characters and actions. Then the artist's work becomes the image of what *endures eternally.* In our way of thinking, however, the artist can give his image validity only for a time, because man as a whole has evolved and is changeable, and not even an individual is fixed or enduring. The same is true of another metaphysical assumption: were our visible world only appearance,[33] as metaphysicians assume, then art would come rather close to the real world; for there would be much similarity between the world of appearance and the artist's world of dream images; the remaining difference would actually enhance the meaning of art rather than the meaning of nature, because art would portray the symmetry, the types and models of nature. But such assumptions are wrong: what place remains for art, then, after this knowledge? Above all, for thousands of years, it has taught us to see every form of life with interest and joy, and to develop our sensibility so that we finally call out, "However it may be, life is good."[34] This teaching of art – to have joy in existence and to regard human life as a part of nature, without being moved too violently, as something that developed through laws – this teaching has taken root in us; it now comes to light again as an all-powerful need for knowledge. We could give art up, but in doing so we would not forfeit what it has taught us to do. Similarly, we have given up religion, but not the emotional intensification and exaltation it led to. As plastic art and music are the standard for the wealth of feeling really earned and won through religion, so the intense and manifold joy in life, which art implants in us, would still demand satisfaction were art to disappear. The scientific man is a further development of the artistic man.

[. . .]

Section 5: Signs of Higher and Lower Culture

224

Ennoblement through degeneration. History[35] teaches us that that part of a people maintains itself best whose members generally share a vital public spirit, due to the similarity of their long-standing, incontrovertible principles, that is, of their common faith. In their case, good, sound custom strengthens them; they are taught to subordinate the individual, and their character is given solidity, at first innately and later through education. The danger in these strong communities, founded on similar, steadfast individual members, is an increasing, inherited stupidity, which follows all stability like a shadow. In such communities, *spiritual progress* depends on those individuals who are less bound, much less certain, and morally weaker; they are men who try new things, and many different things. Because of their weakness, countless such men are destroyed without having much visible effect; but in general, especially if they have descendants, they

---

33 In German: *Erscheinung.*
34 The last line of Goethe's poem "Der Bräutigam" ("The Betrothed").
35 In German: *Geschichte.*

loosen things up, and, from time to time, deliver a wound to the stable element of a community. Precisely at this wounded, weakened place, the common body is *inoculated*, so to speak, with something new; however, the community's overall strength has to be great enough to take this new thing into its bloodstream and assimilate it. Wherever progress is to ensue, deviating natures are of greatest importance. Every progress of the whole must be preceded by a partial weakening. The strongest natures *retain* the type, the weaker ones help to *advance* it. Something similar also happens in the individual. There is rarely a degeneration, a truncation, or even a vice or any physical or moral loss without an advantage somewhere else. In a warlike and restless clan, for example, the sicklier man may have occasion to be alone, and may therefore become quieter and wiser; the one-eyed man will have *one* eye the stronger; the blind man will see deeper inwardly, and certainly hear better. To this extent, the famous theory of the survival of the fittest[36] does not seem to me to be the only viewpoint from which to explain the progress of strengthening of a man or of a race. Rather, two things must coincide: first of all, stable power must increase through minds bound in faith and communal feeling; and secondly, it must be possible to attain higher goals when degenerating natures partially weaken or wound the stable power; it is precisely the weaker nature, as the more delicate and free, that makes progress possible at all. If a people starts to crumble and grow weak at some one place, but is still strong and healthy in general, it can accept being infected with something new, and can incorporate it to its advantage. The task of education is to make the individual so firm and sure that, as a whole being, he can no longer be diverted from his path. But then the educator must wound him, or use the wounds that fate delivers; when pain and need have come about in this way, something new and noble can also be inoculated into the wounded places. His whole nature will take it in, and show the ennoblement later in its fruits. Regarding the state, Machiavelli says that "the form of governments is of very slight importance, although semi-educated people think otherwise. The great goal of politics should be *permanence*, which outweighs anything else, being much more valuable than freedom."[37] Only when permanence is securely established and guaranteed is there any possibility of constant development and ennobling inoculation, which, to be sure, will usually be opposed by the dangerous companion of all permanence: authority.

225

The free spirit a relative concept. A man is called a free spirit if he thinks otherwise than would be expected, based on his origin, environment, class, and position, or based on prevailing contemporary views. He is the exception: bound spirits are the rule; the latter reproach him that his free principles have their origin either in a need to be noticed, or else may even lead one to suspect him of free actions, that is, actions that are irreconcilable with bound morality. Sometimes it is also said that certain free

---

36 As propounded by Darwin in *On the Origin of Species* (1859).
37 Niccolò Machiavelli (1469–1527), Italian political theorist and historian, author of works such as *Il principe* (*The Prince*, 1513), *Discorsi* (*Discourses*, ca. 1519) and *L'Arte della guerra* (*The Art of War*, 1521). The source of Nietzsche's quotation has not been identified.

principles derive from perverseness and eccentricity; but this is only the voice of malice, which does not, itself, believe what it says, but only wants to hurt: for the free
spirit generally has proof of his greater kindness and sharp intellect written so legibly
on his face that bound spirits understand it well enough. But the two other deriva-
tions of free-thinking are meant honestly; and many free spirits do indeed come into
being in one or the other of these ways. But the tenets they arrive at thereby could
still be more true and reliable than the tenets of bound spirits. In the knowledge of
truth, what matters is *having* it, not what made one seek it, or how one found it. If the
free spirits are right, the bound spirits are wrong, whether or not the former came to
truth out of immorality and the others have kept clinging to untruth out of morality.[38]
Incidentally, it is not part of the nature of the free spirit that his views are more correct, but rather that he has released himself from tradition, be it successfully or unsuccessfully. Usually, however, he has truth, or at least the spirit of the search for truth,
on his side: he demands reasons, while others demand faith.

[. . .]

251

Future of science. To the man who works and searches in it, science gives much pleasure;
to the man who *learns* its results, very little. But since all important scientific truths
must eventually become everyday and commonplace, even this small amount of pleasure
ceases; just as we have long ago ceased to enjoy learning the admirable multiplication
tables. Now, if science produces ever less joy in itself and takes ever greater joy in casting suspicion on the comforts of metaphysics, religion, and art, then the greatest source
of pleasure, to which mankind owes almost its whole humanity, is impoverished. Therefore
a higher culture must give man a double brain, two brain chambers, as it were, one
to experience science, and one to experience nonscience. Lying next to one another,
without confusion, separable, self-contained: our health demands this. In the one domain
lies the source of strength, in the other the regulator. Illusions,[39] biases, passions must give
heat; with the help of scientific knowledge, the pernicious and dangerous consequences
of overheating must be prevented. If this demand made by higher culture is not satisfied,
we can almost certainly predict the further course of human development: interest in
truth will cease, the less it gives pleasure; illusion, error, and fantasies, because they
are linked with pleasure, will reconquer their former territory step by step; the ruin
of the sciences and relapse into barbarism follow next. Mankind will have to begin
to weave its cloth from the beginning again, after having, like Penelope, destroyed it
in the night. But who will guarantee that we will keep finding the strength to do so?

[. . .]

270

The art of reading. Every strong orientation is one-sided; it approaches the orientation
of a straight line, and, like it, is exclusive; that is, it does not touch on many other
orientations, as weak parties and natures do in their wavelike vacillation. Thus one
must excuse the philologists for being one-sided. The guild's century-long practice of

38   In this sentence Nietzsche uses the words *Unmoralität* and *Moralität*.
39   In German: *Illusionen*.

producing and preserving texts, as well as explaining them, has finally permitted the discovery of the right methods. The whole Middle Ages was profoundly incapable of a strictly philological explanation, incapable, that is, of the simple wish to understand what the author says. It was something to find these methods; let us not underestimate it! All science has gained continuity and stability only because the art of reading correctly that is, philology, attained its full power.

[. . .]

278

Analogy of the dance. Today we should consider it the decisive sign of great culture if someone possesses the strength and flexibility to pursue knowledge purely and rigorously and, at other times, to give poetry, religion, and metaphysics a handicap, as it were, and appreciate their power and beauty. A position of this sort, between two such different claims, is very difficult, for science urges the absolute dominion of its method, and if this is not granted, there exists the other danger of a feeble vacillation between different impulses. Meanwhile (to open up a view to the solution of this difficulty by means of an analogy, at least) one might remember that *dancing* is not the same thing as staggering wearily back and forth between different impulses. High culture will resemble a daring dance, thus requiring, as we said, much strength and flexibility.

[. . .]

Section 8: A Look at the State

472

Religion and government. As long as the state, or more precisely, the government knows that it is appointed as trustee on behalf of a group of people in their minority, and for their sake considers the question whether religion is to be preserved or eliminated, it will most probably always decide to preserve religion. For religion appeases the individual soul in times of loss, privation, fear, or mistrust, that is, when government feels itself unable to do anything directly to alleviate the private man's inner suffering; even during universal, inevitable, and initially unpreventable misfortunes (famines, financial crises, wars), religion gives the masses a calm, patient and trusting bearing. Wherever the necessary or coincidental failings of a state government, or the dangerous consequences of dynastic interests catch the eye of a man of insight and make him recalcitrant, the uninsightful will think they are seeing the finger of God, and will submit patiently to the directives from *Above* (in which concept, divine and human ways of government are usually merged). Thus the citizens' inner peace and a continuity of development will be preserved. Religion protects and seals the power that lies in the unity of popular sentiment, in identical opinions and goals for all, discounting those rare cases when a priesthood and the state power cannot agree about the price and enter into battle. Usually, the state will know how to win the priests over, because it needs their most private, secret education of souls and knows how to appreciate servants who seem outwardly to represent a quite different interest. Without the help of priests, no power can become "legitimate" even now – as Napoleon understood. Thus, absolute tutelary government and the careful preservation of religion necessarily go together. It is to be presumed that ruling persons and classes will be enlightened about the benefit provided them by religion, and thus feel somewhat superior to it, in that they are using it as a tool: and this is the origin of freethinking. But what if a quite different view of the concept of government, as it is taught in *democratic* states, begins to prevail? If one sees in government nothing but the instrument of popular will, no Above in contrast to a Below, but solely a function of the single sovereign, the people? Then the government can only take the same position toward religion that the people hold; any spread of enlightenment will have to reverberate right into its representatives; it will not be so easy to use or exploit religious energies and comforts for state purposes (unless powerful party leaders occasionally exert an influence similar to that of enlightened despotism). But if the state may no longer draw any use from religion itself, or if the people think so variously about religious matters that the government cannot take uniform, unified measures regarding religion, then the necessary alternative will appear to be to treat religion as a private matter and consign it to the conscience and habits of each individual. At the very first, the result is that religious feeling appears to be strengthened, to the extent that hidden or repressed stirrings of it, which the state had unwittingly or deliberately stifled, now break out and exceed all limits; later, it turns out that religion is overrun with sects, and that an abundance of dragon's teeth had been sown at the moment when religion was made a private affair. Finally, the sight of the strife, and the hostile exposure of all the weaknesses of religious confessions allow no other alternative but that every superior and more gifted man makes irreligiosity his private concern. Then this attitude also prevails in the minds of those who govern, and gives, almost against their will, an antireligious character to the measures they take. As soon as this happens, the people who are still moved by religion, and who used to adore the state as something half-divine or wholly divine, develop an attitude decidedly *hostile to the state*; they attack government measures, try to impede, cross, disturb as much as they can, and because their opposition is so heated, they drive the other party, the irreligious one, into an almost fanatical enthusiasm *for* the state; also contributing secretly to this is the fact that, since they parted from religion, the nonreligious have had a feeling of emptiness and are provisionally trying to create a substitute, a kind of fulfillment, through devotion to the state. After these transitional struggles, which may last a long time, it is finally decided whether the religious parties are still strong enough to resurrect an old state of affairs and turn the wheel back – in which case, the state inevitably falls into the hands of enlightened despotism (perhaps less enlightened and more fearful than before) – or whether the nonreligious parties prevail, undermining and finally thwarting the propagation of their opponents for a few generations, perhaps by means of schools and education. Yet of their enthusiasm for the state will also diminish then. It becomes more and more clear that when religious adoration, which makes the state into a *mysterium*, a transcendent institution, is shaken, so is the reverent and pious relationship to the state. Henceforth, individuals see only the side of it that can be helpful or harmful to them; they press forward with all the means in their power to get an influence over it. But soon this competition becomes too great; men and parties switch too quickly; too impetuously, they throw each other down from the mountain, after they have scarcely arrived at the top. There is no guarantee that any measure a government puts through will endure; people shy away from undertakings that would have to grow quietly over decades or centuries in order to produce ripe fruit. No longer does any-

one feel an obligation toward a law, other than to bow instantaneously to the power
that introduced it; at once, however, people begin to undermine it with a new power,
a new majority yet to be formed. Finally (one can state it with certainty) the distrust
of anything that governs, the insight into the uselessness and irritation of these short-
lived struggles, must urge men to a quite new decision: the abolition of the concept
of the state, the end of the antithesis "private and public." Step by step, private com-
panies incorporate state businesses; even the most stubborn vestige of the old work of
governing (for example, that activity which is supposed to secure private parties against
other private parties) will ultimately be taken care of by private contractors. Neglect,
decline, and *death of the state*, the unleashing of the private person (I am careful not
to say "of the individual") – this is the result of the democratic concept of the state;
this is its mission. If it has fulfilled its task (which, like everything human, includes
much reason and unreason), if all the relapses of the old illness have been overcome,
then a new leaf in the storybook of humanity will be turned; on it one will read all
sorts of strange histories, and perhaps some good things as well. To recapitulate briefly,
the interests of tutelary government and the interests of religion go together hand in
hand, so that if the latter begins to die out, the foundation of the state will also be
shaken. The belief in a divine order of political affairs, in a *mysterium* in the existence
of the state, has a religious origin; if religion disappears, the state will inevitably lose
its old veil of Isis[40] and no longer awaken awe. The sovereignty of the people, seen
closely, serves to scare off even the last trace of magic and superstition contained in
these feelings; modern democracy is the historical form of the *decline of the state*. But
the prospect resulting from this certain decline is not an unhappy one in every respect:
of all their qualities, men's cleverness and selfishness are the best developed; when the
state no longer satisfies the demands of these energies, chaos will be the last thing to
occur. Rather, an invention even more expedient than the state will triumph over the
state. Mankind has already seen many an organizational power die out, for example,
associations by sex, which for thousands of years were much more powerful than the
family, indeed held sway and organized society long before the family existed. We
ourselves are witnessing how the significant legal and political idea of the family, which
once ruled as far as Roman culture reached, is growing ever fainter and feebler. Thus
a later generation will also see the state become meaningless in certain stretches of the
earth – an idea that many men today can hardly contemplate without fear and abhor-
rence. To be sure, to *work* on the spread and realization of this idea is something else
again: one must have a very arrogant opinion of his own reason and only a superficial
understanding of history to set his hand to the plough right now – while there is still
no one who can show us the seeds that are to be strewn afterwards on the ravaged
earth. So let us trust to "men's cleverness and selfishness" that the state will *still* endure
for a good while, and that the destructive efforts of overzealous and rash pretenders
to knowledge will be repulsed!

473

Socialism in respect to its means. Socialism is the visionary younger brother of an almost
decrepit despotism, whose heir it wants to be. Thus its efforts are reactionary in the

---

40 Egyptian fertility goddess, whose cult spread throughout the Roman empire.

deepest sense. For it desires a wealth of executive power, as only despotism had it; indeed, it outdoes everything in the past by striving for the downright destruction of the individual, which it sees as an unjustified luxury of nature, and which it intends to improve into an expedient *organ of the community*. Socialism crops up in the vicinity of all excessive displays of power because of its relation to it, like the typical old social-ist Plato, at the court of the Sicilian tyrant;[41] it desires (and in certain circumstances, furthers) the Caesarean power state of this century, because, as we said, it would like to be its heir. But even this inheritance would not suffice for its purposes; it needs the most submissive subjugation of all citizens to the absolute state, the like of which has never existed. And since it cannot even count any longer on the old religious piety towards the state, having rather always to work automatically to eliminate piety (because it works on the elimination of all existing *states*), it can only hope to exist here and there for short periods of time by means of the most extreme terrorism. Therefore, it secretly prepares for reigns of terror, and drives the word "justice" like a nail into the heads of the semieducated masses, to rob them completely of their reason (after this reason has already suffered a great deal from its semieducation), and to give them a good conscience for the evil game that they are supposed to play. Socialism can serve as a rather brutal and forceful way to teach the danger of all accumulations of state power, and to that extent instill one with distrust of the state itself. When its rough voice chimes in with the battle cry "*As much state as possible*," it will at first make the cry noisier than ever; but soon the opposite cry will be heard with strength the greater: "*As little state as possible.*"

[. . .]

475

The European man and the destruction of nations. Commerce and industry, traffic in books and letters, the commonality of all higher culture, quick changes of locality and land-scape, the present-day nomadic life of all nonlandowners – these conditions necessar-ily bring about a weakening and ultimately a destruction of nations, or at least of European nations; so that a mixed race, that of the European man, has to originate out of all of them, as the result of continual crossbreeding. The isolation of nations due to engen-dered *national* hostilities now works against this goal, consciously or unconsciously, but the mixing process goes on slowly, nevertheless, despite those intermittent counter-currents; this artificial nationalism, by the way, is as dangerous as artificial Catholicism was, for it is in essence a forcible state of emergency and martial law, imposed by the few on the many, and requiring cunning, lies, and force to remain respectable. It is not the self-interest of the many (the people), as one would have it, that urges this nationalism, but primarily the self-interest of certain royal dynasties, as well as that of certain commercial and social classes; once a man has understood this, he should be undaunted in presenting himself as a *good European*, and should work actively on the merging of nations. The Germans, because of their age-old, proven trait of being

---

41   In 388 B.C. Plato visited the court of the Sicilian tyrant Dionysius the Elder in Syracuse, where he returned in 367 and 361 B.C., hoping to realize his political ideals there.

the *nations' interpreter and mediator*, will be able to help in this process. Incidentally, the whole problem of the *Jews* exists only within national states, inasmuch as their energy and higher intelligence, their capital of spirit and will, which accumulated from generation to generation in the long school of their suffering, must predominate to a degree that awakens envy and hatred; and so, in the literature of nearly all present-day nations (and, in fact, in proportion to their renewed nationalistic behavior), there is an increase in the literary misconduct that leads the Jews to the slaughter-house, as scapegoats for every possible public and private misfortune. As soon as it is no longer a matter of preserving nations, but rather of producing the strongest possible mixed European race, the Jew becomes as useful and desirable an ingredient as any other national quantity. Every nation, every man has disagreeable, even dangerous character-istics; it is cruel to demand that the Jew should be an exception. Those character-istics may even be especially dangerous and frightful in him, and perhaps the youthful Jew of the stock exchange is the most repugnant invention of the whole human race. Nevertheless, I would like to know how much one must excuse in the overall account-ing of a people which, not without guilt on all our parts, has had the most sorrowful history of all peoples, and to whom we owe the noblest human being (Christ), the purest philosopher (Spinoza), the mightiest book, and the most effective moral code in the world. Furthermore, in the darkest medieval times, when the Asiatic cloud had settled heavily over Europe, it was the Jewish free-thinkers, scholars, and doctors, who, under the harshest personal pressure, held fast to the banner of enlightenment and intellectual independence, and defended Europe against Asia; we owe to their efforts not least, that a more natural, rational, and in any event unmythical explanation of the world could finally triumph again, and that the ring of culture which now links us to the enlightenment of Greco-Roman antiquity, remained unbroken. If Christianity did everything possible to orientalize the Occident, then Judaism helped substantially to occidentalize it again and again, which, in a certain sense, is to say that it made Europe's history and task into a *continuation of the Greek.*

[. . .]

Section 9: Man Alone with Himself

483

Enemies of truth. Convictions are more dangerous enemies of truth than lies.

[. . .]

486

The one necessary thing. A person must have one or the other: either a disposition which is easygoing by nature, or else a disposition eased by art and knowledge.

490

Idealists' delusion. All idealists imagine that the causes they serve are significantly bet-ter than the other causes in the world; they do not want to believe that if their cause is to flourish at all, it needs exactly the same foul-smelling manure that all other human undertakings require.

499

Friend. Shared joy, not compassion,[42] makes a friend.

[. . .]

508

Out in nature. We like to be out in nature so much because it has no opinion about us.

[. . .]

516

Truth. No one dies of fatal truths nowadays: there are too many antidotes.

[. . .]

519

Truth as Circe.[43] Error has turned animals into men; might truth be capable of turning man into an animal again?

[. . .]

523

Wanting to be loved. The demand to be loved is the greatest kind of arrogance.

[. . .]

553

Lower than the animal. When man howls with laughter, he surpasses all animals by his coarseness.

554

Superficial knowledge. He who speaks a bit of a foreign language has more delight in it than he who speaks it well; pleasure goes along with superficial knowledge.

[. . .]

580

Bad memory. The advantage of a bad memory is that, several times over, one enjoys the same good things for the first time.

[. . .]

---

42 In German: *Mitfreude, nicht Mitleiden.*
43 Circe: daughter of Helios and Perse in Greek mythology, a seductress who, in Homer's *Odyssey* (X. 210ff.), magically transforms half of Odysseus' crew into beasts.

586

The hour-hand of life. Life consists of rare, isolated moments of the greatest significance, and of innumerably many intervals, during which at best the silhouettes of those moments hover about us. Love, springtime, every beautiful melody, mountains, the moon, the sea – all these speak completely to the heart but once, if in fact they ever do get a chance to speak completely. For many men do not have those moments at all, and are themselves intervals and intermissions in the symphony of real life.

[. . .]

589

The first thought of the day. The best way to begin each day well is to think upon awakening whether we could not give at least one person pleasure on this day. If this practice could be accepted as a substitute for the religious habit of prayer, our fellow men would benefit by this change.

[. . .]

609

Age and truth. Young people love what is interesting and odd, no matter how true or false it is. More mature minds love what is interesting and odd about truth. Fully mature intellects, finally, love truth, even when it appears plain and simle, boring to the ordinary person; for they have noticed that truth tends to reveal its highest wisdom in the guise of simplicity.

[. . .]

616

Alienated from the present. There are great advantages in for once removing ourselves distinctly from our time and letting ourselves be driven from its shore back into the ocean of former world views. Looking at the coast from that perspective, we survey for the first time its entire shape, and when we near it again, we have the advantage of understanding it better on the whole than do those who have never left it.

[. . .]

618

A philosophical frame of mind. Generally we strive to acquire *one* emotional stance, *one* viewpoint for all life situations and events: we usually call that being of a philosophical frame of mind. But rather than making oneself uniform, we may find greater value for the enrichment of knowledge by listening to the soft voice of different life situations; each brings its own views with it. Thus we acknowledge and share the life and nature of many by not treating ourselves like rigid, invariable, single individuals.

[. . .]

636

To be sure, there is also quite another category of genius, that of justice; and I can in no way see fit to esteem that kind lower than any philosophical, political, or artistic genius. It is its way to avoid with hearty indignation everything which blinds and confuses our judgment about things; thus it is an *enemy of convictions*, for it wants to give each thing its due, be it living or dead, real or fictive – and to do so it must apprehend it clearly. Therefore it places each thing in the best light and walks all around it with an attentive eye. Finally it will even give its due to its opponent, to blind or shortsighted "conviction" (as men call it; women call it "faith") – for the sake of truth.

14

Daybreak: Thoughts on the Prejudices of Morality (1881)

Book I

9

Concept of morality of custom.[1] – In comparison with the mode of life of whole millennia of mankind we present-day men live in a very immoral age:[2] the power of custom is astonishingly enfeebled and the moral sense so rarefied and lofty it may be described as having more or less evaporated. That is why the fundamental insights into the origin of morality are so difficult for us latecomers, and even when we have acquired them we find it impossible to enunciate them, because they sound so uncouth or because they seem to slander morality! This is, for example, already the case with the *chief proposition*: morality is nothing other (therefore *no more!*) than obedience to customs, of whatever kind they may be; customs, however, are the *traditional* way of behaving and evaluating. In things in which no tradition commands there is no morality; and the less life is determined by tradition, the smaller the circle of morality. The free human being is immoral because in all things he is *determined* to depend upon himself and not upon a tradition: in all the original conditions of mankind, 'evil' signifies the same as 'individual', 'free', 'capricious', 'unusual', 'unforeseen', 'incalculable'. Judged by the standard of these conditions, if an action is performed *not* because tradition commands it but for other motives (because of its usefulness to the individual, for example), even indeed for precisely the motives which once founded the tradition, it is called immoral and is felt to be so by him who performed it: for it was not performed in obedience to tradition. What is tradition? A higher authority which

---

1 In German: *Begriff der Sittlichkeit der Sitte.*
2 In German: *unsittlichen Zeit.* As Nietzsche goes on to make clear, he means that the 'power of custom' (*Sitte*) has grown weak and the "moral sense" (*das Gefühl der Sittlichkeit*), i.e. conformity to customs and traditional ways of living and evaluating, is now something difficult for us to feel and experience. When Nietzsche defines and speaks of morality in this section it is in the sense of tradition and custom (*Sittlichkeit*).

one obeys, not because it commands what is *useful* to us, but because it *commands*. – What distinguishes this feeling in the presence of tradition from the feeling of fear in general? It is fear in the presence of a higher intellect which here commands, of an incomprehensible, indefinite power, of something more than personal – there is *superstition* in this fear. – Originally all education and care of health, marriage, cure of sickness, agriculture, war, speech and silence, traffic with one another and with the gods belonged within the domain of morality: they demanded one observe prescriptions *without thinking of oneself* as an individual. Originally, therefore, everything was custom, and whoever wanted to elevate himself above it had to become lawgiver and medicine man and a kind of demi-god: that is to say, he had to *make customs* – a dreadful, mortally dangerous thing! Who is the most moral man? *First*, he who obeys the law most frequently: who, like the Brahmin, bears a consciousness of the law with him everywhere and into every minute division of time, so that he is continually inventive in creating opportunities for obeying the law. *Then*, he who obeys it even in the most difficult cases. The most moral man is he who *sacrifices* the most to custom: what, however, are the greatest sacrifices? The way in which this question is answered determines the development of several divers kinds of morality; but the most important distinction remains that which divides the morality of *most frequent obedience* from that of the *most difficult* obedience. Let us not deceive ourselves as to the motivation of that morality which demands difficulty of obedience to custom as the mark of morality! Self-overcoming[3] is demanded, *not* on account of the useful consequences it may have for the individual, but so that the hegemony of custom, tradition, shall be made evident in despite of the private desires and advantages of the individual: the individual is to sacrifice himself – that is the commandment of morality of custom. – Those moralists, on the other hand, who, following in the footsteps of Socrates, offer the *individual* a morality[4] of self-control and temperance as a means to his own *advantage*, as his personal key to happiness, *are the exceptions* – and if it seems otherwise to us that is because we have been brought up in their after-effect: they all take a new path under the highest disapprobation of all advocates of morality of custom – they cut themselves off from the community, as immoral men, and are in the profoundest sense evil. Thus to a virtuous Roman of the old stamp every *Christian* who 'considered first of all his *own* salvation' appeared – evil. – Everywhere that a community, and consequently a morality of custom exists, the idea also predominates that punishment for breaches of custom will fall before all on the community: that supernatural punishment whose forms of expression and limitations are so hard to comprehend and are explored with so much superstitious fear. The community can compel the individual to compensate another individual or the community for the immediate injury his action has brought in its train; it can also take a kind of revenge on the individual for having, as a supposed after-effect of his action, caused the clouds and storms of divine anger to have gathered over the community – but it feels the individual's guilt above all as *its own* guilt and bears the punishment as *its own* punishment –: 'customs have grown lax', each wails in his soul, 'if such actions as this are possible'. Every individual action, every individual mode of thought arouses dread; it is impossible to compute what precisely the rarer, choicer, more original spirits in the whole course of history have had to suffer through being felt as evil and dangerous,

3   In German: *Die Selbstüberwindung*.
4   In German: *die Moral*.

indeed through *feeling themselves to be so*. Under the dominion of the morality of custom, originality of every kind has acquired a bad conscience; the sky above the best men is for this reason to this very moment gloomier than it need be.

[. . .]

30

Refined cruelty as virtue. – Here is a morality which rests entirely on the *drive to distinction* – do not think too highly of it! For what kind of a drive is that and what thought lies behind it? We want to make the sight of us *painful* to another and to awaken in him the feeling of envy and of his own impotence and degradation; by dropping on to his tongue a drop of *our* honey, and while doing him this supposed favour looking him keenly and mockingly in the eyes, we want to make him savour the bitterness of his fate. This person has become humble and is now perfect in his humility – seek for those whom he has for long wished to torture with it! you will find them soon enough! That person is kind to animals and is admired on account of it – but there are certain people on whom he wants to vent his cruelty by this means. There stands a great artist: the pleasure he anticipated in the envy of his defeated rivals allowed his powers no rest until he had become great – how many bitter moments has his becoming great not cost the souls of others! The chastity of the nun: with what punitive eyes it looks into the faces of women who live otherwise! how much joy in revenge there is in these eyes! – The theme is brief, the variations that might be played upon it might be endless but hardly tedious – for it is still a far too paradoxical and almost pain-inducing novelty that the morality of distinction is in its ultimate foundation pleasure in refined cruelty. In its ultimate foundation – in this case that means: in its first generation. For when the habit of some distinguishing action is *inherited*, the thought that lies behind it is not inherited with it (thoughts are not hereditary, only feelings): and provided it is not again reproduced by education, even the second generation fails to experience any pleasure in cruelty in connection with it, but only pleasure in the habit as such. *This* pleasure, however, is the first stage of the 'good'.

[. . .]

37

False conclusions from utility. – When one has demonstrated that a thing is of the highest utility, one has however thereby taken not one step towards explaining its origin: that is to say, one can never employ utility to make it comprehensible that a thing must necessarily exist. But it is the contrary judgment that has hitherto prevailed – and even into the domain of the most rigorous science. Even in the case of astronomy, has the (supposed) utility in the way the satellites are arranged (to compensate for the diminished light they receive owing to their greater distance from the sun, so that their inhabitants shall not go short of light) not been advanced as the final objective of this arrangement and the explanation of its origin? It reminds us of the reasoning of Columbus: the earth was made for man, therefore if countries exist they must be inhabited. 'Is it probable that the sun should shine on nothing, and that the nocturnal vigils of the stars are squandered upon pathless seas and countries unpeopled?'

[. . .]

44

Origin and significance. – Why is it that this thought comes back to me again and again and in ever more varied colours? – that *formerly*, when investigators of knowledge sought out the origin of things they always believed they would discover something of incalculable significance for all later action and judgment, that they always *presupposed*, indeed, that the *salvation* of man must depend on *insight into the origin of things*: but that now, on the contrary, the more we advance towards origins, the more our interest diminishes; indeed, that all the evaluations and 'interestedness' we have implanted into things begin to lose their meaning the further we go back and the closer we approach the things themselves. *The more insight we possess into an origin the less significant does the origin appear:* while *what is nearest to us*, what is around us and in us, gradually begins to display colours and beauties and enigmas and riches of significance of which earlier mankind had not an inkling. Formerly, thinkers prowled around angrily like captive animals, watching the bars of their cages and leaping against them in order to smash them down: and *happy* seemed he who through a gap in them believed he saw something of what was outside, of what was distant and beyond.

[. . .]

48

'Know yourself'[5] *is the whole of science.* – Only when he has attained a final knowledge of all things will man have come to know himself. For things are only the boundaries of man.

[. . .]

68

The first Christian.[6] – All the world still believes in the writings of the 'Holy Spirit' or stands in the after-effect of this belief: when one opens the Bible one does so to 'edify' oneself, to discover a signpost of consolation in one's own personal distress, great or small – in short, one reads oneself into and out of it. That it also contains the history of one of the most ambitious and importunate souls, of a mind as superstitious as it was cunning, the history of the apostle Paul – who, apart from a few scholars, knows that? But without this remarkable history, without the storms and confusions of such a mind, of such a soul, there would be no Christianity; we would hardly have heard of a little Jewish sect whose master died on the cross. To be sure: if this history had been understood at the right time, if the writings of Paul had been read, not as the revelations of the 'Holy Spirit', but with a free and honest exercise

5   The inscription on the Temple of Apollo at Delphi.
6   Paul was born in Tarsus into a strict Pharisaic Jewish family under the Hebrew name Saul and became converted to "Paul" after his encounter with the resurrected Jesus on the road to Damascus. The events to which Nietzsche refers in this section are recounted in the New Testament books of Acts and Galatians. In the latter Paul espouses an "inward" style of freedom as the path to salvation and the mark of the true Christian.

of one's own spirit and without thinking all the time of our own personal needs – *really read*, that is to say (but for fifteen hundred years there were no such readers) – Christianity would long since have ceased to exist: for these pages of the Jewish Pascal expose the origin of Christianity as thoroughly as the pages of the French Pascal expose its destiny and that by which it will perish. That the ship of Christianity threw overboard a good part of the Jewish ballast, that it went and was able to go among the heathen – that is a consequence of the history of this one man, of a very tormented, very pitiable, very unpleasant man who also found himself unpleasant. He suffered from a fixed idea, or more clearly from a *fixed question* which was always present to him and would never rest: what is the Jewish *law* really concerned with? and, in particular, what is the *fulfilment of this law*? In his youth he had himself wanted to satisfy it, voracious for this highest distinction the Jews were able to conceive – this people which had taken the fantasy of moral sublimity higher than any other people and which alone achieved the creation of a holy God, together with the idea of sin as an offence against this holiness. Paul had become at once the fanatical defender and chaperone of this God and his law, and was constantly combating and on the watch for transgressors and doubters, harsh and malicious towards them and with the extremest inclination for punishment. And then he discovered in himself that he himself – fiery, sensual, melancholy, malevolent in hatred as he was – *could* not fulfil the law, he discovered indeed what seemed to him the strangest thing of all: that his extravagant lust for power was constantly combating and on the watch for transgressors and goad. Is it really 'carnality' which again and again makes him a transgressor? And not rather, as he later suspected, behind it the law itself, which *must* continually prove itself unfulfillable and with irresistible magic lures on to transgression? But at that time he did not yet possess this way out of his difficulty. Many things lay on his conscience – he hints at enmity, murder, sorcery, idolatry, uncleanliness, drunkenness and pleasure in debauch – and however much he tried to relieve this conscience, and even more his lust for domination, through the extremest fanaticism in revering and defending the law, there were moments when he said to himself: 'It is all in vain! The torture of the unfulfilled law cannot be overcome.' Luther may have felt a similar thing when he wanted in his monastery to become the perfect man of the spiritual ideal: and similarly to Luther, who one day began to hate the spiritual ideal and the Pope and the saints and the whole clergy with a hatred the more deadly the less he dared to admit it to himself – a similar thing happened to Paul. The law was the cross to which he felt himself nailed: how he hated it! how he had to drag it along! how he sought about for a means of *destroying* it – and no longer to fulfil it! And at last the liberating idea came to him, together with a vision, as was bound to happen in the case of this epileptic: to him, the zealot of the law who was inwardly tired to death of it, there appeared on a lonely road Christ with the light of God shining in his countenance, and Paul heard the words: 'Why persecutest thou *me*?' What essentially happened then is rather this: his *mind* suddenly became clear: 'it is *unreasonable*', he says to himself, 'to persecute precisely this Christ! For here is the way out, here is perfect revenge, here and nowhere else do I have and hold the *destroyer of the law*!' Sick with the most tormented pride, at a stroke he feels himself recovered, the moral despair is as if blown away, destroyed – that is to say, *fulfilled*, there on the Cross! Hitherto that shameful *death* had counted with him as the principal argument against the 'Messiahdom' of which the followers of the new teaching spoke: but what if it were *necessary* for the *abolition* of the law! – The tremendous consequences of this notion, this solution of the riddle, whirl before his eyes, all at once he is the happiest of men – the destiny of the Jews – no, of all mankind – seems to him to be tied to this notion, to this second of his sudden enlightenment, he possesses the idea of ideas, the key of keys, the light of lights; henceforth history revolves around him! For from now on he is the teacher of the *destruction of the law*! To die to evil – that means also to die to the law; to exist in the flesh – that means also to exist in the law! To become one with Christ – that means also to become with him the destroyer of the law; to have died with him – that means also to have died to the law! Even if it is still possible to sin, it is no longer possible to sin against the law: 'I am outside the law.' 'If I were now to accept the law again and submit to it I should be making Christ an accomplice of sin', for the law existed so that sins might be committed, it continually brought sin forth as a sharp juice brings forth a disease; God could never have resolved on the death of Christ if a fulfilment of the law had been in any way possible without this death; now not only has all guilt been taken away, guilt as such has been destroyed; now the law is dead, now the carnality in which it dwelt is dead – or at least dying constantly away, as though decaying. Yet but a brief time within this decay! – that is the Christian's lot, before, become one with Christ, he arises with Christ, participates with Christ in divine glory and becomes a 'son of God', like Christ. – With that the intoxication of Paul is at its height, and likewise the importunity of his soul – with the idea of becoming one with Christ all shame, all subordination, all bounds are taken from it, and the intractable lust for power reveals itself as an anticipatory revelling in *divine* glories. – This is the *first Christian*, the inventor of Christianness! Before him there were only a few Jewish sectarians.

[. . .]

Book II

102

The oldest moral judgments. – What really are our reactions to the behaviour of some-one in our presence? – First of all, we see what there is in it *for us* – we regard it only from this point of view. We take *this* effect as the *intention* behind the behaviour – and finally we ascribe the harbouring of such intentions as a *permanent* quality of the person whose behaviour we are observing and thenceforth call him, for instance, 'a harmful person'. Threefold error! Threefold primeval blunder! Perhaps inherited from the animals and their power of judgment! Is the *origin of all morality* not to be sought in the detestable petty conclusions: 'what harms *me* is something *evil* (harmful in itself); what is useful *to me* is something *good* (beneficent and advantageous in itself); what harms me *once or several times* is the inimical as such and in itself; what is useful to me *once or several times* is the friendly as such and in itself'. *O pudenda origo!*[7] Does that not mean; to imagine that the paltry, occasional, often chance *relationship* of another with ourself is his *essence* and most essential being, and to assert that with the whole world and with himself he is capable only of those relationships we have experienced with him once or several times? And does there not repose behind this veritable folly

---

7   Latin: O shameful origin!

the most immodest of all secret thoughts: that, because good and evil are measured according to our reactions, we ourselves must constitute the principle of the good? –

103

There are two kinds of deniers of morality. – 'To deny morality'[8] – this can mean, *first*: to deny that the moral motives[9] which men *claim* have inspired their actions really have done so – it is thus the assertion that morality consists of words and is among the coarser or more subtle deceptions (especially self-deceptions) which men practise, and is perhaps so especially in precisely the case of those most famed for virtue. *Then* it can mean: to deny that moral judgments[10] are based on truths. Here it is admitted that they really are motives of action, but that in this way it is *errors* which, as the basis of all moral judgment, impel men to their moral actions. This is *my* point of view: though I should be the last to deny that *in very many cases* there is some ground for suspicion that the other point of view – that is to say, the point of view of La Rochefoucauld[11] and others who think like him – may also be justified and in any event of great general application. – Thus I deny morality as I deny alchemy, that is, I deny their premises: but I do *not* deny that there have been alchemists who believed in these premises and acted in accordance with them. – I also deny immorality:[12] *not* that countless people *feel* themselves to be immoral, but there is any *true* reason so to feel. It goes without saying that I do not deny – unless I am a fool – that many actions called immoral ought to be avoided and resisted, or that many called moral ought to be done and encouraged – but I think the one should be encouraged and the other avoided *for other reasons than hitherto.* We have to *learn to think differently* – in order at last, perhaps very late on, to attain even more: *to feel differently.*

[. . .]

115

The so-called 'ego'.[13] – Language and the prejudices upon which language is based are a manifold hindrance to us when we want to explain inner processes and drives: because of the fact, for example, that words really exist only for *superlative* degrees of these processes and drives; and where words are lacking, we are accustomed to abandon exact observation because exact thinking there becomes painful; indeed, in earlier times one involuntarily concluded that where the realm of words ceased the realm of existence ceased also. Anger, hatred, love, pity, desire, knowledge, joy, pain – all are names for *extreme* states: the milder, middle degrees, not to speak of the lower degrees which are continually in play, elude us, and yet it is they which weave the web of our character and our destiny. These extreme outbursts – and even the most moderate *conscious* pleasure or displeasure, while eating food or hearing a note, is perhaps, rightly understood, an extreme outburst – very often rend the web apart, and then they constitute

8 In German: *Die Sittlichkeit.*
9 In German: *die sittlichen Motive.*
10 In German: *die sittlichen Urtheile.*
11 See *HH* note 16 above.
12 In German: *die Unsittlichkeit.*
13 In German: *"Ich."*

violent exceptions, no doubt usually consequent on built-up congestions: – and, as such, how easy it is for them to mislead the observer! No less easy than it is for them to mislead the person in whom they occur. *We are none of us* that which we appear to be in accordance with the states for which alone we have consciousness and words, and consequently praise and blame; those cruder outbursts of which alone we are aware make us *misunderstand* ourselves, we draw a conclusion on the basis of data in which the exceptions outweigh the rule, we misread ourselves in this apparently most intelligible of handwriting on the nature of our self. *Our opinion of ourself,* however, which we have arrived at by this erroneous path, the so-called 'ego', is thenceforth a fellow worker in the construction of our character and our destiny. –

[. . .]

119

Experience and invention. – However far a man may go in self-knowledge, nothing however can be more incomplete than his image of the totality of *drives* which constitute his being. He can scarcely name even the cruder ones: their number and strength, their ebb and flood, their play and counterplay among one another, and above all the laws of their *nutriment* remain wholly unknown to him. This nutriment is therefore a work of chance: our daily experiences throw some prey in the way of now this, now that drive, and the drive seizes it eagerly; but the coming and going of these events as a whole stands in no rational relationship to the nutritional requirements of the totality of the drives: so that the outcome will always be twofold – the starvation and stunting of some and the overfeeding of others. Every moment of our lives sees some of the polyp-arms of our being grow and others of them wither, all according to the nutriment which the moment does or does not bear with it. Our experiences are, as already said, all in this sense means of nourishment, but the nourishment is scattered indiscriminately without distinguishing between the hungry and those already possessing a superfluity. And as a consequence of this chance nourishment of the parts, the whole, fully grown polyp will be something just as accidental as its growth has been. To express it more clearly: suppose a drive finds itself at the point at which it desires gratification – or exercise of its strength, or discharge of its strength, or the saturation of an emptiness – these are all metaphors –: it then regards every event of the day with a view to seeing how it can employ it for the attainment of its goal; whether a man is moving, or resting or angry or reading or speaking or fighting or rejoicing, the drive will in its thirst as it were taste every condition into which the man may enter, and as a rule will discover nothing for itself there and will have to wait and go on thirsting: in a little while it will grow faint, and after a couple of days or months of non-gratification it will wither away like a plant without rain. Perhaps this cruelty perpetrated by chance would be more vividly evident if all the drives were as much in earnest as is *hunger,* which is not content with *dream food;* but most of the drives, especially the so-called moral ones, *do precisely this* – if my supposition is allowed that the meaning and value of our *dreams* is precisely to *compensate* to some extent for the chance absence of 'nourishment' during the day. Why was the dream of yesterday full of tenderness and tears, that of the day before yesterday humorous and exuberant, an earlier dream adventurous and involved in a continuous gloomy searching? Why do I in this dream enjoy indescribable beauties of music, why do I in another soar and fly with the joy of an eagle up to distant mountain peaks? These inventions, which give scope and discharge to our drives to tenderness or humorousness or adventurousness or to our desire for music and mountains – and everyone will have his own more striking examples to hand – are interpretations of nervous stimuli we receive while we are asleep, *very free*, very arbitrary interpretations of the motions of the blood and intestines, of the pressure of the arm and the bedclothes, of the sounds made by church bells, weather-cocks, night-revellers and other things of the kind. That this text, which is in general much the same on one night as on another, is commented on in such varying ways, that the inventive reasoning faculty *imagines* today a *cause* for the nervous stimuli so very different from the cause it imagined yesterday, though the stimuli are the same: the explanation of this is that today's prompter of the reasoning faculty was different from yesterday's – a different *drive* wanted to gratify itself, to be active, to exercise itself, to refresh itself, to discharge itself – today this drive was at high flood, yesterday it was a different drive that was in that condition. – Waking life does not have this *freedom* of interpretation possessed by the life of dreams, it is less inventive and unbridled – but do I have to add that when we are awake our drives likewise do nothing but interpret nervous stimuli and, according to their requirements, posit their 'causes'? that there is no *essential* difference between waking and dreaming? that when we compare very different stages of culture we even find that freedom of waking interpretation in the one is in no way inferior to the freedom exercised in the other while dreaming? that our moral judgments and evaluations too are only images and fantasies based on a physiological process unknown to us, a kind of acquired language for designating certain nervous stimuli? that all our so-called consciousness is a more or less fantastic commentary on an unknown, perhaps unknowable, but felt text? – Take some trifling experience. Suppose we were in the market place one day and we noticed someone laughing at us as we went by: this event will signify this or that to us according to whether this or that drive happens at that moment to be at its height in us – and it will be a quite different event according to the kind of person we are. One person will absorb it like a drop of rain, another will shake it from him like an insect, another will try to pick a quarrel, another will examine his clothing to see if there is anything about it that might give rise to laughter, another will be led to reflect on the nature of laughter as such, another will be glad to have involuntarily augmented the amount of cheerfulness and sunshine in the world – and in each case a drive has gratified itself, whether it be the drive to annoyance or to combativeness or to reflection or to benevolence. This drive seized the event as its prey: why precisely this one? Because, thirsty and hungry, it was lying in wait. – One day recently at eleven o'clock in the morning a man suddenly collapsed right in front of me as if struck by lightning, and all the women in the vicinity screamed aloud; I myself raised him to his feet and attended to him until he had recovered his speech – during this time not a muscle of my face moved and I felt nothing, neither fear nor sympathy, but I did what needed doing and went coolly on my way. Suppose someone had told me the day before that tomorrow at eleven o'clock in the morning a man would fall down beside me in this fashion – I would have suffered every kind of anticipatory torment, would have spent a sleepless night, and at the decisive moment instead of helping the man would perhaps have done what he did. For in the meantime all possible drives would have *had time* to imagine the experience and to comment on it. – What then are our experiences? Much *more* that which we put into them than that which they already contain! Or must we go so far as to say: in themselves they contain nothing? To experience is to invent? –

[. . .]

130

Purposes? Will? – We have accustomed ourselves to believe in the existence of two realms, the realm of *purposes* and *will* and the realm of *chance*; in the latter everything happens senselessly, things come to pass without anyone's being able to say why or wherefore. – We stand in fear of this mighty realm of the great cosmic stupidity, for in most cases we experience it only when it falls like a slate from the roof on to that other world of purposes and intentions and strikes some treasured purpose of ours dead. This belief in the two realms is a primeval romance and fable: we clever dwarfs, with our will and purposes, are oppressed by those stupid, arch-stupid giants, chance accidents, overwhelmed and often trampled to death by them – but in spite of all that we would not like to be without the harrowing poetry of their proximity, for these monsters often arrive when our life, involved as it is in the spider's web of purposes, has become too tedious or too filled with anxiety, and provide us with a sublime diversion by for once *breaking* the web – not that these irrational creatures would do so intentionally! Or even notice they had done so! But their coarse bony hands tear through our net as if it were air. – The Greeks called this realm of the incalculable and of sublime eternal narrow-mindedness Moira,[14] and set it around their gods as the horizon beyond which they could neither see nor exert influence: it is an instance of that secret defiance of the gods encountered among many peoples – one worships them, certainly, but one keeps in one's hand a final trump to be used against them; as when the Indians and Persians think of them as being dependent on the *sacrifice* of mortals, so that in the last resort mortals can let the gods go hungry or even starve them to death; or when the harsh, melancholy Scandinavian creates the notion of a coming 'twilight of the gods' and thus enjoys a silent revenge in retaliation for the continual fear his evil gods product in him. Christianity, whose basic feeling is neither Indian nor Persian not Greek nor Scandinavian, acted differently: it bade us to worship the *spirit of power* in the dust and even to kiss the dust itself – the sense of this being that that almighty 'realm of stupidity' was not as stupid as it looked, that it was *we*, rather, who were stupid in failing to see that behind it there stood our dear God who, though his ways were dark, strange and crooked, would in the end 'bring all to glory'. This new fable of a loving god who had hitherto been mistaken for a race of giants or for Moira and who himself span out purposes and nets more refined even than those produced by our own understanding – so that they *had* to seem incomprehensible, indeed unreasonable to it – this fable represented so bold an inversion and so daring a paradox that the ancient world, grown over-refined, could not resist it, no matter how mad and *contradictory* the thing might sound; for, between ourselves, there was a contradiction in it: if our understanding cannot divine the understanding and the purposes of God, whence did it divine this quality of its understanding? and this quality of God's understanding? – In more recent times men have in fact come seriously to doubt whether

14 Originally, *Moira* meant "part" as opposed to the "whole," then one's part in life, hence fate or destiny. See also *BT* note 31 above.

the slate that falls from the roof was really thrown down by 'divine love' – and have again begun to go back to the old romance of giants and dwarfs. Let us therefore *learn*, because it is high time we did so: in our supposed favoured realm of purposes and reason the giants are likewise the rulers! And our purposes and our reason are not dwarfs but giants! And our nets are just as often and just as roughly broken *by us ourselves* as they are by slates from the roof! And all is not purpose that is called purpose, and even less is all will that is called will! And if you want to conclude from this: 'so there is only one realm, that of chance accidents and stupidity?'– one will have to add: yes, perhaps there is only one realm, perhaps there exists neither will nor purposes, and we have only imagined them. Those iron hands of necessity which shake the dice-box of chance play their game for an infinite length of time: so that there *have* to be throws which exactly resemble purposiveness and rationality of every degree. *Perhaps* our acts of will and our purposes are nothing but just such throws – and we are only too limited and too vain to comprehend our extreme limitedness: which consists in the fact that we ourselves shake the dice-box with iron hands, that we ourselves in our most intentional actions do no more than play the game of necessity. Perhaps! – To get out of this *perhaps* one would have to have been already a guest in the underworld and beyond all surfaces, sat at Persephone's[15] table and played dice with the goddess herself.

[. . .]

Book III

163

Contra Rousseau.[16] – If it is true that our civilisation has something pitiable about it, you have the choice of concluding with Rousseau that 'this pitiable civilisation is to blame for our *bad* morality', or against Rousseau that 'our *good* morality is to blame for this pitiableness of our civilisation. Our weak, unmanly, social concepts of good and evil and their tremendous ascendancy over body and soul have finally weakened all bodies and souls and snapped the self-reliant, independent, unprejudiced men, the pillars of a *strong* civilisation: where one still encounters *bad* morality one beholds

15   In Greek mythology the daughter of Zeus and Demeter. One day, when playing with a group of girls in a meadow, she is spotted by Hades-Aidoneus, personification of the underworld. Enchanted by her, Hades causes the earth to open up, rides out in a chariot and steals away with her. She spends a third (or a half) of her time in the underworld, during which Demeter is in mourning and allows no harvest, but is allowed to spend the rest of the time each year on earth, when Demeter allows the harvest: hence the appellations of Persephone as "daughter of the Goddess of the Corn" and "Mistress of the Dead."
16   Jean-Jacques Rousseau (1712–78), Swiss philosopher and writer, author of works such as the epistolary novel *Julie, ou la Nouvelle Héloïse* (*Julie or the New Héloïse*, 1761), the educational treatise in novel form *Émile* (1762 – see *BT* note 40 above), the political treatise *Du contrat social* (*The Social Contract*, 1762) and the autobiographical *Confessions* (1764–70).

the last ruins of these pillars.' Thus paradox stands against paradox! The truth cannot possibly be on both sides: and is it on either of them? Test them and see.

[. . .]

189

On grand politics. – However much utility and vanity, those of individuals as of peoples, may play a part in *grand politics*: the strongest tide which carries them forward is the *need for the feeling of power*, which from time to time streams up out of inexhaustible wells not only in the souls of princes and the powerful but not least in the lower orders of the people. There comes again and again the hour when the masses are *ready* to stake their life, their goods, their conscience, their virtue so as to acquire that higher enjoyment and as a victorious, capriciously tyrannical nation to rule over other nations (or to think it rules). Then the impulses to squander, sacrifice, hope, trust, to be over-daring and to fantasise spring up in such abundance that the ambitious or prudently calculating prince can let loose a war and cloak his crimes in the good conscience of his people. The great conquerors have always mouthed the pathetic language of virtue: they have had around them masses in a condition of elevation who wanted to hear only the most elevated language. Strange madness of moral judgments! When man possesses the feeling of power he feels and calls himself *good*: and it is precisely then that the others upon whom he has to *discharge* his power feel and call him *evil!* – In the fable of the ages of mankind, Hesiod has depicted the same age, that of the Homeric heroes, twice and made *two ages out of one*: from the point of view of those who had to suffer the terrible iron oppression of these adventurous *Gewaltmenschen*,[17] or had heard of it from their forefathers, it appeared *evil*; but the posterity of this knightly generation revered it as the *good* old happy times. In these circumstances, the poet had no other recourse than to do as he did – for he no doubt had around him auditors of both races!

[. . .]

205

Of the people of Israel. – Among the spectacles to which the coming century invites us is the decision as to the destiny of the Jews of Europe. That their die is cast, that they have crossed their Rubicon, is now palpably obvious: all that is left for them is either to become the masters of Europe or to lose Europe as they once a long time ago lost Egypt, where they had placed themselves before a similar either-or. In Europe, however, they have gone through an eighteenth-century schooling such as no other nation of this continent can boast of – and what they have experienced in this terrible time of schooling has benefited the individual to a greater degree than it has the community as a whole. As a consequence of this, the psychological and spiritual resources of the Jews today are extraordinary; of all those who live in Europe they are least liable to resort to drink or suicide in order to escape from some profound dilemma – something the less gifted are often apt to do. Every Jew possesses in the history of his fathers and grandfathers a great fund of examples of the coldest self-possession and endurance in fearful situations, of the subtlest outwitting and exploitation of chance and misfortune;

---

17   German: brutes, men of violence.

their courage beneath the cloak of miserable submission, their heroism in *spernere se sp*erni,[18] surpasses the virtues of all the saints. For two millennia an attempt was made to render them contemptible by treating them with contempt, and by barring to them the way to all honours and all that was honourable, and in exchange thrusting them all the deeper into the dirtier trades – and it is true that they did not grow cleaner in the process. But contemptible? They themselves have never ceased to believe themselves called to the highest things, and the virtues which pertain to all who suffer have likewise never ceased to adorn them. The way in which they honour their fathers and their children, the rationality of their marriages and marriage customs, distinguish them among all Europeans. In addition to all this, they have known how to create for themselves a feeling of power and of eternal revenge out of the very occupations left to them (or to which they were left); one has to say in extenuation even of their usury that without this occasional pleasant and useful torturing of those who despised them it would have been difficult for them to have preserved their own self-respect for so long. For our respect for ourselves is tied to our being able to practise requital, in good things and bad. At the same time, however, their revenge does not easily go too far: for they all possess the liberality, including liberality of soul, to which frequent changes of residence, of climate, of the customs of one's neighbours and oppressors educates men; they possess by far the greatest experience of human society, and even in their passions they practise the caution taught by this experience. They are so sure in their intellectual suppleness and shrewdness that they never, even in the worst straits, need to earn their bread by physical labour, as common workmen, porters, agricultural slaves. Their demeanour still reveals that their souls have never known chivalrous noble sentiments nor their bodies handsome armour: a certain importunity mingles with an often charming but almost always painful submissiveness. But now, since they are unavoidably going to ally themselves with the best aristocracy of Europe more and more with every year that passes, they will soon have created for themselves a goodly inheritance of spiritual and bodily demeanour: so that a century hence they will appear sufficiently noble not to make those they dominate *ashamed* to have them as masters. And that is what matters! That is why it is still too soon for a settlement of their affairs! They themselves know best that a conquest of Europe, or any kind of act of violence, on their part is not to be thought of but they also know that at some future time Europe may fall into their hands like a ripe fruit if they would only just extend them. To bring that about they need, in the meantime, to distinguish themselves in every domain of European distinction and to stand everywhere in the first rank: until they have reached the point at which they themselves determine what is distinguishing. Then they will be called the inventors and signposts of the nations of Europe and no longer offend their sensibilities. And whither shall this assembled abundance of grand impressions which for every Jewish family constitutes Jewish history, this abundance of passions, virtues, decisions, renunciations, struggles, victories of every kind – whither shall it stream out if not at last into great men and great works! Then, when the Jews can exhibit as their work such jewels and golden vessels as the European nations of a briefer and less profound experience could not and cannot produce, when Israel will have transformed its eternal vengeance into an eternal blessing for Europe: then there will again arrive that seventh day on which the ancient Jewish God may

18   Latin: to scorn scorning oneself.

rejoice in himself, his creation and his chosen people – and let us all, all of us, rejoice with him!

206

The impossible class. – Poor, happy and independent! – these things can go together; poor, happy and a slave! – these things can also go together – and I can think of no better news I could give to our factory slaves: provided, that is, they do not feel it to be in general a *disgrace* to be thus used, and *used up*, as a part of a machine and as it were a stopgap to fill a hole in human inventiveness! To the devil with the belief that higher payment could lift from them the *essence* of their miserable condition – I mean their impersonal enslavement! To the devil with the idea of being persuaded that an enhancement of this impersonality within the mechanical operation of a new society could transform the disgrace of slavery into a virtue! To the devil with setting a price on oneself in exchange for which one ceases to be a person and becomes a part of a machine! Are you accomplices in the current folly of the nations – the folly of wanting above all to produce as much as possible and to become as rich as possible? What you ought to do, rather, is to hold up to them the counter-reckoning: how great a sum of *inner* value is thrown away in pursuit of this external goal! But where is your inner value if you no longer know what it is to breathe freely? if you no longer possess the slightest power over yourselves? if you all too often grow weary of yourselves like a drink that has been left too long standing? if you pay heed to the newspapers and look askance at your wealthy neighbour, made covetous by the rapid rise and fall of power, money and opinions? if you no longer believe in philosophy that wears rags, in the free-heartedness of him without needs? if voluntary poverty and freedom from profession and marriage, such as would very well suit the more spiritual among you, have become to you things to laugh at? If, on the other hand, you have always in your ears the flutings of the Socialist pied-pipers whose design is to enflame you with wild hopes? which bid you *to be prepared* and nothing further, prepared day upon day, so that you wait and wait for something to happen from outside and in all other respects go on living as you have always lived – until this waiting turns to hunger and thirst and fever and madness, and at last the day of the *bestia triumphans*[19] dawns in all its glory? – In contrast to all this, everyone ought to say to himself: 'better to go abroad, to seek to become *master* in new and savage regions of the world and above all master over myself; to keep moving from place to place for just as long as any sign of slavery seems to threaten me; to shun neither adventure nor war and, if the worst should come to the worst, to be prepared for death: all this rather than further to endure this indecent servitude, rather than to go on becoming soured and malicious and conspiratorial!' This would be the right attitude of mind: the workers of Europe ought henceforth to declare themselves *as a class* a human impossibility and not, as usually happens, only a somewhat harsh and inappropriate social arrangement; they ought to inaugurate within the European beehive an age of a great swarming-out such as has never been seen before, and through this act of free emigration in the grand manner to protest against the machine, against capital, and against the choice now threatening them of being *compelled* to become either the slave of the state or the slave

19   Latin: triumphant beast.

of a party of disruption. Let Europe be relieved of a fourth part of its inhabitants! They and it will be all the better for it! Only in distant lands and in the undertakings of swarming trains of colonists will it really become clear how much reason and fairness, how much healthy mistrust, mother Europe has embodied in her sons – sons who could no longer endure it with the dull old woman and were in danger of becoming as querulous, irritable and pleasure-seeking as she herself was. Outside of Europe the virtues of Europe will go on their wanderings with these workers; and that which was at home beginning to degenerate into dangerous ill-humour and inclination for crime will, once abroad, acquire a wild beautiful naturalness and be called heroism. – Thus a cleaner air would at last waft over old, over-populated and self-absorbed Europe! No matter if its 'workforce' should be a little depleted! Perhaps it may then be recalled that we grew accustomed to needing many things only when these needs became so *easy* to satisfy – we shall again relinquish some of them! Perhaps we shall also bring in numerous *Chinese*: and they will bring with them the modes of life and thought suitable to industrious ants. Indeed, they might as a whole contribute to the blood of restless and fretful Europe something of Asiatic calm and contemplativeness and – what is probably needed most – Asiatic *perseverance*.

[. . .]

Book V

429

The new passion. – Why do we fear and hate a possible reversion to barbarism? Because it would make people unhappier than they are? Oh no! The barbarians of every age were *happier*: let us not deceive ourselves! – The reason is that our *drive to knowledge* has become too strong for us to be able to want happiness without knowledge or the happiness of a strong, firmly rooted delusion; even to imagine such a state of things is painful to us! Restless discovering and divining has such an attraction for us, and has grown as indispensable to us as is to the lover his unrequited love, which he would at no price relinquish for a state of indifference – perhaps, indeed, we too are *unrequited* lovers! Knowledge has in us been transformed into a passion which shrinks at no sacrifice and at bottom fears nothing but its own extinction; we believe in all honesty that all mankind must believe itself more exalted and comforted under the compulsion and suffering of *this* passion than it did formerly, when envy of the coarser contentment that follows in the train of barbarism had not yet been overcome. Perhaps mankind will even perish of this passion for knowledge! – even this thought has no power over us! But did Christianity ever shun such a thought? Are love and death not brothers? Yes, we hate barbarism – we would all prefer the destruction of mankind to a regression of knowledge! And finally: if mankind does not perish of a *passion* it will perish of a *weakness*: which do you prefer? This is the main question. Do we desire for mankind an end in fire and light or one in the sand? –

[. . .]

432

Investigators and experimenters. – There are no scientific methods which alone lead to knowledge! We have to tackle things experimentally, now angry with them and now

kind, and be successively just, passionate and cold with them. One person addresses
things as a policeman, a second as a father confessor, a third as an inquisitive wanderer.
Something can be wrung from them now with sympathy, now with force; reverence
for their secrets will take one person forwards, indiscretion and roguishness in revealing their secrets will do the same for another. We investigators are, like all conquerors,
discoverers, seafarers, adventurers, of an audacious morality and must reconcile ourselves to being considered on the whole evil.

[. . .]

560

What we are at liberty to do. – One can dispose of one's drives like a gardener and,
though few know it, cultivate the shoots of anger, pity, curiosity, vanity as productively
and profitably as a beautiful fruit tree on a trellis; one can do it with the good or bad
taste of a gardener and, as it were, in the French or English or Dutch or Chinese fashion;
one can also let nature rule and only attend to a little embellishment and tidying-up
here and there; one can, finally, without paying any attention to them at all, let the
plants grow up and fight their fight out among themselves – indeed, one can take
delight in such a wilderness, and desire precisely this delight, though it gives one some
trouble, too. All this we are at liberty to do: but how many know we are at liberty
to do it? Do the majority not *believe* in *themselves* as in complete *fully-developed facts*?
Have the great philosophers not put their seal on this prejudice with the doctrine of
the unchangeability of character?

15

The Gay Science
(1882)

Book I

1

The teachers of the purpose of existence. – Whether I contemplate men with benevolence or with an evil eye, I always find them concerned with a single task, all of them and every one of them in particular: to do what is good for the preservation of the human race. Not from any feeling of love for the race, but merely because nothing in them is older, stronger, more inexorable and unconquerable than this instinct – because this instinct constitutes *the essence* of our species, our herd. It is easy enough to divide our neighbors quickly, with the usual myopia, from a mere five paces away, into useful and harmful, good and evil men; but in any large-scale accounting, when we reflect on the whole a little longer, we become suspicious of this neat division and finally abandon it. Even the most harmful man may really be the most useful when it comes to the preservation of the species; for he nurtures either in himself or in others, through his effects, instincts without which humanity would long have become feeble or rotten. Hatred, the mischievous delight in the misfortunes of others, the lust to rob and dominate, and whatever else is called evil belongs to the most amazing economy of the preservation of the species. To be sure, this economy is not afraid of high prices, of squandering, and it is on the whole extremely foolish. Still it is *proven* that it has preserved our race so far. I no longer know whether you, my dear fellow man and neighbor, are at all *capable* of living in a way that would damage the species; in other words, "unreasonably" and "badly." What *might* have harmed the species may have become extinct many thousands of years ago and may by now be one of those things that are not possible even for God. Pursue your best or your worst desires, and above all perish! In both cases you are probably still in some way a promoter and benefactor of humanity and therefore entitled to your eulogists – but also to your detractors. But you will never find anyone who could wholly mock you as an individual, also in your best qualities, bringing home to you to the limits of truth your boundless, flylike, froglike wretchedness! To laugh at oneself as one would have to laugh in order to laugh *out of the whole truth* – to do that even the best so far lacked sufficient sense for the truth, and the most gifted had too little genius for that. Even laughter may yet have a future. I mean, when the proposition "the species is everything, *one* is always none" has become part of humanity, and this ultimate liberation and irresponsibility has become accessible to all at all times. Perhaps laughter will then have formed an alliance with wisdom, perhaps only "gay science" will then be left. For the present, things are still quite different. For the present, the comedy of existence has not yet "become conscious" of itself. For the present, we still live in the age of tragedy, the age of moralities and religions. What is the meaning of the ever new appearance of these founders of moralities and religions, these instigators of fights over moral valuations, these teachers of remorse and religious wars? What is the meaning of these heroes on this stage? Thus far these have been the heroes, and everything else, even if at times it was all that could be seen and was much too near to us, has always merely served to set the stage for these heroes, whether it was machinery or coulisse or took the form of confidants and valets. (The poets, for example, were always the valets of some morality.) It is obvious that these tragedians, too, promote the interests of the *species*, even if they should believe that they promote the interest of God or work as God's emissaries. They, too, promote the life of the species, *by promoting the faith in life*. "Life is worth living," every one of them shouts; "there is something to life, there is something behind life, beneath it; beware!" From time to time this instinct, which is at work equally in the highest and the basest men – the instinct for the preservation of the species – erupts as reason and as passion of the spirit. Then it is surrounded by a resplendent retinue of reasons and tries with all the force at its command to make us forget that at bottom it is instinct, drive, folly, lack of reasons. Life *shall* be loved, *because* –! Man *shall* advance himself and his neighbor, *because* – ! What names all these Shalls and Becauses receive and may yet receive in the future! In order that what happens necessarily and always, spontaneously and without any purpose, may henceforth appear to be done for some purpose and strike man as rational and an ultimate commandment, the ethical teacher comes on stage, as the teacher of the purpose of existence; and to this end he invents a second, different existence and unhinges by means of his new mechanics the old, ordinary existence. Indeed, he wants to make sure that we do not *laugh* at existence, or at ourselves – or at him: for him, *one* is always one, something first and last and tremendous; for him there are no species, sums, or zeroes. His inventions and valuations may be utterly foolish and overenthusiastic; he may badly misjudge the course of nature and deny its conditions – and all ethical systems hitherto have been so foolish and anti-natural that humanity would have perished of every one of them if it had gained power over humanity – and yet, whenever "the hero" appeared on the stage, something new was attained: the gruesome counterpart of laughter, that profound emotional shock felt by many individuals at the thought: "Yes, I am worthy of living!" Life and I and you and all of us became *interesting* to ourselves once again for a little while. There is no denying that *in the long run* every one of these great teachers of a purpose was vanquished by laughter, reason, and nature: the short tragedy always gave way again and returned into the eternal comedy of existence; and "the waves of uncountable laughter" – to cite Aeschylus – must in the end overwhelm even the greatest of these tragedians. In spite of all this laughter which makes the required corrections, human nature has nevertheless been changed by the ever new appearance of these teachers of the purpose of existence: It now has one additional need – the need for the ever new appearance of such teachers and teachings of a "purpose." Gradually, man has become a fantastic animal that has to fulfill one more condition of existence than any other animal: man *has to* believe, to know, from time to time *why* he exists; his race cannot flourish without a periodic trust in life – without faith in *reason in life*. And again and again the human race will decree from time to time: "There is something at which it is absolutely forbidden henceforth to laugh." The most cautious friend of man will add: "Not only laughter and gay wisdom but the tragic, too, with all its sublime unreason, belongs among the means and necessities of the preservation of the species." – Consequently. Consequently. Consequently. O, do you understand me, my brothers? Do you understand this new law of ebb and flood? There is a time for us, too!

2

The intellectual conscience. – I keep having the same experience and keep resisting it every time. I do not want to believe it although it is palpable: *the great majority of people lacks an intellectual conscience.* Indeed, it has often seemed to me as if anyone calling for an intellectual conscience were as lonely in the most densely populated cities as if he were in a desert. Everybody looks at you with strange eyes and goes right on handling his scales, calling this good and that evil. Nobody even blushes when you intimate that their weights are underweight; nor do people feel outraged; they merely laugh at your doubts. I mean: *the great majority of people* does not consider it contemptible to believe this or that and to live accordingly, without first having given themselves an account of the final and most certain reasons pro and con, and without even troubling themselves about such reasons afterward: the most gifted men and the noblest women still belong to this "great majority." But what is goodheartedness, refinement, or genius to me, when the person who has these virtues tolerates slack feelings in his faith and judgments and when he does not account *the desire for certainty* as his inmost craving and deepest distress – as that which separates the higher human beings from the lower. Among some pious people I found a hatred of reason and was well disposed to them for that; for this at least *betrayed* their bad intellectual conscience. But to stand in the midst of this *rerum concordia discors*[1] and of this whole marvelous uncertainty and rich ambiguity of existence *without questioning*, without trembling with the craving and the rapture of such questioning, without at least hating the person who questions, perhaps even finding him faintly amusing – that is what I feel to be *contemptible*, and this is the feeling for which I look first in everybody. Some folly keeps persuading me that every human being has this feeling, simply because he is human. This is my type of injustice.

[. . .]

4

What preserves the species. – The strongest and most evil spirits have so far done the most to advance humanity: again and again they relumed the passions that were going to sleep – all ordered society puts the passions to sleep – and they reawakened again and again the sense of comparison, of contradiction, of the pleasure in what is new, daring, untried; they compelled men to pit opinion against opinion, model against model. Usually by force of arms, by toppling boundary markers, by violating pieties

1   Latin: discordant concord of things (Horace, *Epistles*, I. 12. 19).

– but also by means of new religions and moralities. In every teacher and preacher of
what is *new* we encounter the same "wickedness" that makes conquerors notorious,
even if its expression is subtler and it does not immediately set the muscles in motion,
and therefore also does not make one that notorious. What is new, however, is always
evil, being that which wants to conquer and overthrow the old boundary markers and
the old pieties; and only what is old is good. The good men are in all ages those who
dig the old thoughts, digging deep and getting them to bear fruit – the farmers of
the spirit. But eventually all land is exploited, and the ploughshare of evil must come
again and again. Nowadays there is a profoundly erroneous moral doctrine that is
celebrated especially in England: this holds that judgments of "good" and "evil" sum
up experiences of what is "expedient" and "inexpedient." One holds that what is called
good preserves the species, while what is called evil harms the species. In truth, however, the evil instincts are expedient, species-preserving, and indispensable to as high
a degree as the good ones; their function is merely different.

[. . .]

7

Something for the industrious. – Anyone who now wishes to make a study of moral matters opens up for himself an immense field for work. All kinds of individual passions
have to be thought through and pursued through different ages, peoples, and great
and small individuals; all their reason and all their evaluations and perspectives on things
have to be brought into the light. So far, all that has given color to existence still lacks
a history. Where could you find a history of love, of avarice, of envy, of conscience,
of pious respect for tradition, or of cruelty? Even a comparative history of law or at
least of punishment is so far lacking completely. Has anyone made a study of different ways of dividing up the day or of the consequences of a regular schedule of work,
festivals, and rest? What is known of the moral effects of different foods? Is there any
philosophy of nutrition? (The constant revival of noisy agitation for and against veg-
etarianism proves that there is no such philosophy.) Has anyone collected men's experiences of living together – in monasteries, for example? Has the dialectic of marriage
and friendship ever been explicated? Have the manners of scholars, of businessmen,
artists, or artisans been studied and thought about? There is so much in them to think
about. Whatever men have so far viewed as the conditions their existence – and all
the reason, passion, and superstition involved in such a view – has this been researched
exhaustively? The most industrious people will find that it involves too much work
simply to observe how differently men's instincts have grown, and might yet grow,
depending on different moral climates. It would require whole generations, and generations of scholars who would collaborate systematically, to exhaust the points of view
and the material. The same applies to the demonstration of the reasons for the differences between moral climates ("why is it that the sun of one fundamental moral
judgment and main standard of value shines here and another one there?"). And it
would be yet another job to determine the erroneousness of all these reasons and the
whole nature of moral judgments to date. If all these jobs were done, the most insidious question of all would emerge into the foreground: whether science can furnish
goals of action after it has proved that it can take such goals away and annihilate them;
and then experimentation would be in order that would allow every kind of heroism
to find satisfaction – centuries of experimentation that might eclipse all the great

projects and sacrifices of history to date. So far, science has not yet built its cyclopic buildings; but the time for that, too, will come.

[. . .]

11

Consciousness. – Consciousness is the last and latest development of the organic and hence also what is most unfinished and unstrong. Consciousness gives rise to countless errors that lead an animal or man to perish sooner than necessary, "exceeding destiny," as Homer puts it.[2] If the conserving association of the instincts were not so very much more power-ful, and if it did not serve on the whole as a regulator, humanity would have to perish of its misjudgments and its fantasies with open eyes, of its lack of thoroughness and its credulity – in short, of its consciousness; rather, without the former, humanity would long have disappeared. Before a function is fully developed and mature it constitutes a danger for the organism, and it is good if during the interval it is subjected to some tyranny. Thus consciousness is tyrannized – not least by our pride in it. One thinks that it constitutes the *kernel* of man; what is abiding, eternal, ultimate, and most original in him. One takes consciousness for a determinate magnitude. One denies its growth and its intermittences. One takes it for the "unity of the organism." This ridiculous over-estimation and misunderstanding of consciousness has the very useful consequence that it prevents an all too fast development of consciousness. Believing that they possess consciousness, men have not exerted themselves very much to acquire it; and things haven't changed much in this respect. To this day the task of *incorporating* knowledge and making it instinctive is only beginning to dawn on the human eye and is not yet clearly discernible; it is a task that is seen only by those who have comprehended that so far we have incorporated only our errors and that all our consciousness relates to errors.

[. . .]

26

What is life? – Life – that is: continually shedding something that wants to die. Life – that is: being cruel and inexorable against everything about us that is growing old and weak – and not only about *us*. Life – that is, then: being without reverence for those who are dying, who are wretched, who are ancient? Constantly being a murderer? – And yet old Moses said: "Thou shalt not kill."

[. . .]

34

Historia abscondita[3] – Every great human being exerts a retroactive force: for his sake all of history is placed in the balance again, and a thousand secrets of the past crawl out of their hiding places – into *his* sunshine. There is no way of telling what may yet become part of history. Perhaps the past is still essentially undiscovered! So many retroactive forces are still needed!

[. . .]

2   See *Iliad* II. 155 and XX. 30, 336.
3   Latin: concealed, secret or unknown history.

54

The consciousness of appearance. – How wonderful and new and yet how gruesome and ironic I find my position via-à-vis the whole of existence in the light of my insight! I have discovered for myself that the human and animal past, indeed the whole primal age and past of all sentient being continues in me to invent, to love, to hate, and to infer. I suddenly woke up in the midst of this dream, but only to the consciousness that I am dreaming and that I must go on dreaming lest I perish – as a somnambulist must go on dreaming lest he fall. What is "appearance" for me now? Certainly not the opposite of some essence: what could I say about any essence except to name the attributes of its appearance! Certainly not a dead mask that one could place on an unknown *x* or remove from it! Appearance is for me that which lives and is effective and goes so far in its self-mockery that it makes me feel that this is appearance and will-o'-the-wisp and a dance of spirits and nothing more – that among all these dreamers, I, too, who "know," am dancing my dance; that the knower is a means for prolonging the earthly dance and thus belongs to the masters of ceremony of existence; and that the sublime consistency and interrelatedness of all knowledge perhaps is and will be the highest means to *preserve* the universality of dreaming and the mutual comprehension of all dreamers and thus also *the continuation*[4] of the dream.

Book II

57

To the realists. – You sober people who feel well armed against passion and fantasies and would like to turn your emptiness into a matter of pride and an ornament: you call yourselves realists and hint that the world really is the way it appears to you. As if reality stood unveiled before you only, and you yourselves were perhaps the best part of it – O you beloved images of Sais![5] But in your unveiled state are not even you still very passionate and dark creatures compared to fish, and still far too similar to an artist in love? And what is "reality" for an artist in love? You are still burdened with those estimates of things that have their origin in the passions and loves of former centuries. Your sobriety still contains a secret and inextinguishable drunkenness. Your love of "reality," for example – oh, that is a primeval "love." Every feeling and sensation contains a piece of this old love; and some fantasy, some prejudice, some unreason, some ignorance, some fear, and ever so much else has contributed to it and worked on it. That mountain there! That cloud there! What is "real" in that? Subtract the

---

4 In German: *die Dauer*, the duration. Throughout this section, Nietzsche's word for "appearance" is *Schein*. See the general introduction to the present volume, note 23.
5 Allusion to Schiller's ballad "Das verschleierte Bild zu Sais" ("The Veiled Image at Sais"). Plutarch reports that in a temple in the Egyptian city of Sais there was a veiled statue of the goddess Isis which bore the inscription: "I am everything that is, that was, and that will be, and no mortal has ever raised my veil." Schiller's ballad tells of an Egyptian youth who, eager to know the Truth, breaks into the temple one night and violates the prohibition by lifting the veil. The next morning, however, he is unable to report what he has seen, and he dies an early death.

phantasm and every human *contribution* from it, my sober friends! If you *can*! If you can forget your descent, your past, your training – all of your humanity and animality. There is no "reality" for us – not for you either, my sober friends. We are not nearly as different as you think, and perhaps our good will to transcend intoxication is as respectable as your faith that you are altogether incapable of intoxication.

58

Only as creators! – This has given me the greatest trouble and still does: to realize that what things *are called* is incomparably more important than what they are. The reputation, name, and appearance, the usual measure and weight of a thing, what it counts for – originally almost always wrong and arbitrary, thrown over things like a dress and altogether foreign to their nature and even to their skin – all this grows from generation unto generation, merely because people believe in it, until it gradually grows to be part of the thing and turns into its very body. What at first was appearance becomes in the end, almost invariably, the essence and is effective as such. How foolish it would be to suppose that one only needs to point out this origin and this misty shroud of delusion in order to *destroy* the world that counts for real, so-called "*reality.*" We can destroy only as creators. – But let us not forget this either: it is enough to create new names and estimations and probabilities in order to create in the long run new "things."

59

We artists. – When we love a woman, we easily conceive a hatred for nature on account of all the repulsive natural functions to which every woman is subject. We prefer not to think of all this; but when our soul touches on these matters for once, it shrugs as it were and looks contemptuously at nature: we feel insulted; nature seems to encroach on our possessions, and with the profanest hands at that. Then we refuse to pay any heed to physiology and decree secretly: "I want to hear nothing about the fact that a human being is something more than *soul and form.*" "The human being under the skin" is for all lovers a horror and unthinkable, a blasphemy against God and love. Well, as lovers still feel about nature and natural functions, every worshiper of God and his "holy omnipotence" formerly felt: everything said about nature by astronomers, geologists, physiologists, or physicians, struck him as an encroachment into his precious possessions and hence as an attack – and a shameless one at that. Even "natural law" sounded to him like a slander against God; really he would have much preferred to see all of mechanics derived from acts of a moral will or an arbitrary will. But since nobody was able to render him this service, he *ignored* nature and mechanics as best he could and lived in a dream. Oh, these men of former times knew how to *dream* and did not find it necessary to go to sleep first. And we men of today still master this art all too well, despite all of our good will toward the day and staying awake. It is quite enough to love, to hate, to desire, simply to feel – and right away the spirit and power of the dream overcome us, and with our eyes open, coldly contemptuous of all danger, we climb up on the most hazardous paths to scale the roofs and spires of fantasy – without any sense of dizziness, as if we had been born to climb, we somnambulists of the day! We artists! We ignore what is natural. We are moonstruck and God-struck. We wander, still as death, unwearied, on heights that we do not see as heights but as plains, as our safety.

60

Women and their action at a distance. – Do I still have ears? Am I all ears and nothing else? Here I stand in the flaming surf whose white tongues are licking at my feet; from all sides I hear howling, threats, screaming, roaring coming at me, while the old earth-shaker[6] sings his aria in the lowest depths, deep as a bellowing bull, while pounding such an earth-shaking beat that the hearts of even these weather-beaten rocky monsters are trembling in their bodies. Then, suddenly, as if born out of nothing, there appears before the gate of this hellish labyrinth, only a few fathoms away – a large sailboat, gliding along as silently as a ghost. Oh, what ghostly beauty! How magically it touches me! Has all the calm and taciturnity of the world embarked on it? Does my happiness itself sit in this quiet place – my happier ego, my second, departed self? Not to be dead and yet no longer alive? A spiritlike intermediate being: quietly observing, gliding, floating? As the boat that with its white sails moves like an immense butterfly over the dark sea. Yes! To move *over* existence! That's it! That would be something! It seems as if the noise here had led me into fantasies. All great noise leads us to move happiness into some quiet distance. When a man stands in the midst of his own noise, in the midst of his own surf of plans and projects, then he is apt also to see quiet, magical beings gliding past him and to long for their happiness and seclusion: *women*. He almost thinks that his better self dwells there among the women, and that in these quiet regions even the loudest surf turns into deathly quiet, and life itself into a dream about life. Yet! Yet! Noble enthusiast, even on the most beautiful sailboat there is a lot of noise, and unfortunately much small and petty noise. The magic and the most powerful effect of women is, in philosophical language, action at a distance, *actio in distans;*[7] but this requires first of all and above all – *distance.*

[. . .]

72

Mothers. – Animals do not think about females as men do; they consider the female the productive being. Paternal love does not exist among them; merely something like love for the children of a beloved and a kind of getting used to them. The females find in their children satisfaction for their desire to dominate, a possession, an occupation, something that is wholly intelligible to them and can be chattered with: the sum of all this is what mother love is; it is to be compared with an artist's love for his work. Pregnancy has made women kinder, more patient, more timid, more pleased to submit; and just so does spiritual pregnancy produce the character of the contemplative type, which is closely related to the feminine character: it consists of male mothers. – Among animals the male sex is considered the beautiful sex.

[. . .]

76

The greatest danger. – If the majority of men had not always considered the discipline of their minds – their "rationality" – a matter of pride, an obligation, and a virtue,

---

6 Epithet for the Greek god Poseidon, who ruled the seas and was thought to be responsible for earthquakes.

7 Latin: action at a distance.

feeling insulted or embarrassed by all fantasies and debaucheries of thought because they saw themselves as friends of "healthy common sense," humanity would have perished long ago. The greatest danger that always hovered over humanity and still hovers over it is the eruption of madness – which means the eruption of arbitrariness in feeling, seeing, and hearing, the enjoyment of the mind's lack of discipline, the joy in human unreason. Not truth and certainty are the opposite of the world of the madman, but the universality and the universal binding force of a faith; in sum, the non-arbitrary character of judgments. And man's greatest labor so far has been to reach agreement about very many things and to submit to a *law of agreement* – regardless of whether these things are true or false. This is the discipline of the mind that mankind has received; but the contrary impulses are still so powerful that at bottom we cannot speak of the future of mankind with much confidence. The image of things still shifts and shuffles continually, and perhaps even more so and faster from now on than ever before. Continually, precisely the most select spirits bristle at this universal binding force – the explorers of *truth* above all. Continually this faith, as *everybody's* faith, arouses nausea and a new lust in subtler minds; and the slow tempo that is here demanded for all spiritual processes, this imitation of the tortoise, which is here recognized as the norm, would be quite enough to turn artists and thinkers into apostates: It is in these impatient spirits that a veritable delight in madness erupts because madness has such a cheerful tempo. Thus the virtuous intellects are needed – oh, let me use the most unambiguous word – what is needed is *virtuous stupidity*, stolid metronomes for the slow spirit, to make sure that the faithful of the great shared faith stay together and continue their dance. It is a first-rate need that commands and demands this. *We others are the exception and the danger* – and we need eternally to be defended. – Well, there actually are things to be said in favor of the exception, *provided that it never wants to become the rule.*

[. . .]

78

What should win our gratitude. – Only artists, and especially those of the theater, have given men eyes and ears to see and hear with some pleasure what each man *is* himself, experiences himself, desires himself; only they have taught us to esteem the hero that is concealed in everyday characters; only they have taught us the art of viewing ourselves as heroes – from a distance and, as it were, simplified and transfigured – the art of staging and watching ourselves. Only in this way can we deal with some base details in ourselves. Without this art we would be nothing but foreground and live entirely in the spell of that perspective which makes what is closest at hand and most vulgar appear as if it were vast, and reality itself. Perhaps one should concede a similar merit to the religion that made men see the sinfulness of every single individual through a magnifying glass, turning the sinner into a great, immortal criminal. By surrounding him with eternal perspectives, it taught man to see himself from a distance and as something past and whole.

[. . .]

99

Schopenhauer's followers. – What happens when barbarians come into contact with a higher culture – the lower culture always accepts first of all the vices, weaknesses, and excesses and only then, on that basis, finds a certain attraction in the higher culture and eventually, by way of the vices and weaknesses that it has acquired, also accepts some of the overflow of what really has value – that can also be observed nearby, without traveling to remote barbarian tribes. Of course, what we see near us is somewhat refined and spiritualized and not quite so palpable. What do Schopenhauer's German followers generally accept first of all from their master? In comparison with his superior culture, they must surely feel barbarous enough to be initially fascinated and seduced by him like barbarians. Is it his sense for hard facts, his good will for clarity and reason, which so often makes him appear so English and un-German? Or the strength of his intellectual conscience that endured a life-long contradiction between Being and Willing, and also compelled him to contradict himself continually in his writings on almost every point? Or his cleanliness in questions about the church and the Christian god? For here his cleanliness was quite unprecedented among German philosophers, and he lived and died "as a Voltairian." Or his immortal doctrines of the intellectuality of intuition, of the a priori nature of the causal law, of the instrumental character of the intellect and the unfreedom of the will? No, none of this enchants his German followers; they do not find it enchanting at all. But Schopenhauer's mystical embarrassments and subterfuges in those places where the factual thinker allowed himself to be seduced and corrupted by the vain urge to be the unriddler of the world; the unprovable doctrine of the *One Will* ("all causes are merely occasional causes of the appearance of the will at this time and at this place" and "the will to life is present, whole and undivided, in every being, including the least – as completely as in all beings that ever have been, are, and shall be, if they were all taken together"); the *denial of the individual* ("all lions are at bottom only one lion"; "the plurality of individuals is mere appearance," even as *development* is mere appearance: he calls Lamarck's[8] idea, "an ingenious but absurd error"); his ecstatic reveries about *genius* ("in aesthetic contemplation, the individual is no longer an individual but the pure, will-less, painless, timeless subject of knowledge"; "as the subject is wholly absorbed in the object that it contemplates, it becomes this object itself"); the nonsense about *pity*, about how it makes possible a break through the *principium individuationis*,[9] and how this is the source of all morality; also such claims as "dying is really the purpose of existence" and "*a priori*, one cannot altogether deny the possibility that magical effects might emanate from one who has died" – these and other such *excesses* and vices of the philosopher are always accepted first of all and turned into articles of faith; for vices and excesses are always aped most easily and require no long training. But let us discuss the most famous living follower of Schopenhauer: Richard Wagner. – What happened to him has happened to many artists: he misinterpreted the characters that he himself had created and misunderstood the philosophy that was implicit in his most characteristic works of art. Until the middle of his life, Richard Wagner allowed himself to be led astray by Hegel. Later, the same thing happened to him a second time when he began to read

8   Jean-Baptiste Lamarck (1744–1829), French naturalist, and one of the founders of modern evolutionary theory with his text *Philosophie zoologique* (*Zoological Philosophy*, 1809), associated with ideas on the inheritance of acquired characteristics and the use and disuse of organs.
9   Latin: principle of individuation. See *On Schopenhauer* note 1 above.

Schopenhauer's doctrine into his characters and to apply to himself such categories as "will," "genius," and "pity." Nevertheless it will remain true that nothing could be more contrary to the spirit of Schopenhauer than what is distinctively Wagnerian in Wagner's heroes: I mean the innocence of the utmost selfishness, the faith in great passion as the good in itself – in one word, what is Siegfried-like in the countenance of his heroes. "All this smells more even of Spinoza than it does of me," Schopenhauer himself might say. Although Wagner would have good reasons to look for some other philosopher rather than Schopenhauer, the spell that this thinker has cast over him has blinded him not only to all other philosophies but even to science itself. More and more, his whole art wants to present itself as a companion piece and supplement to Schopenhauer's philosophy, and more and more explicitly it renounces the loftier ambition of becoming a companion piece and supplement to human knowledge and science. Nor is it only the whole mysterious pomp of this philosophy, which would also have attracted a Cagliostro,[10] but the gestures and passions of the philosophers have always been seductive, too. Wagner is Schopenhauerian, for example, in his exasperation over the corruption of the German language; and if one should applaud his imitation at this point, it should not be overlooked that Wagner's own style suffers rather heavily from all the ulcers and swellings whose sight enraged Schopenhauer; and as for the Wagnerians who write German, Wagnerism is beginning to prove as dangerous as any Hegelisms ever did. Wagner is Schopenhauerian in his hatred of the Jews to whom he is not able to do justice even when it comes to their greatest deed; after all, the Jews are the inventors of Christianity. Wagner is Schopenhauerian in his attempts to understand Christianity as a seed of Buddhism that has been carried far away by the wind, and to prepare a Buddhistic epoch in Europe, with an occasional *rapprochement* with Catholic-Christian formulas and sentiments. Wagner is Schopenhauerian when he preaches mercy in our relations with animals. As we know, Schopenhauer's predecessor at this point was Voltaire who may already have mastered the art that we encounter among his successors – to dress up his hatred against certain things and people as mercy for animals. At least Wagner's hatred of science, which finds expression in his preachment, is certainly not inspired by any spirit of kind-heartedness and benignity – nor indeed, as is obvious, by anything meriting the name of *spirit*. Of course, the philosophy of an artist does not matter much if it is merely an afterthought and does not harm his art. One cannot be too careful to avoid bearing any artist a grudge for an occasional, perhaps very unfortunate and presumptuous masquerade. We should not forget that, without exception, our dear artists are, and have to be to some extent, actors; and without play-acting they would scarcely endure life for any length of time. Let us remain faithful to Wagner in what is *true* and authentic in him – and especially in this, that we, as his disciples, remain faithful to ourselves in what is true and authentic in us. Let him have his intellectual tempers and cramps. Let us, in all fairness, ask what strange nourishments and needs an art like this may require to be able to live and grow. It does not matter that as a thinker he is so often in the wrong; justice and patience are not for *him*. Enough that his life is justified before itself and remains justified – this life which shouts at everyone of us: "Be a man and do

10   Pseudonym of Giuseppe Balsamo (1743–95), Italian adventurer, magician, and alchemist who claimed, among other things, to have the philosopher's stone.

not follow me – but yourself! But yourself!"[11] *Our* life, too, shall remain justified in our own eyes! We, too, shall grow and blossom out of ourselves, free and fearless, in innocent selfishness. And as I contemplate such a human being, these sentences still come to my mind today as formerly: "That passion is better than Stoicism and hypocrisy, that being honest in evil is still better than losing oneself to the morality of tradition, that a free human being can be good as well as evil, but that the unfree human being is a blemish upon nature and has no share in any heavenly or earthly comfort; finally, that everyone who wishes to become free must become free through his own endeavor, and that freedom does not fall into any man's lap as a miraculous gift" (*Richard Wagner in Bayreuth*, p. 94).[12]

[. . .]

107

Our ultimate gratitude to art. – If we had not welcomed the arts and invented this kind of cult of the untrue, then the realization of general untruth and mendaciousness that now comes to us through science – the realization that delusion and error are conditions of human knowledge and sensation – would be utterly unbearable. *Honesty* would lead to nausea and suicide. But now there is a counterforce against our honesty that helps us to avoid such consequences: art as the *good* will to appearance. We do not always keep our eyes from rounding off something and, as it were, finishing the poem; and then it is no longer eternal imperfection that we carry across the river of becoming – then we have the sense of carrying a *goddess*, and feel proud and childlike as we perform this service. As an aesthetic phenomenon existence is still *bearable* for us, and art furnishes us with eyes and hands and above all the good conscience to be *able* to turn ourselves into such a phenomenon. At times we need a rest from ourselves by looking upon, by looking *down* upon, ourselves and, from an artistic distance, laughing *over* ourselves or weeping *over* ourselves. We must discover the *hero* no less than the *fool* in our passion for knowledge; we must occasionally find pleasure in our folly, or we cannot continue to find pleasure in our wisdom. Precisely because we are at bottom grave and serious human beings – really, more weights than human beings – nothing does us as much good as a *fool's cap*: we need it in relation to ourselves – we need all exuberant, floating, dancing, mocking, childish, and blissful art lest we lose the *freedom above things* that our ideal demands of us. It would mean a *relapse* for us, with our irritable honesty, to get involved entirely in morality and, for the sake of the over-severe demands that we make on ourselves in these matters, to become virtuous monsters and scarecrows. We should be *able* also to stand *above* morality[13] – and not only to *stand* with the anxious stiffness of a man who is afraid of slipping and falling any moment, but also to *float* above it and *play*. How then could we possibly dispense

---

11   Goethe added these words as an epigraph to the second (1775) edition of his novel *Die Leiden des jungen Werthers* (*The Sufferings of Young Werther*, 1774), when the hero's suicide inspired young men not only to dress and act like Werther but to shoot themselves as well.
12   Quotation from Nietzsche's own essay of 1876 (*UM* IV. 11). The page reference is to the first edition.
13   In German: *über der Moral*.

with art – and with the fool? – And as long as you are in any way *ashamed* before yourselves, you do not yet belong with us.

Book III

108

New struggles. – After Buddha was dead, his shadow was still shown for centuries in a cave – a tremendous, gruesome shadow. God is dead;[14] but given the way of men, there may still be caves for thousands of years in which his shadow will be shown. – And we – we still have to vanquish his shadow, too.

109

Let us beware. – Let us beware of thinking that the world is a living being. Where should it expand? On what should it feed? How could it grow and multiply? We have some notion of the nature of the organic; and we should not reinterpret the exceedingly derivative, late, rare, accidental, that we perceive only on the crust of the earth and make of it something essential, universal, and eternal, which is what those people do who call the universe an organism. This nauseates me. Let us even beware of believing that the universe is a machine: it is certainly not constructed for one purpose, and calling it a "machine" does it far too much honor. Let us beware of positing generally and everywhere anything as elegant as the cyclical movements of our neighboring stars; even a glance into the Milky Way raises doubts whether there are not far coarser and more contradictory movements there, as well as stars with eternally linear paths, etc. The astral order in which we live is an exception; this order and the relative duration that depends on it have again made possible an exception of exceptions: the formation of the organic. The total character of the world, however, is in all eternity chaos – in the sense not of a lack of necessity but of a lack of order, arrangement, form, beauty, wisdom, and whatever other names there are for our aesthetic anthropomorphisms. Judged from the point of view of our reason, unsuccessful attempts are by all odds the rule, the exceptions are not the secret aim, and the whole musical box repeats eternally its tune which may never be called a melody – and ultimately even the phrase "unsuccessful attempt" is too anthropomorphic and reproachful. But how could we reproach or praise the universe? Let us beware of attributing to it heartlessness and unreason or their opposites: it is neither perfect nor beautiful, nor noble, nor does it wish to become any of these things; it does not by any means strive to imitate man. None of our aesthetic and moral judgments apply to it. Nor does it have any instinct for self-preservation or any other instinct; and it does not observe any laws either. Let us beware of saying that there are laws in nature. There are only necessities: there is nobody who commands, nobody who obeys, nobody who trespasses. Once you know that there are no purposes, you also know that there is no accident; for it is only beside a world of purposes that the word "accident" has meaning. Let us beware of saying that death is opposed to life. The living is merely a type of what is dead, and

---

14   First occurrence of the formulation in Nietzsche's writings. See *GS* 125 for its most significant elaboration.

a very rare type. Let us beware of thinking that the world eternally creates new things. There are no eternally enduring substances; matter is as much of an error as the God of the Eleatics.[15] But when shall we ever be done with our caution and care? When will all these shadows of God cease to darken our minds? When will we complete our de-deification of nature? When may we begin to "*naturalize*" humanity in terms of a pure, newly discovered, newly redeemed nature?

110

Origin of knowledge. – Over immense periods of time the intellect produced nothing but errors. A few of these proved to be useful and helped to preserve the species: those who hit upon or inherited these had better luck in their struggle for themselves and their progeny. Such erroneous articles of faith, which were continually inherited, until they became almost part of the basic endowment of the species, include the following: that there are enduring things; that there are equal things; that there are things, substances, bodies; that a thing is what it appears to be; that our will is free; that what is good for me is also good in itself. It was only very late that such propositions were denied and doubted; it was only very late that truth emerged – as the weakest form of knowledge. It seemed that one was unable to live with it: our organism was prepared for the opposite; all its higher functions, sense perception and every kind of sensation worked with those basic errors which had been incorporated since time immemorial. Indeed, even in the realm of knowledge these propositions became the norms according to which "true" and "untrue" were determined – down to the most remote regions of logic. Thus the *strength* of knowledge does not depend on its degree of truth but on its age, on the degree to which it has been incorporated, on its character as a condition of life. Where life and knowledge seemed to be at odds there was never any real fight, but denial and doubt were simply considered madness. Those exceptional thinkers, like the Eleatics, who nevertheless posited and clung to the opposites of the natural errors, believed that it was possible to *live* in accordance with these opposites: they invented the sage as the man who was unchangeable and impersonal, the man of the universality of intuition who was One and All at the same time, with a special capacity for his inverted knowledge: they had the faith that their knowledge was also the principle of *life*. But in order to claim all of this, they had to *deceive* themselves about their own state: they had to attribute to themselves, fictitiously, impersonality and changeless duration; they had to misapprehend the nature of the knower; they had to deny the role of the impulses in knowledge; and quite generally they had to conceive of reason as a completely free and spontaneous activity. They shut their eyes to the fact that they, too, had arrived at their propositions through opposition to common sense, or owing to a desire for tranquillity, for sole possession, or for dominion. The subtler development of honesty and skepticism eventually made these people, too, impossible; their ways of living and judging were seen to be also dependent upon the primeval impulses and basic errors of all sentient existence. This

15 School of ancient Greek philosophy associated with the teachings of Parmenides (born ca. 510 B.C.) and his followers such as Zeno from Elea and Melissus from Samos; based on a rejection of plurality, change, motion, and so on in favor of an indivisible and unchanging One.

subtler honesty and skepticism came into being wherever two contradictory sentences appeared to be *applicable* to life because *both* were compatible with the basic errors, and it was therefore possible to argue about the higher or lower degree of *utility* for life; also wherever new propositions, though not useful for life, were also evidently not harmful to life: in such cases there was room for the expression of an intellectual play impulse, and honesty and skepticism were innocent and happy like all play. Gradually, the human brain became full of such judgments and convictions, and a ferment, struggle, and lust for power developed in this tangle. Not only utility and delight but every kind of impulse took sides in this fight about "truths." The intellectual fight became an occupation, an attraction, a profession, a duty, something dignified – and eventually knowledge and the striving for the true found their place as a need among other needs. Henceforth not only faith and conviction but also scrutiny, denial, mistrust, and contradiction became a *power*; all "evil" instincts were subordinated to knowledge, employed in her service, and acquired the splendor of what is permitted, honored, and useful – and eventually even the eye and innocence of the *good*. Thus knowledge became a piece of life itself, and hence a continually growing power – until eventually knowledge collided with those primeval basic errors: two lives, two powers, both in the same human being. A thinker is now that being in whom the impulse for truth and those life-preserving errors clash for their first fight, after the impulse for truth has proved to be also a life-preserving power. Compared to the significance of this fight, everything else is a matter of indifference: the ultimate question about the conditions of life has been posed here, and we confront the first attempt to answer this question by experiment. To what extent can truth endure incorporation? That is the question; that is the experiment.

111

Origin of the logical. – How did logic come into existence in man's head? Certainly out of illogic, whose realm originally must have been immense. Innumerable beings who made inferences in a way different from ours perished; for all that, their ways might have been truer. Those, for example, who did not know how to find often enough what is "equal" as regards both nourishment and hostile animals – those, in other words, who subsumed things too slowly and cautiously – were favored with a lesser probability of survival than those who guessed immediately upon encountering similar instances that they must be equal. The dominant tendency, however, to treat as equal what is merely similar – an illogical tendency, for nothing is really equal – is what first created any basis for logic. In order that the concept of substance could originate – which is indispensable for logic although in the strictest sense nothing real corresponds to it – it was likewise necessary that for a long time one did not see nor perceive the changes in things. The beings that did not see so precisely had an advantage over those that saw everything "in flux." At bottom, every high degree of caution in making inferences and every skeptical tendency constitute a great danger for life. No living beings would have survived if the opposite tendency – to affirm rather than suspend judgment, to err and *make up* things rather than wait, to assent rather than negate, to pass judgment rather than be just – had not been bred to the point where it became extraordinarily strong. The course of logical ideas and inferences in our brain today corresponds to a process and a struggle among impulses that are, taken singly, very illogical and unjust. We generally experience only the result of this struggle because this primeval mechanism now runs its course so quickly and is so well concealed.

112

Cause and effect. – "Explanation" is what we call it, but it is "description" that distinguishes us from older stages of knowledge and science. Our descriptions are better – we do not explain any more than our predecessors. We have uncovered a manifold one-after-another where the naive man and inquirer of older cultures saw only two separate things. "Cause" and "effect" is what one says; but we have merely perfected the image of becoming without reaching beyond the image or behind it. In every case the series of "causes" confronts us much more completely, and we infer: first, this and that has to precede in order that this or that may then follow – but this does not involve any *comprehension.* In every chemical process, for example, quality appears as a "miracle," as ever; also, every locomotion; nobody has "explained" a push. But how could we possibly explain anything? We operate only with things that do not exist: lines, planes, bodies, atoms, divisible time spans, divisible spaces. How should explanations be at all possible when we first turn everything into an *image,* our image! It will do to consider science as an attempt to humanize things as faithfully as possible; as we describe things and their one-after-another, we learn how to describe ourselves more and more precisely. Cause and effect: such a duality probably never exists; in truth we are confronted by a continuum out of which we isolate a couple of pieces, just as we perceive motion only as isolated points and then infer it without ever actually seeing it. The suddenness with which many effects stand out misleads us; actually, it is sudden only for us. In this moment of suddenness there is an infinite number of processes that elude us. An intellect that could see cause and effect as a continuum and a flux and not, as we do, in terms of an arbitrary division and dismemberment, would repudiate the concept of cause and effect and deny all conditionality.

[. . .]

117

Herd remorse. – During the longest and most remote periods of the human past, the sting of conscience was not at all what it is now. Today one feels responsible only for one's will and actions, and one finds one's pride in oneself. All our teachers of law start from this sense of self and pleasure in the individual as if this had always been the fount of law. But during the longest period of the human past nothing was more terrible than to feel that one stood by oneself. To be alone, to experience things by oneself, neither to obey nor to rule, to be an individual – that was not a pleasure but a punishment; one was sentenced "to individuality." Freedom of thought was considered discomfort itself. While we experience law and submission as compulsion and loss, it was egoism that was formerly experienced as something painful and as real misery. To be a self and to esteem oneself according to one's own weight and measure – that offended taste in those days. An inclination to do this would have been considered madness; for being alone was associated with every misery and fear. In those days, "free will" was very closely associated with a bad conscience; and the more unfree one's actions were and the more the herd instinct rather than any personal sense found expression in an action, the more moral one felt. Whatever harmed the herd, whether the individual had wanted it or not wanted it, prompted the sting of conscience in the individual – and in his neighbor, too, and even in the whole herd. – There is no point on which we have learned to think and feel more differently.

[. . .]

120

Health of the soul. – The popular medical formulation of morality that goes back to Ariston of Chios,[16] "virtue is the health of the soul," would have to be changed to become useful, at least to read: "*your* virtue is the health of *your* soul." For there is no health as such, and all attempts to define a thing that way have been wretched failures. Even the determination of what is healthy for your *body* depends on your goal, your horizon, your energies, your impulses, your errors, and above all on the ideals and phantasms of your soul. Thus there are innumerable healths of the body; and the more we allow the unique and incomparable to raise its head again, and the more we abjure the dogma of the "equality of men," the more must the concept of a *normal* health, along with a normal diet and the normal course of an illness, be abandoned by medical men. Only then would the time have come to reflect on the health and illness of the *soul*, and to find the peculiar virtue of each man in the health of his soul. In one person, of course, this health could look like its opposite in another person. Finally, the great question would still remain whether we can really dispense with illness – even for the sake of our virtue – and whether our thirst for knowledge and self-knowledge in particular does not require the sick soul as much as the healthy, and whether, in brief, the will to health alone, is not a prejudice, cowardice, and perhaps a bit of very subtle barbarism and backwardness.

121

Life no argument. – We have arranged for ourselves a world in which we can live – by positing bodies, lines, planes, causes and effects, motion and rest, form and content; without these articles of faith nobody now could endure life. But that does not prove them. Life is no argument. The conditions of life might include error.

[. . .]

124

In the horizon of the infinite. – We have left the land and have embarked. We have burned our bridges behind us – indeed, we have gone farther and destroyed the land behind us. Now, little ship, look out! Beside you is the ocean: to be sure, it does not always roar, and at times it lies spread out like silk and gold and reveries of graciousness. But hours will come when you will realize that it is infinite and that there is nothing more awesome than infinity. Oh, the poor bird that felt free and now strikes the walls of this cage! Woe, when you feel homesick for the land as if it had offered more *freedom* – and there is no longer any "land."

16 Stoic philosopher of the third century B.C., who rejected physics, considered dialectical reasoning to be useless, and limited his concerns to ethics.

125

The madman. – Have you not heard of that madman who lit a lantern in the bright morning hours, ran to the market place, and cried incessantly: "I seek God! I seek God!" – As many of those who did not believe in God were standing around just then, he provoked much laughter. Has he got lost? asked one. Did he lose his way like a child? asked another. Or is he hiding? Is he afraid of us? Has he gone on a voyage? emigrated? – Thus they yelled and laughed. The madman jumped into their midst and pierced them with his eyes. "Whither is God?" he cried; "I will tell you. *We have killed him* – you and I. All of us are his murderers. But how did we do this? How could we drink up the sea? Who gave us the sponge to wipe away the entire horizon? What were we doing when we unchained this earth from its sun? Whither is it moving now? Whither are we moving? Away from all suns? Are we not plunging continually? Backward, sideward, forward, in all directions? Is there still any up or down? Are we not straying as through an infinite nothing? Do we not feel the breath of empty space? Has it not become colder? Is not night continually closing in on us? Do we not need to light lanterns in the morning? Do we hear nothing as yet of the noise of the gravediggers who are burying God? Do we smell nothing as yet of the divine decomposition? Gods, too, decompose. God is dead. God remains dead. And we have killed him. "How shall we comfort ourselves, the murderers of all murderers? What was holiest and mightiest of all that the world has yet owned has bled to death under our knives: who will wipe this blood off us? What water is there for us to clean ourselves? What festivals of atonement, what sacred games shall we have to invent? Is not the greatness of this deed too great for us? Must we ourselves not become gods simply to appear worthy of it? There has never been a greater deed; and whoever is born after us – for the sake of this deed he will belong to a higher history than all history hitherto." Here the madman fell silent and looked again at his listeners; and they, too, were silent and stared at him in astonishment. At last he threw his lantern on the ground, and it broke into pieces and went out. "I have come too early," he said then; "my time is not yet. This tremendous event is still on its way, still wandering; it has not yet reached the ears of men. Lightning and thunder require time; the light of the stars requires time; deeds, though done, still require time to be seen and heard. This deed is still more distant from them than the most distant stars – *and yet they have done it themselves.*" It has been related further that on the same day the madman forced his way into several churches and there struck up his *requiem aeternam deo.*[17] Led out and called to account, he is said always to have replied nothing but: "What after all are these churches now if they are not the tombs and sepulchers of God?"

[. . .]

127

Aftereffects of the most ancient religiosity. – Every thoughtless person supposes that will alone is effective; that willing is something simple, a brute datum, underivable, and intelligible by itself. He is convinced that when he does something – strikes something, for

---

17   Latin: grant God eternal rest. Parody of the Order of Mass for the Dead: "Grant [the dead] eternal rest, O Lord."

example – it is he that strikes, and that he did strike because he *willed* it. He does not see any problem here; the feeling of *will* seems sufficient to him not only for the assumption of cause and effect but also for the faith that he *understands* their relationship. He knows nothing of the mechanism of what happened and of the hundredfold fine work that needs to be done to bring about the strike, or of the incapacity of the will in itself to do even the tiniest part of this work. The will is for him a magically effective force; the faith in the will as the cause of effects is the faith in magically effective forces. Now man believed originally that wherever he saw something happen, a will had to be at work in the background as a cause, and a personal, willing being. Any notion of mechanics was far from his mind. But since man believed, for immense periods of time, only in persons (and not in substances, forces, things, and so forth), the faith in cause and effect became for him the basic faith that he applies wherever anything happens – and this it what he still does instinctively: it is an atavism of the most ancient origin. The propositions, "no effect without a cause," "every effect in turn a cause" appear as generalizations of much more limited propositions: "no effecting without willing"; "one can have an effect only on beings that will"; "no suffering of an effect is ever pure and without consequences, but all suffering consists of an agitation of the will" (toward action, resistance, revenge, retribution). But in the pre-history of humanity both sets of propositions were identical: the former were not generalizations of the latter, but the latter were commentaries on the former. When Schopenhauer assumed that all that has being is only a willing, he enthroned a primeval mythology. It seems that he never even attempted an analysis of the will because, like everybody else, he had *faith* in the simplicity and immediacy of all willing – while willing is actually a mechanism that is so well practiced that it all but escapes the observing eye. Against him I posit these propositions: First, for will to come into being an idea of pleasure and displeasure is needed. Second, when a strong stimulus is experienced as pleasure or displeasure, this depends on the *interpretation* of the intellect which, to be sure, generally does this work without rising to our consciousness: one and the same stimulus can be interpreted as pleasure or displeasure. Third, it is only in intellectual beings that pleasure, displeasure, and will are to be found; the vast majority of organisms has nothing of the sort.

[. . .]

264

What we do. – What we do is never understood but always only praised or censured.

265

Ultimate skepsis. – What are man's truths ultimately? Merely his *irrefutable* errors.

266

Where cruelty is needed. – Those who have greatness are cruel to their virtues and to secondary considerations.

267

With a great goal. – With a great goal one is superior even to justice, not only to one's deeds and one's judges.

268

What makes one heroic? – Going out to meet at the same time one's highest suffering and one's highest hope.

269

In what do you believe? – In this, that the weights of all things must be determined anew.

270

What does your conscience say? – "You shall become the person you are."[18]

271

Where are your greatest dangers? – In pity.

272

What do you love in others? – My hopes.

273

Whom do you call bad? – Those who always want to put to shame.

274

What do you consider most humane? – To spare someone shame.

275

What is the seal of liberation? – No longer being ashamed in front of oneself.

Book IV

276

For the new year. – I still live, I still think: I still have to live, for I still have to think. *Sum, ergo cogito: cogito, ergo sum.*[19] Today everybody permits himself the expression of his wish and his dearest thought; hence I, too, shall say what it is that I wish from

18 Motto derived from Pindar's *Second Pythian Victory-Ode* (l. 73): "Become who you are through knowing." Nietzsche later gave *Ecce Homo* the subtitle "How one becomes what one is."

19 Latin: I am, therefore I think: I think, therefore I am. Playful reworking of Descartes' famous principle "I think, therefore I am," in the Latin version from the second of his *Meditations* (1641).

myself today, and what was the first thought to run across my heart this year – what thought shall be for me the reason, warranty, and sweetness of my life henceforth. I want to learn more and more to see as beautiful what is necessary in things; then I shall be one of those who make things beautiful. *Amor fati:*[20] let that be my love henceforth! I do not want to wage war against what is ugly. I do not want to accuse; I do not even want to accuse those who accuse. *Looking away* shall be my only negation. And all in all and on the whole: some day I wish to be only a Yes-sayer.

277

Personal providence. – There is a certain high point in life: once we have reached that, we are, for all our freedom, once more in the greatest danger of spiritual unfreedom, and no matter how much we have faced up to the beautiful chaos of existence and denied it all providential reason and goodness, we still have to pass our hardest test. For it is only now that the idea of a personal providence confronts us with the most penetrating force, and the best advocate, the evidence of our eyes, speaks for it – now that we can see how palpably always everything that happens to us turns out for the best. Every day and every hour, life seems to have no other wish than to prove this proposition again and again. Whatever it is, bad weather or good, the loss of a friend, sickness, slander, the failure of some letter to arrive, the spraining of an ankle, a glance into a shop, a counter-argument, the opening of a book, a dream, a fraud – either immediately or very soon after it proves to be something that "must not be missing"; it has a profound significance and use precisely for *us.* Is there any more dangerous seduction that might tempt one to renounce one's faith in the gods of Epicurus who have no care and are unknown, and to believe instead in some petty deity who is full of care and personally knows every little hair on our head[21] and finds nothing nauseous in the most miserable small service? Well, I think that in spite of all this we should leave the gods in peace as well as the genii who are ready to serve us, and rest content with the supposition that our own practical and theoretical skill in interpreting and arranging events has now reached its high point. Nor should we conceive too high an opinion of this dexterity of our wisdom when at times we are excessively surprised by the wonderful harmony created by the playing of our instrument – a harmony that sounds too good for us to dare to give the credit to ourselves. Indeed, now and then someone plays with us – good old chance; now and then chance guides our hand, and the wisest providence could not think up a more beautiful music than that which our foolish hand produces then.

278

The thought of death. – Living in the midst of this jumble of little lanes, needs, and voices gives me a melancholy happiness: how much enjoyment, impatience, and desire, how much thirsty life and drunkenness of life comes to light every moment! And yet silence will soon descend on all these noisy, living, life-thirsty people. How his shadow

20   Latin: love of [one's] fate. First occurrence of the formulation in Nietzsche's writings.
21   Allusion to Matthew 10: 30 and Luke 12: 7. The contrast Nietzsche is making here is between the gods of Epicurus, who live a happy and contented life with no interest in the human world, and the petty deity of the Gospels.

stands even now behind everyone, as his dark fellow traveler! It is always like the last moment before the departure of an emigrants' ship: people have more to say to each other than ever, the hour is late, and the ocean and its desolate silence are waiting impatiently behind all of this noise – so covetous and certain of their prey. And all and everyone of them suppose that the heretofore was little or nothing while the near future is everything; and that is the reason for all of this haste, this clamor, this out-shouting and overreaching each other. Everyone wants to be the first in this future – and yet death and deathly silence alone are certain and common to all in this future. How strange it is that this sole certainty and common element makes almost no impression on people, and that nothing is further from their minds than the feeling that they form a brotherhood of death. It makes me happy that men do not want at all to think the thought of death! I should like very much to do something that would make the thought of life even a hundred times more appealing to them.

279

Star friendship. – We were friends and have become estranged. But this was right, and we do not want to conceal and obscure it from ourselves as if we had reason to feel ashamed. We are two ships each of which has its goal and course; our paths may cross and we may celebrate a feast together, as we did – and then the good ships rested so quietly in one harbor and one sunshine that it may have looked as if they had reached their goal and as if they had one goal. But then the almighty force of our tasks drove us apart again into different seas and sunny zones, and perhaps we shall never see each other again; perhaps we shall meet again but fail to recognize each other: our exposure to different seas and suns has changed us. That we have to become estranged is the law *above* us; by the same token we should also become more venerable for each other – and the memory of our former friendship more sacred. There is probably a tremendous but invisible stellar orbit in which our very different ways and goals may be *included* as small parts of this path; let us rise up to this thought. But our life is too short and our power of vision too small for us to be more than friends in the sense of this sublime possibility. – Let us then *believe* in our star friendship even if we should be compelled to be earth enemies.

280

Architecture for the search for knowledge. – One day, and probably soon, we need some recognition of what above all is lacking in our big cities: quiet and wide, expansive places for reflection. Places with long, high-ceilinged cloisters for bad or all too sunny weather where no shouting or noise of carriages can reach and where good manners would prohibit even priests from praying aloud – buildings and sites that would altogether give expression to the sublimity of thoughtfulness and of stepping aside. The time is past when the church possessed a monopoly on reflection, when the *vita contemplativa*[22] always had to be first of all a *vita religiosa*;[23] and everything built by the church gives expression to that idea. I do not see how we could remain content with such buildings even if they were stripped of their churchly purposes. The language

22   Latin: contemplative life.
23   Latin: religious life.

spoken by these buildings is far too rhetorical and unfree, reminding us that they are houses of God and ostentatious monuments of some supramundane intercourse; we who are godless could not think *our thoughts* in such surroundings. We wish to see *ourselves* translated into stone and plants, we want to take walks *in ourselves* when we stroll around these buildings and gardens.

[. . .]

283

Preparatory human beings. – I welcome all signs that a more virile, warlike age is about to begin, which will restore honor to courage above all. For this age shall prepare the way for one yet higher, and it shall gather the strength that this higher age will require some day – the age that will carry heroism into the search for knowledge and that will *wage wars* for the sake of ideas and their consequences. To this end we now need many preparatory courageous human beings who cannot very well leap out of nothing, any more than out of the sand and slime of present-day civilization and metropolitanism – human beings who know how to be silent, lonely, resolute, and content and constant in invisible activities; human beings who are bent on seeking in all things for what in them must be *overcome*; human beings distinguished as much by cheerfulness, patience, unpretentiousness, and contempt for all great vanities as by mag-nanimity in victory and forbearance regarding the small vanities of the vanquished; human beings whose judgment concerning all victors and the share of chance in every victory and fame is sharp and free; human beings with their own festivals, their own working days, and their own periods of mourning, accustomed to command with assur-ance but instantly ready to obey when that is called for – equally proud, equally serv-ing their own cause in both cases; more endangered human beings, more fruitful human beings, happier beings! For believe me: the secret for harvesting from existence the greatest fruitfulness and the greatest enjoyment is – to *live dangerously*! Build your cities on the slopes of Vesuvius! Send your ships into uncharted seas! Live at war with your peers and yourselves! Be robbers and conquerors as long as you cannot be rulers and possessors, you seekers of knowledge! Soon the age will be past when you could be content to live hidden in forests like shy deer. At long last the search for knowledge will reach out for its due; it will want to *rule* and *possess*, and you with it!

[. . .]

289

Embark! – Consider how every individual is affected by an overall philosophical justification of his way of living and thinking: he experiences it as a sun that shines especially for him and bestows warmth, blessings, and fertility on him; it makes him independent of praise and blame, self-sufficient, rich, liberal with happiness and good will; inces-santly it refashions evil into good, leads all energies to bloom and ripen, and does not permit the petty weeds of grief and chagrin to come up at all. In the end one exclaims: How I wish that many such new suns were yet to be created! Those who are evil or unhappy and the exceptional human being – all these should also have their philo-sophy, their good right, their sunshine! What is needful is not pity for them. We must learn to abandon this arrogant fancy, however long humanity has hitherto spent learn-ing and practicing it. What these people need is not confession, conjuring of souls, and forgiveness of sins; what is needful is a new *justice*! And a new watchword. And new philosophers. The moral earth, too, is round. The moral earth, too, has its antipodes. The antipodes, too, have the right to exist. There is yet another world to be discovered – and more than one. Embark, philosophers!

290

One thing is needful. – To "give style" to one's character – a great and rare art! It is practiced by those who survey all the strengths and weaknesses of their nature and then fit them into an artistic plan until every one of them appears as art and reason and even weaknesses delight the eye. Here a large mass of second nature has been added; there a piece of original nature has been removed – both times through long practice and daily work at it. Here the ugly that could not be removed is concealed; there it has been reinterpreted and made sublime. Much that is vague and resisted shaping has been saved and exploited for distant views; it is meant to beckon toward the far and immeasurable. In the end, when the work is finished, it becomes evident how the constraint of a single taste governed and formed everything large and small. Whether this taste was good or bad is less important than one might suppose, if only it was a single taste! It will be the strong and domineering natures that enjoy their finest gaiety in such constraint and perfection under a law of their own; the passion of their tremendous will relents in the face of all stylized nature, of all conquered and serving nature. Even when they have to build palaces and design gardens they demur at giving nature freedom. Conversely, it is the weak characters without power over themselves that *hate* the constraint of style. They feel that if this bitter and evil constraint were imposed upon them they would be demeaned; they become slaves as soon as they serve; they hate to serve. Such spirits – and they may be of the first rank – are always out to shape and interpret their environment as *free* nature: wild, arbitrary, fantastic, disorderly, and surprising. And they are well advised because it is only in this way that they can give pleasure to themselves. For one thing is needful: that a human being should *attain* satisfaction with himself, whether it be by means of this or that poetry and art; only then is a human being at all tolerable to behold. Whoever is dissatisfied with himself is continually ready for revenge, and we others will be his victims, if only by having to endure his ugly sight. For the sight of what is ugly makes one bad and gloomy.

[. . .]

301

The fancy of the contemplatives. – What distinguishes the higher human beings from the lower is that the former see and hear immeasurably more, and see and hear thoughtfully – and precisely this distinguishes human beings from animals, and the higher animals from the lower. For anyone who grows up into the heights of humanity the world becomes ever fuller; ever more fishhooks are cast in his direction to capture his interest; the number of things that stimulate him grows constantly, as does the number of different kinds of pleasure and displeasure: The higher human being always becomes at the same time happier and unhappier. But he can never shake off a *delusion*: He fancies that he is a *spectator* and *listener* who has been placed before the great visual and acoustic spectacle that is life; he calls his own nature *contemplative* and overlooks that he himself is really the poet who keeps creating this life. Of course, he is different from the *actor* of this drama, the so-called active type; but he is even less like a mere spectator and festive guest in front of the stage. As a poet, he certainly has *vis contemplativa*[24] and the ability to look back upon his work, but at the same time also and above all *vis creativa*,[25] which the active human being *lacks*, whatever visual appearances and the faith of all the world may say. We who think and feel at the same time are those who really continually *fashion* something that had not been there before: the whole eternally growing world of valuations, colors, accents, perspectives, scales, affirmations, and negations. This poem that we have invented is continually studied by the so-called practical human beings (our actors) who learn their roles and translate everything into flesh and actuality, into the everyday. Whatever has *value* in our world now does not have value in itself, according to its nature – nature is always value-less, but has been *given* value at some time, as a present – and it was *we* who gave and bestowed it. Only we have created the world *that concerns man*! – But precisely this knowledge we lack, and when we occasionally catch it for a fleeting moment we always forget it again immediately; we fail to recognize our best power and under-estimate ourselves, the contemplatives, just a little. We are *neither as proud nor as happy as we might be.*

[. . .]

310

Will and wave. – How greedily this wave approaches, as if it were after something! How it crawls with terrifying haste into the inmost nooks of this labyrinthine cliff! It seems that it is trying to anticipate someone; it seems that something of value, high value, must be hidden there. – And now it comes back, a little more slowly but still quite white with excitement; is it disappointed? Has it found what it looked for? Does it pretend to be disappointed? – But already another wave is approaching, still more greedily and savagely than the first, and its soul, too, seems to be full of secrets and the lust to dig up treasures. Thus live waves – thus live we who will – more I shall not say. So? You mistrust me? You are angry with me, you beautiful monsters? Are you afraid that I might give away your whole secret? Well, be angry with me, arch your dangerous green bodies as high as you can, raise a wall between me and the sun – as you are doing now! Truly, even now nothing remains of the world but green twilight and green lightning. Carry on as you like, roaring with overweening pleasure and malice – or dive again, pouring your emeralds down into the deepest depths, and throw your infinite white mane of foam and spray over them: Everything suits me, for everything suits you so well, and I am so well-disposed toward you for everything; how could I think of betraying you? For – mark my word! – I know you and your secret, I know your kind! You and I – are we not of one kind? – You and I – do we not have *one secret*?

[. . .]

---

24 Latin: contemplative power.
25 Latin: creative power.

319

As interpreters of our experiences. – One sort of honesty has been alien to all founders of religions and their kind: They have never made their experiences a matter of conscience for knowledge. "What did I really experience? What happened in me and around me at that time? Was my reason bright enough? Was my will opposed to all deceptions of the senses and bold in resisting the fantastic?" None of them has asked such questions, nor do any of our dear religious people ask them even now. On the contrary, they thirst after things that *go against reason*, and they do not wish to make it too hard for themselves to satisfy it. So they experience "miracles" and "rebirths" and hear the voices of little angels! But we, we others who thirst after reason, are determined to scrutinize our experiences as severely as a scientific experiment – hour after hour, day after day. We ourselves wish to be our experiments and guinea pigs.

[. . .]

322

Parable. – Those thinkers in whom all stars move in cyclic orbits are not the most profound. Whoever looks into himself as into vast space and carries galaxies in himself, also knows how irregular all galaxies are; they lead into the chaos and labyrinth of existence.

[. . .]

324

In media vita.[26] – No, life has not disappointed me. On the contrary, I find it truer, more desirable and mysterious every year – ever since the day when the great liberator came to me: the idea that life could be an experiment of the seeker for knowledge – and not a duty, not a calamity, not trickery. – And knowledge itself: let it be something else for others; for example, a bed to rest on, or the way to such a bed, or a diversion, or a form of leisure – for me it is a world of dangers and victories in which heroic feelings, too, find places to dance and play. *"Life as a means to knowledge"* – with this principle in one's heart one can live not only boldly but even gaily, and laugh gaily, too. And who knows how to laugh anyway and live well if he does not first know a good deal about war and victory?

325

What belongs to greatness. – Who will attain anything great if he does not find in himself the strength and the will to *inflict* great suffering? Being able to suffer is the least thing; weak women and even slaves often achieve virtuosity in that. But not to perish of internal distress and uncertainty when one inflicts great suffering and hears the cry of this suffering – that is great, that belongs to greatness.

[. . .]

---

26   Latin: in mid-life.

327

Taking seriously. – In the great majority, the intellect is a clumsy, gloomy, creaking machine that is difficult to start. They call it "taking the matter *seriously*" when they want to work with this machine and think well. How burdensome they must find good think- ing! The lovely human beast always seems to lose its good spirits when it thinks well; it becomes "serious." And "where laughter and gaiety are found, thinking does not amount to anything": that is the prejudice of this serious beast against all "gay science." – Well then, let us prove that this is a prejudice.

[. . .]

334

One must learn to love. – This is what happens to us in music: First one has to *learn to hear* a figure and melody at all, to detect and distinguish it, to isolate it and delimit it as a separate life. Then it requires some exertion and good will to *tolerate* it in spite of its strangeness, to be patient with its appearance and expression, and kindhearted about its oddity. Finally there comes a moment when we are *used* to it, when we wait for it, when we sense that we should miss it if it were missing; and now it continues to compel and enchant us relentlessly until we have become its humble and enrap- tured lovers who desire nothing better from the world than it and only it. But that is what happens to us not only in music. That is how we have *learned to love* all things that we now love. In the end we are always rewarded for our good will, our patience, fairmindedness, and gentleness with what is strange; gradually, it sheds its veil and turns out to be a new and indescribable beauty. That is its *thanks* for our hospitality. Even those who love themselves will have learned it in this way; for there is no other way. Love, too, has to be learned.

335

Long live physics! – How many people know how to observe something? Of the few who do, how many observe themselves? "Everybody is farthest away – from himself";[27] all who try the reins know this to their chagrin, and the maxim "know thyself!" addressed to human beings by a god,[28] is almost malicious. That the case of self-observation is indeed as desperate as that is attested best of all by the manner in which *almost every- body* talks about the essence of moral actions – this quick, eager, convinced, and garrulous manner with its expression, its smile, and its obliging ardor! One seems to have the wish to say to you: "But my dear friend, precisely this is my specialty. You have directed your question to the one person who is entitled to answer you. As it happens, there is nothing about which I am as wise as about this. To come to the point: when a human being judges '*this is right*' and then infers '*therefore it must be done,*' and then proceeds to *do* what he has thus recognized as right and designated as necessary – then the essence of his action is *moral.*" But my friend, you are speaking of three actions instead of one. When you judge "this is right," that is an action, too.

27   Reversal of the common German saying "Everyone is closest to himself," i.e. "Charity begins at home."
28   The inscription on the Temple of Apollo at Delphi.

Might it not be possible that one could judge in a moral and in an immoral manner? *Why* do you consider this, precisely this, right? "Because this is what my conscience tells me; and the voice of conscience is never immoral, for it alone determines what is to be moral." But why do you *listen* to the voice of your conscience? And what gives you the right to consider such a judgment true and infallible? For this *faith* – is there no conscience for that? Have you never heard of an intellectual conscience? A conscience behind your "conscience"? Your judgment "this is right" has a pre-history in your instincts, likes, dislikes, experiences, and lack of experiences. "*How* did it originate there?" you must ask, and then also: "What is it that impels me to listen to it?" You can listen to its commands like a good soldier who hears his officer's command. Or like a woman who loves the man who commands. Or like a flatterer and coward who is afraid of the commander. Or like a dunderhead who obeys because no objection occurs to him. In short, there are a hundred ways in which you can listen to your conscience. But that you take this or that judgment for the voice of conscience – in other words, that you feel something to be right – may be due to the fact that you have never thought much about yourself and simply have accepted blindly that what you had been *told* ever since your childhood was right; or it may be due to the fact that what you call your duty has up to this point brought you sustenance and honors – and you consider it "right" because it appears to you as your own "condition of existence" (and that you have a *right* to existence seems irrefutable to you). For all that, the *firmness* of your moral judgment could be evidence of your personal abjectness, of impersonality; your "moral strength" might have its source in your stubbornness – or in your inability to envisage new ideals. And, briefly, if you had thought more subtly, observed better, and learned more, you certainly would not go on calling this "duty" of yours and this "conscience" of yours duty and conscience. Your understanding *of the manner in which moral judgments have originated* would spoil these grand words for you, just as other grand words, like "sin" and "salvation of the soul" and "redemption" have been spoiled for you. – And now don't cite the categorical imperative, my friend! This term tickles my ear and makes me laugh despite your serious presence. It makes me think of the old Kant who had obtained the "thing in itself" *by stealth* – another very ridiculous thing! – and was punished for this when the "categorical imperative" crept stealthily into his heart and led him *astray* – *back* to "God," "soul," "freedom," and "immortality," like a fox who loses his way and goes astray back into his cage. Yet it had been *his* strength and cleverness that had *broken open* the cage! What? You admire the categorical imperative within you? This "firmness" of your so-called moral judgment? This "unconditional" feeling that "here everyone must judge as I do"? Rather admire your *selfishness* at this point. And the blindness, pettiness, and frugality of your selfishness. For it is selfish to experience one's own judgment as a universal law; and this selfishness is blind, petty, and frugal because it betrays that you have not yet discovered yourself nor created for yourself an ideal of your own, your very own – for that could never be somebody else's and much less that of all, all! Anyone who still judges "in this case everybody would have to act like this" has not yet taken five steps toward self-knowledge. Otherwise he would know that there neither are nor can be actions that are the same; that every action that has ever been done was done in an altogether unique and irretrievable way, and that this will be equally true of every future action; that all regulations about actions relate only to their coarse exterior (even the most inward and subtle regulations of all moralities so far); that these regulations may lead to some semblance of sameness, *but really only to some semblance*; that as one contemplates or looks back upon *any* action at all, it is and remains impenetrable; that our opinions about "good" and "noble" and "great" can never be *proved true* by our actions because every action is unknowable; that our opinions, valuations, and tables of what is good certainly belong among the most powerful levers in the involved mechanism of our actions, but that in any particular case the law of their mechanism is indemonstrable. Let us therefore *limit* ourselves to the purification of our opinions and valuations and to the *creation of our own new tables of what is good*, and let us stop brooding about the "moral value of our actions"! Yes, my friends, regarding all the moral chatter of some about others it is time to feel nauseous. Sitting in moral judgment should offend our taste. Let us leave such chatter and such bad taste to those who have nothing else to do but drag the past a few steps further through time and who never live in the present – which is to say the many, the great majority. We, however, *want to become those we are* – human beings who are new, unique, incomparable, who give themselves laws, who create themselves.[29] To that end we must become the best learners and discoverers of everything that is lawful and necessary in the world: we must become *physicists* in order to be able to be *creators* in this sense – while hitherto all valuations and ideals have been based on *ignorance* of physics or were constructed so as to *contradict* it. Therefore: long live physics! And even more so that which *compels* us to turn to physics – our honesty![30]

[. . .]

339

Vita femina.[31] – For seeing the ultimate beauties of a work, no knowledge or good will is sufficient; this requires the rarest of lucky accidents: The clouds that veil these peaks have to lift for once so that we see them glowing in the sun. Not only do we have to stand in precisely the right spot in order to see this, but the unveiling must have been accomplished by our own soul because it needed some external expression and parable, as if it were a matter of having something to hold on to and retain control of itself. But it is so rare for all of this to coincide that I am inclined to believe that the highest peaks of everything good, whether it be a work, a deed, humanity, or nature, have so far remained concealed and veiled from the great majority and even from the best human beings. But what does unveil itself for us, *unveils itself for us once only*. The Greeks, to be sure, prayed: "Everything beautiful twice and even three times!"[32] They implored the gods with good reason, for ungodly reality gives us the beautiful

---

29   In German: *Wir aber wollen Die werden, die wir sind, – die Neuen, die Einmaligen, die Unvergleichbaren, die Sich-selber-Gesetzgebenden, die Sich-selber-Schaffenden.* A more literal translation might render this as: "We, however, *want to become those we are* – the new, the unique, the incomparable, the self-legislating, the self-creating . . ." thus leaving open the question whether Nietzsche here is referring to "human beings" – as the published translations lead us to suppose – or something other and perhaps "more" than human.
30   In German: *Redlichkeit.*
31   Latin: life is a woman.
32   See Plato, *Gorgias* 498e and *Philebus* 59e–60a.

either not at all or once only. I mean to say that the world is overfull of beautiful
things but nevertheless poor, very poor when it comes to beautiful moments and unveil-
ings of these things. But perhaps this is the most powerful magic of life: it is covered
by a veil interwoven with gold, a veil of beautiful possibilities, sparkling with promise,
resistance, bashfulness, mockery, pity, and seduction. Yes, life is a woman.

340

The dying Socrates. – I admire the courage and wisdom of Socrates in everything he did,
said – and did not say. This mocking and enamored monster and pied piper of Athens,
who made the most overweening youths tremble and sob, was not only the wisest
chatterer of all time: he was equally great in silence. I wish he had remained taciturn
also at the last moment of his life; in that case he might belong to a still higher order
of spirits. Whether it was death or the poison or piety or malice – something loosened his tongue at that moment and he said: "O Crito, I owe Asclepius a rooster."
This ridiculous and terrible "last word" means for those who have ears: "O Crito, *life
is a disease.*" Is it possible that a man like him, who had lived cheerfully and like a
soldier in the sight of everyone, should have been a pessimist? He had merely kept a
cheerful mien while concealing all his life long his ultimate judgment, his inmost feeling. Socrates, Socrates *suffered life!* And then he still revenged himself – with this veiled,
gruesome, pious, and blasphemous saying. Did a Socrates need such revenge? Did his
overrich virtue lack an ounce of magnanimity? – Alas, my friends, we must overcome
even the Greeks![33]

341

The greatest weight. – What, if some day or night a demon were to steal after you into
your loneliest loneliness and say to you: "This life as you now live it and have lived
it, you will have to live once more and innumerable times more; and there will be
nothing new in it, but every pain and every joy and every thought and sigh and everything unutterably small or great in your life will have to return to you, all in the same
succession and sequence – even this spider and this moonlight between the trees, and
even this moment and I myself. The eternal hourglass of existence is turned upside
down again and again, and you with it, speck of dust!" Would you not throw yourself down and gnash your teeth and curse the demon who spoke thus? Or have you
once experienced a tremendous moment when you would have answered him: "You

---

33   Asclepius was the god of healing or medicine, and in Athenian custom people would make
a sacrifice to him in hope of a cure. See Plato, *Phaedo* 118; see also *TI* II. 1. Hugh Tredennick
interprets Socrates' final words as follows: "The cock is either a preliminary offering such as
sufferers made before sleeping the night in his precincts with the hope of waking up cured,
or (more probably) a thank-offering for cure effected. In either case Socrates implies – with a
characteristic mixture of humor, paradox and piety – that death is the cure for life" (Plato, *The
Last Days of Socrates*, ed. and trans. Tredennick, 3rd edn [Harmondsworth: Penguin, 1969],
p. 199). Nietzsche interprets the last words as Socrates' revealing a spirit of revenge towards
the time of life. The desire is for the liberation of the soul from its mortal coil and for release
from empirical life into a realm of timeless being.

are a god and never have I heard anything more divine." If this thought gained possession of you, it would change you as you are or perhaps crush you. The question in each and every thing, "Do you desire this once more and innumerable times more?" would lie upon your actions as the greatest weight. Or how well disposed would you have to become to yourself and to life *to crave nothing more fervently* than this ultimate eternal confirmation and seal? –

342

Incipit tragoedia.[34] – When Zarathustra was thirty years old, he left his home and Lake Urmi and went into the mountains. There he enjoyed his spirit and his solitude, and for ten years did not tire of that. But at last his heart changed – and one morning he rose with the dawn, stepped before the sun, and spoke to it thus: "You great star, what would your happiness be if you did not have those for whom you shine? For ten years you have climbed up to my cave: You would have become weary of your light and of the journey had it not been for me and my eagle and my serpent; but we waited for you every morning, took your overflow from you, and blessed you for it. Behold, I am sick of my wisdom, like a bee that has gathered too much honey; I need hands outstretched to receive it; I want to give away and distribute until the wise among men enjoy their folly once again and the poor their riches. For that I must descend to the depths, as you do in the evening when you go behind the sea and still bring light to the underworld, you over-rich star. Like you I must *go under*, as men put it to whom I wish to descend. Bless me then, you calm eye that can look without envy even upon an all too great happiness. Bless the cup that wants to overflow in order that the water may flow from it golden and carry the reflection of your rapture everywhere. Behold, this cup wants to become empty again, and Zarathustra wants to become man again." – Thus Zarathustra began to go under.

34   Latin: the tragedy begins.

16

Notes from 1881

11[141]
The Recurrence[1] of the Same

Outline

1. The incorporation of the fundamental errors.
2. The incorporation of the passions.
3. The incorporation of knowledge and of renunciatory knowledge. (Passion of knowledge)[2]
4. The innocent man. The individual as experiment. The alleviation of life, abasement, enfeeblement – transition.
5. The new *heavy weight: the eternal recurrence of the same*. Infinite importance of our knowing, erring, our habits, ways of living for all that is to come. What shall we do with the *rest* of our lives – we who have spent the majority of our lives in the most profound ignorance? We shall *teach the doctrine* – it is the most powerful means of *incorporating* it in ourselves. Our kind of blessedness, as teachers of the greatest doctrine.

Early August 1881 in Sils-Maria,
6,000 feet above sea level and much higher above all human things! –

On 4) Philosophy of Indifference. What used to be the strongest stimulus now has a quite different effect: it is seen as just a *game* and accepted (the passions and labors),

---

These *Nachlass* notes are taken from Nietzsche's notebook M III 1, in *KSA*, volume 9. Bold type signifies double underlining. Translators are as follows: 11[141]: Duncan Large with Keith Ansell Pearson; 11[143], 11[146], 11[165], 11[220]: Diane Morgan, Keith Ansell Pearson, and Duncan Large; 11[148], 11[158–60], 11[163], 11[213], 11[338]: Keith Ansell Pearson and Duncan Large. For further insight into the M III 1 notebook, see David Farell Krell, "Eternal Recurrence – of the Same? Reading Notebook M III 1," in id., *Infectious Nietzsche* (Bloomington and Indianapolis: Indiana University Press, 1996), pp. 158–77, and Keith Ansell Pearson, "The Eternal Return of the Overhuman: The Weightiest Knowledge and the Abyss of Light," Journal of Nietzsche Studies, 30 (2005), pp. 1–21.

1 In German: *Wiederkunft*. Nietzsche uses this term throughout these notes in preference to its synonym *Wiederkehr*.
2 The terms used for "knowledge" here are, in turn, *Wissen*, *Wissen*, and *Erkenntniss*.

rejected on principle as a life of untruth, but aesthetically enjoyed and cultivated as form and stimulus; we adopt a child's attitude towards what used to constitute the *seriousness of existence*. The seriousness of our striving, though, is to understand everything as becoming, to deny ourselves as individuals, to look into the world through as *many* eyes as possible, to *live in* drives and activities *so as* to create eyes for ourselves, *temporarily* abandoning ourselves to life so as to rest our eye on it temporarily afterwards: to *maintain* the drives as the foundation of all knowing, but to know at what point they become the enemies of knowing: in sum, to **wait and see** how far *knowledge* and *truth* can be **incorporated** – and to what extent a transformation of man occurs when he finally lives only *so as to know*. – This is a consequence of the passion of knowledge: there is *no way of ensuring its existence* except by preserving as well the sources and powers of knowledge, the errors and passions; from the *conflict* between them it draws its sustaining strength. – What will this life look like from the point of view of its sum total of well-being? *A children's game* under the gaze of the wise man, with power over *the latter* **and** *the former* conditions – and over death, if such a thing is not possible. – But now comes the weightiest knowledge, one which prompts the terrible reconsideration of all forms of life: an absolute surplus of pleasure **must** be demonstrable, or else we must choose to destroy ourselves with regard to humanity as a means of destroying humanity. Just this: we have to put the past – our past and that of all humanity – on the scales and *also* outweigh it – no! this piece of human history *will* and must repeat itself eternally; we can leave *that* out of account, we have no influence over it: even if it afflicts our fellow-feeling and biases us against life in general. If we are not to be overwhelmed by it, our compassion must not be great. Indifference needs to have worked away deep inside us, and enjoyment in contemplation, too. Even the misery of future humanity must *not* concern us. But the question is whether *we* still *want to live*: and how!

For thinking over: the various *sublime states* I have experienced, as the basis for the various *chapters* and their materials – regulating the expression, presentation, pathos at work in each chapter – and in this way to obtain an illustration of my ideal, as it were through *addition*. And then to go still higher!

[. . .]

11[143]

"But if everything is necessary, how can I determine my actions?" This thought and belief are a heavy weight pressing down on you alongside every other weight, and more than them. You say that food, location, air, company transform and condition you? Well, your opinions do so even more, since it is they that determine your choice of food, location, air, company. If you incorporate the thought of thoughts within yourself, it will transform you. The question in everything that you want to do: "is it the case that I want to do it countless times?" is the *greatest* weight.

[. . .]

11[146]

Antipathy towards life is rare. We preserve ourselves in it and are in agreement with it even at the end and in difficult circumstances, *not* out of fear of something worse, *not* out of hope for something better, *not* out of habit (which would be boredom), *not* because of occasional pleasure – but out of *variety* and because basically nothing is a *repetition*, rather it reminds us of something we have experienced. The appeal of what is new and yet is reminiscent of the existing taste – like music with much ugliness.

[. . .]

11[148]

The world of forces does not suffer diminution: otherwise in infinite time it would have grown weak and perished. The world of forces suffers no cessation: otherwise this would have been reached, and the clock of existence would have stopped. So the world of forces never reaches equilibrium; it never has a moment of rest; its force and its movement are equally great for all time. Whatever state this world *can* attain, it must have attained it and not once but countless times. Take this moment: it has already been once and many times and it will return as it is with all its forces distributed as now: and so it stands with the moment that gave birth to it and with the moment that is its child. Man! Your whole life will be turned over like an hourglass time and again, and time and again it will run out – one vast minute of time in between, until all the conditions which produced you, in the world's circular course, come together again. Then you will find again every pain and every pleasure and every friend and enemy and every hope and every error and every leaf of grass and every shaft of sunlight, the whole nexus of all things. This ring, in which you are a tiny grain, shines again and again. And in every ring of human existence altogether there is always an hour when – first for one, then for many, then for all – the most powerful thought surfaces, the thought of the eternal recurrence of all things: each time it is for humanity the hour of *midday*.

[. . .]

11[158]

Let us beware of teaching such a doctrine like a sudden religion! It must sink in slowly; entire generations need to build on it and become fruitful – so that it becomes a great tree overshadowing all humanity to come. What are the couple of millennia in which Christianity has survived! For the most powerful thought many millennia are needed – *long, long* must it be small and powerless!

11[159]

Let us impress the image of eternity on *our* life! This thought contains more than all the religions that have taught us to despise this life as something fleeting and to look towards an indeterminate *other* life.

11[160]

This doctrine is mild in its treatment of those who do not believe in it; it has no hells or threats. Anyone who does not believe has a *fleeting* life in the consciousness of it.

[. . .]

11[163]

The political delusion at which I smile in just the same way that my contemporaries smile at the religious delusion of earlier ages, is principally *secularization*, belief in the *world* and a deliberate ignoring of the "beyond" and the "afterworld." Its goal is the well-being of the *fleeting* individual: which is why its fruit is socialism, i.e. *fleeting individuals* want to conquer their happiness through socialization – they have no reason to *wait*, as do human beings with eternal souls and eternal becoming and future improvement. My doctrine says: the task is to live your life in *such* a way that you have to *want* to live again – you will *in any case*! If striving gives you the highest feeling, then strive; if rest gives you the highest feeling, then rest; if fitting in, following, obedience give you the highest feeling, then obey. Only **make sure** *you become aware of* **what** gives you the highest feeling and then stop at *nothing*! *Eternity* is at stake!

[. . .]

11[165]

We want to experience a work of art over and over again! We should fashion our life in this way, so that we have the same wish with each of its parts! This is the main idea! Only at the end will the *doctrine* be presented of the repetition of everything that has been, once the tendency has been implanted to *create* something which can *flourish* a hundred times more strongly in the sunshine of this doctrine!

[. . .]

11[213]

An infinitely new becoming is a contradiction, since it would presuppose an infinitely *growing* force. But *from what* should it grow! Whence its nourishment, its *surplus* of nourishment! The supposition that the universe is an organism conflicts with the *essence of the organic*.

[. . .]

11[220]

The most powerful thought consumes a good deal of energy [*Kraft*] that was previously at the command of other aims: thus it has a *transforming* effect; it creates new laws of movement for energy but no new energy. Therein lies the possibility, however, of determining and ordering individual people's affects differently.

[. . .]

11[338]

Future history: more and more *this* thought will be victorious – and those who do not believe in it must ultimately *die out* in accordance with their nature!

Only those who consider their existence to be capable of eternal repetition will *remain*: with *such ones*, though, a state is *possible* which no utopian has yet reached!

Part IV

Thus Spoke Zarathustra

Introduction

Thus Spoke Zarathustra merits a section to itself because it is a work like no other in the Nietzschean canon. It is undoubtedly Nietzsche's best-known (and bestselling) work – not least because it has proved the greatest inspiration to other writers and artists[1] – but it is not necessarily his best liked, for its singular style is an acquired taste and inevitably polarizes opinion.[2] Its highly figurative language makes it from one point of view the most accessible (because least philosophically technical) of Nietzsche's works, yet by the same token it can also be the most rebarbative and frustrating, for those who approach the text expecting some "straight answers" are destined to be disappointed by Zarathustra's indirections and abstractions. Nor is it "just" the book's style that Nietzsche's readers have found unpalatable, either: he takes advantage of the fictionalized context to deliver himself of some of his most extreme and (consequently) notorious statements – such as the parting words of the little old woman whom Zarathustra meets towards the end of Part I: "'Are you visiting women? Do not forget your whip!'" (*Z* I, "Of Old and Young Women"). As its subtitle suggests, it is a shibboleth, "a book for everyone and no one"; in *Ecce Homo*, Nietzsche even boasts about how inaccessible it is: "to have understood, that is to say *experienced*, six sentences of that book would raise one to a higher level of mortals than 'modern' man could attain to" (*EH* III. 1). With such a hyperbolic comment, though, one realizes just how inordinately fond of his "favorite son" Nietzsche himself was: it best represented his own ideal of what philosophy should be, and in (what would turn out to be) the final phase of his output he increasingly dwelt on the book, quoting from it repeatedly and showering it in superlatives.[3]

1   The best-known example of this is of course Richard Strauss's tone-poem *Also sprach Zarathustra* (1895–6) and the use made of its opening fanfare by Stanley Kubrick in his film *2001: A Space Odyssey* (1968), but the two other most substantial musical interpretations of Nietzsche also set passages from the book: the fourth movement of Gustav Mahler's Third Symphony (also 1895–6) and Frederick Delius's *Mass of Life* (1904–5).
2   For an account of initial distaste from a writer who would later write her dissertation and first monograph on the book, see the opening of Kathleen Higgins, "Reading *Zarathustra*," in Robert C. Solomon and Kathleen M. Higgins (eds), *Reading Nietzsche* (New York and Oxford: Oxford University Press, 1988), pp. 132–51 (p. 132).
3   To gain a sense of just how far Nietzsche would go, see *EH*, Foreword, 4. Later in *Ecce Homo*, in the section devoted to reviewing the book itself, Nietzsche claims to have surpassed Goethe, Shakespeare and Dante (*EH* III, "Z," 6), and comments: "There is no wisdom, no psychology, no art of speech before Zarathustra."

The genesis of the work can be traced very precisely to an event that occurred in early August 1881, during Nietzsche's first summer in the Upper Engadine. Walking along the shore of Lake Silvaplana, he was struck by an overwhelmingly forceful vision of the eternal recurrence of all things. The "inspiration" of this moment is beautifully described in one of *Ecce Homo*'s most lyrical passages (*EH* III, "*Z*," 3), and gave rise to the notebook sketch we have included in our previous section. Nietzsche did not immediately begin work on a book to incorporate this profoundest of truths, though, for he was still in the throes of his "free spirit period" – he had only just received his copy of the newly printed *Daybreak* at the end of July 1881 – and the next 12 months were taken up with the composition and publication of *The Gay Science* (as well as his unsuccessful love affair with Lou Salomé). As the latter work was published, Nietzsche self-consciously brought the "free spirit period" to a close by having printed on its back cover: "With this book we arrive at the conclusion of a series of writings by FRIEDRICH NIETZSCHE whose common goal it is to erect *a new image and ideal of the free spirit*."[4] In the final section of the first edition of *The Gay Science* itself (*GS* 342), he introduces the figure of Zarathustra for the first time in his writings, in a paragraph which acts as a "trailer" for the new project and would become (with minor alterations) the first section of the next book. But it is not until the beginning of the following year, 1883, that Nietzsche finally starts to fulfill the promise of his vision of the eternal recurrence, almost 18 months after his original insight.[5]

Nietzsche composed Part I of *Thus Spoke Zarathustra* in the last ten days of January 1883, while he was staying in Rapallo on the Gulf of Genoa, and posted it to his publisher Schmeitzner on February 14, which turned out to be the day after Richard Wagner died in Venice.[6] Unusually, Schmeitzner did not have the manuscript typeset straight away – ironically, his printer Teubner's presses were tied up with a huge print-run of half a million church hymnals – and it was only after six months of delay that the book was finally published, in late August 1883.[7] By that stage Nietzsche had already completed Part II, which was written during the first two weeks of July 1883, in Sils-Maria, and printed by the beginning of September (but not immediately distributed); Part III followed in the first half of January 1884, when Nietzsche was staying in Nice, and was published in April 1884. Each of the first three parts was written very quickly, in a matter of ten days or two weeks, over a 12-month period. With the publication of Part III – which includes, in "The Convalescent," an overt (if still mediated) declaration of the eternal recurrence doctrine – Nietzsche had finally fulfilled the promise of his 1881 vision and considered the Zarathustra project at an end, but in the winter of 1884 he returned to it and planned three new parts (culminating in Zarathustra's death). The only one of these to be completed was Part IV, the relatively laborious composition of which took up the two months between mid-December 1884 and

4   Cited in William H. Schaberg, *The Nietzsche Canon: A Publication History and Bibliography* (Chicago and London: University of Chicago Press, 1995), p. 86.
5   Nietzsche himself comments on this "elephantine" eighteen-month "pregnancy" in *EH* III, "*Z*," 1.
6   In *Ecce Homo*, typically, he exaggerates the coincidence: "the closing section [. . .] was completed precisely at that sacred hour when Richard Wagner died in Venice" (*EH* III, "*Z*," 1).
7   For full publication details, see Schaberg, *The Nietzsche Canon*, pp. 87–109.

mid-February 1885; a month later he was describing it in a letter to his amanuensis Heinrich Köselitz (Peter Gast) as "the fourth and last part of *Thus Spoke Zarathustra*,"[8] and it was indeed published as such in late April 1885, in a private printing of only 45 copies.

Anyone who approaches *Zarathustra* on the basis of Nietzsche's earlier work will be unprepared for the challenge it presents, for in style and conception it is a radically new departure from the writings of the "free spirit period," befitting Nietzsche's ambitions for a new kind of affirmative philosophy. Many of the elements of the book's style had been embryonically in evidence in the earlier works – the dramatized narrative enframing *The Wanderer and his Shadow* (1880), for example, or the general delight in wordplay and figurative language[9] – but little that has gone before can truly prepare the reader to experience this highly wrought (some would say overwrought) epic prose-poem. In *Ecce Homo* Nietzsche himself claims that had he published the book under a pseudonym no reader would have guessed that he was its author: "Supposing I had baptized my Zarathustra with another name, for example with the name of Richard Wagner, the perspicuity of two millennia would not have sufficed to divine that the author of *Human, All Too Human* is the visionary of Zarathustra . . ." (*EH* II. 4).[10] The name "Richard Wagner" is not chosen at random, of course: we have already noted that the completion of Part I coincided with Wagner's death, and one way of approaching the book – the grandest product of Nietzsche's creative imagination – is to think of it as his tetralogy, his response to *The Ring of the Nibelung*.[11] On this reading, then, whereas in *The Birth of Tragedy* Nietzsche had hailed the new mythology of Wagnerian music-drama as the great hope for the cultural regeneration of Germany, having become disaffected with Wagner – who is parodied as the sorcerer of Part IV ("'O Zarathustra, everything about me is a lie'") – he now undertakes that task of regeneration himself with a "new mythology" of his own. The four (3 + 1) completed parts of the book have also been interpreted as mirroring the practice of the ancient Greek dramatists, whose tragic trilogies were each followed by a comic satyr-play.[12]

8   Letter of March 14, 1885, *KSB* 7:21.
9   On Nietzsche's figurative style, see Malcolm Pasley (ed.), *Nietzsche: Imagery and Thought. A Collection of Essays* (London: Methuen; Berkeley and Los Angeles: University of California Press, 1978), and Sarah Kofman, *Nietzsche and Metaphor*, trans. Duncan Large (London: Athlone Press; Stanford, CA: Stanford University Press, 1993).
10   Ironically, the one book which he had considered publishing under a pseudonym ("Bernhard Cron"), until dissuaded by his publisher, was *Human, All Too Human* itself – the book which had marked the break with the first phase of his writings. Cf. Schaberg, *The Nietzsche Canon*, p. 58f.
11   Cf. Nietzsche's first description of the work, in a letter to Köselitz of February 1, 1883: "With this book I have entered into a new 'Ring'" (*KSB* 6:321). Curt Paul Janz pursues a similar line by investigating the book's "symphonic" structure (*Friedrich Nietzsche: Biographie*, 3 vols [Munich and Vienna: Hanser, 1978–9], vol. 2, pp. 211–21).
12   Cf. Eugen Fink, *Nietzsche's Philosophy*, trans. Goetz Richter (London and New York: Continuum, 2003), and Gary Shapiro, *Nietzschean Narratives* (Bloomington and Indianapolis: Indiana University Press, 1989), p. 97f. In this context we can recall that *GS* 342 is headed "Incipit tragoedia" ("The tragedy begins").

Many other antecedent models have been suggested by commentators, ranging from the *Thousand and One Nights* to Hegel's *Phenomenology*,[13] and the parodying of Plato's Socrates has been frequently remarked.

The book's most obvious model, though, and at the same time (consequently) the target of Nietzsche's most sustained parody, is the Christian New Testament.[14] Nietzsche's relation to models is always ultimately agonistic: a model serves not as an object of veneration and homage (an "idol"), but as an object of emulation, to be surpassed and overcome. Thus although Zarathustra's life is loosely modeled on that of Jesus, the difference between them is marked in the very first paragraph of the Prologue, for whereas Jesus spent only 40 days and 40 nights in the wilderness before beginning his mission at the age of 30, at the same age Zarathustra heads up into the mountains and spends ten years there. Many of Zarathustra's precepts are formulated in direct opposition to the teachings of Jesus, subverting and mocking them, but the most strikingly mock-biblical aspect of the book is its style, for Nietzsche was self-consciously looking to emulate Martin Luther's translation of the Bible (which enjoys the same prestige within the canon of German literature as does the King James Version in English). After completing Part III, for example, he writes in a note from spring 1884: "The language of Luther and the poetic form of the Bible as the basis for a new German *poetry*: – that is *my* invention!" (*KSA* 11:60).[15] Hence the heady brew that is the language of *Zarathustra*: to the love of figurative language and wordplay (bordering here on excess), and the indulgence in parody and paradox, Nietzsche adds the archaisms of Luther's sixteenth-century German and the parabolic style of Jesus' teaching.

It is not from Christian Scripture that Nietzsche derives his title character, though: the historical Zarathustra (Zoroaster to the Greeks) was a prophet and religious teacher who lived in Persia (modern-day Iran) in the sixth century B.C. and founded the dualistic religion that still bears his name, Zoroastrianism, which is based on the perpetual moral struggle between deified forces of good and evil. Nietzsche appropriates the name Zarathustra for a fictional *alter ego* who preaches the overcoming of that opposition and places himself "beyond good and evil," or as *Ecce Homo* puts it:

13   For the *Thousand and One Nights* see Stanley Rosen, *The Mask of Enlightenment: Nietzsche's "Zarathustra"* (Cambridge and New York: Cambridge University Press, 1995), p. 7; for Hegel's *Phenomenology*, see Tracy B. Strong, *Friedrich Nietzsche and the Politics of Transfiguration*, 3rd edn (Urbana and Chicago: University of Illinois Press, 2000), p. 356 n. 25, and Robert Gooding-Williams, *Zarathustra's Dionysian Modernism* (Stanford, CA: Stanford University Press, 2001), pp. 26–31.

14   Cf. Nietzsche's first description of the work to his publisher: "It is a 'poetic composition,' or a fifth 'gospel,' or something for which no name yet exists" (letter of February 13, 1883, *KSB* 6:327).

15   See also his letter to Erwin Rohde from the same period: "it is my theory that with this Z[arathustra] I have brought the German language to a state of perfection. After *Luther* and *Goethe*, a third step had to be taken" (February 22, 1884, in *Selected Letters of Friedrich Nietzsche*, ed. and trans. Christopher Middleton [Chicago and London: University of Chicago Press, 1969; repr. Indianapolis: Hackett, 1996], p. 221). For Nietzsche's relation to Lutheran German more generally, see Duncan Large, "Nietzsche's Use of Biblical Language," *Journal of Nietzsche Studies*, 22 (Autumn 2001), pp. 88–115.

"the self-overcoming of the moralist into his opposite – *into me* – that is what the name Zarathustra means in my mouth" (*EH* IV. 3). Nietzsche was fully aware of Zarathustra's historical role, but the relation of his creation to the historical figure is at best tangential – he makes little attempt, for example, to parody the Zoroastrian scriptures, the *Zendavesta*, in the same way that he parodies the New Testament – for his Zarathustra is ultimately just another mask for himself. But the fictionalization has a purpose, for Nietzsche's Zarathustra is his ideal teacher:[16] as the title of the book suggests, Zarathustra – like Socrates and Jesus – does not write down his teachings but speaks them, and much of the narrative thread of the book (such as it is), has to do with his attempts to attract a suitable audience, to find disciples with "ears to hear," in a phrase frequently borrowed from Jesus. As far as the book's "audience" is concerned, *Thus Spoke Zarathustra* is one of only two books by Nietzsche that announce in their subtitles who they are for: *Human All Too Human: A Book for Free Spirits* had marked the inception of the previous phase in his philosophical development, and now *Thus Spoke Zarathustra: A Book for Everyone and No One* seeks a new audience, a "happy few" who might yet fathom its depths. To give our readers a sporting chance of understanding their six sentences, we have included in our selection "Zarathustra's Prologue" in its entirety, together with a dozen key chapters taken from across the four parts.

The ten sections of "Zarathustra's Prologue" establish a narrative frame for the "Discourses" (*Reden*) to follow. The story begins briskly, with the immediate introduction of the title character (from the perspective of an omniscient narrator – it is ironic that Nietzsche should adopt the classic "God's-eye view"), but the only biographical details we find out are his name and his age: we are given no physical description of Zarathustra, for example, and Nietzsche gives us no indication of a specific place or time in which the narrative is set. Indeed, although this passage reprises section 342 of *The Gay Science* almost verbatim, the reference there to "Lake Urmi" (an actual lake in northwest Iran) is now dropped in favor of a less specific reference to "the lake of his home."[17] The world Zarathustra inhabits is a generic (though clearly pre-industrial), allegorical landscape of unspecified mountains and forests, lakes, seas and islands; similarly, he himself is the only character in the book to be given a proper name, and the rest are given no more than generic descriptions. For all the philosophical realism of Zarathustra's teaching, the mythopoeic narrative is highly *anti-realist* in its literary conventions.

Zarathustra's mission begins, typically, with a pun: addressing the sun in the first section of the Prologue, he announces that he, too, must "go down" (*untergehen*) from his mountain fastness and be among men once more. The first man he encounters is

---

16   On the book's pedagogical purpose, see Richard Schacht, "Zarathustra/*Zarathustra* as Educator," in Peter R. Sedgwick (ed.), *Nietzsche: A Critical Reader* (Oxford: Blackwell, 1995), pp. 222–49, and Laurence Lampert, *Nietzsche's Teaching: An Interpretation of "Thus Spoke Zarathustra"* (New Haven and London: Yale University Press, 1986).

17   Nietzsche's deliberate expunging of any traces of the historical Zarathustra is even clearer when one compares both these passages with the first draft in his notebook of August 1881: "Zarathustra, born by Lake Urmi, left his homeland in his thirtieth year, went into the province of Arya and in the ten years of his solitude in the mountains composed the *Zend-Avesta*" (*KSA* 9:519).

another hermit, a "holy man" or saint (*Heiliger*) who mistrusts mankind and devotes himself to the praise of God, but Zarathustra knows better, and moves on (both literally and metaphorically), wondering: "Could it be possible! This old saint has not yet heard in his forest that *God is dead!*" (Prologue 2). An insight into the eternal recurrence, as we have seen, was Nietzsche's starting-point in conceiving *Thus Spoke Zarathustra*, but the starting-point, the prerequisite for Zarathustra's teaching, is the death of God as it had been announced by the madman in section 125 of *The Gay Science*. Like the madman, Zarathustra now enters the market square to begin his teaching (Prologue 3), and he finds a ready-made audience there in the shape of a crowd waiting to be entertained by a tightrope-walker (or rope-dancer: *Seiltänzer*), so he launches straight into an oration and unburdens himself of the truth he has been so anxious to communicate: "*I teach you the Overman*. Man is something that should be overcome." In the wake of the death of God, humanity needs (to will) a new goal to fill the void, a new ideal to help it reach out and create beyond itself, and Zarathustra baptizes it with the name of "Overman" (*Übermensch*). Crucially, the Overman is an immanent ideal ("the meaning of the earth") who gives the lie to the values derived from belief in an extra-terrestrial, metaphysical deity – happiness, reason, morality, justice, pity – which we must no longer prize but learn to dismiss with "great contempt." Zarathustra has told the holy man in the forest "I love mankind," and in section 4 of the Prologue he explains that what he loves in man is his transitional nature: "what can be loved in man is that he is a *going-across* [*Übergang*] and a *down-going* [*Untergang*]." Like Zarathustra himself, then, man is also destined to *untergehen*, but in order that something better should arise: Zarathustra praises the man who wants to sacrifice himself in the interest of the future advent of the Overman, and contrasts him with "the Last Man, who makes everything small" (Prologue 5), the self-satisfied man who sees no reason to stretch out beyond himself and aim for anything higher, the herd man of cosy contentment who rejoices in the erasure of difference.[18]

With this image of the "Last Man" Zarathustra intends to conjure up a self-evidently dystopian, nightmare vision which will provoke his audience into a reaction of hearty contempt, but the chasm separating him from his audience is made only too plain when the crowd actually prefers this prospect to that of the Overman. Like the madman of GS 125, then, Zarathustra meets with uncomprehending mockery for he has been casting his pearls before swine. He is finally forced to recognize his error and admit that his message is falling on deaf ears, for the unwanted gift that he bears, the fruit of his ten years of solitary contemplation, is the solution to a problem which his listeners do not yet even recognize (they, too, have not yet heard of the death of God). At this point (Prologue 6) the entertainment for which the crowd has been waiting finally begins, and the narrative switches focus away from Zarathustra to the tightrope-walker, who represents a concretization of Zarathustra's earlier metaphor "Man is a rope, fastened between animal and Overman – a rope over an abyss" (Prologue 4). The tightrope-walker fails to make it across to the other side and falls to his death, but Zarathustra salutes his courage and respects him as a kindred spirit, taking away this "first companion" for burial. After a long night's rest, Zarathustra realizes that he needs to change tack and create for himself a new audience, "luring" away from the

18   Cf. Francis Fukuyama, *The End of History and the Last Man* (New York: Free Press, 1992).

herd disciples who are more amenable to his new truths, for he comes as the destroyer
of the old "tables of values" and the creator of new ones (Prologue 9). He is rejoined
by the animals who accompanied him during his years of solitude – the eagle (symbolizing pride) and the snake (symbolizing cleverness)[19] – and after this abortive false start
to his mission begins his "down-going" anew (Prologue 10).

The first of "Zarathustra's Discourses" begins "I name you three metamorphoses
of the spirit," but it is not at all clear who is the "you" he is addressing. This first
chapter ends by telling us that "At that time he was living in the town called The
Pied Cow," and when Zarathustra leaves this town at the end of Part I he is followed
by "many who called themselves his disciples" (Z I, "Of the Bestowing Virtue"),
so we must think of the discourses in Part I as being addressed to a growing band of
followers. The discourses begin with Zarathustra at his most allegorical: taking his cue
from Ovid (and parodying the Hegelian dialectic) he charts the axiological progress
of the shape-shifting "spirit" metamorphosing through three stages. As a camel it is
"the beast of burden, that renounces and is reverent," dutifully acquiescing and shoul-
dering the weight of tradition (like the ass in Part IV, the beast that says "ye-a"); as a
lion (the original "blond beast" – cf. GM I. 11) the spirit defeats and overcomes the
dragon of Judeo-Christian morality – to the "Thou shalt," the "values of a thousand
years," it says "I will!" – but the lion is still too negative and incapable of creating new
values, for which a third phase is required, the innocence of childlike affirmation.
This tripartite allegorical structure can sustain a variety of interpretations: the last phase
is clearly intended to correspond to the advent of the Overman, but the hermit in
the forest acknowledged Zarathustra's own transformation into "a child, an awakened-
one" (Prologue 2), so perhaps the three metamorphoses can be taken to describe
Zarathustra's own personal odyssey, too. Likewise the three phases can be mapped self-
reflexively onto the development of Nietzsche's career thus far, from the camel-like
period of academic philology through the lion-like "free spirit period" to the childlike affirmation of Zarathustra itself.

The child functions as the hope of humanity, but the child also symbolizes ignorance, and "Of the Despisers of the Body" begins by branding as childlike the belief
in the human "soul." This chapter (like "Of the Afterworldsmen," which precedes it)
is principally directed against Christian metaphysics, which downgrades the physical,
material world of "body" in favor of the soul and its "afterworld," failing to realize
that concepts like "soul," "spirit," "I" ("ego"), and "self" are all merely aspects of the
creative body. "Of the Thousand and One Goals" broadens the critique of existing
value-systems to include the moral precepts of the Greeks, Persians, Jews, and
Germans: the plurality of these "ultimate values" relativizes them, for they are all man-
made and anthropomorphic. Values must be interpreted semiotically, symptomatically
(in Nietzsche's later parlance – cf. TI VII. 1), as the result of a struggle, the expression of a fear or a need – of a people's will to power: "A table of values hangs over
every people. Behold, it is the table of its overcomings; behold, it is the voice of its

19 For the significance of Zarathustra's animals, see especially T. J. Reed, "Nietzsche's
Animals: Idea, Image and Influence," in Pasley (ed.), Nietzsche: Imagery and Thought, pp. 159–219,
and Christa Davis Acampora and Ralph R. Acampora (eds), A Nietzschean Bestiary: Becoming Animal
beyond Docile and Brutal (Lanham and Oxford: Rowman & Littlefield, 2004).

will to power." So far there have been a thousand goals, but "the one goal is still lacking" (the Overman). The final chapter in Part I, "Of the Bestowing Virtue," recapitu-
lates a number of themes from the Prologue: Zarathustra extols as the highest virtue
that bestowing or gift-giving (*schenkend*) virtue shown initially by the sun,[20] and urges
his disciples to "stay loyal to the earth," to acknowledge the death of God and prepare the way for the advent of the Overman. By this stage Zarathustra has succeeded
in collecting together a band of disciples, but in order to prevent them becoming just
another ("higher") herd,[21] he now disperses them and withdraws once more, telling
them to lose him and find themselves.

Further years pass before Zarathustra returns in Part II, sensing that "my *doctrine* is
in danger" (Z II, "The Child with the Mirror"). We have included three chapters
from the second half of Part II, beginning with "Of Self-Overcoming," which follows
on from "Of the Thousand and One Goals" in its recognition that all values must be
interpreted in terms of "the will to power, the unexhausted, procreating life-will."
Life itself has told Zarathustra " 'I am that *which must overcome itself again and again*',"
and although self-overcoming may be carried out in the name of "will to truth" or
"will to existence," the fundamental universal of human existence is in fact will to
power. "Of Immaculate Perception" continues the job of unmasking cherished philosophical notions, in this case " 'pure knowledge' " and disinterested contemplation, which
are dismissed as hypocritical concepts that seek to deny their origins in base desire.
"Of Redemption" tackles a much larger theme, what Zarathustra refers to as "*my* most
intolerable burden," namely the problem of the will's relation to time. Christianity
offers man redemption through belief in the risen Christ who took upon himself the
sins of the world; if redemption is to continue to have any meaning after the
(definitive) death of God, then it must involve man in the affirmation of a self-belief,
a belief in the immanent redemption of chance through the imposition of his will.
But the exercise of the creative will is constrained by the existence of an immutable
past beyond its reach, so: "To redeem the past and to transform every 'It was' into an
'I wanted it thus!' – that alone do I call redemption." The key to achieving redemption in this manner, and thus avoiding lapsing into the spirit of resentment and revenge,
is recognizing the power of the creative will to "will backwards," but Zarathustra breaks
off before explaining how that might be possible, for he is not yet ready to reveal the
answer to this greatest conundrum (the affirmation of the truth of the eternal recurrence), so Part II ends with him leaving his disciples and withdrawing once again.

At the beginning of Part III Zarathustra heads out to sea, and the kinship he feels
with the ship's adventurous sailors leads him to reveal to them rather more of his great
secret in the shape of a riddling vision. "Of the Vision and the Riddle" tells of Zarathustra
the solitary climbing in the twilight, accompanied only by the Spirit of Gravity, "my
devil and arch-enemy [. . .] half dwarf, half mole," who mocks him. The two arrive
at the gateway called "Moment" (*Augenblick*), the point at which the two eternities
of past and future converge: the Spirit of Gravity is first to proclaim that " 'time itself

20   On the thematics of gift-giving in the text, see Gary Shapiro, "On Presents and Presence:
The Gift in *Thus Spoke Zarathustra*," in id., *Alcyone: Nietzsche on Gifts, Noise, and Women* (Albany:
State University of New York Press, 1991), pp. 13–51.
21   Cf. *TI* I. 14: "What? you are searching? you would like to multiply yourself by ten, by
a hundred? you are looking for followers? – Look for *zeros!*"

is a circle'," and Zarathustra responds with " 'must we not return eternally?' " No sooner is the secret of the eternal recurrence – Zarathustra's "abysmal thought" (*abgründlicher Gedanke*) – finally hinted at than, by way of confirmation, Zarathustra has an experience of *déjà vu* (strictly speaking, *déjà entendu*). Then the scene shifts, as if in a dream: the Spirit of Gravity disappears, and in his place a young shepherd writhes with a snake in his mouth until, bidden by Zarathustra, he bites the snake's head off and immediately becomes "a transformed being, surrounded with light, *laughing*." Zarathustra offers no interpretation of these events and simply challenges the sailors to solve his riddle, but we have included two chapters from later in Part III which cast further light on it. "Of the Spirit of Gravity" tells us more about the "half dwarf, half mole" who is the enemy of the "bird-like" hero: he champions moral values that are heteronomous and universal (" 'Good for all, evil for all' "), whereas Zarathustra acknowledges the primacy of autonomous personal values and individual taste. No sooner has Zarathustra summoned up his "abysmal thought" once more, at the opening of "The Convalescent" than he is immediately struck down for seven days and is nursed back to health by his animals. It is they who then give the most unadorned account of the doctrine of eternal recurrence, but for that very reason Zarathustra dismisses their account as "a hurdy-gurdy song." He reveals the solution to the riddle of the shepherd and the snake: he himself was the shepherd, and the snake was his "great disgust [*Ekel*] at man," at the prospect of "eternal recurrence even for the smallest!" By overcoming this disgust, biting the head off the snake, Zarathustra is redeemed and proves himself ready to assume his destiny as *"the teacher of the eternal recurrence."*

Part III represents the thematic culmination of the book, so there is inevitably something anti-climactic about Part IV, in which Zarathustra encounters and proselytizes a variety of "Higher Men."[22] We have included the final two chapters, which bring the book as a whole to its conclusion. "The Sleepwalker's Song" rehearses themes from "Of the Vision and the Riddle" and weaves them into a reprise of Nietzsche's "Ode to Joy," "Zarathustra's Roundelay" from Part III (cf. *Z* III, "The Second Dance Song"), building to the most emphatic affirmation of the eternal recurrence in all its horror: "Did you ever say Yes to one joy? O my friends, then you said Yes to *all* woe as well" (*Z* IV, "The Sleepwalker's Song," 10). The following morning Zarathustra receives a sign with the arrival of a new animal, a lion, which persuades him (following the logic of "Of the Three Metamorphoses") that his children are near. The lion's roar scatters the Higher Men from Zarathustra's cave and he realizes that he feels no pity for them, but has overcome this, his "ultimate sin," and become ripe for his work, a new mission.

Thus Spoke Zarathustra was to have no more parts, though, for by 1885 Nietzsche had finally grown impatient with expressing his philosophy through a fictional intermediary. It was time to honor the resolution he had confided in his notebook the previous year: "Resolution: I want to speak, and no longer Zarathustra" (*KSA* 11:83).

---

22 The most exhaustive and authoritative commentary on the text, by Laurence Lampert, considers Part IV briefly in an appendix. Others have treated it more sympathetically, e.g. Kathleen Higgins reads it rather as an exercise in Menippean satire. See, respectively, Lampert, *Nietzsche's Teaching*, pp. 287–311, and Kathleen Marie Higgins, *Nietzsche's "Zarathustra"* (Philadelphia: Temple University Press, 1987), pp. 203–32.

17

Thus Spoke Zarathustra: A Book for Everyone and No One (1883–5)

Zarathustra's Prologue

1

When Zarathustra was thirty years old, he left his home and the lake of his home and went into the mountains. Here he had the enjoyment of his spirit and his solitude and he did not weary of it for ten years. But at last his heart turned – and one morning he rose with the dawn, stepped before the sun, and spoke to it thus:

Great star! What would your happiness be, if you had not those for whom you shine!

You have come up here to my cave for ten years: you would have grown weary of your light and of this journey, without me, my eagle and my serpent.

But we waited for you every morning, took from you your superfluity and blessed you for it.

Behold! I am weary of my wisdom, like a bee that has gathered too much honey; I need hands outstretched to take it.

I should like to give it away and distribute it, until the wise among men have again become happy in their folly and the poor happy in their wealth.

To that end, I must descend into the depths: as you do at evening, when you go behind the sea and bring light to the underworld too, superabundant star!

Like you, I must *go down*[1] – as men, to whom I want to descend, call it.

So bless me then, tranquil eye, that can behold without envy even an excessive happiness!

Bless the cup that wants to overflow, that the waters may flow golden from him and bear the reflection of your joy over all the world!

Behold! This cup wants to be empty again, and Zarathustra wants to be man again.

Thus began Zarathustra's down-going.

---

1 In German: *untergehen*. Three meanings are in play here, and later in the book: not only "go down," but also "set" (as of the sun) and "go under" (be destroyed).

2

Zarathustra went down the mountain alone, and no one met him. But when he entered the forest, an old man, who had left his holy hut to look for roots in the forest, suddenly stood before him. And the old man spoke thus to Zarathustra:

'This wanderer is no stranger to me: he passed by here many years ago. He was called Zarathustra; but he has changed.

'Then you carried your ashes to the mountains: will you today carry your fire into the valleys? Do you not fear an incendiary's punishment?

'Yes, I recognize Zarathustra. His eyes are clear, and no disgust lurks about his mouth. Does he not go along like a dancer?

'How changed Zarathustra is! Zarathustra has become – a child, an awakened-one: what do you want now with the sleepers?

'You lived in solitude as in the sea, and the sea bore you. Alas, do you want to go ashore? Alas, do you want again to drag your body yourself?'

Zarathustra answered: 'I love mankind.'

'Why', said the saint, 'did I go into the forest and the desert? Was it not because I loved mankind all too much?

'Now I love God: mankind I do not love. Man is too imperfect a thing for me. Love of mankind would destroy me.'

Zarathustra answered: 'What did I say of love? I am bringing mankind a gift.'

'Give them nothing,' said the saint. 'Rather take something off them and bear it with them – that will please them best; if only it be pleasing to you!

'And if you want to give to them, give no more than an alms, and let them beg for that!'

'No', answered Zarathustra, 'I give no alms. I am not poor enough for that.'

The saint laughed at Zarathustra, and spoke thus: 'See to it that they accept your treasures! They are mistrustful of hermits, and do not believe that we come to give.

'Our steps ring too lonely through their streets. And when at night they hear in their beds a man going by long before the sun has risen, they probably ask themselves: Where is that thief going?

'Do not go to men, but stay in the forest! Go rather to the animals! Why will you not be as I am – a bear among bears, a bird among birds?'

'And what does the saint do in the forest? asked Zarathustra.

The saint answered: 'I make songs and sing them, and when I make songs, I laugh, weep, and mutter: thus I praise God.

'With singing, weeping, laughing, and muttering I praise the God who is my God. But what do you bring us as a gift?'

When Zarathustra heard these words, he saluted the saint and said: 'What should I have to give you! But let me go quickly, that I may take nothing from you!' And thus they parted from one another, the old man and Zarathustra, laughing as two boys laugh.

But when Zarathustra was alone, he spoke thus to his heart: 'Could it be possible! This old saint has not yet heard in his forest that *God is dead*!' –

3

When Zarathustra arrived at the nearest of the towns lying against the forest, he found in that very place many people assembled in the market square: for it had been announced that a tight-rope walker would be appearing. And Zarathustra spoke thus to the people:

I teach you the Overman.[2] Man is something that should be overcome. What have you done to overcome him?

All creatures hitherto have created something beyond themselves: and do you want to be the ebb of this great tide, and return to the animals rather than overcome man?

What is the ape to men? A laughing-stock or a painful embarrassment. And just so shall man be to the Overman: a laughing-stock or a painful embarrassment.

You have made your way from worm to man, and much in you is still worm. Once you were apes, and even now man is more of an ape than any ape.

But he who is the wisest among you, he also is only a discord and hybrid of plant and of ghost. But do I bid you become ghosts or plants?

Behold, I teach you the Overman.

The Overman is the meaning of the earth. Let your will say: The Overman *shall be* the meaning of the earth!

I entreat you, my brothers, *remain true to the earth*, and do not believe those who speak to you of superterrestrial hopes! They are poisoners, whether they know it or not.

They are despisers of life, atrophying and self-poisoned men, of whom the earth is weary: so let them be gone!

Once blasphemy against God was the greatest blasphemy, but God died, and thereupon these blasphemers died too. To blaspheme the earth is now the most dreadful offence, and to esteem the bowels of the Inscrutable more highly than the meaning of the earth.

Once the soul looked contemptuously upon the body: and then this contempt was the supreme good – the soul wanted the body lean, monstrous, famished. So the soul thought to escape from the body and from the earth.

Oh, this soul was itself lean, monstrous, and famished: and cruelty was the delight of this soul!

But tell me, my brothers: What does your body say about your soul? Is your soul not poverty and dirt and a miserable ease?

In truth, man is a polluted river. One must be a sea, to receive a polluted river and not be defiled.

Behold, I teach you the Overman: he is this sea, in him your great contempt can go under.

What is the greatest thing you can experience? It is the hour of the great contempt. The hour in which even your happiness grows loathsome to you, and your reason and your virtue also.

The hour when you say: 'What good is my happiness? It is poverty and dirt and a miserable ease. But my happiness should justify existence itself!'

The hour when you say: 'What good is my reason? Does it long for knowledge as the lion for its food? It is poverty and dirt and a miserable ease!'

The hour when you say: 'What good is my virtue? It has not yet driven me mad! How tired I am of my good and my evil! It is all poverty and dirt and a miserable ease!'

---

2   In German: *Übermensch*. The translation has been modified from "Superman" to "Overman" throughout.

The hour when you say: 'What good is my justice? I do not see that I am fire and hot coals. But the just man is fire and hot coals!'

The hour when you say: 'What good is my pity? Is not pity the cross upon which he who loves man is nailed? But my pity is no crucifixion!'

Have you ever spoken thus? Have you ever cried thus? Ah, that I had heard you crying thus!

It is not your sin, but your moderation that cries to heaven, your very meanness in sinning cries to heaven!

Where is the lightning to lick you with its tongue? Where is the madness, with which you should be cleansed?

Behold, I teach you the Overman: he is this lightning, he is this madness!

When Zarathustra had spoken thus, one of the people cried: 'Now we have heard enough of the tight-rope walker; let us see him, too!' And all the people laughed at Zarathustra. But the tight-rope walker, who thought that the words applied to him, set to work.

4

But Zarathustra looked at the people and marvelled. Then he spoke thus:

Man is a rope, fastened between animal and Overman – a rope over an abyss.

A dangerous going-across, a dangerous wayfaring, a dangerous looking-back, a dangerous shuddering and staying-still.

What is great in man is that he is a bridge and not a goal; what can be loved in man is that he is a *going-across* and a *down-going*.[3]

I love those who do not know how to live except their lives be a down-going, for they are those who are going across.

I love the great despisers, for they are the great venerators and arrows of longing for the other bank.

I love those who do not first seek beyond the stars for reasons to go down and to be sacrifices: but who sacrifice themselves to the earth, that the earth may one day belong to the Overman.

I love him who lives for knowledge and who wants knowledge that one day the Overman may live. And thus he wills his own downfall.

I love him who works and invents that he may build a house for the Overman and prepare earth, animals, and plants for him: for thus he wills his own downfall.

I love him who loves his virtue: for virtue is will to downfall and an arrow of longing.

I love him who keeps back no drop of spirit for himself, but wants to be the spirit of his virtue entirely: thus he steps as spirit over the bridge.

I love him who makes a predilection and a fate of his virtue: thus for his virtue's sake he will live or not live.

I love him who does not want too many virtues. One virtue is more virtue than two, because it is more of a knot for fate to cling to.

I love him whose soul is lavish, who neither wants nor returns thanks: for he always gives and will not preserve himself.

3   In German: *ein Übergang und ein Untergang.*

I love him who is ashamed when the dice fall in his favour and who then asks: Am I then a cheat? – for he wants to perish.

I love him who throws golden words in advance of his deeds and always performs more than he promised: for he wills his own downfall.

I love him who justifies the men of the future and redeems the men of the past: for he wants to perish by the men of the present.

I love him who chastises his God because he loves his God: for he must perish by the anger of his God.

I love him whose soul is deep even in its ability to be wounded, and whom even a little thing can destroy: thus he is glad to go over the bridge.

I love him whose soul is overfull, so that he forgets himself and all things are in him: thus all things become his downfall.

I love him who is of a free spirit and a free heart: thus his head is only the bowels of his heart, but his heart drives him to his downfall.

I love all those who are like heavy drops falling singly from the dark cloud that hangs over mankind: they prophesy the coming of the lightning and as prophets they perish.

Behold, I am a prophet of the lightning and a heavy drop from the cloud: but this lightning is called Overman. –

5

When Zarathustra had spoken these words he looked again at the people and fell silent. There they stand (he said to his heart), there they laugh: they do not understand me, I am not the mouth for these ears.

Must one first shatter their ears to teach them to hear with their eyes? Must one rumble like drums and Lenten preachers? Or do they believe only those who stammer?

They have something of which they are proud. What is it called that makes them proud? They call it culture, it distinguishes them from the goatherds.

Therefore they dislike hearing the word 'contempt' spoken of them. So I shall speak to their pride.

So I shall speak to them of the most contemptible man: and that is the *Last Man*.[4]

And thus spoke Zarathustra to the people:

It is time for man to fix his goal. It is time for man to plant the seed of his highest hope.

His soil is still rich enough for it. But this soil will one day be poor and weak; no longer will a high tree be able to grow from it.

Alas! The time is coming when man will no more shoot the arrow of his longing out over mankind, and the string of his bow will have forgotten how to twang!

I tell you: one must have chaos in one, to give birth to a dancing star. I tell you: you still have chaos in you.

Alas! The time is coming when man will give birth to no more stars. Alas! The time of the most contemptible man is coming, the man who can no longer despise himself.

Behold! I shall show you the *Last Man*.

---

4   In German: *der letzte Mensch*. The translation has been modified from "Ultimate Man" to "Last Man" throughout.

'What is love? What is creation? What is longing? What is a star?' thus asks the Last Man and blinks.

The earth has become small, and upon it hops the Last Man, who makes everything small. His race is as inexterminable as the flea; the Last Man lives longest.

'We have discovered happiness,' say the Last Men and blink.

They have left the places where living was hard: for one needs warmth. One still loves one's neighbour and rubs oneself against him: for one needs warmth.

Sickness and mistrust count as sins with them: one should go about warily. He is a fool who still stumbles over stones or over men!

A little poison now and then: that produces pleasant dreams. And a lot of poison at last, for a pleasant death.

They still work, for work is entertainment. But they take care the entertainment does not exhaust them.

Nobody grows rich or poor any more: both are too much of a burden. Who still wants to rule? Who obey? Both are too much of a burden.

No herdsman and one herd. Everyone wants the same thing, everyone is the same: whoever thinks otherwise goes voluntarily into the madhouse.

'Formerly all the world was mad,' say the most acute of them and blink.

They are clever and know everything that has ever happened: so there is no end to their mockery. They still quarrel, but they soon make up – otherwise indigestion would result.

They have their little pleasure for the day and their little pleasure for the night: but they respect health.

'We have discovered happiness,' say the Last Men and blink. –

And here ended Zarathustra's first discourse, which is also called 'The Prologue': for at this point the shouting and mirth of the crowd interrupted him, 'Give us this Last Man, O Zarathustra' – so they cried – 'make us into this Last Man! You can have the Overman!' And all the people laughed and shouted. But Zarathustra grew sad and said to his heart:

They do not understand me: I am not the mouth for these ears.

Perhaps I lived too long in the mountains, listened too much to the trees and the streams: now I speak to them as to goatherds.

Unmoved is my soul and bright as the mountains in the morning. But they think me cold and a mocker with fearful jokes.

And now they look at me and laugh: and laughing, they still hate me. There is ice in their laughter.

6

But then something happened that silenced every mouth and fixed every eye. In the meantime, of course, the tight-rope walker had begun his work: he had emerged from a little door and was proceeding across the rope, which was stretched between two towers and thus hung over the people and the market square. Just as he had reached the middle of his course the little door opened again and a brightly-dressed fellow like a buffoon sprang out and followed the former with rapid steps. 'Forward, lame-foot!' cried his fearsome voice, 'forward sluggard, intruder, pallid-face! Lest I tickle you with my heels! What are you doing here between towers? You belong in the tower, you should be locked up, you are blocking the way of a better man than you!' And with each word he came nearer and nearer to him: but when he was only a single pace behind him, there occurred the dreadful thing that silenced every mouth and fixed every eye: he emitted a cry like a devil and sprang over the man standing in his path. But the latter, when he saw his rival thus triumph, lost his head and the rope; he threw away his pole and fell, faster even than it, like a vortex of legs and arms. The market square and the people were like a sea in a storm: they flew apart in disorder, especially where the body would come crashing down.

But Zarathustra remained still and the body fell quite close to him, badly injured and broken but not yet dead. After a while, consciousness returned to the shattered man and he saw Zarathustra kneeling beside him. 'What are you doing?' he asked at length. 'I've known for a long time that the Devil would trip me up. Now he's dragging me to Hell: are you trying to prevent him?'

'On my honour, friend,' answered Zarathustra, 'all you have spoken of does not exist: there is no Devil and no Hell. Your soul will be dead even before your body: therefore fear nothing any more!'

The man looked up mistrustfully. 'If you are speaking the truth,' he said then, 'I leave nothing when I leave life. I am not much more than an animal which has been taught to dance by blows and starvation.'

'Not so,' said Zarathustra. 'You have made danger your calling, there is nothing in that to despise. Now you perish through your calling: so I will bury you with my own hands.'

When Zarathustra had said this the dying man replied no more; but he motioned with his hand, as if he sought Zarathustra's hand to thank him. –

7

In the meanwhile, evening had come and the market square was hidden in darkness: then the people dispersed, for even curiosity and terror grow tired. But Zarathustra sat on the ground beside the dead man and was sunk in thought: thus he forgot the time. But at length it became night and a cold wind blew over the solitary figure. Then Zarathustra arose and said to his heart:

Truly, Zarathustra has had a handsome catch today! He caught no man, but he did catch a corpse.

Uncanny is human existence and still without meaning: a buffoon can be fatal to it.

I want to teach men the meaning of their existence: which is the Overman, the lightning from the dark cloud man.

But I am still distant from them, and my meaning does not speak to their minds. To men, I am still a cross between a fool and a corpse.

Dark is the night, dark are Zarathustra's ways. Come, cold and stiff companion! I am going to carry you to the place where I shall bury you with my own hands.

8

When Zarathustra had said this to his heart he loaded the corpse on to his back and set forth. He had not gone a hundred paces when a man crept up to him and whispered in his ear – and behold! it was the buffoon of the tower who spoke to him. 'Go away from this town, O Zarathustra,' he said. 'Too many here hate you. The good and the just hate you and call you their enemy and despiser; the faithful of the true faith hate you, and they call you a danger to the people. It was lucky for you that they laughed at you: and truly you spoke like a buffoon. It was lucky for you that you made company with the dead dog; by so abasing yourself you have saved yourself for today. But leave this town – or tomorrow I shall jump over you, a living man over a dead one.' And when he had said this, the man disappeared; Zarathustra, however, went on through the dark streets.

At the town gate the gravediggers accosted him: they shone their torch in his face, recognized Zarathustra and greatly derided him. 'Zarathustra is carrying the dead dog away: excellent that Zarathustra has become a gravedigger! For our hands are too clean for this roast. Does Zarathustra want to rob the Devil of his morsel? Good luck then! A hearty appetite! But if the Devil is a better thief than Zarathustra! – he will steal them both, he will eat them both!' And they laughed and put their heads together.

Zarathustra said nothing and went his way. When he had walked for two hours past woods and swamps he had heard too much hungry howling of wolves and he grew hungry himself. So he stopped at a lonely house in which a light was burning.

'Hunger has waylaid me', said Zarathustra, 'like a robber. My hunger has waylaid me in woods and swamps, and in the depth of night.

'My hunger has astonishing moods. Often it comes to me only after mealtimes, and today it did not come at all: where has it been?'

And with that, Zarathustra knocked on the door of the house. An old man appeared; he carried a light and asked: 'Who comes here to me and to my uneasy sleep?'

'A living man and a dead,' said Zarathustra. 'Give me food and drink, I forgot about them during the day. He who feeds the hungry refreshes his own soul: thus speaks wisdom.'

The old man went away, but returned at once and offered Zarathustra bread and wine. 'This is a bad country for hungry people,' he said. 'That is why I live here. Animals and men come here to me, the hermit. But bid your companion eat and drink, he is wearier than you.' Zarathustra answered: 'My companion is dead, I shall hardly be able to persuade him.' 'That is nothing to do with me,' said the old man morosely. 'Whoever knocks at my door must take what I offer him. Eat, and fare you well!'

After that, Zarathustra walked two hours more and trusted to the road and to the light of the stars: for he was used to walking abroad at night and liked to look into the face of all that slept. But when morning dawned, Zarathustra found himself in a thick forest and the road disappeared. Then he laid the dead man in a hollow tree at his head – for he wanted to protect him from the wolves – and laid himself down on the mossy ground. And straightway he fell asleep, weary in body but with a soul at rest.

9

Zarathustra slept long, and not only the dawn but the morning too passed over his head. But at length he opened his eyes: in surprise Zarathustra gazed into the forest and the stillness, in surprise he gazed into himself. Then he arose quickly, like a seafarer who suddenly sees land, and rejoiced: for he beheld a new truth. And then he spoke to his heart thus:

A light has dawned for me: I need companions, living ones, not dead companions and corpses which I carry with me wherever I wish.

But I need living companions who follow me because they want to follow themselves – and who want to go where I want to go.

A light has dawned for me: Zarathustra shall not speak to the people but to companions! Zarathustra shall not be herdsman and dog to the herd!

To lure many away from the herd – that is why I have come. The people and the herd shall be angry with me: the herdsmen shall call Zarathustra a robber.

I say herdsmen, but they call themselves the good and the just. I say herdsmen: but they call themselves the faithful of the true faith.

Behold the good and the just! Whom do they hate most? Him who smashes their tables of values, the breaker, the law-breaker – but he is the creator.

Behold the faithful of all faiths! Whom do they hate the most? Him who smashes their tables of values, the breaker, the law-breaker – but he is the creator.

The creator seeks companions, not corpses or herds or believers. The creator seeks fellow-creators, those who inscribe new values on new tables.

The creator seeks companions and fellow-harvesters: for with him everything is ripe for harvesting. But he lacks his hundred sickles: so he tears off the ears of corn and is vexed.

The creator seeks companions and such as know how to whet their sickles. They will be called destroyers and despisers of good and evil. But they are harvesters and rejoicers.

Zarathustra seeks fellow-creators, fellow-harvesters, and fellow-rejoicers: what has he to do with herds and herdsmen and corpses!

And you, my first companion, fare you well! I have buried you well in your hollow tree, I have hidden you well from the wolves.

But I am leaving you, the time has come. Between dawn and dawn a new truth has come to me.

I will not be herdsman or gravedigger. I will not speak again to the people: I have spoken to a dead man for the last time.

I will make company with creators, with harvesters, with rejoicers: I will show them the rainbow and the stairway to the Overman.

I shall sing my song to the lone hermit and to the hermits in pairs; and I will make the heart of him who still has ears for unheard-of things heavy with my happiness.

I make for my goal, I go my way; I shall leap over the hesitating and the indolent. Thus may my going-forward be their going-down!

10

Zarathustra said this to his heart as the sun stood at noon: then he looked inquiringly into the sky – for he heard above him the sharp cry of a bird. And behold! An eagle was sweeping through the air in wide circles, and from it was hanging a serpent, not like a prey but like a friend: for it was coiled around the eagle's neck.

'It is my animals!' said Zarathustra and rejoiced in his heart.

'The proudest animal under the sun and the wisest animal under the sun – they have come scouting.

'They wanted to learn if Zarathustra was still alive. Am I in fact alive?

'I found it more dangerous among men than among animals; Zarathustra is following dangerous paths. May my animals lead me!'

When Zarathustra had said this he recalled the words of the saint in the forest, sighed, and spoke thus to his heart:

'I wish I were wise! I wish I were wise from the heart of me, like my serpent!

'But I am asking the impossible: therefore I ask my pride always to go along with my wisdom!

'And if one day my wisdom should desert me — ah, it loves to fly away! — then may my pride too fly with my folly!'

Thus began Zarathustra's down-going.

Zarathustra's Discourses

Part I

Of the Three Metamorphoses

I name you three metamorphoses of the spirit: how the spirit shall become a camel, and the camel a lion, and the lion at last a child.

There are many heavy things for the spirit, for the strong, weight-bearing spirit in which dwell respect and awe: its strength longs for the heavy, for the heaviest.

What is heavy? thus asks the weight-bearing spirit, thus it kneels down like the camel and wants to be well laden.

What is the heaviest thing, you heroes? so asks the weight-bearing spirit, that I may take it upon me and rejoice in my strength.

Is it not this: to debase yourself in order to injure your pride? To let your folly shine out in order to mock your wisdom?

Or is it this: to desert our cause when it is celebrating its victory? To climb high mountains in order to tempt the tempter?

Or is it this: to feed upon the acorns and grass of knowledge and for the sake of truth to suffer hunger of the soul?

Or is it this: to be sick and to send away comforters and make friends with the deaf, who never hear what you ask?

Or is it this: to wade into dirty water when it is the water of truth, and not to disdain cold frogs and hot toads?

Or is it this: to love those who despise us and to offer our hand to the ghost when it wants to frighten us?

The weight-bearing spirit takes upon itself all these heaviest things: like a camel hurrying laden into the desert, thus it hurries into its desert.

But in the loneliest desert the second metamorphosis occurs: the spirit here becomes a lion; it wants to capture freedom and be lord in its own desert.

It seeks here its ultimate lord: it will be an enemy to him and to its ultimate God, it will struggle for victory with the great dragon.

What is the great dragon which the spirit no longer wants to call lord and God? The great dragon is called 'Thou shalt'. But the spirit of the lion says 'I will!'

'Thou shalt' lies in its path, sparkling with gold, a scale-covered beast, and on every scale glitters golden 'Thou shalt'.

Values of a thousand years glitter on the scales, and thus speaks the mightiest of all dragons: 'All the values of things – glitter on me.

'All values have already been created, and all created values - are in me. Truly, there shall be no more "I will"!' Thus speaks the dragon.

My brothers, why is the lion needed in the spirit? Why does the beast of burden, that renounces and is reverent, not suffice?

To create new values – even the lion is incapable of that: but to create itself freedom for new creation – that the might of the lion can do.

To create freedom for itself and a sacred No even to duty: the lion is needed for that, my brothers.

To seize the right to new values – that is the most terrible proceeding for a weight-bearing and reverential spirit. Truly, to this spirit it is a theft and a work for an animal of prey.

Once it loved this 'Thou shalt' as its holiest thing: now it has to find illusion and caprice even in the holiest, that it may steal freedom from its love: the lion is needed for this theft.

But tell me, my brothers, what can the child do that even the lion cannot? Why must the preying lion still become a child?

The child is innocence and forgetfulness, a new beginning, a sport, a self-propelling wheel, a first motion, a sacred Yes.

Yes, a sacred Yes is needed, my brothers, for the sport of creation: the spirit now wills *its own* will, the spirit sundered from the world now wins *its own* world.

I have named you three metamorphoses of the spirit: how the spirit became a camel, and the camel a lion, and the lion at last a child. –

Thus spoke Zarathustra. And at that time he was living in the town called The Pied Cow.

[. . .]

Of the Despisers of the Body

I wish to speak to the despisers of the body. Let them not learn differently nor teach differently, but only bid farewell to their own bodies – and so become dumb.

'I am body and soul' – so speaks the child. And why should one not speak like children?

But the awakened, the enlightened man says: I am body entirely, and nothing beside; and soul is only a word for something in the body.

The body is a great intelligence, a multiplicity with one sense, a war and a peace, a herd and a herdsman.

Your little intelligence, my brother, which you call 'spirit',[5] is also an instrument of your body, a little instrument and toy of your great intelligence.

You say 'I' and you are proud of this word. But greater than this – although you will not believe in it – is your body and its great intelligence, which does not say 'I' but performs 'I'.

5   In German: *"Geist."* The word has three basic meanings: spirit, mind, and intellect.

What the sense feels, what the spirit perceives, is never an end in itself. But sense and spirit would like to persuade you that they are the end of all things: they are as vain as that.

Sense and spirit are instruments and toys: behind them still lies the Self. The Self seeks with the eyes of the sense, it listens too with the ears of the spirit.

The Self is always listening and seeking: it compares, subdues, conquers, destroys. It rules and is also the Ego's ruler.[6]

Behind your thoughts and feelings, my brother, stands a mighty commander, an unknown sage – he is called Self. He lives in your body, he is your body.

There is more reason in your body than in your best wisdom. And who knows for what purpose your body requires precisely your best wisdom?

Your Self laughs at your Ego and its proud leapings. 'What are these leapings and flights of thought to me?' it says to itself. 'A by-way to my goal. I am the Ego's leading-string and I prompt its conceptions.'

The Self says to the Ego: 'Feel pain!' Thereupon it suffers and gives thought how to end its suffering – and it is *meant* to think for just that purpose.

The Self says to the Ego: 'Feel joy!' Thereupon it rejoices and gives thought how it may often rejoice – and it is *meant* to think for just that purpose.

I want to say a word to the despisers of the body. It is their esteem that produces this disesteem. What is it that created esteem and disesteem and value and will?

The creative Self created for itself esteem and disesteem, it created for itself joy and sorrow. The creative body created spirit for itself, as a hand of its will.

Even in your folly and contempt, you despisers of the body, you serve your Self. I tell you: your Self itself wants to die and turn away from life.

Your Self can no longer perform that act which it most desires to perform: to create beyond itself. That is what it most wishes to do, that is its whole ardour.

But now it has grown too late for that: so your Self wants to perish, you despisers of the body.

Your Self wants to perish, and that is why you have become despisers of the body! For no longer are you able to create beyond yourselves.

And therefore you are now angry with life and with the earth. An unconscious envy lies in the sidelong glance of your contempt.

I do not go your way, you despisers of the body! You are not bridges to the Overman!

Thus spoke Zarathustra.

[...]

Of the Thousand and One Goals

Zarathustra has seen many lands and many peoples: thus he has discovered the good and evil of many peoples. Zarathustra has found no greater power on earth than good and evil.

No people could live without evaluating; but if it wishes to maintain itself it must not evaluate as its neighbour evaluates.

6   The German terms here for "Self" and "Ego" are *Selbst* and *Ich*.

Much that seemed good to one people seemed shame and disgrace to another: thus I found. I found much that was called evil in one place was in another decked with purple honours.

One neighbour never understood another: his soul was always amazed at his neighbour's madness and wickedness.

A table of values hangs over every people. Behold, it is the table of its overcomings; behold, it is the voice of its will to power.

What it accounts hard it calls praiseworthy; what it accounts indispensable and hard it calls good; and that which relieves the greatest need, the rare, the hardest of all – it glorifies as holy.

Whatever causes it to rule and conquer and glitter, to the dread and envy of its neighbour, that it accounts the sublimest, the paramount, the evaluation and the meaning of all things.

Truly, my brother, if you only knew a people's need and land and sky and neighbour, you could surely divine the law of its overcomings, and why it is upon this ladder that it mounts towards its hope.

'You should always be the first and outrival all others: your jealous soul should love no one, except your friend' – this precept made the soul of a Greek tremble: in following it he followed his path to greatness.

'To speak the truth and to know well how to handle bow and arrow' – this seemed both estimable and hard to that people from whom I got my name – a name which is both estimable and hard to me.[7]

'To honour father and mother and to do their will even from the roots of the soul': another people hung this table of overcoming over itself and became mighty and eternal with it.

'To practise loyalty and for the sake of loyalty to risk honour and blood even in evil and dangerous causes': another people mastered itself with such teaching, and thus mastering itself it became pregnant and heavy with great hopes.

Truly, men have given themselves all their good and evil. Truly, they did not take it, they did not find it, it did not descend to them as a voice from heaven.

Man first implanted values into things to maintain himself – he created the meaning of things, a human meaning! Therefore he calls himself: 'Man', that is: the evaluator.

Evaluation is creation: hear it, you creative men! Valuating is itself the value and jewel of all valued things.

Only through evaluation is there value: and without evaluation the nut of existence would be hollow. Hear it, you creative men!

A change in values – that means a change in the creators of values. He who has to be a creator always has to destroy.

Peoples were the creators at first; only later were individuals creators. Indeed, the individual himself is still the latest creation.

Once the peoples hung a table of values over themselves. The love that wants to rule and the love that wants to obey created together such tables as these.

Joy in the herd is older than joy in the Ego: and as long as the good conscience is called herd, only the bad conscience says: I.

---

7   The people being referred to here are the Persians. The next two paragraphs cover, respectively, the Jews and the Germans.

Truly, the cunning, loveless Ego, that seeks its advantage in the advantage of many – that is not the origin of the herd, but the herd's destruction.

It has always been creators and loving men who created good and evil. Fire of love and fire of anger glow in the names of all virtues.

Zarathustra has seen many lands and many peoples: Zarathustra has found no greater power on earth than the works of these loving men: these works are named 'good' and 'evil'.

Truly, the power of this praising and blaming is a monster. Tell me, who will subdue it for me, brothers? Tell me, who will fasten fetters upon the thousand necks of this beast?

Hitherto there have been a thousand goals, for there have been a thousand peoples. Only fetters are still lacking for these thousand necks, the one goal is still lacking.

Yet tell me, my brothers: if a goal for humanity is still lacking, is there not still lacking – humanity itself? –

Thus spoke Zarathustra.

[. . .]

Of the Bestowing Virtue

1

When Zarathustra had taken leave of the town to which his heart was attached and which was called 'The Pied Cow' there followed him many who called themselves his disciples and escorted him. Thus they came to a cross-road: there Zarathustra told them that from then on he wanted to go alone: for he was a friend of going-alone. But his disciples handed him in farewell a staff, upon the golden haft of which a serpent was coiled about a sun. Zarathustra was delighted with the staff and leaned upon it; then he spoke thus to his disciples:

Tell me: how did gold come to have the highest value? Because it is uncommon and useless and shining and mellow in lustre; it always bestows itself.

Only as an image of the highest virtue did gold come to have the highest value. Gold-like gleams the glance of the giver. Gold-lustre makes peace between moon and sun.

The highest virtue is uncommon and useless, it is shining and mellow in lustre: the highest virtue is a bestowing virtue.

Truly, I divine you well, my disciples, you aspire to the bestowing virtue, as I do. What could you have in common with cats and wolves?

You thirst to become sacrifices and gifts yourselves; and that is why you thirst to heap up all riches in your soul.

Your soul aspires insatiably after treasures and jewels, because your virtue is insatiable in wanting to give.

You compel all things to come to you and into you, that they may flow back from your fountain as gifts of your love.

Truly, such a bestowing love must become a thief of all values; but I call this selfishness healthy and holy.

There is another selfishness, an all-too-poor, a hungry selfishness that always wants to steal, that selfishness of the sick, the sick selfishness.

It looks with the eye of a thief upon all lustrous things; with the greed of hunger it measures him who has plenty to eat; and it is always skulking about the table of the givers.

Sickness speaks from such craving, and hidden degeneration; the thieving greed of this longing speaks of a sick body.

Tell me, my brothers: what do we account bad and the worst of all? Is it not *degeneration*? – And we always suspect degeneration where the bestowing soul is lacking.

Our way is upward, from the species across to the super-species. But the degenerate mind which says 'All for me' is a horror to us.

Our mind flies upward: thus it is an image of our bodies, an image of an advance and elevation.

The names of the virtues are such images of advances and elevations.

Thus the body goes through history, evolving and battling. And the spirit – what is it to the body? The herald, companion, and echo of its battles and victories.

All names of good and evil are images: they do not speak out, they only hint. He is a fool who seeks knowledge from them.

Whenever your spirit wants to speak in images, pay heed; for that is when your virtue has its origin and beginning.

Then your body is elevated and risen up; it enraptures the spirit with its joy, that it may become creator and evaluator and lover and benefactor of all things.

When your heart surges broad and full like a river, a blessing and a danger to those who live nearby: that is when your virtue has its origin and beginning.

When you are exalted above praise and blame, and your will wants to command all things as the will of a lover: that is when your virtue has its origin and beginning.

When you despise the soft bed and what is pleasant and cannot make your bed too far away from the soft-hearted: that is when your virtue has its origin and beginning.

When you are the willers of a single will, and you call this dispeller of need your essential and necessity: that is when your virtue has its origin and beginning.

Truly, it is a new good and evil! Truly, a new roaring in the depths and the voice of a new fountain!

It is power, this new virtue; it is a ruling idea, and around it a subtle soul: a golden sun, and around it the serpent of knowledge.

2

Here Zarathustra fell silent a while and regarded his disciples lovingly. Then he went on speaking thus, and his voice was different:

Stay loyal to the earth, my brothers, with the power of your virtue! May your bestowing love and your knowledge serve towards the meaning of the earth! Thus I beg and entreat you.

Do not let it fly away from the things of earth and beat with its wings against the eternal walls! Alas, there has always been much virtue that has flown away!

Lead, as I do, the flown-away virtue back to earth – yes, back to body and life: that it may give the earth its meaning, a human meaning!

A hundred times hitherto has spirit as well as virtue flown away and blundered. Alas, all this illusion and blundering still dwells in our bodies: it has there become body and will.

A hundred times has spirit as well as virtue experimented and gone astray. Yes, man was an experiment. Alas, much ignorance and error has become body in us!

Not only the reason of millennia – the madness of millennia too breaks out in us. It is dangerous to be an heir.

We are still fighting step by step with the giant Chance, and hitherto the senseless, the meaningless, has still ruled over mankind.

May your spirit and your virtue serve the meaning of the earth, my brothers: and may the value of all things be fixed anew by you. To that end you should be fighters! To that end you should be creators!

The body purifies itself through knowledge; experimenting with knowledge it elevates itself; to the discerning man all instincts are holy; the soul of the elevated man grows joyful.

Physician, heal yourself:[8] thus you will heal your patient too. Let his best healing-aid be to see with his own eyes him who makes himself well.

There are a thousand paths that have never yet been trodden, a thousand forms of health and hidden islands of life. Man and man's earth are still unexhausted and undiscovered.

Watch and listen, you solitaries! From the future come winds with a stealthy flapping of wings; and good tidings go out to delicate ears.

You solitaries of today, you who have seceded from society, you shall one day be a people: from you, who have chosen out yourselves, shall a chosen people spring – and from this chosen people, the Overman.

Truly, the earth shall yet become a house of healing! And already a new odour floats about it, an odour that brings health – and a new hope!

3

When Zarathustra had said these words he paused like one who has not said his last word; long he balanced the staff doubtfully in his hand. At last he spoke thus, and his voice was different:

I now go away alone, my disciples! You too now go away and be alone! So I will have it.

Truly, I advise you: go away from me and guard yourselves against Zarathustra! And better still: be ashamed of him! Perhaps he has deceived you.

The man of knowledge must be able not only to love his enemies but also to hate his friends.

One repays a teacher badly if one remains only a pupil. And why, then, should you not pluck at my laurels?

You respect me; but how if one day your respect should tumble? Take care that a falling statue does not strike you dead!

You say you believe in Zarathustra? But of what importance is Zarathustra? You are my believers: but of what importance are all believers?

You had not yet sought yourselves when you found me. Thus do all believers; therefore all belief is of so little account.

8 Luke 4: 23.

Now I bid you lose me and find yourselves; and only when you have all denied me will I return to you.

Truly, with other eyes, my brothers, I shall then seek my lost ones; with another love I shall then love you.

And once more you shall have become my friends and children of one hope: and then I will be with you a third time, that I may celebrate the great noontide with you.

And this is the great noontide: it is when man stands at the middle of his course between animal and Overman and celebrates his journey to the evening as his highest hope: for it is the journey to a new morning.

Then man, going under, will bless himself; for he will be going over to Overman; and the sun of his knowledge will stand at noontide.

'*All gods are dead: now we want the Overman to live*' – let this be our last will one day at the great noontide! –

Thus spoke Zarathustra.

[. . .]

Part II

Of Self-Overcoming

What urges you on and arouses your ardour, you wisest of men, do you call it 'will to truth'?

Will to the conceivability of all being: that is what *I* call your will!

You first want to *make* all being conceivable: for, with a healthy mistrust, you doubt whether it is in fact conceivable.

But it must bend and accommodate itself to you! Thus will your will have it. It must become smooth and subject to the mind as the mind's mirror and reflection.

That is your entire will, you wisest men; it is a will to power; and that is so even when you talk of good and evil and of the assessment of values.

You want to create the world before which you can kneel: this is your ultimate hope and intoxication.

The ignorant, to be sure, the people – they are like a river down which a boat swims: and in the boat, solemn and disguised, sit the assessments of value.

You put your will and your values upon the river of becoming; what the people believe to be good and evil betrays to me an ancient will to power.

It was you, wisest men, who put such passengers in this boat and gave them splendour and proud names – you and your ruling will!

Now the river bears your boat along: it *has* to bear it. It is of small account if the breaking wave foams and angrily opposes its keel!

It is not the river that is your danger and the end of your good and evil, you wisest men, it is that will itself, the will to power, the unexhausted, procreating life-will.

But that you may understand my teaching about good and evil, I shall relate to you my teaching about life and about the nature of all living creatures.

I have followed the living creature, I have followed the greatest and the smallest paths, that I might understand its nature.

I caught its glance in a hundredfold mirror when its mouth was closed, that its eye might speak to me. And its eye did speak to me.

But wherever I found living creatures, there too I heard the language of obedience. All living creatures are obeying creatures.

And this is the second thing: he who cannot obey himself will be commanded. That is the nature of living creatures.

But this is the third thing I heard: that commanding is more difficult than obeying. And not only because the commander bears the burden of all who obey, and that this burden can easily crush him.

In all commanding there appeared to me to be an experiment and a risk: and the living creature always risks himself when he commands.

Yes, even when he commands himself: then also must he make amends for his commanding. He must become judge and avenger and victim of his own law.

How has this come about? thus I asked myself. What persuades the living creature to obey and to command and to practise obedience even in commanding?

Listen now to my teaching, you wisest men! Test in earnest whether I have crept into the heart of life itself and down to the roots of its heart!

Where I found a living creature, there I found will to power; and even in the will of the servant I found the will to be master.

The will of the weaker persuades it to serve the stronger; its will wants to be master over those weaker still: this delight alone it is unwilling to forgo.

And as the lesser surrenders to the greater, that it may have delight and power over the least of all, so the greatest, too, surrenders and for the sake of power stakes – life.

The devotion of the greatest is to encounter risk and danger and play dice for death.

And where sacrifice and service and loving glances are, there too is will to be master. There the weaker steals by secret paths into the castle and even into the heart of the more powerful – and steals the power.

And life itself told me this secret: 'Behold,' it said, 'I am that *which must overcome itself again and again.*

'To be sure, you call it will to procreate or impulse towards a goal, towards the higher, more distant, more manifold: but all this is one and one secret.

'I would rather perish than renounce this one thing; and truly, where there is perishing and the falling of leaves, behold, there life sacrifices itself – for the sake of power!

'That I have to be struggle and becoming and goal and conflict of goals: ah, he who divines my will surely divines, too, along what *crooked* paths it has to go!

'Whatever I create and however much I love it – soon I have to oppose it and my love: thus will my will have it.

'And you too, enlightened man, are only a path and footstep of my will: truly, my will to power walks with the feet of your will to truth!

'He who shot the doctrine of "will to existence" at truth certainly did not hit the truth: this will – does not exist!

'For what does not exist cannot will; but that which is in existence, how could it still want to come into existence?

'Only where life is, there is also will: not will to life, but – so I teach you – will to power!

'The living creature values many things higher than life itself; yet out of this evaluation itself speaks – the will to power!'

Thus life once taught me: and with this teaching do I solve the riddle of your hearts, you wisest men.

Truly, I say to you: Unchanging good and evil does not exist! From out of themselves they must overcome themselves again and again.

You exert power with your values and doctrines of good and evil, you assessors of values; and this is your hidden love and the glittering, trembling, and overflowing of your souls.

But a mightier power and a new overcoming grow from out your values: egg and egg-shell break against them.

And he who has to be a creator in good and evil, truly, has first to be a destroyer and break values.

Thus the greatest evil belongs with the greatest good: this, however, is the creative good.

Let us *speak* of this, you wisest men, even if it is a bad thing. To be silent is worse; all suppressed truths become poisonous.

And let everything that can break upon our truths – break! There is many a house still to build!

Thus spoke Zarathustra.

[. . .]

Of Immaculate Perception

When the moon rose yesterday I thought it was about to give birth to a sun, it lay on the horizon so broad and pregnant.

But it was a liar with its pregnancy; and I will sooner believe in the man in the moon than in the woman.

To be sure, he is not much of a man, either, this timid night-reveller. Truly, he travels over the roofs with a bad conscience.

For he is lustful and jealous, the monk in the moon, lustful for the earth and for all the joys of lovers.

No, I do not like him, this tomcat on the roofs! All who slink around half-closed windows are repugnant to me!

Piously and silently he walks along on star-carpets: but I do not like soft-stepping feet on which not even a spur jingles.

Every honest man's step speaks out: but the cat steals along over the ground. Behold, the moon comes along catlike and without honesty.

This parable I speak to you sentimental hypocrites, to you of 'pure knowledge'! *I* call you – lustful!

You too love the earth and the earthly: I have divined you well! – but shame and bad conscience is in your love – you are like the moon!

Your spirit has been persuaded to contempt of the earthly, but your entrails have not: *these*, however, are the strongest part of you!

And now your spirit is ashamed that it must do the will of your entrails and follows by-ways and lying-ways to avoid its own shame.

'For me, the highest thing would be to gaze at life without desire and not, as a dog does, with tongue hanging out' – thus speaks your mendacious spirit to itself:

'To be happy in gazing, with benumbed will, without the grasping and greed of egotism – cold and ashen in body but with intoxicated moon-eyes!

'For me, the dearest thing would be to love the earth as the moon loves it, and to touch its beauty with the eyes alone' – thus the seduced one seduces himself.

'And let this be called by me *immaculate* perception of all things: that I desire nothing of things, except that I may lie down before them like a mirror with a hundred eyes.'[9]

Oh, you sentimental hypocrites, you lustful men! You lack innocence in desire: and therefore you now slander desiring!

Truly, you do not love the earth as creators, begetters, men joyful at entering upon a new existence!

Where is innocence? Where there is will to begetting. And for me, he who wants to create beyond himself has the purest will.

Where is beauty? Where I *have to will* with all my will; where I want to love and perish, that an image may not remain merely an image.

Loving and perishing: these have gone together from eternity. Will to love: that means to be willing to die, too. Thus I speak to you cowards!

But now your emasculated leering wants to be called 'contemplation'! And that which lets cowardly eyes touch it shall be christened 'beautiful'! Oh, you befoulers of noble names!

But it shall be your curse, you immaculate men, you of pure knowledge, that you will never bring forth, even if you lie broad and pregnant on the horizon!

Truly, you fill your mouths with noble words: and are we supposed to believe that your hearts are overflowing, you habitual liars?

But *my* words are poor, despised, halting words: I am glad to take what falls from the table at your feast.

Yet with them I can still – tell the truth to hypocrites! Yes, my fish-bones, shells, and prickly leaves shall – tickle hypocrites' noses!

There is always bad air around you and around your feasts: for your lustful thoughts, your lies and secrets are in the air!

Only dare to believe in yourselves – in yourselves and in your entrails! He who does not believe in himself always lies.

You have put on the mask of a god, you 'pure': your dreadful coiling snake has crawled into the mask of a god.

Truly, you are deceivers, you 'contemplative'! Even Zarathustra was once the fool of your divine veneer; he did not guess at the serpent-coil with which it was filled.

Once I thought I saw a god's soul at play in your play, you of pure knowledge! Once I thought there was no better art than your arts!

Distance concealed from me the serpent-filth, and the evil odour, and that a lizard's cunning was prowling lustfully around.

---

9   Allusion to the mythical Greek figure of Argus, a herdsman with a hundred eyes which covered his body, who was set to watch over Io by Hera. Nietzsche frequently alludes to this myth in the context of his epistemological theory of perspectivism – see also *GM* III. 12.

But I *approached* you: then day dawned for me – and now it dawns for you – the moon's love affair had come to an end!

Just look! There it stands, pale and detected – before the dawn!

For already it is coming, the glowing sun – *its* love of the earth is coming! All sun-love is innocence and creative desire!

Just look how it comes impatiently over the sea! Do you not feel the thirst and the hot breath of its love?

It wants to suck at the sea and drink the sea's depths up to its height: now the sea's desire rises with a thousand breasts.

It *wants* to be kissed and sucked by the sun's thirst; it *wants* to become air and height and light's footpath and light itself!

Truly, like the sun do I love life and all deep seas.

And this *I* call knowledge: all that is deep shall rise up – to my height!

Thus spoke Zarathustra.

[. . .]

Of Redemption

As Zarathustra was going across the great bridge one day, the cripples and beggars surrounded him and a hunchback spoke to him thus:

Behold, Zarathustra! The people, too, learn from you and acquire belief in your teaching: but for the people to believe you completely, one thing is still needed – you must first convince even us cripples! Here now you have a fine selection and truly, an opportunity with more than one forelock! You can cure the blind and make the lame walk; and from him who has too much behind him you could well take a little away, too – that, I think, would be the right way to make the cripples believe in Zarathustra!

But Zarathustra replied thus to him who had spoken:

If one takes the hump away from the hunchback, one takes away his spirit – that is what the people teach. And if one gives eyes to the blind man, he sees too many bad things on earth: so that he curses him who cured him. But he who makes the lame man walk does him the greatest harm: for no sooner can he walk than his vices run away with him – that is what the people teach about cripples. And why should Zarathustra not learn from the people, if the people learn from Zarathustra?

But it is the least serious thing to me, since I have been among men, to see that this one lacks an eye and that one an ear and a third lacks a leg, and there are others who have lost their tongue or their nose or their head.

I see and have seen worse things and many of them so monstrous that I should not wish to speak of all of them; but of some of them I should not wish to be silent: and they are, men who lack everything except one thing, of which they have too much – men who are no more than a great eye or a great mouth of a great belly or something else great – I call such men inverse cripples.

And when I emerged from my solitude and crossed over this bridge for the first time, I did not believe my eyes and looked and looked again and said at last: 'That is an ear! An ear as big as a man!' I looked yet more closely: and in fact under the ear there moved something that was pitifully small and meagre and slender. And in truth, the monstrous ear sat upon a little, thin stalk – the stalk, however, was a man! By the use of a magnifying glass one could even discern a little, envious face as well; and one could discern, too, that a turgid little soul was dangling from the stalk. The people told me, however, that the great ear was not merely a man, but a great man, a genius. But I have never believed the people when they talked about great men – and I held to my belief that it was an inverse cripple, who had too little of everything and too much of one thing.

When Zarathustra had spoken thus to the hunchback and to those whose mouthpiece and advocate he was, he turned to his disciples with profound ill-humour and said:

Truly, my friends, I walk among men as among the fragments and limbs of men!

The terrible thing to my eye is to find men shattered in pieces and scattered as if over a battle-field of slaughter.

And when my eye flees from the present to the past, it always discovers the same thing: fragments and limbs and dreadful chances – but no men!

The present and the past upon the earth – alas! my friends – that is *my* most intolerable burden; and I should not know how to live, if I were not a seer of that which must come.

A seer, a willer, a creator, a future itself and a bridge to the future – and alas, also like a cripple upon this bridge: Zarathustra is all this.

And even you have often asked yourselves: Who is Zarathustra to us? What shall we call him? and, like me, you answer your own questions with questions.

Is he a promiser? Or a fulfiller? A conqueror? Or an inheritor? A harvest? Or a ploughshare? A physician? Or a convalescent?

Is he a poet? Or a genuine man? A liberator? Or a subduer? A good man? Or an evil man?

I walk among men as among fragments of the future: of that future which I scan.

And it is all my art and aim, to compose into one and bring together what is fragment and riddle and dreadful chance.

And how could I endure to be a man, if man were not also poet and reader of riddles and the redeemer of chance!

To redeem the past and to transform every 'It was' into an 'I wanted it thus!' – that alone do I call redemption!

Will – that is what the liberator and bringer of joy is called: thus I have taught you, my friends! But now learn this as well: The will itself is still a prisoner.

Willing liberates: but what is it that fastens in fetters even the liberator?

'It was': that is what the will's teeth-gnashing and most lonely affliction is called. Powerless against that which has been done, the will is an angry spectator of all things past.

The will cannot will backwards; that it cannot break time and time's desire – that is the will's most lonely affliction.

Willing liberates: what does willing itself devise to free itself from its affliction and to mock at its dungeon?

Alas, every prisoner becomes a fool! The imprisoned will, too, releases itself in a foolish way.

It is sullenly wrathful that time does not run back; 'That which was' – that is what the stone which it cannot roll away is called.

And so, out of wrath and ill-temper, the will rolls stones about and takes revenge upon him who does not, like it, feel wrath and ill-temper.

Thus the will, the liberator, becomes a malefactor: and upon all that can suffer it takes revenge for its inability to go backwards.

This, yes, this alone is *revenge* itself: the will's antipathy towards time and time's 'It was.'

Truly, a great foolishness dwells in our will; and that this foolishness acquired spirit has become a curse to all human kind.

The spirit of revenge: my friends, that, up to now, has been mankind's chief concern; and where there was suffering, there was always supposed to be punishment.

'Punishment' is what revenge calls itself: it feigns a good conscience for itself with a lie.

And because there is suffering in the willer himself, since he cannot will backwards – therefore willing itself and all life was supposed to be – punishment!

And then cloud upon cloud rolled over the spirit: until at last madness preached: 'Everything passes away, therefore everything deserves to pass aways!'[10]

'And that law of time, that time must devour her children, is justice itself': thus madness preached.

'Things are ordered morally according to justice and punishment. Oh, where is redemption from the stream of things and from the punishment "existence"?' Thus madness preached.

'Can there be redemption when there is eternal justice? Alas, the stone "It was" cannot be rolled away: all punishments, too, must be eternal!' Thus madness preached.

'No deed can be annihilated: how could a deed be undone through punishment? That existence too must be an eternally-recurring deed and guilt, this, this is what is eternal in the punishment "existence"!

'Except the will at last redeem itself and willing become not-willing –': but you, my brothers, know this fable-song of madness!

I led you away from these fable-songs when I taught you: 'The will is a creator.'

All 'It was' is a fragment, a riddle, a dreadful chance – until the creative will says to it: 'But I willed it thus!'

Until the creative will says to it: 'But I will it thus! Thus shall I will it!'

But has it ever spoken thus? And when will this take place? Has the will yet been unharnessed from its own folly?

Has the will become its own redeemer and bringer of joy? Has it unlearned the spirit of revenge and all teeth-gnashing?

And who has taught it to be reconciled with time, and higher things than reconciliation?

The will that is the will to power must will something higher than any reconciliation – but how shall that happen? Who has taught it to will backwards, too?

But at this point of his discourse, Zarathustra suddenly broke off and looked exactly like a man seized by extremest terror. With terrified eyes he gazed upon his disciples; his eyes transpierced their thoughts and their reservations as if with arrows. But after a short time he laughed again and said in a soothed voice:

'It is difficult to live among men because keeping silent is so difficult. Especially for a babbler.'

10 Cf. Goethe, *Faust I*, l. 1339f.

Thus spoke Zarathustra. The hunchback, however, had listened to the conversation and had covered his face the while; but when he heard Zarathustra laugh, he looked up in curiosity, and said slowly:

'But why does Zarathustra speak to us differently than to his disciples?'

Zarathustra answered: 'What is surprising in that? One may well speak in a hunch-backed manner to a hunchback!'

'Very good,' said the hunchback; 'and with pupils one may well tell tales out of school.

'But why does Zarathustra speak to his pupils differently — than to himself?'

Part III

Of the Vision and the Riddle

1

When it became rumoured among the sailors that Zarathustra was on the ship — for a man from the Blissful Islands had gone on board at the same time as he — a great curiosity and expectancy arose. But Zarathustra was silent for two days and was cold and deaf for sorrow, so that he responded neither to looks nor to questions. But on the evening of the second day he opened his ears again, although he still remained silent: for there were many strange and dangerous things to hear on this ship, which had come from afar and had yet further to go. Zarathustra, however, was a friend to all who take long journeys and do not want to live without danger. And behold! in listening his tongue was loosened, and the ice of his heart broke: then he started to speak thus:

To you, the bold venturers and adventurers and whoever has embarked with cun-ning sails upon dreadful seas,

to you who are intoxicated by riddles, who take pleasure in twilight, whose soul is lured with flutes to every treacherous abyss —

for you do not desire to feel for a rope with cowardly hand; and where you can *guess* you hate to *calculate* —

to you alone do I tell this riddle that I *saw* — the vision of the most solitary man.

Lately I walked gloomily through a deathly-grey twilight, gloomily and sternly with compressed lips. Not only one sun had gone down for me.

A path that mounted defiantly through boulders and rubble, a wicked, solitary path that bush or plant no longer cheered: a mountain path crunched under my foot's defiance.

Striding mute over the mocking clatter of pebbles, trampling the stones that made it slip: thus my foot with effort forced itself upward.

Upward — despite the spirit that drew it downward, drew it towards the abyss, the Spirit of Gravity, my devil and arch-enemy.

Upward — although he sat upon me, half dwarf, half mole; crippled, crippling; pour-ing lead-drops into my ear, leaden thoughts into my brain.

'O Zarathustra,' he said mockingly, syllable by syllable, 'you stone of wisdom! You have thrown yourself high, but every stone that is thrown must — fall!

'O Zarathustra, you stone of wisdom, you projectile, you star-destroyer! You have thrown yourself thus high, but every stone that is thrown — must fall!

'Condemned by yourself and to your own stone-throwing: O Zarathustra, far indeed have you thrown your stone, but it will fall back upon *you*!'

Thereupon the dwarf fell silent; and he long continued so. But his silence oppressed me; and to be thus in company is truly more lonely than to be alone!

I climbed, I climbed, I dreamed, I thought, but everything oppressed me. I was like a sick man wearied by his sore torment and reawakened from sleep by a worse dream.

But there is something in me that I call courage: it has always destroyed every discouragement in me. This courage at last bade me stop and say: 'Dwarf! You! Or I!'

For courage is the best destroyer – courage that *attacks*: for in every attack there is a triumphant shout.

Man, however, is the most courageous animal: with his courage he has overcome every animal. With a triumphant shout he has even overcome every pain; human pain, however, is the deepest pain.

Courage also destroys giddiness at abysses: and where does man not stand at an abyss? Is seeing itself not – seeing abysses?

Courage is the best destroyer: courage also destroys pity. Pity, however, is the deepest abyss: as deeply as man looks into life, so deeply does he look also into suffering.

Courage, however, is the best destroyer, courage that attacks: it destroys even death, for it says: 'Was *that* life? Well then! Once more!'

But there is a great triumphant shout in such a saying. He who has ears to hear, let him hear.[11]

2

'Stop, dwarf!' I said. 'I! Or you! But I am the stronger of us two – you do not know my abysmal thought! *That* thought – you could not endure!'

Then something occurred which lightened me: for the dwarf jumped from my shoulder, the inquisitive dwarf! And he squatted down upon a stone in front of me. But a gateway stood just where we had halted.

'Behold this gateway, dwarf!' I went on: 'it has two aspects. Two paths come together here: no one has ever reached their end.

'This long lane behind us: it goes on for an eternity. And that long lane ahead of us – that is another eternity.

'They are in opposition to one another, these paths; they abut on one another: and it is here at this gateway that they come together. The name of the gateway is written above it: "Moment".[12]

'But if one were to follow them further and ever further and further: do you think, dwarf, that these paths would be in eternal opposition?'

'Everything straight lies,' murmured the dwarf disdainfully. 'All truth is crooked, time itself is a circle.'

'Spirit of Gravity!' I said angrily, 'do not treat this too lightly! Or I shall leave you squatting where you are, Lame-foot – and I have carried you *high*!

11   Mark 4: 9; Matthew 11: 15.
12   In German: *"Augenblick"* (literally, "glance of the eye").

'Behold this moment!' I went on. 'From this gateway Moment a long, eternal lane runs *back*: an eternity lies behind us.

'Must not all things that *can* run have already run along this lane? Must not all things that *can* happen *have* already happened, been done, run past?

'And if all things have been here before: what do you think of this moment, dwarf? Must not this gateway, too, have been here – before?

'And are not all things bound fast together in such a way that this moment draws after it *all* future things? *Therefore* – draws itself too?

'For all things that *can* run *must* also run once again *forward* along this long lane.

'And this slow spider that creeps along in the moonlight, and this moonlight itself, and I and you at this gateway whispering together, whispering of eternal things – must we not all have been here before?

'– and must we not return and run down that other lane out before us, down that long, terrible lane – must we not return eternally?'

Thus I spoke, and I spoke more and more softly: for I was afraid of my own thoughts and reservations. Then, suddenly, I heard a dog *howling* nearby.

Had I ever heard a dog howling in that way? My thoughts ran back. Yes! When I was a child, in my most distant childhood:

– then I heard a dog howling in that way. And I saw it, too, bristling, its head raised, trembling in the stillest midnight, when even dogs believe in ghosts:

– so that it moved me to pity. For the full moon had just gone over the house, silent as death, it had just stopped still, a round glow, still upon the flat roof as if upon a forbidden place:

that was what had terrified the dog: for dogs believe in thieves and ghosts. And when I heard such howling again, it moved me to pity again.

Where had the dwarf now gone? And the gateway? And the spider? And all the whispering? Had I been dreaming? Had I awoken? All at once I was standing between wild cliffs, alone, desolate in the most desolate moonlight.

But there a man was lying! And there! The dog, leaping, bristling, whining; then it saw me coming – then it howled again, then it *cried out* – had I ever heard a dog cry so for help?

And truly, I had never seen the like of what I then saw. I saw a young shepherd writhing, choking, convulsed, his face distorted; and a heavy, black snake was hanging out of his mouth.

Had I ever seen so much disgust and pallid horror on a face? Had he, perhaps, been asleep? Then the snake had crawled into his throat – and there it had bitten itself fast.

My hands tugged and tugged at the snake – in vain! they could not tug the snake out of the shepherd's throat. Then a voice cried from me: 'Bite! Bite!

'Its head off! Bite!' – thus a voice cried from me, my horror, my hate, my disgust, my pity, all my good and evil cried out of me with a single cry.

You bold men around me! You venturers, adventurers, and those of you who have embarked with cunning sails upon undiscovered seas! You who take pleasure in riddles!

Solve for me the riddle that I saw, interpret to me the vision of the most solitary man!

For it was a vision and a premonition: *what* did I see in allegory? And *who* is it that must come one day?

Who is the shepherd into whose mouth the snake thus crawled? *Who* is the man into whose throat all that is heaviest, blackest will thus crawl?

The shepherd, however, bit as my cry had advised him; he bit with a good bite! He spat far away the snake's head – and sprang up.

No longer a shepherd, no longer a man – a transformed being, surrounded with light, *laughing*! Never yet one earth had any man laughed as he laughed!

O my brothers, I heard a laughter that was no human laughter – and now a thirst consumes me, a longing that is never stilled.

My longing for this laughter consumes me: oh how do I endure still to live! And how could I endure to die now!

Thus spoke Zarathustra.

[. . .]

Of the Spirit of Gravity

1

My glib tongue – is of the people; I speak too coarsely and warmly for silky rabbits. And my words sound even stranger to all inky fish and scribbling foxes.

My hand – is a fool's hand: woe to all tables and walls and whatever has room left for fool's scribbling, fool's doodling!

My foot – is a horse's foot: with it I trot and trample up hill, down dale, hither and thither over the fields, and am the Devil's own for joy when I am out at a gallop.

My stomach – is it perhaps an eagle's stomach? For it likes lamb's flesh best of all. But it is certainly a bird's stomach.

Nourished with innocent and few things, ready and impatient to fly, to fly away – that is my nature now: how should there not be something of the bird's nature in it!

And especially bird-like is that I am enemy to the Spirit of Gravity: and truly, mortal enemy, arch-enemy, born enemy! Oh where has my enmity not flown and strayed already!

I could sing a song about that – and I *will* sing one, although I am alone in an empty house and have to sing it to my own ears.

There are other singers, to be sure, whose voices are softened, whose hands are eloquent, whose eyes are expressive, whose hearts are awakened, only when the house is full: I am not one of them.

2

He who will one day teach men to fly will have moved all boundary-stones; all boundary-stones will themselves fly into the air to him, he will baptize the earth anew – as 'the weightless'.

The ostrich runs faster than any horse, but even he sticks his head heavily into heavy earth: that is what the man who cannot yet fly is like.

He calls earth and life heavy: and so *will* the Spirit of Gravity have it! But he who wants to become light and a bird must love himself – thus do I teach.

Not with the love of the sick and diseased, to be sure: for with them even self-love stinks!

One must learn to love oneself with a sound and healthy love, so that one may endure it with oneself and not go roaming about – thus do I teach.

Such roaming about calls itself 'love of one's neighbour': these words have been up to now the best for lying and dissembling, and especially for those who were oppressive to everybody.

And truly, to *learn* to love oneself is no commandment for today or for tomorrow. Rather is this art the finest, subtlest, ultimate, and most patient of all.

For all his possessions are well concealed from the possessor; and of all treasure pits, one's own is the last to be digged – the Spirit of Gravity is the cause of that.

Almost in the cradle are we presented with heavy words and values: this dowry calls itself 'Good' and 'Evil'. For its sake we are forgiven for being alive.

And we suffer little children to come to us,[13] to prevent them in good time from loving themselves: the Spirit of Gravity is the cause of that.

And we – we bear loyally what we have been given upon hard shoulders over rugged mountains! And when we sweat we are told: 'Yes, life is hard to bear!'

But only man is hard to bear! That is because he bears too many foreign things upon his shoulders. Like the camel, he kneels down and lets himself be well laden.

Especially the strong, weight-bearing man in whom dwell respect and awe: he has laden too many *foreign* heavy words and values upon himself – now life seems to him a desert!

And truly! Many things that are *one's own* are hard to bear, too! And much that is intrinsic in man is like the oyster, that is loathsome and slippery and hard to grasp –

so that a noble shell with noble embellishments must intercede for it. But one has to learn this art as well: to *have* a shell and a fair appearance and a prudent blindness!

Again, it is deceptive about many things in man that many a shell is inferior and wretched and too much of a shell. Much hidden goodness and power is never guessed at; the most exquisite dainties find no tasters!

Women, or the most exquisite of them, know this: a little fatter, a little thinner – oh, how much fate lies in so little!

Man is difficult to discover, most of all to himself; the spirit often tells lies about the soul. The Spirit of Gravity is the cause of that.

But he has discovered himself who says: This is *my* good and evil: he has silenced thereby the mole and dwarf who says: 'Good for all, evil for all.'

Truly, I dislike also those who call everything good and this world the best of all. I call such people the all-contented.

All-contentedness that knows how to taste everything: that is not the best taste! I honour the obstinate, fastidious tongues and stomachs that have learned to say 'I' and 'Yes' and 'No'.

But to chew and digest everything – that is to have a really swinish nature! Always to say Ye-a[14] – only the ass and those like him have learned that.

Deep yellow and burning red: that is to *my* taste – it mixes blood with all colours. But he who whitewashes his house betrays to me a whitewashed soul.

One loves mummies, the other phantoms; and both alike enemy to all flesh and blood – oh, how both offend my taste! For I love blood.

13   Mark 10: 14.
14   In German: *I-a*. German renders the bray of an ass with "iah," which is very close in sound to "ja" ("yes").

And I do not want to stay and dwell where everyone spews and spits: that is now *my* taste – I would rather live among thieves and perjurers. No one bears gold in his mouth.

More offensive to me, however, are all lickspittles; and the most offensive beast of a man I ever found I baptized Parasite: it would not love, yet wanted to live by love.

I call wretched all who have only one choice: to become an evil beast or an evil tamer of beasts: I would build no tabernacles among these men.

I also call wretched those who always have to *wait* – they offend my taste: all tax-collectors and shopkeepers and kings and other keepers of lands and shops.

Truly, I too have learned to wait, I have learned it from the very heart, but only to wait for *myself*. And above all I have learned to stand and to walk and to run and to jump and to climb and to dance.

This, however, is my teaching: He who wants to learn to fly one day must first learn to stand and to walk and to run and to climb and to dance – you cannot learn to fly by flying!

With rope-ladders I learned to climb to many a window, with agile legs I climbed up high masts: to sit upon high masts of knowledge seemed to me no small happiness –

to flicker like little flames upon high masts: a little light, to be sure, but yet a great comfort to castaway sailors and the shipwrecked!

I came to my truth by diverse paths and in diverse ways: it was not upon a single ladder that I climbed to the height where my eyes survey my distances.

And I have asked the way only unwillingly – that has always offended my taste! I have rather questioned and attempted the ways themselves.

All my progress has been an attempting and a questioning – and truly, one has to *learn* how to answer such questioning! That however – is to my taste:

not good taste, not bad taste, but *my* taste, which I no longer conceal and of which I am no longer ashamed.

'This – is now *my* way: where is yours?' Thus I answered those who asked me 'the way'. For *the* way – does not exist!¹⁵

Thus spoke Zarathustra.

[. . .]

The Convalescent

1

One morning, not long after his return to the cave, Zarathustra sprang up from his bed like a madman, cried with a terrible voice, and behaved as if someone else were lying on the bed and would not rise from it; and Zarathustra's voice rang out in such a way that his animals came to him in terror and from all the caves and hiding-places in the neighbourhood of Zarathustra's cave all the creatures slipped away, flying, flutter-ing, creeping, jumping, according to the kind of foot or wing each had been given. Zarathustra, however, spoke these words:

15   A parting shot at the Jesus who proclaims "I am the way, the truth and the life" (John 14: 6), bringing to an end a sustained anti-Christian chapter.

Up, abysmal thought, up from my depths! I am your cockerel and dawn, sleepy worm: up! up! My voice shall soon crow you awake!

Loosen the fetters of your ears: listen! For I want to hear you! Up! Up! Here is thunder enough to make even the graves listen!

And wipe the sleep and all the dimness and blindness from your eyes! Hear me with your eyes, too: my voice is a medicine even for those born blind.

And once you are awake you shall stay awake for ever. It is not *my* way to awaken great-grandmothers from sleep in order to bid them – go back to sleep![16]

Are you moving, stretching, rattling? Up! Up! You shall not rattle, you shall – speak to me! Zarathustra the Godless calls you!

I, Zarathustra, the advocate of life, the advocate of suffering, the advocate of the circle – I call you, my most abysmal thought!

Ah! you are coming – I hear you! My abyss *speaks*, I have turned my ultimate depth into the light!

Ah! Come here! Give me your hand – ha! don't! Ha, ha! – Disgust, disgust, disgust – woe is me!

2

Hardly had Zarathustra spoken these words, however, when he fell down like a dead man and remained like a dead man for a long time. But when he again came to himself, he was pale and trembling and remained lying down and for a long time would neither eat nor drink. This condition lasted seven days; his animals, however, did not leave him by day or night, except that the eagle flew off to fetch food. And whatever he had collected and fetched he laid upon Zarathustra's bed: so that at last Zarathustra lay among yellow and red berries, grapes, rosy apples, sweet-smelling herbs and pine-cones. At his feet, however, two lambs were spread, which the eagle had, with difficulty, carried off from their shepherd.

At last, after seven days, Zarathustra raised himself in his bed, took a rosy apple in his hand, smelt it, and found its odour pleasant. Then his animals thought the time had come to speak with him.

'O Zarathustra,' they said, 'now you have lain like that seven days, with heavy eyes: will you not now get to your feet again?

'Step out of your cave: the world awaits you like a garden. The wind is laden with heavy fragrance that longs for you; and all the brooks would like to run after you.

'All things long for you, since you have been alone seven days – step out of your cave! All things want to be your physicians!

'Has perhaps a new knowledge come to you, a bitter, oppressive knowledge? You have lain like leavened dough, your soul has risen and overflowed its brim.'

'O my animals,' answered Zarathustra, 'go on talking and let me listen! Your talking is such refreshment: where there is talking, the world is like a garden to me. How sweet it is, that words and sounds of music exist: are words and music not rainbows and seeming bridges between things eternally separated?

'Every soul is a world of its own; for every soul every other soul is an afterworld.

---

16 Allusion to the opening of Act III of Wagner's opera *Siegfried* (1876), where Wotan wakes Erda, the Earth Mother, only to bid her return to sleep shortly afterwards.

'Appearance lies most beautifully among the most alike; for the smallest gap is the most difficult to bridge.

'For me – how could there be an outside-of-me? There is no outside! But we forget that, when we hear music; how sweet it is, that we forget!

'Are things not given names and musical sounds, so that man may refresh himself with things? Speech is a beautiful foolery: with it man dances over all things.

'How sweet is all speech and all the falsehoods of music! With music does our love dance upon many-coloured rainbows.'

'O Zarathustra,' said the animals then, 'all things themselves dance for such as think as we: they come and offer their hand and laugh and flee – and return.

'Everything goes, everything returns; the wheel of existence rolls for ever. Everything dies, everything blossoms anew; the year of existence runs on for ever.

'Everything breaks, everything is joined anew; the same house of existence builds itself for ever. Everything departs, everything meets again; the ring of existence is true to itself for ever.

'Existence begins in every instant; the ball There rolls around every Here. The middle is everywhere. The path of eternity is crooked.'

'O you buffoons and barrel-organs!' answered Zarathustra and smiled again; 'how well you know what had to be fulfilled in seven days:

'and how that monster crept into my throat and choked me! But I bit its head off and spat it away.

'And you – have already made a hurdy-gurdy song of it? I, however, lie here now, still weary from this biting and spitting away, still sick with my own redemption.

'*And you looked on at it all?* O my animals, are you, too, cruel? Did you desire to be spectators of my great pain, as men do? For man is the cruellest animal.

'More than anything on earth he enjoys tragedies, bull-fights, and crucifixions; and when he invented Hell for himself, behold, it was his heaven on earth.

'When the great man cries out, straightway the little man comes running; his tongue is hanging from his mouth with lasciviousness. He, however, calls it his "pity".

'The little man, especially the poet – how zealously he accuses life in words! Listen to it, but do not overlook the delight that is in all accusation!

'Such accusers of life: life overcomes them with a glance of its eye. "Do you love me?" it says impudently; "just wait a little, I have no time for you yet."

'Man is the cruellest animal towards himself; and with all who call themselves "sinners" and "bearers of the Cross" and "penitents" do not overlook the sensual pleasure that is in this complaint and accusation!

'And I myself – do I want to be the accuser of man? Ah, my animals, this alone have I learned, that the wickedest in man is necessary for the best in him,

'that all that is most wicked in him is his best *strength* and the hardest stone for the highest creator; and that man must grow better *and* wickeder:

'To know: Man is wicked; *that* was to be tied to no torture-stake – but I cried as no one had cried before:

'"Alas, that his wickedest is so very small! Alas, that his best is so very small!"

'The great disgust at man – *it* choked me and had crept into my throat: and what the prophet prophesied: "It is all one, nothing is worth while, knowledge chokes."

'A long twilight limps in front of me, a mortally-weary, death-intoxicated sadness which speaks with a yawn.

'"The man of whom you are weary, the little man, recurs eternally" – thus my sadness yawned and dragged its feet and could not fall asleep.

'The human earth became to me a cave, its chest caved in, everything living became to me human decay and bones and mouldering past.

'My sighs sat upon all the graves of man and could no longer rise; my sighs and questions croaked and choked and gnawed and wailed by day and night:

'"Alas, man recurs eternally! The little man recurs eternally!"

'I had seen them both naked, the greatest man and the smallest man: all too similar to one another, even the greatest all too human!

'The greatest all too small! – that was my disgust at man! And eternal recurrence even for the smallest! that was my disgust at all existence!

'Ah, disgust! Disgust! Disgust!' Thus spoke Zarathustra and sighed and shuddered; for he remembered his sickness. But his animals would not let him speak further.

'Speak no further, convalescent!' – thus his animals answered him, 'but go out to where the world awaits you like a garden.

'Go out to the roses and bees and flocks of doves! But go out especially to the song-birds, so that you may learn *singing* from them!

'For convalescents should sing; let the healthy talk. And when the healthy man, too, desires song, he desires other songs than the convalescent.'

'O you buffoons and barrel-organs, do be quiet!' answered Zarathustra and smiled at his animals. 'How well you know what comfort I devised for myself in seven days!

'That I have to sing again – *that* comfort and *this* convalescence did I devise for myself: do you want to make another hurdy-gurdy song out of that, too?'

'Speak no further,' his animals answered once more; 'rather first prepare yourself a lyre, convalescent, a new lyre!

'For behold, O Zarathustra! New lyres are needed for your new songs.

'Sing and bubble over, O Zarathustra, heal your soul with new songs, so that you may bear your great destiny, that was never yet the destiny of any man!

'For your animals well know, O Zarathustra, who you are and must become: behold, *you are the teacher of the eternal recurrence*, that is now *your* destiny!

'That you have to be the first to teach this doctrine – how should this great destiny not also be your greatest danger and sickness!

'Behold, we know what you teach: that all things recur eternally and we ourselves with them, and that we have already existed an infinite number of times before and all things with us.

'You teach that there is a great year of becoming, a colossus of a year: this year must, like an hour-glass, turn itself over again and again, so that it may run down and run out anew:

'so that all these years resemble one another, in the greatest things and in the smallest, so that we ourselves resemble ourselves in each great year, in the greatest things and in the smallest.

'And if you should die now, O Zarathustra: behold, we know too what you would then say to yourself – but your animals ask you not to die yet!

'You would say – and without trembling, but rather gasping for happiness: for a great weight and oppression would have been lifted from you, most patient of men!

'"Now I die and decay," you would say, "and in an instant I shall be nothingness. Souls are as mortal as bodies.

' "But the complex of causes in which I am entangled will recur – it will create me again! I myself am part of these causes of the eternal recurrence.

' "I shall return, with this sun, with this earth, with this eagle, with this serpent – *not* to a new life or a better life or a similar life:

' "I shall return eternally to this identical and self-same life, in the greatest things and in the smallest, to teach once more the eternal recurrence of all things,

' "to speak once more the teaching of the great noontide of earth and man, to tell man of the Overman once more.

' "I spoke my teaching, I broke upon my teaching: thus my eternal fate will have it – as prophet do I perish!

' "Now the hour has come when he who is going down shall bless himself. Thus – *ends* Zarathustra's down-going." ' – –

When the animals had spoken these words they fell silent and expected that Zarathustra would say something to them: but Zarathustra did not hear that they were silent. On the contrary, he lay still with closed eyes like a sleeper, although he was not asleep: for he was conversing with his soul. The serpent and the eagle, however, when they found him thus silent, respected the great stillness around him and discreetly withdrew.

Part IV

The Sleepwalker's Song[17]

Meanwhile, however, one after another had gone out into the open air and the cool, thoughtful night; but Zarathustra himself led the ugliest man by the hand, to show him his nocturnal world and the big, round moon and the silver waterfalls beside his cave. There at last they stood silently together, just a group of old folk, but with comforted, brave hearts and amazed in themselves that it was so well with them on earth; but the mystery of the night drew nearer and nearer their hearts. And Zarathustra thought to himself again: 'Oh, how well they please me now, these Higher Men!' – but he did not say it, for he respected their happiness and their silence. –

Then, however, occurred the most astonishing thing in that long, astonishing day: the ugliest man began once more and for the last time to gurgle and snort, and when he at last came to the point of speech, behold, a question leaped round and pure from his mouth, a good, deep, clear question, which moved the hearts of all who heard it.

'My assembled friends,' said the ugliest man, 'what do you think? For the sake of this day – *I* am content for the first time to have lived my whole life.

'And it is not enough that I testify only this much. It is worth while to live on earth: one day, one festival with Zarathustra has taught me to love the earth.

---

17 In German: *Das Nachtwandler-Lied*. The translation has been modified from "The Intoxicated Song" ("Das trunkne Lied"), the title used for this chapter before the Colli–Montinari editions of the text. At this late stage in Part IV, Zarathustra has gathered around him a motley collection of followers, including "the ugliest man" ("the murderer of God") and various "Higher Men." They have just been celebrating "The Ass Festival."

'"Was *that* – life?" I will say to death. "Very well! Once more!"

'My friends, what do you think? Will you not, like me, say to death: "Was *that* – life? For Zarathustra's sake, very well! Once more!"' – –

Thus spoke the ugliest man; and it was not long before midnight. And what would you think then took place? As soon as the Higher Men had heard his question, they were all at once conscious of their transformation and recovery, and of who had given them these things: then they leaped towards Zarathustra, thanking, adoring, caressing, kissing his hands, each after his own fashion: so that some laughed, some wept. The old prophet, however, danced with pleasure; and even if he was then full of sweet wine, as some narrators believe, he was certainly fuller still of sweet life and had renounced all weariness. There are even those who tell that the ass danced at that time: for not in vain had the ugliest man given it wine to drink. This may be the case, or it may be otherwise; and if in truth the ass did not dance that evening, greater and stranger marvels than the dancing of an ass occurred. In brief, as Zarathustra's saying has it: 'What does it matter!'

2

Zarathustra, however, when this incident with the ugliest man occurred, stood there like one intoxicated: his eyes grew dim, his tongue stammered, his feet tottered. And who could divine what thoughts then passed over Zarathustra's soul? But it seemed that his soul fell back and fled before him and was in remote distances and as if 'upon a high ridge', as it is written,

'wandering like a heavy cloud between past and future.' But gradually, while the Higher Men were holding him in their arms, he came to himself a little and his hands restrained the adoring and anxious throng; yet he did not speak. All at once, however, he swiftly turned his head, for he seemed to hear something: then he laid a finger to his lips and said: '*Come!*'

And at once it grew still and mysterious all around; from the depths, however, there slowly arose the sound of a bell. Zarathustra listened to it, as the Higher Men did; then he laid a finger to his lips a second time and said again: '*Come! Come! Midnight is coming on!*' and his voice had altered. But still he did not move from his place: then it grew yet more still and mysterious, and everything listened, even the ass and Zarathustra's animals of honour, the eagle and the serpent, likewise Zarathustra's cave and the great, cool moon and the night itself. Zarathustra, however, laid his hand to his lips for the third time and said:

Come! Come! Come! Let us walk now! The hour has come: let us walk into the night!

3

You Higher Men, midnight is coming on: so I will say something in your ears, as that old bell says it in my ear,

as secretly, as fearfully, as warmly as that midnight-bell tells it to me, which has experienced more than one man:

which has already counted your fathers' painful heartbeats – ah! ah! how it sighs! how in dreams it laughs! the ancient, deep, deep midnight!

Soft! Soft! Then many a thing can be heard which may not speak by day; but now, in the cool air, when all the clamour of your hearts, too, has grown still, now it speaks, now it is heard, now it creeps into nocturnal, over-wakeful souls: ah! ah! how it sighs! how in dreams it laughs!

do you not hear, how secretly, fearfully, warmly it speaks to you, the ancient, deep, deep midnight?

O Man! Attend!

4

Woe is me! Where has time fled? Did I not sink into deep wells? The world is asleep –

Ah! Ah! The dog howls, the moon is shining. I will rather die, die, than tell you what my midnight-heart is now thinking.

Now I am dead. It is finished. Spider, why do you spin your web around me? Do you want blood? Ah! Ah! The dew is falling, the hour has come

– the hour which chills and freezes me, which asks and asks and asks: 'Who has heart enough for it?

'– who shall be master of the world? Who will say: Thus shall you run, you great and small streams!'

– the hour approaches: O man, you Higher Man, attend! this discourse is for delicate ears, for your ears – *what does deep midnight's voice contend?*

5

I am borne away, my soul dances. The day's task! The day's task! Who shall be master of the world?

The moon is cool, the wind falls silent. Ah! Ah! Have you flown high enough? You dance: but a leg is not a wing.

You good dancers, now all joy is over: wine has become dregs, every cup has grown brittle, the graves mutter.

You have not flown high enough: now the graves mutter: 'Redeem the dead! Why is it night so long? Does the moon not intoxicate us?'

You Higher Men, redeem the graves, awaken the corpses! Alas, why does the worm still burrow? The hour approaches, it approaches,

the bell booms, the heart still drones, the woodworm, the heart's worm, still burrows. Alas! *The world is deep!*

6

Sweet lyre! Sweet lyre! Your sound, your intoxicated, ominous sound, delights me! – from how long ago, from how far away does your sound come to me, from a far distance, from the pools of love!

You ancient bell, you sweet lyre! Every pain has torn at your heart, the pain of a father, the pain of our fathers, the pain of our forefathers; your speech has grown ripe,

ripe like golden autumn and afternoon, like my hermit's heart – now you say: The world itself has grown ripe, the grapes grow brown,

now they want to die, to die of happiness. You Higher Men, do you not smell it? An odour is secretly welling up,

a scent and odour of eternity, an odour of roseate bliss, a brown, golden wine odour of ancient happiness, of intoxicated midnight's dying happiness, which sings: The world is deep: *deeper than day can comprehend!*

7

Let me be! Let me be! I am too pure for you. Do not touch me! Has my world not just become perfect?

My skin is too pure for your hands. Let me be, stupid, doltish, stifling day! Is midnight not brighter?

The purest shall be master of the world; the least known, the strongest, the midnight souls, who are brighter and deeper than any day.

O day, do you grope for me? Do you feel for my happiness? Do you think me rich, solitary, a pit of treasure, a chamber of gold?

O world, do you desire me? Do you think me worldly? Do you think me spiritual? Do you think me divine? But day and world, you are too clumsy,

have cleverer hands, reach out for deeper happiness, for deeper unhappiness, reach out for some god, do not reach out for me:

my unhappiness, my happiness is deep, you strange day, but yet I am no god, no divine Hell: *deep is its woe.*

8

God's woe is deeper, you strange world! Reach out for God's woe, not for me! What am I? An intoxicated, sweet lyre

– a midnight lyre, a croaking bell which no one understands but which *has* to speak before deaf people, you Higher Men! For you do not understand me!

Gone! Gone! Oh youth! Oh noontide! Oh afternoon! Now come evening and midnight; the dog howls, the wind:

is the wind not a dog? It whines, it yelps, it howls. Ah! Ah! how it sighs! how it laughs, how it rasps and gasps, the midnight hour!

How it now speaks soberly, this intoxicated poet! perhaps it has overdrunk its drunkenness? perhaps it has grown over-wakeful? perhaps it ruminates?

it ruminates upon its woe in dreams, the ancient, deep midnight hour, and still more upon its joy. For joy, though woe be deep: *Joy is deeper than heart's agony.*

9

You grape-vine! Why do you praise me? For I cut you! I am cruel, you bleed: what means your praise of my intoxicated cruelty?

'What has become perfect, everything ripe – wants to die!' thus you speak. Blessed, blessed be the vine-knife! But everything unripe wants to live: alas!

Woe says: 'Fade! Be gone, woe!' But everything that suffers wants to live, that it may grow ripe and merry and passionate,

passionate for remoter, higher, brighter things. 'I want heirs,' thus speaks everything that suffers, 'I want children, I do not want *myself.'*

Joy, however, does not want heirs or children, joy wants itself, wants eternity, wants recurrence, wants everything eternally the same.

Woe says: 'Break, bleed, heart! Walk, legs! Wings, fly! Upward! Upward, pain!' Very well! Come on! my old heart: *Woe says: Fade! Go!*

10

What do you think, you Higher Men? Am I a prophet? A dreamer? A drunkard? An interpreter of dreams? A midnight bell?

A drop of dew? An odour and scent of eternity? Do you not hear it? Do you not smell it? My world has just become perfect, midnight is also noonday,

pain is also joy, a curse is also a blessing, the night is also a sun – be gone, or you will learn: a wise man is also a fool.

Did you ever say Yes to one joy? O my friends, then you said Yes to *all* woe as well. All things are chained and entwined together, all things are in love;

if ever you wanted one moment twice, if ever you said: 'You please me, happiness, instant, moment!' then you wanted *everything* to return!

you wanted everything anew, everything eternal, everything chained, entwined together, everything in love, O that is how you *loved* the world,

you everlasting men, loved it eternally and for all time: and you say even to woe: 'Go, but return!' *For all joy wants – eternity!*

11

All joy wants the eternity of all things, wants honey, wants dregs, wants intoxicated midnight, wants graves, wants the consolation of graveside tears, wants gilded sunsets,

what does joy not want! it is thirstier, warmer, hungrier, more fearful, more secret than all woe, it wants *itself*, it bites into *itself*, the will of the ring wrestles within it,

it wants love, it wants hatred, it is superabundant, it gives, throws away, begs for someone to take it, thanks him who takes, it would like to be hated;

so rich is joy that it thirsts for woe, for Hell, for hatred, for shame, for the lame, for the *world* – for it knows, oh it knows this world!

You Higher Men, joy longs for you, joy the intractable, blissful – for your woe, you ill-constituted! All eternal joy longs for the ill-constituted.

For all joy wants itself, therefore it also wants heart's agony! O happiness! O pain! Oh break, heart! You Higher Men, learn this, learn that joy wants eternity,

joy wants the eternity of *all* things, *wants deep, deep, deep eternity!*

12

Have you now learned my song? Have you divined what it means? Very well! Come on! You Higher Men, now sing my roundelay!

Now sing yourselves the song whose name is 'Once more', whose meaning is 'To all eternity!' – sing, you Higher Men, Zarathustra's roundelay!

> *O Man! Attend!*
> *What does deep midnight's voice contend?*
> *'I slept my sleep,*
> *'And now awake at dreaming's end:*
> *'The world is deep,*
> *'Deeper than day can comprehend.*
> *'Deep is its woe,*
> *'Joy – deeper than heart's agony:*
> *'Woe says: Fade! Go!*
> *'But all joy wants eternity,*
> *'Wants deep, deep, deep eternity!'*

The Sign

On the morning after this night, however, Zarathustra sprang up from his bed, girded his loins, and emerged from his cave, glowing and strong, like a morning sun emerging from behind dark mountains.

'Great star,' he said, as he had said once before, 'you profound eye of happiness, what would all your happiness be if you did not have *those* for whom you shine!

'And if they remained in their rooms while you were already awake and had come, giving and distributing: how angry your proud modesty would be!

'Very well! they are still asleep, these Higher Men, while *I* am awake: *they* are not my rightful companions! It is not for them I am waiting in my mountains.

'I want to go to my work, to my day: but they do not understand what are the signs of my morning, my step – is no awakening call for them.

'They are still sleeping in my cave, their dream still chews at my midnights. Yet the ear that listens to *me*, the *obeying* ear, is missing from them.'

Zarathustra had said this to his heart when the sun rose: then he looked inquiringly aloft, for he heard above him the sharp cry of his eagle. 'Very well!' he cried up, 'so do I like it, so do I deserve it. My animals are awake, for I am awake.

'My eagle is awake and, like me, does honour to the sun. With eagle's claws it reaches out for the new light. You are my rightful animals: I love you.

'But I still lack my rightful men!'

Thus spoke Zarathustra; then, however, he suddenly heard that he was surrounded by countless birds, swarming and fluttering – the whirring of so many wings and the throng about his head, however, were so great that he shut his eyes. And truly, it was as if a cloud had fallen upon him, a cloud of arrows discharged over a new enemy. And behold, in this case it was a cloud of love, and over a new friend.

'What is happening to me?' thought Zarathustra, in his astonished heart, and slowly lowered himself on to the great stone that lay beside the exit of his cave. But, as he was clutching about, above and underneath himself, warding off the tender birds, behold, then something even stranger occurred: for in doing so he clutched unawares a thick, warm mane of hair; at the same time, however, a roar rang out in front of him – the gentle, protracted roar of a lion.

'*The sign has come*,' said Zarathustra, and his heart was transformed. And in truth, when it grew clear before him, there lay at his feet a sallow, powerful animal that lovingly pressed its head against his knee and would not leave him, behaving like a dog that has found his old master again. The doves, however, were no less eager than the lion with their love; and every time a dove glided across the lion's nose, the lion shook its head and wondered and laughed.

While this was happening, Zarathustra said but one thing: '*My children are near, my children*,' then he grew quite silent. His heart, however, was loosened, and tears fell from his eyes down upon his hands. And he no longer paid attention to anything, and sat there motionless and no longer warding off the animals. Then the doves flew back and forth and sat upon his shoulder and fondled his white hair and did not weary of tenderness and rejoicing. The mighty lion, however, continually licked the tears that fell down upon Zarathustra's hands, roaring and growling shyly as he did so. Thus did these animals.

All this lasted a long time, or a short time: for, properly speaking, there is *no* time on earth for such things. In the meantime, however, the Higher Men in Zarathustra's cave had awakened and arranged themselves for a procession, that they might go to Zarathustra and offer him their morning greeting: for they had discovered when they awoke that he was no longer among them. But when they reached the door of the cave, and the sound of their steps preceded them, the lion started violently, suddenly turned away from Zarathustra, and leaped up to the cave, roaring fiercely; the Higher Men, however, when they heard its roaring, all cried out as with a single throat and fled back and in an instant had vanished.

But Zarathustra himself, bewildered and spell-bound, raised himself from his seat, gazed about him, stood there amazed, questioned his heart, recollected, and saw he was alone. 'What was it I heard?' he slowly said at last, 'what has just happened to me?'

And at once his memory returned and he comprehended in a glance all that had happened between yesterday and today. 'This here is the stone,' he said and stroked his beard, 'on *this* did I sit yesterday morning; and here did the prophet come to me, and here I first heard the cry which I heard even now, the great cry of distress.

'O you Higher Men, it was of *your* distress that old prophet prophesied to me yesterday morning,

'he tried to seduce and tempt me to your distress: O Zarathustra, he said to me, I have come to seduce you to your ultimate sin.

'To my ultimate sin?' cried Zarathustra and laughed angrily at his own words. '*What* has been reserved for me as my ultimate sin?'

And once more Zarathustra became absorbed in himself and sat himself again on the great stone and meditated. Suddenly, he leaped up –

'*Pity! Pity for the Higher Man!*' he cried out, and his countenance was transformed into brass. 'Very well! *That* – has had its time!

'My suffering and my pity – what of them! For do I aspire after *happiness*? I aspire after my *work*!

'Very well! The lion has come, my children are near, Zarathustra has become ripe, my hour has come!

'This is *my* morning, *my* day begins: *rise up now, rise up, great noontide!*' – –

Thus spoke Zarathustra and left his cave, glowing and strong, like a morning sun emerging from behind dark mountains.

V

The Later Writings

1886–1887

Introduction

This first selection from Nietzsche's later works features writings from 1886–7 and includes selections from two of his most important texts, *Beyond Good and Evil* and *On the Genealogy of Morality*, as well as selections from Book V of *The Gay Science* and Nietzsche's "Lenzer Heide" notebook on European nihilism. In his entry on *Beyond Good and Evil* in *Ecce Homo* Nietzsche tells us that from this point onwards his work is devoted to carrying out the "no-saying" (*neinsagende*) part of his task. By "no-saying" he means the revaluation of values and the "evocation of a day of decision." And he adds, "From now on all my writings are fish-hooks." They are writings, in effect, that seek to seduce. In the texts of his middle period Nietzsche was saying "yes" to the new tasks that he believed now confronted modern human beings, including the incorporation of truth and knowledge (*GS* 110), a new renunciation (*GS* 285), and the purification of their opinions and valuations (*GS* 335). In the texts of his late period he is now articulating a "no-saying" that is centered on the task of performing a critical examination of humanity and of modern values, and demanding a different education and breeding of the human animal (*BGE* 61). The aim is to combat the "degeneration and diminution of man into a perfect herd animal" (*BGE* 203). This requires that we recognize "that man is the *animal that has not yet been established*" and that it is possible for man to be something other than a "sublime deformity" (*BGE* 62).

Beyond Good and Evil is said by Nietzsche to be "in all essentials" a critique of modernity that includes within its range of attack modern science, modern art, and modern politics. Where the vision of *Zarathustra* was that of distant things, the vision of *Beyond Good and Evil* is focused sharply on the modern age, on "what is *around us*." However, Nietzsche holds the two projects and tasks to be intimately related: "In every aspect of the book," he writes in *Ecce Homo*, "above all in its form, one will discover the same *intentional* [*willkürliche*] turning away from the instincts out of which a Zarathustra becomes possible." In a letter to his former Basel colleague Jacob Burckhardt dated September 22, 1886, Nietzsche stresses that *Beyond Good and Evil* says the same things as *Zarathustra* "only in a way that is different – very different."[1] In this letter he draws

---

This introduction draws upon editorial material prepared by Ansell Pearson for a second, revised edition of Nietzsche, *On the Genealogy of Morality* (Cambridge and New York: Cambridge University Press, 2006), trans. Carol Diethe, ed. Keith Ansell Pearson.

1 *Selected Letters of Friedrich Nietzsche*, ed. and trans. Christopher Middleton (Chicago and London: University of Chicago Press, 1969; repr. Indianapolis: Hackett, 1996), p. 255.

attention to the book's chief preoccupations and mentions the "mysterious conditions of any growth in culture," the "extremely dubious relation between what is called the 'improvement' of man (or even 'humanization') and the enlargement of the human type," and, "above all the contradiction between every moral concept and every scientific concept of *life*." *On the Genealogy of Morality* closely echoes these themes and concerns. Nietzsche finds that "all modern judgments about men and things" are smeared with an over-moralistic language; the characteristic feature of modern souls and modern books is to be found in their "moralistic mendaciousness" (*GM* III. 19). Our modern thinking about morals and politics is characterized by a "moral sugariness and falsity" and by "feminism" and "idealism" (*GM* III. 19). We find it hard to encounter and stomach "a single *truth* 'about man'!" (*GM* III. 19).

Nietzsche intended *On the Genealogy of Morality* as a "supplement" and "clarification" to his previous book, *Beyond Good and Evil*. Although it is often prized as his most important and systematic work, Nietzsche himself conceived it as a "small polemical pamphlet," one that might help him sell more copies of his earlier writings.[2] It clearly merits, though, the level of attention it receives from commentators and can justifiably be regarded as one of the key texts of European intellectual modernity. It is a deeply disturbing book that makes for an unnerving and disconcerting read. For shock value no other modern text on the human condition rivals it. Nietzsche himself was well aware of the character of the book. There are moments in the text where he reveals his own sense of shock at what he is discovering about human origins and development, especially the perverse nature of the human animal, the being he calls "the sick animal" (*GM* III. 14): "There is so much in man that is horrifying! . . . The world has been a madhouse for too long!" (*GM* II. 22). In *Ecce Homo* Nietzsche discloses that an "art of surprise" guides each of the three essays that make up the book and admits that they merit being taken as among the "uncanniest" things ever scripted. He then stresses that his god, Dionysus, is also "the god of darkness" (*EH*, "GM"). Indeed, the *Genealogy* is one of the darkest books ever written.

With these two texts, *Beyond Good and Evil* and *On the Genealogy of Morality*, Nietzsche wished to present readers with a set of unpleasant and uncomfortable truths. His aim in doing so was not so much to contribute further to the belittling of man that characterizes so much modern intellectual inquiry, but rather to show the real processes and events that have been at work in our cultural discipline and breeding ("civilization"), and to explore the possibility of a new nobility emerging under modern conditions, in which strong human beings would regain a sense of self-reverence and, through their deeds and self-conquests, "justify" and "redeem" man: "grant me just one glimpse of something perfect . . . happy, powerful, triumphant, which still leaves something to fear! A glimpse of a man who justifies man *himself* . . . and enables us to retain our *faith in mankind*!" Nihilism stems from the fact that the sight of man now makes us tired (*GM* I. 12; see also III. 14). What are Nietzsche's uncomfortable and hard truths about morality? They include the following claims: that what we call "high culture" is based on a deepening and spiritualization of cruelty – European man has not killed off the "wild beast" (*BGE* 229); that what we take to be "spirit" or "mind," as that which distinguishes the human animal from the rest of nature, is the product of a long constraint, involving much violence, arbitrariness, and nonsense (*BGE* 188); that

2   Letter to Peter Gast, July 18, 1887: *Selected Letters*, p. 269.

modern European morality is "herd animal morality" which considers itself to be the
definition of morality and the only morality possible or desirable (*BGE* 202); that the
democratic movement is a decadent form of political organization (*BGE* 203); and
that every enhancement of the type "human being" can only be achieved by a society
that believes in a ladder of hierarchy and differences in value between people (*BGE*
257). The European morality that Nietzsche takes to task is at work for him in various articulations, including the demand for equal rights, the estimation accorded to
unegoistic instincts such as compassion (*Mitleid*), self-denial, and self-sacrifice, and the
utilitarian principle of the happiness of the greatest number. Nietzsche places himself
in opposition to all these values and principles and commits himself to undertaking a
fundamental and far-reaching revaluation of all values. One of his principal criticisms
is directed against the assumption endemic to the modern spirit that that there is a
single morality valid for all. In opposition to this assumption he maintains that "there
is a *hierarchy* between human and human, and therefore between morality and morality as well" (*BGE* 228).

With these two texts Nietzsche wished to offer a new approach to the so-called
"science of morality," a science he considered to be at a clumsy and crude state of
development (*BGE* 186). He wanted to enliven this science by introducing a certain
vitalism into it, one that seeks to draw attention to the importance of questions of
origins and descent, of decisive events, and, perhaps most importantly, of value and
future possibility. In *Beyond Good and Evil* Nietzsche contends that almost all moral
philosophy is "boring and belongs among the sedatives" (*BGE* 228). There is no thinker
in Europe, he further contends, who is prepared to entertain the idea that moral reflection
can be carried out in a dangerous and seductive manner, "that it might involve one's
fate!" (*BGE* 228). Nietzsche argues that in their attempts to account for morality philosophers, "as strange as it may sound," have not developed the suspicion that morality
might be "something problematic"; in effect what they have done is to articulate "an
erudite form of true *belief* in the prevailing morality," and, as a result, their inquiries
remain "a part of the state of affairs within a particular morality" (*BGE* 186).
Nietzsche seeks to develop a genuinely critical approach to morality, in which all kinds
of novel, surprising, and daring questions are posed. Nietzsche does not inquire into
a "moral sense" or a moral faculty[3] – a common intellectual practice in the work
of modern moralists and humanists, such as Francis Hutcheson, Hume, and Kant,
for example – but rather sets out to uncover *the different senses* of morality, that is, the
different "meanings" morality has acquired in the history of human development. His
attempt at a critique involves developing a knowledge of the conditions and circumstances under which values emerged; this will give us an appreciation of the different
"senses" of morality: as symptom, as mask, as sickness, as stimulant, as poison, and so
on. In the *Genealogy* Nietzsche is keen to draw our attention to the importance of a
pre-history of the human animal, the period he calls "the morality of custom" that
pre-dates what we call "world history" and that for him is to be regarded as the
"decisive historical period" which has determined the character of man (*GM* III. 9;
see also *GM* II. 1–2, 9, 19). Nietzsche's contribution to a science of morality is twofold:

3   On the idea of a "moral sense" see Francis Hutcheson, *On the Nature and Conduct of the
Passions with Illustrations of the Moral Sense* (1728), annotated by Andrew Ward (Manchester:
Clinamen Press, 1999).

he seeks to advance the cause of a "natural history" of morals or morality – this is the title of chapter 5 of *Beyond Good and Evil* – and he radicalizes the significance of a "genealogy" of morals or morality. Nietzsche's approach has had a seminal influence on some important developments in the thought of the post-World War II period (the work of Michel Foucault, for example), and we might suppose that Nietzsche can be taken as the originator of these historical and genealogical approaches. This would be an error, however. Nietzsche saw himself as contributing to an approach to morality that was already well established. W. E. H. Lecky's *History of European Morals*, first published in two volumes in 1869, opens with a chapter on the "natural history of morals";[4] and in the *Genealogy* Nietzsche makes it clear on several occasions that certain psychologists and moralists have been doing something we can call "genealogy" (see, for example, *GM* I. 2 and II. 4, 12 – the latter is the key methodological section of the book). He holds, however, that these researchers have not been carrying out a genuinely historical inquiry or engaging in what he calls "real" or effective history (see *GM*, Preface, 7). Such a history will show the human being to be a far stranger animal than we feminized and idealistic moderns could ever suppose. In addition, an examination of the books of moral genealogists would show that, in spite of their novel questioning, they all take morality to be something "given" and place it beyond truly radical questioning.[5] Their questioning is simply not radical and deep enough.

Nietzsche begins the *Genealogy* proper by paying homage to "English psychologists," a group of pioneering researchers who have held a microscope to the soul and, in the process, come up with a new set of truths: "plain, bitter, ugly, foul, unchristian, immoral . . ." (*GM* I. 1).[6] Although Nietzsche goes on to criticize these psychologists for bungling their moral genealogy and for not carrying out a "real" history of morality, we should not lose sight of the fact that he feels a deep affinity with their dedication to the cause of unchristian and immoral truth. The work of these psychologists has its basis in the empiricism of John Locke and in David Hume's new approach to the mind, and seeks to show that so-called complex, intellectual activity emerges out of processes that are,

4   For references to Lecky in Nietzsche see *KSA* 9:473 and 10:240, 258.

5   Hume, for example, writes: "Mankind are so much the same, in all times and places, that history informs us of nothing new or strange in this particular. Its chief use is only to discover the constant and universal principles of human nature, by showing men in all varieties of circumstances and situations, and furnishing us with materials, from which we may form our observations and become acquainted with the regular springs of human action and behaviour": *An Enquiry Concerning Human Understanding* (posthumous 1777 edition), section 8.

6   In the "English psychologists" Nietzsche is referring to quite a diverse body of work, having in mind the work of seminal nineteenth-century thinkers such as Herbert Spencer and the associationist school of psychology. In his *Data of Ethics* (1879) Spencer understands the subject-matter of ethics to be the form that "universal conduct" assumes in the last stages of evolution (for example, the transition from "militant" to "industrial" existence), especially the values of cooperation and mutual aid. Nietzsche makes an important reference to Spencer's text in *KSA* 11:525. For insight into Nietzsche's critical reception of Spencer see Gregory Moore, *Nietzsche, Biology and Metaphor* (Cambridge and New York: Cambridge University Press, 2002), pp. 62–72.

in truth, "stupid," such as the *vis inertiae* of habit and the random coupling or mechanical association of ideas. Although Nietzsche has deep affinities with an empiricist mode of philosophizing, he is highly critical of British empiricism. In the attempt of "English psychologists" to show the real mechanisms of the mind, Nietzsche sees at work not a malicious and mean instinct, and not simply a pessimistic suspicion about the human animal, but the research of proud and generous spirits who have sacrificed much to the cause of truth. He greatly admires the honest craftsmanship of their intellectual labors. He criticizes them, however, for their lack of a real historical sense and for failing to raise questions of value and future legislation. This is why he describes empiricism as having only a "plebeian ambition" (*BGE* 213). At the end of section 4 of the First Essay of the *Genealogy* (not included here) Nietzsche speaks of the "famous case" of Thomas Henry Buckle (1821–62), a Victorian historian of civilization, and claims that the "*plebeianism* of the modern spirit" began in England. This links up with the criticisms he makes, in section 253 of *Beyond Good and Evil*, of "respectable, but mediocre Englishmen," such as the likes of Darwin, Spencer, and John Stuart Mill. What the "English" essentially lack, according to Nietzsche, is "spiritual vision of real *depth* – in short, philosophy." This is why he thinks Hobbes, Hume, and Locke represent a "devaluation of the concept 'philosopher'" (*BGE* 252). Nietzsche can be fruitfully interpreted as developing a *superior* empiricism conceived as a philosophical practice that devotes itself to distinguishing between noble and base ways of thinking and to raising questions of value (that of morality and of truth, for example). Nietzsche refers to the "English" historians of morality in section 345 of *The Gay Science* and spells out what he sees as their fundamental mistake, chiefly that their inquiries do not go deep enough and the problem of the "value" of morality is not raised by them (see also *GM*, Preface, 5). Morality is said by Nietzsche to be the "danger of dangers" because its prejudices contribute to the situation in which the present is lived at the expense of the future (*GM*, Preface, 6). In the entry on the *Genealogy* in *Ecce Homo*, Nietzsche tells us that each of the three essays that make up the book contains a beginning that is calculated to mislead, which intentionally "keeps in suspense," while at the conclusion of each essay "a *new* truth" becomes "visible between thick clouds." Each essay begins coolly and scientifically but at the end of each a reckoning is called for, and this demand concerns the future. At the very end of the First Essay, for example, Nietzsche says that questions concerning the worth of morals and different tables of value can be asked from different angles, and he singles out the question "value *for what?*" as being of special significance. The task of the different sciences of knowledge is to "prepare the way for the future work of the philosopher," which consists in solving the "problem of values" and deciding on their hierarchy. At the end of the Second Essay Nietzsche hints at the overhuman and heralds "the man of the future" who will redeem humanity from the curse of its reigning ideal and from all those things that arise from it, notably nihilism and the will to nothingness.

The Preface to the book is crucial for understanding Nietzsche's intentions. It begins with the enigmatic statement that we knowers, as we moderns like to think of ourselves, are unknown to ourselves, and the nature of these "knowers" is probed in the Third Essay where Nietzsche insists that godless anti-metaphysicians remain "idealists of knowledge" (see, for example, *GM* III. 12 and 24). The task of gaining an adequate comprehension of the present age, so as to perform a critique of modernity, can be compared to the task of acquiring self-knowledge: what is required is that which is most difficult to require, namely, distance and learning how to incorporate truth and knowledge. Nietzsche argues that there are good reasons why "we knowers" are not, in fact, known to ourselves: if we do not know how to search for ourselves, how can we be expected to "know" ourselves (*GM*, Preface, 1)? One problem is that we seek to bring knowledge back "home" (back to a familiar time and place); we wish to see ourselves reflected all the time in all our events and actions. But what we take ourselves to be comes from the very limited conception of time (and of memory) that we have. We want knowledge that is familiar and will not demand too much of our time, or place the demands of time on us. Nietzsche thus raises the question of whether we are serious enough about self-knowledge and whether we can find "enough time" for the task. Finding more time than what is given to us involves emancipating time from the limited and narrow horizon of the present, creating new knowledge through the inventive powers of a critical memory. It is the necessity of the present – and modernity is in large part a cult of the present – that closes off an effective knowledge of the past and unduly limits our conception of the future (on this see also *GS* 380 and the Preface to *CW*). The Preface also makes clear that Nietzsche conceived his project not simply or merely as a contribution to late nineteenth-century naturalism. Nothing less than a "new twist and possible outcome" of the *Dionysian drama on the fate of the "soul"* is what is to be meditated upon and chewed over in our exegetical reading of this book. Here Nietzsche invokes the "comedy of our existence" on the planet, and the Third Essay finds him assuming the role of the comedian of the ascetic ideal and seeking comic effect through all the trickery of the comic, including vulgarity, crudity, and rudeness. Nietzsche says that although he sometimes speaks crudely, he does not wish to be *understood* crudely.

Nietzsche's genealogical inquiry into morality culminates with his extraordinary questioning of the "meaning" of ascetic ideals in the Third Essay. Ascetic ideals are ideals of denial and mortification of the will. Nietzsche couches his inquiry as one into their meaning or significance (*Bedeutung*). It is clear from this final section of the book that his questioning of them is also a questioning of the sense and direction (*Sinn*) of the human will itself. Nietzsche clarifies the specific nature of his inquiry in section 23 of the essay. Here he speaks of the ascetic ideal as a generic term and says that the issue of what it signifies is to be approached through an analysis of "what lies behind, beneath and within it" and "what it expresses in a provisional, indistinct way, laden with question marks and misunderstandings." In short, the task is to bring this ideal to self-knowledge by uncovering what it conceals. Nietzsche holds that this ideal possesses a power; moreover, this power has a monstrosity to it – it has produced a monstrosity of effects that have been "calamitous." He wants to know why it has occupied so much space in human existence and why there has been so little effective resistance to it. He also poses the question of where the "opposing will, in which an *opposing ideal* might express itself" can be found. For Nietzsche the fact that this ideal has been so prevalent in history, and continues to be so, reveals something essential about the human will, a "basic fact," its "horror of a vacuum:" it needs an aim or goal – to the point that "it prefers to will *nothingness* rather than *not* will." Nietzsche is conscious of the fact that with the formulation "will to nothingness" he is deliberately subverting Schopenhauer, for whom willing and nothingness are mutually exclusive conditions. Once we have recognized that incurable suffering and perpetual misery are the essential features of the phenomenon of the will to life and we see the world melt

away with the abolition of this will, then we retain before us only empty nothingness. For Schopenhauer this can become our great consolation. Nietzsche's claim is
that willing something is an inescapable fact of human existence, and that practices of
self-denial, which involve the will turning against itself, remain expressions of willing
(nothingness remains an aim or goal and names something, be it God or Nirvana). On
one level the ascetic ideal seems to express a self-contradiction inasmuch as we seem
to encounter with it life operating against life. Nietzsche argues, however, that viewed
from physiological and psychological angles this amounts to nonsense. In section 13
of the Third Essay he suggests that on closer examination this self-contradiction turns
out to be only apparent; it is "a psychological misunderstanding of something, the real
nature of which was far from being understood." His argument is that the ascetic ideal
has its source or origins in what he calls "the protective and healing instincts of a
degenerating life." The ideal indicates a partial physiological exhaustion in the face of
which "the deepest instincts of life, which have remained intact, continually struggle
with new methods and inventions." The ascetic ideal is not what we might suppose;
it is not, for example, a transcendence of the conditions of life (change, death, becoming) but a struggle with and against them. It amounts, in effect, to a trick or artifice
(*Kunstgriff*) for the preservation of life. Nietzsche holds that the great danger of our
modern human sickness, which is also bound up with an unavoidable fear of man, is
that it will lead not to the promotion of higher and rarer types but to the opposite,
to a leveling out and homogenization in which social and political institutions will
exist simply to contain man. The danger is that we will allow society to nurture a
false sympathy over the human condition. It is not fear of man that we should seek
to overcome, since this can serve as a spur to new experiments and tasks, but rather
nausea at and compassion for him, for this will only produce the " 'last will' of
man, his will to nothingness, nihilism." Nietzsche is fully cognizant of the fact that a
goal cannot be ascribed to human history; rather, a goal can only be put in it. The
problem is not the mere fact that we suffer from life, but that this suffering is in need
of an explanation and justification. He notes that the human animal can even will its
suffering so long as it can be given a meaning and a direction. The interpretation of
suffering developed by the ascetic ideal has succeeded in shutting the door on a suicidal nihilism. It has added new dimensions and layers to suffering by making it deeper
and more internal, creating a suffering that gnaws more intensely at life and bringing
it within the perspective of guilt or moral debt. But this saving of the will has been
won at the expense of the future and led to the cultivation of a hatred of the conditions of human existence. It expresses a fundamental will to nothingness, a "fear of
happiness and beauty" and "a longing to get away from appearance, transience, growth,
death."

It is in the Third Essay that Nietzsche carries out his disconcerting questioning of
truth. We have touched on Nietzsche's critique of the will to truth in our main introduction and so shall limit ourselves here to making only a few key points on this topic.
Nietzsche makes a number of striking claims: that modern knowers and free spirits
remain idealists of knowledge; that these spirits represent the most intellectualized product of the only ideal that has flourished on earth to date, the ascetic ideal; and that
our modern faith in science is a *metaphysical* faith. In calling, *tentatively*, for a "critique"
of the will to truth Nietzsche is not proposing a negative task but a limiting one.
Nietzsche's critical eye is focused on the *unconditional* character of our modern will to

truth and on our belief in the *divine* nature of truth. We moderns overestimate truth; such is our faith in truth we take it to be something that cannot be assessed or criticized (*GM* III. 25). The "truth" that Nietzsche is calling into question in the Third Essay of the *Genealogy of Morality* is the truth which supposes a *metaphysical* valuation, and his startling claim is that modern forms of scientific inquiry, from cosmology to historiography, rest on such a valuation. By "metaphysical" here Nietzsche has in mind such things as the paralogical ideal of knowledge free of presuppositions, a knowledge without a direction, a meaning, and a limit, and a knowledge that renounces interpretation and everything that is essential to it (*GM* III. 24). A *nonmetaphysical* utilization of truth, by contrast, is what we find at work throughout the *Genealogy*. This nonmetaphysical deployment of truth works *alongside* the asceticism of truth-practices that Nietzsche wishes us to call into question but which prove to be so indispensable for his own historical inquiries, including a deep mistrust and skepticism (in *GM* III. 9 Nietzsche lists the drives peculiar to the philosopher and mentions the drives to doubt, to deny, to dare, and to research). That Nietzsche is committed to "truth" and to uncovering "truths" about morality and man should not be doubted. His questioning in the Third Essay is centered on the issue of truth's value and considered from a particular perspective: the need to constitute a new future cultivation for the human and to develop a new justification of man.

We have noted that the *Genealogy of Morality* is a disturbing and dark book. It needs to be pointed out that it is also a dangerous book and demands to be read and taught with the proper degree of intellectual care and responsibility. It contains provocative imagery of "blond beasts" and of the Jewish "slave revolt in morals" which, if not handled carefully, runs the risk of turning Nietzsche into the wrong kind of immoralist. In the Preface Nietzsche mentions the importance of readers familiarizing themselves with his previous books – throughout the *Genealogy* he refers to various sections and aphorisms from them, and occasionally makes partial citations from them. This is significant since it indicates that Nietzsche wished the *Genealogy* not to be read on its own, independently of the rest of his oeuvre, from the publication of *Human, All Too Human* in 1878 to *Beyond Good and Evil* in 1886. The "critique" of morality Nietzsche carries out in the *Genealogy* is a complex one; its nuances are lost if one extracts isolated images and concepts from the argument of the book as a whole. With regard to a number of key phenomena Nietzsche's attention is focused on the complex character of forces that inform phenomena and events, making a historical becoming possible and allowing for things to possess different senses and meanings (in *GM* II. 13 he says that only that which has no history can be defined and draws attention to the "synthesis of meanings" that accrues to any given phenomenon). Throughout the text Nietzsche comments on the essentially ambiguous character of various cultural phenomena, including the priestly form of existence and the bad conscience (see, for example, *GM* I. 6 and II. 16).

It is in *Beyond Good and Evil* and *On the Genealogy of Morality* that we encounter the two most important presentations of the doctrine of the will to power in Nietzsche's published writings (*BGE* 36 and *GM* II. 12; see also *GS* 349). The teaching first appears in his work in the discourse "On Self-Overcoming" in *Zarathustra*; hitherto he has spoken only of "the feeling of power" (in *Daybreak* and in *GS* 13, for example). It is without doubt the doctrine which has generated the most dispute amongst commentators on Nietzsche's work: is he propounding a new ontology and cosmology of forces with his doctrine of will to power and, if so, is he entitled to do so? Some commentators argue that the will to power operates strictly on the level of an empirical psychology, especially human psychology, and are suspicious of treating the will to power as an ontology and cosmology of forces. Others have insisted that the will to power cannot be restricted to the merely empirical or psychological, arguing that it is indeed an ontology and defending Nietzsche's entitlement to one. Commentators suspicious of treating the doctrine of will to power as an ontology argue that there is little basis in Nietzsche for doing so. How coherent is it, for example, for Nietzsche to draw our attention to the anthropomorphic character of our designations of nature, as in section 109 of *The Gay Science*, and then go on to claim that the world in its essence and in all its aspects is will to power? How can we be sure that in this doctrine Nietzsche does not do what he criticizes the Stoics and other modes of thinking for doing, namely, imposing a morality or an ideal on nature (*BGE* 9)? Is the will to power, then, simply a projection of Nietzsche's particular and peculiar evaluative commitments? These are questions with which any conscientious reader of Nietzsche must wrestle.

The majority of Nietzsche's most extensive explorations of the world as will to power are to be found in his *Nachlass* material, selections from which are available in English translation in the volume *The Will to Power*. This is a highly unreliable text put together after Nietzsche's death by his sister and her supporters.[7] It might be proposed that the most prudent approach to adopt with respect to the doctrine of will to power is to pay careful and close attention to what Nietzsche says in his published texts about it – there are two main places where the doctrine is elaborated in methodological terms (*BGE* 36 and *GM* II. 12) – and then allow the notebooks from the 1880s to be used only on the basis of connections one can plausibly make between them and the published texts. However, adopting such a transparently sensible approach as this is not without problems, especially when the complex character of Nietzsche's presentation of his philosophy is taken into account. In his 1971 study the eminent German scholar Wolfgang Müller-Lauter drew attention to those places where Nietzsche complicates the issue of how we are to receive his writings, including a note from 1887 in which he says that he does not write for readers but takes notes only for himself. It is on

---

7   *The Will to Power* was compiled from Nietzsche's notebooks by a group of editors working under Elisabeth's controlling influence. A first edition composed of 483 sections appeared in 1901, and a second edition of 1,067 aphorisms in 1906 (this is the volume we are familiar with in English translation). In Germany a cheap and popular edition was published by Alfred Baeumler, a principal ideologue of National Socialism. Heidegger's reading of Nietzsche is often attacked for placing undue emphasis on Nietzsche's notebooks, but this ignores the fact that he was one of the first to cast suspicion on the volume that bears the title *The Will to Power*. He noted that the *WP* edition gives us a book falsely ascribed to Nietzsche and that it is little more than an arbitrary selection of the notes which predetermines our conception of Nietzsche's philosophy during the period 1883/4–8. See Heidegger, *Nietzsche*, ed. David Farrell Krell, trans. David Farrell Krell et al., 4 vols (San Francisco and London: Harper & Row, 1979–87), vol. 2, p. 152f. See also the remarks Maurice Blanchot makes in his *The Infinite Conversation*, trans. Susan Hanson (Minneapolis and London: University of Minnesota Press, 1993), p. 137ff.

the basis of such disclosures, which can also be found in the published material (see, for example, *BGE* 160), that Müller-Lauter defends Heidegger's contentious view that the "real philosophy" of Nietzsche is not to be found in the published texts, which are merely "foreground," but rather in what he left behind as his posthumous legacy.[8] Nietzsche devised numerous plans for a *magnum opus* which was to bear the title "Will to Power: Attempt at a Revaluation of All Values,"[9] so clearly the principle of the will to power was important to him even if he never articulated it to the extent he wished in his published writings of this period.

Given his rejection of the notion of the thing-in-itself as either unintelligible or useless, why does Nietzsche present his own doctrine of the will to power by articulating it in terms of the "world's intelligible character"[10] in section 36 of *Beyond Good and Evil*? We should be careful not to read his articulation of the will to power in these terms too literally and unimaginatively: there is no doubt that Nietzsche is being provocative and playful in defining his doctrine in these terms at the end of this section. He has argued, in effect, that *supposing* (*gesetzt*) we could view the world from "inside" then the world we would come into contact with and encounter would not be anything radically different from the actual, empirical world of our instincts and affects! So where would the difference reside? Let us pursue this question. It is necessary to appreciate that although Nietzsche can often sound as if he is simply refining Schopenhauer's doctrine, renaming the will to life as will to power and, like Schopenhauer, taking issue with mechanistic modes of explanation, he reformulates the nature and terms of the problem in a number of significant ways. For

---

8   See Wolfgang Müller-Lauter, *Nietzsche: His Philosophy of Contradictions and the Contradictions of his Philosophy*, trans. David J. Parent (Urbana and Chicago: University of Illinois Press, 1999), p. 125ff. Heidegger is frequently misheard on this point. It is not that he arbitrarily privileges Nietzsche's unpublished notebooks and fragments over the published texts: as noted above he voices a deep suspicion about the text *The Will to Power*. What he does is commit himself to a reading of the unpublished material by focusing on Nietzsche's central doctrines, the meaning of which is not self-evident. The result is a necessarily speculative but thought-provoking encounter with Nietzsche and the "West" (the "nihilism" of Western history and metaphysics). Deleuze's reading of Nietzsche was inspired by Heidegger's reading of the problem of nihilism in Nietzsche but took issue with his reading of Nietzsche on the question of Being. See Gilles Deleuze, *Nietzsche and Philosophy*, trans. Hugh Tomlinson (London: Athlone Press; New York: Columbia University Press, 1983), p. 203 n. 30 and p. 220 n. 31.

9   Sometimes the lead title was given over to *Philosophy of Eternal Recurrence*. One of the most complex issues to think through concerns the relation between the doctrines of will to power and eternal recurrence. Heidegger made this task central to his reading of Nietzsche. Deleuze's reading, which is largely inspired by Bergson, is notorious for reading Nietzsche's doctrine not as a doctrine of the return of the same but as a doctrine of selection.

10   For Kant on the distinction between intelligible and sensible character, see *Critique of Pure Reason* A 538/B 566. For Schopenhauer on Kant and "intelligible character," see *WWR* vol. 1, sections 28 and 55. See also the critical comment Nietzsche makes in *GM* III. 12.

Schopenhauer the empirical world merely furnishes a copy of the timeless intelligible world, that is, the empirical makes no real difference and it creates no differences; in Nietzsche, by contrast, the will to power denotes the field of individuating forces and events and is always coterminous with the actual things and individuated bodies that are implicated in this field.

In section 36 of *Beyond Good and Evil*, Nietzsche outlines the doctrine of will to power in terms of a "conscience of method," with the stress placed on the need for an economy of principles, and he makes it clear that the problem he is addressing is not, strictly speaking, one of appearance or representation. He invites us to "perform an experiment," namely, asking whether what is given to us on the level of psychology (the world of our instincts and passions) might not also provide a sufficient explanation for the so-called mechanistic or material world. Nietzsche adds that he does *not* mean the material world taken as a delusion, as appearance (*Schein*) or representation (*Vorstellung*), whether in the sense of Berkeley ("to be is to be perceived") or that of Schopenhauer, "but rather as a world that has the *same reality* that our emotion [*Affekt*] has but in a more rudimentary form" (emphasis added) and conceived "as a kind of instinctual life in which all the organic functions [. . .] are synthetically linked to one another – as a *pre-form* [*Vorform*] of life." This pre-form of life holds all the "potential to develop and differentiate" – and to "spoil and weaken too" – and exists "as a kind of instinctual life."[11] In other words, if we could view the world according to its "intelligible character" and get "inside" it, what we would come into contact with would not be anything radically different from what we encounter in the phenomenal world of our instincts and affects. It would be the same phenomena only existing in a more primitive state. Nietzsche fully acknowledges that his doctrine is an interpretation and a translation (the language of affects is itself caught up in such translation), but he argues that these are at play in all theories of life and knowledge (*BGE* 22). Moreover, the objector to the doctrine of will to power, who objects to it because it is too human and caught up in metaphor, may be objecting too quickly because they insufficiently appreciate the extent to which will to power, conceived as a creative drive, a will to grow and be effective, is the *condition* of all interpretation (*BGE* 22; see also *BGE* 35, which is intriguing in this regard).

Nietzsche holds that an appeal to something like the will to power needs to be made owing to the deficiencies of mechanism, and he makes this appeal in terms of an energetics of life. Mechanical events, he argues, are active only to the extent that energy is a feature of them, and, moreover, this energy cannot simply be construed as the effect of matter but only of "will" (the will to life which is a will to power: an insatiable desire to manifest power, a creative drive for growth and expansion, a releasing of strength, a *pathos*, and so on). In short, we might say that life is characterized by development and differentiation – and this is what, in part, the modern theory of evolution, especially Darwinism, teaches us. *Contra* Darwinism, however,

---

11   The language used in *BGE* 36 is borrowed directly by Nietzsche from a work in embryology and evolutionary thinking by Wilhelm Roux which he read, and took extensive notes from, at various points in the 1880s. For details of his reading of Roux see Müller-Lauter, *Nietzsche*, pp. 161–83.

Nietzsche is arguing that it is insufficient to account for life solely in terms of an exogenous mechanism such as adaptation to external circumstances. Such a conception deprives life of its most important dimension, which he names *Aktivität* (activity). It does this, he contends, by overlooking the primacy of the "spontaneous, expansive, aggressive [. . .] formative forces" that provide life with new directions and new interpretations, and from which adaptation takes place only once these forces have had their effect. He tells us that he lays "stress on this major point of historical method because it runs counter to the prevailing instinct and fashion which would much rather come to terms with absolute randomness, and even the mechanistic senselessness of all events, than the theory that a *power-will* is acted out in all that happens" (*GM* II. 12).

Nietzsche is drawn to the theory of the will to power for a number of reasons, and it forms an important part of his superior empiricism, operating as a principle of value and of legislation. In the *Genealogy* Nietzsche shows a strong commitment to reforming the sciences. He wants the seminal role played by the "active emotions" to be appreciated (*GM* II. 11), and he calls for the natural sciences to resist the "democratic bias" which, in his view, has had a ruinous effect on inquiries into human descent and the human past (*GM* I. 4). We suffer from the "democratic idiosyncrasy" that opposes in principle everything that dominates and wants to dominate (*GM* II. 12). However, a number of critical questions need to be asked of the theory or doctrine of the will to power. For example: can a concept that draws its inspiration from biology and embryology serve as an adequate principle of historical method and cultural critique? Does such a principle not commit the worst errors of "biologism"? What is the status of Nietzsche's claim (*BGE* 259) that the will to power, and all that it entails such as valuing exploitation, domination, and the lust to rule, is the "*original fact*" of all history? Is such a doctrine and principle an example of the recurring penchant of philosophers for over-simplification, which Hume so astutely criticizes? "When a philosopher has once laid hold of a favourite principle, which perhaps accounts for many natural effects, he extends the same principle over the whole creation, and reduces to it every phenomenon, though by the most violent and absurd reasoning."[12]

We have made a generous selection from both *Beyond Good and Evil* and *On the Genealogy of Morality*. From the former we have included nearly all the sections from the opening of the book (including the Preface, with its striking question "assuming truth is a woman – what then?" and the first chapter on the prejudices of the philosophers); some key sections from the chapter on the free spirit, including the presentation of the will to power in section 36; and then sections from the remaining chapters of the book, including his reflections on the relation between religion and philosophy, his attempt to outline a "natural history of morals" that will prepare a "taxonomy of morals" (186), his appeal to the new philosophers of the future (211), his important consideration of the "fundamental will of the spirit," in which man is returned to nature in a complex act of translation (230), and his consideration of the question "what is noble?" (257). From *On the Genealogy of Morality* we have included the Preface in full, some key sections from the First and Third Essays (on the spirit of *ressentiment* and the meaning of the ascetic ideals, respectively), and most of the sections from the Second Essay,

---

12 David Hume, "The Sceptic," in Hume, *Selected Essays* (Oxford and New York: Oxford University Press, 1996), p. 95. For an intelligent reading of the will to power as an ontology, see John Richardson, *Nietzsche's System* (New York and Oxford: Oxford University Press, 1996).

which seeks to trace the origins and development of the bad conscience, as well as indicating its different senses.

In 1887 Nietzsche published a second edition of *The Gay Science* containing a fifth book entitled "We Fearless Ones." He also added a new Preface to the text and an appendix of songs (neither is included here). The book begins with Nietzsche reflecting on the "meaning" of the cheerfulness felt by the free spirits who hear the news that the Christian God is dead. Section 344 is a probing reflection on the "unconditional will to truth" in which Nietzsche contends that modern science is bound to this will and thus rests on a "metaphysical faith." In section 346 he names nihilism as the problem that emerges when European humanity develops a suspicion about itself and the reverences it has relied upon as a way of making existence something that can be endured. We also include important sections on consciousness and the character of our search for, and conception of, knowledge (354 and 355), on the problem of the actor (356 and 361), a long and important paragraph on "What is romanticism?" (370), a section on science as a prejudice and the "meaning" (*Sinn*) of music (373), and sections on what it means to be an emancipated and "good" European in the context of the tremendous changes taking place in culture as a result of the advent of nihilism (377, 380–2).

Around this time Nietzsche drafted various paragraphs on the problem of European nihilism, although extended discussion of this topic features rarely in his published writings. In this section we include a new translation of the "Lenzer Heide" notes on European nihilism, dated June 10, 1887. The notes were composed, in fact, only a few weeks before Nietzsche began writing the *Genealogy* (written in July and August 1887 and published in November of that year). They can be read productively alongside the Third Essay of the *Genealogy*, since what is being examined in both is nihilism and the will to nothingness. For Nietzsche, to be a nihilist in a spiritual and cultural sense is to be in a relatively well-off position. Nihilism necessarily follows from the demise of metaphysics (he insists that nihilism is simply a consequence of humanity's idealism); taken on a psychological level nihilism is a necessary effect of the decline of belief in God. Man's aversion to existence has not become any greater than in previous times, it is simply that we moderns have come to doubt that there is any meaning in suffering and in existence itself. One extreme position is now succeeded by another equally extreme position, one that construes everything as if it were in vain. It is this "in vain" which constitutes the character of "present-day nihilism." The problem is twofold: it involves a mistrust of all previous evaluations that borders on the pathological (all values are now seen as lures that "allow the whole comedy to drag on without ever getting closer to a solution"), and, secondly, "with an 'in vain,' with no aim [*Ziel*] or purpose [*Zweck*], *duration* is the *most paralysing* thought." In short, we understand we are being duped and yet lack the power not to be duped. Eternal recurrence is now construed as a response to this European problem of nihilism: "Let us think this thought in its most terrible form: existence as it is, without sense or aim, but inevitably returning, without a finale in nothingness: 'the eternal return [*die ewige Wiederkehr*]'." The thought, therefore, is a response to the problem of the "in vain" with which we now interpret duration. If the "finale" is taken away and existence is posited without the aid of notions of goal or aim and purpose, we are left confronted with the "nothingness" and the prospect of the *Sinnlose* returning eternally. Nietzsche considers this to be "the most extreme form of nihilism." It is a peculiarly *European* form of Buddhism, and all the *energy* of knowledge compels us to arrive at this position. It is, therefore, on this level, "the *most scientific* of all possible hypotheses. We deny final goals [*Schluss-Ziele*]."

Conceived in these quasi-cosmological terms eternal recurrence becomes an utterly nihilistic thought, a thought that pushes nihilism to its limit. If the need for a meaning and purpose to the universe has hitherto been humankind's greatest problem, then a cult of meaninglessness is hardly a solution to the problem of nihilism (simply because it remains tethered to it). Rather, what is called for is a repositioning of meaning (*Sinn*); this is what Nietzsche seems to be calling for in his critical analysis of the ascetic ideal in the Third Essay of the *Genealogy*. On the level of pathology nihilism is a symptom of those who have turned out badly in life and now find themselves deprived of any consolation. For these unhealthy types – which can be found in all classes, Nietzsche says – the eternal recurrence will be experienced as a curse. These are types who do "no" after existence has lost its meaning and who destroy only in order to be destroyed in return. Their lust for destruction thus has an absurd character to it. They gnash their teeth and fanatically pursue a will to destruction, "*making* everything that is so senseless and aimless be extinguished." Nietzsche envisages a crisis taking place in which different forces will come together and collide and there will be assigned "common tasks to people of opposing mentalities," leading to the initiation of "*a hierarchy* of *forces*." He asks who in this struggle will prove to be the strongest, and states that it is not a matter of numbers or of brute strength. The strongest will be the most moderate ones who do not need extreme dogmas, but can concede a good measure of chance and nonsense and even love it, and who can think of man with a reduction in his value without becoming small and weak in return. These are the ones who are rich in health, equal to the misfortunes of life and therefore less afraid of them, and who are sure of their power. In Nietzsche's marvellous phrase, they "represent with conscious pride the *achievement* of human strength." Nietzsche concludes this notebook on an enigmatic note by asking what the spiritually mature human being would think of eternal recurrence.

18

Beyond Good and Evil: Prelude to a Philosophy of the Future

(1886)

Preface

Assuming that truth is a woman – what then? Is there not reason to suspect that all philosophers, in so far as they were dogmatists, have known very little about women? That if their aim was to charm a female, they have been especially inept and inapt in making advances to truth with such awful seriousness and clumsy insistence? One thing is certain: she has not let herself be charmed – and nowadays every dogmatism stands dejected and dispirited – *if* it is standing at all! For there are those who tauntingly claim that it has fallen, that all dogmatism lies defeated, even more, that it is breathing its last gasp. In all seriousness, there is good reason to hope that all philosophical dogmatizing, however solemn, conclusive, or definite its manner, may have been nothing but the infantile high-mindedness of a beginner. And we may be very near to a time when people will be constantly recognizing anew what in fact it *was* that furnished the cornerstone for those lofty, unconditional philosopher's edifices once built by the dogmatists: some folk superstition from time immemorial (such as the superstition about souls, which even today has not ceased to sow mischief as the superstition about subject and ego); some play on words perhaps, some seductive aspect of grammar, or a daring generalization from very limited, very personal, very human, all-too-human facts. The philosophy of the dogmatists, we may hope, was only a promise reaching across millennia – as astrology used to be, in whose service more effort, money, wit, and patience were probably expended than for any real science to date: it is to astrology and its 'supernatural' pretensions in Asia and Egypt that we owe the grand style in architecture. It seems that in order to inscribe themselves into men's hearts with eternal demands, all great things must first wander the earth as monstrous and fear-inducing caricatures: dogmatic philosophy has been such a caricature, the teachings of Vedanta in Asia, for example, or Platonism in Europe. Let us not be ungrateful towards them, even though we must certainly also admit that of all errors thus far, the most grievous, protracted, and dangerous has been a dogmatist's error: Plato's invention of pure spirit and of transcendental goodness. But now that this error has been overcome, now that Europe is breathing a sigh of relief after this nightmare and in future can at least enjoy a healthier . . . sleep, we, *whose task is wakefulness itself*, have inherited all the energy that has been produced by the struggle against this error. Of course, in order to speak as he did about the spirit and the good, Plato had to set truth on its head and even deny *perspectivity*, that fundamental condition of all life; indeed, in the role of doctor, we may ask: 'What has caused such a canker on the most beautiful plant of antiquity, on Plato? Did that wicked Socrates corrupt him after all? Might Socrates really have been the corrupter of youth? And deserved his hemlock?' But the struggle against Plato, or – to put it more clearly, for the 'common people' – the struggle against thousands of years of Christian-ecclesiastical pressure (for Christianity is Platonism for the 'common people') has created a splendid tension of the spirit in Europe such as the earth has never seen: with this kind of tension in our bow, we can now shoot at the most remote targets. To be sure, Europeans experience this tension as distress, and there have already been two elaborate attempts to loosen the bow, once by means of Jesuitism, and a second time by means of the democratic Enlightenment: with the help of freedom of the press and newspaper reading, these attempts probably did in fact make it harder for the spirit to experience itself as 'distressed'! (The Germans invented gunpowder – my respects! But they also cancelled that out by inventing the press.) But we who are not sufficiently Jesuits, nor democrats, nor even Germans, we *good Europeans* and free, *very* free spirits – we have it still, all the distress of the spirit and all the tension of its bow! And perhaps the arrow, too, the task, who knows? the *target* . . .

Sils-Maria, Upper Engadine
June 1885

Section 1: On the Prejudices of Philosophers

1

The will to truth, which will seduce us yet to many a risky venture, that famous truthfulness about which all philosophers to date have spoken with deference: what manner of questions has this will to truth presented for us! What strange, wicked, questionable questions! It is already a long story, and yet doesn't it seem to be just getting started? Is it any wonder that we finally grow suspicious, lose patience, turn round impatiently? That *we* learn from this Sphinx how to pose questions of our own? *Who* is actually asking us the questions here? *What* is it in us that really wants to 'get at the truth'? It is true that we paused for a long time to question the origin[1] of this will, until finally we came to a complete stop at an even more basic question. We asked about the *value* of this will. Given that we want truth: *why do we not prefer* untruth? And uncertainty? Even ignorance? The problem of the value of truth appeared before us – or did we appear before it? Which of us here is Oedipus? Which the Sphinx? It is a rendezvous, so it seems, of questions and question marks. And would you believe that in the end it seems to us as if the problem had never yet been posed, as if we

---

1   In German: *Ursache*.

were seeing it for the first time, focusing on it, *daring* it? For there is daring to it, and perhaps no daring greater.

2

'How *could* something arise from its opposite? Truth from error, for example? Or the will to truth from the will to deception? Or altruism from egoism? Or the wise man's pure, radiant contemplation from covetous desire? Such origination is impossible; whoever dreams of it is a fool, or worse; those things of highest value must have a different origin,[2] *their own*; they cannot be derived from this perishable, seductive, deceptive, lowly world, from this confusion of desire and delusion! Rather, their basis must lie in the womb of existence, in the imperishable, in the hidden god, in the "thing in itself" – and nowhere else!' Judgements of this kind constitute the typical prejudice by which we can always recognize the metaphysicians of every age; this kind of value judgement is at the back of all their logical proceedings; from out of this 'belief' of theirs, they go about seeking their 'knowledge', which they end by ceremoniously dubbing 'the truth'. The metaphysicians' fundamental belief is *the belief in the opposition of values*. It has never occurred even to the most cautious among them to raise doubts here at the threshold, where doubts would be most necessary, even though they have vowed to themselves: '*de omnibus dubitandum*'.[3] For may there not be doubt, first of all, whether opposites even exist and, second, whether those popular value judgements and value oppositions upon which metaphysicians have placed their seal may be no more than foreground evaluations, temporary perspectives, viewed from out of a corner perhaps, or up from underneath, a perspective from below[4] (to borrow an expression common to painters)? However much value we may ascribe to truth, truthfulness, or altruism, it may be that we need to attribute a higher and more fundamental value to appearance, to the will to illusion,[5] to egoism and desire. It could even be possible that the value of those good and honoured things consists precisely in the fact that in an insidious way *they are related* to those bad, seemingly opposite things, linked, knit together, even identical perhaps. Perhaps! But who is willing to worry about such dangerous Perhapses? We must wait for a new category of philosophers to arrive, those whose taste and inclination are the reverse of their predecessors' – they will be in every sense philosophers of the dangerous Perhaps. And to speak in all seriousness: I see these new philosophers coming.

3

Having long kept a strict eye on the philosophers, and having looked between their lines, I say to myself: the largest part of conscious thinking has to be considered an instinctual activity, even in the case of philosophical thinking; we need a new understanding here, just as we've come to a new understanding of heredity and the 'innate'. Just as the act of birth is scarcely relevant to the entire process and progress of heredity, so 'consciousness' is scarcely *opposite* to the instincts in any decisive sense – most of a

2   In German: *Ursprung*.
3   Latin: everything is to be doubted.
4   In German: *Frosch-Perspektive* (literally, "frog perspective").
5   In German: *Schein*.

philosopher's conscious thinking is secretly guided and channelled into particular tracks by his instincts. Behind all logic, too, and its apparent tyranny of movement there are value judgements, or to speak more clearly, physiological demands for the preservation of a particular kind of life. That a certainty is worth more than an uncertainty, for example, or that appearance⁶ is worth less than 'truth': whatever their regulatory import-ance for *us*, such evaluations might still be nothing but foreground evaluations, a cer-tain kind of *niaiserie*,⁷ as is required for the preservation of beings like us. Given, that is, that man is not necessarily the 'measure of all things'. . .

4

We do not object to a judgement just because it is false; this is probably what is strangest about our new language. The question is rather to what extent the judgement fur-thers life, preserves life, preserves the species, perhaps even cultivates the species; and we are in principle inclined to claim that judgements that are the most false (among which are the synthetic a priori judgements) are the most indispensable to us, that man could not live without accepting logical fictions, without measuring reality by the purely invented world of the unconditional, self-referential, without a continual falsification of the world by means of the number – that to give up false judgements would be to give up life, to deny life. Admitting untruth as a condition of life: that means to resist familiar values in a dangerous way; and a philosophy that dares this has already placed itself beyond good and evil.

[. . .]

6

Little by little I came to understand what every great philosophy to date has been: the personal confession of its author, a kind of unintended and unwitting memoir; and similarly, that the moral (or immoral) aims in every philosophy constituted the actual seed from which the whole plant invariably grew. Whenever explaining how a philosopher's most far-fetched metaphysical propositions have come about, in fact, one always does well (and wisely) to ask first: 'What morality⁸ is it (is *he*) aiming at?' Thus I do not believe that an 'instinct for knowledge' is the father of philosophy, but rather that here as elsewhere a different instinct has merely made use of knowledge (and kNOwledge!)⁹ as its tool. For anyone who scrutinizes the basic human instincts to determine how influential they have been as *inspiring* spirits (or demons and goblins) will find that all the instincts have practised philosophy, and that each one of them would like only too well to represent *itself* as the ultimate aim of existence and as the legitimate *master* of all other instincts. For every instinct is tyrannical; and as *such* seeks to philosophize. Admittedly, things may be different ('better', if you like) with scholars, the truly scientific people; they may really have something like an instinct for know-ledge, some small independent clockwork which, when properly wound up, works

6   In German: *der Schein*.
7   French: foolishness, stupidity.
8   In German: *Moral*.
9   In German: *Verkenntniss*, a neologism and pun on *Erkenntniss* (knowledge), suggesting mis-taken knowledge.

away bravely *without* necessarily involving all the scholar's other instincts. That is why a scholar's real 'interests' generally lie elsewhere entirely, in his family, say, or in the acquisition of wealth, or in politics; indeed it is almost a matter of indifference whether his little machine is located in this branch of science or that, or whether the 'promising' young worker turns out to be a good philologist or a mushroom expert or a chemist: what he eventually becomes does not *distinguish* him. About the philosopher, conversely, there is absolutely nothing that is impersonal; and it is above all his morality which proves decidedly and decisively *who he is* – that is, in what hierarchy the innermost drives of his nature are arranged.

[. . .]

9

You want to *live* 'according to nature'? Oh you noble Stoics, what deceit lies in these words! Imagine a creature constituted like nature, prodigal beyond measure, neutral beyond measure, with no purpose or conscience, with no compassion or fairness, fertile and desolate and uncertain all at once; imagine Indifference itself as a power: how *could* you live according to this indifference? To live – isn't that precisely the desire to be other than this nature? Doesn't life mean weighing, preferring, being unjust, having limits, wanting to be Different? And even if the real meaning of your imperative 'to live according to nature' is 'to live according to life' – how could you do *otherwise*? Why make a principle out of something that you already are and needs must be? The truth is something else entirely: while you pretend to delight in reading the canon of your law from nature, you want the opposite, you curious play-actors and self-deceivers! In your pride you want to dictate your morality, your ideals to nature, incorporate them into nature, of all things; you demand that nature be 'according to Stoics'; you would like to make all existence exist in accordance with your own image alone – for the great and unending glorification and universalization of Stoicism! With all your love of truth, you force yourselves to stare so long, so constantly, so hypnotically at nature that you see it *falsely*, that is, stoically, and you become incapable of seeing it otherwise. And then out of some unfathomable arrogance you conceive the lunatic hope that *because* you know how to tyrannize yourself (Stoicism is self-tyranny), nature too can be tyrannized: for isn't the Stoic a *part* of nature? . . . But this is an old, eternal story: what took place back then with the Stoics is still taking place today, whenever a philosophy begins to believe in itself. It always creates the world according to its own image, it cannot do otherwise; philosophy is this tyrannical drive itself, the most spiritual form of the will to power, to 'creation of the world', to the *causa prima*.[10]

[. . .]

11

People today are trying, it seems to me, to divert attention from Kant's real influence on German philosophy, trying especially to evade what he himself considered his great value. Kant was most proud of his table of categories; holding it in his hands he said, 'This is the most difficult thing that ever could be undertaken for the benefit of metaphysics.' But let us understand what this 'could be' really implies! He was proud

10   Latin: first cause.

of having *discovered* in man a new faculty, the faculty to make synthetic a priori judgements. Granted that he was deceiving himself about his discovery: nevertheless, the development and rapid flowering of German philosophy stem from this pride and from the rivalry of his disciples to discover if at all possible something worthy of even more pride – and in any event 'new faculties'! But let's think about it, it is high time. 'How are synthetic a priori judgements *possible?*' wondered Kant, and what did he answer? They are *facilitated by a faculty*:[11] unfortunately, however, he did not say this in four words, but so cumbersomely, so venerably, and with such an expense of German profundity and ornateness that people misheard the comical *niaiserie allemande*[12] in such an answer. They were ecstatic about this new faculty, in fact, and the rejoicing reached its height when Kant discovered a moral faculty in man as well. (For at that time Germans were still moral, and not yet 'real-political'.) There followed the honeymoon of German philosophy; all the young theologians of the Tübingen Stift[13] headed right for the bushes – they were all looking for 'faculties'. And what all didn't they find, in that innocent, rich, still youthful era of the German spirit when the malicious elf Romanticism was still piping and singing, back when no one yet had learned to distinguish between 'finding' and 'inventing'! They found above all a faculty for the 'extra-sensual': Schelling christened it 'intellectual intuition', thus meeting the dearest desires of his essentially pious-desirous Germans. One can do no greater injustice to this whole arrogant, enthusiastic movement (which was youth itself, however audaciously it may have cloaked itself in grey, senile concepts) than to take it seriously and treat it with anything like moral indignation. Enough, people grew older – the dream vanished. The time came for them to rub their foreheads: they are rubbing them still today. They had been dreaming, and the first among them had been old Kant. 'Facilitated by a faculty' – that's what he had said, or at least that's what he had meant. But what kind of an answer is that? What kind of explanation? Isn't it rather simply repeating the question? How can opium make us sleep? It is 'facilitated by a faculty', the *virtus dormitiva*, answers that doctor in Molière,

> quia est in eo virtus dormitiva
> cujus est natura sensus assoupire.[14]

But answers like these belong in comedy, and for the Kantian question 'How are synthetic a priori judgements possible?' it is high time to substitute another question: 'Why is the belief in such judgements *necessary?*' – it is time to understand that for the purpose of preserving creatures of our kind, we must *believe* that such judgements are true; which means, of course, that they could still be *false* judgements. Or to put it more clearly, and crudely and completely: synthetic a priori judgements should not 'be possible' at all; we have no right to them, in our mouths they are only false judgements. Yet the belief in their truth happens to be necessary as one of

---

11   In German: *Vermöge eines Vermögens*, "by means of a faculty."
12   French: German foolishness.
13   Academy in Tübingen whose pupils included Hegel, Hölderlin, and Schelling.
14   Latin and French: Because it has a sleep-inducing faculty – whose nature is to put the senses to sleep. Spoken by the impostor physician in Molière's *Le Malade imaginaire* (*The Hypochondriac*, 1673).

the foreground beliefs and appearances[15] that constitute the perspective-optics of life. And, finally, remembering the enormous effect that 'German philosophy' exercised throughout Europe (one understands, I hope, why it deserves quotation marks?), let no one doubt that a certain *virtus dormitiva*[16] had a part in it: amidst the noble men of leisure, the moralists, mystics, artists, the partial Christians, and political obscurantists of every nation, people were delighted that German philosophy offered an antidote to the still overpowering sensualism pouring into this century from the previous one, in short: 'sensus assoupire'. . .

12

As regards materialistic atomism, hardly anything has ever been so well refuted; in all Europe there is probably no scholar so unschooled as to want to credit it with serious meaning, apart from a handy everyday usefulness (that is, as a stylistic abbreviation). This we owe primarily to the Pole Boscovich,[17] who along with the Pole Copernicus achieved the greatest victory yet in opposing the appearance[18] of things. For while Copernicus convinced us to believe contrary to all our senses that the earth does *not* stand still, Boscovich taught us to renounce the last thing that 'still stood' about the earth, the belief in 'substance', in 'matter', in the bit of earth, the particle, the atom: no one on earth has ever won a greater triumph over the senses. However, we must go even further and declare war, a merciless war unto the death against the 'atomistic need' that continues to live a dangerous afterlife in places where no one suspects it (as does the more famous 'metaphysical need').[19] The first step must be to kill off that other and more ominous atomism that Christianity taught best and longest: *the atomism of the soul*. If you allow me, I would use this phrase to describe the belief that holds the soul to be something ineradicable, eternal, indivisible, a monad, an atom: science must cast out *this* belief! And confidentially, we do not need to get rid of 'the soul' itself nor do without one of our oldest, most venerable hypotheses, which the bungling naturalists tend to do, losing 'the soul' as soon as they've touched on it. But the way is clear for new and refined versions of the hypothesis about the soul; in future, concepts such as the 'mortal soul' and the 'soul as the multiplicity of the subject' and the 'soul as the social construct of drives and emotions' will claim their rightful place in science. By putting an end to the superstitions that proliferated with nearly tropical abundance around the idea of the soul, the *new* psychologist has of course seemed to cast himself into a new desolation and a new distrust – it may be that the old psychologists had it easier, merrier – but he knows that he is thereby also condemned to *inventing*, and – who knows? – perhaps to *finding*. –

15   In German: *Augenschein*.
16   Latin: sleep-inducing faculty. See note 14 above.
17   Roger Joseph Boscovich (1711–87), mathematician and scientist, author of *Philosophiae naturalis theoria* (*Theory of Natural Philosophy*, 1758). He advanced a theory of dynamism in which nature is to be understood in terms of force and not mass. He was not actually a Pole but born in Ragusa, Dalmatia (present-day Dubrovnik in Croatia), to a Dalmatian father and Italian mother.
18   In German: *Augenschein*.
19   See *WWR*, vol. 2, 1. 17.

13

Physiologists should think twice before deciding that an organic being's primary instinct[20] is the instinct for self-preservation. A living being wants above all else to *release* its strength; life itself is the will to power, and self-preservation is only one of its indirect and most frequent *consequences*. Here as everywhere, in short, we must beware of *superfluous* teleological principles! And this is what the instinct for self-preservation is (which we owe to the inconsistency of Spinoza). Such are the dictates of our method, which in essence demands that we be frugal with our principles.

14

It now may be dawning on five or six thinkers that even physics is only a way of interpreting or arranging the world (if I may say so: according to us!) and *not* a way of explaining the world. But in so far as it relies on our belief in the senses, physics is taken for more than that, and shall long continue to be taken for more, for an explanation. Our eyes and fingers speak for it, appearance[21] and palpability speak for it: to an era with essentially plebeian tastes this is enchanting, persuasive, *convincing*, for it instinctively follows the canonized truth of ever-popular sensualism. What is clear, what 'clarifies'? First, whatever can be seen and touched – you have to take every problem at least that far. Conversely, the magic of the Platonic method consisted precisely in its *resistance to* sensuality, for this was an *aristocratic* method, practised by people who may have enjoyed senses even stronger and more clamorous than those of our contemporaries, but who sought a higher triumph by mastering them, by tossing over this colourful confusion of the senses (the rabble of the senses, as Plato called it) the pale, cold, grey nets of concepts. There was a kind of *enjoyment* in Plato's manner of overpowering and interpreting the world different from the one currently offered us by physicists, including those Darwinists and anti-teleologists among the physiological workers with their principle of the 'least possible energy' and the greatest possible stupidity. 'Where man has nothing more to see and grasp, he has nothing more to seek' – that imperative certainly differs from Plato's, but it may be exactly right for a hardy, industrious future race of machinists and bridge-builders who have only *dirty* work to do.

15

In order to practise physiology with a good conscience, you have to believe that the sense organs are *not* phenomena in the philosophical idealist sense, for then they could not be causes! This is sensualism as a regulative hypothesis at least, if not as an heuristic principle. What's that? And other people are actually saying that the external world is created by our sense organs? But then our body, as part of this external world, would be the creation of our sense organs! But then our very sense organs would be – the creation of our sense organs! It seems to me that this is a complete *reductio ad absurdum*:[22] assuming that the concept *causa sui*[23] is something completely absurd. It follows that the outer world is *not* the creation of our sense organs – ?

20   In German: *Trieb*.
21   In German: *Augenschein*.
22   Latin: reduction to absurdity.
23   Latin: cause of itself.

16

There are still some harmless self-scrutinizers who think that there are 'immediate certainties', as for example, 'I think', or, in Schopenhauer's superstition, 'I will' – as if perception could grasp its object purely and nakedly as the 'thing in itself' without any falsification on the part of the subject or of the object. But I shall repeat a hundred times over that the 'immediate certainty', like 'absolute knowledge' and the 'thing in itself', contains a *contradictio in adjecto*:[24] it's time people freed themselves from the seduction of words! Let the common people think that perception means knowing-to-the-end,[25] the philosopher must say to himself, 'If I analyse the process expressed by the proposition "I think", I get a series of audacious assertions that would be difficult if not impossible to prove; for example, that *I* am the one who is thinking, that there has to be a something doing the thinking, that thinking is an activity and an effect on the part of a being who is thought of as a cause, that an "I" exists, and finally, that we by now understand clearly what is designated as thinking – that I *know* what thinking is. For if I had not already decided it for myself, how could I determine that what is going on is not "willing" or "feeling"? In short, saying "I think" assumes that I am *comparing* my present state with other states that I experience in myself, thereby establishing what it is: because of this reference back to another "knowledge", there is, for me at least, no immediate "certainty" here.' Thus, instead of that 'immediate certainty' that the common people may believe in, the philosopher gets handed a series of metaphysical questions: these are actually the intellect's questions of conscience, such as, 'Where does my concept of thinking come from? Why do I believe in cause and effect? What gives me the right to talk about an "I", and beyond that an "I as cause", and beyond that yet an "I as the cause of thoughts"?' Anyone who dares to answer such metaphysical questions promptly by referring to a kind of epistemological *intuition* (like someone who says, 'I think, and know that this at least is true, real, and certain') will be met with a smile and two question marks by the philosopher of today. 'My dear sir,' the philosopher may suggest, 'it is improbable that you are not in error, but then why must we insist on truth?'

17

As regards the superstition of logicians, I never tire of underlining a quick little fact that these superstitious people are reluctant to admit: namely, that a thought comes when 'it' wants to, and not when 'I' want it to; so it is *falsifying* the facts to say that the subject 'I' is the condition of the predicate 'think'. There is thinking,[26] but to assert that 'there' is the same thing as that famous old 'I' is, to put it mildly, only an assumption, an hypothesis, and certainly not an 'immediate certainty'. And in the end

---

24 Latin: contradiction in the adjective (a logical inconsistency between a noun and its modifier).

25 Because the German prefix *Er-* generally connotes the completion of an action, Nietzsche is playing with the literal meaning of *Erkenntnis* (perception, knowledge) as "knowing-to-the-end," as opposed to *Kenntnis* (informational knowledge).

26 In German: *Es denkt* (literally, "it thinks"). Nietzsche is developing an early critique of the Cartesian *cogito* put forward by the aphorist Georg Christoph Lichtenberg (1742–99).

'there is thinking' is also going too far: even this 'there' contains an *interpretation* of the process and is not part of the process itself. People are concluding here according to grammatical habit: 'Thinking is an activity; for each activity there is someone who acts; therefore – .' Following approximately the same pattern, ancient atomism looked for that particle of matter, the atom, to complement the effective 'energy' that works from out of it; more rigorous minds finally learned to do without this 'little bit of earth' and perhaps some day logicians will even get used to doing without that little 'there' (into which the honest old 'I' has evaporated).

[. . .]

19

Philosophers tend to speak about the will as if everyone in the world knew all about it; Schopenhauer even suggested that the will was the only thing we actually do know, know through and through, know without additions or subtractions. But I continue to think that even in this case Schopenhauer was only doing what philosophers simply tend to do: appropriating and exaggerating a *common prejudice*. As I see it, the act of willing is above all something *complicated*, something that has unity only as a word – and this common prejudice of using only one word has overridden the philosophers' caution (which was never all that great anyway). So let us be more cautious for once, let us be 'unphilosophical'. Let us say that in every act of willing there is first of all a multiplicity of feelings, namely the feeling of the condition we are moving *away* from and the feeling of the condition we are moving *towards*; the feeling of this 'away' and this 'towards'; and then a concomitant feeling in the muscles that, without our actually moving 'arms and legs', comes into play out of a kind of habit, whenever we 'will'. Second, just as we must recognize feeling, and indeed many kinds of feeling, as an ingredient of the will, so must we likewise recognize thinking: in every act of will there is a commanding thought, and we must not deceive ourselves that this thought can be separated off from 'willing', as if we would then have any will left over! Third, the will is not merely a complex of feelings and thoughts, it is above all an *emotion*,[27] and in fact the *emotion* of command. What is called 'freedom of the will' is essentially the emotion of superiority felt towards the one who must obey: 'I am free, "he" must obey.' This consciousness lies in every will, as does also a tense alertness, a direct gaze concentrated on one thing alone, an unconditional assessment that 'now we must have this and nothing else', an inner certainty that obedience will follow, and everything else that goes along with the condition of giving commands. A person who *wills*: this person is commanding a Something in himself that obeys, or that he thinks is obeying. But let us now consider the strangest thing about the will, about this multifarious thing that the common people call by one word alone. In any given case, we both command *and* obey, and when we obey we know the feelings of coercion, pressure, oppression, resistance, and agitation that begin immediately after the act of will. On the other hand, we are in the habit of ignoring or overlooking this division by means of the synthetic concept 'I'. Thus, a whole series of erroneous conclusions and therefore of false assessments of the will itself has been appended to willing in such a way that the person who wills now believes with complete faith that

27 In German: *ein Affekt*.

willing *is enough* for action. Because in the vast majority of cases, willing has only occurred when there is also the *expectation* that the effect of the command – that is obedience, action – will follow, this *impression* has been translated into the feeling that there is a *necessary effect*; suffice it to say, the person willing thinks with some degree of certainty that will and action are somehow one: he attributes his success in carrying out his willing to the will itself and in this way enjoys an increase in that feeling of power that accompanies any kind of success. 'Freedom of the will' – that is the word for that complex pleasurable condition experienced by the person willing who commands and simultaneously identifies himself with the one who executes the command – as such he can share in enjoying a triumph over resistance, while secretly judging that it was actually his will that overcame that resistance. Thus the person willing adds to his pleasurable feeling as commander the pleasurable feelings of the successful executing instrument, the serviceable 'underwill' or under-soul (our body after all is nothing but a social structure of many souls). *L'effet c'est moi*:[28] what is occurring here occurs in every well-structured happy community where the ruling class identifies with the successes of the community as a whole. As we have said, every act of willing is simply a matter of commanding and obeying, based on a social structure of many 'souls'; for this reason a philosopher should claim the right to comprehend willing from within the sphere of ethics:[29] ethics, that is, understood as the theory of hierarchical relationships among which the phenomenon 'life' has its origins.

20

That individual philosophical concepts are not something isolated, something unto themselves, but rather grow up in reference and relatedness to one another; that however suddenly and arbitrarily they seem to emerge in the history of thought, they are as much a part of one system as are the branches of fauna on one continent: this is revealed not least by the way the most disparate philosophers invariably fill out one particular basic schema of *possible* philosophies. Under some unseen spell they always run around the same orbit: however independent they may feel, one from the other, with their will to criticism or to system, something in them is leading them, driving them all to follow one another in a certain order – an inborn taxonomy and affinity of concepts. In truth their thinking is much less an act of discovery than an act of recognizing anew, remembering anew, a return back home to a distant, ancient universal economy of the soul from out of which those concepts initially grew: philosophizing is thus a kind of atavism of the highest order. This easily explains the strange family resemblance of all Indian, Greek, and German philosophizing. Wherever linguistic affinity, above all, is present, everything necessary for an analogous development and sequence of philosophical systems will inevitably be on hand from the beginning, thanks to the shared philosophy of grammar (I mean thanks to being unconsciously ruled and guided by similar grammatical functions), just as the way to certain other possibilities for interpreting the world will seem to be blocked. Philosophers from the Ural-Altaic linguistic zone (where the concept of the subject is least developed) will most probably look

28   French: I am the effect. A play on *L'état, c'est moi* ("I am the state"), the claim made by Louis XIV (1638–1715).
29   In German: *Moral*.

differently 'into the world' and will be found on other paths than Indo-Germans or
Muslims: and in the last analysis, the spell of certain grammatical functions is the spell
of *physiological* value judgements and conditions of race. This by way of a rejection of
Locke's superficiality[30] concerning the origin of ideas.

21

The *causa sui*[31] is the best internal contradiction ever devised, a kind of logical freak
or outrage: but because of man's excessive pride we have come to be deeply and terribly entangled with this particular nonsense. The yearning for 'freedom of the will'
in the superlative metaphysical sense that unfortunately still prevails in the minds of
the half-educated, the yearning to bear complete and final responsibility for one's own
actions and to relieve God, the world, one's ancestors, coincidence, society from it –
this is really nothing less than being that same *causa sui* and, with a daring greater than
Münchhausen's,[32] dragging yourself by your hair out of the swamp of nothingness and
into existence. Now, if someone can see through the cloddish simplicity of this famous
concept 'free will' and eliminate it from his mind, I would then ask him to take his
'enlightenment' a step further and likewise eliminate from his head the opposite of
the non-concept 'free will': I mean the 'unfree will' which amounts to a misuse of
cause and effect. One should not make the mistake of *concretizing* 'cause' and 'effect'
as do the natural scientists (and whoever else today naturalizes in their thinking . . .),
in conformity with the prevalent mechanistic foolishness that pushes and tugs at
the cause until it 'has an effect'; 'cause' and 'effect' should be used only as pure *concepts*, as conventional fictions for the purpose of description or communication,
and *not* for explanation. In the 'in itself' there is nothing of 'causal associations', of
'necessity', of 'psychological constraint'; the effect does *not* follow 'upon the cause',
no 'law' governs it. *We* alone are the ones who have invented causes, succession, recipro-
city, relativity, coercion, number, law, freedom, reason, purpose; and if we project, if
we mix this world of signs into things as if it were an 'in itself', we act once more as
we have always done, that is, *mythologically*. The 'unfree will' is mythology: in real life
it is only a matter of *strong* and *weak* wills. Whenever a thinker sniffs out coercion,
necessity, obligation, pressure, constraint in any 'causal connection' or 'psychological
necessity', it is almost always a symptom of where his own inadequacy lies: to feel this
particular way is revealing – the person is revealing himself. And if I have observed
correctly, the 'constraint of the will' is always conceived as a problem from two completely opposite standpoints, but always in a profoundly *personal* way: the one group
will not hear of relinquishing their 'responsibility', their belief in *themselves*, their personal right to take *their* credit (the vain races are of this type); conversely, the other
group wants to be responsible for nothing, guilty of nothing, and out of their inner
self-contempt they yearn to *cast off* their own selves one way or another. When this

---

30   Reference to Locke's *Essay Concerning Human Understanding* (1690).
31   Latin: cause of itself.
32   Karl Friedrich Hieronymus, Freiherr von Münchhausen (1720–97), the prevaricating
adventurer-hero of Rudolf Erich Raspe's *Baron Münchhausen's Narrative of his Marvellous Travels
and Campaigns in Russia*, published in London in 1785 and translated into German in 1786.

latter group writes books nowadays, they tend to take up the cause of criminals; a sort of socialistic compassion is their nicest disguise. And indeed, it is surprising how much prettier the fatalism of the weak-willed can look when it presents itself as 'la religion de la souffrance humaine';[33] that is what *it* means by 'good taste'.

22

If you'll forgive me, an old philologist who can't give up the wickedness of pointing out examples of bad interpretative practice, the 'lawfulness of nature' that you physicists speak about so proudly, as if . . . – this only exists by grace of your interpretations, your bad 'philology'; it is not a factual matter, not a 'text', but rather no more than a naive humanitarian concoction, a contortion of meaning that allows you to succeed in accommodating the democratic instincts of the modern soul! 'Equality before the law is everywhere – nature is no different and no better than we are' – this amiable ulterior thought once again masks the plebeian's enmity towards everything privileged and autocratic, as well as a new and more subtle atheism. 'Ni dieu, ni maître'[34] – that's what you folks want, too. So, 'long live the law of nature!' Isn't that right? But as I say, this is interpretation, not text; and someone could come along with the opposite intention and interpretative skill who, looking at the very same nature and referring to the very same phenomena, would read out of it the ruthlessly tyrannical and unrelenting assertion of power claims. Such an interpreter would put to you the universality and unconditionality in all 'will to power' in such a way that virtually every word, even the word 'tryanny', would ultimately appear useless or at least only as a modifying, mitigating metaphor – as too human. Yet this philosopher, too, would end by making the same claims for his world as you others do for yours, namely that its course is 'necessary' and 'predictable', *not* because laws are at work in it, but rather because the laws are absolutely *lacking*, and in every moment every power draws its final consequence. And given that he too is just interpreting – and you'll be eager to raise that objection, won't you? – then, all the better.

23

Until now, all psychology has been brought to a stop by moral prejudices and fears: it has not dared to plumb these depths. If we may take previous writing as a symptom of what has also been suppressed, then no one in his thoughts has even brushed these depths as I have, as a morphology and *evolutionary theory of the will to power*. The force of moral prejudices has reached far into the most spiritual world, a world apparently cold and without premiss – and it has obviously had a harmful, inhibiting, blinding, distorting effect. A real physio-psychology must struggle with the unconscious resistances in the heart of the researcher, the 'heart' is working against it; a conscience that is still strong and hearty will be distressed and annoyed even by a theory of the reciprocal conditionality of 'good' and 'bad' instincts,[35] which seems to be a kind of subtle immorality – and even more by a theory of the derivation of all good drives

---

33 French: the religion of human suffering.
34 French: neither God nor master.
35 In German: *Triebe*.

from bad ones. But granted that a person takes the emotions[36] of hatred, envy, greed, power hunger as conditions for living, crucial and fundamental to the universal economy of life and therefore in need of intensifying if life is to be intensified, he is also a person who suffers from such an orientation in judgement as if he were seasick. And yet even this hypothesis is by no means the strangest or most painful one in this enormous, virtually new realm of dangerous insights – and in truth there are a hundred good reasons for everyone to stay away from it if he – *can*! On the other hand, once your ship has strayed onto this course: well then! All right! Grit your teeth bravely! Open your eyes! Keep your hand at the helm! – we are going to be travelling *beyond* morality,[37] and by daring to travel there we may in the process stifle or crush whatever remnant of morality we have left – but what do *we* matter! Never yet has a *deeper* world of insight been opened to bold travellers and adventurers; and the psychologist who makes this kind of 'sacrifice' (it is *not* the *sacrifizio dell'intelletto*,[38] quite the contrary!) may demand at least that psychology be recognized once again as the queen of the sciences, which the other sciences exist to serve and anticipate. For psychology has once again become the way to basic issues.

Section 2: The Free Spirit

24

O sancta simplicitas![39] How strangely simplified and false are people's lives! Once we have focused our eyes on this wonder, there is no end to the wonderment! See how we have made everything around us bright and free and light and simple! Weren't we clever to give our senses free access to everything superficial, to give our minds a divine craving for headlong leaps and fallacies! How we have managed from the beginning to cling to our ignorance, in order to enjoy a life of almost inconceivable freedom, thoughtlessness, carelessness, heartiness, cheerfulness – to enjoy life! And only upon this foundation of ignorance, now as firm as granite, could our science be established, and our will to knowledge only upon the foundation of a much more powerful will, the will to no knowledge, to uncertainty,[40] to untruth – not as the opposite of the former will, but rather – as its refinement! For even if *language*, in this case as in others, cannot get past its own unwieldiness and continues to speak of oppositions where there are really only degrees and many fine differences of grade; even if we the knowing also find the words in our mouths twisted by the ingrained moral hypocrisy that is now part of our insuperable 'flesh and blood', now and then we understand what has happened, and laugh at how even the very best science would keep us trapped in this *simplified*, thoroughly artificial, neatly concocted, neatly falsified world, how

---

36   In German: *die Affkete*.
37   In German: *über die Moral weg*.
38   Italian: sacrifice of the intellect. Part of the duty owed by Jesuits who take the vow of obedience.
39   Latin: O holy simplicity!
40   Nietzsche here is playing with various terms derived from the word *wissen* (to know): *die Unwissenheit* (ignorance), *die Wissenschaft* (science), *das Nicht-wissen* (not knowing), and *das Ungewisse* (uncertainty).

the best science loves error whether it will or not, because science, being alive, – loves life!

25

After such a light-hearted introduction, it is time to attend to a serious word, one that is addressed to the most serious of people. Be on guard, all you philosophers and lovers of knowledge, and beware of turning into martyrs! Beware of suffering 'for the sake of truth'! Beware even of defending yourselves! You will ruin all the innocence and fine objectivity of your conscience; you will become obstinate in the face of objections and red rags; you will grow stupid, brutish, and bullish if in your fight against danger, defamation, accusations, expulsion, and even baser consequences of enmity you will ultimately have to play the role of defenders of truth on earth as well: as if 'truth' were such a meek and hapless woman as to need defenders! And especially such as you, gentlemen, you knights of the most sorrowful countenance,[41] you intellectual idlers and cobweb-spinners! In the end you know very well that it does not matter whether *you* are proved right, and likewise that no philosopher to date has been proved right, and that there is probably more value for truth in every little question mark that you place at the end of your mottoes and favourite doctrines (and occasionally after your own selves) than in all your dignified gestures and your playing the trump before plaintiffs and lawcourts! Take the side exit instead! Flee to hidden spaces! And wear your mask and your subtlety so that people will not be able to tell you apart! Or will fear you a little! And please don't forget the garden, the garden with the golden trellises! And keep people around you who are like a garden – or like music over the waters at that evening hour when day is already turning into memory: choose the *good* solitude, the free, wanton, weightless solitude that also gives you the right to remain good, in some sense at least. How venomous, how wily, how bad one becomes in every long war that cannot be waged in the open! How *personal* one becomes by holding fears for a long time, by watching long for enemies, possible enemies! Despite their most spiritual disguises and perhaps without even knowing it, these outcasts of society, these long-term fugitives, hunters' prey – and also the enforced hermits, the Spinozas or Giordano Brunos[42] – always end by becoming elegant avengers and poisoners (just excavate the foundation of Spinoza's ethics and theology!) – not to mention the foolish moral indignation that is the unfailing sign of a philosopher whose philosophical humour has deserted him. The philosopher's martyrdom, his 'sacrifice for truth', forces into the light whatever was lurking in him of the propagandist and the actor; and if it is true that people have regarded him with only an artistic curiosity until now, we can certainly understand why they would have the dangerous wish to see him in his degeneracy for once (degenerated to a 'martyr', to a playhouse and courthouse ranter). When we make such a wish, however, we have to be clear *what* it is that we will get to see: merely a satyr play, merely a farcical epilogue, merely the continuing proof that the actual, long tragedy *is over* – assuming that every philosophy, as it was taking shape, was one long tragedy. –

41   Allusion to the eponymous hero of Cervantes' *Don Quixote* (1615).
42   Giordano Bruno (1548–1600), anti-dogmatic Italian philosopher and astronomer, burned as a heretic in Rome at the hands of the Inquisition.

26

Every exceptional person instinctively seeks out his fortress, his secrecy, where he is *delivered* from the crowd, the multitude, the majority, where he is allowed to forget the rule of 'humanity', being the exception to it; in one case, however, an even stronger instinct pushes him, as a person of great and exceptional knowledge, towards this rule. Anyone who interacts with other people without occasionally displaying all the colours of distress (green and grey with disgust, annoyance, compassion, gloom, loneliness) is surely not a man of higher taste; but if on the other hand he declines to assume this whole dispiriting burden and keeps evading it by remaining, as described above, tucked away peaceful and proud in his fortress, then one thing is certain: he is not made for, not destined for, knowledge. For if he were, he would some day have to say to himself, 'To hell with my good taste! The rule is more interesting than the exception, more interesting than I, the exception!' – and he would go *down*, and above all, go 'into'. The study of the *average* man is a long, serious study, requiring much in the way of disguise, self-discipline, intimacy, bad company (every company is bad company except that of one's equals); it makes up a necessary part of every philosopher's biography, and it is perhaps the most unpleasant, worst-smelling part, most rife with disappointment. But if he has the good fortune that befits a fortunate child of knowledge, he will encounter others who in fact shorten and lighten his task: I mean the so-called cynics, those people who simply acknowledge what is animal-like, common, the 'rule' about themselves and yet still have enough spirituality and excitability to need to speak about themselves and their kind *in front of witnesses* – sometimes these people even wallow around in books, as in their own mire. It is only in the form of cynicism that common souls come near to being honest; and the higher man must open his ears to every kind of cynicism, whether crude or subtle, and must congratulate himself whenever he is lucky enough to hear a shameless joker or scholarly satyr raise his voice. There are even cases that mix enchantment with the disgust, when a whim of nature joins genius to such a prying goat and ape, as in the case of the Abbé Galiani,[43] the most profound, acute, and perhaps dirtiest man of his century – he was much more profound than Voltaire and therefore a good deal more taciturn. As I suggested, it is more common that the scholarly head is set upon an ape's body, a subtle exceptional mind above a common heart – with doctors and the physiologists of morality we find it especially often. And whenever someone speaks about human beings not bitterly, but neutrally, as if he were talking about a belly with two different needs and a head with but one; whenever someone sees, looks for, and *wants* to see only hunger, sexual desire, and vanity, as if these were the only true motives for human behaviour; whenever, in short, someone speaks 'badly' about human beings (and not even *wickedly*), then the lover of knowledge must pay close and careful attention – he must keep his ears open in general, whenever people speak without indignation. For the indignant man and whoever else uses his own teeth to mutilate and dismember himself (or God or society in place of himself) may stand higher than the laughing and self-satisfied satyr in moral terms, but in every other sense he

---

43   Ferdinando Galiani (1728–87), Italian economist who developed a theory of value based on utility and scarcity.

represents the more common, more inconsequential, more uninstructive case. And only the indignant tell so many *lies*. −

[. . .]

29

Only a very few people can be independent: it is a prerogative of the strong. And when independence is attempted by someone who has the right to it, but does not *need* it, we have proof that this man is probably not only strong, but bold to the point of recklessness. He ventures into a labyrinth, he multiplies life's inevitable dangers a thousandfold, and not the least among these is the absence of any person to see how and where he is going astray, becoming isolated, being rent apart piece by piece in the cave of some Minotaur of the conscience. Assuming that such a person perishes, he perishes so far away from the understanding of human beings that they do not feel it or feel for him − and he cannot go back again! Not even to the pity of humans!

[. . .]

32

During the longest age of human history − it is called the prehistoric age − an action's value or lack of value was determined by its consequences: the action itself was taken into consideration as little as its origin. More or less as in China today, where a child's distinction or disgrace reflects back on the parent, the retroactive force of the success or failure of an action determined whether people thought well or badly of it. Let us call this period mankind's *pre-moral* period: at this time no one had heard of the imperative 'know thyself!' During the last ten thousand years, however, over large stretches of the earth, people have little by little reached the point of determining the value of an action not by its consequences but by its origins. Taken as a whole, this was a great event, a considerable refinement in perceptions and standards, with the unconscious influence of the dominance of aristocratic values and the belief in 'origins'[44] still persisting. It was the badge of a period that we may designate in the narrower sense as the *moral*[45] period, and it signals the first attempt at self-knowledge. Instead of consequences, origins:[46] what a reversal of perspective! And most certainly a reversal achieved only after long struggles and hesitations! Along with it, to be sure, came an ominous new superstition, a peculiar narrowness of interpretation took hold: the origin of an action was interpreted in the most precise terms as itself originating in an *intention*; everyone was united in the belief that the value of an action lay in the value of its intention. Intention as the entire source and past history of an action: almost right up into modern times this prejudice has determined how moral judgements have been made on earth, praising, blaming, judging, philosophizing. But now that human beings are again gaining a deeper self-awareness, shouldn't we weigh another reversal and fundamental shift in values − might we not be standing at the threshold of a period that, to put it negatively, would at first have to be described as *extra-moral*?[47] Is not

44   In German: *Herkunft*.
45   In German: *moralische*.
46   In German: *Herkunft*.
47   In German: *aussermoralische*.

the suspicion growing, at least among us immoralists, that an action's decisive value is demonstrated precisely by that part of it that is *not intentional*; do we not suspect that all of an action's intentionality, everything that can be seen or known about it, that can be 'conscious' about it, is still part of its surface and skin – which, like all skin, reveals something, but *hides* even more? In short, we believe that the intention is but a sign or a symptom, first of all requiring interpretation, and furthermore that it is a sign with so many meanings that as a consequence it has almost none in and of itself; we believe that morality[48] in its earlier sense, intention-morality, was a prejudice, something precipitous or perhaps preliminary, something of the order of astrology or alchemy, but in any event something that must be overcome. The overcoming of morality, or even (in a certain sense) the self-overcoming of morality:[49] let that be the name for the long, clandestine work that was kept in reserve for the most subtle and honest (and also the most malicious) people of conscience today, living touchstones of the human heart. –

[. . .]

34

No matter what philosophical standpoint we may take these days, looking out from any position, the *erroneousness* of the world we think we are living in is the most certain and concrete thing our eyes can fasten on: we find a host of reasons for it, reasons that might tempt us to speculate about a deceptive principle in the 'nature of things'. But anyone who would try to claim that the falsity of the world is due to our thought process, to our 'intellect' (an honourable way out, taken by every conscious or unconscious *advocatus dei*[50]), anyone who takes this world with all its space, time, form, movement, to be falsely *inferred*, would at the very least have good reason to end by distrusting the thought process itself – for wouldn't this thought process have made us the victims of the greatest hoax ever? And what guarantee would we have that it wouldn't go on doing what it has always done? In all seriousness, there is something touching and awe-inspiring in the innocence of thinkers that allows them even nowadays to request *honest* answers from their consciousness: about whether it is 'substantial', for example, or why it insists on keeping the outside world at such a distance, and all sorts of other questions of that kind. The faith in 'immediate certainties' is *morally* naive, and does honour to us philosophers, but – we are not supposed to be '*only* moral' after all! In any but moral terms, our faith in immediate certainties is stupid, and does us no great honour! Maybe it is true that in bourgeois life an ever-ready distrust is taken as a sign of 'bad character' and therefore classified as imprudence: here where we are, beyond the bourgeois world and its Yes's and No's – what is there to keep us from being imprudent and saying that the philosopher has a veritable *right* to his 'bad character', as the creature who so far has always been most made a fool of on earth – these days he has a *duty* to be distrustful, to squint out as maliciously as he can from the bottom of every abyss of doubt. Please forgive me for

48   In German: *Moral*.
49   In German: *Die Überwindung der Moral . . . die Selbstüberwindung der Moral*.
50   Latin: God's advocate. A play on the more common phrase *advocatus diaboli* (devil's advocate).

the joking tone of this sad caricature: for a while now, I myself have learned to think differently about deceiving and being deceived, learned to assess them differently, so I am always ready to take a few pokes at the philosophers' blind rage at being deceived. Why *not*? It is nothing but a moral prejudice to consider truth more valuable than appearance;[51] it is, in fact, the most poorly proven assumption in the world. We should admit at least this much: there would be no life at all if not on the basis of perspectivist assessments and apparentnesses;[52] and if one wanted to do away with the 'apparent world'[53] entirely, as some valiantly enthusiastic and foolish philosophers want to do, well then, assuming that people like *you* could do that – then at the very least there would be nothing left of your 'truth', either! Really, why should we be forced to assume that there is an essential difference between 'true' and 'false' in the first place? Isn't it enough to assume that there are degrees of apparentness[54] and, so to speak, lighter and darker shadows and hues of appearance – different *valeurs*,[55] to use the language of painters? Why should the world *that is relevant to us* not be a fiction? And if someone asks, 'But mustn't a fiction have an author?' shouldn't we answer him bluntly, '*Why?*' Mustn't this 'mustn't' be part of the fiction, too, perhaps? Aren't we allowed to be a little bit ironic, not only about predicates and objects, but also about subjects? Shouldn't the philosopher be able to rise above a faith in grammar? My respects to governesses, but isn't it about time that philosophers renounced the religion of governesses?

35

O Voltaire! O humanity! O hogwash! 'Truth' and the *search* for truth are no trivial matter; and if a person goes about searching in too human a fashion ('il ne cherche le vrai que pour faire le bien'[56]), I'll bet he won't find anything!

36

Assuming that nothing real is 'given' to us apart from our world of desires and passions, assuming that we cannot ascend or descend to any 'reality' other than the reality of our instincts[57] (for thinking is merely an interrelation of these instincts, one to the other), may we not be allowed to perform an experiment and ask whether this 'given' also provides a *sufficient* explanation for the so-called mechanistic (or 'material') world? I do not mean the material world as a delusion, as 'appearance' or 'representation'[58] (in the Berkeleian or Schopenhauerian sense), but rather as a world

---

51 In German: *Schein*.
52 In German: *perspektivischer Schätzungen und Scheinbarkeiten*. The translation has been modified from "appearances" to "apparentnesses."
53 In German: *die "scheinbare Welt."*
54 In German: *Stufen der Scheinbarkeit*. The translation has been modified from "apparency" to "apparentness."
55 French: values.
56 French: "he seeks truth only to do good."
57 In German: *Triebe*.
58 The German words are: *Täuschung*, "*Schein*," "*Vorstellung*."

with the same level of reality that our emotion[59] has – that is, as a more rudimentary form of the world of emotions, holding everything in a powerful unity, all the potential of the organic process to develop and differentiate (and spoil and weaken, too, of course), as a kind of instinctual life[60] in which all the organic functions (self-regulation, adaptation, alimentation, elimination, metabolism) are synthetically linked to one another – as a *pre-form* of life?[61] In the end, we are not only allowed to perform such an experiment, we are commanded to do so by the conscience of our *method*. We must not assume that there are several sorts of causality until we have tested the possibility that one alone will suffice, tested it to its furthest limits (to the point of nonsense, if you'll allow me to say so). We cannot evade this morality of method today: it follows 'by definition', as a mathematician would say. The question is ultimately whether we really recognize that the will can *effect* things, whether we believe in the causality of the will: if we do (and to believe in *this* is basically to believe in causality itself), we *must* experiment to test hypothetically whether the causality of the will is the only causality. A 'will' can have an effect only upon another 'will', of course, and not upon 'matter' (not upon 'nerves', for example): one must dare to hypothesize, in short, that wherever 'effects' are identified, a will is having an effect upon another will – and that all mechanical events, in so far as an energy is active in them, are really the energy of the will, the effect of the will. Assuming, finally, that we could explain our entire instinctual life as the development and differentiation of *one* basic form of the will (namely the will to power, as *my* tenet would have it); assuming that one could derive all organic functions from this will to power and also find in it the solution to the problem of procreation and alimentation (it is all one problem), then we would have won the right to designate *all* effective energy unequivocally as: the *will to power*. The world as it is seen from the inside, the world defined and described by its 'intelligible character' – would be simply 'will to power' and that alone. –

37

'What's that? But doesn't that mean, to speak in the vernacular, that God's been disproved, but not the devil?' On the contrary! On the contrary, my friends! And who the devil's forcing you to speak in the vernacular! –

[...]

40

Everything deep loves a mask; the very deepest things even have a hatred for image and parable. Wouldn't an *antithesis* be a more fitting disguise if the shame of a god were to walk abroad? A questionable question: it would be strange if some mystic had not already dared to ask himself something like it. There are experiences of such a delicate nature that it is well to conceal them by a coarse act and make them unrecognizable; there are actions of love and extravagant generosity after which nothing is more advisable than to take a stick and thrash the eyewitness, thus to cloud his

---

59   In German: *Affekt.*
60   In German: *Triebleben.*
61   In German: *Vorform des Lebens.* The translation has been modified from "preliminary form" to "pre-form."

memory. Some people know how to cloud and abuse their own memories, to take revenge on this one confidant, at least: shame is inventive. It is not the worst things that cause us the worst shame: wicked cunning is not the only thing behind a mask – there is so much kindness in cunning. I could imagine that a man who had something precious and fragile to hide might roll through life as rough and round as an old green heavily banded wine barrel: that is how his refined shame would have it. A man whose shame is deep will encounter even his destinies and delicate choices upon roads that few people ever find and whose existence must be kept from his neighbours and closest friends: his mortal danger is hidden from their eyes, and also his regained mortal confidence. This secretive one, whose instincts bid him speak in order to silence and be silent, who is inexhaustible in evading communication, this person *wants* and demands that in his stead a mask inhabit the hearts and minds of his friends; and should it be that this is something he does not want, then one day his eyes will be opened to the fact that a mask of him is there nevertheless, and that that is good. Every deep spirit needs a mask: not only that, around every deep spirit a mask is continually growing, thanks to the constantly false, that is to say, *shallow* interpretations of his every word, his every step, every sign of life that he gives. –

[. . .]

42

A new category of philosophers is on the rise: I shall be so bold as to christen them with a name that is not without its dangers. As I divine them, as they allow themselves to be divined (for it is part of their nature to *want* to remain a riddle in some respects), these philosophers of the future might rightfully – perhaps also wrongfully – be described as *experimenters*. And this name too is ultimately only an experiment, and, if you like, a temptation.[62]

43

Are they new friends of 'truth', these approaching philosophers? Probably so, for until now all philosophers have loved their truths. But it is certain that they will not be dogmatists. It would surely go against their pride, and also against their good taste, if their truth had to be a truth for everyone else, too – this has been the secret wish and ulterior thought in all earlier dogmatic endeavours. 'My judgement is *my* judgement: no one else has a right to it so easily', as a philosopher of the future might say. We have to rid ourselves of the bad taste of wanting to agree with many others. 'Good' is no longer good if our neighbour takes the word into his mouth. So how could there possibly be 'common goods'! The term contradicts itself: anything that is common never has much value. In the end things will have to be as they are and always have been: the great things are left to the great, the abysses to the profound, tenderness and thrills to the sensitive, and to sum it up in a few words, everything extraordinary to the extraordinary.

[. . .]

62   A play on *Versuch* (experiment) and *Versuchung* (temptation). Nietzsche often exploits this pun, especially in *Zarathustra*.

Section 3: The Religious Disposition

55

The great ladder of religious cruelty has many rungs, but three of them are the most important. In earlier times, people offered their god sacrifices of human beings, perhaps even those whom they loved best: to this group belong those first sacrifices of all prehistoric religions, and also the Emperor Tiberius' sacrifice in the Mithras Grotto[63] on the Isle of Capri, that most terrifying of all Roman anachronisms. Later, in humanity's moral epoch, people sacrificed to their God the strongest instincts[64] that they possessed, their 'nature'; *this* is the celebratory joy that shines in the terrible glance of the ascetic, of a man living rapturously contrary to nature. Finally: what was left to sacrifice? Didn't people finally have to sacrifice everything comforting, sacred, curative, all hope, all faith in hidden harmony, in future bliss and justice? Didn't they have to sacrifice God himself, and, out of self-directed cruelty, worship stone, stupidity, heaviness, fate, nothingness? To sacrifice God for the sake of nothingness – the paradoxical mystery of this final cruelty has been reserved for the generation that is just now emerging – and all of us already know something about it.

56

Anyone who has struggled for a long time, as I have, with a mysterious desire to think down to the depths of pessimism and redeem it from the half-Christian, half-German narrowness and simplicity with which it has most recently been portrayed, namely in the form of Schopenhauerian philosophy; anyone who has truly looked with an Asiatic and super-Asiatic eye into – and underneath – the most world-denying of all possible ways of thinking (beyond good and evil and no longer helplessly deluded, like Buddha and Schopenhauer, by morality) – this person may, without really intending it, have opened his eyes to the opposite ideal: to the ideal of the most audacious, lively, and world-affirming human being, one who has learned not only to accept and bear that which has been and is, but who also wants to have it over again, *just as it was and is*, throughout all eternity, calling out insatiably *da capo*,[65] not only to himself, but to the whole drama, the whole spectacle, and not only to a spectacle, but ultimately to the one who has need of just this spectacle – and makes it necessary, because he continually has need of himself – and makes himself necessary – Well? And wouldn't this then be – *circulus vitiosus deus?*[66]

57

As his intellectual sight and insight grow stronger, the distances and, as it were, the space surrounding a man increase: his world becomes more profound; new stars, new

---

63   The Roman emperor Tiberius (42 B.C.–A.D. 37) is said to have conducted human sacrifices here after A.D. 27.
64   In German: *Instinkte*.
65   Italian: from the beginning. Term used in music to indicate a repeat; the context here is the Overman affirming the eternal recurrence.
66   Latin: God as vicious circle.

images and riddles keep coming into view. Perhaps all the things that trained his mind's eye to see more acutely and profoundly were nothing but occasions for training, playthings for children and childish people. Perhaps the most solemn concepts, those that have triggered the greatest struggles and suffering, the concepts 'God' and 'sin', will some day seem no more important to us than the toys and pains of childhood seem to an old man – and perhaps the 'old man' will then need a different toy and a different pain – still so much a child, an eternal child!

[. . .]

59

Whoever has looked deeply into the world will surely divine what wisdom there is in human superficiality. It is the instinct of preservation that teaches us to be fleet, light, and false. Now and then, in philosophers or artists, one finds a passionate and exaggerated worship of 'pure forms': no one should doubt that a person who so *needs* the surface must once have made an unfortunate grab *underneath* it. Perhaps these burnt children, the born artists who find their only joy in trying to *falsify* life's image (as if taking protracted revenge against it –), perhaps they may even belong to a hierarchy: we could tell the degree to which they are sick of life by how much they wish to see its image adulterated, diluted, transcendentalized, apotheosized – we could count the *homines religiosi*[67] among the artists, as their *highest* class. For thousands of years, a deep, suspicious fear of an incurable pessimism has forced people to cling to a religious interpretation of existence: this instinctual fear senses that they might gain possession of the truth *too soon*, before they have become strong enough for it, tough enough, artist enough . . . When viewed thus, piety, a 'life with God', would appear to be the most exquisite end product of the *fear* of truth; the worshipful artist's intoxication at the most persistent of all falsifications; the will to truth-reversal, to untruth at any price. Perhaps there has never yet been a more powerful device for beautifying even mankind than piety itself: it can turn humans so completely into art, surface, opalescence, kindness, that we no longer suffer when we look at them.

[. . .]

61

The philosopher as *we* understand him, we free spirits – as a person with the most wide-ranging responsibility, whose conscience encompasses mankind's overall development: this philosopher, in his efforts to improve education and breeding, will make use of religions just as he makes use of the political and economic circumstances of his time. The influence that can be exerted with the help of religion is an influence for selecting and breeding, and is always necessarily as destructive as it is creative and formative; depending on the sort of people who come under the spell and protection of religion, its influence can be manifold and diverse. For those who are strong and independent, prepared and predestined to command, who embody the intellect and the art of a governing race, religion is one further means to overcome obstacles, to learn to rule: as a bond that ties together rulers and subjects, revealing and surrendering to the former the consciences of the latter, their hidden and innermost secret,

67 Latin: religious men.

the wish to escape the bonds of obedience. And if, because of their high spirituality, a few of these nobly-born natures are inclined to a more removed and contemplative life, reserving for themselves only the most subtle form of authority (over selected disciples or brothers of the order), they can use religion as a means to ensure their repose when confronted with the noisy exertions of the *cruder* type of authority, and their purity when confronted with the *necessary* filth of every kind of political activity. That is how the Brahmans understood it, for example: with the help of a religious organization, they gave themselves the power to appoint the kings for the common people, while they themselves remained apart and outside, feeling that their own duties were more important than those of royalty. Meanwhile, religion also gives guidance and an opportunity to prepare for eventual authority and command to a portion of the governed, to those slowly rising classes and ranks whose successful marriage patterns have ensured that the strong desire of their will, their will to self-rule, is always growing. Religion can offer them enough incitements and temptations to go the ways of higher spirituality, to test their feelings of great self-control, silence, and solitude: asceticism and puritanism are the virtually indispensable means to educate and improve a race that wants to overcome its origin in the rabble and work itself up to eventual authority. To the ordinary people, finally, to the vast majority who exist to serve and be generally useful and *must* exist only to that end, religion offers an inestimable contentment with their own situation and nature, an ongoing peace of heart, improved obedience, joy and sorrow shared with their own kind, and something in the way of transfiguration and beautification, something that justifies their everyday lives, all the baseness, all the semi-animal poverty of their souls. Being religious and finding a religious significance to life sheds sunshine on these constantly afflicted people, even enabling them to bear the sight of themselves; it has the same effect that Epicurean philosophy tends to have on a higher class of sufferer: refreshing, purifying, *exploiting* suffering, as it were, and ultimately even sanctifying and justifying it. There is perhaps nothing so admirable about Christianity and Buddhism as their skill in showing even the lowliest people how piety can place them within an illusory higher order of things and thus enable them to remain content with the real order, within which they certainly live a harsh (and this harshness is exactly what's needed!) life.

62

But finally, of course, to reckon up the bad side of religions like these and expose their sinister danger: there is always a dear and terrible price to pay whenever religions hold sway *not* as the philosopher's means to breed and educate, but rather on their own and *absolutely*, when they claim to be an ultimate end, rather than one means among others. Among humans as among every other species of animal, there is a surplus of deformed, sick, degenerating, frail, necessarily suffering individuals; even among humans and even considering that man is the *animal that has not yet been established*, successful cases are always the exception, the rare exception. But even worse: the higher the nature of a particular type, the greater the probability that any representative individual of that type *will not thrive*: randomness, the law of meaninglessness in the overall economy of mankind, is seen at its most terrible in its destructive effect on higher individuals, whose needs in life are subtle, manifold, and difficult to calculate. Now how do the two above-mentioned greatest religions treat this *surplus* of failed cases? They try to preserve, try to keep alive, whatever can somehow be retained of them, indeed they take their side on principle, as religions *for the suffering*; according to these religions, all the people who suffer from life as from an illness are in the right, and they would like to ensure that any other experience of life be considered wrong and rendered impossible. However greatly one might like to value such indulgent and supportive solicitude, in that it has also included and continues to include among the suffering the highest species of humans, who until now have almost always suffered the most: nevertheless, in the last analysis, earlier religions, namely *absolute* religions are among the main reasons that the species 'human' has been stuck on a lower rung of development – they have preserved too much of what *ought to perish*. They have given us priceless gifts; and who is so richly endowed with gratitude that he would not become poor in thanking Christianity's 'spiritual people', for example, for what they have already done for Europe! And yet, after they have offered comfort to the suffering, courage to the oppressed and desperate, and been a staff and support to the dependent; after they have lured those inwardly ravaged and driven mad away from society into cloisters and spiritual prisons: what more should they have to do to work with such conviction and a good conscience for the preservation of everything sick and suffering, that is to say, to work in deed and in truth for the *degeneration of the European race*? Turn all evaluations *upside down* – *that* is what they had to do! And shatter the strong, debilitate the great hopes, question any joy in beauty, take everything autocratic, masculine, triumphant, tyrannical, all the instincts that belong to the highest and best-formed species of 'human', and twist them into doubt, pangs of conscience, self-destruction, indeed reverse all love for earthly things and for mastery of the earth into a hatred of the earth and the earthly – *that* is the task the Church set for itself and had to set for itself, until 'unworldliness', 'asceticism', and 'the higher man' fused together in its estimation into *one* feeling. Assuming that one were able to survey the strangely painful comedy of European Christianity, as coarse as it is refined, with the mocking and disinterested eye of an Epicurean god, I think there would be no end to the astonishment and laughter: doesn't it seem that for eighteen centuries one will alone has ruled over Europe, set on making man into a *sublime deformity*? But if someone with the opposite needs, no longer an Epicurean, but with some divine hammer in his hand, were to come up to this almost capriciously degenerate and stunted man that is the European Christian (Pascal,[68] for example), would he not have to cry out in anger, in pity, in horror: 'Oh you fools, you presumptuous pitying fools, see what you have done! Was this a work for your hands! See how you have hacked up my most beautiful stone and bungled it! How could *you* presume to do such a thing!' That is to say: Christianity has been the most disastrous form of human presumption yet. Humans who were neither high-minded nor tough enough to claim the power to work *on mankind* as its shaping artist; humans who were neither strong nor far-sighted enough to exercise a sublime self-control and *let* the foreground law of thousands of failures and defeats hold sway; humans who were not noble enough to see the unfathomably diverse hierarchy in the gulf between human and human – *these* are the people who have controlled Europe's destiny so far, with their 'equal in the eyes of God', until they have bred a diminished, almost ludicrous species, a herd animal, something good-natured, sickly, and mediocre, today's European . . .

68   See *On Truth and Lies* note 14 above.

Section 4: Epigrams and Interludes

63

A true teacher doesn't take anything seriously except in relation to his pupils – not even himself.

64

'Knowledge for its own sake' – that is the last snare set by morality, tangling us up in it again completely.

[. . .]

68

'I have done that,' says my memory. I cannot have done that – says my pride and remains unshakeable. Finally – memory yields.

[. . .]

70

If a person has character, he also has his typical experience that happens again and again.

[. . .]

73

One who reaches his ideal has by so doing gone beyond it.

[. . .]

75

The degree and nature of a person's sexuality extends into the highest pinnacle of his spirit.

[. . .]

79

A heart that knows it is loved, but does not itself love, reveals its sediment – its bottom rises to the top.

[. . .]

82

'To pity everyone' – that would be to chastise and tyrannize *yourself*, my dear neighbour! –

[. . .]

85

Men and women have the same emotions, but at a different tempo: that is why men and women never cease to misunderstand one another.

[. . .]

88

We begin to distrust very clever people when they become embarrassed.

89

Dreadful experiences make us wonder whether the person who experiences them may not be something dreadful.

[. . .]

94

A man's maturity: having rediscovered the seriousness that he had as a child, at play.

[. . .]

96

We should depart from life as Odysseus parted from Nausicaa – with a blessing, but not in love.

[. . .]

98

When we teach our conscience to do tricks, it kisses us even as it bites.

[. . .]

108

There is no such thing as moral phenomena, but only a moral interpretation of phenomena . . .

[. . .]

116

The great periods of our life occur when we gain the courage to rechristen what is bad about us as what is best.

[. . .]

123

Even cohabitation has been corrupted – by marriage.

[. . .]

127

All proper women find that science is inimical to their modesty. It makes them feel as if someone wanted to take a look under their skin – or worse! under their clothes and make-up.

128

The more abstract the truth you wish to teach us, the more you must entice our senses into learning it.

[. . .]

131

The sexes deceive themselves about one another: as a result, they basically honour and love only themselves (or their ideal of themselves, to express it more kindly –). Thus men want women to be peaceful – but women especially are *by their very nature* unpeaceful, like cats, however well they have learned to give the impression of peacefulness.

[. . .]

134

Our senses are the first origin of all credibility, all good conscience, all apparent truth.

[. . .]

136

One person seeks a midwife for his thoughts, another seeks to act as midwife: the origin of a good conversation.

[. . .]

139

In revenge and in love, women are more barbaric than men.

[. . .]

146

Anyone who fights with monsters should take care that he does not in the process become a monster. And if you gaze for long into an abyss, the abyss gazes back into you.

[. . .]

150

Around a hero everything becomes a tragedy, around a demigod everything becomes a satyr play; and around God everything becomes – what do you think? perhaps the 'world'? –

[. . .]

153

What is done out of love always takes place beyond good and evil.

[. . .]

156

Madness is rare in individuals – but in groups, political parties, nations, epochs, it is the rule.

157

The thought of suicide is a powerful solace: it helps us through many a bad night.

[. . .]

160

We no longer love our knowledge enough, once we have communicated it.

[. . .]

163

Love exposes the great and hidden qualities in the lover – what is rare and exceptional about him: to that extent it easily conceals what is ordinary.

[. . .]

177

In speaking about 'truthfulness', perhaps no one yet has been sufficiently truthful.

[. . .]

Section 5: Towards a Natural History of Morals

186

The moral sensibility in Europe these days is as subtle, mature, differentiated, sensitive, refined, as the relevant 'science of morality'[69] is still young, raw, clumsy, and crude: an attractive antithesis which is sometimes revealed in the person of the moralist himself. Even the term 'science of morality', considering what it describes, is much too arrogant and offends *good* taste – which always tends to prefer more modest terms. We should sternly admit to ourselves *what* will be required in the long term, *what* the only right course is for the moment: that is, to gather the material, establish the concepts, and organize the abundance of subtle feelings and distinctions in the area of values, as they live, grow, procreate, and perish; and perhaps we should also attempt to illustrate the more frequently recurring forms of this living crystallization – in preparation for a *taxonomy* of morals.[70] True, such modesty has not so far been the rule. The moment philosophers were concerned with morality as a science, all of them, with a ridiculous stiff solemnity, demanded of themselves something much greater, more ambitious, more solemn: they wanted to *account for* morality – and every philosopher to date has thought that he has done so; morality itself, however, was taken as a 'given'. In their clumsy pride, how remote they were from the seemingly modest task of description, forgotten in dust and decay, although even the most delicate hands and senses could hardly be delicate enough for it! Precisely because the moral philosophers knew moral *facta*[71] only roughly, in arbitrary excerpts or random condensations, knew them as the morality of their neighbourhood, say, or of their class, their Church, the *Zeitgeist*,[72] their climate or region; precisely because they were not well informed about peoples, epochs, past histories and were not even particularly curious about them, they never

---

69   In German: *"Wissenschaft der Moral."*
70   In German: *Typenlehre der Moral.*
71   Latin: facts.
72   German: spirit of the time.

did catch sight of the real problems of morality – all of which come to light only by comparing *many* moralities. As strange as it may sound, in every previous 'science of morality' the problem of morality itself was *missing*; there was no suspicion that it might be something problematic. What the philosophers called 'accounting for morality'[73] and expected of themselves was, viewed in the right light, only an erudite form of true *belief* in the prevailing morality, a new medium for *expressing* it, and thus itself a part of the state of affairs within a particular morality. Indeed, in the last analysis it was a way of forbidding that this morality *might be* construed as a problem – and in any event it was the opposite of a testing, analysing, doubting, dissecting of their partic- ular belief. Just listen, for example, to the almost admirable innocence with which Schopenhauer portrays his own task, and draw your conclusions as to the scientific nature of a 'science' whose past masters still talk like children or old women: 'The principle', he writes in *The Fundamental Problems of Morality*, 'the axiom about whose content all moralists *really* agree, neminem laede, immo omnes, quantum potes, juva[74] – that is *really* the tenet that all moralists endeavour to account for – the *real* foundation of morality, which people have been seeking for thousands of years like the philosophers' stone.' To be sure, it may be very difficult to account for the tenet he cites (everyone knows that Schopenhauer himself was not successful in doing so), and anyone who has ever thoroughly appreciated how tastelessly false and sentimental this tenet is in a world whose essence is the will to power, may want to be reminded that Schopenhauer, although he was a pessimist, *really* – played the flute . . . Every day, after dinner: just read what his biographer says about this. And by the way, may we not inquire whether a pessimist who denies God and the world, but *stops short* at the prob- lem of morality, says Yes to morality, to a *laede-neminem* morality and plays the flute: well then? is this person really – a pessimist?

187

Apart from whatever value there may be in assertions such as 'a categorical impera- tive exists within us', we can still ask what such an assertion tells us about the person asserting it. There are moral codes that are meant to justify their author to other peo- ple; other codes are meant to soothe the author and allow him to be content with himself. Some are intended to nail him to the cross and humiliate him, others to exact vengeance for him, or hide him, or transfigure him and set him above and beyond. One moral code serves its author to forget, another to make others forget him or for- get something about him. One sort of moralist would like to exercise his power and creative whims upon mankind; a different sort, and perhaps Kant himself, uses his moral code to announce: 'What is honourable about me is that I can obey – and it *should* be no different for you than for me!' In short, moral codes too are only a *sign lan- guage of emotions*.[75]

---

73   In German: *"Begründung der Moral."*
74   Latin: harm no one; rather help everyone as much as you can. Quotation from section 6 of the second essay of Schopenhauer's *Die beiden Grundprobleme der Ethik* (*The Two Fundamental Problems of Ethics*, 1841), which contained his essays *On the Freedom of the Human Will* and *On the Basis of Morality*.
75   In German: *Zeichensprache der Affekte.*

188

Every moral code, in opposition to *laisser-aller*,[76] is an example of tyranny against 'nature',
and against 'reason', too: but that cannot be an objection to it, or else we would have
to turn around and decree on the basis of some other moral code that all kinds of
tyranny and unreason were impermissible. The essential, invaluable thing about every
moral code is that it is one long coercion: in order to understand Stoicism or Port-
Royal[77] or Puritanism, just think of the coercion that every language has employed
up till now in achieving its strength and freedom – the coercion of metre, the tyranny
of rhyme and rhythm. How much trouble the poets and orators of every people (not
to exclude certain contemporary prose writers, in whose ear an unshakeable conscience
resides) have put themselves to – 'for the sake of folly', as utilitarian fools say, thus
fancying themselves clever; 'in subservience to tyrannical laws', as anarchists say, thus
imagining themselves 'free', even freethinking. But the strange fact is that everything on earth that exists or has existed by way of freedom, subtlety, daring, dance,
and perfect sureness, whether it be in ideas, or in governance, or in oratory and rhetoric, in the arts as well as in manners, has developed only by virtue of the 'tyranny
of such despotic laws'; and seriously, it is very likely that *this* is what is 'nature' and
'natural' – and *not* that *laisser-aller*! Every artist knows how far from the feeling of
anything-goes his 'most natural' condition is, the free ordering, arranging, deciding,
shaping that occurs in his moments of 'inspiration' – and how delicately and strictly,
especially at such moments, he obeys the thousandfold laws whose very exactness and
rigour make mockery of all conceptual formulations (even the most solid concept, by
comparison, has something muzzy, multifarious, ambiguous –). To repeat, it seems that
the essential thing, both 'in heaven and on earth', is that there be a protracted period
of unidirectional *obedience*: in the long run, that is how something emerged and emerges
that makes life on earth worth living: virtue, for example, or art, music, dance, reason,
spirituality – something transfiguring, elegant, wild, and divine. The long constraint
of the spirit; the reluctant coercion in the communicability of thoughts; the thinker's
self-imposed discipline to think within guidelines set up by court or Church, or according to Aristotelian assumptions; the long-standing spiritual will to interpret every event
according to a Christian scheme and to rediscover and justify the Christian God in
every chance incident – all this violence, arbitrariness, harshness, horror, nonsense has
turned out to be the means by which the European spirit was bred to be strong, ruthlessly curious, and beautifully nimble. Admittedly, much irreplaceable energy and spirit
had to be suppressed, suffocated, and spoiled in the process (for here as everywhere
'nature' reveals her true colours in all her extravagant and *indifferent* grandeur, which
is infuriating but also noble). For thousands of years European thinkers thought only
in order to prove something (today on the other hand we are sceptical of any thinker
who 'has something to prove'). They already knew in advance what was *supposed* to
emerge as a result of their most rigorous meditation, rather as once in Asian astrology,
or as is still the case today in harmless Christian-ethical interpretations of immediate
personal experiences 'for the glory of God' or 'for the soul's salvation'. This kind of

76   French: letting things go.
77   French Jansenism, as practiced at the abbey and school of Port-Royal near Paris, founded
in the seventeenth century.

tyranny, this despotism, this stern, grandiose stupidity *educated* the spirit: it would seem
that slavery, both in the cruder and the finer sense, is also the indispensable means to
discipline and cultivate[78] the spirit. Whichever moral code we inspect in that light, its
'nature' teaches us to hate the excessive freedom of *laisser-aller* and instils a need for
limited horizons, for immediate tasks – it teaches us to *narrow our perspective*, and thus
in a certain sense, to be stupid, as a precondition for life and growth. 'Thou shalt
obey, obey somebody, and for a long time: *or else* you will perish and lose your last
remnant of self-respect' – this seems to me to be nature's moral imperative, and to be
sure it is neither 'categorical', as old Kant demanded (hence the 'or else' –), nor is
it addressed to individuals (what should it care about individuals!), but rather to peoples, races, epochs, classes, and above all to the whole animal 'human', to human beings
in general.

[. . .]

197

People completely misunderstand predatory animals and predatory people (Cesare Borgia,[79]
for example), they misunderstand 'nature' as long as they persist in examining these
most healthy of all tropical plants and brutes (as nearly all moralists till now have done)
to find their fundamental 'diseased state' or inborn 'hell'. Doesn't it seem that moralists hate the jungle and the tropics? And that the 'tropical person' must be discredited
at all costs, whether as a disease or degeneration in mankind or else as his own self-
punishing hell? Why should this be so? To favour the 'moderate regions'? The moderate people? The 'moral' people? The mediocre people? – Notes for a chapter on
'morals as timidity'.

[. . .]

202

Let us immediately say once again what we have already said a hundred times, for
nowadays ears are reluctant to hear such truths – *our* truths. We know perfectly well
how offensive it sounds when someone counts man among the animals plain and simple, without metaphorical intent; but we will almost be accounted a *criminal* for always
using expressions such as 'herd', 'herd instincts', and the like when speaking about
people of 'modern ideas'. What's the use! We can't do otherwise, for this is just what
our new insight is about. We discovered that Europe, and those countries dominated
by a European influence, are now of one mind in all their key moral judgements: it
is obvious that Europeans nowadays *know* that which Socrates thought he did not know,
and what that famous old serpent once promised to teach – people 'know' what is good
and evil. It must sound harsh and trouble the ears, then, if we insist over and over that
it is the instinct of man the herd animal that thinks it knows, that glorifies itself
and calls itself good whenever it allots praise or blame. This instinct has had a breakthrough, has come to predominance, has prevailed over the other instincts and continues to do so as a symptom of the increasing process of physiological approximations

78 In German: *Zucht und Züchtung*.
79 Cesare Borgia (1476–1507), cardinal, soldier, statesman, and duke of the Romagna.
Admired by Nietzsche as the embodiment of Renaissance *virtù*.

and resemblances. *Morality*[80] *in Europe today is herd animal morality* – and thus, as we understand things, it is only one kind of human morality next to which, before which, after which many others, and especially *higher* moralities, are or should be possible. But this morality defends itself with all its strength against such 'possibilities', against such 'should be's'. Stubbornly and relentlessly it says, 'I am Morality itself, and nothing else is!' Indeed, with the help of a religion that played along with and flattered the most sublime desires of the herd animal, we have reached the point of finding an ever more visible expression of this morality even in political and social structures: the *democratic* movement is Christianity's heir. But its tempo is still far too slow and sleepy for the overeager, for patients or addicts of this above-mentioned instinct, as we can tell from the increasingly frantic howl, the ever more widely bared teeth of the anarchist dogs who now roam the alleys of European culture. They appear to be in conflict with the peaceably industrious democrats or ideologues of revolution, and even more with the foolish philosophasts and brotherhood enthusiasts who call themselves socialists and want a 'free society'; but in reality they are united with those others in their fundamental and instinctive enmity towards every form of society other than *autonomous* herds (right up to the point of even rejecting the concepts 'master' and 'servant' – *ni dieu ni maître*[81] is a socialist motto); united in their tough resistance to every exceptional claim, every exceptional right and privilege (and thus ultimately to *all* rights, for no one needs 'rights' any longer when everyone is equal); united in their distrust of any justice that punishes (as if it were a rape of the weaker party, unjust towards the *necessary* consequence of all earlier society); but also just as united in their religion of pity, in their empathy, wherever there are feelings, lives, or suffering (reaching down to the animal or up to 'God' – the eccentric notion of 'pity for God' suits a democratic age); united one and all in their impatient cry for pity, in their mortal hatred of any suffering,[82] in their almost feminine incapacity to remain a spectator to it, to *allow* suffering; united in the involuntary depression and decadence which seems to hold Europe captive to a threatening new Buddhism; united in their belief in a morality of *communal* pity, as if it were Morality itself, the summit, the *conquered* summit of humankind, the only hope for the future, comfort in the present, the great redemption from all past guilt – united together in their belief in community as a *redeemer*, and thus a belief in the herd, a belief in 'themselves'. . .

203

We who hold a different belief – we who consider the democratic movement not merely a decadent form of political organization, but a decadent (that is to say, diminished) form of the human being, one that mediocritizes[83] him and debases his value: what can *we* set our hopes on? On *new philosophers*, we have no other choice; on spirits that are strong and original enough to give impetus to opposing value judgements and to revalue, to reverse 'eternal values'; on forerunners, on men of the future,

80   In German: *Moral*. This is the term Nietzsche uses throughout this section.
81   See note 34 above.
82   The German terms used here for "pity" and "suffering" are, respectively, *Mitleiden* (literally, "suffering with") and *Leiden*.
83   In German: *Vermittelmässigung*. Nietzsche's neologism.

who in the present will forge the necessary link to force a thousand-year-old will onto *new* tracks. They will teach humans that their future is their *will*, that the future depends on their human will, and they will prepare the way for great risk-taking and joint experiments in discipline and breeding in order to put an end to that terrible reign of nonsense and coincidence that until now has been known as 'history' (the nonsense about the 'greatest number' is only its most recent form). To accomplish this, new kinds of philosophers and commanders will eventually be necessary, whose image will make all the secretive, frightful, benevolent spirits that have existed in the world look pale and dwarfish. The image of such leaders is what hovers before *our* eyes – may I say it aloud, you free spirits? The circumstances that would have to be in part created, in part exploited to give rise to these leaders; the probable paths and tests by which a soul would grow so great and powerful that it would feel *compelled* to accomplish these projects; a revaluation of values, under whose new hammer and pressure the conscience would be transformed into steel, the heart into bronze, so that they could bear the weight of such responsibility; the indispensability of such leaders; on the other hand, the terrible danger that they might not arrive or might go astray and degenerate – those are really the things that concern and worry *us* – do you know that, you free spirits? – those are the distant oppressive thoughts and thunderstorms that pass across the sky of *our* life. There are few pains so raw as to have once observed, understood, sympathized while an extraordinary man strayed from his path or degenerated: but a person with the rare vision to see the general danger that 'man' himself *is degenerating*, who has recognized as we have the tremendous randomness that thus far has been at play in determining the future of mankind (a play that has been guided by no one's hand, not even by 'God's finger!'), who has guessed the fate that lies hidden in all the stupid innocence and blissful confidence of 'modern ideas', and even more in the entire Christian-European morality: this person suffers from an anxiety that cannot be compared to any other. With one single glance he grasps everything that *mankind could be bred to be* if all its energies and endeavours were gathered together and heightened; with all the knowledge of his conscience, he knows how mankind's greatest possibilities have as yet been untapped, and how many mysterious decisions and new paths the human type has already encountered – he knows better yet, from his most painful memory, what kind of wretched things have usually caused the finest example of an evolving being to shatter, break apart, sink down, become wretched. The *overall degeneration of man*, right down to what socialist fools and flatheads call their 'man of the future' (their ideal!); this degeneration and diminution of man into a perfect herd animal (or, as they call it, man in a 'free society'); this bestialization of man into a dwarf animal with equal rights and claims is *possible*, no doubt about that! Anyone who has thought this possibility through to its end knows no disgust but other people – and also, perhaps, a new *project*! . . .

Section 6: We Scholars

210

If, then, in the portrait of the philosophers of the future, some one trait makes us wonder whether they will have to be sceptics in the sense suggested above, we would still be describing only one thing about them – and *not* them themselves. They would be every bit as justified in calling themselves critics; and surely they will be men who experiment. By the name that I have dared to call them[84] I have already expressly underlined their acts of experimenting and their joy in experimenting: did I do this because these critics in body and soul like to make use of experiments in new, perhaps extended, perhaps more dangerous senses? Will they, in their passion for knowledge, take their daring and painful experiments farther than the soft and spoiled taste of a democratic century can sanction? There can be no doubt that these coming men will be least able to forgo those important and not inconsiderable qualities that distinguish the critic from the sceptic; I mean the certainty of standards, the conscious use of a unified method, shrewd courage, independence, and a capacity for self-reliance. Indeed, in private they admit to a *joy* in saying No and in dissecting; they admit to a certain cruel concentration that knows how to wield the knife surely and subtly, even when the heart is bleeding. They will be *harsher* (and perhaps not always only towards themselves) than humane people may wish. They will not get involved with 'truth' just for the sake of 'liking' it or so that it can 'exalt' or 'inspire' them; rather, they will have only slight faith that it is actually *truth* that elicits these emotional pleasures. They will smile, these stern spirits, should somebody say to them, 'That thought exalts me: how can it not be true?' Or, 'That work delights me: how can it not be beautiful?' Or, 'That artist makes me greater: how can he not be great?' They greet all such enthusiasm, idealism, femininity, hermaphroditism not only with a smile, but with a real disgust, and if anyone were to follow them right into their secret heart's chamber, he would be hard put to discover there any intention of reconciling 'Christian sentiment' with 'ancient taste', let alone with 'modern parliamentarianism' (a reconciliation that is said to occur even in the philosophers of our very insecure and thus very conciliatory age). Critical discipline and such habits as lead to neatness and rigour in matters of the spirit: these philosophers of the future will not only demand them of themselves, but might even make a display of them as their type of adornment – nevertheless they will not yet want to be called critics. They deem it no little insult to philosophy to decree, as people nowadays like to do, that 'Philosophy is criticism and critical science[85] – and that is all it is!' Although this evaluation of philosophy may enjoy the approval of all the positivists in France and Germany (and it may even have flattered the heart and taste of *Kant*: just think of the titles of his major works), our new philosophers will say nevertheless that critics are the tools of the philosopher, and precisely because they are tools they are a long way from being philosophers themselves! The great Chinaman of Königsberg, too, was only a great critic.

211

I must insist that we finally stop mistaking philosophical workers or learned people in general for philosophers – in this regard especially, we should give strictly 'to each his own', and not too much to the former or much too little to the latter. The education of the true philosopher may require that he himself once pass through all the

---

84   See *BGE* 42.
85   In German: *Kritik und kritische Wissenschaft.*

stages at which his servants, the learned workers of philosophy, remain – *must* remain. Perhaps he even needs to have been a critic and a sceptic and a dogmatist and an historian, and in addition a poet and collector and traveller and puzzle-solver and moralist and seer and 'free spirit' and nearly all things, so that he can traverse the range of human values and value-feelings and *be able* to look with many kinds of eyes and consciences from the heights into every distance, from the depths into every height, from the corners into every wide expanse. But all these are only the preconditions for his task: the task itself calls for something else – it calls for him to *create values*. It is the task of those philosophical workers in the noble mould of Kant and Hegel to establish and press into formulae some large body of value judgements (that is, previous value-*assumptions*, value-creations that have become dominant and are for a time called 'truths'), whether in the realm of *logic* or of *politics* (morals) or of *aesthetics*. It is incumbent upon these researchers to describe clearly, conceivably, intelligibly, manageably everything that has already taken place and been assessed, to abbreviate everything that is lengthy, even 'time' itself, and to *subdue* the entire past: a tremendous and wondrous task, the execution of which can surely satisfy any refined pride or tenacious will. *But true philosophers are commanders and lawgivers.* They say, 'This is the way it *should* be!' Only they decide about mankind's Where to? and What for? and to do so they employ the preparatory work of all philosophical workers, all subduers of the past. With creative hands they reach towards the future, and everything that is or has existed becomes their means, their tool, their hammer. Their 'knowing' is *creating*, their creating is law-giving, their will to truth is – *will to power*. Do philosophers like these exist today? Have philosophers like these ever existed? Don't philosophers like these *have* to exist? . . .

212

More and more, I tend to think that because the philosopher is *necessarily* a man of tomorrow and the day after tomorrow, he has always been and has *had* to be in conflict with his Today: in every instance, Today's ideal was his enemy. Until now, all these extraordinary furtherers of humankind who are called philosophers (and who themselves rarely felt like lovers of wisdom, but more like disagreeable fools and dangerous question marks) have found their task, their difficult, unwanted, unrefusable task, but ultimately also the greatness of their task, in being the bad conscience of their age. By taking a vivisecting knife to the breast of the *virtues of their age*, they revealed their own secret: their knowledge of a *new* human greatness, a new, untrodden path to human aggrandizement. Time and again they uncovered how much hypocrisy, smugness, casual acquiescence, how much falsehood was hidden under the best-honoured examples of their contemporary morality, how much virtue was *obsolete*; time and again they said, 'We must go there, out there, where all of *you* today are least at home.' Faced with a world of 'modern ideas' that would like to confine everyone to a corner and to a 'speciality', the philosopher (if philosophers could exist today) would be forced to find human greatness, the concept of 'greatness' precisely in man's breadth and variety, in his wholeness in diversity: in fact, he would assign value and rank according to how many and how many sorts of things one person could bear, could take upon himself, by how *far* a person could extend his responsibility. These days, the spirit of the times and the virtue of the times are weakening and diluting the will; nothing is so fashionable as weakness of will. Thus it is precisely strength of will, harshness, and a capacity for lengthy decisions that are integral to the philosopher's ideal concept of 'greatness'. This is as appropriate as was the opposite doctrine (the ideal of a stupid, renunciatory, submissive, selfless humanity) in an opposite period, one that, like the sixteenth century, suffered from the pent-up energy of the will and from the wildest floods and tidal waves of selfishness. At the time of Socrates, everyone's instinct was weary, and conservative old Athenians let themselves go ('for happiness' as they claimed, for pleasure as they behaved), still pronouncing the same splendid words that their lives had long failed to justify. At that time, *irony* may have been necessary for greatness of soul, that malicious, Socratic certainty of the old doctor and plebeian who cut mercilessly into his own flesh, as he did into the flesh and heart of the 'noble', with a gaze that said clearly enough, 'Don't dissemble in front of me! Here – we are equal!' In Europe today, by contrast, it is only the herd animal who is honoured and bestows honour; 'equal rights' can all too easily be transformed into equality of wrong (I mean, into a shared struggle against everything rare, strange, privileged, against the higher human, the higher soul, the higher duty, the higher responsibility, the creative abundance of power and elegance). And so these days, being noble, wanting to be for oneself, managing to be different, standing alone and needing to live independently are integral to the concept of 'greatness'; and the philosopher will reveal something of his own ideal when he asserts, 'The greatest person should be the one who can be most lonely, most hidden, most deviant, the man beyond good and evil, the master of his virtues, abundantly rich in will. This is what *greatness* should mean: the ability to be both multifarious and whole, both wide and full.' And to ask it once again: nowadays, is – greatness *possible*?

[. . .]

Section 7: Our Virtues

225

Whether it be hedonism, pessimism, utilitarianism, eudemonism – all of these ideas that measure the value of things according to *pleasure* or *suffering*, that is to say, according to secondary states and side-effects, are foreground ideas, and naive. Anyone conscious of having *creative* energies and an artist's conscience will look down on them not without mockery, but also not without pity. Pity for all of *you*! although it is not pity in your sense, to be sure. It is not pity for social 'misery', for 'society' and its sick and injured, for the perennially depraved and downtrodden who lie around us everywhere; even less is it pity for the grumbling, oppressed, rebellious ranks of slaves who are looking to be masters (which they call 'being free'). *Our* pity is a more elevated, more far-sighted pity – we see how *human beings* are being reduced, how all of *you* are reducing them! And there are moments when we look at *your* pity especially with an indescribable anxiety, when we defend ourselves against this pity – when we find your seriousness more dangerous than any frivolity. If possible (and no 'if possible' can be more crazy) you want *to abolish suffering*! And we? – it seems that *we* want it to be, if anything, worse and greater than before! Well-being in your sense of the word – that certainly is no goal, it seems to us to be an *end*! A condition that would immediately make people ludicrous and contemptible – make us *wish* their downfall! The discipline of suffering, *great* suffering – don't you know that this discipline *alone* has created all human greatness to date? The tension of the soul in unhappiness, which cultivates its strength; its horror at the sight of the great destruction; its inventiveness and bravery in bearing, enduring, interpreting, exploiting unhappiness, and whatever in the way of depth, mystery, mask, spirit, cleverness, greatness the heart has been granted – has it not been granted them through suffering, through the discipline of great suffering? In the human being, *creature* and *creator* are united: the human being is matter, fragment, excess, clay, filth, nonsense, chaos; but the human being is also creator, sculptor, hammer-hardness, observer-divinity, and the Seventh Day – do you understand this opposition? Do you understand that *your* pity is for the 'creature in the human being', that which must be formed, broken, forged, torn, burned, annealed, purified – that which necessarily has to *suffer* and *should* suffer? And *our* pity – do you not understand whom our *reversed* pity is intended for, when it resists your pity as the worst of all possible self-indulgences and weaknesses? Pity *versus* pity, then! But to repeat, there are more important problems than all those concerning pleasure and suffering and pity; and any philosophy that confines itself only to these is naive.

[. . .]

229

In those advanced eras that are rightfully proud of their humanity, there remains so much fear, so much *superstitious* fear of the 'wild, savage beast' which they are so particularly proud of having tamed, that even palpable truths remain unspoken for hundreds of years as if by agreement because they would seem to instil new life into that wild, finally dispatched beast. Perhaps I am risking something by letting a truth like that escape me: let others round it up again and give it enough to drink of the 'milk of pious thinking'[86] so that it lies down again quiet and forgotten in its old corner. People should learn to understand cruelty differently and open their eyes; people should finally learn to be impatient, so that presumptuous, fat errors no longer wander about, virtuous and cheeky, like the errors concerning tragedy, for example, that have been fattened up by old and new philosophers. Almost everything that we call 'high culture' is based on the deepening and spiritualizing of *cruelty* – this is my tenet. That 'wild beast' has not been killed off at all, it lives and thrives, it has only – made a divinity of itself. It is cruelty that constitutes the painful voluptuousness of tragedy; whatever pleasing effect is to be found in so-called tragic pity or in anything sublime in fact, right up to the highest and most delicate shivers of metaphysics, gets its sweetness solely because it is blended with the ingredient of cruelty. What the Roman in his arena, the Christian in his raptures before the cross, the Spaniard confronting the stake or the bullfight, the Japanese of today who rushes to see tragic theatre, the working-class Parisian who is nostalgic for bloody revolutions, the female Wagnerian who lets *Tristan und Isolde* wash over her with her will exposed – what all these people are enjoying, what they aspire to drink in with mysterious ardour is the spiced brew of the great Circe 'Cruelty'. Of course, we have to get rid of that foolish psychology of earlier times that held that cruelty arises only at the sight of *another* person's suffering: there is also abundant, over-abundant pleasure in our own suffering, in making

---

86   From Schiller's play *Wilhelm Tell* (IV. iii), and recalling Shakespeare's phrase "the milk of human kindness" in *Macbeth* (I. v).

ourselves suffer. And wherever a person can be persuaded to deny himself in a *religious* sense, or to mutilate himself in the manner of Phoenicians and ascetics, or in general to become contrite, desensualized, decorporealized, to feel the puritan spasm of penitence, to dissect the conscience and make a Pascalian *sacrifizio dell'intelletto*,[87] he is covertly being tempted and urged forward by his cruelty, by that dangerous shiver of cruelty turned *against himself*. Finally, let us consider that even the man who seeks knowledge, by forcing his spirit to know things *contrary* to the inclination of his mind and often enough also contrary to the wishes of his heart (that is, saying No where he would like to say Yes, where he would like to love and adore) functions as an artist and transfigurer of cruelty; whenever we take on anything deeply and thoroughly, it is already a rape, a wanting to do harm to the fundamental will of the spirit, a will that is constantly drawn to appearances and surfaces – in every desire for knowledge there is already a drop of cruelty.

230

Perhaps what I have said about a 'fundamental will of the spirit' will not be immediately transparent: permit me to explain. That imperious something that the common people call 'spirit' wants to be the master, in itself and around itself, and to feel its mastery: it has the will to go from multiplicity to simplicity, a will that binds together, subdues, a tyrannical and truly masterful will. In this regard, its needs and capacities are the same as those the physiologists claim for everything that lives, grows, and reproduces. The spirit's energy[88] in appropriating what is foreign to it is revealed by its strong tendency to make the new resemble the old, to simplify multiplicity, to overlook or reject whatever is completely contradictory; the spirit likewise arbitrarily underlines, emphasizes, or distorts certain qualities and contours in everything that is foreign to it or of the 'outer world'. Its intention in doing so is to incorporate new 'experiences', to fit new things into old orders – to grow, then; and more specifically, to *feel* growth, to feel an increase in strength. This same will is served by an apparently opposite instinct[89] of the spirit: a sudden decision for ignorance, for arbitrary conclusions, a closing of the shutters, inwardly saying No to this thing or that, a refusal to let things draw near, a kind of defensive posture against much potential knowledge, being content with darkness, with a limited horizon, saying Yes to ignorance and affirming it; all this activity is necessary according to the degree of the spirit's appropriating energy, its digestive energy, to keep to the same metaphor – and indeed the 'spirit' really resembles nothing so much as a stomach. Likewise relevant here is the spirit's occasional will to allow itself to be deceived, accompanied perhaps by the mischievous intuition that things are *not* this way or that, that we are just allowing them to be taken this way or that; a joy in every uncertainty and ambivalence; an exulting self-satisfaction in the arbitrary confinement and privacy of a nook, in things that are all too close, in foreground things, in what has been enlarged, reduced, slanted, prettified; a self-satisfaction in the arbitrariness of all these expressions of power. Also relevant here, finally, is the spirit's not inconsiderable readiness to deceive other spirits and go among

87   See note 38 above.
88   In German: *Kraft.*
89   In German: *Trieb.*

them in disguises, that constant pressure and stress of a creating, shaping, transforming energy; it enables the spirit to enjoy its multiple masks and slynesses, and also its feeling of security – its Protean arts are just what defend and hide it best! *This* will to appearance,[90] to simplification, to masks, to cloaks, in short, to the surface (for every surface is a cloak) is *countered* by the sublime tendency of the man in search of knowledge to take and to *want* to take things deeply, multifariously, profoundly, as a kind of cruelty of intellectual conscience and aesthetic taste that every courageous thinker will recognize in himself, if he has spent an appropriate amount of time in tempering and sharpening his self-critical eye and if he is accustomed both to severe discipline and to severe words. He will say, 'There is something cruel in the propensity of my spirit' – let virtuous and amiable people try to talk him out of it! In truth, it would sound nicer if people could talk about us, whisper about us, praise us (the free, *very* free spirits) for 'excessive honesty', say, instead of for cruelty. And might *that* really be what they will praise us for – when we are dead? Meanwhile (for there is still time until then) there is probably no one as disinclined as we to deck ourselves out in such spangled, sparkly moral language: all our previous work has soured us to the cheerful pomposity of just this kind of taste. They are beautiful, glittering, jingling, festive words: honesty, love of truth, love of wisdom, sacrifice for knowledge, the heroism of truthfulness – there is something about them that makes one swell with pride. But we hermits and marmots, we have long ago convinced ourselves in all the privacy of our hermit's conscience, that even this worthy linguistic ostentation belongs with the old adornments, the mendacious trash and gold dust of unconscious human vanity, and that even under this kind of flattering paint and concealing gilt the horrible original text *homo natura*[91] must still be glimpsed. For to return man to nature; to master the many conceited and gushing interpretations and secondary meanings that have heretofore been scribbled and painted over that eternal original text *homo natura*; to ensure that henceforth man faces man in the same way that currently, grown tough within the discipline of science, he faces the *other* nature, with unfrightened Oedipus-eyes and plugged Odysseus-ears, deaf to the seductive melodies of the old metaphysical birdcatchers who have too long been piping at him, 'You are more! You are greater! You are of a different origin!' – that may be a strange and crazy project, but it is a *project* – who could deny that! Why have we chosen it, this crazy project? Or to ask it another way, 'Why bother with knowledge?' Everyone will ask us about it. And we, pressed in this way, we who have asked ourselves just the same thing a hundred times over, we have found and do find no better answer . . .

[. . .]

Section 8: Peoples and Fatherlands

242

Whether we seek the distinctiveness of today's Europeans in what we call 'civilization' or 'humanization' or 'progress', or whether we withhold our praise or blame and simply use the political term: Europe's *democratic* movement – behind all the moral

90   In German: *Schein*.
91   Latin: natural man.

and political foregrounds that such terms describe, a tremendous *physiological* process is occurring and continually gaining momentum. Europeans are coming to resemble one another more and more, and are more and more free of the conditions that would give rise to races connected by climate and class. They are increasingly independent of any *particular* environment that might inscribe its identical demands into their bodies and souls over the course of centuries – that is to say, an essentially supernatural and nomadic type of man is slowly emerging, one that is distinguished, physiologically speaking, by having a maximum of adaptive skills and powers. This process of the *evolving European*, which can be delayed by great relapses in tempo but may as a result very well grow with new force and depth (like the Storm and Stress of 'national feeling' still raging even now, for example, or the recent emergence of Anarchism): this process probably ends with results that were least anticipated by its naive sponsors and apologists, the apostles of 'modern ideas'. The same new conditions that typically give rise to ordinary and mediocre men (serviceable, industrious, diversely useful and handy herd-animal men) are also those most suited to producing exceptional men of the most dangerous and attractive qualities. For while it is quite impossible for this adaptability (which tries out ever-changing conditions and starts a new project in every generation, almost in every decade) to promote the *powerfulness* of the type; and while such future Europeans will probably give the overall impression of being diverse, loquacious, weak-willed, and extremely handy workers who *need* a master, a commander, like their daily bread; and while, finally, the democratization of Europe will end by procreating a type that has been developed in the subtlest sense to be *slaves* – the *strong* man, in the individual and exceptional case, will have to turn out even stronger and richer than he ever would have done before, owing to the impartiality of his training, owing to the tremendous diversity of his activities, arts, and masks. That is to say, the democratization of Europe is at the same time an involuntary contrivance for the breeding of *tyrants* – understanding the word in every sense, even the most spiritual.

[. . .]

250

What does Europe owe to the Jews? Many things, both good and bad, and one thing above all, at once the best and the worst: the grand moral style, the horror and majesty of everlasting demands, everlasting meanings, the whole sublime romanticism of moral questions – and thus the most attractive, insidious, and choice part of those kaleidoscopic shifts and seductions to life in whose afterglow the sky of our European culture, its evening sky is now flickering – perhaps flickering out. For this, we artists among the spectators and philosophers look to the Jews with – gratitude.

251

If a people suffers, *wants* to suffer from national nervous fever and political ambition, it must be expected that various clouds and disturbances will pass across its spirit, little attacks of acquired stupidity, in short. With today's Germans, for example, it is now the anti-French stupidity, now the anti-Jewish, now the anti-Polish, now the Christian-Romantic, now the Wagnerian, now the Teutonic, now the Prussian (just think of those pitiful historians, those Sybels and Treitschkes[92] with their heavily bandaged heads), and whatever else they are called, these little becloudings of the German spirit and conscience. May I be forgiven that I too, during a short, hazardous stay in a very infected area, did not remain entirely spared by the disease and, like everyone, began to think about things that were none of my business: the first sign of political infection. About the Jews, for example: just listen. I have never yet met a German who might have been well disposed to Jews; and however unconditionally all careful and political people may reject real anti-Semitism, even their care and politics are not really directed at the type of feeling per se, but rather at its dangerous extremes, especially if these extreme feelings are expressed reprehensibly or tastelessly – we must not deceive ourselves about that. That Germany has *more than enough* Jews, that German stomachs, German blood have found it difficult (and will continue to find it difficult) to deal with even this amount of 'Jew' (which the Italian, the Frenchman, the Englishman have dealt with, thanks to their stronger digestions): a general instinct states this in clear language, and we must listen to that instinct and act accordingly. 'Do not allow any new Jews to enter! And bar especially those doors that face East (and also towards Austria)!' Thus decrees the instinct of a people whose kind is still weak and inchoate, making it easily vulnerable to obliteration or elimination by a stronger race. But the Jews are without doubt the strongest, toughest, and purest race now living in Europe; they know how to succeed under even the worst conditions (better in fact than under favourable ones) by means of certain virtues that we today would like to label vices – they owe it above all to their resolute faith that has no need to feel ashamed at 'modern ideas'. They change, *if* they change, only in the way the Russian Empire makes its conquests: like an empire that takes its time and did not just develop overnight – that is to say, according to the principle 'As slowly as possible!' Any thinker who has Europe's future on his conscience must in any proposal he makes about that future take the Jews into account like the Russians, as they are obviously the surest and most likely elements in the great game and struggle of forces. What we in Europe today call a 'nation' and what is actually more of a *res facta* than *nata* (sometimes even easily confounded with a *res ficta et picta*)[93] is certainly something evolving, young, easily displaced, not yet a race, let alone the sort of *aere perennius*[94] that is the Jewish kind: these 'nations' should refrain from becoming the Jews' hot-headed enemies or competitors! If they wanted to (or if they were forced to it, as the anti-Semites seem to want them to be), the Jews *could* gain the upper hand, could in fact quite literally rule over Europe, that much is clear – just as clear as the fact that they are *not* planning or working towards that end. For the time being, what they want and wish for, even with a certain urgency, is rather to be wholly absorbed by Europe, into Europe; they yearn to be established, legitimate, respected somewhere at last, and to set an end to their nomadic life as 'wandering Jews'. And we should heed and welcome this strong desire (that in itself may already express a softening of Jewish instincts) – in that spirit it might be proper and useful to reprimand all the anti-Semitic loudmouths in the

92   Heinrich von Sybel (1817–95) and Heinrich von Treitschke (1834–91), the two most significant political historians of their day.
93   *res facta . . . nata . . . res ficta et picta*. Latin: something man-made . . . born . . . something invented and painted.
94   Latin: more enduring than bronze (Horace, *Odes*, III. 30).

land. We should welcome them with great caution, with selectivity, more or less as the English nobility does. It is obvious that the stronger and better-established types of the new German (an aristocratic officer from the March of Brandenburg, for example) could have to do with them most freely. It might be of diverse interest to see whether his inherited skill in commanding and obeying (the aforementioned province is the classic case for both at the moment) could be added to, bred together with their genius for money and patience (and especially some of their spirit and spirituality, both of which are sadly wanting in the aforementioned place). But this is where I should interrupt the cheerful Germanizing of my oration, for I am already touching on my *serious* concern, the 'European problem' as I understand it, the breeding of a new caste to rule over Europe.

252

They are not a philosophical race, these Englishmen: Bacon represents an *attack* on the philosophical spirit in general; Hobbes, Hume, and Locke a century-long degradation and devaluation of the concept 'philosopher'. Kant rose and raised himself up to rebel *against* Hume; Schelling had the *right* to say of Locke: 'je méprise Locke'.[95] In their struggle against the doltish mechanistic English ideas about the world, Hegel and Schopenhauer (along with Goethe) were in agreement, those two inimical brother geniuses of philosophy who strove towards opposite poles of the German spirit and thereby did wrong by each other as only brothers can. Carlyle,[96] that rhetorician and quasi-actor, that tasteless, addlepated Carlyle knew well enough what England lacks and has always lacked; behind passionate masks he tried to hide what he knew about himself, which was what Carlyle *lacked*: real spiritual *power*, spiritual vision of real *depth* – in short, philosophy. Typically, this kind of unphilosophical race adheres strictly to Christianity: it *needs* to be disciplined by Christian 'moralizing' and humanization. Because Englishmen are gloomier, more sensual, wilful, and brutal than Germans, the coarser of the two, they are also more pious: they are simply more *in need* of Christianity. In this English Christianity, finer noses will even sense a genuine English after-smell of spleen and alcoholic excess, to cure which they have good reason to use Christianity – a subtler poison, that is, to counteract a cruder; and in clumsy peoples a subtler form of poison is progress indeed, a step on the way to spiritualization. English clumsiness and boorish solemnity are most successfully disguised or (more accurately) explained and reinterpreted by Christian gesture and prayer and the singing of psalms; and truly, in a drunken and profligate beast who has been taught to make moral grunts, once by the power of Methodism and again more recently by the 'Salvation Army', a penitent's spasm really may be the relatively highest 'human' achievement that it can aspire to: this much we can easily admit. But what also offends us about the most human Englishman is his lack of music, to speak metaphorically (and non-metaphorically): in the movements of his body and soul he has no tempo, no dance, not even a desire for tempo and dance, for 'music'. Just listen to him speak; just look at how the most beautiful Englishwomen *walk* – there are no more beautiful doves or swans in any land on earth, but when all is said and done: just listen to them sing! But I am demanding too much . . .

95   French: I despise Locke.
96   Thomas Carlyle (1795–1881), Scottish essayist and historian.

253

There are truths best perceived by mediocre minds, because they are most suited to them; there are truths that have charms and seductive powers only for mediocre spirits: we are being forced just now to embrace this perhaps unpleasant tenet, ever since the spirit of respectable, but mediocre Englishmen (I am thinking of Darwin, John Stuart Mill, and Herbert Spencer) has begun to gain the upper hand in the middle region of European taste. Indeed, who would question that it is occasionally useful for *these* kinds of spirits to be dominant? It would be a mistake to expect lofty-natured, daring spirits to be especially adept at ascertaining lots of common little facts and forcing them into conclusions: rather, as they are exceptions themselves, they do not even start out in any propitious relationship to 'rules'. In the end they have more to do than merely to perceive, and that is to *be* something new, to *signify* something new, and to *represent* new values! The chasm between knowledge and ability is perhaps greater and also more sinister than we think: a person of ability in the grand style, a creative person may have to be a person lacking in knowledge – while making scientific discoveries in the manner of Darwin, on the other hand, might require a certain narrowness, dryness, and diligent meticulousness, in short, something English. Finally, let us not forget that there has already been a time when the English, a profoundly average people, caused the European spirit to sink into an overall depression: what we call 'modern ideas' or 'eighteenth-century ideas' or 'French ideas' (that is, what the *German* spirit opposed with deep revulsion) had an English origin, there can be no doubt about that. The French were just the apes and actors of these ideas, also their best soldiers, as well as their first and most complete, unfortunate *victims*: the damnable Anglomania of 'modern ideas' has made the *âme française*[97] so thin and haggard that we can scarcely credit our memory of its sixteenth and seventeenth centuries, with their deep, passionate strength, their inventive elegance. But we must cling fiercely to this tenet of historical fairness and defend it against the moment and appearances: European *noblesse*[98] (in feeling, taste, custom – in short, in every great sense of the word) is *France's* invention and accomplishment, while European commonness, the plebeianism of modern ideas is – *England's*.

[...]

Section 9: What Is Noble?

257

In the past, every elevation of the type 'human being' was achieved by an aristocratic society – and this will always be the case: by a society that believes in a great ladder of hierarchy and value differentiation between people and that requires slavery in one sense or another. Without the *grand feeling of distance* that grows from inveterate class differences, from the ruling caste's constant view downwards onto its underlings and tools, and from its equally constant practice in obeying and commanding, in holding down and holding at arm's length – without this grand attitude, that other, more

97   French: French soul.
98   French: aristocratic nobility.

mysterious attitude could never exist, that longing for ever greater distances within the soul itself, the development of ever higher, rarer, more far-flung, extensive, spacious inner states, in short, the elevation of the type 'human being', the continual 'self-overcoming of the human',[99] to use a moral formula in a supra-moral sense. To be sure, we must not give in to any humanitarian delusions about these aristocratic societies' historical origins (that is, about the preconditions for that elevation of the type 'human'): the truth is harsh. Let us not mince words in describing to ourselves the *beginnings* of every previous higher culture on earth! People who still had a nature that was natural, barbarians in every terrible sense of the word, predatory humans, whose strength of will and desire for power were still unbroken, threw themselves upon the weaker, more well-behaved, peaceable, perhaps trading or stockbreeding races, or upon old, crumbling cultures whose remaining life-force was flickering out in a brilliant fireworks display of wit and depravity. At the beginning, the noble caste was always the barbarian caste: its dominance was not due to its physical strength primarily, but rather to its spiritual – these were the *more complete* human beings (which at every level also means the 'more complete beasts').

[. . .]

259

To refrain from injuring, abusing, or exploiting one another; to equate another person's will with our own: in a certain crude sense this can develop into good manners between individuals, if the preconditions are in place (that is, if the individuals have truly similar strength and standards and if they are united within one single social body). But if we were to try to take this principle further and possibly even make it the *basic principle of society*, it would immediately be revealed for what it is: a will to *deny* life, a principle for dissolution and decline. We must think through the reasons for this and resist all sentimental frailty: life itself *in its essence* means appropriating, injuring, overpowering those who are foreign and weaker; oppression, harshness, forcing one's own forms on others, incorporation, and at the very least, at the very mildest, exploitation – but why should we keep using this kind of language, that has from time immemorial been infused with a slanderous intent? Even that social body whose individuals, as we have just assumed above, treat one another as equals (this happens in every healthy aristocracy) must itself, if the body is vital and not moribund, do to other bodies everything that the individuals within it refrain from doing to one another: it will have to be the will to power incarnate, it will want to grow, to reach out around itself, pull towards itself, gain the upper hand – not out of some morality or immorality,[100] but because it is *alive*, and because life simply *is* the will to power. This, however, more than anything else, is what the common European consciousness resists learning; people everywhere are rhapsodizing, even under the guise of science, about future social conditions that will have lost their 'exploitative character' – to my ear that sounds as if they were promising to invent a life form that would refrain from all organic functions. 'Exploitation' is not part of a decadent or imperfect, primitive society: it is part of the *fundamental nature* of living things, as its fundamental organic function; it is a

---

99   In German: *"Selbst-Überwindung des Menschen."*
100   In German: *Moralität oder Immoralität.*

consequence of the true will to power, which is simply the will to life. Assuming that this is innovative as theory – as reality it is the *original fact* of all history: let us at least be this honest with ourselves!

260

While perusing the many subtler and cruder moral codes that have prevailed or still prevail on earth thus far, I found that certain traits regularly recurred in combination, linked to one another – until finally two basic types were revealed and a fundamental difference leapt out at me. There are *master moralities* and *slave moralities*.[101] I would add at once that in all higher and more complex cultures, there are also apparent attempts to mediate between the two moralities, and even more often a confusion of the two and a mutual misunderstanding, indeed sometimes even their violent juxtaposition – even in the same person, within one single breast. Moral value distinctions have emerged either from among a masterful kind, pleasantly aware of how it differed from those whom it mastered, or else from among the mastered, those who were to varying degrees slaves or dependants. In the first case, when it is the masters who define the concept 'good', it is the proud, exalted states of soul that are thought to distinguish and define the hierarchy. The noble person keeps away from those beings who express the opposite of these elevated, proud inner states: he despises them. Let us note immediately that in this first kind of morality the opposition 'good' and 'bad' means about the same thing as 'noble' and 'despicable' – the opposition 'good' and '*evil*' has a different origin. The person who is cowardly or anxious or petty or concerned with narrow utility is despised; likewise the distrustful person with his constrained gaze, the self-disparager, the craven kind of person who endures maltreatment, the importunate flatterer, and above all the liar: all aristocrats hold the fundamental conviction that the common people are liars. 'We truthful ones' – that is what the ancient Greek nobility called themselves. It is obvious that moral value distinctions everywhere are first attributed to *people* and only later and in a derivative fashion applied to *actions*: for that reason moral historians commit a crass error by starting with questions such as: 'Why do we praise an empathetic action?' The noble type of person feels *himself* as determining value – he does not need approval, he judges that 'what is harmful to me is harmful per se', he knows that he is the one who causes things to be revered in the first place, he *creates values*. Everything that he knows of himself he reveres: this kind of moral code is self-glorifying. In the foreground is a feeling of fullness, of overflowing power, of happiness in great tension, an awareness of a wealth that would like to bestow and share – the noble person will also help the unfortunate, but not, or not entirely, out of pity, but rather from the urgency created by an excess of power. The noble person reveres the power in himself, and also his power over himself, his ability to speak and to be silent, to enjoy the practice of severity and harshness towards himself and to respect everything that is severe and harsh. 'Wotan placed a harsh heart within my breast,' goes a line in an old Scandinavian saga: that is how it is written from the heart of a proud Viking – and rightly so. For this kind of a person is proud

---

101   In German: *Herren-Moral und Sklaven-Moral.* Nietzsche first introduces this contrast in *HH* 45, and it plays a major role in *GM* I. Throughout this section he uses the terms *Moral* and *Moralität.*

not to be made for pity; and so the hero of the saga adds a warning: 'If your heart is not harsh when you are young, it will never become harsh.' The noble and brave people who think like this are the most removed from that other moral code which sees the sign of morality in pity or altruistic behaviour or *désintéressement*;[102] belief in ourselves, pride in ourselves, a fundamental hostility and irony towards 'selflessness' – these are as surely a part of a noble morality as caution and a slight disdain towards empathetic feelings and 'warm hearts'. It is the powerful who *understand* how to revere, it is their art form, their realm of invention. Great reverence for old age and for origins (all law is based upon this twofold reverence), belief in ancestors and prejudice in their favour and to the disadvantage of the next generation – these are typical in the morality of the powerful; and if, conversely, people of 'modern ideas' believe in progress and 'the future' almost by instinct and show an increasing lack of respect for old age, that alone suffices to reveal the ignoble origin of these 'ideas'. Most of all, however, the master morality is foreign and embarrassing to current taste because of the severity of its fundamental principle: that we have duties only towards our peers, and that we may treat those of lower rank, anything foreign, as we think best or 'as our heart dictates' or in any event 'beyond good and evil' – pity and the like should be thought of in this context. The ability and duty to feel enduring gratitude or vengefulness (both only within a circle of equals), subtlety in the forms of retribution, a refined concept of friendship, a certain need for enemies (as drainage channels for the emotions of envy, combativeness, arrogance – in essence, in order to be a good *friend*): these are the typical signs of a noble morality, which, as we have suggested, is not the morality of 'modern ideas' and is therefore difficult to sympathize with these days, also difficult to dig out and uncover. It is different with the second type of morality, *slave morality*. Assuming that the raped, the oppressed, the suffering, the shackled, the weary, the insecure engage in moralizing, what will their moral value judgements have in common? They will probably express a pessimistic suspicion about the whole human condition, and they might condemn the human being along with his condition. The slave's eye does not readily apprehend the virtues of the powerful: he is sceptical and distrustful, he is *keenly* distrustful of everything that the powerful revere as 'good' – he would like to convince himself that even their happiness is not genuine. Conversely, those qualities that serve to relieve the sufferers' existence are brought into relief and bathed in light: this is where pity, a kind, helpful hand, a warm heart, patience, diligence, humility, friendliness are revered – for in this context, these qualities are most useful and practically the only means of enduring an oppressive existence. Slave morality is essentially a morality of utility. It is upon this hearth that the famous opposition 'good' and '*evil*' originates – power and dangerousness, a certain fear-inducing, subtle strength that keeps contempt from surfacing, are translated by experience into evil. According to slave morality, then, the 'evil' person evokes fear; according to master morality, it is exactly the 'good' person who evokes fear and wants to evoke it, while the 'bad' person is felt to be despicable. The opposition comes to a head when, in terms of slave morality, a hint of condescension (it may be slight and well intentioned) clings even to those whom this morality designates as 'good', since within a slave mentality a good person must in any event be *harmless*: he is good-natured,

---

102   French: disinterestedness.

easily deceived, perhaps a bit stupid, a *bonhomme*.[103] Wherever slave morality gains the upper hand, language shows a tendency to make a closer association of the words 'good' and 'stupid'. A last fundamental difference: the longing for *freedom*, an instinct[104] for the happiness and nuances of feeling free, is as necessarily a part of slave morals and morality as artistic, rapturous reverence and devotion invariably signal an aristocratic mentality and judgement. From this we can immediately understand why *passionate* love (our European speciality) absolutely must have a noble origin: the Provençal poet-knights are acknowledged to have invented it, those splendid, inventive people of the '*gai saber*'[105] to whom Europe owes so much – virtually its very self.

[. . .]

284

To go through life with tremendous, proud calmness; always beyond . . . To feel or not to feel our emotions, our Pros and Cons, as we see fit, to condescend to them for hours at a time; to *sit upon* them, as we do upon a horse, and often an ass – for we need to know how to capitalize on their stupidity as well as their fire. To hold on to our three hundred foreground reasons; also our dark glasses, for there are times when no one may look into our eyes, and even less into our 'reasons'. And to choose to keep company with that roguish and cheerful vice Courtesy. And to remain master of our four virtues: courage, insight, sympathy, solitude. For we think solitude is a virtue, a sublime, exceeding need for cleanliness, born from knowing what unavoidably unclean things must transpire when people touch one another ('in company'). Somehow, somewhere, sometime, every commonality makes us – 'common'.

285

The greatest events and thoughts (but the greatest thoughts are the greatest events) are the last to be understood: the generations that live contemporaneously with these events do not *experience* them: they live past them. Something similar takes place as in the heavens. The light of the farthest stars is the last to reach human beings; and until it has arrived, people *deny* that out there, there are – stars. 'How many centuries does a spirit need in order to be understood?' – that, too, is a measuring stick; with it, too, we can create the sort of hierarchy and etiquette required – for spirit and star.

286

'Up here the view is clear, the spirit exalted.'[106] But there is an opposite kind of person who is likewise at the top and likewise has a clear view – but looks *down*.

287

What is noble? What meaning does the word 'noble' still have for us today? As the rule of the rabble begins, under this heavy, cloudy sky that makes everything opaque and leaden, how is a noble person revealed, by what do we recognize him? It is not

---

103   French: simple man.
104   In German: *Instinkt*.
105   Provençal: "gay science."
106   See Goethe, *Faust II*, l. 11990f.

his actions that identify him (actions are always ambiguous, always unfathomable). Nor is it his 'works'. There are plenty of artists and scholars these days whose works reveal that they are motivated by a great desire to be noble: but just this very need *for* nobility is fundamentally different from the needs of the noble soul itself, and virtually the eloquent and dangerous sign of its absence. It is not works, it is *faith* that is decisive here and establishes a hierarchy, to take up an old religious formula again in a new and deeper sense: some fundamental certainty of a noble soul about itself, something that cannot be sought or found or, perhaps, lost. *The noble soul reveres itself.*

[. . .]

289

We always hear something of the echo of desolation in a hermit's writings, something of the whispering tone and shy, roundabout glance of solitude; out of his mightiest words, even out of his screams, we still hear the sound of a new and dangerous sort of silence, silencing. Anyone who has sat alone, in intimate dissension and dialogue with his soul, year in and year out, by day and by night; anyone whose cave (which might be a labyrinth, but also a gold mine) has turned him into a cave-bear or a treasure-digger or a treasure-keep and dragon; this person's ideas will themselves finally take on a characteristic twilight colour, an odour fully as much of the depths as of decay, something uncommunicative and stubborn that gusts coldly at every passer-by. The hermit does not believe that any philosopher (given that all philosophers have always first been hermits) ever expressed his true and final opinions in books: don't we write books precisely in order to hide what we keep hidden? Indeed, he will doubt whether a philosopher is even *capable* of 'final and true' opinions, whether at the back of his every cave a deeper cave is lying, is bound to lie – a wider, stranger, richer world over every surface, an abyss behind his every ground, beneath his every 'grounding'.[107] Every philosophy is a foreground philosophy – this is a hermit's judgement: 'There is something arbitrary about the fact that *he* stopped just here, looked back, looked around, that he did not dig deeper *just here*, but set down his spade – and there is also something suspicious about it.' Every philosophy also *conceals* a philosophy; every opinion is also a hiding place, every word also a mask.

290

Every deep thinker is more afraid of being understood than of being misunderstood. In the latter case his vanity may suffer; but in the former it will be his heart, his sympathy, forever saying, 'Oh, why do all of *you* also want to have it as hard as I?'

291

Human beings (complex, mendacious, artificial, impenetrable animals, and disturbing to other animals less because of their strength than because of their cunning and cleverness) invented the good conscience so that they could begin to enjoy their souls by *simplifying* them; and all of morality is one long, bold falsification that enables us to take what pleasure we can in observing the soul. From this vantage point, there may be much *more* to the concept of 'art' than we usually think.

---

107   The German terms used here for "abyss," "ground," and "grounding" are, respectively, *Abgrund, Gründe,* and *Begründung.*

292

A philosopher: that is a person who is constantly experiencing, seeing, hearing, suspecting, hoping, dreaming extraordinary things; who is struck by his own thoughts as if they came from outside, from above or below, as *his* sort of happenings and lightning bolts; who may even be himself a thunderstorm, going about pregnant with new lightning; an ominous person, ringed round by roaring and rumbling, gaping and sinister. A philosopher: alas, a being who often runs away from himself, is often afraid of himself – but too curious not to 'come to himself' eventually . . .

[. . .]

295

The genius of the heart, a heart of the kind belonging to that great secretive one, the tempter god and born Pied Piper of the conscience whose voice knows how to descend into the underworld of every soul, who does not utter a word or send a glance without its having a crease and aspect that entices, whose mastery consists in part in knowing how to seem – and seem not what he is, but rather what those who follow him take as one *more* coercion to press ever closer to him, to follow him ever more inwardly and completely: the genius of the heart that silences everything loud and self-satisfied and teaches it how to listen; that smoothes out rough souls and gives them a taste of a new longing (to lie still like a mirror so that the deep sky can mirror itself upon them); the genius of the heart, that teaches the foolish and over-hasty hand to hesitate and to grasp more daintily; that guesses the hidden and forgotten treasure, the drop of kindness and sweet spirituality lying under thick, turbid ice and is a divining rod for every speck of gold that has long lain buried in some dungeon of great mud and sand; the genius of the heart, from whose touch everyone goes forth the richer, neither reprieved nor surprised, not as if delighted or depressed by another's goodness, but rather richer in themselves, newer than before, opened up, breathed upon and sounded out by a warm wind, more unsure, perhaps, more brooding, breakable, broken, but full of hopes that still remain nameless, full of new willing and streaming, full of new not-willing and back-streaming . . . but my friends, what am I doing? Who is it that I am telling you about? Have I forgotten myself so much that I have not even told you his name? Unless, of course, you have already guessed who this questionable spirit and god may be, who demands this kind of *praise*. Like everyone who since childhood has always been on the road and abroad, I too have had some strange and not necessarily harmless spirits run across my path, but especially the one I was just speaking about; and he has come again and again, the god *Dionysus*, no less, that great ambiguous tempter god, to whom, as you know, I once offered my first-born in all secrecy and reverence.[108] It seems to me that I was the last to *sacrifice* to him, for I found no one who understood what I was doing then. Meanwhile I learned much, all too much more about this god's philosophy and, as I mentioned, from mouth to mouth – I, the last disciple and initiate of the god Dionysus, may I now be finally

---

108   Reference to *The Birth of Tragedy*. In the post-*Zarathustra* period Nietzsche increasingly identifies with Dionysus, a process culminating in the last words of *Ecce Homo* and the final letters. See *EH* IV. 9 and *Four Letters* note 22 below.

allowed to begin to give you, my friends, a little taste, as much as I am permitted, of this philosophy? In an undertone, of course: for we are talking about much that is secret, new, strange, curious, uncanny. Just the very fact that Dionysus is a philosopher and that gods can philosophize too, seems to be something new and not without its dangers, perhaps making philosophers suspicious – you, my friends, have less to object to, unless the news should come too late and at the wrong hour: for they've informed me that you do not like to believe in God or gods these days. And perhaps to tell my tale candidly, I must go further than the severity of your listening habits would always like? Certainly the god I named went further in such dialogues, much further, and always kept many steps ahead of me . . . Indeed, if I were permitted to follow the human custom and call him by beautiful, ceremonious, splendid, virtuous names, I would have to speak in very grand terms about his courage as an explorer and discoverer, his daring eloquence, truthfulness, and love of wisdom. But this kind of a god has no use for all this worthy pomp and rubbish. 'Keep this,' he would say, 'for yourself and your own kind and whoever else may need it! I – have no reason to cover my nakedness!' Do you think that this kind of godhead and philosopher may be lacking in shame? Thus, he once said, 'In certain cases I love human beings' (and he was alluding to Ariadne, who was present); 'to me, human beings are pleasant, brave, inventive animals who do not have their equal on earth; they can find their way in any labyrinth. I am well disposed towards them: I often think about how I can help them go forward and make them stronger, deeper, and more evil than they are.' 'Stronger, deeper, and more evil?' I asked, frightened. 'Yes,' he said once again, 'stronger, deeper, and more evil – more beautiful, too.' And at that the tempter god smiled his halcyon smile, as if he had just uttered a charming compliment. This shows us two things at once: shame is not the only thing that this godhead lacks; and there are generally good reasons to assume that in some respects all the gods could do with some human schooling. We humans are – more human . . .'[109]

296

Oh, what are you really, all of you, my written and depicted thoughts! Not so long ago, you were still so colourful, young, and malicious, so full of thorns and covert spices that you made me sneeze and laugh – and now? You've already cast off your novelty and some of you, I fear, are at the point of becoming truths: they already look so immortal, so heart-breakingly righteous, so boring! And was it not ever thus? What things do we really write down and depict, we mandarins with our Chinese brush, we immortalizers of things that *can* be written, what things are really left for us to paint, after all? Alas, only that which is about to wither and beginning to smell rank! Alas, only exhausted, retreating storms and late, yellowed feelings! Alas, only birds that have flown themselves weary, flown astray, and have let themselves be caught in someone's hand – *our* hand! We immortalize what cannot live or fly any longer, weary and crumbling things all! And it is only for your *afternoon*, my written and depicted thoughts, that I still have paint, much paint perhaps, many colourful tender words and fifty yellows and browns and greens and reds – but they will not help anyone to guess how you looked in your morning, you sudden sparks and miracles of my solitude, my old, beloved – *wicked* thoughts!

109   In German: *Wir Menschen sind – menschlicher.*

19

The Gay Science, Book V (1887)

343

The meaning of our cheerfulness. – The greatest recent event – that "God is dead," that the belief in the Christian god has become unbelievable – is already beginning to cast its first shadows over Europe. For the few at least, whose eyes – the *suspicion* in whose eyes is strong and subtle enough for this spectacle, some sun seems to have set and some ancient and profound trust has been turned into doubt; to them our old world must appear daily more like evening, more mistrustful, stranger, "older." But in the main one may say: The event itself is far too great, too distant, too remote from the multitude's capacity for comprehension even for the tidings of it to be thought of as having *arrived* as yet. Much less may one suppose that many people know as yet *what* this event really means – and how much must collapse now that this faith has been undermined because it was built upon this faith, propped up by it, grown into it; for example, the whole of our European morality. This long plenitude and sequence of breakdown, destruction, ruin, and cataclysm that is now impending – who could guess enough of it today to be compelled to play the teacher and advance proclaimer of this monstrous logic of terror, the prophet of a gloom and an eclipse of the sun whose like has probably never yet occurred on earth? Even we born guessers of riddles who are, as it were, waiting on the mountains, posted between today and tomorrow, stretched in the contradiction between today and tomorrow, we firstlings and premature births of the coming century, to whom the shadows that must soon envelop Europe really *should* have appeared by now – why is it that even we look forward to the approaching gloom without any real sense of involvement and above all without any worry and fear for *ourselves*? Are we perhaps still too much under the impression of the *initial consequences* of this event – and these initial consequences, the consequences for *ourselves*, are quite the opposite of what one might perhaps expect: They are not at all sad and gloomy but rather like a new and scarcely describable kind of light, happiness, relief, exhilaration, encouragement, dawn. Indeed, we philosophers and "free spirits" feel, when we hear the news that "the old god is dead," as if a new dawn shone on us; our heart overflows with gratitude, amazement, premonitions, expectation. At long last the horizon appears free to us again, even if it should not be bright; at long last our ships may venture out again, venture out to face any danger; all the daring of the lover of knowledge is permitted again; the sea, *our* sea, lies open again; perhaps there has never yet been such an "open sea." –

344

How we, too, are still pious. – In science convictions have no rights of citizenship, as one says with good reason. Only when they decide to descend to the modesty of hypotheses, of a provisional experimental point of view, of a regulative fiction, they may be granted admission and even a certain value in the realm of knowledge – though always with the restriction that they remain under police supervision, under the police of mistrust. – But does this not mean, if you consider it more precisely, that a conviction may obtain admission to science only when it *ceases* to be a conviction? Would it not be the first step in the discipline of the scientific spirit that one would not permit oneself any more convictions? Probably this is so; only we still have to ask: *To make it possible for this discipline to begin*, must there not be some prior conviction – even one that is so commanding and unconditional that it sacrifices all other convictions to itself? We see that science also rests on a faith; there simply is no science "without presuppositions." The question whether *truth* is needed must not only have been affirmed in advance, but affirmed to such a degree that the principle, the faith, the conviction finds expression: "*Nothing* is needed *more* than truth, and in relation to it everything else has only second-rate value." This unconditional will to truth – what is it? Is it the will *not to allow oneself to be deceived*? Or is it the will *not to deceive*? For the will to truth could be interpreted in the second way, too – if only the special case "I do not want to deceive myself" is subsumed under the generalization "I do not want to deceive." But why not deceive? But why not allow oneself to be deceived? Note that the reasons for the former principle belong to an altogether different realm from those for the second. One does not want to allow oneself to be deceived because one assumes that it is harmful, dangerous, calamitous to be deceived. In this sense, science would be a long-range prudence, a caution, a utility; but one could object in all fairness: How is that? Is wanting not to allow oneself to be deceived really less harmful, less dangerous, less calamitous? What do you know in advance of the character of existence to be able to decide whether the greater advantage is on the side of the unconditionally mistrustful or of the unconditionally trusting? But if both should be required, much trust *as well as* much mistrust, from where would science then be permitted to take its unconditional faith or conviction on which it rests, that truth is more important than any other thing, including every other conviction? Precisely this conviction could never have come into being if both truth and untruth constantly proved to be useful, which is the case. Thus – the faith in science, which after all exists undeniably, cannot owe its origin to such a calculus of utility; it must have originated *in spite of* the fact that the disutility and dangerousness of "the will to truth," of "truth at any price" is proved to it constantly. "At any price": how well we understand these words once we have offered and slaughtered one faith after another on this altar! Consequently, "will to truth" does *not* mean "I will not allow myself to be deceived" but – there is no alternative – "I will not deceive, not even myself"; *and with that we stand on moral ground*. For you only have to ask yourself carefully, "Why do you not want to deceive?" especially if it should seem – and it does seem! – as if life aimed at semblance, meaning error, deception, simulation, delusion, self-delusion, and when the great sweep of life has actually always shown itself to be on the side of the most unscrupulous *polytropoi*.[1]

---

1 Greek: "much-turned," i.e. much-traveled, versatile, cunning, or manifold. Applied to Odysseus in the first line of Homer's *Odyssey*.

Charitably interpreted, such a resolve might perhaps be a quixotism, a minor slightly mad enthusiasm; but it might also be something more serious, namely, a principle that is hostile to life and destructive. – "Will to truth" – that might be a concealed will to death. Thus the question "Why science?" leads back to the moral problem: *Why have morality at all* when life, nature, and history are "not moral"? No doubt, those who are truthful in that audacious and ultimate sense that is presupposed by the faith in science *thus affirm another world* than the world of life, nature, and history; and insofar as they affirm this "other world" – look, must they not by the same token negate its counterpart, this world, *our* world? – But you will have gathered what I am driving at, namely, that it is still a *metaphysical faith* upon which our faith in science rests – that even we seekers after knowledge today, we godless anti-metaphysicians still take our fire, too, from the flame lit by a faith that is thousands of years old, that Christian faith which was also the faith of Plato, that God is the truth, that truth is divine. – But what if this should become more and more incredible, if nothing should prove to be divine any more unless it were error, blindness, the lie – if God himself should prove to be our most enduring lie? –

345

Morality[2] *as a problem.* – The lack of personality always takes its revenge: A weakened, thin, extinguished personality that denies itself is no longer fit for anything good – least of all for philosophy. "Selflessness" has no value either in heaven or on earth. All great problems demand *great love*, and of that only strong, round, secure spirits who have a firm grip on themselves are capable. It makes the most telling difference whether a thinker has a personal relationship to his problems and finds in them his destiny, his distress, and his greatest happiness, or an "impersonal" one, meaning that he can do no better than to touch them and grasp them with the antennae of cold, curious thought. In the latter case nothing will come of it; that much one can promise in advance, for even if great problems should allow themselves to be *grasped* by them they would not permit frogs and weaklings to *hold on* to them; such has been their taste from time immemorial – a taste, incidentally, that they share with all redoubtable females. Why is it then that I have never yet encountered anybody, not even in books, who approached morality in this personal way and who knew morality as a problem, and this problem as his own personal distress, torment, voluptuousness, and passion? It is evident that up to now morality was no problem at all but, on the contrary, precisely that on which after all mistrust, discord, and contradiction one could agree – the hallowed place of peace where our thinkers took a rest even from themselves, took a deep breath, and felt revived. I see nobody who ventured a *critique* of moral valuations; I miss even the slightest attempts of scientific curiosity, of the refined, experimental imagination of psychologists and historians that readily anticipates a problem and catches it in flight without quite knowing what it has caught. I have scarcely detected a few meager preliminary efforts to explore the *history of the origins* of these feelings and valuations (which is something quite different from a critique and again different from a history of ethical systems). In one particular case I have done everything to encourage a sympathy and talent for this kind of history – in vain, as it seems to me today.[3] These historians of

---

2   In German: *Moral*.
3   Allusion to Paul Rée. See *HH* notes 19–20 above.

morality (mostly Englishmen) do not amount to much. Usually they themselves are still quite unsuspectingly obedient to one particular morality and, without knowing it, serve that as shield-bearers and followers – for example, by sharing that popular superstition of Christian Europe which people keep mouthing so guilelessly to this day, that what is characteristic of moral actions is selflessness, self-sacrifice, or sympathy and pity. Their usual mistaken premise is that they affirm some consensus of the nations, at least of tame nations, concerning certain principles of morals, and then they infer from this that these principles must be unconditionally binding also for you and me; or, conversely, they see the truth that among different nations moral valuations are *necessarily* different and then infer from this that *no* morality is at all binding. Both procedures are equally childish. The mistake made by the more refined among them is that they uncover and criticize the perhaps foolish opinions of a people about their morality, or of humanity about all human morality – opinions about its origin, religious sanction, the superstition of free will, and things of that sort – and then suppose that they have criticized the morality itself. But the value of a command "thou shalt" is still fundamentally different from and independent of such opinions about it and the weeds of error that may have overgrown it – just as certainly as the value of a medication for a sick person is completely independent of whether he thinks about medicine scientifically or the way old women do. Even if a morality has grown out of an error, the realization of this fact would not as much as touch the problem of its value. Thus nobody up to now has examined the *value* of that most famous of all medicines which is called morality; and the first step would be – for once to *question* it. Well then, precisely this is our task. –

346

Our question mark. – But you do not understand this? Indeed, people will have trouble understanding us. We are looking for words; perhaps we are also looking for ears. Who are we anyway? If we simply called ourselves, using an old expression, godless, or unbelievers, or perhaps immoralists, we do not believe that this would even come close to designating us: We are all three in such an advanced stage that one – that *you*, my curious friends – could never comprehend how we feel at this point. Ours is no longer the bitterness and passion of the person who has torn himself away and still feels compelled to turn his unbelief into a new belief, a purpose, a martyrdom. We have become cold, hard, and tough in the realization that the way of this world is anything but divine; even by human standards it is not rational, merciful, or just. We know it well, the world in which we live is ungodly, immoral, "inhuman"; we have interpreted it far too long in a false and mendacious way, in accordance with the wishes of our reverence, which is to say, according to our *needs*. For man is a reverent animal. But he is also mistrustful; and that the world is *not* worth what we thought it was, that is about as certain as anything of which our mistrust has finally got hold. The more mistrust, the more philosophy. We are far from claiming that the world is worth *less*; indeed it would seem laughable to us today if man were to insist on inventing values that were supposed to *excel* the value of the actual world. This is precisely what we have turned our backs on as an extravagant aberration of human vanity and unreason that for a long time was not recognized as such. It found its final expression in modern pessimism, and a more ancient and stronger expression in the teaching of Buddha; but it is part of Christianity also, if more doubtfully and ambiguously so but not for that reason any less seductive. The whole pose of "man *against* the world," of man as a "world-negating" principle, of man as the measure of the value of things, as judge of the world who in the end places existence itself upon his scales and finds it wanting – the monstrous insipidity of this pose has finally come home to us and we are sick of it. We laugh as soon as we encounter the juxtaposition of "man *and* world," separated by the sublime presumption of the little word "and." But look, when we laugh like that, have we not simply carried the contempt for man one step further? And thus also pessimism, the contempt for that existence which is knowable by *us*? Have we not exposed ourselves to the suspicion of an opposition – an opposition between the world in which we were at home up to now with our reverences that perhaps made it possible for us to *endure* life, and another world *that consists of us* – an inexorable, fundamental, and deepest suspicion about ourselves that is more and more gaining worse and worse control of us Europeans and that could easily confront coming generations with the terrifying Either/Or: "Either abolish your reverences or – *yourselves!*" The latter would be nihilism; but would not the former also be – nihilism? – This is *our* question mark.

[. . .]

349

Once more the origin of scholars. – The wish to preserve oneself is the symptom of a condition of distress, of a limitation of the really fundamental instinct of life which aims at *the expansion of power* and, wishing for that, frequently risks and even sacrifices self-preservation. It should be considered symptomatic when some philosophers – for example, Spinoza who was consumptive – considered the instinct of self-preservation decisive and *had* to see it that way; for they were individuals in conditions of distress. That our modern natural sciences have become so thoroughly entangled in this Spinozistic dogma (most recently and worst of all, Darwinism with its incomprehensibly onesided doctrine of the "struggle for existence") is probably due to the origins of most natural scientists: In this respect they belong to the "common people"; their ancestors were poor and undistinguished people who knew the difficulties of survival only too well at firsthand. The whole of English Darwinism breathes something like the musty air of English overpopulation, like the smell of the distress and overcrowding of small people. But a natural scientist should come out of his human nook; and in nature it is not conditions of distress that are *dominant* but overflow and squandering, even to the point of absurdity. The struggle for existence is only an *exception*, a temporary restriction of the will to life. The great and small struggle always revolves around superiority, around growth and expansion, around power – in accordance with the will to power which is the will of life.

[. . .]

354

On the "genius of the species." – The problem of consciousness (more precisely, of becoming conscious of something) confronts us only when we begin to comprehend how we could dispense with it; and now physiology and the history of animals place us at the beginning of such comprehension (it took them two centuries to catch up with *Leibniz's* suspicion which soared ahead). For we could think, feel, will, and remember, and we could also "act" in every sense of that word, and yet none of all this would have to "enter our consciousness" (as one says metaphorically). The whole of life would be possible without, as it were, seeing itself in a mirror. Even now, for that matter, by far the greatest portion of our life actually takes place without this mirror effect; and this is true even of our thinking, feeling, and willing life, however offensive this may sound to older philosophers. *For what purpose*, then, any consciousness at all when it is in the main *superfluous*? Now, if you are willing to listen to my answer and the perhaps extravagant surmise that it involves, it seems to me as if the subtlety and strength of consciousness always were proportionate to a man's (or animal's) *capacity for communication*, and as if this capacity in turn were proportionate to the *need for communication*. But this last point is not to be understood as if the individual human being who happens to be a master in communicating and making understandable his needs must also be most dependent on others in his needs. But it does seem to me as if it were that way when we consider whole races and chains of generations: Where need and distress have forced men for a long time to communicate and to understand each other quickly and subtly, the ultimate result is an excess of this strength and art of communication – as it were, a capacity that has gradually been accumulated and now waits for an heir who might squander it. (Those who are called artists are these heirs; so are orators, preachers, writers – all of them people who always come at the end of a long chain, "late born" every one of them in the best sense of that word and, as I have said, by their nature squanderers.) Supposing that this observation is correct, I may now proceed to the surmise that *consciousness has developed only under the pressure of the need for communication*; that from the start it was needed and useful only between human beings (particularly between those who commanded and those who obeyed); and that it also developed only in proportion to the degree of this utility. Consciousness is really only a net of communication between human beings; it is only as such that it had to develop; a solitary human being who lived like a beast of prey would not have needed it. That our actions, thoughts, feelings, and movements enter our own consciousness – at least a part of them – that is the result of a "must" that for a terribly long time lorded it over man. As the most endangered animal, he *needed* help and protection, he needed his peers, he had to learn to express his distress and to make himself understood; and for all of this he needed "consciousness" first of all, he needed to "know" himself what distressed him, he needed to "know" how he felt, he needed to "know" what he thought. For, to say it once more: Man, like every living being, thinks continually without knowing it; the thinking that rises to *consciousness* is only the smallest part of all this – the most superficial and worst part – for only this conscious thinking *takes the form of words, which is to say signs of communication*, and this fact uncovers the origin of consciousness. In brief, the development of language and the development of consciousness (*not* of reason but merely of the way reason enters consciousness) go hand in hand. Add to this that not only language serves as a bridge between human beings but also a mien, a pressure, a gesture. The emergence of our sense impressions into our own consciousness, the ability to fix them and, as it were, exhibit them externally, increased proportionately with the need to communicate them to *others* by means of signs. The human being inventing signs is at the same time the human being who becomes ever more keenly conscious of himself. It was only as a social animal that man acquired self-consciousness – which he is still in the process of doing, more and more. My idea is, as you see, that consciousness does not really belong to man's individual existence but rather to his social or herd nature; that, as follows from this, it has developed subtlety only insofar as this is required by social or herd utility. Consequently, given the best will in the world to understand ourselves as individually as possible, "to know ourselves," each of us will always succeed in becoming conscious only of what is not individual but "average." Our thoughts themselves are continually governed by the character of consciousness – by the "genius of the species" that commands it – and translated back into the perspective of the herd. Fundamentally, all our actions are altogether incomparably personal, unique, and infinitely individual; there is no doubt of that. But as soon as we translate them into consciousness *they no longer seem to be*. This is the essence of phenomenalism and perspectivism as *I* understand them: Owing to the nature of *animal consciousness*, the world of which we can become conscious is only a surface- and sign-world, a world that is made common and meaner; whatever becomes conscious *becomes* by the same token shallow, thin, relatively stupid, general, sign, herd signal; all becoming conscious involves a great and thorough corruption, falsification, reduction to superficialities, and generalization. Ultimately, the growth of consciousness becomes a danger; and anyone who lives among the most conscious Europeans even knows that it is a disease. You will guess that it is not the opposition of subject and object that concerns me here: This distinction I leave to the epistemologists who have become entangled in the snares of grammar (the metaphysics of the people). It is even less the opposition of "thing-in-itself" and appearance; for we do not "know" nearly enough to be entitled to any such distinction. We simply lack any organ for knowledge, for "truth": we "know" (or believe or imagine) just as much as may be *useful* in the interests of the human herd, the species; and even what is here called "utility" is ultimately also a mere belief, something imaginary, and perhaps precisely that most calamitous stupidity of which we shall perish some day.

355

The origin of our concept of "knowledge." – I take this explanation from the street. I heard one of the common people say, "he knew me right away." Then I asked myself: What is it that the common people take for knowledge? What do they want when they want "knowledge"? Nothing more than this: Something strange is to be reduced to something *familiar*. And we philosophers – have we really meant *more* than this when we have spoken of knowledge? What is familiar means what we are used to so that we no longer marvel at it, our everyday, some rule in which we are stuck, anything at all in which we feel at home. Look, isn't our need for knowledge precisely this need for the familiar, the will to uncover under everything strange, unusual, and questionable something that no longer disturbs us? Is it not the *instinct of fear* that bids us to know? And is the jubilation of those who attain knowledge not the jubilation over the restoration of a sense of security? Here is a philosopher who fancied that the world was "known" when he had reduced it to the "idea."[4] Was it not because the "idea" was so familiar to him and he was so well used to it – because he hardly was afraid of the "idea" any more? How easily these men of knowledge are satisfied! Just have a look at their principles and their solutions of the world riddle with this in mind!

4   In German: "*Idee*."

When they find something in things – under them, or behind them – that is unfortunately quite familiar to us, such as our multiplication tables or our logic, or our willing and desiring – how happy they are right away! For "what is familiar is known": on this they are agreed. Even the most cautious among them suppose that what is familiar is at least *more easily knowable* than what is strange, and that, for example, sound method demands that we start from the "inner world," from the "facts of consciousness," because this world is *more familiar to us*. Error of errors! What is familiar is what we are used to; and what we are used to is most difficult to "know" – that is, to see as a problem; that is, to see as strange, as distant, as "outside us." The great certainty of the natural sciences in comparison with psychology and the critique of the elements of consciousness – one might almost say, with the *unnatural* sciences – is due precisely to the fact that they choose for their object what is *strange*, while it is almost contradictory and absurd to even *try* to choose for an object what is not-strange.

356

How things will become ever more "artistic" in Europe. – Even today, in our time of transition when so many factors cease to compel men, the care to make a living still compels almost all male Europeans to adopt a particular *role*, their so-called occupation. A few retain the freedom, a merely apparent freedom, to choose this role for themselves; for most men it is chosen. The result is rather strange. As they attain a more advanced age, almost all Europeans confound themselves with their role; they become the victims of their own "good performance"; they themselves have forgotten how much accidents, moods, and caprice disposed of them when the question of their "vocation" was decided – and how many other roles they might perhaps have been *able* to play; for now it is too late. Considered more deeply, the role has actually *become* character; and art, nature. There have been ages when men believed with rigid confidence, even with piety, in their predestination for precisely this occupation, precisely this way of earning a living, and simply refused to acknowledge the element of accident, role, and caprice. With the help of this faith, classes, guilds, and hereditary trade privileges managed to erect those monsters of social pyramids that distinguish the Middle Ages and to whose credit one can adduce at least one thing: durability (and duration is a first-rate value on earth). But there are opposite ages, really democratic, where people give up this faith, and a certain cocky faith and opposite point of view advance more and more into the foreground – the Athenian faith that first becomes noticeable in the Periclean age, the faith of the Americans today that is more and more becoming the European faith as well: The individual becomes convinced that he can do just about everything and *can manage almost any role*, and everybody experiments with himself, improvises, makes new experiments, enjoys his experiments; and all nature ceases and becomes art. After accepting this *role faith* – an artist's faith, if you will – the Greeks, as is well known, went step for step through a rather odd metamorphosis that does not merit imitation in all respects: *They really became actors.* As such they enchanted and overcame all the world and finally even "the power that had overcome the world" (for the *Graeculus histrio*[5] vanquished Rome, and *not*, as innocents usually say, Greek culture). But what I fear, what is so palpable that today one could grasp it with one's

5   Latin: little Greek actor. *Graeculus* was a term used ironically by the Romans.

hands, if one felt like grasping it, is that we modern men are even now pretty far along on the same road; and whenever a human being begins to discover how he is playing a role and how he *can* be an actor, he *becomes* an actor. With this a new human flora and fauna emerge that could never have grown in more solid and limited ages; or at least they would be left there "below" under the ban and suspicion of lacking honor. It is thus that the maddest and most interesting ages of history always emerge, when the "actors," *all* kinds of actors, become the real masters. As this happens, another human type is disadvantaged more and more and finally made impossible; above all, the great "architects": The strength to build becomes paralyzed; the courage to make plans that encompass the distant future is discouraged; those with a genius for organization become scarce: who would still dare to undertake projects that would require thousands of years for their completion? For what is dying out is the fundamental faith that would enable us to calculate, to promise, to anticipate the future in plans of such scope, and to sacrifice the future to them – namely, the faith that man has value and meaning only insofar as he is *a stone in a great edifice*; and to that end he must be *solid* first of all, a "stone" – and above all not an actor! To say it briefly (for a long time people will still keep silent about it): What will not be built any more henceforth, and *cannot* be built any more, is – a society in the old sense of that word; to build that, everything is lacking, above all the material. *All of us are no longer material for a society*; this is a truth for which the time has come. It is a matter of indifference to me that at present the most myopic, perhaps most honest, but at any rate noisiest human type that we have today, our good socialists, believe, hope, dream, and above all shout and write almost the opposite. Even now one reads their slogan for the future "free society" on all tables and walls. Free society? Yes, yes! But surely you know, gentlemen, what is required for building that? Wooden iron! The well-known wooden iron. And it must not even be wooden.

357

On the old problem: "What is German?" – Recapitulate in your mind the real achievements of philosophical thinking that one owes to Germans. Is there any legitimate sense in which one might give the credit for these achievements to the whole race? May we say that they are at the same time the product of "the German soul," or at least symptoms of that in the sense in which, say, Plato's ideomania, his almost religious madness about Forms, is usually taken also for an event and testimony of "the Greek soul"? Or should the opposite be the truth? Might they be just as individual, just as much *exceptions* from the spirit of the race as was, for example, Goethe's paganism with a good conscience? Or as is Bismarck's Machiavellism with a good conscience, his so-called "*Realpolitik*," among Germans? Might our philosophers actually contradict the *need* of "the German soul"? In short, were the German philosophers really – philosophical *Germans*? I recall three cases. First, *Leibniz's* incomparable insight that has been vindicated not only against Descartes but against everybody who had philosophized before him – that consciousness is merely an *accidens*[6] of representation[7]

---

6 Latin: accidental property.
7 In German: *Vorstellung*. The translation has been modified from "experience" to "representation."

and *not* its necessary and essential attribute; that, in other words, what we call consciousness constitutes only one state of our spiritual and psychic world (perhaps a pathological state) and *not by any means the whole of it*. The profundity of this idea has not been
exhausted to this day. Is there anything German in this idea? Is there any reason for
surmising that no Latin could easily have thought of this reversal of appearances?
For it is a reversal. Let us recall, secondly, *Kant's* tremendous question mark that he
placed after the concept of "causality" – without, like Hume, doubting its legitimacy
altogether. Rather, Kant began cautiously to delimit the realm within which this concept makes sense (and to this day we are not done with this fixing of limits). Let us
take, thirdly, the astonishing stroke of *Hegel*, who struck right through all our logical
habits and bad habits when he dared to teach that species concepts develop *out of each
other*. With this proposition the minds of Europe were preformed for the last great
scientific movement, Darwinism – for without Hegel there could have been no Darwin.
Is there anything German in this Hegelian innovation which first introduced the
decisive concept of "development" into science? Yes, without any doubt. In all three
cases we feel that something in ourselves has been "uncovered" and guessed, and we
are grateful for it and at the same time surprised. Each of these three propositions is a
thoughtful piece of German self-knowledge, self-experience, self-understanding. "Our
inner world is much richer, more comprehensive, more concealed," we feel with Leibniz.
As Germans, we doubt with Kant the ultimate validity of the knowledge attained by
the natural sciences and altogether everything that *can* be known *causaliter*,[8] whatever
is know*able* immediately seems to us less valuable on that account. We Germans are
Hegelians even if there never had been any Hegel, insofar as we (unlike all Latins)
instinctively attribute a deeper meaning and greater value to becoming and development than to what "is"; we hardly believe in the justification of the concept of "being"
– and also insofar as we are not inclined to concede that our human logic is logic as
such or the only kind of logic (we would rather persuade ourselves that it is merely
a special case and perhaps one of the oddest and most stupid cases). It would be a
fourth question whether *Schopenhauer*, too, with his pessimism – that is, the problem
of the *value of existence* – had to be precisely a German. I believe not. The event after
which this problem was to be expected for certain – an astronomer of the soul could
have calculated the very day and hour for it – the decline of the faith in the Christian
god, the triumph of scientific atheism, is a generally European event in which all races
had their share and for which all deserve credit and honor. Conversely, one might
charge precisely the Germans – those Germans who were Schopenhauer's contemporaries – that they *delayed* this triumph of atheism most dangerously for the longest
time. Hegel in particular was its delayer par excellence, with his grandiose attempt to
persuade us of the divinity of existence, appealing as a last resort to our sixth sense,
"the historical sense." As a philosopher, Schopenhauer was the *first* admitted and
inexorable atheist among us Germans: This was the background of his enmity against
Hegel. The ungodliness of existence was for him something given, palpable, indisputable; he always lost his philosopher's composure and became indignant when he saw
anyone hesitate or mince matters at this point. This is the locus of his whole integrity;
unconditional and honest atheism is simply the *presupposition* of the way he poses his
problem, being a triumph achieved finally and with great difficulty by the European

8 Latin: causally.

conscience, being the most fateful act of two thousand years of discipline for truth that in the end forbids itself the *lie* in faith in God. You see what it was that really triumphed over the Christian God: Christian morality itself, the concept of truthfulness that was understood ever more rigorously, the father confessor's refinement of the Christian conscience, translated and sublimated into a scientific conscience, into intellectual cleanliness at any price. Looking at nature as if it were proof of the goodness and governance of a god; interpreting history in honor of some divine reason, as a continual testimony of a moral world order and ultimate moral purposes; interpreting one's own experiences as pious people have long enough interpreted theirs, as if everything were providential, a hint, designed and ordained for the sake of the salvation of the soul – that is *all over* now, that has man's conscience *against* it, that is considered indecent and dishonest by every more refined conscience – mendaciousness, feminism, weakness, and cowardice. In this severity, if anywhere, we are *good* Europeans and heirs of Europe's longest and most courageous self-overcoming.[9] As we thus reject the Christian interpretation and condemn its "meaning" like counterfeit, Schopenhauer's question immediately comes to us in a terrifying way: *Has existence any meaning at all?* It will require a few centuries before this question can even be heard completely and in its full depth. What Schopenhauer himself said in answer to this question was – forgive me – hasty, youthful, only a compromise, a way of remaining – remaining stuck – in precisely those Christian-ascetic moral perspectives in which one had *renounced faith* along with the faith in God. But he *posed* the question – as a good European, as I have said, and *not* as a German. Or is it possible that at least the manner in which the Germans appropriated Schopenhauer's question proves that the Germans did have an inner affinity, preparation, and *need* for his problem? That after Schopenhauer one thought and printed things in Germany, too – by the way, late enough – about the problem he had posed, is certainly not sufficient to decide in favor of such an inner affinity. One might rather adduce the peculiar *ineptitude* of this post-Schopenhauerian pessimism *against* this thesis. Obviously, the Germans did not behave in this affair as if they had been in their own element. This is not by any means an allusion to Eduard von Hartmann.[10] On the contrary, to this day I have not shaken off my old suspicion that he is too *apt* for us. I mean that he may have been a wicked rogue from the start who perhaps made fun not only of German pessimism – but in the end he might even "bequeath" to the Germans in his will how far it was possible even in the age of foundations to make fools of them. But let me ask you: Should we perhaps consider that old humming-top Bahnsen[11] as a credit to the Germans, seing how voluptuously he revolved his life long around his real-dialectical misery and his "personal tough luck"? Perhaps precisely this is German? (I herewith recommend his writings for the purpose for which I have used them myself, as an anti-pessimistic diet, especially on account of their *elegantiae psychologicae*;[12] they should, I think, be effective even for the most constipated bowels and mind.) Or could one count such

---

9   In German: *Selbstüberwindung*.

10   Eduard von Hartmann (1842–1906), German philosopher, author of *Die Philosophie des Unbewussten* (*Philosophy of the Unconscious*, 1869).

11   Julius Bahnsen (1830–81) published books on characterology, philosophy of history, and the tragic as the law of the world.

12   Latin: psychological elegance.

dilettantes and old spinsters as that mawkish apostle of virginity, Mainländer,[13] as a genuine German? In the last analysis he probably was a Jew (all Jews become mawkish when they moralize). Neither Bahnsen nor Mainländer, not to speak of Eduard von Hartmann, gives us any clear evidence regarding the question whether Schopenhauer's pessimism, his horrified look into a de-deified world that had become stupid, blind, mad, and questionable, his *honest* horror, was not merely an exceptional case among Germans but a *German* event. Everything else that one sees in the foreground – our bold politics and our cheerful fatherlandishness which resolutely enough consider all matters with a view to a not very philosophical principle ("*Deutschland, Deutschland über alles*"), which means *sub specie speciei*,[14] namely the German species, bears emphatic witness of the opposite. No, the Germans of today are *no* pessimists. And Schopenhauer was a pessimist, to say it once more, as a good European and *not* as a German. –

[. . .]

360

Two kinds of causes that are often confounded. – This seems to me to be one of my most essential steps and advances: I have learned to distinguish the cause of acting from the cause of acting in a particular way, in a particular direction, with a particular goal. The first kind of cause is a quantum of dammed-up energy that is waiting to be used up somehow, for something, while the second kind is, compared to this energy, something quite insignificant, for the most part a little accident in accordance with which this quantum "discharges" itself in one particular way – a match versus a ton of powder. Among these little accidents and "matches" I include so-called "purposes" as well as the even much more so-called "vocations": They are relatively random, arbitrary, almost indifferent in relation to the tremendous quantum of energy that presses, as I have said, to be used up somehow. The usual view is different: People are accustomed to consider the goal (purposes, vocations, etc.) as the *driving force*, in keeping with a very ancient error; but it is merely the *directing* force – one has mistaken the helmsman for the steam. And not even always the helmsman, the directing force. Is the "goal," the "purpose" not often enough a beautifying pretext, a self-deception of vanity after the event that does not want to acknowledge that the ship is *following* the current into which it has entered accidentally? that it "wills" to go that way *because it – must*? that is has a direction, to be sure, but – no helmsman at all? We still need a critique of the concept of "purpose."

361

On the problem of the actor. – The problem of the actor has troubled me for the longest time. I felt unsure (and sometimes still do) whether it is not only from this angle that one can get at the dangerous concept of the "artist" – a concept that has so far been

13 Philipp Mainländer, pseudonym of Philipp Batz (1841–76). His *Philosophie der Erlösung* (*Philosophy of Redemption*, 1876–7) makes much of the will to death, of virginity, and of suicide; he himself died by his own hand.
14 Latin: from the point of view of the species. Allusion to Spinoza's phrase *sub specie aeternitatis* (from the point of view of eternity, *Ethics*, V. 22).

treated with unpardonable generosity. Falseness with a good conscience; the delight in simulation exploding as a power that pushes aside one's so-called "character," flooding it and at times extinguishing it; the inner craving for a role and mask, for *appearance*; an excess of the capacity for all kinds of adaptations that can no longer be satisfied in the service of the most immediate and narrowest utility – all of this is perhaps not *only* peculiar to the actor? Such an instinct will have developed most easily in families of the lower classes who had to survive under changing pressures and coercions, in deep dependency, who had to cut their coat according to the cloth, always adapting themselves again to new circumstances, who always had to change their mien and posture, until they learned gradually to turn their coat with *every* wind and thus virtually to *become* a coat – and masters of the incorporated and inveterate art of eternally playing hide-and-seek, which in the case of animals is called mimicry – until eventually this capacity, accumulated from generation to generation, becomes domineering, unreasonable, and intractable, an instinct that learns to lord it over other instincts, and generates the actor, the "artist" (the zany, the teller of lies, the buffoon, fool, clown at first, as well as the classical servant, Gil Blas;[15] for it is in such types that we find the pre-history of the artist and often enough even of the "genius"). In superior social conditions, too, a similar human type develops under similar pressures; only in such cases the histrionic instinct is usually barely kept under control by another instinct; for example, in the case of "diplomats." Incidentally, I am inclined to believe that a good diplomat would always be free to become a good stage actor if he wished – if only he were "free." As for the *Jews*, the people who possess the art of adaptability par excellence, this train of thought suggests immediately that one might see them virtually as a world-historical arrangement for the production of actors, a veritable breeding ground for actors. And it really is high time to ask: What good actor today is *not* – a Jew? The Jew as a born "man of letters," as the true master of the European press, also exercises his power by virtue of his histrionic gifts; for the man of letters is essentially an actor: He plays the "expert," the "specialist." Finally, *women*. Reflect on the whole history of women: do they not *have* to be first of all and above all else actresses? Listen to physicians who have hypnotized women; finally, love them – let yourself be "hypnotized by them"! What is always the end result? That they "put on something" even when they take off everything. Woman is so artistic.

[. . .]

369

Our side by side. – Don't we have to admit to ourselves, we artists, that there is an uncanny difference within us between our taste and our creative power? They stand oddly side by side, separately, and each grows in its own way. I mean, they have altogether different degrees and *tempi* of old, young mature, mellow, and rotten. A musician, for example, might create his life long what is utterly at odds with what his refined listener's ear and listener's heart esteem, enjoy, and prefer – and he need not even be aware of this contradiction. As our almost painfully frequent experience shows,

---

15   Eponymous hero of the picaresque novel (3 vols, 1715–35) by Alain-René Lesage (1668–1747). The son of humble Spanish parents, the hero is sent off at age 17 with little money, but after several adventures becomes rich and influential.

one's taste can easily grow far beyond the reach of the taste of one's powers, and this need not at all paralyze these powers and keep them from continued productivity. But the opposite can happen, too – and this is what I should like to call to the attention of artists. Consider a continually creative person, a "mother" type in the grand sense, one who knows and hears nothing any more except about the pregnancies and deliveries of his spirit, one who simply lacks the time to reflect on himself and his work and to make comparisons, one who no longer has any desire to assert his taste and who simply forgets it, without caring in the least whether it still stands, or lies, or falls – such a person might perhaps eventually produce works *that far excel his own judgment*, so that he utters stupidities about them and himself – utters them and believes them. This seems to me to be almost the norm among fertile artists – nobody knows a child less well than its parents do – and it is true even in the case, to take a tremendous example, of the whole world of Greek art and poetry: it never "knew" what it did.[16]

370

What is romanticism? – It may perhaps be recalled, at least among my friends, that initially I approached the modern world with a few crude errors and overestimations and, in any case, hopefully. Who knows on the basis of what personal experiences, I understood the philosophical pessimism of the nineteenth century as if it were a symptom of a superior force of thought, of more audacious courage, and of more triumphant *fullness* of life than had characterized the eighteenth century, the age of Hume, Kant, Condillac,[17] and the sensualists. Thus tragic insight appeared to me as the distinctive *luxury* of our culture, as its most precious, noblest, and most dangerous squandering, but, in view of its over-richness, as a *permissible* luxury. In the same way, I reinterpreted German music for myself as if it signified a Dionysian power of the German soul: I believed that I heard in it the earthquake through which some primeval force that had been dammed up for ages finally liberated itself – indifferent whether everything else that one calls culture might begin to tremble. You see, what I failed to recognize at that time both in philosophical pessimism and in German music was what is really their distinctive character – their *romanticism*. *What is romanticism?* – Every art, every philosophy may be viewed as a remedy and an aid in the service of growing and struggling life; they always presuppose suffering and sufferers. But there are two kinds of sufferers: first, those who suffer from the *over-fullness of life* – they want a Dionysian art and likewise a tragic view of life, a tragic insight – and then those who suffer from the *impoverishment of life* and seek rest, stillness, calm seas, redemption from themselves through art and knowledge, or intoxication, convulsions, anaesthesia, and madness. All romanticism in art and insight corresponds to the dual needs of the latter type, and that included (and includes) Schopenhauer as well as Richard Wagner, to name the two most famous and pronounced romantics whom I *misunderstood* at that time – *not*, incidentally, to their disadvantage, as one need not hesitate in all fairness to admit. He that is richest in the fullness of life, the Dionysian god and man, cannot only afford the sight of the terrible and questionable but even the terrible deed

16 Allusion to Jesus' words on the cross: "Father, forgive them; for they know not what they do" (Luke 23: 34).
17 Etienne Bonnot, abbé de Condillac (1714–80), French empiricist philosopher.

and any luxury of destruction, decomposition, and negation. In his case, what is evil, absurd, and ugly seems, as it were, permissible, owing to an excess of procreating, fertilizing energies that can still turn any desert into lush farmland. Conversely, those who suffer most and are poorest in life would need above all mildness, peacefulness, and goodness in thought as well as deed – if possible, also a god who would be truly a god for the sick, a healer and savior; also logic, the conceptual understandability of existence – for logic calms and gives confidence – in short, a certain warm narrowness that keeps away fear and encloses one in optimistic horizons. Thus I gradually learned to understand Epicurus, the opposite of a Dionysian pessimist; also the "Christian" who is actually only a kind of Epicurean – both are essentially romantics – and my eye grew ever sharper for that most difficult and captious form of *backward inference* in which the most mistakes are made: the backward inference from the work to the maker, from the deed to the doer, from the ideal to those who *need it*, from every way of thinking and valuing to the commanding need behind it. Regarding all aesthetic values I now avail myself of this main distinction: I ask in every instance, "is it hunger or superabundance that has here become creative?" At first glance, another distinction may seem preferable – it is far more obvious – namely the question whether the desire to fix, to immortalize, the desire for *being* prompted creation, or the desire for destruction, for change, for future, for *becoming*. But both of these kinds of desire are seen to be ambiguous when one considers them more closely; they can be interpreted in accordance with the first scheme that is, as it seems to me, preferable. The desire for *destruction*, change, and becoming can be an expression of an overflowing energy that is pregnant with future (my term for this is, as is known, "Dionysian"); but it can also be the hatred of the ill-constituted, disinherited, and underprivileged, who destroy, *must* destroy, because what exists, indeed all existence, all being, outrages and provokes them. To understand this feeling, consider our anarchists closely. The will to *immortalize* also requires a dual interpretation. It can be prompted, first, by gratitude and love; art with this origin will always be an art of apotheoses, perhaps dithyrambic like Rubens,[18] or blissfully mocking like Hafiz,[19] or bright and gracious like Goethe, spreading a Homeric light and glory over all things. But it can also be the tyrannic will of one who suffers deeply, who struggles, is tormented, and would like to turn what is most personal, singular, and narrow, the real idiosyncrasy of his suffering, into a binding law and compulsion – one who, as it were, revenges himself on all things by forcing his own image, the image of his torture, on them, branding them with it. This last version is *romantic pessimism* in its most expressive form, whether it be Schopenhauer's philosophy of will or Wagner's music – romantic pessimism, the last *great* event in the fate of our culture. (That there still *could* be an altogether different kind of pessimism, a classical type – this premonition and vision belongs to me as inseparable from me, as my *proprium* and *ipsissimum*;[20] only the word "classical" offends my ears, it is far too trite and has become round and indistinct. I call this pessimism of the future – for it comes! I see it coming! – *Dionysian* pessimism.)

[. . .]

18   Sir Peter Paul Rubens (1577–1640), Flemish Baroque painter.
19   Muhammad Shams al-Din (ca. 1326–90), Persian lyric poet, popular in Germany owing to Goethe's fondness for his work.
20   Latin: my own and my ownmost (or quintessence).

372

Why we are no idealists. – Formerly philosophers were afraid of the senses. Have we perhaps unlearned this fear too much? Today all of us are believers in the senses, we philosophers of the present and the future, *not* in theory but in praxis, in practice. They, however, thought that the senses might lure them away from their own world, from the cold realm of "ideas," to some dangerous southern island where they feared that their philosopher's virtues might melt away like snow in the sun. Having "wax in one's ears" was then almost a condition of philosophizing; a real philosopher no longer listened to life insofar as life is music; he *denied* the music of life – it is an ancient philosopher's superstition that all music is sirens' music.[21] We today are inclined to make the opposite judgment (which actually could be equally wrong), namely that *ideas* are worse seductresses than our senses, for all their cold and anemic appearance, and not even in spite of this appearance: they have always lived on the "blood" of the philosopher, they always consumed his senses and even, if you will believe us, his "heart." These old philosophers were heartless; philosophizing was always a kind of vampirism. Looking at these figures, even Spinoza, don't you have a sense of something profoundly enigmatic and uncanny? Don't you notice the spectacle that unrolls before you, how they *become ever paler* – how desensualization is interpreted more and more ideally? Don't you sense a long concealed vampire in the background who begins with the senses and in the end is left with, and leaves, mere bones, mere clatter? I mean categories, formulas, *words* (for, forgive me, what was left of Spinoza, *amor intellectualis dei*,[22] is mere clatter and no more than that: What is *amor*, what *deus*, if there is not a drop of blood in them?). In sum: All philosophical idealism to date was something like a disease, unless it was, as it was in Plato's case, the caution of an over-rich and dangerous health, the fear of *over-powerful* senses, the prudence of a prudent Socratic. – Perhaps we moderns are merely not healthy enough *to be in need of* Plato's idealism? And we are not afraid of the senses because –

373

"Science"[23] *as a prejudice.* – It follows from the laws of the order of rank that scholars, insofar as they belong to the spiritual middle class, can never catch sight of the really great problems and question marks; moreover, their courage and their eyes simply do not reach that far – and above all, their needs which led them to become scholars in the first place, their inmost assumptions and desires that things might be such and such, their fears and hopes all come to rest and are satisfied too soon. Take, for example, that pedantic Englishman, Herbert Spencer.[24] What makes him "enthuse" in his

---

21   In Homer's *Odyssey* (XII), Odysseus stops the ears of his companions with wax to keep them from hearing the sirens' song as their ship approaches the sirens' island, and he has himself bound to the mast.

22   Latin: intellectual love of God. Quotation from Spinoza, *Ethics*, V. 32, Corollary.

23   In German: *"Wissenschaft."* See *On Truth and Lies* note 13 above.

24   A leading English social thinker (1820–1903) and one of the most influential evolutionists of the Victorian era (it is Spencer who coined the phrase "survival of the fittest"). An apostle of *laissez-faire* individualism, he combined evolutionary theory with utilitarianism, believing that

way and then leads him to draw a line of hope, a horizon of desirability – that eventual reconciliation of "egoism and altruism" about which he raves – almost nauseates the likes of us; a human race that adopted such Spencerian perspectives as its ultimate perspectives would seem to us worthy of contempt, of annihilation! But the mere fact that he had to experience as his highest hope something that to others appears and may appear only as a disgusting possibility poses a question mark that Spencer would have been incapable of foreseeing. It is no different with the faith with which so many materialistic natural scientists rest content nowadays, the faith in a world that is supposed to have its equivalent and its measure in human thought and human valuations – a "world of truth" that can be mastered completely and forever with the aid of our square little reason. What? Do we really want to permit existence to be degraded for us like this – reduced to a mere exercise for a calculator and an indoor diversion for mathematicians? Above all, one should not wish to divest existence of its *rich ambiguity*:[25] that is a dictate of good taste, gentlemen, the taste of reverence for everything that lies beyond your horizon. That the only justifiable interpretation of the world should be one in which *you* are justified because one can continue to work and do research scientifically in *your* sense (you really mean, mechanistically?) – an interpretation that permits counting, calculating, weighing, seeing, and touching, and nothing more – that is a crudity and naiveté, assuming that it is not a mental illness, an idiocy. Would it not be rather probable that, conversely, precisely the most superficial and external aspect of existence – what is most apparent, its skin and sensualization – would be grasped first – and might even be the only thing that allowed itself to be grasped? A "scientific" interpretation of the world, as you understand it, might therefore still be one of the *most stupid* of all possible interpretations of the world, meaning that it would be one of the poorest in meaning. This thought is intended for the ears and consciences of our mechanists who nowadays like to pass as philosophers and insist that mechanics is the doctrine of the first and last laws on which all existence must be based as on a ground floor. But an essentially mechanical world would be an essentially *meaningless*[26] world. Assuming that one estimated the *value* of a piece of music according to how much of it could be counted, calculated, and expressed in formulas: how absurd would such a "scientific" estimation of music be! What would one have comprehended, understood, grasped of it? Nothing, really nothing of what is "music" in it!

human history would eventually culminate in an ideal state in which egoism and altruism were reconciled. There are a number of criticisms of Spencer to be found in Nietzsche's writings, and it seems as if Nietzsche took him to be the representative of English Darwinism. While it is true that Spencer transformed the new evolutionism into a social doctrine, this aspect of his work is, according to current research, better described as "social Lamarckism" rather than "social Darwinism" (on Lamarck, see GS [Books I–IV] note 8 above). It is a liberal ideology of progress through struggle that places the emphasis on the individual having the power to adapt itself to a new environment through its own efforts, with nature seen as rewarding hard work, thrift, and initiative. At the time of the attempt in the 1880s to purge Darwinism of its Lamarckian element, Spencer never abandoned his support for Lamarckism and wrote in defense of the inheritance of acquired characteristics.

25 In German: *seines vieldeutigen Charakters* (literally, "its polysemic character").
26 In German: *sinnlose*.

374

Our new "infinite." – How far the perspective character of existence extends or indeed whether existence has any other character than this; whether existence without interpretation, without "sense," does not become "nonsense"; whether, on the other hand, all existence is not essentially actively engaged in *interpretation* – that cannot be decided even by the most industrious and most scrupulously conscientious analysis and self-examination of the intellect; for in the course of this analysis the human intellect cannot avoid seeing itself in its own perspectives, and *only* in these. We cannot look around our own corner: it is a hopeless curiosity that wants to know what other kinds of intellects and perspectives there *might* be; for example, whether some beings might be able to experience time backward, or alternately forward and backward (which would involve another direction of life and another concept of cause and effect). But I should think that today we are at least far from the ridiculous immodesty that would be involved in decreeing from our corner that perspectives are permitted only from this corner. Rather has the world become "infinite" for us all over again, inasmuch as we cannot reject the possibility that *it may include infinite interpretations*. Once more we are seized by a great shudder; but who would feel inclined immediately to deify again after the old manner this monster of an unknown world? And to worship the unknown henceforth as "the Unknown One"? Alas, too many *ungodly* possibilities of interpretation are included in the unknown, too much devilry, stupidity, and foolishness of interpretation – even our own human, all too human folly, which we know.

[. . .]

377

We who are homeless. – Among Europeans today there is no lack of those who are entitled to call themselves homeless in a distinctive and honorable sense: it is to them that I especially commend my secret wisdom and *gaya scienza*. For their fate is hard, their hopes are uncertain; it is quite a feat to devise some comfort for them – but what avail? We children of the future, how *could* we be at home in this today? We feel disfavor for all ideals that might lead one to feel at home even in this fragile, broken time of transition; as for its "realities," we do not believe that they will *last*. The ice that still supports people today has become very thin; the wind that brings the thaw is blowing; we ourselves who are homeless constitute a force that breaks open ice and other all too thin "realities." We "conserve" nothing; neither do we want to return to any past periods; we are not by any means "liberal"; we do not work for "progress"; we do not need to plug up our ears against the sirens who in the market place sing of the future: their song about "equal rights," "a free society," "no more masters and no servants" has no allure for us. We simply do not consider it desirable that a realm of justice and concord should be established on earth (because it would certainly be the realm of the deepest leveling and *chinoiserie*);[27] we are delighted with all who love, as we do, danger, war, and adventures, who refuse to compromise, to be captured, reconciled, and castrated; we count ourselves among conquerors; we think about the necessity for new orders, also for a new slavery – for every strengthening and enhancement of the

27 In German: *Chineserei.*

human type also involves a new kind of enslavement. Is it not clear that with all this we are bound to feel ill at ease in an age that likes to claim the distinction of being the most humane, the mildest, and the most righteous age that the sun has ever seen? It is bad enough that precisely when we hear these beautiful words we have the ugliest suspicions. What we find in them is merely an expression – and a masquerade – of a profound weakening, of weariness, of old age, of declining energies. What can it matter to us what tinsel the sick may use to cover up their weakness? Let them parade it as their *virtue*; after all, there is no doubt that weakness makes one mild, oh so mild, so righteous, so inoffensive, so "humane"! The "religion of pity" to which one would like to convert us – oh, we know the hysterical little males and females well enough who today need precisely this religion as a veil and make-up. We are no humanitarians; we should never dare to permit ourselves to speak of our "love of humanity"; our kind is not actor enough for that. Or not Saint-Simonist[28] enough, not French enough. One really has to be afflicted with a *Gallic* excess of erotic irritability and enamored impatience to approach in all honesty the whole of humanity with one's lust! Humanity! Has there ever been a more hideous old woman among all old women – (unless it were "truth": a question for philosophers)? No, we do not love humanity; but on the other hand we are not nearly "German" enough, in the sense in which the word "German" is constantly being used nowadays, to advocate nationalism and race hatred and to be able to take pleasure in the national scabies of the heart and blood poisoning that now leads the nations of Europe to delimit and barricade themselves against each other as if it were a matter of quarantine. For that we are too openminded, too malicious, too spoiled, also too well informed, too "traveled": we far prefer to live on mountains, apart, "untimely," in past or future centuries, merely in order to keep ourselves from experiencing the silent rage to which we know we should be condemned as eyewitnesses of politics that are desolating the German spirit by making it vain and that is, moreover, *petty* politics:[29] to keep its own creation from immediately falling apart again, is it not finding it necessary to plant it between two deadly hatreds? *must* it not desire the eternalization of the European system of a lot of petty states? We who are homeless are too manifold and mixed racially and in our descent, being "modern men," and consequently do not feel tempted to participate in the mendacious racial self-admiration and racial indecency that parades in Germany today as a sign of a German way of thinking and that is doubly false and obscene among the people of the "historical sense." We are, in one word – and let this be our word of honor – *good Europeans*, the heirs of Europe, the rich, oversupplied, but also overly obligated heirs of thousands of years of European spirit. As such, we have also outgrown Christianity and are averse to it – precisely because we have grown out of it, because our ancestors were Christians who in their Christianity were uncompromisingly upright: for their faith they willingly sacrificed possessions and position, blood and fatherland. We – do the same. For what? For our unbelief? For every kind of unbelief? No, you know better than that, friends! The hidden Yes in you is stronger than all Nos and Maybes that afflict you and your age like a disease; and when

---

28   Claude-Henri de Rouvroy, comte de Saint-Simon (1760–1825), leading representative of French utopian socialism.
29   In German: *kleine Politik* (literally, "small politics").

you have to embark on the sea, you emigrants, you, too, are compelled to this by –
a *faith*!

[. . .]

380

"The wanderer" speaks. – If one would like to see our European morality for once as
it looks from a distance, and if one would like to measure it against other moralities,
past and future, then one has to proceed like a wanderer who wants to know how
high the towers in a town are: he *leaves* the town. "Thoughts about moral prejudices,"
if they are not meant to be prejudices about prejudices, presuppose a position *outside*
morality, some point beyond good and evil to which one has to rise, climb, or fly –
and in the present case at least a point beyond *our* good and evil, a freedom from
everything "European," by which I mean the sum of the imperious value judgments
that have become part of our flesh and blood. That one *wants* to go precisely out
there, up there, may be a minor madness, a peculiar and unreasonable "you must" –
for we seekers for knowledge also have our idiosyncrasies of "unfree will" – the question is whether one really *can* get up there. This may depend on manifold conditions.
In the main the question is how light or heavy we are – the problem of our "specific
gravity." One has to be *very light* to drive one's will to knowledge into such a distance
and, as it were, beyond one's time, to create for oneself eyes to survey millennia and,
moreover, clear skies in these eyes. One must have liberated oneself from many things
that oppress, inhibit, hold down, and make heavy precisely us Europeans today. The
human being of such a beyond who wants to behold the supreme measures of value
of his time must first of all "overcome"[30] this time in himself – this is the test of his
strength – and consequently not only his time but also his prior aversion and contradiction *against* this time, his suffering from this time, his un-timeliness, his *romanticism*.

381

On the question of being understandable. – One does not only wish to be understood
when one writes; one wishes just as surely *not* to be understood. It is not by any
means necessarily an objection to a book when anyone finds it impossible to understand: perhaps that was part of the author's intention – he did not want to be understood by just "anybody." All the nobler spirits and tastes select their audience when
they wish to communicate; and choosing that, one at the same time erects barriers
against "the others." All the more subtle laws of any style have their origin at this
point: they at the same time keep away, create a distance, forbid "entrance," understanding, as said above – while they open the ears of those whose ears are related to
ours. And let me say this among ourselves and about my own case: I don't want either
my ignorance or the liveliness of my temperament to keep me from being understandable
for *you*, my friends – not the liveliness, however much it compels me to tackle a
matter swiftly to tackle it at all. For I approach deep problems like cold baths: quickly
into them and quickly out again. That one does not get to the depths that way, not
deep enough down, is the superstition of those afraid of the water, the enemies of
cold water; they speak without experience. The freezing cold makes one swift. And

30   In German: *"überwinden."*

to ask this incidentally: does a matter necessarily remain ununderstood and unfathomed merely because it has been touched only in flight, glanced at, in a flash? Is it absolutely imperative that one settles down on it? that one has brooded over it as over an egg? *Diu noctuque incubando*,[31] as Newton said of himself? At least there are truths that are singularly shy and ticklish and cannot be caught except suddenly – that must be *surprised* or left alone. Finally, my brevity has yet another value: given such questions as concern me, I must say many things briefly in order that they may be heard still more briefly. For, being an immoralist, one has to take steps against corrupting innocents – I mean, asses and old maids of both sexes whom life offers nothing but their innocence. Even more, my writings should inspire, elevate, and encourage them to be virtuous. I cannot imagine anything on earth that would be a merrier sight than inspired old asses and maids who feel excited by the sweet sentiments of virtue; and "this I have seen" – thus spoke Zarathustra. So much regarding brevity. Matters stand worse with my ignorance which I do not try to conceal from myself. There are hours when I feel ashamed of it – to be sure, also hours when I feel ashamed of feeling ashamed. Perhaps all of us philosophers are in a bad position nowadays regarding knowledge: science keeps growing, and the most scholarly among us are close to discovering that they know too little. But it would be still worse if it were different – and we knew *too much*; our task is and remains above all not to mistake ourselves for others. We *are* something different from scholars, although it is unavoidable for us to be also, among other things, scholarly. We have different needs, grow differently, and also have a different digestion: we need more, we also need less. How much a spirit needs for its nourishment, for this there is no formula; but if its taste is for independence, for quick coming and going, for roaming, perhaps for adventures for which only the swiftest are a match, it is better for such a spirit to live in freedom with little to eat than unfree and stuffed. It is not fat but the greatest possible suppleness and strength that a good dancer desires from his nourishment – and I would not know what the spirit of a philosopher might wish more to be than a good dancer. For the dance is his ideal, also his art, and finally also his only piety, his "service of God."

382

The great health. – Being new, nameless, hard to understand, we premature births of an as yet unproven future need for a new goal also a new means – namely, a new health, stronger, more seasoned, tougher, more audacious, and gayer than any previous health. Whoever has a soul that craves to have experienced the whole range of values and desiderata to date, and to have sailed around all the coasts of this ideal "mediterranean"; whoever wants to know from the adventures of his own most authentic experience how a discoverer and conqueror of the ideal feels, and also an artist, a saint, a legislator, a sage, a scholar, a pious man, a soothsayer, and one who stands divinely apart in the old style – needs one thing above everything else: the *great health* – that one does not merely have but also acquires continually, and must acquire because one gives it up again and again, and must give it up. And now, after we have long been on our way in this manner, we argonauts of the ideal, with more daring perhaps than is prudent, and have suffered shipwreck and damage often enough, but are, to repeat

31   Latin: By incubating it day and night.

it, healthier than one likes to permit us, dangerously healthy, ever again healthy – it will seem to us as if, as a reward, we now confronted an as yet undiscovered country whose boundaries nobody has surveyed yet, something beyond all the lands and nooks of the ideal so far, a world so overrich in what is beautiful, strange, questionable, terrible, and divine that our curiosity as well as our craving to possess it has got beside itself – alas, now nothing will sate us any more! After such vistas and with such a burning hunger in our conscience and science,[32] how could we still be satisfied *with present-day man?* It may be too bad but it is inevitable that we find it difficult to remain serious when we look at his worthiest goals and hopes, and perhaps we do not even bother to look any more. Another ideal runs ahead of us, a strange, tempting, dangerous ideal to which we should not wish to persuade anybody because we do not readily concede *the right to it* to anyone: the ideal of a spirit who plays naively – that is, not deliberately but from overflowing power and abundance – with all that was hitherto called holy, good, untouchable, divine; for whom those supreme things that the people naturally accept as their value standards, signify danger, decay, debasement, or at least recreation, blindness, and temporary self-oblivion; the ideal of a human, superhuman well-being and benevolence that will often appear *inhuman* – for example, when it confronts all earthly seriousness so far, all solemnity in gesture, word, tone, eye, morality, and task so far, as if it were their most incarnate and involuntary parody – and in spite of all of this, it is perhaps only with him that *great seriousness* really begins, that the real question mark is posed for the first time, that the destiny of the soul changes, the hand moves forward, the tragedy *begins*.

32   In German: *Wissen und Gewissen.*

Der europäische Nihilismus

Lenzer Heide d. 10. Juni 1887

20

European Nihilism
(1887)

Lenzer Heide[1]   10 June 1887

1

What *advantages* did the Christian morality hypothesis offer?

1) it conferred on man an absolute *value*, in contrast to his smallness and contingency in the flux of becoming and passing away
2) it served the advocates of God to the extent that, despite suffering and evil, it let the world have the character of *perfection* – including "freedom" – and evil appeared full of *sense*
3) it posited[2] a *knowledge* [*Wissen*] of absolute values in man and thus gave him *adequate knowledge* [*Erkenntniss*] of precisely the most important thing

it prevented man from despising himself as man, from taking against life, from despairing of knowing [*Erkennen*]: it was a *means of preservation* – in sum: morality was the great *antidote* against practical and theoretical *nihilism*.

These *Nachlass* notes, translated by Duncan Large, are taken from Nietzsche's notebook N VII 3. They have been published twice in the Colli–Montinari *Kritische Gesamtausgabe* of Nietzsche's works: initially (as 5[71]) in vol. VIII/1, pp. 215–21 (*KSA* 12:211–17), and more recently in vol. IX/3, pp. 13–24. The latter volume is accompanied by a CD-ROM with a complete facsimile of the notebook (see opening page reproduced opposite), on which translation choices have been based when the two transcriptions were occasionally at variance. (In *WP* these notes are split up and appear as sections 4, 5, 114 and the long section 55.) The paragraph numbering is Nietzsche's; bold type signifies double underlining.

1   Village about 40 miles north of Sils-Maria, in southeast Switzerland.
2   Reading *setzte* (against both *Kritische Gesamtausgabe* transcriptions, which have *setzt*, "posits").

2

But among the forces nurtured by morality was *truthfulness*: *this* ultimately turns on morality, discovers its *teleology*, the *partiality* of its viewpoint – and now the *insight* into this long-ingrained mendacity, which one despairs of throwing off, acts precisely as a stimulus. To nihilism. We now notice in ourselves needs, implanted by the long-held morality interpretation, which now appear to us as needs to untruth: conversely it is on them that the value for which we bear to live seems to depend. This antagonism – *not* valuing what we know [*erkennen*], and no longer being *permitted* to value what we would like to hoodwink ourselves with – results in a disintegration process.

3

In fact we no longer need an antidote against the *first* nihilism so much: life is no longer so uncertain, contingent, senseless in our Europe. Such an immense *multiplication* of the *value* of man, of the value of evil etc. is not so necessary now; we can stand a significant *reduction* in this value and concede a good deal of nonsense and chance: the *power* that man has achieved now permits a *reduction* in the disciplinary measures, of which the moral interpretation was the strongest. "God" is much too extreme a hypothesis.

4

But extreme positions are replaced not by moderate ones, rather by equally extreme but *opposite* ones. And so the belief in the absolute immorality of nature, in purposelessness and senselessness, is the psychologically necessary *affect* once belief in God and an essentially moral order can no longer be sustained. Nihilism now appears, *not* because aversion to existence is greater than before, but because people have begun to mistrust any "sense" in evil, even in existence. *One* interpretation has collapsed, but because it was considered *the* interpretation, it appears as though there is no sense in existence whatsoever, as though everything is *in vain*.

5

It remains to be demonstrated that this "in vain!" is the character of our present-day nihilism. Mistrust of our previous evaluations increases, leading to the question "aren't all 'values' lures which allow the whole comedy to drag on without ever getting closer to a solution?" With an "in vain," with no aim or purpose, *duration* is the *most paralysing* thought, especially when one realizes one is being duped but is powerless to prevent oneself being duped.

6

Let us think this thought in its most terrible form: existence as it is, without sense or aim, but inevitably returning, without a finale in nothingness: "the eternal return."[3]

---

3   In German: "*die ewige Wiederkehr*." Elsewhere in these notes (sections 7, 13, 14, 16) Nietzsche always uses *Wiederkunft*, translated as "recurrence."

This is the most extreme form of nihilism: nothingness (the "senseless") eternally!

European form of Buddhism: energy of knowledge [*Wissen*] and strength *forces* one into such a belief. It is the *most scientific* of all possible hypotheses. We deny final goals: if existence had one, it would have to have been reached.

7

Thus we can understand that an antithesis to pantheism is being striven for here: since "everything perfect, divine, eternal" forces one *likewise into a belief in the "eternal recurrence."* Query: does morality make this pantheistic affirmation of all things impossible, too? At bottom, after all, only the moral God has been overcome. Does it make any sense to imagine a god "beyond good and evil"? Would a pantheism in *this* sense be possible? If we remove finality from the process, can we *nevertheless* still affirm the process? – This would be the case if something within that process were being *achieved* at its every moment – and always the same.

Spinoza reached such an affirmative position, to the extent that every moment has a *logical* necessity: and with the logicality of his fundamental instinct he was triumphant that the world was constituted in *such* a manner.

8

But his case is just an individual case. *Every fundamental characteristic* at the basis of *every* event, as expressed in every event, would need to impel any individual who felt it was *his* fundamental characteristic to welcome triumphantly every moment of existence in general. It would need this fundamental characteristic in oneself to be felt precisely as good, valuable, with pleasure.

9

Now *morality* has protected life from despair and the leap into nothingness in the kind of people and classes who were violated and oppressed by *people*: for it is powerlessness in the face of people, *not* powerlessness in the face of nature, that generates the most desperate embitterment against existence. Morality has treated the powerful, the violent, the "masters" in general as the enemies against whom the common man must be protected, *i.e. first of all encouraged, strengthened.* Consequently morality has taught to *hate* and *despise* most profoundly what is the fundamental characteristic of the rulers: *their will to power.* To abolish, deny, break down this morality: that would mean providing the most hated drive with an *opposite* sensation and evaluation. If the sufferer, the oppressed man *lost his belief* in having a *right* to his contempt for the will to power, he would enter the stage of hopeless desperation. This would be the case if this trait were essential to life, if it turned out that even that "will to morality" was just concealing this "will to power," that even that hatred and contempt is still a power-will [*Machtwille*]. The oppressed man would realize that he is *in the same boat* as the oppressor and that he has no *prerogative* over him, no *higher status* than him.

10

Rather *the other way around*! There is nothing about life that has value except the degree of power – assuming, of course, that life itself is the will to power. Morality protected from nihilism *those who turned out badly* by granting *everyone* an infinite value, a metaphysical value, and placing them in an order which did[4] not correspond to that of worldly power and hierarchy: it taught submissiveness, humility etc. *Provided that the belief in this morality collapses*, those who turned out badly would no longer have their consolation – and they would *perish*.

11

This *perishing* presents itself as a – *self-ruination*, as an instinctive selection of that which *must destroy. Symptoms* of this self-destruction by those who turned out badly: self-vivisection, poisoning, intoxication, romanticism, above all the instinctive need for actions which make *deadly enemies* of the powerful (– as if one were breeding one's own executioners); the *will to destruction* as the will of an even deeper instinct, the instinct of self-destruction, of the *will into nothingness*.

12

Nihilism as a symptom of the fact that those who turned out badly have no consolation left: that they destroy in order to be destroyed, that, relieved of morality, they no longer have any reason to "surrender themselves" – that they position themselves on the territory of the opposing principle and *want power* for themselves, too, by *forcing* the powerful to be their executioners. This is the European form of Buddhism: *doing no*, after all existence has lost its "sense."

13

It is not that "distress," for example, has got greater: on the contrary! "God, morality, submissiveness" were remedies on terribly deep levels of misery: *active nihilism* appears when the conditions are, relatively speaking, much more favorably disposed. For morality to be felt to have been overcome already presupposes quite a degree of spiritual culture; this in turn presupposes relative prosperity. A certain spiritual fatigue – reaching the point of hopeless scepticism directed *against* philosophers[5] as a result of the long struggle between philosophical opinions – likewise characterizes the by no means *lowly* standing of these nihilists. Think of the situation in which Buddha appeared. The doctrine of the eternal recurrence would have *erudite* presuppositions (such as the teacher Buddha[6] had, e.g. concept of causality etc.).

14

Now what does "turned out badly" mean? Above all *physiologically*: no longer politically. The *unhealthiest* kind of man in Europe (of all classes) is the ground of this nihilism:

---

4   Reading *stimmte* (with *Kritische Gesamtausgabe* vol. IX/3; vol. VIII/1 has *stimmt*, "does").
5   Reading *Philosophen* (with *Kritische Gesamtausgabe* vol. IX/3; vol. VIII/1 has *Philosophie*, "philosophy").
6   Reading *der Lehrer Buddha* (with *Kritische Gesamtausgabe* vol. IX/3; vol. VIII/1 has *die Lehre Buddha<s>*, "Buddha's doctrine").

they will feel that belief in the eternal recurrence is a *curse* which, once you are struck by it, makes you no longer baulk at any action; not being passively extinguished, but *making* everything that is so senseless and aimless be extinguished: although it is only a spasm, a blind rage on realizing that everything has existed for eternities – including this moment of nihilism and lust for destruction. – The **value** *of such a crisis* is that it *cleanses*, that it forces together related elements and makes them ruin each other, that it allocates common tasks to people of opposing mentalities – also bringing to light the weaker, more insecure among them and thus initiating *a hierarchy* of *forces* from the point of view of health: acknowledging commanders as commanders, obeyers as obeyers. At one remove from all existing social orders, of course.

15

Who will prove to be the *strongest* in this? The most moderate, those who have no *need* of extreme dogmas, those who not only concede but love a good measure of chance and nonsense, those who can conceive of man with a significant reduction in his value without thereby becoming small and weak: the richest in health who can cope with the most misfortunes and so have no great fear of misfortunes – men who *are sure of their power* and represent with conscious pride the *achievement* of human strength.

16

How would such a man think of the eternal recurrence? –

21

On the Genealogy
of Morality: A Polemic
(1887)

Preface

1

We are unknown to ourselves, we knowers, even to ourselves, and there is a good reason for this. We have never looked for ourselves, – so how are we ever supposed to *find* ourselves? How right is the saying: 'Where your treasure is, there will your heart be also';[1] *our* treasure is where the hives of our knowledge are. As born winged-insects and intellectual honey-gatherers we are constantly making for them, concerned at heart with only one thing – to 'bring something home'. As far as the rest of life is concerned, the so-called 'experiences', – who of us ever has enough seriousness for them? or enough time? I fear we have never really been 'with it' in such matters: our heart is simply not in it – and not even our ear! On the contrary, like somebody divinely absent-minded and sunk in his own thoughts who, the twelve strokes of midday having just boomed into his ears, wakes with a start and wonders 'What hour struck?', sometimes we, too, *afterwards* rub our ears and ask, astonished, taken aback, 'What did we actually experience then?' or even, 'Who *are* we, in fact?' and afterwards, as I said, we count all twelve reverberating strokes of our experience, of our life, of our *being* – oh! and lose count . . . We remain strange to ourselves out of necessity, we do not understand ourselves, we *must* confusedly mistake who we are, the motto 'everyone is furthest from himself'[2] applies to us for ever, – we are not 'knowers' when it comes to ourselves . . .

2

– My thoughts on the *descent*[3] of our moral prejudices – for that is what this polemic is about – were first set out in a sketchy and provisional way in the collection of

1 Matthew 6: 21.
2 See *GS* (Books I–IV) note 27 above.
3 In German: *Herkunft.*

aphorisms entitled *Human, All Too Human: A Book for Free Spirits*, which I began to write in Sorrento during a winter in which I was able to pause, as a walker pauses, to take in the vast and dangerous land through which my mind had hitherto travelled. This was in the winter of 1876–7; the thoughts themselves go back further. They were mainly the same thoughts which I shall be taking up again in the present essays – let us hope that the long interval has done them good, that they have become riper, brighter, stronger and more perfect! The fact *that* I still stick to them today, and that they themselves in the meantime have stuck together increasingly firmly, even growing into one another and growing into one, makes me all the more blithely confident that from the first, they did not arise in me individually, randomly or sporadically but as stemming from a single root, from a *fundamental will* to knowledge deep inside me which took control, speaking more and more clearly and making ever clearer demands. And this is the only thing proper for a philosopher. We have no right to stand out *individually*: we must not either make mistakes or hit on the truth individually. Instead, our thoughts, values, every 'yes', 'no', 'if' and 'but' grow from us with the same inevitability as fruits borne on the tree – all related and referring to one another and a testimonial to one will, one health, one earth, one sun. – Do *you* like the taste of our fruit? – But of what concern is that to the trees? And of what concern is it to *us* philosophers? . . .

3

With a characteristic scepticism to which I confess only reluctantly – it relates to *morality*[4] and to all that hitherto people have celebrated as morality –, a scepticism which sprang up in my life so early, so unbidden, so unstoppably, and which was in such conflict with my surroundings, age, precedents and lineage that I would almost be justified in calling it my '*a priori*', – my curiosity and suspicion were bound to fix on the question of *what origin*[5] our terms good and evil actually have. Indeed, as a thirteen-year-old boy, I was preoccupied with the problem of the origin of evil: at an age when one's heart was 'half-filled with childish games, half-filled with God',[6] I dedicated my first literary childish game, my first philosophical essay, to this problem – and as regards my 'solution' to the problem at that time, I quite properly gave God credit for it and made him the *father* of evil. Did my '*a priori*' want *this* of me? That new, immoral, or at least immoralistic '*a priori*': and the oh-so-anti-Kantian, so enigmatic 'categorical imperative'[7] which spoke from it and to which I have, in the meantime, increasingly lent an ear, and not just an ear? . . . Fortunately I learnt, in time, to separate theological from moral prejudice and I no longer searched for the origin of evil *beyond* the world. Some training in history and philosophy, together with my innate fastidiousness with regard to all psychological problems, soon transformed my problem into another: under what conditions did man invent the value judgments good and evil? *and what value do they themselves have?* Have they up to now obstructed or promoted

---

4 In German: *die Moral*.

5 In German: *Ursprung*.

6 Goethe, *Faust I*, l. 3781f.

7 "Act only on that maxim through which you can at the same time will that it become a general law" – Kant, *Grundlegung zur Metaphysik der Sitten* (*Groundwork of the Metaphysics of Morals*, 1785), 1.

human flourishing? Are they a sign of distress, poverty and the degeneration of life? Or, on the contrary, do they reveal the fullness, vitality and will of life, its courage, its confidence, its future? To these questions I found and ventured all kinds of answers, I distinguished between epochs, peoples, grades of rank between individuals, I focused my inquiry, and out of the answers there developed new questions, investigations, conjectures, probabilities until I had my own territory, my own soil, a whole silently growing and blossoming world, secret gardens, as it were, the existence of which nobody must be allowed to suspect . . . Oh! how *happy* we are, we knowers, provided we can keep quiet for long enough! . . .

4

I was given the initial stimulation to publish something about my hypotheses on the origin of morality[8] by a clear, honest and clever, even too-clever little book, in which I first directly encountered the back-to-front and perverse kind of genealogical hypotheses, actually the *English* kind, which drew me to it – with that power of attraction which everything contradictory and antithetical has. The title of the little book was *The Origin of Moral Sensation*; its author was Dr Paul Rée; the year of its publication 1877. I have, perhaps, never read anything to which I said 'no', sentence by sentence and deduction by deduction, as I did to this book: but completely without annoyance and impatience. In the work already mentioned which I was working on at the time, I referred to passages from this book more or less at random, not in order to refute them – what business is it of mine to refute! – but, as befits a positive mind, to replace the improbable with the more probable and in some circumstances to replace one error with another. As I said, I was, at the time, bringing to the light of day those hypotheses on descent to which these essays are devoted, clumsily, as I am the first to admit, and still inhibited because I still lacked my own vocabulary for these special topics, and with a good deal of relapse and vacillation. In particular, compare what I say about the dual pre-history of good and evil in *Human, All Too Human*, section 45 (namely in the sphere of nobles and slaves); likewise section 136 on the value and descent of ascetic morality; likewise sections 96 and 99 and volume II, section 89 on the 'Morality of Custom', that much older and more primitive kind of morality which is *toto coelo*[9] removed from the altruistic evaluation (which Dr Rée, like all English genealogists, sees as the moral method of valuation *as such*); likewise section 92, *The Wanderer*, section 26, and *Daybreak*, section 112, on the descent of justice as a balance between two roughly equal powers (equilibrium as the pre-condition for all contracts and consequently for all law); likewise *The Wanderer*, sections 22 and 33 on the descent of punishment, the deterrent [*terroristisch*] purpose of which is neither essential nor inherent (as Dr Rée thinks: – instead it is introduced in particular circumstances and is always incidental and added on).

5

Actually, just then I was preoccupied with something much more important than the nature of hypotheses, mine or anybody else's, on the origin of morality (or, to be more

8   In German: *Ursprung der Moral.*
9   Latin: completely, utterly.

exact: the latter concerned me only for one purpose, to which it is one route among many). For me it was a question of the *value* of morality, – and here I had to confront my great teacher Schopenhauer, to whom that book of mine spoke as though he were still present, with its passion and its hidden contradiction (– it, too, being a 'polemic'). I dealt especially with the value of the 'unegoistic', the instincts[10] of pity, self-denial, self-sacrifice which Schopenhauer had for so long gilded, deified and transcendentalized until he was finally left with them as those 'values as such' on the basis of which he *said 'no'* to life and to himself as well. But against *these* very instincts I gave vent to an increasingly deep mistrust, a scepticism which dug deeper and deeper! Precisely here I saw the *great* danger to mankind, its most sublime temptation and seduction – temptation to what? to nothingness? – precisely here I saw the beginning of the end, standstill, mankind looking back wearily, turning its will *against* life, and the onset of the final sickness becoming gently, sadly manifest: I understood the morality of pity, casting around ever wider to catch even philosophers and make them ill, as the most uncanny symptom of our European culture which has itself become uncanny, as its detour to a new Buddhism? to a new Euro-Buddhism? to – *nihilism?* . . . This predilection for and over-valuation of pity that modern philosophers show is, in fact, something new: up till now, philosophers were agreed as to the *worthlessness* of pity. I need only mention Plato, Spinoza, La Rochefoucauld and Kant, four minds as different from one another as it is possible to be, but united on one point: their low opinion of pity. –

6

This problem of the *value* of pity and of the morality of pity (– I am opposed to the disgraceful modern softness of feeling –) seems at first to be only an isolated phenomenon, a lone question mark; but whoever pauses over the question and *learns* to ask, will find what I found: – that a vast new panorama opens up for him, a possibility makes him giddy, mistrust, suspicion and fear of every kind spring up, belief in morality, every kind of morality, wavers, – finally, a new demand becomes articulate. So let us give voice to this *new demand*: we need a *critique* of moral values, *the value of these values should itself, for once, be examined* – and so we need to know about the conditions and circumstances under which the values grew up, developed and changed (morality as result, as symptom, as mask, as tartuffery, as sickness, as misunderstanding; but also morality as cause, remedy, stimulant, inhibition, poison), since we have neither had this knowledge up till now nor even desired it. People have taken the *value* of these 'values' as given, as factual, as beyond all questioning; up till now, nobody has had the remotest doubt or hesitation in placing higher value on 'the good man' than on 'the evil', higher value in the sense of advancement, benefit and prosperity for man in general (and this includes man's future). What if the opposite were true? What if a regressive trait lurked in 'the good man', likewise a danger, an enticement, a poison, a narcotic, so that the present lived *at the expense of the future?* Perhaps in more comfort and less danger, but also in a smaller-minded, meaner manner? . . . So that morality itself were to blame if man, as species, never reached his *highest* potential *power and splendour?* So that morality itself was the danger of dangers? . . .

---

10 In German: *Instinkte.*

7

Suffice it to say that since this revelation, I had reason to look around for scholarly, bold, hardworking colleagues (I am still looking). The vast, distant and hidden land of morality – of morality as it really existed and was really lived – has to be journeyed through with quite new questions and as it were with new eyes: and surely that means virtually *discovering* this land for the first time? . . . If, on my travels, I thought about the above-mentioned Dr Rée, amongst others, this was because I was certain that, judging from the questions he raised, he himself would have to adopt a more sensible method if he wanted to find the answers. Was I mistaken? At any rate, I wanted to focus this sharp, unbiased eye in a better direction, the direction of a real *history of morality*,[11] and to warn him, while there was still time, against such English hypothesis-mongering *into the blue*. It is quite clear which colour is a hundred times more important for a genealogist than blue: namely *grey*, which is to say, that which can be documented, which can actually be confirmed and has actually existed, in short, the whole, long, hard-to-decipher hieroglyphic script of man's moral past! *This* was unknown to Dr Rée; but he had read Darwin: – and so, in his hypotheses, the Darwinian beast and the ultra-modern, humble moral weakling who 'no longer bites' politely shake hands in a way that is at least entertaining, the latter with an expression of a certain good-humoured and cultivated indolence on his face, in which even a grain of pessimism and fatigue mingle: as if it were really not worth taking all these things – the problems of morality – so seriously. Now I, on the contrary, think there is nothing which more *rewards* being taken seriously; the reward being, for example, the possibility of one day being allowed to take them *gaily*. That gaiety, in fact, or to put it into my parlance, that *gay science* – is a reward: a reward for a long, brave, diligent, subterranean seriousness for which, admittedly, not everyone is suited. The day we can say, with conviction: 'Forwards! even our old morality would make a *comedy!*' we shall have discovered a new twist and possible outcome for the Dionysian drama of the 'fate of the soul' –: and he'll make good use of it, we can bet, he, the grand old eternal writer of the comedy of our existence! . . .

8

– If anyone finds this work incomprehensible and hard on the ears, I do not think the fault necessarily lies with me. It is clear enough, assuming, as I do, that people have first read my earlier works without sparing themselves some effort: because they really are not easy to approach. With regard to my *Zarathustra*, for example, I do not acknowledge anyone as an expert on it if he has not, at some time, been both profoundly wounded and profoundly delighted by it, for only then may he enjoy the privilege of sharing, with due reverence, the halcyon element from which the book was born and its sunny brightness, spaciousness, breadth and certainty. In other cases, the aphoristic form causes difficulty: this is because this form is *not taken seriously enough* these days. An aphorism, properly stamped and moulded, has not been 'deciphered' just because it has been read out; on the contrary, this is just the beginning of its proper *interpretation*,[12] and for this, an art of interpretation is needed. In the third essay

11   In German: *wirklichen Historie der Moral*.
12   In German: *Auslegung*.

of this book I have given an example of what I mean by 'interpretation' in such a case: – this treatise is a commentary on the aphorism that precedes it. I admit that you need one thing above all in order to practise the requisite *art* of reading, a thing which today people have been so good at forgetting – and so it will be some time before my writings are 'readable' –, you almost need to be a cow for this one thing and certainly *not* a 'modern man': it is *rumination* . . .

Sils–Maria, Upper Engadine
July 1887.

First Essay: 'Good and Evil,' 'Good and Bad'

1

– These English psychologists, who have to be thanked for having made the only attempts so far to write a history of the emergence of morality,[13] – provide us with a small riddle in the form of themselves; in fact, I admit that as living riddles they have a significant advantage over their books – *they are actually interesting!* These English psychologists – just what do they want? You always find them at the same task, whether they want to or not, pushing the *partie honteuse*[14] of our inner world to the foreground, and look-ing for what is really effective, guiding and decisive for our development where man's intellectual pride would least *wish* to find it (for example, in the *vis inertiae*[15] of habit, or in forgetfulness, or in a blind and random coupling of ideas, or in something purely passive, automatic, reflexive, molecular and thoroughly stupid) – what is it that actually drives these psychologists in precisely *this* direction all the time? Is it a secret, malicious, mean instinct to belittle man, which is perhaps unacknowledged? Or perhaps a pessimistic suspicion, the mistrust of disillusioned, surly idealists who have turned poisonous and green? Or a certain subterranean animosity and *rancune*[16] towards Christianity (and Plato), which has perhaps not even passed the threshold of the consciousness? Or even a lewd taste for the strange, for the painful paradox, for the dubious and nonsensical in life? Or finally – a bit of everything, a bit of meanness, a bit of gloominess, a bit of anti-Christianity, a bit of a thrill and need for pepper? . . . But people tell me that they are just old, cold, boring frogs crawling round men and hopping into them as if they were in their element, namely a *swamp*. I am resistant to hearing this and, indeed, I do not believe it; and if it is permissible to wish where it is impossible to know, I sincerely hope that the reverse is true, – that these analysts holding a microscope to the soul are actually brave, generous and proud animals, who know how to control their own plea-sure and pain and have been taught to sacrifice desirability to truth, *every* truth, even a plain, bitter, ugly, foul, unchristian, immoral truth . . . Because there are such truths. –

2

So you have to respect the good spirits which preside in these historians of morality! But it is unfortunately a fact that *historical spirit* itself is lacking in them, they have

---

13   In German: *Entstehungsgeschichte der Moral.*
14   French: shameful part.
15   Latin: force of inactivity.
16   French: rancor.

been left in the lurch by all the good spirits of history itself! As is now established philosophical practice, they all think in a way that is *essentially* unhistorical; this can't be doubted. The idiocy of their moral genealogy is revealed at the outset when it is a question of conveying the descent of the concept and judgment of 'good'. 'Originally' – they decree – 'unegoistic acts were praised and called good by their recipients, in other words, by the people to whom they were *useful*; later, everyone *forgot* the origin of the praise and because such acts had always been *routinely* praised as good, people began also to experience them as good – as if they were something good as such'. We can see at once: this first deduction contains all the typical traits of idiosyncratic English psychologists, – we have 'usefulness', 'forgetting', 'routine' and finally 'error', all as the basis of a respect for values of which the higher man has hitherto been proud, as though it were a sort of general privilege of mankind. This pride *must be* humbled, this valuation devalued: has that been achieved? . . . Now for me, it is obvious that the real breeding-ground for the concept 'good' has been sought and located in the wrong place by this theory: the judgment 'good' does *not* emanate from those to whom goodness is shown! Instead it has been 'the good' themselves, meaning the noble, the mighty, the high-placed and the high-minded, who saw and judged themselves and their actions as good, I mean first-rate, in contrast to everything lowly, low-minded, common and plebeian. It was from this *pathos of distance* that they first claimed the right to create values and give these values names: usefulness was none of their concern! The standpoint of usefulness is as alien and inappropriate as it can be to such a heated eruption of the highest rank-ordering and rank-defining value judgments: this is the point where feeling reaches the opposite of the low temperatures needed for any calculation of prudence or reckoning of usefulness, – and not just for once, for one exceptional moment, but permanently. The pathos of nobility and distance, as I said, the continuing and predominant feeling of complete and fundamental superiority of a higher ruling kind in relation to a lower kind, to those 'below' – *that* is the origin of the antithesis 'good' and 'bad'. (The seigneurial privilege of giving names even allows us to conceive of the origin of language itself as a manifestation of the power of the rulers: they say 'this *is* so and so', they set their seal on everything and every occurrence with a sound and thereby take possession of it, as it were.) It is because of this origin that the word 'good' is *not* absolutely necessarily attached to 'unegoistic' actions: as the superstition of these moral genealogists would have it. On the contrary, it is only with a *decline* of aristocratic value-judgments that this whole antithesis between 'egoistic' and 'unegoistic' forces itself more and more on man's conscience, – it is, to use my language, the *herd instinct* which, with that, finally gets its word in (and makes *words*). And even then it takes long enough for this instinct to become sufficiently dominant for the valuation of moral values to become enmeshed and embedded in the antithesis (as is the case in contemporary Europe, for example: the prejudice which takes 'moral', 'unegoistic' and '*désintéressé*'[17] as equivalent terms already rules with the power of a 'fixed idea' and mental illness).

[. . .]

17   French: disinterested.

6

If the highest caste is at the same time the *clerical* caste and therefore chooses a title for its overall description which calls its priestly function to mind, this does not yet constitute an exception to the rule that the concept of political superiority always resolves itself into the concept of psychological superiority (although this may be the occasion giving rise to exceptions). This is an example of the first juxtaposition of 'pure' and 'impure' as signs of different estates; and later 'good' and 'bad' develop in a direction which no longer refers to social standing. In addition, people should be wary of taking these terms 'pure' and 'impure' too seriously, too far or even symbolically: all ancient man's concepts were originally understood – to a degree we can scarcely imagine – as crude, coarse, detached, narrow, direct and in particular *unsymbolic*. From the outset the 'pure man' was just a man who washed, avoided certain foods which cause skin complaints, did not sleep with the filthy women from the lower orders and had a horror of blood, – nothing more, not much more! And yet the very nature of an essentially priestly aristocracy shows how contradictory valuations could become dangerously internalized and sharpened, precisely in such an aristocracy at an early stage; and in fact clefts were finally driven between man and man which even an Achilles of free-thinking would shudder to cross. From the very beginning there has been something *unhealthy* about these priestly aristocracies and in the customs dominant there, which are turned away from action and which are partly brooding and partly emotionally explosive, resulting in the almost inevitable bowel complaints and neurasthenia which have plagued the clergy down the ages; but as for the remedy they themselves found for their sickness, – surely one must say that its after-effects have shown it to be a hundred times more dangerous than the disease it was meant to cure? People are still ill from the after-effects of these priestly quack-cures! For example, think of certain diets (avoidance of meat), of fasting, sexual abstinence, the flight 'into the desert' (Weir-Mitchell's bed-rest, admittedly without the subsequent overfeeding and weight-gain which constitute the most effective antidote to all hysteria brought on by the ascetic ideal): think, too, of the whole metaphysics of the clergy, which is antagonistic towards the senses, making men lazy and refined, think, too, of their Fakir-like and Brahmin-like self-hypnotizing – Brahminism as crystal ball and fixed idea – and the final, all-too-comprehensible general disenchantment with its radical cure, *nothingness* (or God: – the yearning for a *unio mystica*[18] with God is the Buddhist yearning for nothingness, Nirvâna – and no more!) Priests make *everything* more dangerous, not just medicaments and healing arts but pride, revenge, acumen, debauchery, love, lust for power, virtue, sickness; – in any case, with some justification one could add that man first became an *interesting animal* on the foundation of this *essentially dangerous* form of human existence, the priest, and that the human soul became *deep* in the higher sense and turned *evil* for the first time – and of course, these are the two basic forms of man's superiority, hitherto, over other animals! . . .

7

– You will have already guessed how easy it was for the priestly method of valuation to split off from the chivalric-aristocratic method and then to develop further into the

18   Latin: mystical union.

opposite of the latter; this receives a special impetus when the priestly caste and warrior caste confront one another in jealousy and cannot agree on the prize of war. The chivalric-aristocratic value-judgments are based on a powerful physicality, a blossoming, rich, even effervescent good health which includes the things needed to maintain it, war, adventure, hunting, dancing, jousting and everything else that contains strong, free, happy action. The priestly-aristocratic method of valuation – as we have seen – has different criteria: woe betide it when it comes to war! As we know, priests make the most *evil enemies* – but why? Because they are the most powerless. Out of this powerlessness, their hate swells into something huge and uncanny to a most intellectual and poisonous level. The greatest haters in world history, and the most intelligent [*die geistreichsten Hasser*], have always been priests: – nobody else's intelligence [*Geist*] stands a chance against the intelligence [*Geist*] of priestly revenge. The history of mankind would be far too stupid a thing if it had not had the intellect [*Geist*] of the powerless injected into it: – let us take the best example straight away. Nothing which has been done on earth against 'the noble', 'the mighty', 'the masters' and 'the rulers', is worth mentioning compared with what *the Jews* have done against them: the Jews, that priestly people, which in the last resort was able to gain satisfaction from its enemies and conquerors only through a radical revaluation of their values, that is, through an act of the most *deliberate revenge* [*durch einen Akt der geistigsten Rache*]. Only this was fitting for a priestly people with the most entrenched priestly vengefulness. It was the Jews who, rejecting the aristocratic value equation (good = noble = powerful = beautiful = happy = blessed) ventured, with awe-inspiring consistency, to bring about a reversal and held it in the teeth of their unfathomable hatred (the hatred of the powerless), saying, 'Only those who suffer are good, only the poor, the powerless, the lowly are good; the suffering, the deprived, the sick, the ugly, are the only pious people, the only ones saved, salvation is for them alone, whereas you rich, the noble and powerful, you are eternally wicked, cruel, lustful, insatiate, godless, you will also be eternally wretched, cursed and damned!' . . . We know *who* became heir to this Jewish revaluation . . . With regard to the huge and incalculably disastrous initiative taken by the Jews with this most fundamental of all declarations of war, I recall the words I wrote on another occasion (*Beyond Good and Evil*, section 195) – namely, that *the slaves' revolt in morality*[19] begins with the Jews: a revolt which has two thousand years of history behind it and which has only been lost sight of because – it was victorious . . .

8

– But you don't understand that? You don't have eyes for something which needed two millennia to achieve victory? . . . There is nothing surprising about that: all *long* things are difficult to see, to see round. But *that* is what happened: from the trunk of the tree of revenge and hatred, Jewish hatred – the deepest and most sublime, indeed a hatred which created ideals and changed values, the like of which has never been seen on earth – there grew something just as incomparable, a *new love*, the deepest and most sublime kind of love: – and what other trunk could it have grown out of? . . . But don't make the mistake of thinking that it had grown forth as a denial of the

---

19 In German: *Sklavenaufstand in der Moral*.

thirst for revenge, as the opposite of Jewish hatred! No, the reverse is true! This love grew out of the hatred, as its crown, as the triumphant crown expanding ever wider in the purest brightness and radiance of the sun, the crown which, as it were, in the realm of light and height, was pursuing the aims of that hatred, victory, spoils, seduction with the same urgency with which the roots of that hatred were burrowing ever more thoroughly and greedily into everything that was deep and evil. This Jesus of Nazareth, as the embodiment of the gospel of love, this 'redeemer' bringing salvation and victory to the poor, the sick, to sinners – was he not seduction in its most sinister and irresistible form, seduction and the circuitous route to just those very *Jewish* values and innovative ideals? Did Israel not reach the pinnacle of her sublime vengefulness via this very 'redeemer', this apparent opponent of and disperser of Israel? Is it not part of a secret black art of a truly *great* politics of revenge, a far-sighted, subterranean revenge, slow to grip and calculating, that Israel had to denounce her actual instrument of revenge before all the world as a mortal enemy and nail him to the cross so that 'all the world', namely all Israel's enemies, could safely nibble at this bait? And could anyone, on the other hand, using all the ingenuity of his intellect, think up a more *dangerous* bait? Something to equal the enticing, intoxicating, benumbing, corrupting power of that symbol of the 'holy cross', to equal that horrible paradox of a 'God on the Cross', to equal that mystery of an unthinkable final act of extreme cruelty and self-crucifixion of God for the *salvation of mankind*? . . . At least it is certain that *sub hoc signo*[20] Israel, with its revenge and revaluation of all former values, has triumphed repeatedly over all other ideals, all *nobler* ideals.

9

– 'But why do you talk about *nobler* ideals! Let's bow to the facts: the people have won – or "the slaves", the "plebeians", "the herd", or whatever you want to all them – if the Jews made this come about, good for them! No people ever had a more world-historic mission. "The Masters" are deposed; the morality of the common people has triumphed. You might take this victory for blood-poisoning (it did mix the races up) – I do not deny it; but undoubtedly this intoxication has *succeeded*. The "salvation" of the human race (I mean, from "the Masters") is well on course; everything is being made appreciably Jewish, Christian or plebeian (never mind the words!). The passage of this poison through the whole body of mankind seems unstoppable, even though its tempo and pace, from now on, might tend to be slower, softer, quieter, calmer – there is no hurry . . . With this in view, does the church still have a *vital* role, indeed, does it have a right to exist? Or could one do without it? *Quaeritur.*[21] It seems that the Church rather slows down and blocks the passage of poison instead of accelerating it? Well, that might be what makes it useful . . . Certainly it is by now crude and boorish, something which is repugnant to a more tender intellect, to a truly modern taste. Should not the church at least try to be more refined? . . . Nowadays it alienates, more than it seduces . . . Who amongst us would be a free-thinker if it were not for the Church? We loathe the Church, *not* its poison . . . Apart from the Church, we too love the poison . . .' – This is the epilogue by a 'free-thinker' to my speech, an

---

20 Latin: under this sign.
21 Latin: That is the question.

honest animal as he clearly shows himself to be, and moreover a democrat; he had listened to me up to that point, and could not stand listening to my silence. As a matter of fact, there is much for me to keep silent about at this point. –

10

The beginning of the slaves' revolt in morality occurs when **ressentiment** itself turns creative and gives birth to values: the *ressentiment* of those beings who, being denied the proper response of action, compensate for it only with imaginary revenge. Whereas all noble morality grows out of a triumphant saying 'yes' to itself, slave morality says 'no' on principle to everything that is 'outside', 'other', 'non-self': and *this* 'no' is its creative deed. This reversal of the evaluating glance – this *inevitable* orientation to the outside instead of back onto itself – is a feature of *ressentiment*: in order to come about, slave morality first has to have an opposing, external world, it needs, physiologically speaking, external stimuli in order to act at all, – its action is basically a reaction. The opposite is the case with the noble method of valuation: this acts and grows sponta- neously, seeking out its opposite only so that it can say 'yes' to itself even more thank- fully and exultantly, – its negative concept 'low', 'common', 'bad' is only a pale contrast created after the event compared to its positive basic concept, saturated with life and passion, 'We the noble, the good, the beautiful and the happy!' When the noble method of valuation makes a mistake and sins against reality, this happens in relation to the sphere with which it is *not* sufficiently familiar, a true knowledge of which it has indeed rigidly resisted: in some circumstances, it misjudges the sphere it despises, that of the common man, the rabble; on the other hand, we should bear in mind that the distortion which results from the feeling of contempt, disdain and superciliousness, always assuming that the image of the despised person is *distorted*, remains far behind the distortion with which the entrenched hatred and revenge of the powerless man attacks his opponent – in effigy of course. Indeed, contempt has too much negligence, nonchalance, complacency and impatience, even too much personal cheerfulness mixed into it, for it to be in a position to transform its object into a real caricature and monster. Nor should one fail to hear the almost kindly nuances which the Greek nobility, for example, places in all words which it uses to distinguish itself from the rabble; a sort of sympathy, consideration and indulgence incessantly permeates and sugars them, with the result that nearly all words referring to the common man remain as expressions for 'unhappy', 'pitiable' (compare δειλός, δείλαιος, πονηρός, μοχθηρός,[22] the last two actually designating the common man as slave worker and beast of burden) – and on the other hand, 'bad', 'low' and 'unhappy' have never ceased to reverberate in the Greek ear in a tone in which 'unhappy' predominates: this is a legacy of the old, nobler, aristocratic method of valuation, which does not deny itself even in contempt (– philologists will remember the sense in which οἴζυρός,[23] ἄνολβος,[24]

---

22   Greek: *deilos*, cowardly, low-born, miserable, worthless; *deilaios*, wretched, paltry; *poneros*, wretched, worthless, base, cowardly; *mochtheros*, wretched, miserable, worthless, etc.
23   "Oi" is an interjection expressive of pain. A person whose life gives ample occasion for the use of this interjection is *oizuros* (pitiable, miserable).
24   Greek: *anolbos*, poor, unfortunate, luckless.

τλήμων,[25] δυϛτυχεῖν,[26] ξυμφοϱά[27] are used). The 'well-born' *felt* they were 'the happy'; they did not need first of all to construct their happiness artificially by looking at their enemies, or in some cases by talking themselves into it, *lying themselves into it* (as all men of *ressentiment* are wont to do); and also, as complete men bursting with strength and therefore *necessarily* active, they knew they must not separate happiness from action, – being active is by necessity counted as part of happiness (this is the etymological derivation of εὖ πϱάττειν)[28] – all very much the opposite of 'happiness' at the level of the powerless, the oppressed, and those rankled with poisonous and hostile feelings, for whom it manifests itself as essentially a narcotic, an anaesthetic, rest, peace, 'sabbath', relaxation of the mind and stretching of the limbs, in short as something *passive*. While the noble man is confident and frank with himself (γενναῖος,[29] 'of noble birth', underlines the nuance 'upright' and probably 'naïve' as well), the man of *ressentiment* is neither upright nor naïve, nor honest and straight with himself. His soul *squints*; his mind loves dark corners, secret paths and back-doors, everything secretive appeals to him as being *his* world, *his* security, *his* comfort; he knows all about keeping quiet, not forgetting, waiting, temporarily humbling and abasing himself. A race of such men of *ressentiment* will inevitably end up *cleverer* than any noble race, and will respect cleverness to a quite different degree as well: namely, as a condition of existence of the first rank, whilst the cleverness of noble men can easily have a subtle aftertaste of luxury and refinement about it: – precisely because in this area, it is nowhere near as important as the complete certainty of function of the governing *unconscious* instincts, nor indeed as important as a certain lack of cleverness, such as a daring charge at danger or at the enemy, or those frenzied sudden fits of anger, love, reverence, gratitude and revenge by which noble souls down the ages have recognized one another. When *ressentiment* does occur in the noble man himself, it is consumed and exhausted in an immediate reaction, and therefore it does not *poison*, on the other hand, it does not occur at all in countless cases where it is unavoidable for all who are weak and powerless. To be unable to take his enemies, his misfortunes and even his *misdeeds* seriously for long – that is the sign of strong, rounded natures with a superabundance of a power which is flexible, formative, healing and can make one forget (a good example from the modern world is Mirabeau, who had no recall for the insults and slights directed at him and who could not forgive, simply because he – forgot). A man like this shakes from him, with one shrug, many worms which would have burrowed into another man; here and here alone is it possible, assuming that this is possible at all on earth – truly to '*love* your enemies'.[30] How much respect a noble man has for his enemies! – and a respect of that sort is a bridge to love . . . For he insists on having his enemy to himself, as a mark of distinction, indeed he will tolerate as enemies none other than such as have nothing to be despised and a *great deal* to be honoured! Against this, imagine 'the enemy' as conceived of by the man of *ressentiment* – and here we

25   Greek: *tlemon*, endurance, suffering.
26   Greek: *dystychein*, unlucky, unhappy, unfortunate.
27   Greek: *xymphora*, chance, accident, misfortune.
28   Greek: *eu prattein*, an ambiguous term similar to the English 'do well,' i.e. engage in some activity successfully or 'fare well.'
29   Greek: *gennaios*, noble, high-minded.
30   Cf. Matthew 5: 43. The translation has been modified from 'neighbour' to 'enemies.'

have his deed, his creation: he has conceived of the 'evil enemy', '*the evil one*' as a basic idea to which he now thinks up a copy and counterpart, the 'good one' – himself! . . .

11

Exactly the opposite is true of the noble man who conceives of the basic idea 'good' by himself, in advance and spontaneously, and only then creates a notion of 'bad'! This 'bad' of noble origin and that 'evil' from the cauldron of unassuaged hatred – the first is an afterthought, an aside, a complementary colour, whilst the other is the original, the beginning, the actual *deed* in the conception of slave morality – how different are the two words 'bad' and 'evil', although both seem to be the opposite for the same concept, 'good'! But it is *not* the same concept 'good'; on the contrary, one should ask *who* is actually evil in the sense of the morality of *ressentiment*. The stern reply is: *precisely* the 'good' person of the other morality, the noble, powerful, dominating man, but re-touched, re-interpreted and re-viewed through the poisonous eye of *ressentiment*. Here there is one point which we would be the last to deny: anyone who came to know these 'good men' as enemies came to know nothing but '*evil enemies*', the same people who are so strongly held in check by custom, respect, habit, gratitude and even more through spying on one another and through peer-group jealousy, who, on the other hand, behave towards one another by showing such resourcefulness in consideration, self-control, delicacy, loyalty, pride and friendship, – they are not much better than uncaged beasts of prey in the world outside where the strange, the foreign, begin. There they enjoy freedom from every social constraint, in the wilderness they compensate for the tension which is caused by being closed in and fenced in by the peace of the community for so long, they *return* to the innocent conscience of the wild beast, as exultant monsters, who perhaps go away having committed a hideous succession of murder, arson, rape and torture, in a mood of bravado and spiritual equilibrium as though they had simply played a student's prank, convinced that poets will now have something to sing about and celebrate for quite some time. At the centre of all these noble races we cannot fail to see the blond beast of prey, the magnificent *blond beast* avidly prowling round for spoil and victory; this hidden centre needs release from time to time, the beast must out again, must return to the wild: – Roman, Arabian, Germanic, Japanese nobility, Homeric heroes, Scandinavian Vikings – in this requirement they are all alike. It was the noble races which left the concept of 'barbarian' in their traces wherever they went; even their highest culture betrays the fact that they were conscious of this and indeed proud of it (for example, when Pericles, in that famous funeral oration, tells his Athenians, 'Our daring has forced a path to every land and sea, erecting timeless memorials to itself everywhere for good *and ill*').[31] This 'daring' of the noble races, mad, absurd and sudden in the way it manifests itself, the unpredictability and even the improbability of their undertakings – Pericles singles out the ῥαθυμία[32] of the Athenians for praise – their unconcern and scorn for safety, body, life, comfort, their shocking cheerfulness, and depth of delight in all destruction, in all the debauches of victory and cruelty – all this, for those who suffered under it, was summed up in the image of the 'barbarian',

---

31   Thucydides, *History of the Peloponnesian War*, II. 39ff.
32   Greek: *rhathymia*, indifference, rashness.

the 'evil enemy', perhaps the 'Goth' or the 'Vandal'. The deep and icy mistrust which the German arouses as soon as he comes to power, which we see again even today – is still the aftermath of that inextinguishable horror with which Europe viewed the raging of the blond Germanic beast for centuries (although between the old Germanic peoples and us Germans there is scarcely an idea in common, let alone a blood relationship). I once remarked on Hesiod's dilemma[33] when he thought up the series of cultural eras and tried to express them in gold, silver and iron: he could find no other solution to the contradiction presented to him by the magnificent but at the same time so shockingly violent world of Homer than to make two eras out of one, which he now placed one behind the other – first the era of heroes and demigods from Troy and Thebes, as that world which remained in the memory of the noble races which had their ancestors in it; then the iron era, as that same world appeared to the descendants of the downtrodden, robbed, ill-treated, and those carried off and sold: as an era of iron, hard, as I said, cold, cruel, lacking feeling and conscience, crushing everything and coating it with blood. Assuming that what is at any rate believed as 'truth' were indeed true, that it is the *meaning of all culture*[34] to breed a tame and civilized animal, a *household pet*, out of the beast of prey 'man', then one would undoubtedly have to view all instinctive reaction and instinctive *ressentiment*, by means of which the noble races and their ideals were finally wrecked and overpowered, as the actual *instruments of culture*; which, however, is not to say that the *bearers* of these instincts were themselves representatives of the culture. Instead, the opposite would be not only probable – no! it is *visible* today! These bearers of oppressive, vindictive instincts, the descendants of all European and non-European slavery, in particular of all pre-Aryan population – represent the *decline* of mankind! These 'instruments of culture' are a disgrace to man, more a grounds for suspicion of, or an argument against, 'culture' in general! We may be quite justified in retaining our fear of the blond beast at the centre of every noble race and remain on our guard: but who would not, a hundred times over, prefer to fear if he can admire at the same time, rather than *not* fear, but thereby permanently retain the disgusting spectacle of the failed, the stunted, the wasted away and the poisoned? And is that not *our* fate? What constitutes *our* aversion to 'man' today? – for we *suffer* from man, no doubt about that. – *Not* fear; rather, the fact that we have nothing to fear from man; that 'man' is first and foremost a teeming mass of worms; that the 'tame man', who is incurably mediocre and unedifying, has already learnt to view himself as the aim and pinnacle, the meaning of history,[35] the 'higher man'; – yes, the fact that he has a certain right to feel like that in so far as he feels distanced from the superabundance of failed, sickly, tired and exhausted people of whom today's Europe is beginning to reek, and in so far as he is at least relatively successful, at least still capable of living, at least saying 'yes' to life . . .

12

– At this juncture I cannot suppress a sigh and one last hope. What do I find absolutely intolerable? Something which I just cannot cope alone with and which suffocates me and makes me feel faint? Bad air! Bad air! That something failed comes

33 Hesiod, *Works and Days*, 143ff.
34 In German: *der Sinn aller Cultur.*
35 In German: *Sinn der Geschichte.*

near me, that I have to smell the bowels of a failed soul! . . . Apart from that, what cannot be borne in the way of need, deprivation, bad weather, disease, toil, solitude? Basically we can cope with everything else, born as we are to an underground and battling existence; again and again we keep coming up to the light, again and again we experience our golden hour of victory, – and then there we stand, the way we were born, unbreakable, tense, ready for new, more difficult and distant things, like a bow which is merely stretched tauter by affliction. – But from time to time grant me – assuming that there are divine benefactresses beyond good and evil – a glimpse, grant me just one glimpse of something perfect, completely finished, happy, powerful, triumphant, which still leaves something to fear! A glimpse of a man who justifies man *himself*, a stroke of luck, an instance of a man who makes up for and redeems man, and enables us to retain our *faith in mankind!* . . . For the matter stands like so: the stunting and levelling of European man conceals *our* greatest danger, because the sight of this makes us tired . . . Today we see nothing that wants to expand, we suspect that things will just continue to decline, getting thinner, better-natured, cleverer, more comfortable, more mediocre, more indifferent, more Chinese, more Christian – no doubt about it, man is getting 'better' all the time . . . Right here is where the destiny of Europe lies – in losing our fear of man we have also lost our love for him, our respect for him, our hope in him and even our will to be man. The sight of man now makes us tired – what is nihilism today if it is not *that*? . . . We are tired of *man* . . .

13

– But let us return: the problem of the *other* origin of 'good', of good as thought up by the man of *ressentiment*, demands its solution. – There is nothing strange about the fact that lambs bear a grudge towards large birds of prey: but that is no reason to blame the large birds of prey for carrying off the little lambs. And if the lambs say to each other, 'These birds of prey are evil; and whoever is least like a bird of prey and most like its opposite, a lamb, – is good, isn't he?', then there is no reason to raise objections to this setting-up of an ideal beyond the fact that the birds of prey will view it somewhat derisively, and will perhaps say, '*We* don't bear any grudge at all towards these good lambs, in fact we love them, nothing is tastier than a tender lamb.' – It is just as absurd to ask strength *not* to express itself as strength, *not* to be a desire to overthrow, crush, become master, to be a thirst for enemies, resistance and triumphs, as it is to ask weakness to express itself as strength. A quantum of force is just such a quantum of drive, will, action, in fact it is nothing but this driving, willing and acting, and only the seduction of language (and the fundamental errors of reason petrified within it), which construes and misconstrues all actions as conditional upon an agency, a 'subject', can make it appear otherwise. And just as the common people separates lightning from its flash and takes the latter to be a *deed*, something performed by a subject, which is called lightning, popular morality separates strength from the manifestations of strength, as though there were an indifferent substratum behind the strong person which had the *freedom* to manifest strength or not. But there is no such substratum; there is no 'being' behind the deed, its effect and what becomes of it; 'the doer' is invented as an afterthought, – the doing is everything. Basically, the common people double a deed; when they see lightning, they make a doing-a-deed out of it: they posit the same event, first as cause and then as its effect. The scientists do no better when they say 'force moves, force causes' and such like, – all our science, in spite of its coolness and freedom from emotion, still stands exposed to the seduction of language and has not ridded itself of the changelings foisted upon it, the 'subjects' (the atom is, for example, just such a changeling, likewise the Kantian 'thing-in-itself'): no wonder, then, if the entrenched, secretly smouldering emotions of revenge and hatred put this belief to their own use and, in fact, do not defend any belief more passionately than that *the strong are free* to be weak, and the birds of prey are free to be lambs: – in this way, they gain the right to make the birds of prey *responsible* for being birds of prey . . . When the oppressed, the downtrodden, the violated say to each other with the vindictive cunning of powerlessness: 'Let us be different from evil people, let us be good! And a good person is anyone who does not rape, does not harm anyone, who does not attack, does not retaliate, who leaves the taking of revenge to God, who keeps hidden as we do, avoids all evil and asks little from life in general, like us who are patient, humble and upright' – this means, if heard coolly and impartially, nothing more than 'We weak people are just weak; it is good to do nothing *for which we are not strong enough*' – but this grim state of affairs, this cleverness of the lowest rank which even insects possess (which play dead, in order not to 'do too much' when in great danger), has, thanks to the counterfeiting and self-deception of power-lessness, clothed itself in the finery of self-denying, quiet, patient virtue, as though the weakness of the weak were itself – I mean its *essence*, its effect, its whole unique, unavoidable, irredeemable reality – a voluntary achievement, something wanted, chosen, a *deed*, an *accomplishment*. This type of man *needs* to believe in an unbiased 'subject' with freedom of choice, because he has an instinct of self-preservation and self-affirmation in which every lie is sanctified. The reason the subject (or, as we more colloquially say, the *soul*) has been, until now, the best doctrine on earth, is perhaps because it facilitated that sublime self-deception whereby the majority of the dying, the weak and the oppressed of every kind could construe weakness itself as freedom, and their particular mode of existence as an *accomplishment*.

[. . .]

16

Let us draw to a close. The two *opposing* values 'good and bad', 'good and evil' have fought a terrible battle for thousands of years on earth; and although the latter has been dominant for a long time, there is still no lack of places where the battle remains undecided. You could even say that, in the meantime, it has reached ever greater heights but at the same time has become ever deeper and more intellectual: so that there is, today, perhaps no more distinguishing feature of the *'higher nature'*, the intellectual nature, than to be divided in this sense and really and truly a battle ground for these opposites. The symbol of this fight, written in a script which has hitherto remained legible throughout human history, is 'Rome against Judea, Judea against Rome': – up to now there has been no greater event than *this* battle, *this* question, *this* contradiction of mortal enemies. Rome saw the Jew as something contrary to nature, as though he were its polar opposite, a monster; in Rome, the Jew was looked upon as *convicted* of hatred against the whole of mankind:[36] rightly, if one is right in linking the well being

---

36 In the *Annals* (XV. 44), Tacitus describes "those popularly called 'Christians'" as "con-victed of hatred against the whole human species"; in the *Histories* (V. 5), he claims that the Jews show benevolence to one another, but exhibit hatred of all the rest of the world.

and future of the human race with the unconditional rule of aristocratic values, Roman values. What, on the other hand, did the Jews feel about Rome? We can guess from a thousand indicators; but it is enough to call once more to mind the Apocalypse of John, the wildest of all outbursts ever written which revenge has on its conscience. (By the way, we must not underestimate the profound consistency of Christian instinct in inscribing this book of hate to the disciple of love, the very same to whom it attributed that passionately ecstatic gospel –: there is some truth in this, however much literary counterfeiting might have been necessary to the purpose.) So the Romans were the strong and noble, stronger and nobler than anybody hitherto who had lived or been dreamt of on earth; their every relic and inscription brings delight, provided one can guess *what* it is that is doing the writing there. By contrast, the Jews were a priestly nation of *ressentiment par excellence*, possessing an unparalleled genius for popular morality: compare peoples with similar talents, such as the Chinese or the Germans, with the Jews, and you will realize who are first rate and who are fifth. Which of them has *prevailed* for the time being, Rome or Judea? But there is no trace of doubt: just consider whom you bow down to in Rome itself, today, as though to the embodiment of the highest values – and not just in Rome, but over nearly half the earth, everywhere where man has become tame or wants to become tame, to *three Jews*, as we know, and *one Jewess* (to Jesus of Nazareth, Peter the Fisherman, Paul the Carpet-Weaver and the mother of Jesus mentioned first, whose name was Mary). This is very remarkable: without a doubt Rome has been defeated. However, in the Renaissance there was a brilliant, uncanny reawakening of the classical ideal, of the noble method of valuing everything: Rome itself woke up, as though from suspended animation, under the pressure of the new, Judaic Rome built over it, which looked like an ecumenical synagogue and was called 'Church': but Judea triumphed again at once, thanks to that basically proletarian (German and English) *ressentiment*–movement which people called the Reformation, including its inevitable consequence, the restoration of the church, – as well as the restoration of the ancient, tomb-like silence of classical Rome. In an even more decisive and profound sense than then, Judea once again triumphed over the classical ideal with the French Revolution: the last political nobility in Europe, that of the *French* seventeenth and eighteenth centuries, collapsed under the *ressentiment*-instincts of the rabble, – the world had never heard greater rejoicing and more uproarious enthusiasm! True, the most dreadful and unexpected thing happened in the middle: the ancient ideal itself appeared *bodily* and with unheard-of splendour before the eye and conscience of mankind, and once again, stronger, simpler and more penetrating than ever, in answer to the old, mendacious *ressentiment* slogan of *priority for the majority*, of man's will to baseness, abasement, levelling, decline and decay, there rang out the terrible and enchanting counter-slogan: *priority for the few*! Like a last signpost to the *other* path, Napoleon appeared as a man more unique and late-born for his times than ever a man had been before, and in him, the problem of the *noble ideal itself* was made flesh – just think *what* a problem that is: Napoleon, this synthesis of *monster* [*Unmensch*] and *Overman* . . .

17

– Was it over after that? Was that greatest among all conflicts of ideals placed *ad acta*[37] for ever? Or just postponed, postponed indefinitely? . . . Won't there have to be an even more terrible flaring up of the old flame, one prepared much longer in advance? And more: shouldn't one desire *that* with all one's strength? or will it, even? or even promote it? . . . Whoever, like my readers, now starts to ponder these points and reflect further, will have difficulty coming to a speedy conclusion, – reason enough, then, for me to come to a conclusion myself, assuming that it has been sufficiently clear for some time what I *want*, what I actually want with that dangerous slogan which is written on the spine of my last book, *Beyond Good and Evil* . . . at least this does *not* mean 'Beyond Good and Bad.' – –

Note

I take the opportunity presented to me by this essay, of publicly and formally expressing a wish which I have only expressed in occasional conversations with scholars up till now: that is, that some Faculty of Philosophy should do the great service of promoting the study of *the history of morality* by means of a series of academic prize essays: – perhaps this book might serve to give a powerful impetus in such a direction. With regard to such a possibility, I raise the following question for consideration: it merits the attention of philologists and historians as well as those who are actually philosophers by profession:

'What signposts does linguistics, especially the study of etymology, give to the history of the evolution of moral concepts?'

 – On the other hand, it is just as essential to win the support of physiologists and doctors for these problems (on the *value* of all previous valuations): we can leave it to the professional philosophers to act as advocates and mediators in this, once they have completely succeeded in transforming the originally so reserved and suspicious relationship between philosophy, physiology and medicine into the most cordial and fruitful exchange. Indeed, every table of values, every 'thou shalt' known to history or the study of ethnology, needs first and foremost a *physiological* elucidation and interpretation, rather than a psychological one; and all of them await critical study from medical science. The question: what is this or that table of values and 'morals' *worth*? needs to be asked from different angles; in particular, the question 'value for *what*?' cannot be examined too finely. Something, for example, which obviously had value with regard to the longest possible life-span of a race (or to the improvement of its abilities to adapt to a particular climate, or to maintaining the greatest number) would not have anything like the same value if it was a question of developing a stronger type. The good of the majority and the good of the minority are conflicting moral stand-points: we leave it to the naïvety of English biologists to view the first as higher in value as *such* . . . *All* sciences must, from now on, prepare the way for the future work of the philosopher: this work being understood to mean that the philosopher has to solve the *problem of values* and that he has to decide on the *hierarchy of values*. –

37   Latin: shelved, filed away.

Second Essay: 'Guilt,' 'Bad Conscience,' and Related Matters

1

To breed an animal *which is permitted to make promises*[38] – is that not precisely the para-doxical task which nature has set herself with regard to humankind? is it not the real problem *of* humankind? . . . The fact that this problem has been solved to a large degree must seem all the more surprising to the person who can fully appreciate the oppos-ing force, *forgetfulness*. Forgetfulness is not just a *vis inertiae*,[39] as superficial people believe, but is rather an active ability to suppress, positive in the strongest sense of the word, to which we owe the fact that what we simply live through, experience, take in, no more enters our consciousness during digestion (one could call it spiritual ingestion) than does the thousand-fold process which takes place with our physical consumption of food, our so-called ingestion. To shut the doors and windows of consciousness for a while; not to be bothered by the noise and battle with which our underworld of serviceable organs work with and against each other; a little peace, a little *tabula rasa*[40] of consciousness to make room for something new, above all for the nobler functions and functionaries, for ruling, predicting, predetermining (our organism runs along oligarchic lines, you see) – that, as I said, is the benefit of active forgetfulness, like a doorkeeper or guardian of mental order, rest and etiquette: from which we can immediately see how there could be no happiness, cheerfulness, hope, pride, *immedi-acy*, without forgetfulness. The person in whom this apparatus of suppression is dam-aged, so that it stops working, can be compared (and not just compared –) to a dyspeptic; he cannot 'cope' with anything . . . And precisely this necessarily forgetful animal, in whom forgetting is a strength, representing a form of *robust* health, has bred for him-self a counter-device, memory, with the help of which forgetfulness can be suspended in certain cases, – namely in those cases where a promise is to be made: consequently, it is by no means merely a passive inability to be rid of an impression once it has made its impact, nor is it just indigestion caused by giving your word on some occasion and finding you cannot cope, instead it is an active *desire* not to let go, a desire to keep on desiring what has been, on some occasion, desired, really it is the *will's memory*: so that a world of strange new things, circumstances and even acts of will may be placed quite safely in between the original 'I will', 'I shall do' and the actual discharge of the will, its *act*, without breaking this long chain of the will. But what a lot of pre-conditions there are for this! In order to have that degree of control over the future, man must first have learnt to distinguish between what happens by accident and what by design, to think causally, to view the future as the present and anticipate it, to grasp with certainty what is end and what is means, in all, to be able to calculate, compute – and before he can do this, man himself will really have to become *reliable, regular, automatic* [*notwendig*], even in his own self-image, so that he, as someone making a promise is, is answerable for his own *future*!

38   In German: *das versprechen darf*. The translation has been modified from "is able" to "is permitted."
39   See note 15 above.
40   Latin: blank tablet.

2

That is precisely what constitutes the long history of the origins of *responsibility*.[41] The particular task of breeding an animal which is permitted to make a promise includes, as we have already understood, as precondition and preparation, the more immediate task of first *making* man to a certain degree undeviating [*notwendig*], uniform, a peer amongst peers, orderly and consequently predictable. The immense amount of labour involved in what I have called the 'morality of custom' [see *Daybreak*, I, 9; 14; 16], the actual labour of man on himself during the longest epoch of the human race, his whole *prehistoric* labour,[42] is explained and justified on a grand scale, in spite of the hardness, tyranny, stupidity and idiocy it also contained, by this fact: with the help of the morality of custom and the social straitjacket, man was *made* truly predictable. Let us place ourselves, on the other hand, at the end of this immense process where the tree actually bears fruit, where society and its morality of custom finally reveal what they were simply *the means to*: we then find the *sovereign individual* as the ripest fruit on its tree, like only to itself, having freed itself from the morality of custom,[43] an autonomous, supra-ethical individual[44] (because 'autonomous' and 'ethical' are mutually exclusive), in short, we find a man with his own, independent, durable will, who *is permitted to make a promise* — and has a proud consciousness quivering in every muscle of *what* he has finally achieved and incorporated, an actual awareness of power and freedom, a feeling that man in general has reached completion. This man who is now free and who really is *permitted* to make a promise, this master of the *free* will, this sovereign — how could he remain ignorant of his superiority over everybody who is not permitted to make a promise or answer for himself, how much trust, fear and respect he arouses — he '*merits*' all three — and how could he, with his self-mastery, not realise that he has necessarily been given mastery over circumstances, over nature and over all creatures with a less durable and reliable will? The 'free' man, the possessor of a durable, unbreakable will, thus has his own *standard of value*: in the possession of such a will: viewing others from his own standpoint, he respects or despises; and just as he will necessarily respect his peers, the strong and the reliable (those *with the right* to give their word), — that is everyone who makes promises like a sovereign, ponderously, seldom, slowly, and is sparing with his trust, who *confers an honour* when he places his trust, who gives his word as something which can be relied on, because he is strong enough to remain upright in the face of mishap or even 'in the face of fate' —: so he will necessarily be ready to kick the febrile whippets who make a promise when they have no right to do so, and will save the rod for the liar who breaks his word in the very moment it passes his lips. The proud realization of the extraordinary privilege of *responsibility*, the awareness of this rare freedom and power over himself and his destiny, has penetrated him to the depths and become an instinct, his dominant instinct: — what will he call his dominant instinct, assuming that he needs a word for it? No doubt about the answer: this sovereign man calls it his *conscience* . . .

41   In German: *Geschichte der Herkunft der Verantwortlichkeit.*
42   In German: *vorhistorische Arbeit.* The translation has been modified from 'labour *before history*' to '*prehistoric* labour.'
43   In German: *Sittlichkeit der Sitte.*
44   In German: *das autonome übersittliche Individuum.*

3

His conscience? . . . We can presume, in advance, that the concept 'conscience', which we meet here in its highest, almost disconcerting form, already has a long history and metamorphosis behind it. To be answerable for oneself, and proudly, too, and therefore to *be permitted to say 'yes'* to oneself – is, as I said, a ripe fruit, but also a *late* fruit: – how long must this fruit have hung, bitter and sour, on the tree! And for even longer there was nothing to see of this fruit, – nobody could have promised it would be there, although it is certain that everything about the tree was ready and growing towards it! – 'How do you give a memory to the animal, man? How do you impress something upon this partly dull, partly idiotic, inattentive mind, this personification of forgetfulness, so that it will stick?' . . . This age-old question was not resolved with gentle solutions and methods, as can be imagined; perhaps there is nothing more terrible and strange in man's pre-history than his *technique of mnemonics*. 'A thing must be burnt in so that it stays in the memory: only something which continues *to hurt* stays in the memory' – that is a proposition from the oldest (and unfortunately the longest-lived) psychology on earth. You almost want to add that wherever on earth you still find ceremonial, solemnity, mystery, gloomy shades in the lives of men and peoples, something of the dread with which everyone, everywhere, used to make promises, give pledges and commendation, is *still working*: the past, the most prolonged, deepest, hardest past, breathes on us and rises up in us when we become 'solemn'. When man decided he had to make a memory for himself, it never happened without blood, torments and sacrifices: the most horrifying sacrifices and forfeits (the sacrifice of the first born belongs here), the most disgusting mutilations (for example, castration), the cruellest rituals of all religious cults (and all religions are, at their most fundamental, systems of cruelty) – all this has its origin in that particular instinct which discovered that pain was the most powerful aid to mnemonics. The whole of asceticism belongs here as well: a few ideas have to be made ineradicable, ubiquitous, unforgettable, 'fixed', in order to hypnotize the whole nervous and intellectual system through these 'fixed ideas' – and ascetic procedures and lifestyles are a method of freeing those ideas from competition with all other ideas, of making them 'unforgettable'. The worse man's memory has been, the more dreadful his customs have appeared; in particular, the harshness of the penal law gives a measure of how much trouble it had in conquering forgetfulness, and *preserving* a few primitive requirements of social life in the minds of these slaves of the mood and desire of the moment. We Germans certainly do not regard ourselves as a particularly cruel or hard-hearted people, still less as particularly irresponsible and happy-go-lucky; but you only have to look at our old penal code in order to see how difficult it was on this earth to breed a 'nation of thinkers' (by which I mean: *the* nation in Europe which still contains the maximum of reliability, solemnity, tastelessness and sobriety, qualities which give it the right to breed all sorts of European mandarin). These Germans made a memory for themselves with dreadful methods, in order to master their basic plebeian instincts and the brutal crudeness of the same: think of old German punishments such as stoning (– even the legend drops the millstone on the guilty person's head), breaking on the wheel (a unique invention and speciality of German genius in the field of punishment!), impaling, ripping apart and trampling to death by horses ('quartering'), boiling of the criminal in oil or wine (still in the fourteenth and fifteenth centuries), the popular flaying ('cutting strips'), cutting out flesh from the breast; and, of course, coating the wrong-doer with honey and leaving him to the flies in the scorching sun. With the aid of such images and procedures, man was eventually able to retain five or six 'I-don't-want-to's' in his memory, in connection with which a *promise* had been made, in order to enjoy the advantages of society – and there you are! With the aid of this sort of memory, people finally came to 'reason'! – Ah, reason, solemnity, mastering of emotions, this really dismal thing called reflection, all these privileges and splendours man has: what a price had to be paid for them! how much blood and horror lies at the basis of all 'good things'! . . .

4

How, then, did that other 'dismal thing', the consciousness of guilt,[45] all 'bad conscience', come into the world? – And with this we return to our genealogists of morality. I'll say it again – or maybe I haven't said it yet? – they are no good. No more than five spans of their own, merely 'modern' experience; no knowledge and no will to know the past; still less an instinct for history, a 'second sight' which is so necessary at this point – and yet they go in for the history of morality: of course, this must logically end in results which have a more than brittle relationship to the truth. Have these genealogists of morality up to now ever remotely dreamt that, for example, the main moral concept '*Schuld*' ('guilt') descends from the very material concept of '*Schulden*' ('debts')? Or that punishment, as *retribution*, evolved quite independently of any assumption about freedom or lack of freedom of the will? – and this to the point where a *high* degree of humanization had first to be achieved, so that the animal 'man' could begin to differentiate between those much more primitive nuances 'intentional',

45   In German: *das Bewusstsein der Schuld*. In the Second Essay of *GM* Nietzsche is concerned to trace how a sense of debt (*Schuld*) was transmuted into a moralized guilt (*Schuld*) and the Diethe translation of *GM* II. 4 attempts to make this transparent. It is a mistake to suppose that 'bad conscience' and 'consciousness of guilt' are entirely equivalent (one can have a bad conscience, a consciousness of debt, without the deep sense of guilt that is part of Christian ideas of debt and obligation). Initially, then, Nietzsche has to address the question of how the bad conscience first arose, before addressing the question of how this conscience became bound up with a consciousness of *moral* guilt. Hence in section 4 he speaks of the 'main moral concept' of guilt descending from the 'material concept' of debts. This point is then reiterated in the opening of section 6, and the train of thought is picked up again and further elaborated in section 8. The topic is then returned to in section 16 and Nietzsche's analysis makes it clear that 'bad conscience' is to be distinguished, in terms of its pre-history, from any sense of moralized guilt. Bad conscience is taken to be an 'illness' that man contracts through the pressure of the most fundamental change he undergoes, 'that change whereby he finally found himself imprisoned within the confines of society and peace.' In section 17 Nietzsche argues that the change was not a gradual and voluntary one, nor is it to be understood in evolutionary terms of an 'organic assimilation into new circumstances'; rather, it represents a 'leap' and a 'compulsion.' In its beginnings, then, bad conscience denotes a situation where an aggressive and expansive instinct for freedom is no longer able to discharge itself but is forced back, repressed, and held within. In section 21 Nietzsche finally turns to addressing head-on how concepts of guilt/debt and duty became subject to a moralization and what this entails. He reads this development ingeniously in the context of his previous argument about the creditor–debtor relationship constituting the material foundation of concepts of debt/guilt and obligation.

'negligent', 'accidental', 'of sound mind' and their opposites, and take them into account when dealing out punishment. That inescapable thought, which is now so cheap and apparently natural, and which has had to serve as an explanation of how the sense of justice came about at all on earth, 'the criminal deserves to be punished *because* he could have acted otherwise', is actually an extremely late and refined form of human judgment and inference; whoever thinks it dates back to the beginning is laying his coarse hands on the psychology of primitive man in the wrong way. Throughout most of human history, punishment has *not* been meted out *because* the miscreant was held responsible for his act, therefore it was *not* assumed that the guilty party alone should be punished: – but rather, as parents still punish their children, it was out of anger over some wrong which had been suffered, directed at the perpetrator, – but this anger was held in check and modified by the idea that every injury has its *equivalent* which can be paid in compensation, if only through the *pain* of the person who injures. And where did this primeval, deeply-rooted and perhaps now ineradicable idea gain its power, this idea of an equivalence between injury and pain? I have already let it out: in the contractual relationship between *creditor* and *debtor*, which is as old as the very conception of a 'legal subject' and itself refers back to the basic forms of buying, selling, bartering, trade and traffic.

5

To be sure, thinking about these contractual relationships, as can be expected from what has gone before, arouses all kinds of suspicion and hostility towards the primitive men who created them or permitted them. Precisely here, *promises are made*; precisely here, the person making the promise has to have a memory *made* for him: precisely here, we can guess, is a repository of hard, cruel, painful things. The debtor, in order to inspire confidence that the promise of repayment will be honoured, in order to give a guarantee of the solemnity and sanctity of his promise, and in order to etch the duty and obligation of repayment into his conscience, pawns something to the creditor by means of the contract in case he does not pay, something which he still 'possesses' and controls, for example, his body, or his wife, or his freedom, or his life (or, in certain religious circumstances, even his after-life, the salvation of his soul, finally, even his peace in the grave: as in Egypt, where the corpse of a debtor found no peace from the creditor even in the grave – and this peace meant a lot precisely to the Egyptians). But in particular, the creditor could inflict all kinds of dishonour and torture on the body of the debtor, for example, cutting as much flesh off as seemed appropriate for the debt: – from this standpoint there were everywhere, early on, estimates which went into horrifyingly minute and fastidious detail, *legally* drawn up estimates for individual limbs and parts of the body. I regard it as definite progress and proof of a freer, more open-handed calculation, of a *more Roman* pricing of justice, when Rome's code of the Twelve Tables decreed that it did not matter how much or how little a creditor cut off in such a circumstance, '*si plus minusve secuerunt, ne fraude esto*'.[46] Let's be quite clear about the logic of this whole matter of compensation: it is strange enough. The equivalence is provided by the fact that instead of an advantage directly making up for the wrong (so, instead of compensation in money, land or possessions of any kind),

---

46   Latin: "If they have cut off more or less, let that not be considered a crime."

a sort of *pleasure* is given to the creditor as repayment and compensation, – the pleasure of having the right to exercise power over the powerless without a thought, the pleasure *'de faire le mal pour le plaisir de le faire'*,[47] the enjoyment of violating: an enjoyment which is prized all the higher, the lower and baser the position of the creditor in the social scale, and which can easily seem a delicious titbit to him, even foretaste of higher rank. Through punishment of the debtor, the creditor takes part in the *rights of the masters*: at last he, too, shares the elevated feeling of despising and maltreating someone as an 'inferior' – or at least, when the actual power of punishment, of exacting punishment, is already transferred to the 'authorities', of *seeing* the debtor despised and maltreated. So, then, compensation is made up of a warrant for and entitlement to cruelty. –

6

In *this* sphere of legal obligations then, we find the breeding-ground of the moral conceptual world of 'guilt', 'conscience', 'duty', 'sacred duty', – all began with a thorough and prolonged blood-letting, like the beginning of all great things on earth. And may we not add that this world has really never quite lost a certain odour of blood and torture? (not even with old Kant: the categorical imperative smells of cruelty . . .) In the same way, it was here that the uncanny and perhaps inextricable link-up between the ideas of 'guilt and suffering' as first crocheted together. I ask again: to what extent can suffering be a compensation for 'debts'? To the degree that *to make* someone suffer is pleasure in its highest form, and to the degree that the injured party received an extraordinary counter-pleasure in exchange for the injury and distress caused by the injury: to *make* someone suffer, – a true *feast*, something which, as I mentioned, rose in price the more it contrasted with the rank and social position of the creditor. I say all this in speculation: because such subterranean things are difficult to fathom out, besides being embarrassing; and anyone who clumsily tries to interject the concept 'revenge' has merely obscured and darkened his own insight, rather than clarified it (– revenge itself just leads us back to the same problem: 'how can it be gratifying to make someone suffer?'). It seems to me that the delicacy and even more the tartuffery of tame house-pets (meaning modern man, meaning us) revolts against a truly forceful realization of the degree to which *cruelty* is part of the festive joy of the ancients and, indeed, is an ingredient in nearly every pleasure they have; on the other hand, how naively and innocently their need for cruelty appears, and how fundamental is that 'disinterested malice' (or, to use Spinoza's words, the *sympathia malevolens*)[48] they assume is a *normal* human attribute –: making it something to which conscience says a hearty '*yes*'! A more piercing eye would perhaps be able to detect, even now, plenty of these most primitive and basic festive joys of man; in *Beyond Good and Evil*, VII, section 229 (earlier in *Daybreak*, I, sections 18, 77, 113) I pointed a wary finger at the ever-growing intellectualization and 'deification' of cruelty, which runs though the whole history of higher culture (and indeed, constitutes it in an important sense). At all events, not so long ago it was unthinkable to hold a royal wedding or full-scale

---

47   French: "of doing evil for the pleasure of doing it." Quotation from Prosper Mérimée, *Lettres à une inconnue* (*Letters to an Unknown Girl*, 1874), I. 8.
48   Latin: ill-willing sympathy.

festival for the people without executions, tortures or perhaps an *auto-da-fé*, similarly, no noble household was without creatures on whom people could discharge their malice and cruel taunts with impunity – think of Don Quixote, for example, at the court of the Duchess:[49] today we read the whole of *Don Quixote* with a bitter taste in the mouth, it is almost an ordeal, which would make us seem very strange and incomprehensible to the author and his contemporaries, – they read it with a clear conscience as the funniest of books, it made them nearly laugh themselves to death). To see somebody suffer is nice, to make somebody suffer even nicer – that is a hard proposition, but an ancient, powerful, human-all-too-human proposition to which, by the way, even the apes might subscribe: as people say, in thinking up bizarre cruelties they anticipate and, as it were, act out a 'demonstration' of what man will do. No cruelty, no feast: that is what the oldest and longest period in human history teaches us – and punishment, too, has such very strong *festive* aspects! –

[. . .]

8

The feeling of guilt, of personal obligation, to pursue our train of inquiry again, originated, as we saw, in the oldest and most primitive personal relationship there is, in the relationship of buyer and seller, creditor and debtor: here person met person for the first time, and *measured himself* person against person. No form of civilization has been discovered which is so low that it did not display something of this relationship. Fixing prices, setting values, working out equivalents, exchanging – this preoccupied man's first thoughts to such a degree that in a certain sense it *constitutes* thought: the most primitive kind of cunning was bred here, as was also, presumably, the first appearance of human pride, man's sense of superiority over other animals. Perhaps our word 'man' (*manas*)[50] expresses something of *this* first sensation of self-confidence: man designated himself as the being who measures values, who values and measures, as the 'calculating animal as such'. Buying and selling, with their psychological trappings, are older even than the beginnings of any social form of organization or association: it is much more the case that the germinating sensation of barter, contract, debt, right, duty, compensation was simply *transferred* from the most rudimentary form of the legal rights of persons to the most crude and elementary social units (in their relations with similar units), together with the habit of comparing power with power, of measuring, of calculating. Now the eye was focused in this direction in any case: and with the ponderous consistency characteristic of the ancients' way of thinking, which, though difficult to get started, never deviated once it was moving, man soon arrived at the great generalization, 'Every thing has its price: *everything* can be compensated for' – the oldest, most naïve canon of morals relating to *justice*, the beginning of all 'good naturedness', 'equity', all 'good will', all 'objectivity' on earth. Justice at this first level is the good will, between those who are roughly equal, to come to terms with each other, to 'come to an understanding' again by means of a settlement – and, in connection with those who are less powerful, to *force* them to reach a settlement amongst themselves. –

49   See *Don Quixote*, II, chs 31–7.
50   Sanskrit: mind (understanding or conscious will).

9

Still measuring with the standard of pre-history (a pre-history which, by the way, exists at all times or could possibly re-occur): the community has the same basic relationship to its members as the creditor to the debtor. You live in a community, you enjoy the benefits of a community (oh, what benefits! sometimes we underestimate them today), you live a sheltered, protected life in peace and trust, without any worry of suffering certain kinds of harm and hostility to which the man *outside*, the 'man without peace', is exposed – a German understands what 'misery', *êlend*,[51] originally means –, you make pledges and take on obligations to the community with just that harm and hostility in mind. What happens *if* you do not? The community, the cheated creditor, will make you pay up as best it can, you can be sure of that. The immediate damage done by the offender is what we are talking about least: quite apart from this, the lawbreaker is a 'breaker', somebody who has broken his contract and his word *to the whole*, in connection with all the valued features and amenities of communal life which he has shared up till now. The lawbreaker is a debtor who not only fails to repay the benefits and advances granted to him, but also actually assaults the creditor: so, from now on, as is fair, he is not only deprived of all these valued benefits, – he is now also reminded *how important these benefits are*. The anger of the injured creditor, the community, makes him return to the savage and outlawed state from which he was sheltered hitherto: he is cast out – and now any kind of hostile act can be perpetrated on him. 'Punishment' at this level of civilization is simply a copy, a *mimus*, of normal behaviour towards a hated, disarmed enemy who has been defeated, and who has not only forfeited all rights and safeguards, but all mercy as well; in fact, the rules of war and the victory celebration of *vae victis!*[52] in all their mercilessness and cruelty: – which explains the fact that war itself (including the warlike cult of the sacrificial victim) has given us all *forms* in which punishment manifests itself in history.

10

As a community grows in power, it ceases to take the offence of the individual quite so seriously, because these do not seem to be as dangerous and destabilizing for the survival of the whole as they did earlier: the wrong-doer is no longer 'deprived of peace' and cast out, nor can the general public vent their anger on him with the same lack of constraint, – instead the wrong-doer is carefully shielded by the community from this anger, especially from that of the immediate injured party, and given protection. A compromise with the anger of those immediately affected by the wrong-doing; and therefore an attempt to localize the matter and head off further or more widespread participation and unrest; attempts to work out equivalents and settle the matter (*compositio*); above all, the will, manifesting itself ever more distinctly, to treat every offence as being something which *can be paid off*, so that, at least to a certain degree, the wrong-doer is *isolated* from his deed – these are the characteristics imprinted more and more clearly into penal law in its further development. As the power and self-confidence of a community grows, its penal law becomes more

---

51   Literally "other country," i.e. banishment, exile.
52   Latin: woe to the vanquished! (Livy, *History of Rome*, V. 48).

lenient; if the former is weakened or endangered, harsher forms of the latter will re-emerge. The 'creditor' always becomes more humane as his wealth increases; finally, the *amount* of his wealth determines how much injury he can sustain without suffering from it. It is not impossible to imagine society *so conscious of its power* that it could allow itself the noblest luxury available to it, – that of letting its malefactors go *unpunished*. 'What do I care about my parasites', it could say, 'let them live and flourish: I am strong enough for all that!' . . . Justice, which began by saying 'Everything can be paid off, everything must be paid off', ends by turning a blind eye and letting off those unable to pay, – it ends, like every good thing on earth, by *sublimating itself*. The self-sublimation of justice:[53] we know what a nice name it gives itself – *mercy*; it remains, of course, the prerogative of the most powerful man, better still, his way of being beyond the law.[54]

[. . .]

12

Now another word on the origin and purpose of punishment – two problems which are separate, or ought to be: unfortunately people usually throw them together. How have the moral genealogists reacted so far in this matter? Naïvely, as is their wont –: they highlight some 'purpose' in punishment, for example, revenge or deterrence, then innocently place the purpose at the start, as *causa fiendi*[55] of punishment, and – have finished. But 'purpose in law' is the last thing we should apply to the history of the emergence of law: on the contrary, there is no more important proposition for all kinds of historical research than that which we arrive at only with great effort but which we really *should* reach, – namely that the origin of the emergence of a thing and its ultimate usefulness, its practical application and incorporation into a system of ends, are *toto coelo*[56] separate; that anything in existence, having somehow come about, is continually interpreted anew, requisitioned anew, transformed and redirected to a new purpose by a power superior to it; that everything that occurs in the organic world consists of *overpowering*, *dominating*, and in their turn, overpowering and dominating consist of re-interpretation, adjustment, in the process of which their former 'meaning' [*Sinn*] and 'purpose' must necessarily be obscured or completely obliterated. No matter how perfectly you have understood the *usefulness* of any physiological organ (or legal institution, social custom, political usage, art form or religious rite) you have not yet thereby grasped how it emerged: uncomfortable and unpleasant as this may sound to more elderly ears, – for people down the ages have believed that the obvious purpose of a thing, its utility, form and shape are its reason for existence, the eye is made to see, the hand to grasp. So people think punishment has evolved for the purpose of punishing. But every purpose and use is just a *sign* that the will to power has achieved mastery over something less powerful, and has impressed upon it its own idea [*Sinn*] of a use function; and the whole history of a 'thing', an organ, a tradition can to this extent be a continuous chain of signs, continually revealing new interpretations and adaptations, the causes of which need not be connected even amongst themselves, but rather sometimes just follow and replace one another at random. The 'development'

---

53   In German: *Diese Selbstaufhebung der Gerechtigkeit.*
54   In German: *Jenseits des Rechts.*
55   Latin: cause of the coming into being.
56   See note 9 above.

of a thing, a tradition, an organ is therefore certainly not its *progressus* towards a goal, still less is it a logical *progressus*, taking the shortest route with least expenditure of energy and cost, – instead it is a succession of more or less profound, more or less mutually independent processes of subjugation exacted on the thing, added to this the resistances encountered every time, the attempted transformations for the purpose of defence and reaction, and the results, too, of successful countermeasures. The form is fluid, the 'meaning' [*Sinn*] even more so . . . It is no different inside any individual organism: every time the whole grows appreciably, the 'meaning' [*Sinn*] of the individual organs shifts, – sometimes the partial destruction of organs, the reduction in their number (for example, by the destruction of intermediary parts) can be a sign of increasing vigour and perfection. To speak plainly: even the partial *reduction in usefulness*, decay and degeneration, loss of meaning [*Sinn*] and functional purpose, in short death, make up the conditions of true *progressus*: always appearing, as it does, in the form of the will and way to *greater power* and always emerging victorious at the cost of countless smaller forces. The amount of 'progress' can actually be *measured* according to how much has had to be sacrificed to it; man's sacrifice *en bloc* to the prosperity of one single *stronger* species of man – that *would be* progress . . . – I lay stress on this major point of historical method, especially as it runs counter to just that prevailing instinct and fashion which would much rather come to terms with absolute randomness, and even the mechanistic senselessness of all events, than the theory that a *power-will* is acted out in all that happens. The democratic idiosyncracy of being against everything that dominates and wants to dominate, the modern *misarchism* (to coin a bad word for a bad thing) has gradually shaped and dressed itself up as intellectual, most intellectual, so much so that it already, today, little by little penetrates the strictest, seemingly most objective sciences, and is *allowed* to do so; indeed, I think it has already become master of the whole of physiology and biology, to their detriment, naturally, by spiriting away their basic concept, that of actual *activity*. On the other hand, the pressure of this idiosyncracy forces 'adaptation' into the foreground, which is a second-rate activity, just a reactivity, indeed life itself has been defined as an increasingly efficient inner adaptation to external circumstances (Herbert Spencer). But this is to misunderstand the essence of life, its *will to power*, we overlook the prime importance which the spontaneous, aggressive, expansive, re-interpreting, re-directing and formative forces have, which 'adaptation' follows only when they have had their effect; in the organism itself, the dominant role of these highest functionaries, in whom the life-will is active and manifests itself, is denied. One recalls what Huxley reproached Spencer with, – his 'administrative nihilism': but we are dealing with *more* than 'administration' . . .

13

– To return to our topic, namely *punishment*, we have to distinguish between two of its aspects: one is its relative *permanence*, a traditional usage, a fixed form of action, a 'drama', a certain strict sequence of procedures, the other is its *fluidity*, its meaning [*Sinn*], purpose and expectation, which is linked to the carrying out of such procedures. And here, without further ado, I assume, *per analogiam*,[57] according to the major point of historical method just developed, that the procedure itself will be something older, predating its use as punishment, that the latter was only *inserted* and interpreted

57 Latin: by analogy.

into the procedure (which had existed for a long time though it was thought of in a different way), in short, that the matter is *not* to be understood in the way our naïve moral and legal genealogists assumed up till now, who all thought the procedure had been *invented* for the purpose of punishment, just as people used to think that the hand had been invented for the purpose of grasping. With regard to the other element in punishment, the fluid one, its 'meaning', the concept 'punishment' presents, at a very late stage of culture (for example, in Europe today), not just one meaning but a whole synthesis of 'meanings' [*Sinnen*]: the history of punishment up to now in general, the history of its use for a variety of purposes, finally crystallizes in a kind of unity which is difficult to dissolve back into its elements, difficult to analyse and, this has to be stressed, is absolutely *undefinable*. (Today it is impossible to say precisely *why* people are actually punished: all concepts in which an entire process is semiotically concentrated defy definition; only something which has no history can be defined.) At an earlier stage, however, the synthesis of 'meanings' appeared much easier to undo and shift; we can still make out how, in every single case, the elements of the synthesis change valence and alter the order in which they occur so that now this, then that element stands out and dominates, to the detriment of the others, indeed, in some circumstances one element (for example, the purpose of deterrence) seems to overcome all the rest. To at least give an impression of how uncertain, belated and haphazard the 'meaning' of punishment is, and how one and the same procedure can be used, interpreted and adapted for fundamentally different projects: you have here a formula which suggested itself to me on the basis of relatively restricted and random material. Punishment as a means of rendering harmless, of preventing further harm. Punishment as payment of a debt to the creditor in any form (even one of emotional compensation). Punishment as a means of isolating a disturbance of balance, to prevent further spread of the disturbance. Punishment as a means of inspiring the fear of those who determine and execute punishment. Punishment as a sort of counter-balance to the privileges which the criminal has enjoyed up till now (for example, by using him as a slave in the mines). Punishment as a rooting-out of degenerate elements (sometimes a whole branch, as in Chinese law: whereby it becomes a means of keeping the race pure or maintaining a social type). Punishment as a festival, in the form of violating and mocking an enemy, once he is finally conquered. Punishment as an *aide mémoire*, either for the person suffering the punishment – so called 'reform', or for those who see it carried out. Punishment as payment of a fee stipulated by the power which protects the wrongdoer from the excesses of revenge. Punishment as a compromise with the natural state of revenge, in so far as the latter is still nurtured and claimed as a privilege by more powerful clans. Punishment as a declaration of war and a war measure against an enemy of peace, law, order, authority, who is fought as dangerous to the life of the community, in breach of the contract on which the community is founded, as a rebel, a traitor and breaker of the peace, with all the means which war can provide. –

[. . .]

16

At this point I can no longer avoid giving a first, preliminary expression to my own theory on the origin of 'bad conscience': it is not easy to get a hearing for this hypothesis and it needs to be pondered, watched and slept on. I look on bad conscience as a serious illness to which man was forced to succumb by the pressure of the most fundamental of all changes which he experienced, – that change whereby he finally found himself imprisoned within the confines of society and peace. It must have been no different for this semi-animal, happily adapted to the wilderness, war, the wandering life and adventure than it was for the sea animals when they were forced to either become land animals or perish – at one go, all instincts were devalued and 'suspended'. Now they had to walk on their paws and 'carry themselves' whereas they had been carried by the water up till then: a terrible heaviness bore down on them. They felt they were clumsy at performing the simplest task, they did not have their familiar guide any more for this new, unknown world, those regulating impulses which unconsciously led them to safety – the poor things were reduced to relying on think-ing, inference, calculation, and the connecting of cause with effect, that is, to relying on their 'consciousness', that most impoverished and error-prone organ! I do not think there has ever been such a feeling of misery on earth, such a leaden discomfort, – and meanwhile, the old instincts had not suddenly ceased to make their demands! But it was difficult and seldom possible to give in to them: they mainly had to seek new and as it were underground gratifications. All instincts which are not discharged out-wardly *turn inwards* – this is what I call the *internalization* of man: with it there now evolves in man what will later be called his 'soul'. The whole inner world, originally stretched thinly as though between two layers of skin, was expanded and extended itself and gained depth, breadth and height in proportion to the degree that the exter-nal discharge of man's instincts was *obstructed*. Those terrible bulwarks with which state organizations protected themselves against the old instincts of freedom – punishments are a primary instance of this kind of bulwark – had the result that all those instincts of the wild, free, roving man were turned backwards, *against man himself*. Animosity, cruelty, the pleasure of pursuing, raiding, changing and destroying – all this was pitted against the person who had such instincts: *that* is the origin of 'bad conscience'. Lacking external enemies and obstacles, and forced into the oppressive narrowness and con-formity of custom, man impatiently ripped himself apart, persecuted himself, gnawed at himself, gave himself no peace and abused himself, this animal who battered himself raw on the bars of his cage and who is supposed to be 'tamed'; man, full of emptiness and torn apart with homesickness for the desert, has had to create from within himself an adventure, a torture-chamber, an unsafe and hazardous wilderness – this fool, this prisoner consumed with longing and despair, became the inventor of 'bad conscience'. With it, however, the worst and most insidious illness was intro-duced, one from which mankind has not yet recovered, man's sickness of *man*, of *him-self*: as the result of a forcible breach with his animal past, a simultaneous leap and fall into new situations and conditions of existence, a declaration of war against all the old instincts on which, up till then, his strength, pleasure and formidableness had been based. Let us immediately add that, on the other hand, the prospect of an animal soul turning against itself, taking a part against itself, was something so new, profound, unheard-of, puzzling, contradictory *and momentous* [*Zukunftsvolles*] on earth that the whole character of the world changed in an essential way. Indeed, a divine audience was needed to appreciate the spectacle which began then, but the end of which is not yet in sight, – a spectacle too subtle, too wonderful, too paradoxical to be allowed to be played senselessly unobserved on some ridiculous planet! Since that time, man has been *included* among the most unexpected and exciting throws of dice played by Heraclitus' 'great child', call him Zeus or fate,[58] – he arouses interest, tension, hope, almost certainty for himself, as though something were being announced through him, were being prepared, as though man were not an end but just a path, an episode, a bridge, a great promise. . . .

17

The first assumption in my theory on the origin of bad conscience is that the alteration was not gradual and voluntary and did not represent an organic assimilation into new circumstances but was a breach, a leap, a compulsion, a fate which nothing could ward off, which occasioned no struggle, not even any *ressentiment*. A second assumption, however, is that the shaping of a population, which had up till now been unrestrained and shapeless, into a fixed form, as happened at the beginning with an act of violence, could only be concluded with acts of violence, – that consequently the oldest 'state' emerged as a terrible tyranny, as a repressive and ruthless machinery, and continued working until the raw material of people and semi-animals had been finally not just kneaded and made compliant, but *shaped*. I used the word 'state': it is obvious who is meant by this – some pack of blond beasts of prey, a conqueror and master race, which, organized on a war footing, and with the power to organize, unscrupulously lays its dreadful paws on a populace which, though it might be vastly greater in number, is still shapeless and shifting. In this way, the 'state' began on earth: I think I have dispensed with the fantasy which has it begin with a 'contract'. Whoever can command, whoever is a 'master' by nature, whoever appears violent in deed and gesture – what is he going to care about contracts! Such beings cannot be reckoned with, they come like fate, without cause, reason, consideration or pretext, they appear just as lightning appears, too terrible, sudden, convincing and 'other' even to be hated. What they do is to create and imprint forms instinctively, they are the most involuntary, unconscious artists there are: – where they appear, soon something new arises, a structure of domination that *lives*, in which parts and functions are differentiated and co-related, in which there is absolutely no room for anything which does not first acquire 'meaning' with regard to the whole. They do not know what guilt, responsibility, consideration are, these born organizers; they are ruled by that terrible inner artist's egoism which has a brazen countenance and sees itself justified to all eternity by the 'work', like the mother in her child. *They* are not the ones in whom 'bad conscience' grew; that is obvious – but it would not have grown *without* them, this ugly growth would not be there if a huge amount of freedom had not been driven from the world, or at least driven from sight and, at the same time, made *latent* by the pressure of their hammer blows and artists' violence. This *instinct of freedom*, forcibly made latent – we have already seen how – this instinct of freedom forced back, repressed, incarcerated within itself and finally able to discharge and unleash itself only against itself: that, and that alone, is *bad conscience* in its beginnings.

[. . .]

---

58   Heraclitus (Diels–Kranz edn), fragment 52.

21

So much for a brief and rough preliminary outline of the connection between the concepts 'debt'[59] and 'duty' and religious precepts: I have so far intentionally set aside the actual moralization of these concepts (the way they are pushed back into conscience; more precisely, the way *bad* conscience is woven together with the concept of God), and at the conclusion of the last section I actually spoke as though this moralization did not exist, consequently, as though these concepts would necessarily come to an end once the basic premise no longer applied, the belief in our "creditor", in God. The facts diverge from this in a terrible way. With the moralization of the concepts debt and duty and their relegation to *bad* conscience, we have, in reality, an attempt to *reverse* the direction of the development I have described, or at least halt its movement: now the prospect for a once-and-for-all payment *is to be* foreclosed, out of pessimism, now our glance *is to* bounce and recoil disconsolately off an iron impossibility, now those concepts 'debt' and 'duty' *are to be* reversed – but against *whom*? It is indisputable: firstly against the 'debtor', in whom bad conscience now so firmly establishes itself, eating into him, broadening out and growing, like a polyp, so wide and deep that in the end, with the impossibility of expiating the guilt, is conceived the impossibility of discharging the penance, the idea that it cannot be paid off ("*eternal* punishment") –; ultimately, however, against the 'creditor', and here we should think of the *causa prima*[60] of man, the beginning of the human race, of his ancestor who is now burdened with a curse ('Adam', 'original sin', 'the will in bondage') or of nature, from whose womb man originated and to whom the principle of evil is imputed (diabolization of nature) or of existence in general, which is left standing as *inherently worthless* (a nihilistic turning-away from existence, the desire for nothingness or desire for the 'antithesis', to be other, Buddhism and such like) – until, all at once, we confront the paradoxical and horrifying expedient through which a martyred humanity has sought temporary relief, *Christianity's* stroke of genius: none other than God sacrificing himself for man's guilt, none other than God paying himself back, God as the only one able to redeem man from what, to man himself, has become irredeemable – the creditor sacrificing himself for his debtor, out of *love* (would you credit it? –), out of love for the debtor! . . .

22

You will already have guessed *what* has really gone on with all this and *behind* all this: that will to torment oneself, that suppressed cruelty of animal man who has been frightened back into himself and given an inner life, incarcerated in the 'state' to be tamed, and has discovered bad conscience so that he can hurt himself, after the *more natural* outlet of this wish to hurt had been blocked, – this man of bad conscience has seized on religious precept in order to provide his self-torture with its most horrific hardness and sharpness. Guilt towards *God*: this thought becomes an instrument of torture. In 'God' he seizes upon the ultimate antithesis he can find to his real and irredeemable animal instincts, he re-interprets these self-same animal instincts as guilt before God

59   The translation of *Schuld* has been modified from "guilt" to "debt." See note 45 above.
60   Latin: first cause.

(as animosity, insurrection, rebellion against the 'master', the 'father', the primeval ancestor and beginning of the world), he pitches himself into the contradiction of 'God' and 'Devil', he emits every 'no' which he says to himself, nature, naturalness and the reality of his being as a 'yes', as existing, living, real, as God, as the holiness of God, as God-the-Judge, as God-the-Hangman, as the beyond, as eternity, as torture without end, as hell, as immeasurable punishment and guilt. We have here a sort of madness of the will showing itself in mental cruelty which is absolutely unparalleled: man's *will* to find himself guilty and condemned without hope of reprieve, his *will* to think of himself as punished, without the punishment ever measuring up to the crime, his *will* to infect and poison the fundamentals of things with the problem of punishment and guilt in order to cut himself off, once and for all, from the way out of this labyrinth of 'fixed ideas', this *will* to set up an ideal – that of a 'holy God' –, in order to be palpably convinced of his own absolute worthlessness in the face of this ideal. Alas for this crazy, pathetic beast man! What ideas he has, what perversity, what hysterical non-sense, what *bestiality of thought* immediately erupts, the moment he is prevented, if only gently, from being a *beast in deed*! . . . This is all almost excessively interesting, but there is also a black, gloomy, unnerving sadness to it as well, so that one has to force one-self to forego peering for too long into these abysses. Here is *sickness*, without a doubt, the most terrible sickness ever to rage in man: – and whoever is still able to hear (but people have no ear for it nowadays! –) how the shout of *love* has rung out during this night of torture and absurdity, the shout of most yearning rapture, of salvation through *love*, turns away, gripped by an unconquerable horror . . . There is so much in man that is horrifying! . . . The world has been a madhouse for too long! . . .

<h1 style="text-align:center">23</h1>

That should be enough, once and for all, about the descent of the 'holy God'. – That the conception of gods does not, *as such*, necessarily lead to that deterioration of the imagination which we had to think about for a moment, that there are *nobler* ways of making use of the invention of gods than man's self-crucifixion and self-abuse, ways in which Europe excelled during the last millennia, – this can fortunately be deduced from any glance at the *Greek gods*, these reflections of noble and proud men in whom the *animal* in man felt deified, did *not* tear itself apart and did *not* rage against itself! These Greeks, for most of the time, used their gods expressly to keep 'bad con-science' at bay so that they could carry on enjoying their freedom of soul: therefore, the opposite of the way Christendom made use of its God. They went *very far* in this, these marvellous, lion-hearted children; and no less an authority than the Homeric Zeus gives them to understand that they are making it too easy for themselves. 'Strange!', he says on one occasion – he is talking about the case of Aegisthus, a *very* bad case –

> *Strange how much the mortals complain about the gods! We alone cause evil, they claim, but they themselves through folly, bring about their own distress, even contrary to fate!*[61]

Yet we can immediately hear and see that even this Olympian observer and judge has no intention of bearing them a grudge for this and thinking ill of them: 'How *foolish*

---

61   *Odyssey*, I. 32–4.

they are' is what he thinks when the mortals misbehave, – 'foolishness', 'stupidity', a little 'mental disturbance', this much even the Greeks of the strongest, bravest period *allowed* themselves as a reason for much that was bad or calamitous: – foolishness, *not* sin! you understand? . . . But even this mental disturbance was a problem – 'Yes, how is this possible? Where can this have actually have come from with minds like *ours*, we men of high lineage, happy, well-endowed, high-born, noble and virtuous?' – for centuries, the noble Greek asked himself this in the face of any incomprehensible atrocity or crime with which one of his peers had sullied himself. 'A *god* must have confused him', he said to himself at last, shaking his head . . . This solution is *typical* for the Greeks . . . In this way, the gods served to justify man to a certain degree, even if he was in the wrong they served as causes of evil – they did not, at that time, take the punishment on themselves, but rather, as is *nobler*, the guilt . . .

24

– I shall conclude with three question marks, that much is plain. 'Is an ideal set up or destroyed here?' you might ask me . . . But have you ever asked yourselves properly how costly the setting up of *every* ideal on earth has been? How much reality always had to be vilified and misunderstood in the process, how many lies had to be sanctified, how much conscience had to be troubled, how much 'god' had to be sacrificed every time? If a shrine is to be set up, a *shrine has to be destroyed*: that is the law – show me an example where this does not apply! . . . We moderns have inherited millennia of conscience-vivisection and animal-torture inflicted on ourselves: we have had most practice in it, are perhaps artists in the field, in any case it is our *raffinement* and the indulgence of our taste. For too long, man has viewed his natural inclinations with an 'evil eye', so that they finally came to be intertwined with 'bad conscience' in him. A reverse experiment should be possible *in principle* – but who has sufficient strength? – by this, I mean an intertwining of bad conscience with *perverse* inclinations, all those other-worldly aspirations, alien to the senses, the instincts, to nature, to animals, in short all the ideals which up to now have been hostile to life and have defamed the world. To whom should we turn with *such* hopes and claims today? . . . We would have none other than the *good* men against us; and, as is fitting, the lazy, the complacent, the vain, the zealous, the tired . . . What is more deeply offensive to others and separates us more profoundly from them than allowing them to realize something of the severity and high-mindedness with which we treat ourselves? And again – how co-operative and pleasant everyone is towards us, as soon as we do as everyone else does and 'let ourselves go' like everyone else! . . . For that purpose, we would need *another* sort of spirit than those we are likely to encounter in this age: spirits which are strengthened by wars and victories, for which conquest, adventure, danger and even pain have actually become a necessity; they would also need to be acclimatised to thinner air higher up, to winter treks, ice and mountains in every sense, they would need a sort of sublime nastiness [*Bosheit*] itself, a final, very self-assured wilfulness of insight which belongs to great health, in brief and unfortunately, they would need precisely this *great health*! . . . Is this at all possible today? . . . But some time, in a stronger age than this mouldy, self-doubting present day, he will have to come to us, the *redeeming* man of great love and contempt, the creative spirit who is pushed out of any position 'outside' or 'beyond' by his surging strength again and again, whose solitude will be misunderstood by the people as though it were flight *from* reality –: whereas it is just his way of being absorbed, buried and immersed in reality so that from it, when he emerges into the light again, he can return with the *redemption* of this reality: redeem it from the curse which its ideal has placed on it up till now. This man of the future will redeem us not just from the ideal held up till now, but also from the things *which will have to arise from it*, from the great nausea, the will to noth-ingness, from nihilism, that stroke of midday and of great decision which makes the will free again, which gives earth its purpose and man his hope again, this Antichrist and anti-nihilist, this conqueror of God and of nothingness – *he must come one day* . . .

25

– But what am I saying? Enough! Enough! At this point just one thing is proper, silence: otherwise I shall be misappropriating something which belongs to another, younger man, one 'with more future', one stronger than me – something to which *Zarathustra* alone is entitled, *Zarathustra the Godless* . . .

Third Essay: What Do Ascetic Ideals Mean?

Carefree, mocking, violent – this is how wisdom wants *us*: she is a woman, all she ever loves is a warrior.

Thus Spoke Zarathustra

1

What do ascetic ideals mean? – With artists, nothing, or too many different things; with philosophers and scholars, something like a nose and sense for the most favourable con-ditions of higher intellectuality [*Geistigkeit*]; with women, at most, one *more* seductive charm, a little *morbidezza* on fair flesh, the angelic expression on a pretty, fat animal; with physiological causalities and the disgruntled (with the *majority* of mortals), an attempt to see themselves as 'too good' for this world, a saintly form of debauchery, their chief weapon in the battle against long-drawn-out pain and boredom; with priests, the actual priestly faith, their best instrument of power and also the "ultimate" sanction of their power; with saints, an excuse to hibernate at last, their *novissima gloriæ cupido*,[62] their rest in nothingness ('God'), their form of madness. *That* the ascetic ideal has meant so much to man reveals a basic fact of human will, its *horror vacui*;[63] it needs an aim –, and it prefers to will *nothingness* rather than *not* will. – Do I make myself understood? . . . Have I made myself understood? . . . '*Absolutely not, sir!*' – So let us start at the beginning.

[. . .]

10

In the same book (section 42[64]), I examined in what kind of esteem the earliest race of contemplative men had to live, – widely despised when they were not feared! –

62   Latin: desire for glory last. Quotation from Tacitus, *Histories*, IV. 6: 'the desire for glory, which is the last thing they will rid themselves of.'
63   Latin: horror of emptiness.
64   Reference to Nietzsche's earlier text, *Daybreak*.

and how *heavily* that esteem weighed down on them. Without a doubt: contemplation first appeared in the world in disguise, with an ambiguous appearance, an evil
heart and often with an anxiety-filled head. All that was inactive, brooding and unwar-
like in the instincts of contemplative men surrounded them with a deep mistrust for
a long time: against which they had no other remedy than to arouse a pronounced
fear of themselves. And the old Brahmins, for example, certainly knew how to do that!
The earliest philosophers knew how to give their life and appearance a meaning, support and setting which would encourage people to learn to *fear* them: on closer inspection, from an even more fundamental need, namely in order to fear and respect themselves.
Because they found in themselves all their value judgments turned *against* themselves,
they had to fight off every kind of suspicion and resistance to the 'philosopher in themselves'. As men living in a terrible age, they did this with terrible methods: cruelty
towards themselves, imaginative forms of self-mortification – these were the main methods for these power-hungry hermits and thought-innovators, for whom it was necessary to violate the gods and tradition in themselves so they could *believe* in their own
innovations. I remind you of the famous story about King Viçvamitra, who gained
such a sense of power and self-confidence from a thousand-year-long self-martyrdom
that he undertook to build a *new heaven*: the uncanny symbol in the oldest philosopher's tale on earth, and also in the most recent, – anybody who has ever built a 'new
heaven', only mustered the power he needed through his *own hell*. . . . Let us set out
the whole state of affairs briefly: the philosophic spirit has always had to disguise and
cocoon itself among *previously established* types of contemplative man, as a priest, magician, soothsayer, religious man in general, in order for its existence *to be possible* at all:
the ascetic ideal served the philosopher for a long time as outward appearance, an a precondition of existence, – he had to *play* that part [*darstellen*] in order to be a philosopher, he had to *believe* in it in order to be able to play it [*um es darstellen zu können*].
The peculiarly withdrawn attitude of the philosophers, denying the world, hating life,
doubting the senses, desensualized, which has been maintained until quite recently to
the point where it almost counted for the *philosophical attitude as such*, – this is primarily a result of the desperate conditions under which philosophy evolved and exists
at all: that is, philosophy would have been *absolutely impossible* for most of the time on
earth without an ascetic mask and suit of clothes, without an ascetic misconception
of itself. To put it vividly and clearly: the *ascetic priest* has until the most recent times
displayed the vile and dismal form of a caterpillar, which was the only one philosophers were allowed to adopt and creep round in. . . . Have things really *changed*? Has
the brightly coloured, dangerous winged-insect, the 'spirit' which the caterpillar
concealed, really thrown off the monk's habit and emerged into the light, thanks to
a more sunny, warmer and more enlightened world? Is there enough pride, daring,
courage, self-confidence, will of spirit [*Wille des Geistes*], will to take responsibility,
freedom of will, for 'the philosopher' on earth to be really – *possible*? . . .

11

Only now that we have the *ascetic priest* in sight can we seriously get to grips with
our problem: what does the ascetic ideal mean? – only now does it become 'serious':
after all, we are face to face with the actual *representative of seriousness*. 'What is the
meaning of all seriousness?' – this even more fundamental question is perhaps on our

lips already: a question for physiologists, as is proper, but one which we skirt round for the moment. The ascetic priest not only rests his faith in that ideal, but his will, his power, his interest as well. His *right* to exist stands and falls with that ideal: hardly surprising, then, that we encounter a formidable opponent in him, providing, of course, that we are opposed to that ideal? Such an opponent who fights for his life against people who deny that ideal? . . . On the other hand it is *prima facie* not very likely that such a biased attitude to our problem would be of much use in attempting to solve it; the ascetic priest will hardly be the happiest defender of his own ideal, for the same reason that a woman always fails when she wants to justify 'woman as such', – there can be no question of his being the most objective assessor and judge of the controversy raised here. So, it is more a case of our having to help him – that much is obvious – to defend himself well against us than of our having to fear being refuted too well by him . . . The idea we are fighting over here is the *valuation* of our lives by the ascetic priest: he relates this (together with all that belongs to it, 'nature', 'the world', the whole sphere of what becomes and what passes away), to a quite different kind of existence which is opposed to it and excludes it *unless* it should turn against itself and *deny itself*: in this case, the case of the ascetic life, life counts as a bridge to that other existence. The ascetic treats life as a wrong path which he has to walk along back-wards, till he reaches the point where he starts; or, like a mistake which can only be set right by action – *ought* to be set right: he *demands* that we should accompany him, and when he can, he imposes *his* valuation of existence. What does this mean? Such a monstrous method of valuation is not inscribed in the records of human history as an exception and curiosity: it is one of the most wide-spread and long-lived facts there are. Read from a distant planet, the majuscule script of our earthly existence would perhaps seduce the reader to the conclusion that the earth was the ascetic planet *par excellence*, an outpost of discontented, arrogant and nasty creatures who harboured a deep disgust for themselves, for the world, for all life and hurt themselves as much as possible out of pleasure in hurting: – probably their only pleasure. Let us consider how regularly and universally the ascetic priest makes his appearance in almost any age; he does not belong to any race in particular; he thrives everywhere; he comes from every social class. Not that he breeds and propagates his method of valuation through heredity: the opposite is the case, – a deep instinct forbids him to procreate, broadly speaking. It must be a necessity of the first rank which makes this species con-tinually grow and prosper when it is *hostile to life*, – *life itself must have an interest* in preserving such a self-contradictory type. For an ascetic life is a self-contradiction: here an unparalleled *ressentiment* rules, that of an unfulfilled instinct and power-will which wants to be master, not over something in life, but over life itself and its deepest, strongest, most profound conditions; here, an attempt is made to use power to block the sources of the power; here, the green eye of spite turns on physiological growth itself, in par-ticular the manifestation of this in beauty and joy; while satisfaction is *looked for* and found in failure, decay, pain, misfortune, ugliness, voluntary deprivation, destruction of selfhood, self-flagellation and self-sacrifice. This is all paradoxical in the extreme: we are faced with a dissidence [*Zwiespältigkeit*] which *wills* itself to be dissident [*zwiespältig*], which *relishes* itself in this affliction and becomes more self-assured and triumphant to the same degree as its own condition, the physiological capacity to live, *decreases*. 'Triumph precisely in the final agony': the ascetic ideal has always fought under this exagger-ated motto; in this seductive riddle, this symbol of delight and anguish, it recognized its brightest light, its salvation, its ultimate victory. *Crux, nux, lux*[65] – with the ascetic ideal, these are all one. –

12

Assuming that such an incorporate will to contradiction and counter-nature can be made to *philosophize*: on what will it vent its inner arbitrariness? On that which is experienced most certainly to be true and real: it will look for *error* precisely where the actual instinct of life most unconditionally judges there to be truth. For example, it will demote physicality to the status of illusion like the ascetics of the Vedânta philosophy did, similarly pain, plurality, the whole conceptual antithesis 'subject' and 'object' – errors, nothing but errors! To renounce faith in one's own ego, to deny one's own 'reality' to oneself – what a triumph! – and not just over the senses, over appearance, a much higher kind of triumph, an act of violation and cruelty inflicted on *reason*: a voluptuousness which reaches its peak when the ascetic self-contempt and self-ridicule of reason decrees: 'there *is* a realm of truth and being, but reason is firmly *excluded* from it!' . . . (By the way: even in the Kantian concept of 'the intelligible character of things',[66] something of this lewd ascetic conflict [*Zwiespältigkeit*] still lingers, which likes to set reason against reason: 'intelligible character' means, in Kant, a sort of quality of things about which all that the intellect can comprehend is that it is, for the intellect – *completely incomprehensible*.) – Finally, as knowers, let us not be ungrateful towards such resolute reversals of familiar perspectives and valuations with which the mind has raged against itself for far too long, apparently to wicked and useless effect: to see differently, and to *want* to see differently to that degree, is no small discipline and preparation of the intellect for its future 'objectivity' – the latter understood not as 'contemplation [*Anschauung*] without interest' (which is, as such, a non-concept and an absurdity), but as *having in our power* our 'pros' and 'cons': so as to be able to engage and disengage them so that we can use the *difference* in perspectives and affective interpretations for knowledge. From now on, my philosophical colleagues, let us be more wary of the dangerous old conceptual fairy-tale which has set up a 'pure, will-less, painless, timeless, subject of knowledge', let us be wary of the tentacles of such contradictory concepts as 'pure reason', 'absolute spirituality', 'knowledge as such': – here we are asked to think an eye which cannot be thought at all, an eye turned in no direction at all, an eye where the active and interpretative powers are to be suppressed, absent, but through which seeing still becomes a seeing-something, so it is an absurdity and non-concept of eye that is demanded. There is *only* a perspective seeing, *only* a perspective 'knowing'; the *more* affects we allow to speak about a thing, the *more* eyes, various eyes we are able to use for the same thing, the more complete will be our 'concept' of the thing, our 'objectivity'. But to eliminate the will completely and turn off all the emotions without exception, assuming we could: well? would that not mean to *castrate* the intellect? . . .

---

65   Latin: Cross, nut, light. The meaning is unclear unless "nux" is a misprint for "nox" (night) or unless the Greek word (= "night") is intended.
66   Kant, *Critique of Pure Reason*, B 564ff. Cf. Nietzsche's reworking of "intelligible character" in *BGE* 36.

13

But to return. A self-contradiction such as that which seems to occur in the ascetic, 'life *against* life', is – so much is obvious – seen from the physiological, not just the psychological standpoint, simply nonsense. It can only be *apparent*; it has to be a sort of provisional expression, an explanation, formula, adjustment, a psychological mis-understanding of something, the real nature of which was far from being understood, was far from being able to be designated as it is *in itself*, – a mere word wedged into an old *gap* in human knowledge. Allow me to present the real state of affairs in con-trast to this: *the ascetic ideal springs from the protective and healing instincts of a degenerating life* which uses every means to maintain itself and struggles for its existence; it indi-cates a partial physiological inhibition and exhaustion against which the deepest instincts of life, which have remained intact, continually struggle with new methods and inventions. The ascetic ideal is one such method: the situation is therefore the precise opposite of what the worshippers of this ideal imagine, – in it and through it, life struggles with death and *against* death, the ascetic ideal is a trick for the *preserva-tion* of life. The fact that, as history tells us, this ideal could rule man and become powerful to the extent that it did, especially everywhere where the civilization and taming of man took place, reveals a major fact, the *sickliness* of the type of man who has lived up till now, at least of the tamed man, the physiological struggle of man with death (to be more exact: with disgust at life, with exhaustion and with the wish for the 'end'). The ascetic priest is the incarnate wish for being otherwise, being else-where, indeed, he is the highest pitch of this wish, its essential ardour and passion: but the *power* of his wishing is the fetter which binds him here, precisely this is what makes him a tool, who now has to work to create more favourable circumstances for our being here and being man, – it is precisely with this *power* that he makes the whole herd of failures, the disgruntled, the under-privileged, the unfortunate, and all who suffer from themselves, retain their hold on life by instinctively placing himself at their head as their shepherd. You take my meaning already: this ascetic priest, this apparent enemy of life, this *negative man*, – he actually belongs to the really great forces in life which *conserve* and *create the positive* . . . What causes this sickliness? For man is more ill, uncertain, changeable and unstable than any other animal, without a doubt, – he is *the* sick animal: what is the reason for this? Certainly he had dared more, innovated more, braved more, challenged fate more than all the rest of the animals taken together: he, the great experimenter with himself, the unsatisfied and insatiable, struggling for supreme control against animals, nature and gods, – man, the still-unconquered eternal-futurist who finds no more rest from the pressure of his own strength, so that his future mercilessly digs into the flesh of every present like a spur: – how could such a courageous and rich animal not be the most endangered as well, of all sick animals the one most seriously ill, and for longest? . . . Man is often enough fed up, there are whole epidemics of this state of being fed up (– like the one around 1348, at the time of the Dance of Death): but even this nausea, this weariness, this fatigue, this disgust with himself – everything manifests itself so powerfully in him that it immediately becomes a new fetter. His 'no' which he says to life brings a wealth of more tender 'yeses' to light as though by magic; and even when he *wounds* himself, this master of destruc-tion, self-destruction, – afterwards it is the wound itself which forces him *to live* . . .

[. . .]

16

You can now guess what, in my opinion, the healing instinct of life has at least *tried* to do through the ascetic priest and what purpose was served by a temporary tyranny of such paradoxical and paralogical concepts as 'guilt', 'sin', 'sinfulness', 'corruption', 'damnation': to make the sick *harmless* to a certain degree, to bring about the self-destruction of the incurable, to direct the less ill strictly towards themselves, to give their *ressentiment* a backwards direction ('one thing is needful'[67] –) and in this way to *exploit* the bad instincts of all sufferers for the purpose of self-discipline, self-surveillance and self-overcoming. It goes without saying that 'medication' of this sort, mere affect-medication, cannot possibly yield a real *cure* in the physiological sense; we do not even have the right to claim that in this instance, the instinct of life in any way expects or intends a cure. On the one hand, the sick packed together and organized (– the word 'church' is the most popular name for it), on the other hand a sort of provisional safeguarding of those in better health, the physically better-developed, thus the opening of a *cleft* between healthy and sick – and for a long time that was all! And it was a great deal! It was a *very great deal!* . . . [In this essay I proceed, as you see, on the assumption, which I do not first have to justify with regard to readers of the kind I need: that 'sinfulness' in man is not a fact, but rather the interpreta-tion of a fact, namely a physiological upset, – the latter seen from a perspective of morals and religion which is no longer binding on us. The fact that someone *feels* 'guilty', 'sinful', by no means proves that he is right in feeling this way; any more than someone is healthy just because he feels healthy. Just remember the notorious witch-trials: at the time, the most perspicacious and humane judges did not doubt that they were dealing with guilt; the witches *themselves did not doubt it,* – and yet there was no guilt. To expand upon that assumption: even 'psychic suffering' does not seem to be a fact to me at all, but simply an interpretation (causal interpretation) of facts which could not up to now be formulated exactly: thus, as something which is still completely in the air and has no scientific standing – actually just a fat word in place of a spindly question mark. If someone cannot cope with his 'psychic suffering', this does *not* stem from his psyche, to speak crudely; more probably from his stomach (I did say I would speak crudely: which does not in any way signify a desire for it to be heard crudely, understood crudely . . .). A strong and well-formed man digests his experi-ences (including deeds and misdeeds) as he digests his meals, even when he has hard lumps to swallow. If he 'cannot cope' with an experience, this sort of indigestion is as much physiological as any other – and often in fact just one of the consequences of that other – with such a point of view we can, between ourselves, still be the fero-cious opponents of all materialism . . .]

[. . .]

24

– And now consider the rarer cases of which I spoke, the last idealists we have today amongst philosophers and scholars: do we perhaps have, in them, the sought-for *opponents* of ascetic ideals, the latter's *counter-idealists*? In fact, they *believe* they are these

67 Luke 10: 42.

'unbelievers' (because that is what they all are); that seems to be their last remnant of faith, to be opponents of this ideal, so serious are they on this score, so passionate is their every word and gesture: − does what they believe therefore need to be *true*? . . . We 'knowers' are positively mistrustful of any kind of believers; our mistrust has gradually trained us to conclude the opposite to what was formerly concluded: to infer a certain weakness in the possible proofs of what is believed, or even its *implausibility* whenever the strength of the faith in it becomes prominent. Even we do not deny that faith 'brings salvation':[68] *precisely for that reason* we deny that faith *proves* anything, − a strong faith which brings salvation is grounds for suspicion of the object of its faith, it does not establish truth, it establishes a certain probability − of *deception*. What now is the position in this case? − These 'no'-sayers and outsiders of today, those who are absolute in one thing, their demand for intellectual rigour [*Sauberkeit*], these hard, strict, abstinent, heroic minds who make up the glory of our time, all these pale atheists, Antichrists, immoralists, nihilists, these sceptics, ephectics, *hectics* of the mind [*des Geistes*] (they are one and all the latter in a certain sense), these last idealists of knowledge in whom, alone, intellectual conscience dwells and is embodied these days, − they believe they are all as liberated as possible from the ascetic ideal, these 'free, *very* free spirits': and yet, I will tell them what they themselves cannot see − because they are standing too close to themselves − this ideal is quite simply *their* ideal as well, they themselves represent it nowadays, and perhaps no one else, they themselves are its most intellectualized product, its most advanced front-line troops and scouts, its most insidious, delicate and elusive form of seduction: − if I am at all able to solve riddles, I wish to claim to do so with *this* pronouncement! . . . These are very far from being *free* spirits: *because they still believe in truth*. . . . When the Christian Crusaders in the East fell upon that invincible order of Assassins, the order of free spirits *par excellence*, the lowest rank of whom lived a life of obedience the like of which no monastic order has ever achieved, somehow or other they received an inkling of that symbol and watchword which was reserved for the highest ranks alone as their *secretum*: 'nothing is true, everything is permitted' . . . Certainly *that* was *freedom* of the mind [*des Geistes*], *with that* the termination of the belief in truth was *announced*. . . . Has a European or a Christian free-thinker [*Freigeist*] ever strayed into this proposition and the labyrinth of its *consequences*? Has he ever got to know the Minotaur in this cave by *direct experience*? . . . I doubt it; indeed, I know otherwise: − nothing is stranger to these people who are absolute in one thing, these *so-called* 'free spirits', than freedom and release in that sense, in no respect are they more firmly bound; precisely in their faith in truth they are more rigid and more absolute than anyone else. Perhaps I am too familiar with all this: that venerable philosopher's abstinence to which a faith like that commits one, that stoicism of the intellect which, in the last resort, denies itself the 'no' just as strictly as the 'yes', that *will* to stand still before the factual, the *factum* **brutum**, that fatalism of '*petits faits*'[69] (*ce petit faitalisme*,[70] as I call it) in which French scholarship now seeks a kind of moral superiority over the German, that renunciation of any interpretation (of forcing, adjusting, shortening, omitting, filling-out, inventing, falsifying and everything else *essential* to interpretation) − on the whole, this expresses the asceticism of

68   Luke 1: 45; John 20: 29.
69   French: little facts.
70   French: this petty factualism.

virtue just as well as any denial of sensuality (it is basically just a *modus* of this denial). However, the *compulsion* towards it, that unconditional will to truth, is *faith in the ascetic ideal itself*, even if, as an unconscious imperative, – make no mistake about it, – it is the faith in a *metaphysical* value, a value *as such of truth* as vouched for and confirmed by that ideal alone (it stands and falls by that ideal). Strictly speaking, there is no 'presuppositionless' knowledge, the thought of such a thing is unthinkable, paralogical: a philosophy, a 'faith' always has to be there first, for knowledge to win from it a direction, a meaning, a limit, a method, a *right* to exist. (Whoever understands it the other way round and, for example, tries to place philosophy 'on a strictly scientific foundation', first needs to stand not only philosophy *on its head* but truth itself as well: the worst offence against decency which can occur in relation to two such respectable ladies!) [. . .] At this point we need to stop and take time to reflect. Science itself now *needs* a justification (which is not at all to say that there is one for it). On this question, turn to the most ancient and most modern philosophies: all of them lack a consciousness of the extent to which the will to truth itself needs a justification, here is a gap in every philosophy – how does it come about? Because the ascetic ideal has so far been *master* over all philosophy, because truth was set as being, as God, as the highest authority itself, because truth was not *allowed* to be a problem. Do you understand this 'allowed to be'? – From the very moment that faith in the God of the ascetic ideal is denied, *there is a new problem as well*: that of the *value* of truth. – The will to truth needs a critique – let us define our own task with this –, the value of truth is tentatively to be *called into question* . . . (Anyone who finds this put too briefly is advised to read that section of *Gay Science* with the title 'To what extent even we are still pious' (section 344) better still, the whole fifth book of that work, similarly the Preface to *Daybreak*.)

25

No! Do not come to me with science[71] when I am looking for the natural antagonist to the ascetic ideal, when I ask: 'Where is the opposing will in which its *opposing ideal* expresses itself?' Science is not nearly independent enough for that, in every respect it first needs a value-ideal, a value-creating power, *serving* which it *is allowed to believe* in itself, – science itself never creates values. Its relationship to the ascetic ideal is certainly not yet inherently antagonistic; indeed, it is much more the case, in general, that it still represents the driving force in the inner evolution of that ideal. Its contradiction and struggle are, on closer inspection, directed not at the ideal itself but at its outworks, its apparel and disguise, at the way the ideal temporarily hardens, solidifies, becomes dogmatic – it liberates what life is in it by denying what is exoteric in this ideal. Both of them, science and the ascetic ideal, are still on the same foundation – I have already explained –; that is to say, both overestimate truth (more correctly: they share the same faith that truth can*not* be assessed or criticized), and this makes them both *necessarily* allies, – so that, if they must be fought, they can only be fought and called into question together. A depreciation of the value of the ascetic ideal inevitably brings about a depreciation of the value of science: one must keep one's eyes open and prick up one's ears for this in time! (*Art*, let me say at the outset, since I shall deal with this at length some day, – art, in which *lying* sanctifies itself

71 In German: *Wissenschaft*.

and the *will to deception* has good conscience on its side, is much more fundamentally opposed to the ascetic ideal than science is: this was sensed instinctively by Plato, the greatest enemy of art Europe has yet produced. Plato *versus* Homer:[72] that is complete, genuine antagonism – on the one hand, the sincerest 'transcendentalist', the great slanderer of life, on the other hand, its involuntary idolater, the *sunny* nature. Artistic servitude in the service of the ascetic ideal is thus the specific form of artistic *corruption*, unfortunately one of the most common: for nothing is more corruptible than an artist.) And when we view it physiologically, too, science rests on the same base as the ascetic ideal: the precondition of both the one and the other is a certain *impoverishment of life*, – the emotions cooled, the tempo slackened, dialectics in place of instinct, *solemnity* stamped on faces and gestures (solemnity, that most unmistakable sign of a more sluggish metabolism and of a struggling, more toiling life). Look at the epochs in the life of a people during which scholars predominated: they are times of exhaustion, often of twilight, of decline, – gone are the overflowing energy, the certainty of life, the certainty as to the *future*. The preponderance of the mandarins never indicates anything good: any more than the rise of democracy, international courts of arbitration instead of wars, equal rights for women, the religion of pity and everything else that is a symptom of life in decline. (Science conceived as a problem: what does science mean? – compare the Preface to *The Birth of Tragedy* on this.) No! – open your eyes! – this 'modern science' is, for the time being, the *best* ally for the ascetic ideal, for the simple reason that it is the most unconscious, involuntary, secret and subterranean! The 'poor in spirit'[73] and the scientific opponents of this ideal have up till now played the same game (by the way, beware of thinking that they are its opposite, i.e. the *rich* in spirit: – they are *not* that, I called them the hectics of spirit). These famous *victories* of the latter: undoubtedly they are victories – but over what? The ascetic ideal was decidedly not conquered, it was, on the contrary, made stronger, I mean more elusive, more spiritual, more insidious by the fact that science constantly and unsparingly detached and broke off a wall or outwork which had attached itself to it and *coarsened* its appearance. Do you really think that, for example, the defeat of theological astronomy meant a defeat of that ideal? . . . Has man perhaps become *less in need* of a transcendental solution to the riddle of his existence because this existence has since come to look still more arbitrary, idle, and dispensable in the *visible* order of things? Has not man's self-deprecation, his *will* to self-deprecation, been unstoppably on the increase since Copernicus? Gone, alas, is his faith in his dignity, uniqueness, irreplaceableness in the rank-ordering of beings, – he has become *animal*, literally, unqualifiedly and unreservedly an animal, man who in his earlier faiths was almost God ('child of God', 'man of God') . . . Since Copernicus, man seems to have been on a downward path, – now he seems to be rolling faster and faster away from the centre – where to? into nothingness? into the *piercing* sensation of his nothingness'? – Well! that would be the straight path – to the *old* idea? . . . *All* science (and not just astronomy alone, the humiliating and degrading effects of which Kant singled out for the remarkable confession that 'it destroys my importance'[74] . . .), all science, natural as well as *unnatural* – this is the name I would give to the self-critique of knowledge

72   See Plato, *Republic*, especially Books II, III, and X.
73   Matthew 5: 3.
74   Kant, *Critique of Pure Reason*, A 289.

– is seeking to talk man out of his former self-respect as though this were nothing but a bizarre piece of self-conceit; you could almost say that its own pride, its own austere form of stoical ataraxy,[75] consisted in maintaining this laboriously won *self-contempt* of man as his last, most serious claim to self-respect (in fact, rightly so: for the person who feels contempt is always someone who 'has not forgotten how to respect' ...) Does this really *work against* the ascetic ideal? Do people in all seriousness still really believe, (as theologians imagined for a while), that, say, Kant's *victory* over theological conceptual dogmatism ('God', 'soul', 'freedom', 'immortality') damaged that ideal? – we shall not, for the moment, concern ourselves with whether Kant himself had anything like that in view. What is certain is that every sort of transcendentalist since Kant has had a winning hand, – they are emancipated from the theologians: what good luck! – he showed them the secret path on which, from now on, they could, independently, and with the best scientific decorum, pursue 'their heart's desires'. Likewise: who would blame the agnostics if, as worshippers of the unknown and the secret, they worship *the question mark* itself as God. (Xaver Doudan[76] on one occasion speaks of the ravages caused by '*l'habitude d'admirer l'inintelligible au lieu de rester tout simplement dans l'inconnu*';[77] he thinks the ancients avoided this.) Suppose that everything man 'knows' does not satisfy his desires but instead contradicts them and arouses horror, what a divine excuse it is to be permitted to lay the guilt for this at the door of 'knowing' rather than 'wishing'! ... 'There is no knowing: *consequently* – there is a God': what a new *elegantia syllogismi*![78] What a *triumph* for the ascetic ideal! –

[...]

27

– Enough! Enough! Let us leave these curiosities and complexities of the most modern spirit, which have as many ridiculous as irritating aspects: *our* problem, indeed, can do without them, the problem of the *meaning* of the ascetic ideal, – what has that to do with yesterday and today! These things will be addressed by me more fully and seriously in another connection (with the title 'On the History of European Nihilism'; for which I refer you to a work I am writing, **The Will to Power**: *Attempt at a Revaluation of all Values*). The only reason I have alluded to this is that the ascetic ideal has, for the present, even in the most spiritual sphere, only one type of real enemy and *injurer*: these are the comedians of this ideal – because they arouse mistrust. Everywhere else where spirit is at work in a rigorous, powerful and honest way, it now completely lacks an ideal – the popular expression for this abstinence is 'atheism' –: *except for its will to truth*. But this will, this *remnant* of an ideal, if you believe me, is that ideal itself in its strictest, most spiritual formulation, completely esoteric, totally stripped of externals, and thus not so much its remnant as its *kernel*. Unconditional, honest atheism (– *that* alone is the air we more spiritual men of the age breathe!) is therefore *not* opposed to the ascetic ideal as it appears to be; instead, it is only one of

75 "Tranquility of the soul," from the Greek *ataraxia* (impassiveness).
76 Ximenes [*sic*] Doudan (1800–72), French politician and author of several posthumously published volumes, including *Mélanges* (*Mixed Writings and Letters*, 1876–7).
77 French: "the habit of *admiring* the unintelligible rather than simply remaining in the dark."
78 Latin: elegant form of inference.

the ideal's last phases of development, one of its final forms and inherent logical conclusions, – it is the awe-inspiring *catastrophe* of a two-thousand-year discipline in truth-telling, which finally forbids itself the *lie entailed in the belief in God*. (The same process of development in India, completely independently, which therefore proves something; the same ideal forcing the same conclusion; the decisive point was reached five centuries before the European era began, with Buddha or, more precisely: already with the Sankhya philosophy which Buddha then popularized and made into a religion.) *What*, strictly speaking, has actually *conquered* the Christian God? The answer is in my *Gay Science* (section 357): 'Christian morality itself, the concept of truthfulness which was taken more and more seriously, the confessional punctiliousness of Christian conscience, translated and sublimated into scientific conscience, into intellectual purity at any price. Regarding nature as though it were a proof of God's goodness and providence; interpreting history in honour of divine reason, as a constant testimonial to an ethical world order and ethical ultimate purpose; explaining all one's own experiences in the way pious folk have done for long enough, as though everything were providence, a sign, intended, and sent for the salvation of the soul: now all that is *over*, it has conscience *against* it, every sensitive conscience sees it as indecent, dishonest, as a pack of lies, feminism, weakness, cowardice, – this severity makes us *good Europeans* if anything does, and heirs to Europe's most protracted and bravest self-overcoming!'[79] . . . All great things bring about their own demise through an act of self-sublimation:[80] that is the law of life,[81] the law of *necessary* 'self-overcoming'[82] in the essence of life, – the lawgiver himself is always ultimately exposed to the cry: '*patere legem, quam ipse tulisti*'.[83] In this way, Christianity *as a dogma* was destroyed by its own morality, in the same way Christianity *as a morality* must also be destroyed, – we stand on the threshold of *this* occurrence. After Christian truthfulness has drawn one conclusion after another, it will finally draw the *strongest conclusion*, that *against* itself; this will, however, happen when it asks itself, '*What does all will to truth mean?*' . . . and here I touch on my problem again, on our problem, my *unknown* friends (– because I don't *know* of any friend as yet): what meaning does *our* being have, if it were not that that will to truth has become conscious of itself *as a problem* in us? . . . Without a doubt, from now on, morality will be *destroyed* by the will to truth's becoming-conscious-of-itself: that great drama in a hundred acts reserved for Europe in the next two centuries, the most terrible, most dubious drama but perhaps also the one most rich in hope . . .

28

Except for the ascetic ideal: man, the *animal* man, had no meaning up to now. His existence on earth had no purpose; 'What is man for, actually?' – was a question without an answer; there was no *will* for man and earth; behind every great human destiny sounded the even louder refrain 'in vain!' *This* is what the ascetic ideal meant: something was *missing*, there was an immense *lacuna* around man, – he himself could think of no justification or explanation or affirmation, he *suffered* from the problem

---

79 In German: *Selbstüberwindung.*
80 In German: *Selbstaufhebung.*
81 In German: *das Gesetz des Lebens.*
82 In German: *"Selbstüberwindung."*
83 Latin: "submit to the law you have yourself made."

of what he meant. Other things made him suffer too, in the main he was a *sickly* animal: but suffering itself was *not* his problem, but the fact that there was no answer to the question he screamed, 'Suffering for *what?*' Man, the bravest animal and most prone to suffer, does *not* deny suffering as such: he *wills* it, he even seeks it out, provided he is shown a *meaning* for it, a *purpose* of suffering. The meaningless of suffering, *not* the suffering, was the curse which has so far blanketed mankind, – and *the ascetic ideal offered man a meaning!* Up to now it was the only meaning, but any meaning at all is better than no meaning at all; the ascetic ideal was, in very respect, the ultimate '*faute de mieux*'[84] *par excellence*. Within it, suffering was given an *interpretation*; the enormous emptiness seemed filled; the door was shut on all suicidal nihilism. The interpretation – without a doubt – brought new suffering with it, deeper, more internal, more poisonous suffering, suffering that gnawed away more intensely at life: it brought all suffering within the perspective of *guilt* . . . But in spite of all that – man was *saved*, he had a *meaning*, from now on he was no longer like a leaf in the breeze, the plaything of the absurd, of 'non-sense'; from now on he could *will* something, – no matter what, why and how he did it at first, the *will itself was saved*. It is absolutely impossible for us to conceal what was actually expressed by that whole willing, which was given its direction by the ascetic ideal: this hatred of the human, and even more of the animalistic, even more of the material, this horror of the senses, of reason itself, this fear of happiness and beauty, this longing to get away from appearance, transience, growth, death, wishing, longing itself – all that means, let us dare to grasp it, a *will to nothingness*, an aversion to life, a rebellion against the most fundamental prerequisites of life, but it is and remains a *will!* . . . And, to conclude by saying what I said at the beginning: man still prefers to will *nothingness*, than *not* will . . .

84   French: for lack of anything better.

1888–1889

Introduction

The final year of Nietzsche's philosophically active life, 1888, was uncommonly fruitful, even by his exacting standards. Since the publication of his first book, *The Birth of Tragedy*, in 1872, he had published on average exactly one new book per year:[1] 1888 saw a marked acceleration in output and he completed no fewer than six books, of which we have included excerpts from four in our final section. These are all shorter works – the longest of them, *Ecce Homo*, is only 120 pages in the standard German edition – but they vary greatly in philosophical scope, in form and in tone. *Twilight of the Idols* and *Ecce Homo* are both works of considerable ambition, providing relatively disparate but highly condensed overviews of Nietzsche's preoccupations throughout his career thus far; *The Case of Wagner* and *The Anti-Christ*, by contrast, are more narrowly focused polemics on specific themes, "through-composed" single arguments of the kind Nietzsche had not produced since the *Untimely Meditations* a decade and a half before. The two works from which we have not included material here, *Nietzsche contra Wagner* and the *Dithyrambs of Dionysus*, are re-edited compilations of earlier material on which Nietzsche worked at the very end of this *annus mirabilis*, in December 1888 and the first days of January 1889, immediately before his definitive collapse into insanity.

With the benefit of hindsight it is easy to view Nietzsche's works of 1888 as a glorious final flourishing before the descent into darkness, but we must bear in mind that Nietzsche himself was far from imagining them as any kind of swan-song. On the contrary, he wrote the works of 1888 in high-spirited anticipation of the momentous impact he was shortly to have on the world by publishing a great summation of his philosophical ideas. This *magnum opus* was the project on which he had been working in the background since the time of *Zarathustra* in 1884, amassing a great many preparatory notes towards what he generally referred to as *The Will to Power*. The story of the works of 1888 is intimately bound up with the gradual abandonment of that project – in the course of the year it was retitled and reconceived as *Revaluation of All Values* (*Umwerthung aller Werthe*) before being definitively shelved shortly before Nietzsche's mental collapse[2] – but its prospect haunted him till the end. As he was

---

1   A total of 16 books in 16 years – not counting the reprints of the mid-1880s, occasional pieces, his musical composition *Hymn to Life*, etc. For an exhaustive listing of all Nietzsche's works, see William H. Schaberg, *The Nietzsche Canon: A Publication History and Bibliography* (Chicago and London: University of Chicago Press, 1995).
2   See Mazzino Montinari, "Nietzsche's Unpublished Writings from 1885 to 1888; or, Textual Criticism and the Will to Power," in *Reading Nietzsche*, trans. Greg Whitlock (Urbana and Chicago: University of Illinois Press, 2003), pp. 80–103.

writing the works of 1888, then, Nietzsche considered them products of an interim period, situated between the "philosophy of the future" pronounced by Zarathustra and its fulfillment in the great work to come.[3] In a letter of September 14, 1888 to his friend Paul Deussen, for example, he describes *The Case of Wagner* and *Twilight of the Idols* as "only recuperations in the midst of an immeasurably difficult and decisive task which, *when it is understood*, will split humanity into two halves";[4] similarly, he begins the Foreword to *Ecce Homo* with a justification for writing his autobiography on the grounds that "I must shortly approach mankind with the heaviest demand that has ever been made on it."

For Nietzsche himself, then, in 1888 his main task still lay ahead, and he looked forward to its fulfillment with relish, buoyed by some of the best health he had enjoyed in years.[5] Janus-faced, though, Nietzsche looked backwards as well: in preparation for the earth-shatteringly affirmative philosophy to come, he was concerned to settle his accounts and draw a line under as many as possible of his philosophical antagonisms, bringing to a conclusion the period of negativity inaugurated by *Beyond Good and Evil*, the "no-saying" (*neinsagend*) part of his task. Not surprisingly, then, the majority of these 1888 works are (like *On the Genealogy of Morality*) polemics, and parodic in intent,[6] less concerned with introducing new themes than with reaching definitive formulations of earlier positions in order to rebuff the staunchest of his philosophical opponents – most notably Richard Wagner, his compatriots the Germans in general,[7] and Christianity.

The Case of Wagner: A Musicians' Problem

The year 1888 may have turned out to be one of final reckonings, but Nietzsche began it working intensively on material intended for *The Will to Power*, and continued doing so till late summer. He was diverted from the task of preparing his *magnum opus* in February and March of 1888 when some correspondence with his most musical friend, Heinrich Köselitz (Peter Gast), on the subject of the music of Richard Wagner prompted him to address once more in writing (in late April and May) the cultural significance of his erstwhile mentor, five years after Wagner's death and more extensively than at any time since his first book, *The Birth of Tragedy*, over a decade and a half before.

---

3   Cf. *TI* IX. 51: "I have given humanity the most profound book it possesses, my *Zarathustra*: I shall shortly give it the most independent one. –"

4   *Selected Letters of Friedrich Nietzsche*, ed. and trans. Christopher Middleton (Chicago and London: University of Chicago Press, 1969; repr. Indianapolis: Hackett, 1996), p. 311.

5   Again with hindsight, one can readily interpret this as the state of euphoria which often precedes the onset of tertiary syphilis.

6   For an excellent introduction to Nietzsche's work through the lens of this theme, see Sander L. Gilman, *Nietzschean Parody: An Introduction to Reading Nietzsche* (Bonn: Bouvier Verlag Herbert Grundmann, 1976).

7   We have omitted most of this anti-German material from our selections. Those interested in following up this strand in Nietzsche's late work should turn in particular to the two postscripts in *The Case of Wagner*, the section "What the Germans Lack" in *Twilight of the Idols*, and the section on *The Case of Wagner* in *EH* III.

In his first book Nietzsche had hailed Wagnerian music-drama as the greatest hope for Germany's cultural regeneration, but already by the mid-1870s he had broken with Wagner. He faced considerable difficulty in completing the fourth of the *Untimely Meditations*, *Richard Wagner in Bayreuth* (1876), such was the extent of his growing disaffection; the inaugural Bayreuth Festival in the summer of 1876 – from which he fled, racked by psychosomatic illness – proved a decisive breaking-point, and the two men met for the last time shortly afterwards, in October of 1876. Their next works sealed their division by demonstrating to each other the radically different directions in which they were moving: at the beginning of 1878 Wagner sent Nietzsche the text of *Parsifal*, and a few months later Nietzsche sent him a copy of *Human, All Too Human*; in *Ecce Homo* (in a typical embellishment of the truth) Nietzsche heightens the dramatic effect of the exchange by imagining the two texts crossing in the post like crossed swords (*EH* III, "HH," 5). Nietzsche's criticisms of Wagner remained relatively restrained until after the latter's death in February 1883; then Part IV of *Thus Spoke Zarathustra* contains a thinly veiled portrait of the composer in the figure of the Sorcerer who acts out the part of "the penitent of the spirit," and *Parsifal*, in particular, is taken to task in both *Beyond Good and Evil* (256 – "*Rome's faith in all but name!*") and the Third Essay of *On the Genealogy of Morality* (*GM* III. 2–4), where it provides an object lesson in the artist's wayward pursuit of the "ascetic ideal." Just as *On the Genealogy of Morality* had been written "by way of clarification and supplement" to *Beyond Good and Evil*, so *The Case of Wagner* follows on from this earlier portrait of Wagner in *On the Genealogy of Morality*, and by 1888 the gloves are well and truly off.[8]

In German, Nietzsche's title *Der Fall Wagner* is richly polysemic, suggesting a legal "case" (Wagner's arraignment) as well as the "sinful" Wagner's "fall" *and* the "falling off" of his decadence. The dominant meaning, though, is that of a medical "case history," with Dr Nietzsche treating Wagner as a paradigmatic pathology. The text is thus the most prominent example of the medical idiom to which Nietzsche resorts very frequently in his last works. Wagner here is denounced as the archetypal "artist of decadence," "*the modern artist par excellence*" (*CW* 5), his neurotic, hysterical, histrionic art "a sickness." As Nietzsche admits in the Preface, though, Wagner is "one of my sicknesses," and he does not shrink from addressing his own personal implication in the Wagnerian project. This attack on Wagner, then, is also, at the same time, a self-critique: Nietzsche candidly admits his own decadence, but seeks to mitigate it in two ways. Firstly, retrospectively generalizing from his own experience he makes an encounter with Wagner, the epitome of modernity, into a necessary, fateful stage in the personal development of any philosopher worthy of the name. Secondly, he presents his own break with Wagner as an overcoming of the "sickness" of Wagnerism and, in a spirit of self-heroicizing which will culminate in *Ecce Homo*, celebrates it as the successful achievement of a self-overcoming, the assertion of a contrary taste. Just at the point where Wagner "condescended to become German" (*EH* III. 5), Nietzsche himself switched his allegiance to French culture (cf. the end of *BGE* 254), for Paris

---

8 The vehemence of Nietzsche's attacks in *The Case of Wagner* came as a surprise to those Wagnerians who had ceased to follow his output after *Richard Wagner in Bayreuth*, so at the end of 1888 he assembled *Nietzsche contra Wagner* from his texts of the previous decade, in order to demonstrate that the "divine malice" of *The Case of Wagner* was no flash in the pan.

is the capital of contemporary decadence, home not only to its greatest exponents but, crucially, to its most perceptive analysts, too. Indeed the analysis of "literary decadence" included in section 7 of *The Case of Wagner* is borrowed wholesale from an essay by the Parisian novelist and critic Paul Bourget on the poet Charles Baudelaire.

The most signal mobilization of French culture against Wagner in *The Case of Wagner* is in the name of Georges Bizet, composer of the opera *Carmen*, whose lightness of touch Nietzsche holds up against the (German, all too German) turgidity of Wagner's music at the opening of the text. In a letter to his friend Carl Fuchs from the end of December 1888, though, Nietzsche admits to using this opposition merely for tactical effect: "What I say about Bizet, you should not take seriously; the way I am, Bizet does not matter to me at all. But as an ironic *antithesis* to Wagner, it has a strong effect."[9] It would be a mistake, then, to read *The Case of Wagner* (and, for that matter, *Nietzsche contra Wagner*), as evidence of a simple tipping of the balance in Nietzsche's relationship with Wagner from love to hate, for this relationship remained ambivalent to the last. It is quite clear, for example, that Nietzsche's allegiance to Wagner's *music* remained unshakeable: in his late letters and *Ecce Homo* (II. 6) he praises *Tristan and Isolde* as "Wagner's *non plus ultra*," and in *The Case of Wagner* he can even write of *Parsifal*: "I admire this work; I wish I had written it myself" (*CW*, "Second Postscript"). He knows too well that his youthful encounter with this artistic genius and surrogate father figure was too important in his own development – what he will call in *Ecce Homo* the drama of "becoming what he is" – just to shrug off and turn his back on the relationship; true to his philosophical principles he admits at the end of the "Epilogue": "This essay is inspired [. . .] by gratitude."

Twilight of the Idols; or, How to Philosophize with a Hammer

Although *The Case of Wagner* is subtitled "Turinese Letter of May 1888," Nietzsche continued tinkering with the text – in particular, appending two "Postscripts" and an "Epilogue" – till August. By this stage, as usual, he was summering in Sils-Maria, but unusually he was finding great difficulty in advancing his plans for *The Will to Power*, facing unwonted periods of writer's block, till a breakthrough came at the end of that month, when he finally abandoned the project and recast it as a new four-volume masterwork to be called *Revaluation of All Values* (*Umwerthung aller Werthe*). This ushered in the febrile activity of the last few months of 1888, beginning with a draft of a new book which he completed in little more than a week and had already dispatched to his publisher a fortnight before *The Case of Wagner* was eventually published, on September 22, 1888. The working title of this new book, "Idleness of a Psychologist" ("Müssiggang eines Psychologen"), emphasized its nature as a welcome release, a recuperation from the "great task" that still lay ahead, but Köselitz persuaded him to change the title to something more grandiose, and the book became *Twilight of the Idols*.

The final title, a parody of *Twilight of the Gods* (the final music-drama in Wagner's tetralogy *The Ring of the Nibelung*), leads the reader to expect another anti-Wagnerian polemic, but such an impression is misleading, for Wagner is mentioned only three times in the text, and in passing. Instead, the Wagnerian parody is just a clever hook on which to hang a critique of myriad "idols" – would-be "eternal truths" decking

---

9   *Selected Letters of Friedrich Nietzsche*, p. 340.

themselves out as worshipful deities but which the hammer-wielding psychologist Nietzsche can sound out as hollow, prior to their destruction (cf. the Preface). In *Twilight of the Idols*, Nietzsche manages to encapsulate his main mature themes within a remarkably short compass: it represents the culmination of the "free spirit" strain in his thinking and was intended by Nietzsche himself as a kind of primer in his philosophy thus far; hence at various points he seeks to "ease comprehension" (*TI* III. 6). Both philosophically and stylistically it is the most wide-ranging of these works of 1888; indeed stylistically it is the most varied of *all* his texts. We have included the first six chapters in their entirety as well as substantial excerpts from three of the remaining five.

Inspired by the French *moralistes*, Nietzsche had included chapters composed of pithy epigrams in several of his previous works (see especially our selection from *Beyond Good and Evil* section 4, "Epigrams and Interludes"), but *Twilight of the Idols* is the only one of his books in which such a chapter is placed first, reinforcing the fact that Nietzsche here wants to be appreciated primarily as a psychologist. As before, many of these "Maxims and Barbs" are technical *tours de force*, masterpieces of concision; they are also (uncoincidentally) at the same time some of his most famous and memorable *aperçus* (e.g. "Whatever does not kill me makes me stronger," *TI* I. 8; "The will to system is a lack of integrity," *TI* I. 26). However, we have also included some of the epigrams from this chapter which it is much more difficult for the modern reader to find admirable, namely some of his throwaway remarks belittling women (*TI* I. 27–8), for one cannot (and should not seek to) deny that in this respect, too, he is "a child of his time" (*CW*, Preface). Nietzsche may have been recuperated for modern feminism,[10] but he remained an implacable opponent of the first feminist movement in Germany and could not resist making such casually misogynistic remarks as these.

Twilight opens with a loose collection of aphorisms, but this is followed by a closely knit single-thread argument about "The Problem of Socrates" (*TI* II). Here Nietzsche returns to the bugbear of *The Birth of Tragedy*, but subtly revises his previous argument and views Socrates now in a different light, as the *symptom* of Greek cultural decadence rather than its cause (this chapter has much in common with the similarly symptomatological approach to Wagner in *The Case of Wagner*). After this highly personalized attack on Socrates for introducing dialectics into philosophy and making a "tyrant out of reason" (*TI* II. 10), Nietzsche devotes the third chapter of the book to further reflections on "Reason in Philosophy," attacking the quasi-fetishistic worship of rationality at all costs, seen as the occupational hazard of philosophy hitherto which has resulted in the dehistoricization and dematerialization of the great majority of philosophical concepts – "unity, identity, duration, substance, cause, materiality, Being" (*TI* III. 5). Nietzsche's critique of the dematerializing tendency in metaphysics, and defense of the real world of empirical sense-perception, reaches a mischievous culmination in the next chapter, "How the 'Real World' Finally Became a Fable" (*TI* IV), of which Heidegger remarked: "here, in a magnificent moment of vision, the entire realm of Nietzsche's thought is permeated by a new and singular brilliance."[11]

---

10 See especially Kelly Oliver and Marilyn Pearsall (eds), *Feminist Interpretations of Friedrich Nietzsche* (University Park: Pennsylvania State University Press, 1998).

11 Heidegger, "Nietzsche's Overturning of Platonism," in *Nietzsche*, ed. David Farrell Krell, trans. David Farrell Krell et al., 4 vols (San Francisco and London: Harper & Row, 1979–87), vol. 1, p. 202.

At an early stage in the composition of *Twilight of the Idols* Nietzsche decided to hold back the majority of his material on Christianity to form the nucleus of a separate text (*The Anti-Christ* – see below), so that "Morality as Anti-Nature" (*TI* V) is left as the main attack on Christian morality in this text. Following on from the Third Essay of the *Genealogy*, Christian morality is here condemned as decadent, anti-instinctual, anti-natural, "inimical to life" (*TI* V. 1), even if "we immoralists and anti-Christians" (*TI* V. 3) still deem it necessary to uphold it as an enemy (and, to that extent, respect it). Of "The Four Great Errors" in the next chapter (*TI* VI), the greatest is the first, the common misconception about causality – "confusing the *consequence with the cause*" (*TI* VI. 1) – from which the remaining three are derived. We suffer from a "causal drive" (*TI* VI. 5), Nietzsche tells us here, which impels us to explain actions in terms of erroneous "inner facts" such as "will," "mind," and "subject" which are but illusions populating our fabricated "'inner world'" (*TI* VI. 3). "Morality and religion belong entirely under the *psychology of error*" (*TI* VI. 6): developing the argument of the Second Essay of the *Genealogy*, Nietzsche argues that the myth of "free will" derives from Christian theology's desire to make people responsible for their actions and thus foster guilt, which in turn derives from the ("slavish") desire to blame and punish (*TI* VI. 7). Instead, he proposes as his own counter-explanation a kind of fatalism: "*No one is the result of his own intention, his own will, his own purpose*" (*TI* VI. 8). Those who seek to bring about the moral "improvement" of humanity, then, have set themselves an absurd, anti-natural task and should recognize instead that "Morality is merely sign language, merely symptomatology" (*TI* VII. 1). Morality is a semiotics (in the original, medical sense of the word), a surface phenomenon requiring meta-level interpretation in accordance with a different, superior set of extra-moral values "beyond good and evil."

By far the longest, most disparate and wide-ranging chapter in *Twilight* is "Reconnaissance Raids of an Untimely Man," of which we have included a substantial selection here. In two linked paragraphs (*TI* IX. 10–11), Nietzsche revisits the meaning of the Apollonian/Dionysian opposition crucial to *The Birth of Tragedy*, and revises it (both are now "conceived as types of intoxication," whereas in *The Birth of Tragedy* this applied only to the Dionysian). He restates his anti-Darwinism, setting his theory of will to power against Darwin's "struggle for existence" (*TI* IX. 14), and in an extended sequence dealing with aesthetics (*TI* IX. 19–24) he rejects the (Christian, Kantian, Schopenhauerian) conception of the "disinterested" perception of beauty as "nihilistic," arguing instead that "Art is the great stimulant to life" (*TI* IX. 24) and (unusually) using Plato to reinforce his contention that man's aesthetic sense is in fact the product of a drive which is both anthropomorphic and sexualized.[12] The artist is "a genius of communication" (*TI* IX. 24) and can therefore presumably avoid the self-vulgarization which ordinary language-use entails (*TI* IX. 26). Included among the "Reconnaissance Raids" are a number of important aphorisms concerned with contemporary political structures and movements. "Christian and Anarchist" (*TI* IX. 34) argues that the two types have much in common in that they seek to place moral *blame* (on themselves or others respectively) for their misfortunes: in the parlance of

12   Freud will follow on from Nietzsche's conclusion here and consider the mechanism of "sublimation" by which higher culture arises out of the unconscious drives not sanctioned by society. See, in particular, *Civilization and its Discontents*.

On the Genealogy of Morality they are both classically creatures of *ressentiment*. Two further linked paragraphs (*TI* IX. 38–9) subject modern liberal institutions to an incisive critique: Nietzsche argues that they are based on a paradox, since they are born of *il*liberalism and need to be fought for to be achieved in the first place. What is more, "The whole of the West has lost those instincts from which institutions grow, from which *future* grows" (*TI* IX. 39): to found an institution is to live for the future, and decadent modern man cannot think that far ahead (cannot *feel* that far ahead in his instincts). It is not possible to turn back the clock; the only possibility that remains for humanity is to go "*step by step further in décadence*" (*TI* IX. 43), and the only ("redemptive") hope is that the accumulated energy of the herd might yet explode (*TI* IX. 44) to produce exceptional individuals, great squanderers (like Zarathustra), geniuses such as Napoleon or Goethe (*TI* IX. 48–9).

Nietzsche sees in Goethe a fellow disciple of the god Dionysus, and in our final two paragraphs from *Twilight of the Idols* – taken from the penultimate chapter, "What I Owe the Ancients" – he expands further on what he understands by the Dionysian (*TI* X. 4–5). He revisits the terrain of *The Birth of Tragedy* – where he had proposed a radically innovative understanding of the importance to ancient Greek culture of the orgiastic, life-affirming Dionysian energies (see the introduction to Part II) – and boasts that even his former Basel colleague and renowned historian of Greek culture Jacob Burckhardt deferred to his conception of this phenomenon, that even Goethe failed to understand correctly the function of the Dionysian in Greek culture. Nietzsche signs off here as not just "the last disciple of the philosopher Dionysus" but as "the teacher of the eternal recurrence" (*TI* X. 5): at the last he grafts on to this book a piece of Zarathustran wisdom, one of the "grand doctrines" (like will to power and perspectivism) which are otherwise little in evidence here. But he leaves the final word to Zarathustra himself, and brings the book as a whole to its conclusion with a short excerpt from "Of Old and New Law-Tables" (*TI* XI; cf. *Z* III).

The Anti-Christ: Curse on Christianity

The anti-Christian implications of Nietzsche's intense self-identification with a pagan, pre-Christian god are fully developed in his next text, *The Anti-Christ*, the first 24 paragraphs of which he originally intended using in *Twilight* before hiving them off to a separate text.[13] *The Anti-Christ* represents Nietzsche's final reckoning with Christianity, its starkest condemnation in his writings and thus the culmination of the spiritual odyssey embarked upon by this Protestant pastor's son a quarter-century before. He had begun to doubt his ancestral faith by his late teens, had stopped taking communion and abandoned his studies in theology at Bonn University in 1865, but it is not until the "middle period" that his antipathy towards religion in general, and Christianity in particular, really begins to have an impact on his writings. The "free spirit" (*freier Geist*) is also a "freethinker" (*Freigeist*), as Nietzsche makes perfectly plain by dedicating the first edition of *Human, All Too Human* to the most notable Enlightenment critic of Christianity, Voltaire, whose anti-clerical rallying-cry "écrasez

---

13 The intimate relation between the two texts is confirmed by *Ecce Homo*, where Nietzsche comments on *The Anti-Christ* in the section ostensibly devoted to *Twilight* alone.

l'infâme!" ("crush the infamous thing!") he will take up again much later, at the conclusion of *Ecce Homo* (*EH* IV. 8).

The title of this new work could hardly be more bellicose, but, once again, it is also ambiguous and potentially misleading, for Nietzsche is not identifying with Satan as the personal antagonist of Jesus Christ. The German title (*Der Antichrist*) also signifies "The Anti-Christian," which makes a better translation, since Nietzsche here has little interest in the figure of Jesus and is much more concerned to attack the Church, the perverted brainchild of "the first Christian" (*D* 68), Paul.[14] Nietzsche had already taken his critique of Christianity very far in the Second Essay of *On the Genealogy of Morality*, with its characterization of the Judeo-Christian priest figure as a historical bogeyman, bent on exerting his power by "taming" man's natural instincts and turning him against himself, into a piece of "anti-nature," but in *The Anti-Christ* Nietzsche will take his condemnation yet further. At the outset he adopts the detached vantage point of the "Hyperborean" outsider (*AC* 1) from which to draw up his charge sheet: Christianity has waged war on the higher type, we are told, sapping his strength and domesticating him through pity (Zarathustra's besetting sin). Christianity has instituted the reign of nihilistic values (*AC* 6); a religion of *décadence*, of the weak, it has a depressive effect that drains vitality – the "physiological reality" of Christianity is a degeneration of the instincts (*AC* 30). Previous German philosophy, and Kant in particular, has been seduced by the insidious "spirituality" of Christian virtues (*AC* 11); instead, as a corrective Nietzsche proposes "our" rather less lofty view of man as the most cunning, sickliest, most interesting of animals (*AC* 13–14). The Christian God is the apotheosis of nihilism, "the will to nothingness sanctified" (*AC* 18), and monotheism is merely an excuse for creative barrenness – "almost two millennia and not a single new God!" (*AC* 19). Nietzsche contrasts Christianity unfavorably with the "hygienic" practice of Buddhism (*AC* 20–3, not included here), but emphasizes the fact that it had its origin in Judaism (*AC* 24), with its perverse tendency to falsify concepts and invert them into contradictions of their natural values (as analyzed in the First Essay of *On the Genealogy of Morality*, which is explicitly cross-referenced here).

It is only at this point in the development of the argument of *The Anti-Christ* that Nietzsche finally turns to the figure of Jesus, considered typologically as redeemer. Jesus is not a hero, Nietzsche argues here, but rather the "symbolist *par excellence*" (*AC* 32): a childlike figure akin to Wagner's Parsifal (the "pure fool"), Nietzsche's Jesus represents the triumph of metaphysical non-entities like "the 'kingdom of God'" (*AC* 34) over the realm of the real. Nietzsche clearly shows a more than grudging respect for the achievements of this Jewish holy man, and reserves his contempt rather for the Church that was founded in his name, since "one constructed the *Church* out of the antithesis to the Gospel" (*AC* 36) in a deliberate misunderstanding of Jesus' symbolism and perversion of his truths. Jesus himself was the only true Christian, and he died on the cross (*AC* 39); after him came Paul (*AC* 42), "the genius of hatred," the archetypal Judaic priest who founded the new religion of Christianity as an expression of his personal *ressentiment*, spirit of revenge and pursuit of power. As a result, Christian belief is a self-delusion and the enemy of truth, defined as intellectual honesty (*AC* 50). In the final paragraphs of the text (*AC* 59–62), Nietzsche's tone turns elegiac as he

14   On Nietzsche's rejection of Christianity more generally, see Walter Kaufmann, "Nietzsche's Repudiation of Christ," in id., *Nietzsche: Philosopher, Psychologist, Anti-Christ*, 4th edn (Princeton and London: Princeton University Press, 1974), ch. 12.

wistfully considers the great cultural achievements on which Christianity foreclosed: "Christianity robbed us of the harvest of the culture of the ancient world, it later went on to rob us of the harvest of the culture of *Islam*" (*AC* 60); moreover, thanks to the Lutheran Reformation which revitalized the Church, "The Germans have robbed Europe of the last great cultural harvest Europe had to bring home – of the harvest of *Renaissance*" (*AC* 61). The Renaissance was European culture's most recent attempt to restore the noble values of antiquity and it was cruelly aborted, so a new revaluation is required, a "revaluation of all values" which will dispose of Christianity, this "immortal blemish of mankind" (*AC* 62), once and for all.

With this stirring call to arms Nietzsche brought *The Anti-Christ* to a close on September 30, 1888, describing it in the Preface to *Twilight of the Idols* as "the first book of the *Revaluation of All Values*." Over the next couple of months, though, his plans for the book changed and he began to envisage it instead as synonymous with the *Revaluation of All Values* project *tout court*. Then finally, just before his mental collapse in January 1889, he changed plans one last time and crossed out the subtitle "Attempt at a Revaluation of All Values" on the title page of the manuscript, substituting "Curse on Christianity." At this point, in other words, what Nietzsche had begun four years earlier as a projected *magnum opus* (*The Will to Power*, then the *Revaluation*) was finally laid to rest.

Ecce Homo: How One Becomes What One Is

In December 1872 Nietzsche had given Cosima Wagner his "Five Prefaces to Five Unwritten Books" in manuscript as a birthday present; on his own forty-fourth birthday, October 15, 1888, he already had two books in the pipeline (*Twilight of the Idols* and *The Anti-Christ*), yet this did not prevent him from starting a third, an autobiography, as a birthday present to himself. As with the other texts of this period, he wrote *Ecce Homo* very quickly, in a frenzy of inspiration, and completed the first draft in less than three weeks. From its blasphemous title ("Behold the Man" – a self-application of Pontius Pilate's words as he reveals Jesus to the mob in the Vulgate version of John 19: 5) to its final confrontation, "*Dionysus against the Crucified*" (*EH* IV. 9), the text continues to mine the same vein of anti-Christian sentiment as that which preceded it. What is more, like *Twilight of the Idols; or, How to Philosophize with a Hammer*, the subtitle to *Ecce Homo*, "how one becomes what one is," conjures up a kind of instruction manual – but this time Nietzsche is presenting himself as an aid to *self*-help, *self*-education in others (the Zarathustran truth quoted at the end of the Foreword). We have included the complete Foreword and excerpts from all four chapters.

Taken together, the texts of 1888 are certainly Nietzsche's most personal in tone, but *Ecce Homo* takes the art of confessional self-affirmation to new heights, and what strikes its reader – even just from perusing the chapter titles – is the outrageous immodesty of its author. In itself, such a deliberately provocative attitude can be read as an attack on modesty as a Christian virtue (and has been read in this way by Sarah Kofman in her magisterial two-volume commentary on the text).[15] *Ecce Homo* makes the most

---

15 See Sarah Kofman, "Explosion I: Of Nietzsche's *Ecce Homo*," trans. Duncan Large, *Diacritics*, 24/4 (Winter 1994), pp. 51–70, repr. in *Nietzsche: Critical Assessments*, ed. Daniel W. Conway with Peter S. Groff, 4 vols (London and New York: Routledge, 1998), vol. 1, pp. 218–41.

extravagant claims for the "I" whom it invokes, but we must be careful not to be taken in by the rhetoric of the text and to observe instead a basic principle of literary criticism, respecting the distance between the author and the character he creates, even if that character speaks in the first person. Nietzsche himself tells us (paradoxically, in one of his writings): "I am one thing, my writings are another" (*EH* III. 1), but as Alexander Nehamas points out, "Nietzsche himself [. . .] is a creature of his own texts"; he makes an "effort to create an artwork out of himself, a literary character who is a philosopher,"[16] and nowhere is this effort more in evidence than in *Ecce Homo*. In another inevitable paradox, then, what appears to be the most self-revelatory of texts is in fact the most obfuscatory and self-mythopoeic. It is certainly highly unconventional – Michael Tanner goes so far as to write: "Almost certainly it is the most bizarre example of [autobiography] ever penned."[17] Not only does it flaunt its partiality, but it lacks the usual scaffolding of dates and places (and, for the most part, other characters); in its obsessive concern with how this particular character "became what he was" the text is at times positively autistic.

No sooner has the Foreword opened by claiming that it is now imperative for Nietzsche to say who he is than he proceeds to explain who he is *not*, and in the final section of the Foreword – as so often in these late texts (cf. *TI* XI) – he speaks indirectly by adopting the mask of his "favorite son" and quoting at length from his fictional creation Zarathustra. After these initial feints, the text "proper" opens (equally coyly) with a riddle, but one which does at least introduce the key theme of these late writings, the question of *décadence*. As in *Twilight of the Idols*, Nietzsche writes here as a psychophysiologist, but this time he is subjecting himself to a meticulous auto-examination in order to determine how his own constitution measures up against his new extramoral yardsticks of health and sickness, life-affirmation and life-denial. Nietzsche here returns to the theme of the Preface to *The Case of Wagner*: he frankly admits to his own *décadence* but claims also to have within him the healthiest of instincts towards the overcoming of *décadence*, to be a self-healing physician who has "turned out well" – and it is in this that his "wisdom" lies (*EH* I. 2). In the controversial third paragraph of "Why I Am So Wise" – initially suppressed by Nietzsche's sister Elisabeth and reinstated only in 1969 by Nietzsche's editor Mazzino Montinari[18] – he indulges in a bout of wishful thinking and allows himself to be seduced by a fantasy genealogy (since proven to be false) according to which "I am a pure-blooded Polish nobleman, in whom there is no drop of bad blood, least of all German" (*EH* I. 3). In the other paragraph we have included from this chapter, he warns against the deleterious effects of *ressentiment* on the metabolism and offers as his patent remedy "Russian fatalism": "To accept oneself as a fate, not to desire oneself 'different'" (*EH* I. 6). Such a prescription will recur at several key points over the rest of the text.

"Why I Am So Clever" is a testament to Nietzsche's tastes, and to the importance he attaches to taste itself, in all its guises – "not good taste, not bad taste, but *my* taste,

16 Alexander Nehamas, *Nietzsche: Life as Literature* (Cambridge, MA and London: Harvard University Press, 1985), p. 8.

17 See his introduction to Nietzsche, *Ecce Homo*, trans. R. J. Hollingdale, 2nd edn (Harmondsworth: Penguin, 1992), pp. vii–xvii (p. vii).

18 See Montinari, "A New Section in Nietzsche's *Ecce Homo*," in *Reading Nietzsche*, pp. 103–26.

which I no longer conceal and of which I am no longer ashamed" (*Z* III, "Of the Spirit of Gravity"). He documents in minute detail his preferences in food (Piedmontese cuisine), drink (no alcohol or coffee) and recreation (lots of exercise), but also his taste in places to live (which must have dry air), reading matter (preferably French, though he has a soft spot for the works of Heinrich Heine and Shakespeare) and music (three surprisingly generous paragraphs on Wagner). We have included the final three paragraphs in this chapter, when – just at the point where the reader might lose patience and wonder why on earth Nietzsche considers it so important to parade such details before us – he draws back from the minutiae of his tastes and derives some more general principles, including an answer to the question raised by the subtitle of the book, "how one becomes what one is." In this chapter Nietzsche gives us a self-definition through his particular tastes, at the same time emphasizing the importance of *having* tastes at all (of being selective) and of *knowing* one's tastes, for it is only on that basis that one can know what is best for one's metabolism and avoid everything else. Such is Nietzsche's recipe for "spiritual" health (in reality, for healthy intestines): his "instinct for self-defense" recognizes the primacy of the principle of the conservation of energy. "Becoming what one is" is a question of discovering and then "owning" oneself (*being* a self, an individual),[19] encapsulated at the end of the chapter in a restatement of the principle of "Russian fatalism" in terms of *amor fati* (cf. *GS* 276–7): "My formula for greatness in a human being is *amor fati*: that one wants nothing to be other than it is, not in the future, not in the past, not in all eternity. Not merely to endure that which happens of necessity, still less to dissemble it [. . .] but to *love* it" (*EH* II. 10).

The third chapter of *Ecce Homo*, "Why I Write Such Good Books," is mainly devoted to passing under review Nietzsche's earlier works, but we have included its first five paragraphs, in which he discusses their reception and the style of their writing. He freely admits that his earlier work has generally been misunderstood but, undaunted, turns this into a badge of honor and argues that his "good books" have simply not yet found the right readers – "some are born posthumously" (*EH* III. 1). He clearly has very high expectations of his readers and wants to be read by only the choicest few kindred spirits who might be able to appreciate the virtues of his writing on account of shared personal experience: he does have a handful of such admirers, he claims, but they are not to be found in Germany (*EH* III. 2–3). Nietzsche's best critic is himself, then, and only he can hope to give an appraisal of his own works which is adequate to the quality of their achievement: in a veritable orgy of self-praise, he claims for himself "the most manifold art of style any man has ever had at his disposal" (*EH* III. 4) and reasserts his unparalleled psychological acuity (*EH* III. 5).

For the final chapter Nietzsche returns to the question of fate, fatalism, and *amor fati* in order to explain "Why I Am a Destiny." With the celebrated remark "I am not a man, I am dynamite" (*EH* IV. 1) he turns squarely to face the future and announces the great cataclysms which he imagines will be associated with his name once the impact of his philosophy (and in particular the *Revaluation of All Values*, which at this stage he is still anticipating) has at last been fully felt. Again we have included the final three paragraphs, in which the chapter, and the book as a whole, builds up to its climax with Nietzsche's repeated refrain "have I been understood?" In the last resort,

19   Cf. the existential challenge of the eternal return: becoming individual *in order to* be able to return eternally.

then, although he claims not to want to be understood by the modern age, that does not stop him spelling out his message as plainly as he can, and for his ultimate self-definition he returns once again to his anti-Christian immoralism: "What defines me, what sets me apart from all the rest of mankind, is that I have *unmasked* Christian morality" (*EH* IV. 7).

Four Letters

Nietzsche concludes *Ecce Homo* by identifying with "Dionysus against the Crucified" (*EH* IV. 9), and only a few weeks later this (still metaphorical) identification with a divinity would tip over into the insane megalomania that marks the series of letters and postcards he wrote immediately after his mental collapse, in the first few days of January 1889. We conclude our selection with one of these, but it is preceded by three other of Nietzsche's late letters, to give something of a taste of Nietzsche as correspondent. In total the standard German edition of his correspondence collects together almost 3,000 items, and it is notable that during the extraordinarily prolific final year of his philosophically active life he was also at his most prolific as a letter-writer. The letters we have included all supplement the autobiographical material of *Ecce Homo*: the first, to Georg Brandes (April 10, 1888), is part of Nietzsche's late correspondence with the Danish admirer who gave him his first academic recognition by lecturing on his philosophy at the University of Copenhagen. In response to a request, Nietzsche sends Brandes a curriculum vitae which is particularly interesting for its various embellishments of the truth. Karl Knortz was an American journalist planning to write an essay on him, so Nietzsche, similarly, sent him appraisals of his works (June 21, 1888), including a no-holds-barred appreciation of *Zarathustra* as "the profoundest work in the German tongue, also the most perfect in its language." The letter to Franz Overbeck (October 18, 1888) conveys the great excitement and sense of everything coming to fruition which gripped Nietzsche at the time he began *Ecce Homo*; the letter to Jacob Burckhardt (dated January 6, 1889) is his last letter of all, a clear testament to his tragic "transfiguration." Even such a letter is not without philosophical interest, though, for one of the claims Nietzsche advances in it – "at root every name in history is I" – is but a hyperbolic form of the tendency to identify with historical figures which he has shown throughout his career.

One of the greatest ironies of Nietzsche's fate is that his mental collapse should have been followed by the rapid establishment of the "Nietzsche legend," the "Nietzsche cult," and the "Nietzsche industry." As far as Nietzsche himself was concerned, though, and to speak with Hamlet's last words (one of his favorite quotations), "The rest is silence." What followed the end of his intellectual career was over a decade of mental and physical degeneration before his eventual death at the dawn of a new century which would finally begin to embark on the task of understanding itself with the aid of his work.

22

The Case of Wagner:
A Musicians' Problem
(1888)

ridendo dicere *severum*[1]

Preface

I have granted myself some small relief. It is not merely pure malice when I praise Bizet in this essay at the expense of Wagner. Interspersed with many jokes, I bring up a matter that is no joke. To turn my back on Wagner was for me a fate; to like anything at all again after that, a triumph. Perhaps nobody was more dangerously attached to – grown together with – Wagnerizing; nobody tried harder to resist it; nobody was happier to be rid of it. A long story! – You want a word for it? – If I were a moralist, who knows what I might call it? Perhaps self-overcoming. – But the philosopher has no love for moralists. Neither does he love pretty words.

What does a philosopher demand of himself first and last? To overcome his time in himself, to become "timeless." With what must he therefore engage in the hardest combat? With whatever marks him as the child of his time. Well, then! I am, no less than Wagner, a child of this time; that is, a decadent: but I comprehended this, I resisted it. The philosopher in me resisted.

Nothing has preoccupied me more profoundly than the problem of decadence – I had reasons. "Good and evil" is merely a variation of that problem. Once one has developed a keen eye for the symptoms of decline, one understands morality, too – one understands what is hiding under its most sacred names and value formulas: impoverished life, the will to the end, the great weariness. Morality negates life. For such a task I required a special self-discipline: to take sides against everything sick in me, including Wagner, including Schopenhauer, including all of modern "humaneness." – A profound estrangement, cold, sobering up – against everything that is of this time, everything timely – and most desirable of all, the eye of Zarathustra, an eye that beholds the

---

1 Latin: through what is laughable say what is sombre. Variation of Horace's *ridentem dicere verum, quid vetat* ("What forbids us to tell the truth, laughing?"), *Satires*, I. 24.

whole fact of man at a tremendous distance – below. For such a goal – what sacrifice wouldn't be fitting? what "self-overcoming"?[2] what "self-denial"?

My greatest experience was a recovery. Wagner is merely one of my sicknesses.

Not that I wish to be ungrateful to this sickness. When in this essay I assert the proposition that Wagner is harmful, I wish no less to assert for whom he is nevertheless indispensable – for the philosopher. Others may be able to get along without Wagner; but the philosopher is not free to do without Wagner. He has to be the bad conscience of his time: for that he needs to understand it best. But confronted with the labyrinth of the modern soul, where could he find a guide more initiated, a more eloquent prophet of the soul, than Wagner? Through Wagner modernity speaks most intimately, concealing neither its good nor its evil – having forgotten all sense of shame. And conversely: one has almost completed an account of the value of what is modern once one has gained clarity about what is good and evil in Wagner. I understand perfectly when a musician says today: "I hate Wagner, but I can no longer endure any other music." But I'd also understand a philosopher who would declare: "Wagner sums up modernity. There is no way out, one must first become a Wagnerian."

1

Yesterday I heard – would you believe it? – Bizet's masterpiece, for the twentieth time. Again I stayed there with tender devotion; again I did not run away. This triumph over my impatience surprises me. How such a work makes one perfect! One becomes a "masterpiece" oneself. Really, every time I heard *Carmen* I seemed to myself more of a philosopher, a better philosopher, than I generally consider myself: so patient do I become, so happy, so Indian, so settled. – To sit five hours: the first stage of holiness! May I say that the tone of Bizet's orchestra is almost the only one I can still endure? That other orchestral tone which is now the fashion, Wagner's, brutal, artificial, and "innocent" at the same time – thus it speaks all at once to the three senses of the modern soul – how harmful for me is this Wagnerian orchestral tone! I call it *sirocco*. I break out into a disagreeable sweat. *My* good weather is gone.

This music seems perfect to me. It approaches lightly, supplely, politely. It is pleasant, it does not *sweat*. "What is good is light; whatever is divine moves on tender feet": first principle of my aesthetics. This music is evil, subtly fatalistic: at the same time it remains popular – its subtlety belongs to a race, not to an individual. It is rich. It is precise. It builds, organizes, finishes: thus it constitutes the opposite of the polyp in music, the "infinite melody." Have more painful tragic accents ever been heard on the stage? How are they achieved? Without grimaces. Without counterfeit. Without the *lie* of the great style. Finally, this music treats the listener as intelligent, as if himself a musician – and is in this respect, too, the counterpart of Wagner, who was, whatever else he was, at any rate the most *impolite* genius in the world (Wagner treats us as if – he says something so often – till one despairs – till one believes it).

Once more: I become a better human being when this Bizet speaks to me. Also a better musician, a better *listener*. Is it even possible to listen better? – I actually bury my ears under this music to hear its causes. It seems to me I experience its genesis – I tremble before dangers that accompany some strange risk; I am delighted by strokes of good fortune of which Bizet is innocent. – And, oddly, deep down I don't think

---

2   In German: "*Selbst-Überwindung.*"

of it, or don't know how much I think about it. For entirely different thoughts are meanwhile running through my head. Has it been noticed that music liberates the spirit? gives wings to thought? that one becomes more of a philosopher the more one becomes a musician? – The gray sky of abstraction rent as if by lightning; the light strong enough for the filigree of things; the great problems near enough to grasp; the world surveyed as from a mountain. – I have just defined the pathos of philosophy. – And unexpectedly answers drop into my lap, a little hail of ice and wisdom, of *solved* problems. – Where am I? – Bizet makes me fertile. Whatever is good makes me fertile. I have no other gratitude, nor do I have any other *proof* for what is good. –

[. . .]

5

To *the artist of decadence:* there we have the crucial words. And here my seriousness begins. I am far from looking on guilelessly while this decadent corrupts our health – and music as well. Is Wagner a human being at all? Isn't he rather a sickness? He makes sick whatever he touches – *he has made music sick* –

A typical decadent who has a sense of necessity in his corrupted taste, who claims it as a higher taste, who knows how to get his corruption accepted as law, as progress, as fulfillment.

And he is not resisted. His seductive force increases tremendously, smoke clouds of incense surround him, the misunderstandings about him parade as "gospel" – he hasn't by any means converted only the *poor in spirit.*[3]

I feel the urge to open the windows a little. Air! More air![4] –

That people in Germany should deceive themselves about Wagner does not surprise me. The opposite would surprise me. The Germans have constructed a Wagner for themselves whom they can revere: they have never been psychologists; their gratitude consists in misunderstanding. But that people in Paris, too, deceive themselves about Wagner, though there they are hardly anything anymore except psychologists! And in St. Petersburg, where they guess things that aren't guessed even in Paris! How closely related Wagner must be to the whole of European decadence to avoid being experienced by them as a decadent. He belongs to it: he is its protagonist, its greatest name. – One honors oneself when raising him to the clouds. For that one does not resist him, this itself is a sign of decadence. The instincts are weakened. What one ought to shun is found attractive. One puts to one's lips what drives one yet faster into the abyss. Is an example desired? One only need observe the regimen that those suffering from anemia or gout or diabetes prescribe for themselves. Definition of a vegetarian: one who requires a corroborant diet. To sense that what is harmful is harmful, to be *able* to forbid oneself something harmful, is a sign of youth and vitality. The exhausted are *attracted* by what is harmful: the vegetarian by vegetables. Sickness itself can be a stimulant to life: only one has to be healthy enough for this stimulant. Wagner increases exhaustion: that is why he attracts the weak and exhausted. Oh, the rattlesnake-happiness of the old master when he always saw precisely "the little children" coming unto him![5]

---

3 Allusion to Matthew 5: 3.
4 Goethe's last words are said to have been "Light! More light!"
5 Allusion to Matthew 19: 14, Mark 10: 14, Luke 18: 16.

I place this perspective at the outset: Wagner's art is sick. The problems he presents on the stage – all of them problems of hysterics – the convulsive nature of his affects, his overexcited sensibility, his taste that required ever stronger spices, his instability which he dressed up as principles, not least of all the choice of his heroes and heroines – consider them as physiological types (a pathological gallery!) – all of this taken together represents a profile of sickness that permits no further doubt. *Wagner est une névrose.*[6] Perhaps nothing is better known today, at least nothing has been better studied, than the Protean character of degeneration that here conceals itself in the chrysalis of art and artist. Our physicians and physiologists confront their most interesting case in Wagner, at least a very complete case. Precisely because nothing is more modern than this total sickness, this lateness and overexcitement of the nervous mechanism, Wagner is *the modern artist par excellence*, the Cagliostro of modernity. In his art all that the modern world requires most urgently is mixed in the most seductive manner: the three great *stimulantia* of the exhausted – the *brutal*, the *artificial*, and the *innocent* (idiotic).

Wagner represents a great corruption of music. He has guessed that it is a means to excite weary nerves – and with that he has made music sick. His inventiveness is not inconsiderable in the art of goading again those who are weariest, calling back into life those who are half dead. He is a master of hypnotic tricks, he manages to throw down the strongest like bulls. Wagner's *success* – his success with nerves and consequently women – has turned the whole world of ambitious musicians into disciples of his secret art. And not only the ambitious, the *clever*, too. – Only sick music makes money today; our big theaters subsist on Wagner.

[. . .]

7

Enough! Enough! My cheerful strokes, I fear, may have revealed sinister reality all too clearly – the picture of a decay of art, a decay of the artists as well. The latter, the decay of a character, could perhaps find preliminary expression in this formula: the musician now becomes an actor, his art develops more and more as a talent to *lie.* I shall have an opportunity (in a chapter of my main work, entitled "Toward a Physiology of Art")[7] to show in more detail how this over-all change of art into histrionics is no less an expression of physiological degeneration (more precisely, a form of hystericism) than every single corruption and infirmity of the art inaugurated by Wagner: for example, the visual restlessness which requires one continually to change one's position. One doesn't understand a thing about Wagner as long as one finds in him merely an arbitrary play of nature, a whim, an accident. He was no "fragmentary," "hapless," or "contradictory" genius, as people have said. Wagner was something *perfect,* a typical decadent in whom there is no trace of "free will" and in whom every feature is necessary. If anything in Wagner is interesting it is the logic with which a physiological defect makes move upon move and takes step upon step as practice and procedure, as innovation in principles, as a crisis in taste.

For the present I merely dwell on the question of *style.* – What is the sign of every *literary decadence?* That life no longer dwells in the whole. The word becomes sovereign and leaps out of the sentence, the sentence reaches out and obscures the

6   French: Wagner is a neurosis.
7   Nietzsche is referring here to his planned work *The Will to Power: Attempt at a Revaluation of all Values.*

meaning of the page, the page gains life at the expense of the whole – the whole is no longer a whole. But this is the simile of every style of *decadence*: every time, the anarchy of atoms, disgregation of the will, "freedom of the individual," to use moral terms – expanded into a political theory, "*equal* rights for all." Life, *equal* vitality, the vibration and exuberance of life pushed back into the smallest forms; the rest, *poor* in life. Everywhere paralysis, arduousness, torpidity *or* hostility and chaos: both more and more obvious the higher one ascends in forms of organization. The whole no longer lives at all: it is composite, calculated, artificial, and artifact. –

Wagner begins from a hallucination – not of sounds but of gestures. Then he seeks the sign language of sounds for them. If one would admire him, one should watch him at work at this point: how he separates, how he gains small units, how he animates these, severs them, and makes them visible. But this exhausts his strength: the rest is no good. How wretched, how embarrassed, how amateurish is his manner of "development," his attempt to at least interlard what has not grown out of each other. His manners recall those of the *frères* de Goncourt, who are quite generally pertinent to Wagner's style: one feels a kind of compassion for so much distress. That Wagner disguised as a principle his incapacity for giving organic form, that he establishes a "dramatic style" where we merely establish his incapacity for any style whatever, this is in line with a bold habit that accompanied Wagner through his whole life: he posits a principle where he lacks a capacity (– very different in this respect, incidentally, from the old Kant who preferred *another* boldness: wherever he lacked a principle he posited a special human "capacity").[8] Once more: Wagner is admirable and gracious only in the invention of what is smallest, in spinning out the details. Here one is entirely justified in proclaiming him a master of the first rank, as our greatest *miniaturist* in music who crowds into the smallest space an infinity of sense and sweetness. His wealth of colors, of half shadows, of the secrecies of dying light spoils one to such an extent that afterward almost all other musicians seem too robust. If one would believe me one should have to derive the highest conception of Wagner not from what is liked about him today. That has been invented to persuade the masses; from that we recoil as from an all too impudent fresco. Of what concern to *us* is the *agaçant*[9] brutality of the *Tannhäuser* Overture. Or the circus of *Walküre*? Whatever of Wagner's music has become popular also apart from the theater shows dubious taste and corrupts taste. The *Tannhäuser* March I suspect of *bonhommerie*;[10] the overture of *The Flying Dutchman* is noise about nothing;[11] the *Lohengrin* Prelude furnished the first example, only too insidious, only too successful, of hypnotism by means of music (– I do not like whatever music has no ambition beyond persuasion of the nerves). But quite apart from the *magnétiseur*[12] and fresco-painter Wagner, there is another Wagner who lays aside small gems: our greatest melancholiac in music, full of glances, tendernesses, and comforting words in which nobody has anticipated him, the master in tones of a heavy-hearted and drowsy happiness. A lexicon of Wagner's most intimate words, all of them short things of five to fifteen measures, all of it music *nobody knows*. – Wagner had the virtue of decadents: pity. –

8   In German: *ein "Vermögen."* See *BGE* 11.
9   French: provocative.
10   French: good-naturedness.
11   The standard German translation of Shakespeare's *Much Ado about Nothing* is *Viel Lärm um Nichts* ("Much Noise about Nothing").
12   French: hypnotist.

23

Twilight of the Idols; or, How to Philosophize with a Hammer (1888)

Maxims and Barbs[1]

1

Psychology finds work for idle hands to do. What? does that make psychology a – devil?

2

Even the bravest of us only rarely has the courage for what he actually *knows* . . .

3

To live alone you must be an animal or a god – says Aristotle.[2] He left out the third case: you must be both – *a philosopher* . . .

4

'All truth is simple.' – Is that not a compound lie? –

[. . .]

8

From the Military School of Life. – Whatever does not kill me makes me stronger.

[. . .]

10

Do not be cowardly towards your actions! Do not abandon them after the event! – Remorse is indecent.

---

1 In German: *Pfeile*, literally "arrows," but also with the connotation of "barbed remarks."
2 Aristotle, *Politics*, 1253a.

11

Can an *ass* be tragic? – Perishing under a load you can neither bear nor shed? . . .
The case of the philosopher.

12

If you have your *why?* for life, then you can get along with almost any *how?* – Man
does *not* strive for happiness; only the English do that.

13

Man created woman – but from what? From a rib of his God – of his 'ideal' . . .
[. . .]

15

Posthumous people – like me, for example – are less well understood than timely ones,
but better *heard*. More strictly: we are never understood – and *hence* our authority . . .
[. . .]

18

Anyone who cannot manage to invest his will in things at least invests them with a
meaning: i.e. he believes there is already a will in them (principle of 'belief').
[. . .]

24

To search for beginnings you turn into a crab. The historian looks backwards; in the
end he even *believes* backwards.
[. . .]

26

I mistrust all systematists and avoid them. The will to system is a lack of integrity.

27

People think woman is profound – why? because you can never get to the bottom of
her. Woman is not even shallow.

28

If a woman has manly virtues you should run away from her; and if she has no manly
virtues she runs away herself.
[. . .]

42

Those were steps for me; I climbed up by way of them – and so had to pass beyond
them. But they thought I wanted to sit down and rest on them . . .

43

What does it matter that *I* turn out to be right! I *am* too often right. – And he who laughs longest today also laughs last.

44

Formula for my happiness: a yes, a no, a straight line, a *goal* . . .

The Problem of Socrates

1

Throughout the ages the wisest of men have passed the same judgement on life: *it is no good* . . . Always and everywhere their mouths have been heard to produce the same sound – a sound full of doubt, full of melancholy, full of weariness of life, full of resistance to life. Even Socrates said as he was dying: 'Life is one long illness: I owe the saviour Asclepius a cock.'[3] Even Socrates had had enough of it. – What does this *prove*? What does this *point to*? – In former times people would have said (– oh they did say it, and loudly enough, with our pessimists in the vanguard!): 'There must be at least something true here! The *consensus sapientium*[4] proves the truth.' – Shall we still speak in such terms today? *can* we do so? 'There must be at least something *sick* here' is the answer *we* give: these wisest of every age,[5] we should look at them from close to! Were they all perhaps no longer steady on their feet? belated? doddery? *décadents*? Would wisdom perhaps appear on earth as a raven excited by a faint whiff of carrion? . . .

2

I myself was first struck by this impertinent thought, that the great wise men are *declining types*, in the very case where it meets with its strongest opposition from scholarly and unscholarly prejudice: I recognized Socrates and Plato as symptoms of decay, as tools of the Greek dissolution, as pseudo-Greek, as anti-Greek (*Birth of Tragedy*, 1872). That *consensus sapientium* – I have realized it more and more – proves least of all that they were right in what they agreed on: it proves rather that they themselves, these wisest of men, were somehow in *physiological* agreement in order to have – to *have* to have – the same negative attitude towards life. Judgements, value judgements on life, whether for or against, can ultimately never be true: they have value only as symptoms, they can be considered only as symptoms – in themselves such judgements are foolish. We must really stretch out our fingers and make the effort to grasp this astonishing *finesse, that the value of life cannot be assessed*.[6] Not by a living person because he

3 See *GS* (Books I–IV) note 33 above.
4 Latin: consensus of the wise.
5 Allusion to Goethe's 'Kophtisches Lied' ('Cophtic Song'), 1. 3: "All the wisest of every age."
6 Allusion to Eugen Dühring's (1833–1921) book *Der Werth des Lebens* (*The Value of Life*, 1865).

is an interested party, indeed even the object of dispute, and not the judge; nor by a dead person, for a different reason. For a philosopher to see a problem in the *value* of life is thus even an objection against him, a question mark against his wisdom, a piece of unwisdom. – What? so all these great wise men were not only *décadents*, they were not even wise? – But I return to the problem of Socrates.

3

Socrates belonged by extraction to the lowest of the people: Socrates was rabble, We know, we can even still see, how ugly he was.[7] But ugliness, in itself an objection, is to Greek practically a refutation. Was Socrates actually really a Greek? Ugliness is often enough the expression of a cross-bred development *stunted* by cross-breeding. If not, then it appears as a development in *decline*. The anthropologists among criminologists tell us that the typical criminal is ugly: *monstrum in fronte, monstrum in animo.*[8] But the criminal is a *décadent*, Was Socrates a typical criminal? – This would at least not be contradicted by that famous physiognomic judgement which sounded so rebarbative to Socrates' friends. When a foreigner who was an expert on faces came through Athens, he told Socrates to his face that he *was* a *monstrum* – that he was harbouring all the bad vices and desires. To which Socrates answered simply: 'You know me, sir!'[9]

4

Socrates' *décadence* is signalled not only by the avowed chaos and anarchy of his instincts: it is also signalled by the superfetation of the logical and that *jaundiced malice* which is his hallmark. Let us also not forget those auditory hallucinations which, as 'Socrates' Demon',[10] have taken on a religious interpretation. Everything about him is exaggerated, *buffo*, caricature; everything is at the same time concealed, ulteriorly motivated, subterranean. I am seeking to understand what was the idiosyncrasy[11] which gave rise to that Socratic equation, reason = virtue = happiness: that most bizarre of all equations which, in particular, has all the instincts of the older Hellene ranged against it.

5

With Socrates, Greek taste switches over in favour of dialectics: what is actually going on here? Above all it means a *noble* taste is defeated; with dialectics the rabble comes out on top. Before Socrates, dialectical manners were disapproved of in polite society: they were seen as bad manners because they were revealing. The young were warned

7   On Socrates' ugliness, see the speech by Alcibiades in Plato's *Symposium* 215b.

8   Latin: a monster in the face, a monster in the soul.

9   The incident is recorded in Cicero, *Tusculan Disputations*, IV. 80.

10   In the account Plato gives of his trial, Socrates describes the experience as follows: "I am subject to a divine or supernatural experience . . . It began early in my childhood – a sort of voice which comes to me; and when it comes it always dissuades me form what I am proposing to do, and never urges me on" (*Apology*, 31c–d). See also *BT* note 77 above.

11   The primary sense of "idiosyncrasy" here is medico-physiological ("physical constitution peculiar to a person").

against them. People also mistrusted any such presentation of one's reasons. Respectable things, like respectable people, do not wear their reasons on their sleeves like that. It is indecent to show all five fingers. Anything which needs first to have itself proved is of little value. Wherever it is still good manners to be authoritative, and people do not 'justify' but command, the dialectician is a kind of buffoon: he is laughed at and not taken seriously. – Socrates was the buffoon who *got himself taken seriously*: what was actually going on here?

6

You choose dialectics only when you have no other means. You know that using it provokes mistrust, and that it is not very convincing. Nothing is easier to dismiss than the effect a dialectician produces: the experience of any assembly where speeches are made is proof of that. It can only be an *emergency defence* in the hands of those who have no other weapons left. You must need to *force* your being in the right out of people: otherwise you do not use it. That is why the Jews were dialecticians; Reynard the Fox[12] was one: what? and Socrates was one, too? –

7

– Is Socrates' irony an expression of revolt? of the rabble's resentment? as one of the oppressed does he enjoy his own ferocity in the knife-thrusts of the syllogism? does he *avenge* himself on the noble men he fascinates? – As a dialectician you have a merciless tool in your hand; you can play the tyrant with it; you reveal by conquering. The dialectician leaves it to his opponent to prove he is not an idiot: he infuriates him and makes him helpless at the same time. The dialectician *disempowers* his opponent's intellect. – What? is dialectics just a form of *revenge* for Socrates?

8

I have indicated how Socrates could be repulsive: the fact that he *did* fascinate people needs all the more explaining. – For one thing he discovered a new kind of *agon* and was its first fencing master for the noble circles of Athens. He fascinated people by stirring up the agonal drive[13] of the Hellenes – he introduced a variation into the wrestling match between young men and youths. Socrates was also a great *eroticist*.

9

But Socrates sensed still more. He saw *behind* his noble Athenians; he realized that *his* case, his oddity of a case, was already unexceptional. The same kind of degenerescence was silently preparing itself everywhere: old Athens was coming to an end. – And Socrates understood that the whole world *needed* him – his method, his cure, his personal trick of self-preservation . . . Everywhere the instincts were in anarchy; everywhere people were a few steps away from excess: the *monstrum in animo* was the

---

12 In German: *Reineke Fuchs*. The eponymous hero of Goethe's epic poem (1794), where the fabled character twice escapes death through his cunning "dialectical" speeches.
13 In German: *Trieb*.

general danger. 'The drives want to play the tyrant; we must invent a *counter-tyrant* who is stronger' . . . When that physiognomist had revealed to Socrates who he was – a den of all the bad desires – the great ironist said one more thing which gives the key to him. 'This is true,' he said, 'but I became *master* of all of them.' *How* did Socrates become master of *himself*? His was basically only the extreme case, only the most overt example of what was at that stage starting to become a general need: the fact that no one was master of himself any more, that the instincts were turning *against* each other. He fascinated people by being this extreme case – his terrifying ugliness marked him out to every eye: it goes without saying that he exerted an even greater fascination as the answer, the solution, the apparent *cure* for this case. –

10

If it is necessary to make a tyrant out of *reason*, as Socrates did, then there must be no little danger that something else might play the tyrant. At that time people sensed in rationality a *deliverance*; neither Socrates nor his 'invalids' were free to be rational – it was *de rigueur*,[14] it was their *last* available means. The fanaticism with which the whole of Greek thought throws itself on rationality betrays a crisis: they were in danger, they had just *one* choice: either perish or – be *absurdly rational* . . . The moralism of Greek philosophers from Plato onwards is pathologically conditioned: likewise their appreciation of dialectics. Reason = virtue = happiness means simply: we must imitate Socrates and establish permanent *daylight* to combat the dark desires – the daylight of reason. We must be clever, clear, bright at all costs; any yielding to the instincts, to the unconscious, leads *downwards* . . .

11

I have indicated how Socrates fascinated people: he appeared to be a physician, a saviour. Is it still necessary to demonstrate the error which lay in his belief in 'rationality at all costs'? It is a self-deception on the part of philosophers and moralists to believe that in waging war on *décadence* they are already emerging from it. It is beyond their power to emerge from it: whatever they choose as their means, their deliverance, is itself just another expression of *décadence* – they *alter* its expression, but they do not get rid of it. Socrates was a misunderstanding; *the entire morality of improvement, Christianity's included, was a misunderstanding* . . . The harshest daylight, rationality at all costs, life bright, cold, cautious, conscious, instinct-free, instinct-resistant: this itself was just an illness, a different illness – and definitely not a way back to 'virtue', 'health', happiness . . . To *have to* fight against the instincts – this is the formula for décadence: so long as life is *ascendant*, happiness equals instinct. –

12

– Did he himself understand this, that cleverest of all self-out-witters? Did he ultimately tell himself this, in the *wisdom* of his courage unto death? . . . Socrates *wanted* to die – it was not Athens but *he* himself who administered the cup of poison; he forced Athens into it . . . 'Socrates is no physician,' he said quietly to himself: 'death alone is the physician here . . . Socrates himself has simply had a long illness . . .'

14   French: inescapable.

'Reason' in Philosophy

1

You ask me what are all the idiosyncrasies of the philosophers? . . . For one thing their lack of historical sense, their hatred of the very idea of becoming, their Egypticism. They think they are doing a thing an *honour* when they dehistoricize it, *sub specie aeterni*[15] – when they make a mummy out of it. All that philosophers have been handling for thousands of years is conceptual mummies; nothing real has ever left their hands alive. They kill things and stuff them, these servants of conceptual idols, when they worship – they become a mortal danger to everything when they worship. Death, change, age, as well as procreation and growth, are objections – even refutations – for them. Whatever is, does not *become*; whatever becomes, *is* not . . . Now they all believe, even to the point of desperation, in being. But because they cannot gain possession of it they look for reasons as to why it is being withheld from them. 'There must be some pretence, some deception going on, preventing us from perceiving being: wheres the deceiver hiding?' – 'We've got him', they cry in rapturous delight, 'it's our sensuousness! These senses, *which are otherwise so immoral, too*, they are deceiving us about the *real* world. Moral: free yourself from sense-deception, from becoming, history, lies – history is nothing but belief in the senses, belief in lies. Moral: say no to anything which believes in the senses, to the whole of the rest of humanity: they are all just "the populace". Be a philosopher, be a mummy, represent monotono-theism by miming a gravedigger! – And above all away with the *body*, this pitiful *idée fixe* of the senses! afflicated with every logical error there is, refuted, even impossible, though it is cheeky enough to act as if it were real!' . . .

2

I shall set apart, with great respect, the name of *Heraclitus*. If the rest of the philosophical populace rejected the evidence of the senses because they showed multiplicity and change, he rejected their evidence because they showed things as if they had duration and unity. Heraclitus, too, did the senses an injustice. They do not lie either in the way that the Eleatics[16] believe, or as he believed – they do not lie at all. What we *make* of their evidence is what gives rise to the lie, for example the lie of unity, the lie of materiality, of substance, of duration . . . 'Reason' is what causes us to falsify the evidence of the senses. If the senses show becoming, passing away, change, they do not lie . . . But Heraclitus will always be right that Being is an empty fiction. The 'apparent' world[17] is the only one: the 'real world'[18] has just been *lied on* . . .

3

– And what fine instruments of observation we have in our senses! This nose, for example, of which not one philosopher has yet spoken in reverence and gratitude, is

---

15   Latin: from the point of view of eternity. See *GS* (Book V) note 14 above.
16   See *GS* (Books I–IV) note 15 above.
17   In German: *die "scheinbare" Welt.*
18   In German: *die "wahre Welt."*

nevertheless actually the most delicate instrument we have at our command: it can register minimal differences in movement which even the spectroscope fails to register. We possess science nowadays precisely to the extent that we decided to *accept* the evidence of the senses – when we were still learning to sharpen them, arm them, think them through to the end. The rest is abortion and not-yet-science: to wit, metaphysics, theology, psychology, theory of knowledge. *Or* the science of forms, the theory of signs: like logic and that applied logic, mathematics. Reality is nowhere to be found in them, not even as a problem; nor does the question arise as to what actual value a sign-convention like logic has. –

4

The *other* idiosyncrasy of the philosophers is no less dangerous: it consists in mistaking the last for the first. They put what comes at the end – unfortunately! for it should not come anywhere! – the 'highest concepts', i.e. the most general, emptiest concepts, the last wisp of evaporating reality, at the beginning *as* the beginning. This is once again simply the expression of their kind of reverence: the higher *is not allowed* to grow out of the lower, *is not allowed* to have grown at all . . . Moral: everything first-rate must be *causa sui*.[19] If it is descended from something else, this is seen as an objection and brings its value into question. All the supreme values are first-rate; all the highest concepts – being, the absolute, the good, the true, the perfect – none of them can have become, so they *must* be *causa sui*. Equally, though, none of them can differ from the others or conflict with them . . . Hence their astounding notion of 'God' . . . The last, thinnest, emptiest, is put first, as cause in itself, as *ens realissimum*[20] . . . Oh that humanity had to take seriously the brain-feverish fantasies spun out by the sick! – And it has paid dearly for it! . . .

5

– Let us finally set against this the different way in which *we* (– I say we out of politeness . . .) contemplate the problem of error and appearance. In former times people took alteration, change, becoming in general as proof of appearance, as a sign that there must be something there leading us astray. Nowadays, conversely – and precisely in so far as the prejudice called 'reason' compels us to establish unity, identity, duration, substance, cause, materiality, Being – we see ourselves to a certain extent tangled up in error, *forced* into error; as sure as we are, on the basis of stringent checking, *that* the error is here. It is no different from the movements of the great stars: in their case error has our eye as its constant advocate, here it has our *language*. Language is assigned by its emergence to the time of the most rudimentary form of psychology: we become involved in a crude fetishism when we make ourselves conscious of the basic premises of the metaphysics of language, in plain words: of *reason*. *This* is what sees doer and deed everywhere: it believes in the will as cause in general; it believes in the 'I', in the I as Being, in the I as substance, and *projects* the belief in the I-substance onto all things – only then does it *create* the concept 'thing' . . . Being is thought in, *foisted in* everywhere as cause; only following on from the conception 'I'

19 Latin: cause of itself.
20 Latin: the most real being. Term applied by scholastic philosophers to God.

is the concept 'Being' derived . . . At the beginning stands the great disaster of an error that the will is something *at work* – that will is a *capacity* . . . Nowadays we know that it is just a word . . . Very much later, in a world a thousand times more enlightened, philosophers were surprised to realize how *assured*, how subjectively *certain* they were in handling the categories of reason – which, they concluded, could not come from the empirical world, since the empirical world stands in contradiction to them. *So where do they come from?* – And in India as in Greece they made the same mistake: 'we must once have been at home in a higher world (– instead of *in a very much lower one*: which would have been the truth!), we must have been divine *because* we have reason!' . . . In fact nothing has had a more naïve power of persuasion so far than the error of Being, as formulated, for example, by the Eleatics: for it has on its side every word, every sentence we speak! – Even the opponents of the Eleatics still succumbed to the seduction of their concept of Being: among others Democritus, when he invented his *atom* . . . 'Reason' in language: oh what a deceitful old woman![21] I am afraid we are not getting rid of God because we still believe in grammar . . .

6

People will be grateful to me for condensing such an essential new insight into four theses: this way I am easing comprehension; this way I am inviting contradiction.

First Proposition. The reasons which have been given for designating 'this' world as apparent actually account for its reality — any *other* kind of reality is absolutely unprovable.

Second Proposition. The characteristics which have been given to the 'true Being' of things are the characteristics of non-Being, of *nothingness* – the 'real world' has been constructed from the contradiction of the actual world: an apparent world, indeed, to the extent that it is merely a *moral-optical* illusion.

Third Proposition. Concocting stories about a world 'other' than this one is utterly senseless, unless we have within us a powerful instinct to slander, belittle, cast suspicion on life: in which case we are *avenging* ourselves on life with the phantasmagoria of 'another', 'better' life.

Fourth Proposition. Dividing the world into a 'real' one and an 'apparent' one, whether in the manner of Christianity, or of Kant (a *crafty* Christian, when all's said and done), is but a suggestion of *décadence* – a symptom of *declining* life . . . The fact that the artist values appearance more highly than reality is no objection to this proposition. For 'appearance' here means reality *once more*, only selected, strengthened, corrected . . . The tragic artist is *no* pessimist – on the contrary, he says *yes* to all that is questionable and even terrible; he is *Dionysian* . . .

How the 'Real World' Finally Became a Fable

History[22] of an error

1. The real world attainable for the wise man, the pious man, the virtuous man – he lives in it, *he is it*.

---

21   Nietzsche here is exploiting the fact that the grammatical gender of the word for "reason" in German (*die Vernunft*) is feminine.

22   In German: *Geschichte*, which means both history and story/tale.

(Most ancient form of the idea, relatively clever, simple, convincing. Paraphrase of the proposition: 'I, Plato, *am* the truth.')

2. The real world unattainable for now, but promised to the wise man, the pious man, the virtuous man ('to the sinner who repents').

(Progress of the idea: it becomes more cunning, more insidious, more incomprehensible – *it becomes a woman*, it becomes Christian . . .)

3. The real world unattainable, unprovable, unpromisable, but the mere thought of it a consolation, an obligation, an imperative.

(The old sun in the background, but seen through mist and scepticism; the idea become sublime, pale, Nordic, Königsbergian.)[23]

4. The real world – unattainable? At any rate unattained. And since unattained also *unknown*. Hence no consolation, redemption, obligation either: what could something unknown oblige us to do? . . .

(Break of day. First yawn of reason. Cock-crow of positivism.)

5. The 'real world' – an idea with no further use, no longer even an obligation – an idea become useless, superfluous, *therefore* a refuted idea: let us do away with it!

(Broad daylight; breakfast; return of *bon sens*[24] and cheerfulness; Plato's shameful blush; din from all free spirits.)

6. The real world – we have done away with it: what world was left? the apparent one, perhaps? . . . But no! *with the real world we have also done away with the apparent one!*

(Noon; moment of the shortest shadow; end of the longest error; pinnacle of humanity; INCIPIT ZARATHUSTRA.)

Morality as Anti-Nature

1

All passions have a period in which they are merely fateful, in which they draw their victims down by weight of stupidity – and a later, very much later one, in which they marry the spirit, 'spiritualize' themselves. In former times, because of the stupidity of passion, people waged war on passion itself: they plotted to destroy it – all the old moral monsters are in complete agreement that 'il faut tuer les passions'.[25] The most famous formula for this can be found in the New Testament, in that Sermon on the Mount where, incidentally, things are by no means viewed *from on high*. Here it is said, for example, with reference to sexuality, 'if thine eye offend thee, pluck it out':[26] fortunately no Christian acts according to this precept. *Destroying* the passions and desires merely in order to avoid their stupidity and the disagreeable consequences of their stupidity seems to us nowadays to be itself simply an acute form of stupidity. We no longer marvel at dentists who *pull out* teeth to stop them hurting . . . On the other

---

23 Kant lived all his life in Königsberg, then in East Prussia and now Kaliningrad in Russia.
24 French: good sense.
25 French: "one must kill the passions."
26 Matthew 18: 9, Mark 9: 47.

hand, to be fair, it should be admitted that there was no way in which, on the soil from which Christianity grew up, the concept of '*spiritualization* of passion' could even be conceived. For the first church, as is well known, fought *against* the 'intelligent' on the side of the 'poor in spirit':[27] how could one expect from it an intelligent war on passion? – The church fights against passion with every kind of excision: its method, its 'cure', is *castratism*. It never asks 'how does one spiritualize, beautify, deify a desire?' – in disciplining, it has put the emphasis throughout the ages on eradication (of sensuality, pride, the urge to rule, to possess, to avenge). – But attacking the passions at the root means attacking life at the root: the practice of the church is *inimical to life* . . .

2

The same means – castration, eradication – are instinctively chosen by those fighting against a desire who are too weak-willed, too degenerate to be able to set themselves a measure in it: by those types who need La Trappe,[28] metaphorically speaking (and non-metaphorically –), some definitive declaration of enmity, a *gulf* between themselves and a passion. Only the degenerate find radical means indispensable; weakness of will, more specifically the inability *not* to react to a stimulus, is itself simply another form of degenerescence. Radical enmity, mortal enmity against sensuality, remains a thought-provoking symptom: it justifies you in speculating about the overall condition of such an excessive. – This enmity, this hatred reaches its peak, moreover, only when such types are no longer steadfast enough even for a radical cure, for renouncing their 'devil'. If you survey the whole history of priests and philosophers, and artists, too: it is *not* the impotent who have said the most poisonous things against the senses; *nor* is it the ascetics, but the impossible ascetics, those who could have done with being ascetics . . .

3

The spiritualization of sensuality is called *love*: it is a great triumph over Christianity. A further triumph is our spiritualization of *enmity*. This consists in our profound understanding of the value of having enemies: in short, our doing and deciding the converse of what people previously thought and decided. Throughout the ages the church has wanted to destroy its enemies: we, we immoralists and anti-Christians, see it as to our advantage that the church exists . . . Even in the field of politics enmity has nowadays become more spiritual – much cleverer, much more thoughtful, much *gentler*. Almost every party sees that its interest in self-preservation is best served if its opposite number does not lose its powers; the same is true of great politics. A new creation in particular, such as the new Reich, needs enemies more than it does friends: only by being opposed does it feel necessary; only by being opposed does it *become* necessary . . . Our behaviour towards our 'inner enemy' is no different: here, too, we have spiritualized enmity; here, too, we have grasped its *value*. One is *fruitful* only at the price of being rich in opposites; one stays *young* only on condition that the soul does not have a stretch and desire peace . . . Nothing has become more alien to us than that desideratum of old, 'peace of soul', the *Christian* desideratum; nothing makes

27   Matthew 5: 3.
28   The Cistercian monastery in Normandy which gave its name to the Trappist order, founded in 1664 and noted for its austere rules.

us less envious than ruminant morality and the luxuriant happiness of a good conscience. Renouncing war means renouncing *great* life . . . In many cases, of course, 'peace of soul' is simply a misunderstanding – something *else* which is just unable to give itself a more honest name. Without digression or prejudice, a few cases. 'Peace of soul' can be, for example, a rich animality radiating gently out into the moral (or religious) domain. Or the onset of tiredness, the first shadow which evening, any kind of evening, casts. Or a sign that the air is moist, that southerly winds are drawing close. Or unwitting gratitude for successful digestion (sometimes called 'love of humanity'). Or the falling quiet of a convalescent as he finds everything tastes good again and waits . . . Or the state which follows the powerful satisfaction of our ruling passion, the sense of well-being at being uncommonly sated. Or the infirmity of our will, our desires, our vices. Or laziness persuaded by vanity to dress itself up in moral garb. Or the advent of certainty, even terrible certainty, after a long period of tension and torment at the hands of uncertainty. Or the expression of maturity and mastery in the midst of doing, creating, affecting, willing; breathing easily, 'freedom of the will' *achieved* . . . *Twilight of the idols*: who knows? perhaps also just a kind of 'peace of soul' . . .

4

– I shall make a principle into a formula. All naturalism in morality, i.e. every *healthy* morality, is governed by a vital instinct – one or other of life's decrees is fulfilled through a specific canon of 'shalls' and 'shall nots', one or other of the obstructions and hostilities on life's way is thus removed. *Anti-natural* morality, i.e. almost every morality which has hitherto been taught, revered, and preached, turns on the contrary precisely *against* the vital instincts – it is at times secret, at times loud and brazen in *condemning* these instincts. In saying 'God looks at the heart'[29] it says no to the lowest and highest of life's desires, and takes God to be an *enemy of life* . . . The saint, in whom God is well pleased,[30] is the ideal castrato . . . Life ends where the 'kingdom of God' *begins* . . .

5

Once you have grasped the heinousness of such a revolt against life, which has become almost sacrosanct in Christian morality, then fortunately you have also grasped something else: the futile, feigned, absurd; *lying* nature of such a revolt. A condemnation of life on the part of the living remains in the last resort merely the symptom of a specific kind of life: the question as to whether it is justifiable or not simply does not arise. You would need to be situated *outside* life, and at the same time to know life as well as someone – many people, everyone – who has lived it, to be allowed even to touch on the problem of the *value* of life: reason enough for realizing that the problem is an inaccessible problem to us. Whenever we speak of values, we speak under the inspiration – from the perspective – of life: life itself forces us to establish values; life itself evaluates through us *when* we posit values . . . It follows from this that even that *anti-nature of a morality* which conceives of God as the antithesis and condemnation of life is merely a value judgement on the part of life – *which* life? *what* kind of

29   Cf. Luke 16: 15: "God knoweth your hearts."
30   Cf. Matthew 12: 18: "my beloved, in whom my soul is well pleased."

life? – But I have already given the answer: declining, weakened, tired, condemned life. Morality as it has hitherto been understood – and formulated by Schopenhauer, lastly, as 'denial of the will to life' – is the *décadence instinct* itself making an imperative out of itself: it says: '*perish!*' – it is the judgement of the condemned . . .

6

Let us finally consider what naïvety it is in general to say 'man *should* be such and such!' Reality shows us a delightful abundance of types, the richness that comes from an extravagant play and alternation of forms: to which some wretched loafer of a moralist says: 'no! man should be *different*'? . . . He even knows how man should be, this maundering miseryguts: he paints himself on the wall and says '*ecce homo!*'[31] . . . But even when the moralist turns just to the individual and says to him: '*you* should be such and such!' he does not stop making a fool of himself. The individual is a piece of fate from top to bottom, one more law, one more necessity for all that is to come and will be. Telling him to change means demanding that everything should change, even backwards . . . And indeed there have been consistent moralists who wanted man to be different, namely virtuous; they wanted him to be in their image, namely a miseryguts: to which end they *denied* the world! No minor madness! No modest kind of immodesty! . . . Morality, in so far as it *condemns* – in itself, and *not* in view of life's concerns, considerations, intentions – is a specific error on which we should not take pity, a *degenerate's idiosyncrasy* which has wrought untold damage! . . . We who are different, we immoralists, on the contrary, have opened our hearts to all kinds of understanding, comprehending, *approving*. We do not readily deny; we seek our honour in being *affirmative*. More and more our eyes have been opened to that economy which still needs and can exploit all that is rejected by the holy madness of the priest, of the priest's *sick* reason; to that economy in the law of life which can gain advantage even from the repulsive species of the miseryguts, the priest, the virtuous man – *what* advantage? – But we ourselves, we immoralists are the answer here . . .

The Four Great Errors

1

Error of Confusing Cause and Consequence. – There is no error more dangerous than that of confusing the *consequence with the cause*: I call it the real ruination of reason. Nevertheless this error is among the most long-standing and recent of humanity's habits: it is even sanctified by us, and bears the name 'religion', 'morality'. *Every* proposition which religion and morality formulate contains it; priests and moral legislators are the originators of this ruination of reason. – I shall take one example: everyone knows the book by the famous Cornaro,[32] in which he recommends his meagre diet as a

---

31   Latin: 'Behold the man!' – the words of Pilate as he presents Jesus to the mob (John 19: 5). Also an allusion to the German expression 'to paint the Devil on the wall,' meaning 'to think the worst.'

32   Lodovico (Luigi) Cornaro (1467–1566), Italian writer whose bestselling *Discorsi della vita sobria* (*Discourses on a Life of Temperance*, 1558) was translated into German as 'The Art of Reaching a Great and Healthy Age.'

recipe for a long and happy life – and a virtuous one, too. Few books have been read so much; even now in England many thousands of copies of it are printed annually. I have no doubt that hardly any book (with due exception for the Bible) has done as much damage, *shortened* as many lives as this well-intentioned *curiosum*. The reason: confusion of the consequence with the cause. The worthy Italian gentleman saw in his diet the *cause* of his long life: whereas the precondition for a long life – extraordinarily slow metabolism, low consumption – was the cause of his meagre diet. He was not free to eat a little *or* a lot; his frugality was *not* an act of 'free will': he fell ill if he ate any more. But anyone who is not a carp[33] finds it not only good but necessary to eat *properly*. A scholar in *our* day, with his rapid consumption of nervous energy, would destroy himself on Cornaro's regimen. *Crede experto.*[34] –

2

The most general formula underlying every religion and morality is: 'Do this and that, stop this and that – then you will be happy! Or else . . .' Every morality, every religion *is* this imperative – I call it the great original sin of reason, *immortal unreason*. In my mouth that formula is transformed into its inversion – *first* example of my 'revaluation of all values': a well-balanced person, a 'happy man', *has* to do certain actions and instinctively shies away from others; he carries over the order which his physiology represents into his relations with people and things. In a formula: his virtue is the *consequence* of his happiness . . . A long life, numerous progeny, are *not* the reward for virtue; instead, virtue is itself that slowing down of the metabolism which among other things also brings a long life, numerous progeny, in short *Cornarism* in its wake. – The church and morality say: 'a race, a people is destroyed by vice and extravagance.' My *restored* reason says: if a people is destroyed, if it physiologically degenerates, then this is *followed* by vice and extravagance (i.e. the need for ever stronger and more frequent stimuli, familiar to every exhausted type). This young man grows prematurely pale and listless. His friends say: such and such an illness is to blame. I say: *the fact that* he fell ill, *the fact that* he could not withstand the illness, was already the consequence of an impoverished life, of hereditary exhaustion. The newspaper reader says: this party will destroy itself by such a mistake. My *higher* politics says: a party which makes such mistakes is already finished – its instinct is no longer sure. Every mistake, in every sense, results from a degeneration of instinct, a disgregation of the will – which is almost a definition of the *bad*. Everything *good* is instinct – and therefore easy, necessary, free. Effort is an objection; a god is typologically different from a hero (in my language: *light* feet the foremost attribute of divinity).

3

Error of a False Causality. – People throughout the ages have believed they knew what a cause is: but where did we get our knowledge, more precisely our belief that we know? From the realm of the celebrated 'inner facts', not one of which has so far turned out to be real. We believed that we ourselves, in the act of willing, were causes; we thought that we were at least catching causality there *in the act*. Likewise people

33   That is, toothless.
34   Latin: Believe the expert! Quotation from Silius Italicus, *Punica*, VII. 395.

were in no doubt that all the *antecedentia* of an action, its causes, were to be sought in consciousness and would be rediscovered there if sought – as 'motives': otherwise they would not have been free *to do* it, responsible *for* it. Finally, who would have denied that a thought is caused? that the 'I' causes the thought? . . . Of these three 'inner facts', by which causality seemed to be authenticated, the first and most convincing one is that of the *will as cause*; the conception of a consciousness ('mind') as cause and, later still, of the 'I' (the 'subject') as cause came only afterwards, once the causality of the will had been established as given, as *empirical* . . . Since then we have thought better of all this. Nowadays we no longer believe a word of it. The 'inner world' is full of illusions and jack-o'-lanterns: the will is one of them. The will no longer moves anything, and therefore no longer explains anything either – it simply accompanies events, and can even be absent. The so-called 'motive': another error. Merely a surface phenomenon of consciousness, an accessory to the act, which does more to conceal the *antecedentia* of an act than to represent them. And as for the I! It has become a fable, a fiction, a play on words: it has completely given up thinking, feeling, and willing! . . . What is the result? There are no mental causes at all! All the apparently empirical evidence for them has gone to the devil! *That* is the result! – And we had subjected this 'empirical evidence' to a pretty piece of abuse; we had *created* the world on the basis of it as a world of causes, a world of will, a spirit world . . . The most ancient and long-established psychology was at work here, and it did absolutely nothing else: in its eyes every event was an action, every action the result of a will; in its eyes the world became a multiplicity of agents, an agent (a 'subject') foisting itself onto every event. Man's three 'inner facts', the things he believed in most firmly – the will, the mind, the I – were projected out of himself: he derived the concept of Being from the concept of the I, and posited the existence of 'things' after his own image, after his concept of the I as cause. No wonder if, later on, he only ever rediscovered in things *what he had put in them*. – The thing itself, to say it again, the concept of thing: just a reflection of the belief in the I as cause . . . And even your atom, my dear mechanicians and physicists, how much error, how much rudimentary psychology still remains in your atom! Not to speak of the 'thing in itself', the *horrendum pudendum*[35] of the metaphysicians! The error of confusing the mind as cause with reality! And made the measure of reality! And called *God*! –

4

Error of Imaginary Causes. – To take dreams as my starting point: a specific sensation, for example one which results from a distant cannon-shot, has a cause foisted onto it after the event (often a complete little novel, in which the dreamer himself is the main character). Meanwhile the sensation persists, in a kind of resonance: it is as if it waits for the causal drive to allow it to step into the foreground – now no longer as chance, but as 'meaning'. The cannon-shot makes its appearance in a *causal* way, in an apparent reversal of time. The later thing, the motivation, is experienced first, often together with a hundred details which pass by like lightning, and the shot follows . . . What has happened? The ideas which a certain state *generated* have been mistakenly understood as its cause. – In fact we do the same thing in waking life. Most of our general feelings

---

35   Latin: terrible shameful part.

– every kind of inhibition, pressure, excitation, explosion in the play and counter-play of the organs, such as the state of the *nervus sympathicus*[36] in particular – stimulate our causal drive: we want a *reason* for having *such and such* a feeling, for feeling bad or feeling good. We are never satisfied with simply establishing the fact *that* we have such and such a feeling: we license this fact – become *conscious* of it – only *when* we have given it a kind of motivation. – Memory, which in such cases comes into operation without our knowledge, fetches up earlier, similar states and the causal interpretations entwined with them – *not* their causality. Of course the belief that the ideas, the con-comitant processes in consciousness, were the causes, is fetched up by memory, too. Thus we become *used* to a specific causal interpretation which, in truth, inhibits any *inquiry* into causes and even rules it out.

5

Psychological Explanation for This. – Tracing something unknown back to something known gives relief, soothes, satisfies, and furthermore gives a feeling of power. The unknown brings with it danger, disquiet, worry – one's first instinct is to *get rid of* these awkward conditions. First principle: any explanation is better than none. Because it is basically just a question of wanting to get rid of oppressive ideas, we are not exactly strict with the means we employ to get rid of them: the first idea which can explain the unknown as known feels so good that it is 'held to be true'. Proof of *pleasure* ('strength') as criterion of truth. – The causal drive is therefore determined and stim-ulated by the feeling of fear. The 'why?' is intended, if at all possible, not so much to yield the cause in its own right as rather a *kind of cause* – a soothing, liberating, relief-giving cause. The fact that something already *known*, experienced, inscribed in the memory is established as a cause, is the first consequence of this need. The new, the unexperienced, the alien is ruled out as a cause. So it is not just a kind of expla-nation which is sought as cause, but a *select* and *privileged* kind of explanation, the kind which has allowed the feeling of the alien, new, unexperienced to be dispelled most quickly and most often – the *most usual* explanations. – Result: one way of positing causes becomes increasingly prevalent, is concentrated into a system and ultimately emerges as *dominant*, i.e. simply ruling out *other* causes and explanations. – The banker's first thoughts are of 'business', the Christian's of 'sin', the girl's of her love.

6

The Entire Realm of Morality and Religion Belongs Under This Concept of Imaginary Causes. – 'Explanation' for *unpleasant* general feelings. They are determined by beings which are hostile to us (evil spirits: most famous case – misunderstanding of hysterics as witches). They are determined by actions which cannot be sanctioned (the feeling of 'sin', of 'sinfulness', foisted onto a physiological unease – one can always find reasons to be dissatisfied with oneself). They are determined as punishments, as a repayment for something we should not have done, should not have *been* (impudently generalized by Schopenhauer into a proposition which reveals morality as it really is, as the poisoner and slanderer of life: 'Every great pain, whether bodily or mental, states what

36   Latin: sympathetic nervous system.

we deserve; for it could not come to us if we did not deserve it' – *World as Will and Representation*). They are determined as the consequences of thoughtless actions which turned out badly (– the emotions, the senses posited as cause, as 'to blame'; physiological crises interpreted with the help of *other* crises as 'deserved'). – 'Explanation' for *pleasant* general feelings. These are determined by trust in God. They are determined by the awareness of good works (the so-called 'good conscience', a physiological state which sometimes looks so similar to successful digestion that one could confuse the two). They are determined by the successful outcome of undertakings (– naïvely false conclusion: the successful outcome of an undertaking gives a hypochondriac or a Pascal no pleasant general feelings at all). They are determined by faith, charity, hope – the Christian virtues.[37] – In truth all these so-called explanations are states which *result* from something, a kind of translation of feelings of pleasure or displeasure into the wrong dialect: one is in a position to hope *because* one's basic physiological feeling is strong and rich again; one trusts in God *because* one is calmed by a feeling of plenitude and strength. – Morality and religion belong entirely under the *psychology of error*: in every single case cause and effect are confused; or truth is confused with the effect of what is *believed* to be true; or a state of consciousness is confused with the causality of this state.

7

Error of Free Will. – We no longer have any sympathy nowadays for the concept 'free will': we know only too well what it is – the most disreputable piece of trickery the theologians have produced, aimed at making humanity 'responsible' in their sense, i.e. at *making it dependent on them* . . . I shall give here simply the psychology behind every kind of making people responsible. – Wherever responsibilities are sought, it is usually the instinct for *wanting to punish and judge* that is doing the searching. Becoming is stripped of its innocence once any state of affairs is traced back to a will, to intentions, to responsible acts: the doctrine of the will was fabricated essentially for the purpose of punishment, i.e. of *wanting to find guilty*. The old psychology as a whole, the psychology of the will, presupposes the fact that its originators, the priests at the head of ancient communities, wanted to give themselves the *right* to impose punishments – or give God the right to do so . . . People were thought of as 'free' so that they could be judged and punished – so that they could become *guilty*: consequently every action *had* to be thought of as willed, the origin of every action as located in consciousness (– thus the *most fundamental* piece of counterfeiting *in psychologicis*[38] became the principle of psychology itself). Nowadays, since we are engaged in a movement in the *opposite* direction, since we immoralists especially are seeking with all our strength to eliminate the concepts of guilt and punishment again and to cleanse psychology, history, nature, social institutions and sanctions of them, there is in our view no more radical opposition than that which comes from the theologians who, with their concept of the 'moral world order', persist in plaguing the innocence of becoming with 'punishment' and 'guilt'. Christianity is a metaphysics of the hangman . . .

---

37   Cf. I Corinthians 13: 13: "And now abideth faith, hope, charity, these three; but the greatest of these is charity."
38   Latin: in psychological matters.

8

What can *our* doctrine be, though? – That no one *gives* man his qualities, neither God, nor society, nor his parents and ancestors, nor *man himself* (– the nonsense of the last idea rejected here was taught as 'intelligible freedom' by Kant, perhaps already by Plato, too). *No one* is responsible for simply being there, for being made in such and such a way, for existing under such conditions, in such surroundings. The fatality of one's being cannot be derived from the fatality of all that was and will be. *No one* is the result of his own intention, his own will, his own purpose; *no one* is part of an experiment to achieve an 'ideal person' or an 'ideal of happiness' or in 'ideal of morality' – it is absurd to want to *discharge* one's being onto some purpose or other. *We* invented the concept 'purpose': in reality, 'purpose' is *absent* . . . One is necessary, one is a piece of fate, one belongs to the whole, one *is* in the whole – there is nothing which could judge, measure, compare, condemn our Being, for that would mean judging, measuring, comparing, condemning the whole . . . *But there is nothing apart from the whole!* That no one is made responsible any more, that a kind of Being cannot be traced back to a *causa prima*,[39] that the world is no unity, either as sensorium or as 'mind', *this alone is the great liberation* – this alone re-establishes the *innocence* of becoming . . . The concept 'God' has been the greatest *objection* to existence so far . . . We deny God, we deny responsibility in God: *this* alone is how we redeem the world. –

The 'Improvers' of Humanity

1

People are familiar with my call for the philosopher to place himself *beyond* good and evil – to have the illusion of moral judgement *beneath* him. This call results from an insight which I was the first to formulate: *that there are no moral facts at all*. Moral judgement has this in common with religious judgement, that it believes in realities which do not exist. Morality is merely an interpretation of certain phenomena, more precisely a *mis*interpretation. Moral judgement pertains, like religious judgement, to a level of ignorance on which the very concept of the real, the distinction between the real and the imaginary, is still lacking: so that 'truth', on such a level, designates nothing but what we nowadays call 'illusions'. In this respect moral judgement should never be taken literally: as such it is only ever an absurdity. But as a *semiotics* it remains inestimable: it reveals, at least to anyone who knows, the most valuable realities of cultures and interiorities which did not *know* enough to 'understand' themselves. Morality is merely sign language, merely symptomatology: you must already know *what* is going on in order to profit by it.

[. . .]

Reconnaissance Raids of an Untimely Man

10

What is the meaning of the conceptual opposition I introduced into aesthetics, between *Apollonian* and *Dionysian*, both conceived as types of intoxication? –

39   Latin: first cause, God as prime mover.

Apollonian intoxication keeps the eye in particular aroused, so that it receives vision-ary power. The painter, the sculptor, the epic poet are visionaries *par excellence*. In the Dionysian state, on the other hand, the whole system of the emotions is aroused and intensified: so that it discharges its every means of expression at one stroke, at the same time forcing out the power to represent, reproduce, transfigure, transform, every kind of mime and play-acting. The essential thing remains the ease of the metamor-phosis, the inability *not* to react (– as with certain hysterics who also enter into *any* role at the slightest sign). It is impossible for Dionysian man not to understand every suggestion; he overlooks no emotional sign, he has the instinct for understanding and sensing in the highest degree, just as he possesses the art of communication in the highest degree. He adopts every skin, every emotion: he is constantly transforming himself. – Music, as we understand it nowadays, is likewise a total arousal and discharge of the emotions, and yet it is merely the remnant of a much fuller world of emotional expression, a mere *residuum* of Dionysian histrionism. To make music possible as a speci-alized art-form a number of the senses, above all the kinaesthetic sense, were made inactive (at least relatively so: for to a certain extent all rhythm still speaks to our mus-cles): with the result that man no longer immediately imitates and represents with his body everything he feels. Nevertheless *that* is the truly Dionysian state of normality, at any rate the original state; with music it slowly becomes more specific at the expense of the most closely related faculties.

11

The actor, the mime, the dancer, the musician, the lyric poet are fundamentally related in their instincts and are actually one, but have gradually specialized and separated off from one another – even to the point of contradiction. The lyric poet stayed united with the musician the longest; the actor with the dancer. – The *architect* represents neither a Dionysian nor an Apollonian state: here it is the great act of will, the will which removes mountains,[40] the intoxication of the great will, that is demanding to become art. The most powerful people have always inspired the architects; the archi-tect has always been influenced by power. In a building, pride, victory over gravity, the will to power should make themselves visible; architecture is a kind of power-eloquence in forms, at times persuading, even flattering, at times simply commanding. The highest feeling of power and assuredness is expressed in anything which has *great style*. Power which no longer needs to prove itself; which disdains to please; which is loath to answer; which feels no witness around it; which lives oblivious of the fact that there is opposition to it; which reposes in *itself*, fatalistically, a law among laws: *this* is what speaks of itself in great style. –

[. . .]

14

Anti-Darwin. – As far as the famous 'struggle for *life*' is concerned, it seems to me for the moment to be more asserted than proven. It occurs, but it is the exception; life as a whole is *not* a state of crisis or hunger, but rather a richness, a luxuriance, even

40   Cf. I Corinthians 13: 2: "and though I have all faith, so that I could remove mountains, and have not charity, I am nothing."

an absurd extravagance – where there is a struggle, there is a struggle for *power* . . .
Malthus should not be confused with nature. – But given that there is this struggle –
and indeed it does occur – it unfortunately turns out the opposite way to what the
school of Darwin wants, to what one perhaps *ought* to join with them in wanting: i.e.
to the detriment of the strong, the privileged, the fortunate exceptions. Species do
not grow in perfection: time and again the weak become the masters of the strong –
for they are the great number, they are also *cleverer* . . . Darwin forgot intelligence (–
that is English!), *the weak are more intelligent* . . . You must have need of intelligence in
order to gain it – you lose it if you no longer have need of it. Anyone who has strength
dispenses with intelligence (– 'let it go!' people think in today's Germany, 'for the
Reich must still be ours' . . .). By 'intelligence' it is clear that I mean caution, patience,
cunning, disguise, great self-control, and all that is mimicry (which last includes a large
part of so-called virtue).

[. . .]

19

Beautiful and Ugly. – Nothing is more qualified, let us say *more limited*, than our feeling for the beautiful. If you tried to think of it in isolation from the pleasure humanity
takes in itself, you would immediately lose the ground beneath your feet. The 'beautiful in itself' is merely a word, not even a concept. In beautiful things, man posits
himself as the measure of perfection; in exceptional cases he worships himself in them.
A species cannot *help* saying yes to itself alone in this way. Its *most deep-seated* instinct,
for self-preservation and self-expansion, radiates out even from such sublimities. Man
thinks the world itself is overwhelmed with beauty – he *forgets* he is its cause. He alone
has bestowed beauty on it – oh! but a very human, all-too-human beauty . . . Basically
man mirrors himself in things, he thinks anything that reflects his image back to him
is beautiful: the judgement 'beautiful' is *the vanity of his species* . . . Now the sceptic
might find a slight suspicion whispering in his ear the question: is the world really
beautified just because man takes it to be beautiful? He has *anthropomorphized* it: that
is all. But we have no guarantee, none at all, that it is man who should be singled
out to provide the model of the beautiful. Who knows how he might look in the
eyes of a higher arbiter of taste? Perhaps audacious? perhaps amused at himself? perhaps a little arbitrary? . . . 'Oh Dionysus, you divinity, why are you tugging at my ears?'
Ariadne once asked her philosophical paramour during one of those famous dialogues
on Naxos,[41] 'I find your ears rather humorous, Ariadne: why aren't they even longer?'

20

Nothing is beautiful, only man is beautiful: all aesthetics rests on this naïvety; it is its
first truth. Let us immediately add its second: nothing is ugly except *degenerating* man
– thus the realm of aesthetic judgement is delimited. – In physiological terms everything ugly weakens and saddens man. It reminds him of decay, danger, powerlessness;
it actually makes him lose strength. You can measure the effect of ugly things with a
dynamometer. Whenever man gets depressed, he senses something 'ugly' is nearby.

41   In Greek mythology, Bacchus (Dionysus) successfully woos Ariadne on the island of Naxos
after she has been abandoned there by her former lover Theseus.

His feeling of power, his will to power, his courage, his pride – all are diminished by ugliness and increased by beauty . . . In both cases *we reach a conclusion*, the premises for which accumulate in immense abundance in our instinct. Ugly things are understood as signs and symptoms of degenerescence: anything which serves as the slightest reminder of degenerescence produces in us the judgement 'ugly'. Any sign of exhaustion, of heaviness, of age, of tiredness; any kind of constraint, a cramp, a paralysis; above all the whiff, the colour, the form of dissolution, of decomposition, even in the ultimate rarefaction into a symbol – all produce the same reaction, the value judgement 'ugly'. A *hatred* springs up here: who is man hating here? But there is no doubt: the *decline of his type*. His hatred here stems from the most deep-seated instinct of the species; in this hatred there is shuddering horror, caution, profundity, far-sightedness – it is the most profound hatred there is. That is why art is *profound* . . .

21

Schopenhauer. – Schopenhauer, the last German to be worth considering (– to be a *European* event like Goethe, Hegel, Heinrich Heine, and *not just* a local, 'national' one), is to the psychologist a case of the first order: namely as a brilliantly malicious attempt to bring to bear in the service of a nihilistic devaluation of all life precisely the counter-examples, the great self-affirmations of the 'will to life', the exuberance-forms of life. He interpreted in turn *art*, heroism, genius, beauty, great fellow-feeling, knowledge, the will to truth, tragedy as consequences of the 'denial' of the 'will', or the need to deny it – the greatest piece of psychological counterfeiting in history, Christianity excepted. On closer inspection he is simply the heir to Christian interpretation in this: except that he also managed to *approve* of what Christianity had *rejected* – the great cultural facts of humanity – in a Christian, i.e. nihilistic sense (– namely as paths to 'redemption', as prefigurations of 'redemption', as stimulants of the need for 'redemption' . . .)

22

I shall take one specific case. Schopenhauer speaks of *beauty* with a melancholy passion – but why? Because he sees in it a *bridge* which takes us further on, or makes us thirst to go further on . . . It is to him a momentary redemption from the 'will' – it tempts us into redemption for ever . . . In particular he praises it as redeeming us from the 'focus of the will', from sexuality – in beauty he sees the procreative drive *denied* . . . Strange fellow! There is someone contradicting you, and I am afraid it is nature. *Why* is there any beauty in sound, colour, fragrance, rhythmic movement in nature? What is it that *forces out* beauty? – Fortunately there is also a philosopher contradicting him. No lesser authority than the divine Plato (– as Schopenhauer himself calls him) maintains a different proposition: that all beauty stimulates procreation[42] – that this is precisely the *proprium* of its effect, from the most sensual right up to the most spiritual . . .

23

Plato goes further. With an innocence which requires a Greek and not a 'Christian', he says there would be no Platonic philosophy at all were there not such beautiful

---

42   Cf. Plato, *Symposium*, 206b–d.

youths in Athens: only on seeing them is the philosopher's soul sent into an erotic frenzy from which it will not rest until it has planted the seed of all lofty things in such a beautiful soil.[43] Another strange fellow! – you cannot believe your ears, if indeed you can believe Plato. At least you can sense that they philosophized *differently* in Athens, above all in public. Nothing is less Greek than the conceptual cobwebbery of a hermit, *amor intellectualis dei*[44] after the manner of Spinoza. Philosophy after the manner of Plato would need to be defined as more of an erotic competition, as a development and internalization of the agonal gymnastics of old and its *preconditions* . . . What was it that ultimately grew out of this philosophical erotics of Plato's? A new art-form of the Greek *agon*, dialectics. – I would point out, *contra* Schopenhauer and in Plato's favour, that all the higher culture and literature of *classical* France, too, grew up on the soil of sexual interest. You can search everywhere in it for gallantry, the senses, sexual competition, 'woman' – and you will never search in vain . . .

24

L'art pour l'art.[45] – The struggle against purpose in art is always a struggle against the *moralizing* tendency in art, against its subordination to morality. *L'art pour l'art* means: 'the devil take morality!' But even this enmity betrays the overwhelming force of prejudice. Once you take away from art the purpose of preaching morality and improving humanity, the result is still a far cry from art as completely purposeless, aimless, senseless, in short *l'art pour l'art* – a worm biting its own tail. 'Better no purpose at all than a moral purpose!' – thus speaks pure passion. But a psychologist asks: what does all art do? does it not praise? does it not glorify? does it not select? does it not emphasize? In all these ways it *strengthens* or *weakens* certain value judgements . . . Is this just incidental? a coincidence? something from which the artist's instinct remains completely detached? Or rather: is it not a prerequisite for the artist *to be able* . . . ? Is his most deep-seated instinct for art, or is it not rather for the meaning of art, *life*, for a *desideratum of life*? – Art is the great stimulant to life: how could one conceive of it as purposeless, aimless, *l'art pour l'art*? – One question remains: art also reveals much that is ugly, harsh, questionable in life – does it not thereby seem to remove the suffering from life? – And indeed there have been philosophers who have given it this meaning: 'freeing oneself from the will' was what Schopenhauer taught as the overall purpose of art, 'fostering a mood of resignation' was what he admired as the great benefit of tragedy.[46] – But this, as I have already indicated, is a pessimist's perspective and an 'evil eye' – we must appeal to the artists themselves. *What does the tragic artist communicate about himself*? Is it not precisely the state of *fearlessness* in the face of the fearful and questionable that he shows? – This state is itself highly desirable: anyone who knows it honours it with the highest honours. He communicates it, he *must* communicate it, so long as he is an artist, a genius of communication. Bravery and

---

43   Cf. Plato, *Phaedrus*, 249c–256e.
44   Latin: intellectual love of God. Quotation from Spinoza, *Ethics*, V. 32, Corollary.
45   French: Art for art's sake. Slogan coined in 1818 by the French philosopher and politician Victor Cousin, and adopted as a creed by many writers of the later nineteenth century, such as Baudelaire and Flaubert in France.
46   See *WWR*, vol. 1, bk. 3, especially section 51.

unrestrained feeling in the face of a powerful enemy, or noble hardship, or a problem which makes one shudder with horror – it is this *triumphant* state that the tragic artist selects and glorifies. Faced with tragedy, the warlike element in our souls celebrates its Saturnalia;[47] anyone who is used to suffering, who seeks out suffering, the *heroic* person praises his existence through tragedy – to him alone the tragedian offers a draught of this sweetest cruelty. –

[. . .]

26

We stop appreciating ourselves enough when we communicate. Our actual experiences are not in the least talkative. They could not express themselves even if they wanted to. For they lack the words to do so. When we have words for something we have already gone beyond it. In all speech there is a grain of contempt. Language, it seems, was invented only for average, middling, communicable things. The speaker *vulgarizes* himself as soon as he speaks. – From a morality for deaf-mutes and other philosophers.

[. . .]

33

Natural Value of Egoism. – Selfishness is worth as much as the physiological value of whoever is exhibiting it: it can be worth a great deal; it can be worthless and contemptible. Every single person can be considered from the point of view of whether he represents the ascendant or descendent line of life. A decision on this point gives you a criterion for the value of his selfishness. If he represents the line ascendant then his value is indeed extraordinary – and for the sake of the totality of life, which takes a step *further* with him, extreme care may even be taken in maintaining and creating the optimum conditions for him. For the single person – the 'individual', as the people and the philosophers have understood him thus far – is an error: he is nothing by himself, no atom, no 'ring in the chain', nothing which has simply been inherited from the past – he is the whole single line of humanity up to and including himself . . . If he represents a development downwards, a falling-off, a chronic degeneration, or illness (– illnesses are by and large already the consequences of a falling-off, *not* the causes of it), then he is worth little, and in all fairness he should *detract* as little as possible from those who turned out well. He is merely a parasite on them . . .

34

Christian and Anarchist. – When the anarchist, as the mouthpiece of social strata *in decline*, waxes indignant and demands 'rights', 'justice', 'equal rights', then he is just feeling the pressure of his lack of culture, which is incapable of understanding *why* he is actually suffering – *what* he is poor in, in life . . . There is a powerful causal drive within him: someone must be to blame for his feeling bad . . . And 'waxing indignant' itself does him good, too; all poor devils take pleasure in grumbling – it gives a little rush of power. Even a complaint, making a complaint, can give life some spice and make

47 See *On Truth and Lies* note 16 above.

it endurable: there is a small dose of *revenge* in every complaint; people blame those who are different from themselves for the fact that they feel bad, possibly even for their badness – as though it were an injustice, an *illicit* privilege. 'If I'm *canaille*,[48] then so should you be': this is the logic on which revolutions are based. – Complaining is never any good: it stems from weakness. Whether people attribute their feeling bad to others or to *themselves* – socialists do the former, Christians, for example, the latter – it makes no real difference. What they have in common, let us say what is *unworthy* about them, too, is that someone is supposed to be *to blame* for their suffering – in short, that the sufferer prescribes himself the honey of revenge for his suffering. The objects of this need for revenge, a need for *pleasure*, are contingent causes: the sufferer will find grounds everywhere for venting his petty revenge – if he is a Christian, to say it again, then he will find them in *himself* . . . The Christian and the anarchist – both are *décadents*. – But even when the Christian condemns, slanders, denigrates the '*world*', he does so from the same instinct from which the socialist worker condemns, slanders, denigrates *society*: the 'last judgement' itself is still the sweet consolation of revenge – the revolution which the socialist worker is also awaiting, only taken somewhat further in thought . . . The 'hereafter' itself – why have a hereafter if it is not a means to denigrate this life? . . .

[. . .]

38

My Idea of Freedom. – The value of a thing sometimes depends not on what we manage to do with it, but on what we pay for it – what it *costs* us. Let me give an example. Liberal institutions stop being liberal as soon as they have been set up: afterwards there is no one more inveterate or thorough in damaging freedom than liberal institutions. Now we know *what* they achieve: they undermine the will to power, they are the levelling of mountain and valley elevated to the status of morality, they make things petty, cowardly, and hedonistic – with them the herd animal triumphs every time. Liberalism: in plain words *herd-animalization* . . . While these same institutions are still being fought for, they produce quite different effects: then they are actually powerful promoters of freedom. On closer inspection, it is war that produces these effects, war waged *for* liberal institutions, which as war allows the *illiberal* instincts to persist. And war is an education in freedom. For what is freedom! Having the will to be responsible to oneself. Maintaining the distance which divides us off from each other. Becoming more indifferent towards hardship, harshness, privation, even life itself. Being prepared to sacrifice people to one's cause – oneself included. Freedom means that the manly instincts which delight in war and victory rule over other instincts, for example the instincts for 'happiness'. The *liberated* man – and the liberated *spirit* even more so – tramples over the contemptible kind of well-being that shopkeepers, Christians, cows, women, Englishmen, and other democrats dream about. The free man is a *warrior*. – How is freedom measured, in individuals as well as nations? By the resistance which must be overcome, the effort it costs to stay *on top*. The highest type of free men would need to be sought in the place where the greatest resistance is constantly being overcome: a short step away from tyranny, right on the threshold of the danger of servitude. This is psychologically true, if one understands here by 'tyrants' pitiless and

48   French: riff-raff.

terrible instincts which require the maximum of authority and discipline to deal with them – finest type Julius Caesar – and it is also politically true, if one simply takes a walk through history. The nations which were worth something, *became* worth something, never did so under liberal institutions: it was *great danger* that turned them into something worthy of respect, the kind of danger without which we would not know our instruments, our virtues, our defences and weapons, our *spirit* – which *forces* us to be strong . . . *First* principle: you must need to be strong, or else you will never become it. – Those great hothouses for strong, for the strongest kind of people there has yet been – the aristocratic communities such as Rome and Venice – understood freedom in exactly the same sense as I understand the word freedom: as something which one can have and *not* have, which one can *want*, which one can *conquer* . . .

39

Critique of Modernity. – Our institutions are no longer any good: this is universally accepted. But it is not their fault, it is *ours*. Once we have lost all the instincts from which institutions grow, we lose the institutions themselves because *we* are no longer good enough for them. Democratism has always been the form taken by organizing energy in decline: in *Human, All Too Human.*[49] I already characterized modern democracy, along with its inadequacies like 'German Reich', as the *form of the state's decay.* For there to be institutions there must be a kind of will, instinct, imperative, which is anti-liberal to the point of malice: the will to tradition, to authority, to centuries of responsibility to come, the will to *solidarity* of generational chains stretching forwards and backwards *in infinitum*. If this will is there, then something like the *imperium Romanum*[50] is founded: or like Russia, the *only* power nowadays which has endurance, which can wait, which still has promise – Russia, the conceptual opposite of Europe's pitiful petty-statery and nervousness, which has reached a critical condition with the founding of the German Reich . . . The whole of the West has lost those instincts from which institutions grow, from which *future* grows: nothing perhaps goes against the grain of its 'modern spirit' so much. People live for today, they live very quickly – they live very irresponsibly: and this is precisely what is called 'freedom'. The thing that *makes* institutions into institutions is despised, hated, rejected: people think they are in danger of a new form of slavery whenever the word 'authority' is even just uttered. *Décadence* has penetrated the value-instinct of our politicians and political parties to such an extent that *they instinctively prefer* anything which dissolves things, which hastens the end . . . Witness *modern marriage.* Modern marriage has patently lost all its rationality: and yet this is no objection to marriage, rather to modernity. The rationality of marriage lay in the sole legal responsibility of the husband: this is what gave marriage its centre of gravity; whereas nowadays it has a limp in both legs. The rationality of marriage lay in the principle of its indissolubility: this gave it an accent which, set against the contingencies of feeling, passion, and the moment, could *make itself heard.* Likewise it lay in the responsibility of families for the choice of husband and wife. The increasing indulgence shown towards *love*-matches has practically eliminated the basis for marriage, the thing which *makes* it an institution in the first place. An

---

49   See *HH* 472.
50   Latin: Roman empire.

institution can never ever be founded on an idiosyncrasy; marriage, as I have already said, can *not* be founded on 'love' – it is founded on the sexual drive, on the drive to own (wife and child as property), on the *drive to rule*, which is constantly organizing for itself the smallest structure of rule, the family, which *needs* children and heirs in order to keep a physiological hold, too, on the measure of power, influence, wealth it has achieved, in order to prepare for long-term tasks, for instinctual solidarity between centuries. Marriage as an institution already encompasses the affirmation of the greatest, most enduring organizational form: if society itself cannot *guarantee* itself as a whole unto the most distant generations, then there is no sense in marriage at all. – Modern marriage has *lost* its sense – consequently it is being abolished. –

[. . .]

43

A Word in the Conservatives' Ear. – What we did not know before, what we know today, could know today – a *regression*, an about-turn of any kind or to any extent, is just not possible. At least we physiologists know this. But all the priests and moralists have believed it is – they *wanted* to bring humanity, *crank* humanity back to an *earlier* measure of virtue. Morality has always been a Procrustean bed.[51] Even the politicians have imitated the preachers of virtue in this respect: even today there are still parties which dream of the crab-like *retrogression* of all things as their goal. But no one is free to be a crab. It is no use: we *have* to go forwards, i.e. *step by step further in* décadence (– this being *my* definition of modern 'progress' . . .). You can *check* this development and, by checking it, dam up, accumulate degeneration itself, making it more vehement and *sudden*: no more can be done. –

44

My Idea of Genius. – Great men, like periods of greatness, are explosives storing up immense energy; historically and physiologically speaking, their precondition is always that they be collected, accumulated, saved, and preserved for over a long period – that there be a long period without explosions. Once the tension in the mass becomes too great, then the most accidental stimulus is enough to bring 'genius', 'action', a great destiny into the world. What, then, do the environment, the age, the 'spirit of the age', 'public opinion' have to do with it! – Take the case of Napoleon. Revolutionary France, and pre-Revolutionary France even more so, would have produced the opposite type to Napoleon: indeed it *did* produce it. And because Napoleon was *different*, the heir to a stronger, longer-lasting, older civilization than the one which was going to pieces and up in smoke in France, he became master there – he *was* the sole master there. Great people are necessary, the age in which they appear is incidental; if they almost always become master of it, then this is simply because they are stronger and older, and result from a longer period of accumulation. The relationship between a genius and his age is like that between strong and weak, or old and young: the age is always comparatively much younger, thinner, more immature, more insecure, more

---

51   Polypemon, or Procrustes (Greek for "stretcher"), was a legendary Greek robber who would lay travelers on his bed: if they were too long for it he would cut their limbs shorter; if they were too short he would stretch them to make them fit.

childish. – The fact that people think *very differently* about this in France today (in Germany, too: but that means nothing), the fact that the theory of *milieu*,[52] a real neurotics' theory, has become sacrosanct and almost scientific there, and is believed in even among physiologists, 'does not smell good'; it makes one sad to think about it. – In England, too, they understand things no differently, but no one will be saddened by that. The English have only two ways of accommodating the genius and the 'great man': either *democratically*, after the manner of Buckle,[53] or *religiously*, after the manner of Carlyle. The *danger* that lies in great people and periods of greatness is extraordinary; every kind of exhaustion, and sterility, follow in their footsteps. The great person is an end; the period of greatness, for example the Renaissance, is an end. The genius – in his works, in his deeds – is necessarily a squanderer: his greatness lies in his *expenditure* . . . The instinct for self-preservation is, so to speak, unhinged; the overwhelming pressure of the energies streaming out from him forbids him any such care and caution. People call this 'self-sacrifice'; they praise his 'heroism', his indifference towards his own well-being, his devotion to an idea, a great cause, a fatherland: all of these are misunderstandings . . . He streams out, he overflows, he consumes himself, he does not spare himself – fatefully, fatally, involuntarily, just as a river bursts its banks involuntarily. But because we owe a great deal to such explosives, we have given them a great deal in return, too, for example a kind of *higher morality* . . . For that is how humanity expresses its gratitude: it *misunderstands* its benefactors. –

[. . .]

48

Progress in My Sense. – Even I speak of a 'return to nature', although it is actually not a going back but a *coming up* – up into high, free, even fearful nature and naturalness, the kind which plays – is *entitled* to play – with great tasks . . . To use an *analogy*: Napoleon was a piece of 'return to nature' as I understand it (for example *in rebus tacticis*,[54] and even more so, as army officers know, in matters strategic). – But Rousseau – where did *he* actually want to go back to? Rousseau, that first modern man, idealist and *canaille* in one person, who needed moral 'dignity' in order to stand the sight of himself; sick with unbridled vanity and unbridled self-contempt. Even this abortion, who lodged himself on the threshold of the new age, wanted a 'return to nature' – where, to repeat my question, did Rousseau want to go back to? – I still hate Rousseau *in* the Revolution: it is the world-historic expression of that duplicity of idealist and *canaille*. The bloody farce with which this Revolution played itself out, its 'immorality', is of little concern to me: what I hate is its Rousseauesque *moral* – the so-called 'truths' of the Revolution, through which it is still having an effect and winning over everything shallow and mediocre. The doctrine of equality! . . . But there is no more venomous poison in existence: for it *appears* to be preached by justice itself, when it is actually the *end* of justice . . . 'Equality to the equal; inequality to the unequal' – *that* would be

---

52   The theory that one's surroundings are more important than heredity in the formation of one's character. Its main exponents were August Comte and Hippolyte Taine.
53   Henry Thomas Buckle (1821–62), English cultural historian, whom Nietzsche also criticizes in *GM* (I. 4).
54   Latin: in tactical matters.

true justice speaking: and its corollary, 'never make the unequal equal'. Because that doctrine of equality was surrounded by so much horror and bloodshed, this 'modern idea' *par excellence* was given a kind of glory and fiery glow, so that the Revolution as *spectacle* seduced even the noblest of minds. Ultimately that is no reason to respect it the more. – I can see only one man who experienced it as it must be experienced, with *revulsion* – Goethe . . .

49

Goethe – not a German event but a European one: a magnificent attempt to overcome the eighteenth century by a return to nature, by a coming-*up* to the naturalness of the Renaissance, a kind of self-overcoming on the part of that century. – He bore its strongest instincts in himself: sentimentality, nature-idolatry, the anti-historical, the idealistic, the unreal and revolutionary (– the last being merely a form of the unreal). He made use of history, natural science, antiquity, as well as Spinoza, and of practical activity above all; he surrounded himself with nothing but closed horizons; he did not divorce himself from life but immersed himself in it; he never lost heart, and took as much as possible upon himself, above himself, into himself. What he wanted was *totality*; he fought against the disjunction of reason, sensuality, feeling, will (– preached in the most repulsively scholastic way by *Kant*, Goethe's antipode), he disciplined himself into a whole, he *created* himself . . . In the midst of an age disposed to unreality, Goethe was a convinced realist: he said yes to all that was related to him in this respect – he had no greater experience than that *ens realissimum*[55] called Napoleon. Goethe conceived of a strong, highly educated man, adept in all things bodily, with a tight rein on himself and a reverence for himself, who can dare to grant himself the whole range and richness of naturalness, who is strong enough for this freedom; the man of tolerance, not out of weakness, but out of strength, because he knows how to turn to his advantage what would destroy the average type; the man to whom there is no longer anything forbidden except *weakness*, whether it be called vice or virtue . . . Such a *liberated* spirit stands in the midst of the universe with a joyful and trusting fatalism, with *faith* in the fact that only what is individual is reprehensible, that everything is redeemed and affirmed in the whole – *he no longer denies* . . . But such a faith is the highest of all possible faiths; I have baptized it with the name of *Dionysus*. –

[. . .]

What I Owe the Ancients

4

I was the first person who, in order to understand the more ancient Hellenic instinct, when it was still rich and even overflowing, took seriously that marvellous phenomenon which bears the name of Dionysus: it can be explained only by an *excess* of strength. Anyone investigating the Greeks, like that most profound connoisseur of their culture alive today, Jakob Burckhardt in Basle, knew at once that this was an achievement: Burckhardt inserted into his *Culture of the Greeks* his own section on this phenomenon. If you want the opposite, then you should look at the almost laughable instinctual

---

55   See note 20 above.

poverty of German philologists when they approach the Dionysian. In particular the famous Lobeck,[56] who crawled into this world of secret states with the respectful self-assuredness of a worm which has dried out between books, and convinced himself this made him scientific, so much so that he was nauseatingly thoughtless and childish – applying all his erudition, Lobeck gave us to understand that all these curiosities really did not amount to anything. In truth, he tells us, the priests may well have informed the participants in such orgies about a few things of some value: for example, that wine excites lust, that it is possible for people to live off fruit, that plants blossom in the spring and wither in the autumn. As far as that disconcerting wealth of rites, symbols, and myths of orgiastic origin is concerned, with which the ancient world is quite literally overgrown, Lobeck takes it as an opportunity to become even a shade wittier: 'If the Greeks', he says (*Aglaophamus* i. 672), 'had nothing else to do, then they laughed, leapt, and rushed around, or, since from time to time man is also so inclined, they sat down, wept, and wailed. *Others* then came along later and looked for some kind of reason for their remarkable nature; and so, in order to explain these customs, those countless festival legends and myths were created. On the other hand it was believed that that *droll activity* which now took place on festival days also belonged necessarily to the festival ceremony, and it was held to be an indispensable part of the divine service.' – This is contemptible twaddle, and no one will take people like Lobeck seriously for a moment. We are affected quite differently when we test the concept of 'Greek' which Winckelmann[57] and Goethe shaped for themselves, and find it incompatible with the element from which Dionysian art grows – the orgiastic. In fact I have no doubt that Goethe would have excluded anything like this in principle from the possibilities of the Greek soul. *Hence Goethe did not understand the Greeks.* For only in the Dionysian mysteries, in the psychology of the Dionysian state, is the *basic fact* of the Hellenic instinct expressed – its 'will to life'. *What* did the Hellene guarantee for himself with these mysteries? *Eternal* life, the eternal return of life; the future heralded and consecrated in the past; the triumphant yes to life over and above death and change; *true* life as the totality living on through procreation, through the mysteries of sexuality. That is why for the Greeks the *sexual* symbol was the venerable symbol in itself, the true profundity inherent in the whole of ancient piety. Every particular about the act of procreation, of pregnancy, of birth evoked the loftiest and solemnest of feelings. In the doctrine of the mysteries *pain* is sanctified: the 'woes of the woman in labour' sanctify pain in general – all becoming and growing, everything that vouchsafes the future, *presupposes* pain . . . For the eternal joy of creation to exist, for the will to life to affirm itself eternally, the 'torment of the woman in labour' *must* also exist eternally . . . The word 'Dionysus' means all of this: I know of no higher symbolism than this *Greek* symbolism, the symbolism of the Dionysia.[58] In it the most profound instinct of life, the instinct for the future of life, for the eternity of life, is felt in a religious way – the very path to life, procreation, is felt to be the *holy* path

56   Christian August Lobeck (1781–1860), German classical philologist.
57   Johann Joachim Winckelmann (1717–68), German archaeologist and historian of ancient art, one of Goethe's early influences.
58   Various Athenian festivals held in honor of Dionysus which included sacrifices and dramatic performances as well as the tasting of the new wine, the parading of sculpted phalluses, symbolic marriages, and orgies.

. . . Only when Christianity came along, with its fundamental resentment *against* life, was sexuality turned into something impure: it threw *filth* at the beginning, at the precondition for our life . . .

5

The psychology of the orgiastic as an overflowing feeling of life and strength, within which even pain still has a stimulating effect, gave me the key to the concept of *tragic* feeling, which has been misunderstood as much by Aristotle as, more especially, by our pessimists. Tragedy is so far from providing any proof of the pessimism of the Hellenes in Schopenhauer's sense that it should rather be seen as its decisive refutation and *counter-example*. Saying yes to life, even in its strangest and hardest problems; the will to life rejoicing in the *sacrifice* of its highest types to its own inexhaustibility – *this* is what I called Dionysian, *this* is what I sensed as the bridge to the psychology of the *tragic* poet. *Not* freeing oneself from terror and pity, not purging oneself of a dangerous emotion through its vehement discharge – such was Aristotle's understanding of it – but, over and above terror and pity, *being oneself* the eternal joy of becoming – that joy which also encompasses the *joy of destruction* . . . And so again I am touching on the point from which I once started out – the *Birth of Tragedy* was my first revaluation of all values: so again I am taking myself back to the ground from which my willing, my *ability* grows – I, the last disciple of the philosopher Dionysus – I, the teacher of the eternal recurrence . . .

24

The Anti-Christ:
Curse on Christianity
(1888)

1

– Let us look one another in the face. We are Hyperboreans[1] – we know well enough
how much out of the way we live. 'Neither by land nor by sea shalt thou find the
road to the Hyperboreans': Pindar already knew that of us.[2] Beyond the North, beyond
the ice, beyond death – *our* life, *our* happiness. . . . We have discovered happiness, we
know the road, we have found the exit out of whole millennia of labyrinth. Who *else*
has found it? – Modern man perhaps? – 'I know not which way to turn; I am everything that knows not which way to turn' – sighs modern man. . . . It was from *this*
modernity that we were ill – from lazy peace, from cowardly compromise, from the
whole virtuous uncleanliness of modern Yes and No. This tolerance and *largeur*[3] of
heart which 'forgives' everything because it 'Understands' everything is sirocco to us.
Better to live among ice than among modern virtues and other south winds! . . . We
were brave enough, we spared neither ourselves nor others: but for long we did not
know *where* to apply our courage. We became gloomy, we were called fatalists. *Our*
fatality – *was* the plenitude, the tension, the blocking-up of our forces. We thirsted
for lightning and action, of all things we kept ourselves furthest from the happiness
of the weaklings, from 'resignation'. . . . There was a thunderstorm in our air, the nature
which we are grew dark – *for we had no road*. Formula of our happiness: a Yes, a No,
a straight line, a *goal* . . .

2

What is good? – All that heightens the feeling of power, the will to power, power
itself in man.

---

1   In Greek mythology, a race dwelling beyond the north wind (Boreas) in a country of warmth
and plenty.
2   See Pindar, *Pythian Odes*, X. 29–30.
3   French: breadth, generosity.

What is bad? – All that proceeds from weakness.

What is happiness? – The feeling that power *increases* – that a resistance is overcome.

Not contentment, but more power; *not* peace at all, but war; *not* virtue, but proficiency (virtue in the Renaissance style, *virtù*, virtue free of moralic acid).[4]

The weak and ill-constituted shall perish: first principle of *our* philanthropy. And one shall help them to do so.

What is more harmful than any vice? – Active sympathy for the ill-constituted and weak – Christianity . . .

3

The problem I raise here is not what ought to succeed mankind in the sequence of species (– the human being is a *conclusion* –): but what type of human being one ought to *breed*, ought to *will*, as more valuable, more worthy of life, more certain of the future.

This more valuable type has existed often enough already: but as a lucky accident, as an exception, never as *willed*. *He* has rather been the most feared, he has hitherto been virtually *the* thing to be feared – and out of fear the reverse type has been willed, bred, *achieved*: the domestic animal, the herd animal, the sick animal man – the Christian . . .

4

Mankind does *not* represent a development of the better or the stronger or the higher in the way that is believed today. 'Progress' is merely a modern idea, that is to say a false idea. The European of today is of far less value than the European of the Renaissance; onward development is not by *any* means, by any necessity the same thing as elevation, advance, strengthening.

In another sense there are cases of individual success constantly appearing in the most various parts of the earth and from the most various cultures in which a *higher type* does manifest itself: something which in relation to collective mankind is a sort of overman. Such chance occurrences of great success have always been possible and perhaps always will be possible. And even entire races, tribes, nations can under certain circumstances represent such a *lucky hit*.

5

One should not embellish or dress up Christianity: it has waged a *war to the death* against this *higher* type of man, it has excommunicated all the fundamental instincts of this type, it has distilled evil, the *Evil One*, out of these instincts – the strong human being as the type of reprehensibility, as the 'outcast'. Christianity has taken the side of everything weak, base, ill-constituted, it has made an ideal out of *opposition* to the preservative instincts of strong life; it has depraved the reason even of the intellectually strongest natures by teaching men to feel the supreme values of intellectuality as sinful, as misleading, as *temptations*. The most deplorable example: the depraving of Pascal, who believed his reason had been depraved by original sin while it had only been depraved by his Christianity! –

4   In German: *moralinfreie Tugend*.

6

It is a painful, a dreadful spectacle which has opened up before me: I have drawn back the curtain on the *depravity* of man. In my mouth this word is protected against at any rate one suspicion: that it contains a moral accusation of man. It is – I should like to underline the fact again – free of any *moralic acid*: and this to the extent that I find that depravity precisely where hitherto one most consciously aspired to 'virtue', to 'divinity'. I understand depravity, as will already have been guessed, in the sense of *décadence*: my assertion is that all the values in which mankind at present summarizes its highest desideratum are *décadence values*.

I call an animal, a species, an individual depraved when it loses its instincts, when it chooses, when it *prefers* what is harmful to it. A history of the 'higher feelings', of the 'ideals of mankind' – and it is possible I shall have to narrate it – would almost also constitute an explanation of *why* man is so depraved.

I consider life itself instinct for growth, for continuance, for accumulation of forces, for *power*: where the will to power is lacking there is decline. My assertion is that this will is *lacking* in all the supreme values of mankind – that values of decline, *nihilistic* values hold sway under the holiest names.

7

Christianity is called the religion of *pity*.[5] – Pity stands in antithesis to the tonic emotions which enhance the energy of the feeling of life: it has a depressive effect. One loses force when one pities. The loss of force which life has already sustained through suffering is increased and multiplied even further by pity. Suffering itself becomes contagious through pity; sometimes it can bring about a collective loss of life and life-energy which stands in an absurd relation to the quantum of its cause (– the case of the death of the Nazarene). This is the first aspect; but there is an even more important one. If one judges pity by the value of the reactions which it usually brings about, its mortally dangerous character appears in a much clearer light. Pity on the whole thwarts the law of evolution, which is the law of *selection*. It preserves what is ripe for destruction; it defends life's disinherited and condemned; through the abundance of the ill-constituted of all kinds which it *retains* in life it gives life itself a gloomy and questionable aspect. One has ventured to call pity a virtue (– in every *noble* morality it counts as weakness –); one has gone further, one has made of it *the* virtue, the ground and origin of all virtue – only, to be sure, from the viewpoint of a nihilistic philosophy which inscribed *Denial of Life* on its escutcheon – a fact always to be kept in view. Schopenhauer was within his rights in this: life is denied, made *more worthy of denial* by pity – pity is *practical* nihilism. To say it again, this depressive and contagious instinct thwarts those instincts bent on preserving and enhancing the value of life: both as a *multiplier* of misery and as a *conservator* of everything miserable it is one of the chief instruments for the advancement of *décadence* – pity persuades to *nothingness*! . . . One does not say 'nothingness': one says 'the Beyond'; or 'God'; or '*true* life'; or Nirvana, redemption, blessedness. . . . This innocent rhetoric from the domain of religio-moral idiosyncrasy at once appears *much less innocent* when one grasps *which* tendency is

---

5   In German: *Mitleiden* (literally, "suffering with").

here draping the mantle of sublime words about itself: the tendency *hostile to life*. Schopenhauer was hostile to life: *therefore* pity became for him a virtue. . . . Aristotle, as is well known, saw in pity a morbid and dangerous condition which one did well to get at from time to time with a purgative: he understood tragedy as a purgative. From the instinct for life one would indeed have to seek some means of puncturing so morbid and dangerous an accumulation of pity as that represented by the case of Schopenhauer (and unfortunately also by our entire literary and artistic *décadence* from St Petersburg to Paris, from Tolstoy to Wagner), so that it might *burst*. . . . Nothing in our unhealthy modernity is more unhealthy than Christian pity. To be physician *here*, to be inexorable *here*, to wield the knife *here* – that pertains to *us*, that is *our* kind of philanthropy, with that are *we* philosophers, we Hyperboreans! –

[. . .]

11

A word against Kant as *moralist*. A virtue has to be *our* invention, *our* most personal defence and necessity: in any other sense it is merely a danger. What does not condition our life *harms* it: a virtue merely from a feeling of respect for the concept 'virtue', as Kant desired it, is harmful. 'Virtue', 'duty', 'good in itself', impersonal and universal – phantoms, expressions of decline, of the final exhaustion of life, of Königsbergian Chinadom. The profoundest laws of preservation and growth demand the reverse of this: that each one of us should devise *his own* virtue, *his own* categorical imperative. A people perishes if it mistakes *its own* duty for the concept of duty in general. Nothing works more profound ruin than any 'impersonal' duty, any sacrifice to the Moloch of abstraction. – Kant's categorical imperative[6] should have been felt as *mortally dangerous*! . . . The theologian instinct alone took it under its protection! – An action compelled by the instinct of life has in the joy of performing it the proof it is a *right* action: and that nihilist with Christian-dogmatic bowels understands joy as an *objection*. . . . What destroys more quickly than to work, to think, to feel without inner necessity, without a deep personal choice, without *joy*? as an automaton of 'duty'? It is virtually a *recipe* for *décadence*, even for idiocy. . . . Kant became an idiot. – And that was the contemporary of *Goethe*! This fatal spider counted as the *German* philosopher – still does! I take care not to say what I think of the Germans. . . . Did Kant not see in the French Revolution the transition from the inorganic form of the state to the *organic*? Did he not ask himself whether there was an event which could be explained in no other way than by a moral predisposition on the part of mankind, so that with it the 'tendency of man to seek the good' would be *proved* once and for all? Kant's answer: 'The Revolution is that.' The erring instinct in all and everything, *anti-naturalness* as instinct, German *décadence* as philosophy – *that is Kant*! –

[. . .]

13

Let us not undervalue this: *we ourselves*, we free spirits, are already a 'revaluation of all values', an *incarnate* declaration of war and victory over all ancient conceptions of 'true'

6   See *GM* note 7 above.

and 'untrue'. The most valuable insights are the last to be discovered; but the most valuable insights are *methods*. *All* the methods, *all* the prerequisites of our present-day scientificality have for millennia been the objects of the profoundest contempt: on their account one was excluded from associating with 'honest' men – one was considered an 'enemy of God', a despiser of truth, a man 'possessed'. As a practitioner of science one was Chandala. . . . We have had the whole pathos of mankind against us – its conception of what truth *ought* to be, what the service of truth *ought* to be; every 'thou shalt' has hitherto been directed *against* us. . . . Our objectives, our practices, our quiet, cautious, mistrustful manner – all this appeared utterly unworthy and contemptible to mankind. – In the end one might reasonably ask oneself whether it was not really an *aesthetic* taste which blinded mankind for so long: it desired a *picturesque* effect from truth, it desired especially that the man of knowledge should produce a powerful impression on the senses. It was our *modesty* which offended their taste the longest. . . . Oh, how well they divined that fact, those turkey-cocks of God –

14

We have learned better. We have become more modest in every respect. We no longer trace the origin of man in the 'spirit', in the 'divinity', we have placed him back among the animals. We consider him the strongest animal because he is the most cunning: his spirituality is a consequence of this. On the other hand, we guard ourselves against a vanity which would like to find expression even here: the vanity that man is the great secret objective of animal evolution. Man is absolutely not the crown of creation: every creature stands beside him at the same stage of perfection. . . . And even in asserting that we assert too much: man is, relatively speaking, the most unsuccessful animal, the sickliest, the one most dangerously strayed from its instincts – with all that, to be sure, the most *interesting*! – As regards the animals, Descartes was the first who, with a boldness worthy of reverence, ventured to think of the animal as a *machine*: our whole science of physiology is devoted to proving this proposition. Nor, logically, do we exclude man, as even Descartes did: our knowledge of man today is real knowledge precisely to the extent that it is knowledge of him as a machine. Formerly man was presented with 'free will' as a dowry from a higher order: today we have taken even will away from him, in the sense that will may no longer be understood as a faculty. The old word 'will' only serves to designate a resultant, a kind of individual reaction which necessarily follows a host of partly contradictory, partly congruous stimuli – the will no longer 'effects' anything, no longer 'moves' anything. . . . Formerly one saw in man's consciousness, in his 'spirit', the proof of his higher origin, his divinity; to make himself *perfect* man was advised to draw his senses back into himself in the manner of the tortoise, to cease to have any traffic with the earthly, to lay aside his mortal frame: then the chief part of him would remain behind, 'pure spirit'. We have thought better of this too: becoming-conscious, 'spirit', is to us precisely a symptom of a relative imperfection of the organism, as an attempting, fumbling, blundering, as a toiling in which an unnecessarily large amount of nervous energy is expended – we deny that anything can be made perfect so long as it is still made conscious. 'Pure spirit' is pure stupidity: if we deduct the nervous system and the senses, the 'mortal frame', *we miscalculate* – that's all! . . .

[. . .]

18

The Christian conception of God – God as God of the sick, God as spider, God as spirit – is one of the most corrupt conceptions of God arrived at on earth: perhaps it even represents the low-water mark in the descending development of the God type. God degenerated to the *contradiction of life*, instead of being its transfiguration and eternal *Yes*! In God a declaration of hostility towards life, nature, the will to life! God the formula for every calumny of 'this world', for every lie about 'the next world'! In God nothingness deified, the will to nothingness sanctified! . . .

19

That the strong races of northern Europe have not repudiated the Christian God certainly reflects no credit on their talent for religion – not to speak of their taste. They ought to have felt *compelled* to have done with such a sickly and decrepit product of *décadence*. But there lies a curse on them for not having had done with it: they have taken up sickness, old age, contradiction into all their instincts – since then they have failed to *create* a God! Almost two millennia and not a single new God! But still, and as if existing by right, like an ultimate and maximum of the God-creating force, of the *creator spiritus* in man, this pitiable God of Christian monotono-theism! This hybrid of the void, conceptualism and contradiction, this picture of decay, in which all *décadence* instincts, all cowardliness and weariness of soul have their sanction! –

[. . .]

24

I only touch on the problem of the *origin*[7] of Christianity here. The *first* proposition towards its solution is: Christianity can be understood only by referring to the soil out of which it grew – it is *not* a counter-movement against the Jewish instinct, it is actually its logical consequence, one further conclusion of its fear-inspiring logic. In the Redeemer's formula: 'Salvation is of the Jews'.[8] – The *second* proposition is: the psychological type of the Galilean is still recognizable – but only in a completely degenerate form (which is at once a mutilation and an overloading with foreign traits) could it serve the end to which it was put, that of being the type of a *redeemer* of mankind. –

The Jews are the most remarkable nation of world history because, faced with the question of being or not being, they preferred, with a perfectly uncanny conviction, being *at any price*: the price they had to pay was the radical *falsification* of all nature, all naturalness, all reality, the entire inner world as well as the outer. They defined themselves *counter* to all those conditions under which a nation was previously able to live, was *permitted* to live; they made of themselves an antithesis to *natural* conditions – they inverted religion, religious worship, morality, history, psychology one after the other in an irreparable way into the *contradiction of their natural values*. We encounter the same phenomenon again and in unutterably vaster proportions, although only as a copy – the Christian Church, in contrast to the 'nation of saints', renounces all claim

---

7   In German: *Entstehung*.
8   John 4: 22.

to originality. For precisely this reason the Jews are the most *fateful* nation in world history; their after-effect has falsified mankind to such an extent that today the Christian is able to feel anti-Jewish without realizing he is the *ultimate consequence of the Jews*.

In my *Genealogy of Morality* I introduced for the first time the psychology of the antithetical concepts of a *noble* morality and a *ressentiment* morality, the latter deriving from a *denial* of the former: but this latter corresponds totally to Judeo-Christian morality. To be able to reject all that represents the *ascending* movement of life, well-constitutedness, power, beauty, self-affirmation on earth, the instinct of *ressentiment* here become genius had to invent *another* world from which that *life-affirmation* would appear evil, reprehensible as such. Considered psychologically, the Jewish nation is a nation of the toughest vital energy which, placed in impossible circumstances, voluntarily, from the profoundest shrewdness in self-preservation, took the side of all *décadence* instincts – *not* as being dominated by them but because it divined in them a power by means of which one can prevail *against* 'the world'. The Jews are the counterparts of *décadents*: they have been compelled to *act* as *décadents* to the point of illusion, they have known, with a *non plus ultra* of histrionic genius, how to place themselves at the head of all *décadence* movements (– as the Christianity of *Paul* –) so as to make of them something stronger than any party *affirmative* of life. For the kind of man who desires to attain power through Judaism and Christianity, the *priestly* kind, *décadence* is only a *means*: this kind of man has a life-interest in making mankind *sick* and in inverting the concepts 'good' and 'evil', 'true' and 'false' in a mortally dangerous and world-calumniating sense. –

[. . .]

32

I resist, to repeat it, the incorporation of the fanatic into the type of the redeemer: the word *impérieux*[9] alone which Renan[10] employs already *annuls* the type. The 'glad tidings' are precisely that there are no more opposites; the kingdom of Heaven belongs to *children*; the faith which here finds utterance is not a faith which has been won by struggle – it is there, from the beginning, it is as it were a return to childishness in the spiritual domain. The occurrence of retarded puberty undeveloped in the organism as a consequence of degeneration is familiar at any rate to physiologists. – Such a faith is not angry, does not censure, does not defend itself: it does not bring 'the sword' – it has no idea to what extent it could one day cause dissention. It does not prove itself, either by miracles or by rewards and promises, and certainly not 'by the Scriptures': it is every moment its own miracle, its own reward, its own proof, its own 'kingdom of God'. Neither does this faith formulate itself – it *lives*, it resists formulas. Chance, to be sure, determines the environment, the language, the preparatory schooling of a particular configuration of concepts: primitive Christianity employs *only* Judeo-Semitic concepts (– eating and drinking at communion belong here, concepts

---

9   French: imperious.

10   Ernest Renan (1823–92), French historian, author of a popular *Vie de Jésus* (*Life of Jesus*, 1863) and six further volumes constituting the *Histoire des origines du Christianisme* (*History of the Origins of Christianity*, 1863–83), also including *L'Antéchrist* (*The Antichrist*, 1873).

so sadly abused, like everything Jewish, by the Church). But one must be careful not to see in this anything but a sign-language, a semeiotic, an occasion for metaphors. It is precisely on condition that nothing he says is taken literally that this anti-realist can speak at all. Among Indians he would have made use of Sankhyam concepts, among Chinese those of Lao-tse – and would not have felt the difference. – One could, with some freedom of expression, call Jesus a 'free spirit' – he cares nothing for what is fixed: the word *killeth*, everything fixed *killeth*. The concept, the *experience* 'life' in the only form he knows it is opposed to any kind of word, formula, law, faith, dogma. He speaks only of the inmost thing: 'life' or 'truth' or 'light' is his expression for the inmost thing – everything else, the whole of reality, the whole of nature, language itself, possesses for him merely the value of a sign, a metaphor. – On this point one must make absolutely no mistake, however much Christian, that is to say *ecclesiastical* prejudice, may tempt one to do so: such a symbolist *par excellence* stands outside of all religion, all conceptions of divine worship, all history, all natural science, all experience of the world, all acquirements, all politics, all psychology, all books, all art – his 'knowledge' is precisely the *pure folly* of the fact *that* anything of this kind exists. He has not so much as heard of *culture*, he does not need to fight against it – he does not deny it. . . . The same applies to the *state*, to society and the entire civic order, to *work*, to war – he never had reason to deny 'the world', he had no notion of the ecclesiastical concept 'world'. . . . *Denial* is precisely what is totally impossible for him. – Dialectics are likewise lacking, the idea is lacking that a faith, a 'truth' could be proved by reasons (– *his* proofs are inner 'lights', inner feelings of pleasure and self-affirmations, nothing but 'proofs by potency' –). Neither *can* such a doctrine argue: it simply does not understand that other doctrines exist, *can* exist, it simply does not know how to imagine an opinion contrary to its own. . . . Where it encounters one it will, with the most heartfelt sympathy, lament the 'blindness' – for it sees the 'light' – but it will make no objection . . .

[. . .]

34

[. . .]

The 'kingdom of Heaven' is a condition of the heart – not something that comes 'upon the earth' or 'after death'. The entire concept of natural death is *lacking* in the Gospel: death is not a bridge, not a transition, it is lacking because it belongs to quite another world, a merely apparent world useful only for the purpose of symbolism. The 'hour of death' is *not* a Christian concept – the 'hour', time, physical life and its crises, simply do not exist for the teacher of the 'glad tidings'. . . . The 'kingdom of God' is not something one waits for; it has no yesterday or tomorrow, it does not come 'in a thousand years' – it is an experience within a heart; it is everywhere, it is nowhere . . .

[. . .]

39

– To resume, I shall now relate the *real* history of Christianity. – The word 'Christianity' is already a misunderstanding – in reality there has been only one Christian, and he died on the Cross. The 'Evangel' *died* on the Cross. What was called 'Evangel' from this moment onwards was already the opposite of what *he* had lived: '*bad* tidings', a *dysangel*. It is false to the point of absurdity to see in a 'belief', perchance the belief in redemption through Christ, the distinguishing characteristic of the Christian: only Christian *practice*, a life such as he who died on the Cross *lived*, is Christian. . . . Even today, *such* a life is possible, for *certain* men even necessary: genuine, primitive Christianity will be possible at all times. . . . *Not* a belief but a doing, above all a *not*-doing of many things, a different *being*. . . . States of consciousness, beliefs of any kind, holding something to be true for example – every psychologist knows this – are a matter of complete indifference and of the fifth rank compared with the value of the instincts: to speak more strictly, the whole concept of spiritual causality is false. To reduce being a Christian, Christianness, to a holding something to be true, to a mere phenomenality of consciousness, means to negate Christianness. *In fact there have been no Christians at all.* The 'Christian', that which has been called Christian for two millennia, is merely a psychological self-misunderstanding. Regarded more closely, that which has ruled in him, *in spite of* all his 'faith', has been *merely* the instincts – and what instincts! 'Faith' has been at all times, with Luther for instance, only a cloak, a pretext, a *screen*, behind which the instincts played their game – a shrewd *blindness* to the dominance of *certain* instincts. . . . 'Faith' – I have already called it the true Christian *shrewdness* – one has always *spoken* of faith, one has always *acted* from instinct. . . . The Christian's world of ideas contains nothing which so much as touches upon actuality: on the other hand, we have recognized in instinctive hatred *for* actuality the driving element, the only driving element in the roots of Christianity. What follows therefrom? That here, *in psychologicis* also, error is radical, that is to say determinant of the essence, that is to say *substance*. *One* concept removed, a single reality substituted in its place – and the whole of Christianity crumbles to nothing! – From a lofty standpoint, this strangest of all facts, a religion not only determined by errors but inventive and even possessing genius *only* in harmful, *only* in life-poisoning and heart-poisoning errors, remains a *spectacle for the gods* – for those divinities which are at the same time philosophers and which I encountered, for example, during those celebrated dialogues on Naxos. In the hour when their *disgust* leaves them (– *and* leaves us!) they become grateful for the spectacle of the Christian: perhaps it is only for the sake of *this* curious case that the pathetic little star called Earth deserves a divine glance and divine participation. . . . For let us not undervalue the Christian: the Christian, false *to the point of innocence*, far surpasses the ape – with respect to Christians a well-known theory of descent becomes a mere compliment . . .

[. . .]

42

One sees *what* came to an end with the death on the Cross: a new, an absolutely primary beginning to a Buddhistic peace movement, to an actual and *not* merely promised *happiness on earth*. For this remains – I have already emphasized it – the basic distinction between the two *décadence* religions: Buddhism makes no promises but keeps them, Christianity makes a thousand promises but *keeps none*. – On the heels of the 'glad tidings' came the *worst of all*: those of Paul. In Paul was embodied the antithetical type to the 'bringer of glad tidings', the genius of hatred, of the vision of hatred, of the inexorable logic of hatred. *What* did this dysangelist not sacrifice to his hatred! The redeemer above all: he nailed him to *his* Cross. The life, the example, the teaching, the death, the meaning and the right of the entire Gospel – nothing was left once this hate-obsessed false-coiner had grasped what alone he could make use of. *Not* the reality, *not* the historical truth! . . . And once more the priestly instinct of the Jew per- petrated the same great crime against history – it simply erased the yesterday and the day before yesterday of Christianity, *it devised for itself a history of primitive Christianity*. More: it falsified the history of Israel over again so as to make this history seem the pre-history of *its* act: all the prophets had spoken of *its* 'redeemer'. . . . The Church subsequently falsified even the history of mankind into the pre-history of Christianity. . . . The type of the redeemer, the doctrine, the practice, the death, the meaning of the death, even the sequel to the death – nothing was left untouched, nothing was left bearing even the remotest resemblance to reality. Paul simply shifted the centre of gravity of that entire existence *beyond* this existence – in the *lie* of the 'resurrected' Jesus. In fact he could make no use at all of the redeemer's life – he needed the death on the Cross *and* something in addition. . . . To regard as honest a Paul whose home was the principal centre of Stoic enlightenment when he makes of a hallucination the *proof* that the redeemer is *still* living, or even to believe his story *that* he had this hallucination, would be a real *niaiserie*[11] on the part of a psychologist: Paul willed the end, *consequently* he willed the means. . . . What he himself did not believe was believed by the idiots among whom he cast *his* teaching. – *His* requirement was *power*, with Paul the priest again sought power – he could employ only those concepts, teach- ings, symbols with which one tyrannizes over masses, forms herds. *What* was the only thing Mohammed later borrowed from Christianity? The invention of Paul, his means for establishing a priestly tyranny, for forming herds: the belief in immortality – *that is to say the doctrine of 'judgement'*. . .

[. . .]

50

– At this point I cannot absolve myself from giving an account of the psychology of 'belief', of 'believers', for the use, as is only reasonable, of precisely the 'believers' them- selves. If there is today still no lack of those who do not know how *indecent* it is to 'believe' – or a sign of *décadence*, of a broken will to live – well, they will know it tomorrow. My voice reaches even the hard-of-hearing. – It appears, if I have not misheard, that there exists among Christians a kind of criterion of truth called 'proof by potency'. 'Belief makes blessed: *therefore* it is true.' – One might here object straight- away that this making-blessed itself is not proved but only *promised*: blessedness condi- tional upon 'believing' – one *shall* become blessed *because* one believes. . . . But *that* what the priest promises the believer for a 'Beyond' inaccessible to any control actually occurs, how could *that* be proved? – The alleged 'proof by potency' is there- fore at bottom only a further belief that the effect which one promises oneself from the belief will not fail to appear. In a formula: 'I believe that belief makes blessed – consequently it is true'. – But with that we have already reached the end of the argument. This 'consequently' would be the *absurdum* itself as a criterion of truth. – But if, with no little indulgence, we suppose that the fact that belief makes blessed be

11   French: piece of foolishness.

regarded as proved (– *not* merely desired, *not* merely promised by the somewhat suspect mouth of a priest): would blessedness – more technically, *pleasure* – ever be a
proof of truth? So little that it provides almost the counterproof, at any rate the strongest
suspicion against 'truth', when feelings of pleasure enter into the answer to the question 'what is true?' The proof by 'pleasure' is a proof *of* pleasure – that is all; when
on earth was it established that *true* judgements give more enjoyment than false ones
and, in accordance with a predetermined harmony, necessarily bring pleasant feelings
in their train? – The experience of all severe, all profound intellects teaches *the reverse*.
Truth has had to be fought for every step of the way, almost everything else dear to
our hearts, on which our love and our trust in life depend, has had to be sacrificed
to it. Greatness of soul is needed for it: the service of truth is the hardest service. –
For what does it mean to be *honest* in intellectual things? That one is stern towards
one's heart, that one despises 'fine feelings', that one makes every Yes and No a question of conscience! – Belief makes blessed: *consequently* it lies. . .

[. . .]

59

The whole labour of the ancient world *in vain*: have no words to express my feelings
at something so dreadful. – And considering its labour was a preparation, that only
the substructure for a labour of millennia had, with granite self-confidence, been
laid, the whole *meaning* of the ancient world in vain! . . . Why did the Greeks exist?
Why the Romans? – Every prerequisite for an erudite culture, all the scientific *methods*
were already there, the great, the incomparable art of reading well had already been
established – the prerequisite for a cultural tradition, for a uniform science; natural
science, in concert with mathematics and mechanics, was on the best possible road –
the *sense for facts*, the last-developed and most valuable of all the senses, had its schools
and its tradition already centuries old! Is this understood? Everything *essential* for
setting to work had been devised – methods, one must repeat ten times, *are* the essential, as well as being the most difficult, as well as being that which has habit and
laziness against it longest. What we have won back for ourselves today with an unspeakable amount of self-constraint – for we all still have bad instincts, the Christian instincts,
somewhere within us – the free view of reality, the cautious hand, patience and seriousness in the smallest things, the whole *integrity* of knowledge – was already there!
already more than two millennia ago! *And* good and delicate taste and tact! *Not* as
brain training! *Not* as 'German' culture with the manners of ruffians! But as body, as
gesture, as instinct – in a word, as reality. . . . *All in vain!* Overnight merely a memory!
– Greeks! Romans! nobility of instinct, of taste, methodical investigation, genius for
organization and government, the faith in, the *will* to a future for mankind, the great
Yes to all things, visibly present to all the senses as the *Imperium Romanum*,[12] grand
style no longer merely art but become reality, truth, *life*. . . . And not overwhelmed
overnight by a natural event! Not trampled down by Teutons and other such clod-
hoppers! But ruined by cunning, secret, invisible, anaemic vampires! Not conquered
– only sucked dry! . . . Covert revengefulness, petty envy become *master!* Everything
pitiful, everything suffering from itself, everything tormented by base feelings, the whole

---

12   Latin: Roman empire.

ghetto-world of the soul suddenly *on top*! – One has only to read any of the Christian agitators, Saint Augustine for example, to realize, to *smell*, what dirty fellows had therewith come out on top. One would be deceiving oneself utterly if one presupposed a lack of intelligence of any sort on the part of the leaders of the Christian movement – oh they are shrewd, shrewd to the point of holiness, these Church Fathers! What they lack is something quite different. Nature was neglectful when she made them – she forgot to endow them with even a modest number of respectable, decent, *cleanly* instincts. . . . Between ourselves, they are not even men. . . . If Islam despises Christianity, it is a thousand times right to do so: Islam presupposes *men* . . .

60

Christianity robbed us of the harvest of the culture of the ancient world, it later went on to rob us of the harvest of the culture of *Islam*. The wonderful Moorish cultural world of Spain, more closely related to *us* at bottom, speaking more directly to our senses and taste, than Greece and Rome, was *trampled down* (– I do not say by what kind of feet –): why? because it was noble, because it owed its origin to manly instincts, because it said Yes to life even in the rare and exquisite treasures of Moorish life! . . . Later on, the Crusaders fought against something they would have done better to lie down in the dust before – a culture compared with which even our nineteenth century may well think itself very impoverished and very 'late'. – They wanted booty, to be sure: the Orient was rich. . . . But let us not be prejudiced! The Crusades – higher piracy, that is all! German knighthood, Viking knighthood at bottom, was there in its element: the Church knew only too well what German knighthood can be *had* for. . . . The German knights, always the 'Switzers' of the Church, always in the service of all the bad instincts of the Church – but *well paid*. . . . That it is precisely with the aid of German swords, German blood and courage, that the Church has carried on its deadly war against everything noble on earth! A host of painful questions arise at this point. The German aristocracy is virtually *missing* in the history of higher culture: one can guess the reason. . . . Christianity, alcohol – the two *great* means of corruption. . . . For in itself there should be no choice in the matter when faced with Islam and Christianity, as little as there should when faced with an Arab and a Jew. The decision is given in advance; no one is free to choose here. One either *is* Chandala or one is *not*. . . . 'War to the knife with Rome! Peace, friendship with Islam': this is what that great free spirit, the genius among German emperors, Friedrich the Second, felt, this is what he *did*. What? does a German have to be a genius, a free spirit, before he can have *decent* feelings? How a German could ever have felt *Christian* escapes me . . .

61

Here it is necessary to touch on a memory a hundred times more painful for Germans. The Germans have robbed Europe of the last great cultural harvest Europe had to bring home – of the harvest of *Renaissance*. Is it at last understood, is there a *desire* to understand, *what* the Renaissance was? The *revaluation of Christian values*, the attempt, undertaken with every expedient, with every instinct, with genius of every kind, to bring about the victory of the opposing values, the *noble* values . . . Up till now *this* has been the only great war, there has been no more decisive interrogation than that conducted by the Renaissance – the question it asks is the question *I* ask – : neither has there been a form of *attack* more fundamental, more direct, and more strenuously delivered on the entire front and at the enemy's centre! To attack at the decisive point, in the very seat of Christianity, to set the *noble* values on the throne, which is to say to set them *into* the instincts, the deepest needs and desires of him who sits thereon. . . . I see in my mind's eye a *possibility* of a quite unearthly fascination and splendour – it seems to glitter with a trembling of every refinement of beauty, there seems to be at work in it an art so divine, so diabolically divine, that one might scour the millennia in vain for a second such possibility; I behold a spectacle at once so meaningful and so strangely paradoxical it would have given all the gods of Olympus an opportunity for an immortal roar of laughter – *Cesare Borgia as Pope*. . . . Am I understood? . . . Very well, *that* would have been a victory of the only sort *I* desire today –: Christianity would thereby have been *abolished*![13] – What happened? A German monk, Luther, went to Rome. This monk, all the vindictive instincts of a failed priest in him, fulminated in Rome *against* the Renaissance. . . . Instead of grasping with profound gratitude the tremendous event which had taken place, the overcoming of Christianity in its very *seat* – his hatred grasped only how to nourish itself on this spectacle. The religious man thinks only of himself. – What Luther saw was the *corruption* of the Papacy, while precisely the opposite was palpably obvious: the old corruption, the *peccatum originale*, Christianity *no* longer sat on the Papal throne! Life sat there instead! the triumph of life! the great Yes to all lofty, beautiful, daring things! . . . And Luther *restored the Church*: he attacked it. . . . The Renaissance – an event without meaning, a great *in vain*! – Oh these Germans, what they have already cost us! In vain – that has always been the *work* of the Germans. – The Reformation; Leibniz; Kant and so-called German philosophy; the Wars of 'Liberation'; the *Reich* – each time an in vain for something already in existence, for something *irretrievable*. . . . They are *my* enemies, I confess it, these Germans: I despise in them every kind of uncleanliness of concept and value, of *cowardice* in the face of every honest Yes and No. For almost a millennium they have twisted and tangled everything they have laid their hands on, they have on their conscience all the half-heartedness – three-eighths-heartedness! – from which Europe is sick – they also have on their conscience the uncleanest kind of Christianity there is, the most incurable kind, the kind hardest to refute, Protestantism. . . . If we never get rid of Christianity, the *Germans* will be to blame. . .

62

– With that I have done and pronounce my judgement. I *condemn* Christianity, I bring against the Christian Church the most terrible charge any prosecutor has ever uttered. To me it is the extremest thinkable form of corruption, it has had the will to the ultimate corruption conceivably possible. The Christian Church has left nothing untouched by its depravity, it has made of every value a disvalue, of every truth a lie, of every kind of integrity a vileness of soul. People still dare to talk to me of its 'humanitarian' blessings! To *abolish* any state of distress whatever has been profoundly

---

13   Nietzsche is encouraged in this speculation by similar reflections from Jacob Burckhardt in *Die Cultur der Renaissance in Italien* (*The Civilisation of the Renaissance in Italy*, 1860).

inexpedient to it: it has lived on states of distress, it has *created* states of distress in order to eternalize *itself*. . . . The worm of sin, for example: it was only the Church which enriched mankind with this state of distress! – 'Equality of souls before God', this falsehood, this *pretext* for the *rancune* of all the base-minded, this explosive concept which finally became revolution, modern idea and the principle of the decline of the entire social order – is *Christian* dynamite. . . . 'Humanitarian' blessings of Christianity! To cultivate out of *humanitas* a self-contradiction, an art of self-violation, a will to falsehood at any price, an antipathy, a contempt for every good and honest instinct! These are the blessings of Christianity! – Parasitism as the *sole* practice of the Church; with its ideal of green-sickness, of 'holiness' draining away all blood, all love, all hope for life; the Beyond as the will to deny reality of every kind; the Cross as the badge of recognition for the most subterranean conspiracy there has ever been – a conspiracy against health, beauty, well-constitutedness, bravery, intellect, *benevolence* of soul, *against life itself* . . .

Wherever there are walls I shall inscribe this eternal accusation against Christianity upon them – I can write in letters which make even the blind see. . . . I call Christianity the *one* great curse, the *one* great intrinsic depravity, the *one* great instinct for revenge for which no expedient is sufficiently poisonous, secret, subterranean, *petty* – I call it the *one* immortal blemish of mankind . . .

And one calculates *time* from the *dies nefastus*[14] on which this fatality arose – from the *first* day of Christianity! – *Why not rather from its last?* – *From today?* – Revaluation of all values!

14   Latin: unlucky day.

25

Ecce Homo: How One Becomes What One Is (1888)

Foreword

1

Seeing that I must shortly approach mankind with the heaviest demand that has ever been made on it, it seems to me indispensable to say *who I am*. This ought really to be known already: for I have not neglected to 'bear witness' about myself. But the disparity between the greatness of my task and the *smallness* of my contemporaries has found expression in the fact that I have been neither heard nor even so much as seen. I live on my own credit, it is perhaps merely a prejudice that I am alive at all? . . . I need only to talk with any of the 'cultured people' who come to the Ober-Engadin in the summer to convince myself that I am *not* alive . . . Under these circumstances there exists a duty against which my habit, even more the pride of my instincts revolts, namely to say: *Listen to me! far I am thus and thus. Do not, above all, confound me with what I am not!*

2

I am, for example, absolutely not a bogey-man, not a moral-monster – I am even an antithetical nature to the species of man hitherto honoured as virtuous. Between ourselves, it seems to me that precisely this constitutes part of my pride. I am a disciple of the philosopher Dionysos, I prefer to be even a satyr rather than a saint. But you have only to read this writing. Perhaps I have succeeded in giving expression to this antithesis in a cheerful and affable way – perhaps this writing had no point at all other than to do this. The last thing *I* would promise would be to 'improve' mankind. I erect no new idols; let the old idols learn what it means to have legs of clay. *To overthrow idols* (my word for 'ideals') – that rather is my business. Reality has been deprived of its value, its meaning, its veracity to the same degree as an ideal world has been *fabricated* . . . The 'real world' and the 'apparent world' – in plain terms: the *fabricated* world and reality . . . The *lie* of the ideal has hitherto been the curse on reality, through it mankind itself his become mendacious and false down to its deepest instincts – to the point of worshipping the *inverse* values to those which alone could guarantee it prosperity, future, the exalted *right* to a future.

3

– He who knows how to breathe the air of my writings knows that it is an air of the heights, a *robust* air. One has to be made for it, otherwise there is no small danger one will catch cold. The ice is near, the solitude is terrible – but how peacefully all things lie in the light! how freely one breathes! how much one feels *beneath* one! – Philosophy, as I have hitherto understood and lived it, is a voluntary living in ice and high mountains – a seeking after everything strange and questionable in existence, all that has hitherto been excommunicated by morality. From the lengthy experience afforded by such a wandering in the *forbidden* I learned to view the origin of moralizing and idealizing very differently from what might be desirable: the *hidden* history of the philosophers, the psychology of their great names came to light for me. – How much truth can a spirit *bear*, how much truth can a spirit *dare*? that became for me more and more the real measure of value. Error (– belief in the ideal –) is not blindness, error is *cowardice* . . . Every acquisition, every step forward in knowledge is the *result* of courage, of severity towards oneself, of cleanliness with respect to oneself . . . I do not refute ideals, I merely draw on gloves in their presence . . . *Nitimur in vetitum*:[1] in this sign my philosophy will one day conquer, for what has hitherto been forbidden on principle has never been anything but the truth. –

4

– Within my writings my *Zarathustra* stands by itself. I have with this book given mankind the greatest gift that has ever been given it. With a voice that speaks across millennia, it is not only the most exalted book that exists, the actual book of the air of the heights – the entire fact man lies at a tremendous distance *beneath* it – it is also the *profoundest*, born out of the innermost abundance of truth, an inexhaustible well into which no bucket descends without coming up filled with gold and goodness. Here there speaks no 'prophet', none of those gruesome hybrids of sickness and will to power called founders of religions. One has above all to *hear* correctly the tone that proceeds from this mouth, this halcyon tone, if one is not to do pitiable injustice to the meaning of its wisdom. 'It is the stillest words which bring the storm, thoughts that come on doves' feet guide the world –'[2]

> The figs are falling from the trees, they are fine and sweet: and as they fall their red skins split. I am a north wind to ripe figs.
> Thus, like figs, do these teachings fall to you, my friends: now drink their juice and eat their sweet flesh! It is autumn all around and clear sky and afternoon –[3]

Here there speaks no fanatic, here there is no 'preaching', here *faith* is not demanded: out of an infinite abundance of light and depth of happiness there falls drop after drop,

---

1 Latin: We strive after the forbidden (Ovid, *Amores*, III. 4. 17).
2 Quotation from *Z* II, "The Stillest Hour."
3 Quotation from *Z* II, "On the Blissful Islands."

word after word – a tender slowness of pace is the tempo of these discourses. Such things as this reach only the most select; it is an incomparable privilege to be a listener here; no one is free to have ears for Zarathustra . . . With all this, is Zarathustra not a *seducer*? . . . But what does he himself say when for the first time he again goes back into his solitude? Precisely the opposite of that which any sort of 'sage', 'saint', 'world-redeemer' and other *décadent* would say in such a case . . . He does not only speak differently, he *is* different . . .

I now go away alone, my disciples! You too now go away and be alone! So I will have it.

Go away from me and guard yourselves against Zarathustra! And better still: be ashamed of him! Perhaps he has deceived you.

The man of knowledge must be able not only to love his enemies but also to hate his friends.

One repays a teacher badly if one remains only a pupil. And why, then, should you not pluck at my laurels?

You respect me; but how if one day your respect should tumble? Take care that a falling statue does not strike you dead!

You say you believe in Zarathustra? But of what importance is Zarathustra? You are my believers: but of what importance are all believers?

You had not yet sought yourselves when you found me. Thus do all believers; therefore all belief is of so little account.

Now I bid you lose me and find yourselves; and only *when you have all denied me* will I return to you . . .[4]

FRIEDRICH NIETZSCHE

Why I Am So Wise

1

The fortunateness of my existence, its uniqueness perhaps, lies in its fatality: to express it in the form of a riddle, as my father I have already died, as my mother I still live and grow old. This twofold origin, as it were from the highest and the lowest rung of the ladder of life, at once *décadent* and *beginning* – this if anything explains that neutrality, that freedom from party in relation to the total problem of life which perhaps distinguishes me. I have a subtler sense for signs of ascent and decline than any man has ever had, I am the teacher *par excellence* in this matter – I know both, I am both. – My father died at the age of thirty-six: he was delicate, lovable and morbid, like a being destined to pay this world only a passing visit – a gracious reminder of life rather than life itself. In the same year in which his life declined mine too declined: in the thirty-sixth year of my life I arrived at the lowest point of my vitality – I still lived, but without being able to see three paces in front of me. At that time – it was 1879 – I relinquished my Basel professorship, lived through the summer like a shadow in St Moritz and the following winter, the most sunless of my life, *as* a shadow in Naumburg.

4   Quotation from *Z* I, "Of the Bestowing Virtue."

This was my minimum: 'The Wanderer and his Shadow' came into existence during the course of it. I undoubtedly knew all about shadows in those days . . . In the following winter, the first winter I spent in Genoa, that sweetening and spiritualization which is virtually inseparable from an extreme poverty of blood and muscle produced 'Daybreak'. The perfect brightness and cheerfulness, even exuberance of spirit reflected in the said work is in my case compatible not only with the profoundest physiological weakness, but even with an extremity of pain. In the midst of the torments which attended an uninterrupted three-day headache accompanied by the laborious vomiting of phlegm – I possessed a dialectical clarity *par excellence* and thought my way very cold-bloodedly through things for which when I am in better health I am not enough of a climber, not refined, not *cold* enough. My readers perhaps know the extent to which I regard dialectics as a symptom of *décadence*, for example in the most famous case of all: in the case of Socrates. – All morbid disturbances of the intellect, even that semi-stupefaction consequent on fever, have remained to this day totally unfamiliar things to me, on their nature and frequency I had first to instruct myself by scholarly methods. My blood flows slowly. No one has ever been able to diagnose fever in me. A doctor who treated me for some time as a nervous case said at last: 'No! there is nothing wrong with your nerves, it is only I who am nervous.' Any kind of local degeneration absolutely undemonstrable; no organically originating stomach ailment, though there does exist, as a consequence of general exhaustion, a profound weakness of the gastric system. Condition of the eyes, sometimes approaching dangerously close to blindness, also only consequence, not causal: so that with every increase in vitality eyesight has also again improved. – Convalescence means with me a long, all too long succession of years – it also unfortunately means relapse, deterioration, periods of a kind of *décadence*. After all this do I need to say that in questions of *décadence* I am *experienced*? I have spelled it out forwards and backwards. Even that filigree art of grasping and comprehending in general, that finger for nuances, that psychology of 'looking around the corner' and whatever else characterizes me was learned only then, is the actual gift of that time in which everything in me became more subtle, observation itself together with all the organs of observation. To look from a morbid perspective towards *healthier* concepts and values, and again conversely to look down from the abundance and certainty of *rich* life into the secret labour of the instinct of *décadence* – that is what I have practised most, it has been my own particular field of experience, in this if in anything I am a master. I now have the skill and knowledge to *invert perspectives*: first reason why a 'revaluation of values' is perhaps possible at all to me alone. –

2

Setting aside the fact that I am a *décadent*, I am also its antithesis. My proof of this is, among other things, that in combating my sick conditions I always instinctively chose the *right* means: while the *décadent* as such always chooses the means harmful to him. As *summa summarum*[5] I was healthy, as corner, as speciality I was *décadent*. That energy for absolute isolation and detachment from my accustomed circumstances, the way I compelled myself no longer to let myself be cared for, served, *doctored* – this betrayed an unconditional certainty of instinct as to *what* at that time was needful above all else.

5   Latin: as a totality.

I took myself in hand, I myself made myself healthy again: the precondition for this – every physiologist will admit it – is that *one is fundamentally healthy*. A being who is typically morbid cannot become healthy, still less can he make himself healthy; conversely, for one who is typically healthy being sick can even be an energetic *stimulant* to life, to more life. Thus in fact does that long period of sickness seem to me *now*: I discovered life as it were anew, myself included, I tasted all good and even petty things in a way that others could not easily taste them – I made out of my will to health, to *life*, my philosophy . . . For pay heed to this: it was in the years of my lowest vitality that I *ceased* to be a pessimist: the instinct for self-recovery *forbade* to me a philosophy of indigence and discouragement . . . And in what does one really recognize that someone has *turned out well*! In that a human being who has turned out well does our senses good: that he is carved out of wood at once hard, delicate and sweet-smelling. He has a taste only for what is beneficial to him; his pleasure, his joy ceases where the measure of what is beneficial is overstepped. He divines cures for injuries, he employs ill chances to his own advantage; what does not kill him makes him stronger. Out of everything he sees, hears, experiences he instinctively collects together *his* sum: he is a principle of selection, he rejects much. He is always in *his* company, whether he traffics with books, people or landscapes: he does honour when he *chooses*, when he *admits*, when he *trusts*. He reacts slowly to every kind of stimulus, with that slowness which a protracted caution and a willed pride have bred in him – he tests an approaching stimulus, he is far from going out to meet it. He believes in neither 'misfortune' nor in 'guilt': he knows how to *forget* – he is strong enough for everything to *have* to turn out for the best for him. Very well, I am the *opposite* of a *décadent*: for I have just described *myself*.

3

I consider the fact that I had such a father as a great privilege: the peasants he preached to – for, after he had lived for several years at the court of Altenburg, he was a preacher in his last years – said that the angels must look like he did. And with this I touch on the question of race. I am a pure-blooded Polish nobleman, in whom there is no drop of bad blood, least of all German. When I look for my profoundest opposite, the incalculable pettiness of the instincts, I always find my mother and my sister – to be related to such *canaille* would be a blasphemy against my divinity. The treatment I have received from my mother and my sister, up to the present moment, fills me with inexpressible horror: there is an absolutely hellish machine at work here, operating with infallible certainty at the precise moment when I am most vulnerable – at my highest moments . . . for then one needs all one's strength to counter such a poisonous viper . . . physiological contiguity renders such a *disharmonia praestabilita*[6] possible . . . But I confess that the deepest objection to the 'Eternal Recurrence', my real idea from the abyss, is always my mother and my sister. – But even as a Pole I am a monstrous atavism. One would have to go back centuries to find this noblest of races that the earth has ever possessed in so instinctively pristine a degree as I present it. I have, against everything that is today called *noblesse*, a sovereign feeling of distinction – I

---

6 Latin: pre-established disharmony. Parody of Leibniz's concept of the "pre-established harmony" of God's creation.

wouldn't award to the young German Kaiser the honour of being my coachman. There is one single case where I acknowledge my equal – I recognize it with profound gratitude. Frau Cosima Wagner is by far the noblest nature; and, so that I shouldn't say one word too few, I say that Richard Wagner was by far the most closely related man to me . . . The rest is silence[7] . . . All the prevalent notions of degrees of kinship are physiological nonsense in an unsurpassable measure. The Pope still deals today in this nonsense. One is least related to one's parents: it would be the most extreme sign of vulgarity to be related to one's parents. Higher natures have their origins infinitely farther back, and with them much had to be assembled, saved and hoarded. The great individuals are the oldest: I don't understand it, but Julius Caesar could be my father – or Alexander, this Dionysos incarnate . . . At the very moment that I am writing this the post brings me a Dionysos-head.

[. . .]

6

Freedom from *ressentiment*, enlightenment over *ressentiment* – who knows the extent to which I ultimately owe thanks to my protracted sickness for this too! The problem is not exactly simple: one has to have experienced it from a state of strength and a state of weakness. If anything whatever has to be admitted against being sick, being weak, it is that in these conditions the actual curative instinct, that is to say the *defensive and offensive instinct* in man becomes soft. One does not know how to get free of anything, one does not know how to have done with anything, one does not know how to thrust back – everything hurts. Men and things come importunately close, events strike too deep, the memory is a festering wound. Being sick *is* itself a kind of *ressentiment*. – Against this the invalid has only one great means of cure – I call it *Russian fatalism*, that fatalism without rebellion with which a Russian soldier for whom the campaign has become too much at last lies down in the snow. No longer to take anything at all, to receive anything, to take anything *into* oneself – no longer to react at all . . . The great rationality of this fatalism, which is not always the courage to die but can be life-preservative under conditions highly dangerous to life, is reduction of the metabolism, making it slow down, a kind of will to hibernation. A couple of steps further in this logic and one has the fakir who sleeps for weeks on end in a grave . . . Because one would use oneself up too quickly *if* one reacted at all, one no longer reacts: this is the logic. And nothing burns one up quicker than the affects of *ressentiment*. Vexation, morbid susceptibility, incapacity for revenge, the desire, the thirst for revenge, poison-brewing in any sense – for one who is exhausted this is certainly the most disadvantageous kind of reaction: it causes a rapid expenditure of nervous energy, a morbid accretion of excretions, for example of gall into the stomach. *Ressentiment* is the forbidden *in itself* for the invalid – *his* evil: unfortunately also his most natural inclination. – This was grasped by that profound physiologist Buddha. His 'religion', which one would do better to call a *system of hygiene* so as not to mix it up with such pitiable things as Christianity, makes its effect dependent on victory over *ressentiment*: to free the soul of *that* – first step to recovery. 'Not by enmity is enmity ended, by friendship is enmity ended': this stands at the beginning of Buddha's teaching – it is

7 Hamlet's dying words in Shakespeare's play, and one of Nietzsche's favorite quotations.

not morality that speaks thus, it is physiology that speaks thus. – *Ressentiment*, born of weakness, to no one more harmful than to the weak man himself – in the opposite case, where a rich nature is the presupposition, a *superfluous* feeling to stay master of which is almost the proof of richness. He who knows the seriousness with which my philosophy has taken up the struggle against the feelings of vengefulness and vindictiveness even into the theory of 'free will' – my struggle against Christianity is only a special instance of it – will understand why it is precisely here that I throw the light on my personal bearing, my *sureness of instinct* in practice. In periods of *décadence* I forbade them to myself as harmful; as soon as life was again sufficiently rich and proud for them I forbade them to myself as *beneath* me. That 'Russian fatalism' of which I spoke came forward in my case in the form of clinging tenaciously for years on end to almost intolerable situations, places, residences, company, once chance had placed me in them – it was better than changing them, than *feeling* them as capable of being changed – than rebelling against them . . . In those days I took it deadly amiss if I was disturbed in this fatalism, if I was forcibly awakened from it – and to do this was in fact every time a deadly dangerous thing. – To accept oneself as a fate, not to desire oneself 'different' – in such conditions this is *great rationality* itself.

[. . .]

Why I Am So Clever

8

In all this – in selection of nutriment, of place and climate, of recreation – there commands an instinct of self-preservation which manifests itself most unambiguously as an instinct for *self-defence*. Not to see many things, not to hear them, not to let them approach one – first piece of ingenuity, first proof that one is no accident but a necessity. The customary word for this self-defensive instinct is *taste*. Its imperative commands, not only to say No when Yes would be a piece of 'selflessness', but also to say *No as little as possible*. To separate oneself, to depart from that to which No would be required again and again. The rationale is that defensive expenditures, be they never so small, become a rule, a habit, lead to an extraordinary and perfectly superfluous impoverishment. Our *largest* expenditures are our most frequent small ones. Warding off, not letting come close, is an expenditure – one should not deceive oneself over this – a strength *squandered* on negative objectives. One can merely through the constant need to ward off become too weak any longer to defend oneself. – Suppose I were to step out of my house and discover, instead of calm and aristocratic Turin, the German provincial town: my instinct would have to blockade itself so as to push back all that pressed upon it from this flat and cowardly world. Or suppose I discovered the German metropolis, that built vice where nothing grows, where every kind of thing, good and bad, is dragged in. Would I not in face of it have to become a *hedgehog*? – But to have spikes is an extravagance, a double luxury even if one is free to have no spikes but *open* hands . . .

Another form of sagacity and self-defence consists in *reacting as seldom as possible* and withdrawing from situations and relationships in which one would be condemned as it were to suspend one's 'freedom', one's initiative, and become a mere reagent. I take as a parable traffic with books. The scholar, who really does nothing but 'trundle' books – the philologist at a modest assessment about 200 a day – finally loses altogether the ability to think for himself. If he does not trundle he does not think. He *replies* to a stimulus (– a thought he has read) when he thinks – finally he does nothing but react. The scholar expends his entire strength in affirmation and denial, in criticizing what has already been thought – he himself no longer thinks . . . The instinct for self-defence has in his case become soft; otherwise he would defend himself against books. The scholar – a *décadent*. – This I have seen with my own eyes: natures gifted, rich and free already in their thirties 'read to ruins', mere matches that have to be struck if they are to ignite – emit 'thoughts'. – Early in the morning at the break of day, in all the freshness and dawn of one's strength, to read a *book* – I call that vicious! –

9

At this point I can no longer avoid actually answering the question *how one becomes what one is*. And with that I touch on the masterpiece in the art of self-preservation – of *selfishness* . . . For assuming that the task, the vocation, the *destiny* of the task exceeds the average measure by a significant degree, there would be no greater danger than to catch sight of oneself *with* this task. That one becomes what one is presupposes that one does not have the remotest idea *what* one is. From this point of view even the *blunders* of life – the temporary sidepaths and wrong turnings, the delays, the 'modesties', the seriousness squandered on tasks which lie outside *the* task – have their own meaning and value. They are an expression of a great sagacity, even the supreme sagacity: where *nosce te ipsum*[8] would be the recipe for destruction, self-forgetfulness, self-*misunderstanding*, self-diminution, -narrowing, -mediocratizing becomes reason itself. Expressed morally: love of one's neighbour, living for others and other things *can* be the defensive measure for the preservation of the sternest selfishness. This is the exceptional case in which I, contrary to my rule and conviction, take the side of the 'selfless' drives: here they work in the service of *selfishness*, *self-cultivation*. – The entire surface of consciousness – consciousness *is* a surface – has to be kept clear of any of the great imperatives. Even the grand words, the grand attitudes must be guarded against! All of them represent a danger that the instinct will 'understand itself' too early –. In the meantime the organizing 'idea' destined to rule grows and grows in the depths – it begins to command, it slowly leads *back* from sidepaths and wrong turnings, it prepares *individual* qualities and abilities which will one day prove themselves indispensable as means to achieving the whole – it constructs the *ancillary* capacities one after the other before it gives any hint of the dominating task, of the 'goal', 'objective', 'meaning'. – Regarded from this side my life is simply wonderful. For the task of a *revaluation of values* more capacities perhaps were required than have dwelt together in one individual, above all antithetical capacities which however are not allowed to disturb or destroy one another. Order of rank among capacities; distance; the art of dividing without making inimical; mixing up nothing, 'reconciling' nothing; a tremendous multiplicity which is none the less the opposite of chaos – this has been the precondition, the protracted secret labour and artistic working of my instinct. The magnitude of its *higher protection* was shown in the fact I have at no time had the remotest

8   Latin: know thyself. See *BT* note 47 above.

idea what was growing within me – that all my abilities one day *leapt forth* suddenly ripe, in their final perfection. I cannot remember ever having taken any trouble – no trace of *struggle* can be discovered in my life, I am the opposite of an heroic nature. To 'want' something, to 'strive' after something, to have a 'goal', a 'wish' in view – I know none of this from experience. Even at this moment I look out upon my future – a *distant* future! – as upon a smooth sea: it is ruffled by no desire. I do not want in the slightest that anything should become other than it is; I do not want myself to become other than I am . . . But that is how I have always lived. I have harboured no desire. Someone who after his forty-fourth year can say he has never striven after *honours*, after *women*, after *money*! – Not that I could not have had them . . . Thus, for example, I one day became a university professor – I had never had the remotest thought of such a thing, for I was barely twenty-four years old. Thus two years earlier I was one day a philologist: in the sense that my *first* philological work, my beginning in any sense, was requested by my teacher Ritschl for his 'Rheinisches Museum' (*Ritschl* – I say it with respect – the only scholar gifted with genius whom I have encountered up to the present day. He was characterized by that pleasant depravity which distinguishes us Thuringians and which can render even a German sympathetic – to get to the truth we even prefer to go by secret paths. I should not with these words like to have in any way undervalued my close compatriot, the *sagacious* Leopold von Ranke . . .)

10

– I shall be asked why I have really narrated all these little things which according to the traditional judgement are matters of indifference: it will be said that in doing so I harm myself all the more if I am destined to fulfil great tasks. Answer: these little things – nutriment, place, climate, recreation, the whole casuistry of selfishness – are beyond all conception of greater importance than anything that has been considered of importance hitherto. It is precisely here that one has to begin to *learn anew*. Those things which mankind has hitherto pondered seriously are not even realities, merely imaginings, more strictly speaking *lies* from the bad instincts of sick, in the profoundest sense injurious natures – all the concepts 'God', 'soul', 'virtue', 'sin', 'the Beyond', 'truth', 'eternal life' . . . But the greatness of human nature, its 'divinity', has been sought in them . . . All questions of politics, the ordering of society, education have been falsified down to their foundations because the most injurious men have been taken for great men – because contempt has been taught for the 'little' things, which is to say for the fundamental affairs of life . . . Now, when I compare myself with the men who have hitherto been honoured as *pre-eminent* men the distinction is palpable. I do not count these supposed 'pre-eminent men' as belonging to mankind at all – to me they are the refuse of mankind, abortive offspring of sickness and vengeful instincts: they are nothing but pernicious, fundamentally incurable monsters who take revenge on life . . . I want to be the antithesis of this: it is my privilege to possess the highest subtlety for all the signs of healthy instincts. Every morbid trait is lacking in me; even in periods of severe illness I did not become morbid; a trait of fanaticism will be sought in vain in my nature. At no moment of my life can I be shown to have adopted any kind of arrogant or pathetic posture. The pathos of attitudes does *not* belong to greatness; whoever needs attitudes at all is *false* . . . Beware of all picturesque men! – Life has been easy for me, easiest when it demanded of me the most difficult things. Anyone who saw me during the seventy days of this autumn when I was uninterruptedly creating nothing but things of the first rank which no man will be able to do again or has done before, bearing a responsibility for all the coming millennia, will have noticed no trace of tension in me, but rather an overflowing freshness and cheerfulness. I never ate with greater relish, I never slept better. – I know of no other way of dealing with great tasks than that of *play*: this is, as a sign of greatness, an essential precondition. The slightest constraint, the gloomy mien, any kind of harsh note in the throat are all objections to a man, how much more to his work! . . . One must have no nerves . . . To *suffer* from solitude is likewise an objection – I have always suffered only from the 'multitude' . . . At an absurdly early age, at the age of seven, I already knew that no human word would ever reach me: has anyone ever seen me sad on that account? – Still today I treat everyone with the same geniality, I am even full of consideration for the basest people: in all this there is not a grain of arrogance, of secret contempt. He whom I despise *divines* that I despise him: through my mere existence I enrage everything that has bad blood in its veins . . . My formula for greatness in a human being is *amor fati*:[9] that one wants nothing to be other than it is, not in the future, not in the past, not in all eternity. Not merely to endure that which happens of necessity, still less to dissemble it – all idealism is untruthfulness in the face of necessity – but to *love* it . . .

Why I Write Such Good Books

1

I am one thing, my writings are another. – Here, before I speak of these writings themselves, I shall touch on the question of their being understood or *not* understood. I shall do so as perfunctorily as is fitting: for the time for this question has certainly not yet come. My time has not yet come, some are born posthumously. – One day or other institutions will be needed in which people live and teach as I understand living and teaching: perhaps even chairs for the interpretation of Zarathustra will be established. But it would be a complete contradiction of myself if I expected ears *and hands* for *my* truths already today: that I am not heard today, that no one today knows how to take from me, is not only comprehensible; it even seems to me right. I do not want to be taken for what I am not – and that requires that I do not take myself for what I am not. To say it again, little of 'ill will' can be shown in my life; neither would I be able to speak of barely a single case of 'literary ill will'. On the other hand all too much of *pure folly*! . . . It seems to me that to take a book of mine into his hands is one of the rarest distinctions anyone can confer upon himself – I even assume he removes his shoes when he does so – not to speak of boots . . . When Doctor Heinrich von Stein[10] once honestly complained that he understood not one word of my Zarathustra, I told him that was quite in order: to have understood, that is to say *experienced*, six sentences of that book would raise one to a higher level of mortals than 'modern' man could attain to. How *could* I, with *this* feeling of distance, even want

9   Latin: love of [one's] fate.
10   Heinrich von Stein (1857–87), German philosopher and writer.

the 'modern men' I know – to read me! – My triumph is precisely the opposite of Schopenhauer's – I say 'non *legor*, non *legar*'.[11] – Not that I should like to underestimate the pleasure which the *innocence* in the rejection of my writings has given me. This very summer just gone, at a time when, with my own weighty, too heavily weighty literature, I was perhaps throwing all the rest of literature off its balance, a professor of Berlin University kindly gave me to understand that I ought really to avail myself of a different form: no one read stuff like mine. – In the end it was not Germany but Switzerland which offered me the two extreme cases. An essay of Dr V. Widmann[12] in the *Bund* on 'Beyond Good and Evil' under the title 'Nietzsche's Dangerous Book', and a general report on my books as a whole on the part of Herr Karl Spitteler,[13] also in the *Bund*, constitute a maximum in my life – of what I take care not to say . . . The latter, for example, dealt with my Zarathustra as an *advanced exercise in style*, with the request that I might later try to provide some content; Dr Widmann expressed his respect for the courage with which I strive to abolish all decent feelings. – Through a little trick of chance every sentence here was, with a consistency I had to admire, a truth stood on its head: remarkably enough, all one had to do was to 'revalue all values' in order to hit the nail on the head with regard to me – instead of hitting my head with a nail . . . All the more reason for me to attempt an explanation. – Ultimately, no one can extract from things, books included, more than he already knows. What one has no access to through experience one has no ear for. Now let us imagine an extreme case: that a book speaks of nothing but events which lie outside the possibility of general or even of rare experience – that it is the *first* language for a new range of experiences. In this case simply nothing will be heard, with the acoustical illusion that where nothing is heard there *is* nothing . . . This is in fact my average experience and, if you like, the *originality* of my experience. Whoever believed he had understood something of me had dressed up something out of me after his own image – not uncommonly an antithesis of me, for instance an 'idealist'; whoever had understood nothing of me denied that I came into consideration at all. – The word 'overman' to designate a type that has turned out supremely well, in antithesis to 'modern' men, to 'good' men, to Christians and other nihilists – a word which, in the mouth of a Zarathustra, the *destroyer* of morality, becomes a very thoughtful word – has almost everywhere been understood with perfect innocence in the sense of those values whose antithesis makes its appearance in the figure of Zarathustra: that is to say as an 'idealistic' type of higher species of man, half 'saint', half 'genius' . . . Other learned cattle caused me on its account to be suspected of Darwinism; even the 'hero cult' of that great unconscious and involuntary counterfeiter Carlyle which I rejected so maliciously has been recognized in it. He into whose ear I whispered he ought to look around rather for a Cesare Borgia than for a Parsifal did not believe his ears. – That I am utterly incurious about discussions of my books, especially by newspapers, will have to be forgiven me. My friends, my publishers know this and do not speak to me about

---

11   Latin: "I *am* not read; I *shall not* be read." Schopenhauer's formulation is "Legor et legar" in the preface to the second edition of his treatise *Über den Willen in der Natur* (*On the Will in Nature*, 1854).

12   Joseph Viktor Widmann (1842–1911), Swiss writer.

13   Karl Spitteler (1845–1924), Swiss writer, awarded the Nobel Prize for Literature in 1919.

such things. In a particular instance I once had a sight of all the sins that had been committed against a single book – it was 'Beyond Good and Evil'; I could tell a pretty story about that. Would you believe it that the 'Nationalzeitung' – a Prussian newspaper, for my foreign readers – I myself read, if I may say so, only the Journal des Débats – could in all seriousness understand the book as a 'sign of the times', as the real genuine *Junker philosophy* for which the 'Kreuzzeitung' merely lacked the courage? . . .

2

This was said for Germans: for I have readers everywhere else – nothing but *choice* intelligences of proved character brought up in high positions and duties; I have even real geniuses among my readers. In Vienna, in St Petersburg, in Stockholm, in Copenhagen, in Paris and New York – I have been discovered everywhere: I have *not* been in Europe's flatland Germany . . . And to confess it, I rejoice even more over my non-readers, such as have never heard either my name or the word philosophy; but wherever I go, here in Turin for example, every face grows more cheerful and benevolent at the sight of me. What has flattered me the most is that old market-women take great pains to select together for me the sweetest of their grapes. That is *how far* one must be a philosopher . . . It is not in vain that the Poles are called the French among the Slavs. A charming Russian lady would not mistake for a moment where I belong. I cannot succeed in becoming solemn, the most I can achieve is embarrassment . . . To think German, to feel German – I can do everything, but *that* is beyond my powers . . . My old teacher Ritschl went so far as to maintain that I conceived even my philological essays like a Parisian *romancier* – absurdly exciting. In Paris itself there is astonishment over '*toutes mes audaces et finesses*'[14] – the expression is Monsieur Taine's –; I fear that with me there is up to the highest forms of the dithyramb an admixture of that salt which never gets soggy – 'German' – *esprit* . . . I cannot do otherwise, so help me God! Amen. – We all know, some even know from experience, what a longears is. Very well, I dare to assert that I possess the smallest ears. This is of no little interest to women – it seems to me they feel themselves better understood by me? . . . I am the *anti-ass par excellence* and therewith a world-historical monster – I am, in Greek and not only in Greek, the *Anti-Christ* . . .

3

I know my privileges as a writer to some extent; in individual cases it has been put to me how greatly habituation to my writings 'ruins' taste. One can simply no longer endure other books, philosophical ones least of all. To enter this noble and delicate world is an incomparable distinction – to do so one absolutely must not be a German; it is in the end a distinction one has to have earned. But he who is related to me through *loftiness* of will experiences when he reads me real ecstasies of learning: for I come from heights no bird has ever soared to, I know abysses into which no foot has ever yet strayed. I have been told it is impossible to put a book of mine down – I even disturb the night's rest . . . There is altogether no prouder and at the same time more exquisite kind of book than my books – they attain here and there the highest

14 French: "all my boldness and subtleties."

thing that can be attained on earth, cynicism; one needs the most delicate fingers as well as the bravest fists if one is to master them. Any infirmity of soul excludes one from them once and for all, any dyspepsia, even, does so: one must have no nerves, one must have a joyful belly. Not only does the poverty, the hole-and-corner air of a soul exclude it from them – cowardice, uncleanliness, secret revengefulness in the entrails does so far more: a word from me drives all bad instincts into the face. I have among my acquaintances several experimental animals on whom I bring home to myself the various, very instructively various reactions to my writings. Those who want to have nothing to do with their contents, my so-called friends for example, become 'impersonal': they congratulate me on having 'done it' again – progress is apparent, too, in a greater cheerfulness of tone . . . The completely vicious 'spirits', the 'beautiful souls',[15] the thoroughly and utterly mendacious have no idea at all what to do with these books – consequently they see the same as *beneath* them, the beautiful consistency of all 'beautiful souls'. The horned cattle among my acquaintances, mere Germans if I may say so, give me to understand they are not always of my opinion, though they are sometimes . . . I have heard this said even of Zarathustra . . . Any 'feminism' in a person, or in a man, likewise closes the gates on me: one will never be able to enter this labyrinth of daring knowledge. One must never have spared oneself, *harshness* must be among one's habits, if one is to be happy and cheerful among nothing but hard truths. When I picture a perfect reader, I always picture a monster of courage and curiosity, also something supple, cunning, cautious, a born adventurer and discoverer. Finally: I would not know how to say better to whom at bottom alone I speak than Zarathustra has said it: *to whom* alone does he want to narrate his riddle?

> To you, the bold venturers and adventurers, and whoever has embarked with cunning sails upon dreadful seas,
> to you who are intoxicated with riddles, who take pleasure in twilight, whose soul is lured with flutes to every treacherous abyss –
> for you do not desire to feel for a rope with cowardly hand; and where you can *guess* you hate to *calculate* . . .[16]

4

I shall at the same time also say a general word on my *art of style*. To *communicate* a state, an inner tension of pathos through signs, including the tempo of these signs – that is the meaning of every style; and considering that the multiplicity of inner states is in my case extraordinary, there exists in my case the possibility of many styles – altogether the most manifold art of style any man has ever had at his disposal. Every style is *good* which actually communicates an inner state, which makes no mistake as to the signs, the tempo of the signs, the *gestures* – all rules of phrasing are art of gesture. My instinct is here infallible. – Good style *in itself* – a piece of pure folly, mere 'idealism', on a par with the 'beautiful *in itself*', the 'good *in itself*', the 'thing *in itself*'

---

15 German: *"schöne Seelen."* Term from Winckelmann (see *TI* note 57 above) popularized by Goethe's novel *Wilhelm Meisters Lehrjahre* (*Wilhelm Meister's Apprenticeship*, 1795), Book VI of which is entitled "Bekenntnisse einer schönen Seele" ("Confessions of a Beautiful Soul").
16 Quotation from *Z* III, "Of the Vision and the Riddle."

... Always presupposing there are ears – that there are those capable and worthy of a similar pathos, that those are not lacking to whom one *ought* to communicate one-self. – My Zarathustra for example is at present still looking for them – alas! he will have to look for a long time yet! One has to be *worthy* of assaying him ... And until then there will be no one who comprehends the *art* which has here been squandered: no one has ever had more of the new, the unheard-of, the really new-created in artistic means to squander. That such a thing was possible in the German language remained to be proved: I myself would previously have most hotly disputed it. Before me one did not know what can be done with the German language – what can be done with language as such. The art of *grand* rhythm, the *grand style* of phrasing, as the expression of a tremendous rise and fall of sublime, of superhuman passion, was first discovered by me; with a dithyramb such as the last of the *third* Zarathustra, entitled 'The Seven Seals', I flew a thousand miles beyond that which has hitherto been called poesy.

5

– That out of my writings there speaks a *psychologist* who has not his equal, that is perhaps the first thing a good reader will notice – a reader such as I deserve, who reads me as good old philologists read their Horace. The propositions over which everybody is in fundamental agreement – not to speak of everybody's philosophers, the moralists and other hollow-heads and cabbage-heads – appear with me as naive blunders: for example that belief that 'unegoistic' and 'egoistic' are antitheses, while the *ego* itself is merely a 'higher swindle', an 'ideal'. There are *neither* egoistic *nor* unegoistic actions: both concepts are psychologically nonsense. Or the proposition 'man strives after happiness' ... Or the proposition 'happiness is the reward of virtue' ... Or the proposition 'pleasure and displeasure are opposites' ... The Circe of mankind, morality, has falsified all *psychologica* to its very foundations – has *moralized* it – to the point of the frightful absurdity that love is supposed to be something 'unegoistic' ... One has to be set firmly upon *oneself*, one has to stand bravely upon one's own two legs, otherwise one *cannot* love at all. In the long run the little women know that all too well: they play the deuce with selfless, with merely objective men ... Dare I venture in addition to suggest that I *know* these little women? It is part of my Dionysian endowment. Who knows? perhaps I am the first psychologist of the eternal-womanly. They all love me – an old story: excepting the *abortive* women, the 'emancipated' who lack the stuff for children. – Happily I am not prepared to be torn to pieces: the complete woman tears to pieces when she loves ... I know these amiable maenads ... Ah, what a dangerous, creeping, subterranean little beast of prey it is! And so pleasant with it! ... A little woman chasing after her revenge would over-run fate itself. – The woman is unspeakably more wicked than the man, also cleverer; goodness in a woman is already a form of *degeneration* ... At the bottom of all so-called 'beautiful souls' there lies a physiological disadvantage – I shall not say all I could or I should become medicynical. The struggle for *equal* rights is even a symptom of sickness: every physician knows that. – The more a woman is a woman the more she defends herself tooth and nail against rights in general: for the state of nature, the eternal *war* between the sexes puts her in a superior position by far. – Have there been ears for my definition of love? it is the only one worthy of a philosopher. Love – in its methods war, in its foundation the mortal hatred of the sexes. Has my answer been heard to the question how one cures – 'redeems' – a woman? One makes a child for her. The woman has need of children, the man is always only the means: thus spoke Zarathustra. – 'Emancipation of woman' – is the instinctive hatred of the woman who has *turned out ill*, that is to say is incapable of bearing, for her who has turned out well – the struggle against 'man' is always only means, subterfuge, tactic. When they elevate *themselves* as 'woman in herself', as 'higher woman', as 'idealist' woman, they want to *lower* the general level of rank of woman; no surer means for achieving that than grammar school education, trousers and the political rights of voting cattle. At bottom the emancipated are the *anarchists* in the world of the 'eternal-womanly',[17] the under-privileged whose deepest instinct is revenge . . . An entire species of the most malevolent 'idealism' – which, by the way, also occurs in men, for example in the case of Henrik Ibsen, that typical old maid – has the objective of *poisoning* the good conscience, the naturalness in sexual love . . . And so as to leave no doubt as to my opinion in this matter, which is as honest as it is strict, I would like to impart one more clause of my moral code against *vice*: with the word vice I combat every sort of anti-nature or, if one likes beautiful words, idealism. The clause reads: 'The preaching of chastity is a public incitement to anti-nature. Every expression of contempt for the sexual life, every befouling of it through the concept "impure", is *the* crime against life – is the intrinsic sin against the holy spirit of life.'

[. . .]

Why I Am a Destiny

1

I know my fate. One day there will be associated with my name the recollection of something frightful – of a crisis like no other before on earth, of the profoundest collision of conscience, of a decision evoked *against* everything that until then had been believed in, demanded, sanctified. I am not a man, I am dynamite. – And with all that there is nothing in me of a founder of a religion – religions are affairs of the rabble, I have need of washing my hands after contact with religious people . . . I do not *want* 'believers', I think I am too malicious to believe in myself, I never speak to masses . . . I have a terrible fear I shall one day be pronounced *holy*: one will guess why I bring out this book *beforehand*; it is intended to prevent people from making mischief with me . . . I do not want to be a saint, rather even a buffoon . . . Perhaps I am a buffoon . . . And none the less, or rather *not* none the less – for there has hitherto been nothing more mendacious than saints – the truth speaks out of me. – But my truth is *dreadful*: for hitherto the *lie* has been called truth. – *Revaluation of all values*: this is my formula for an act of supreme coming-to-oneself on the part of mankind which in me has become flesh and genius. It is my fate to have to be the first *decent* human being, to know myself in opposition to the mendaciousness of millennia . . . I was the first to *discover* the truth, in that I was the first to sense – *smell* – the lie as lie . . . My genius is in my nostrils . . . I contradict as has never been contradicted and am none the less the opposite of a negative spirit. I am a *bringer of good tidings* such as there has never been, I know tasks from such a height that any conception of them

17   Allusion to the closing lines of Goethe's *Faust II*, "The eternal-womanly / Draws us on," to which Nietzsche often refers ironically.

has hitherto been lacking; only after me is it possible to hope again. With all that I am necessarily a man of fatality. For when truth steps into battle with the lie of millennia we shall have convulsions, an earthquake spasm, a transposition of valley and mountain such as has never been dreamed of. The concept politics has then become completely absorbed into a war of spirits, all the power-structures of the old society have been blown into the air – they one and all reposed on the lie: there will be wars such as there have never yet been on earth. Only after me will there be *grand politics* on earth.

[. . .]

7

Have I been understood? – What defines me, what sets me apart from all the rest of mankind, is that I have *unmasked* Christian morality. That is why I needed a word which would embody the sense of a challenge to everyone. Not to have opened its eyes here sooner counts to me as the greatest piece of uncleanliness which humanity has on its conscience, as self-deception become instinct, as a fundamental will *not* to observe every event, every cause, every reality, as false-coinage *in psychologicis*[18] to the point of crime. Blindness in the face of Christianity is the *crime par excellence* – the crime *against life* . . . The millennia, the peoples, the first and the last, the philosophers and the old women – except for five or six moments of history, me as the seventh – on this point they are all worthy of one another. The Christian has hitherto been *the* 'moral being', a curiosity without equal – and, *as* 'moral being', more absurd, mendacious, vain, frivolous, *harmful to himself* than even the greatest despiser of mankind could have allowed himself to dream. Christian morality – the most malicious form of the will to the lie, the actual Circe of mankind: that which has *ruined* it. It is *not* error as error which horrifies me at the sight of this, *not* the millennia-long lack of 'good will', of discipline, of decency, of courage in spiritual affairs which betrays itself in its victory – it is the lack of nature, it is the utterly ghastly fact that *anti-nature* itself has received the highest honours as morality, and has hung over mankind as law, as categorical imperative! . . . To blunder to this extent, *not* as an individual, *not* as a people, but as mankind! . . . That contempt has been taught for the primary instincts of life; that a 'soul', a 'spirit' has been *lyingly invented* in order to destroy the body; that one teaches that there is something unclean in the precondition of life, sexuality; that the evil principle is sought in that which is most profoundly necessary for prosperity, in *strict* selfishness (- the very word is slanderous!); that on the other hand one sees in the typical signs of decline and contradictoriness of instinct, in the 'selfless', in loss of centre of gravity, in 'depersonalization' and 'love of one's neighbour' (– *lust for* one's neighbour!) the *higher* value, what am I saying! *value in itself*! . . . *What*! could mankind itself be in *décadence*? has it always been? – What is certain is that it has been *taught* only *décadence* values as supreme values. The morality of unselfing is the morality of decline *par excellence*, the fact 'I am perishing' translated into the imperative 'you all *shall* perish' – and *not only* into the imperative! . . . This sole morality which has hitherto been taught, the morality of unselfing, betrays a will to the end, it *denies* the very foundations of life. – Let us here leave the possibility open that it is not mankind which is degenerating but only that parasitic species of man the *priest*, who with the aid of morality has lied himself up to being the determiner of mankind's values – who

---

18 Latin: in psychological matters.

divines in Christian morality his means to *power* . . . And that is in fact *my* insight: the teachers, the leaders of mankind, theologians included, have also one and all been *décadents*: *thence* the revaluation of all values into the inimical to life, *thence* morality . . . *Definition of morality*: morality – the idiosyncrasy of *décadents* with the hidden intention of *avenging themselves on life* – and successfully. I set store by *this* definition. –

8

– Have I been understood? – I have not just now said a word that I could not have said five years ago through the mouth of Zarathustra. – The *unmasking* of Christian morality is an event without equal, a real catastrophe. He who exposes it is a *force majeure*, a destiny – he breaks the history of mankind into two parts. One lives *before* him, one lives *after* him . . . The lightning-bolt of truth struck precisely that which formerly stood highest: he who grasps *what* was then destroyed had better see whether he has anything at all left in his hands. Everything hitherto called 'truth' is recognized as the most harmful, malicious, most subterranean form of the lie; the holy pretext of 'improving' mankind as the cunning to *suck out* life itself and to make it anaemic. Morality as *vampirism* . . . He who unmasks morality has therewith unmasked the valuelessness of all values which are or have been believed in; he no longer sees in the most revered, even *canonized* types of man anything venerable, he sees in them the most fateful kind of abortion, fateful *because they exercise fascination* . . . The concept 'God' invented as the antithetical concept to life – everything harmful, noxious, slanderous, the whole mortal enmity against life brought into one terrible unity! The concept 'the Beyond', 'real world' invented so as to deprive of value the *only* world which exists – so as to leave over no goal, no reason, no task for our earthly reality! The concept 'soul', 'spirit', finally even 'immortal soul', invented so as to despise the body, so as to make it sick – 'holy' – so as to bring to all the things in life which deserve serious attention, the questions of nutriment, residence, cleanliness, weather, a horrifying frivolity! Instead of health 'salvation of the soul' – which is to say a *folie circulaire*[19] between spasms of atonement and redemption hysteria! The concept 'sin' invented together with the instrument of torture which goes with it, the concept of 'free will', so as to confuse the instincts, so as to make mistrust of the instincts into second nature! In the concept of the 'selfless', of the 'self-denying' the actual badge of *décadence*, being *lured* by the harmful, no longer being *able* to discover where one's advantage lies, self-destruction, made the sign of value in general, made 'duty', 'holiness', the 'divine' in man! Finally – it is the most fearful – in the concept of the *good* man common cause made with everything weak, sick, ill-constructed, suffering from itself, all that *which ought to perish* – the law of *selection* crossed, an ideal made of opposition to the proud and well-constituted, to the affirmative man, to the man certain of the future and guaranteeing the future – the latter is henceforth called the *evil man* . . . And all this was believed in *as morality*! – *Ecrasez l'infâme!*[20] –

9

– Have I been understood? – *Dionysos against the Crucified* . . .

19   French: recursive madness.
20   French: Crush the infamous thing! Quotation from Voltaire, Letter to d'Alembert, November 28, 1762.

26

Four Letters
(1888–9)

To Georg Brandes   Turin (Italy), *poste restante*,
                                      April 10, 1888

But, *verehrter Herr*,[1] what a surprise! Where did you find the courage to consider speaking in public about a *vir obscurissimus!*[2] . . . Do you perhaps believe that I am known in my own dear country? I am treated there as if I were something way-out and absurd, something that one need not for the time being *take seriously* . . . Obviously you sense that I do not take my compatriots seriously either: and how could I today, now that German *Geist*[3] has become a *contradictio in adjecto!*[4] – I am most grateful to you for the photograph. Unfortunately nothing of the kind is to be had from my side: the last pictures I had are in the possession of my married sister in South America.

I enclose a small curriculum vitae, the first I have written.

As regards the chronology of the particular books, you will find it on the back flyleaf of *Beyond Good and Evil*. Perhaps you no longer have that page.

The Birth of Tragedy was written between the summer of 1870 and the winter of 1871 (finished in Lugano, where I was living with Field Marshal Moltke's family).

The *Untimely Meditations*, between 1872 and summer, 1875 (there should have been thirteen of these; my health fortunately said No!).

What you say about *Schopenhauer as Educator* gives me pleasure. This little essay serves me as a signal of recognition: the man to whom it says nothing personal will probably not be further interested in me. It contains the basic scheme according to which I have so far lived; it is a rigorous promise.

Human, All Too Human with its two continuations, summer, 1876–79. *Daybreak*, 1880. The *Gay Science*, January, 1882. *Zarathustra*, 1883–85 (each part in about ten days). Perfect state of a "man inspired." All parts conceived on strenuous marches; absolute certainty, as if every thought were being called out to me. At the same time as the writing, the greatest physical elasticity and fullness –).

1   German: dear Sir.
2   Latin: most obscure man.
3   German: spirit, mind, intellect.
4   See *BGE* note 24 above.

Beyond Good and Evil, summer, 1885, in the Oberengadin and the following winter in Nice.

The *Genealogy* resolved on, written down, and the clean copy sent to the Leipzig printer between July 10 and 30, 1887. (Of course there are *philologica* by me too. But that does not concern either of us anymore.)

I am at the moment giving Turin a trial; I mean to stay here until June 5, and then go to the Engadin. Weather so far hard and bad as in winter. But the city superbly quiet and flattering to my instincts. The loveliest sidewalks in the world.

Greetings from your grateful and devoted   Nietzsche

A wretched pity that I do not understand either Danish or Swedish.

Curriculum vitae. I was born on October 15, 1844, on the battlefield of Lützen. The first name I heard was that of Gustav Adolf. My forebears were Polish aristocrats (Niëzky); it seems that the type has been well preserved, despite three German "mothers."[5] Abroad, I am usually taken for a Pole; even this last winter the aliens' register in Nice had me inscribed *comme Polonais*.[6] I have been told that my head and features appear in paintings by Matejko.[7] My grandmother was associated with the Goethe–Schiller circle in Weimar; her brother became Herder's successor as superintendent-general of the churches in the duchy of Weimar. I had the good fortune to be a pupil at the distinguished *Schulpforta*, which produced so many men of note (Klopstock, Fichte, Schlegel, Ranke, and so on, and so on) in German literature. We had teachers who would have done honor to any University (or have done so). I was a student at Bonn, and later in Leipzig; In his old age, Ritschl, in those days the foremost classical scholar in Germany, picked me out almost from the start. At the age of twenty-two I was contributing to the *Literarisches Zentralblatt* (Zarncke). The establishment of a classical society at Leipzig, which exists to this day, was my doing. In the winter of 1868–69 the University of Basel offered me a professorship; I did not even have my doctorate. Subsequently the University of Leipzig gave me the doctorate, in a very honorable fashion, without any examination, without even a dissertation. From Easter, 1869, until 1879 I was at Basel; I had to give up my German citizenship, because as an officer (mounted artillery) I would have been drafted too frequently and disturbed in my academic duties. Nevertheless, I am versed in the use of two weapons: saber and cannon – and, perhaps, one other . . . At Basel everything went very well, in spite of my youth; it happened, especially with examinations for doctorate, that the examinee was older than the examiner. It was my great good fortune that friendly relations developed between Jakob Burckhardt and myself, a very unusual thing for this very hermetic and aloof thinker. An even greater good fortune that, from the beginning of my life at Basel, I became indescribably intimate with Richard and Cosima Wager, who were then living on the estate at Tribschen near Lucerne, as on an island cut off from all their earlier associations. For several years we shared all our great and small

---

5   That is, three generations of maternal forebears: great-grandmother, grandmother, and mother. Nietzsche's Polish ancestry has since been disproved.
6   French: as a Pole.
7   Jan Matejko (1838–93), Poland's leading nineteenth-century artist, noted for his monumental historical pictures. It was Nietzsche's friend Resa von Schirnhofer who saw the likeness.

experiences – there was limitless confidence between us. (In Wagner's *Collected Writings*, volume 7, you will find an "epistle" from him to me, written when the *Birth of Tragedy* appeared). Through this relationship I met a wide circle of interesting men (and "man-esses") – actually almost everyone sprouting between Paris and Petersburg. Around 1876 my health grew worse. I spent a winter in Sorrento then, with my old friend Baroness Meysenbug (*Memoirs of an Idealist*) and the congenial Dr. Rée. My health did not improve. There were extremely painful and obstinate headaches which exhausted all my strength. They increased over long years, to reach a climax at which pain was habitual, so that any given year contained for me two hundred days of pain. The malaise must have had an entirely local cause – there was no neuropathological basis for it at all. I have never had any symptoms of mental disturbance – not even fever, no fainting. My pulse was as slow as that of the first Napoleon (= 60). My specialty was to endure the extremity of pain, *cru, vert*,[8] with complete lucidity for two or three days in succession, with continuous vomiting of mucus. Rumors have gone around that I am in a madhouse (have even died there). Nothing could be further from the truth. During this terrible period my mind even attained maturity: as testimony, the *Daybreak*, which I wrote in 1881 during a winter of unbelievable misery in Genoa, far from doctors, friends, and relatives. The book is, for me, a kind of "dynamometer" – I wrote it when my strength and health were at a minimum. From 1882 on, very slowly to be sure, my health was in the ascendant again: the crisis was passed (my father died very young, at exactly the age at which I myself was nearest to death). Even today I have to be extremely cautious; a few climatic and meteorological conditions are indispensable. It is not by choice – it is by necessity – that I spend the summers in the Oberengadin, the winters on the Riviera . . . Recently my sickness has done me the greatest service: it has liberated me, it has restored to me the courage to be myself . . . Also I am, by instinct, a courageous animal, even a military one. The long resistance has exasperated my pride a little. Am I a philosopher? What does that matter!

To Karl Knortz[9]

Sils Maria, Oberengadin,
June 21, 1888

Hochgeehrter Herr:
The arrival of two works of your pen, for which I am grateful to you, seems to vouch for your having in the meantime received my writings. The task of giving you some picture of myself, as a thinker, or as a writer and poet, seems to me extraordinarily difficult. The first major attempt of this kind was made last winter by the excellent Dane Dr. Georg Brandes, who will be known to you as a literary historian. He gave, at the University of Copenhagen, a longish course of lectures about me, entitled "The German Philosopher Friedrich Nietzsche," the success of which, as I have been informed from there, must have been brilliant. He imparted to an audience of three hundred persons a lively interest in the audacity of the questions which I have posed and, as

---

8   French: raw, green.
9   Karl Knortz (1841–1918), American journalist who was planning an essay on Nietzsche, and went on to publish four pamphlets on him, in German, between 1898 and 1913.

he says himself, he has made my name a topic of conversation throughout the north. In other respects, I have a more hidden circle of listeners and readers, to which also a few Frenchmen, like M. Taine, belong. It is my inmost conviction that these problems of mine – this whole position of an "Immoralist" – is still far too premature for the present day, still far too unprepared. The thought of advertising myself is utterly alien to me personally; I have not lifted a finger with that end in view.

Of my *Zarathustra*, I tend to think that it is the profoundest work in the German tongue, also the most perfect in its language. But for others to feel this will require whole generations to *catch up with* the inner experiences from which that work could arise. I would almost like to advise you to begin with the latest works, which are the most far-reaching and important ones (*Beyond Good and Evil* and *Genealogy of Morality*). To me, personally, the middle books are the most congenial, *Daybreak* and *The Gay Science* (they are the most personal).

The *Untimely Meditations*, youthful writings in a certain sense, deserve the closest attention for my development. In *Völker, Zeiten und Menschen*, by Karl Hillebrand, there are a few very good essays on the first *Untimely Meditations*. The piece against Strauss raised a great storm; the piece on Schopenhauer, which I especially recommend that you read, shows how an energetic and instinctively affirmative mind can accept the most salutory impulses even from a pessimist. With Richard Wagner and Frau Cosima Wagner, I enjoyed for several years, which are among the most valuable in my life, a relationship of deep confidence and inmost concord. If I am now one of the opponents of the Wagnerite movement, there are, needless to say, no mean motives behind this. In Wagner's *Collected Works*, volume nine (if I remember rightly) there is a letter to me which testifies to our relationship.

My pretension is that my books are of the first rank by virtue of their wealth of psychological experience, their fearlessness in face of the greatest dangers, and their sublime candor. I fear no comparison as far as the art of presentation in them and their claims to artistry are concerned. A love of long duration binds me to the German language – a secret intimacy, a deep reverence. Reason enough for reading hardly any books written in this language today.

I am, dear sir, yours truly, Professor Dr. Nietzsche

To Franz Overbeck   Turin, October 18, 1888

Dear friend:

Yesterday, with your letter in my hand, I took my usual afternoon walk outside Turin. The clearest October light everywhere: the glorious avenue of trees, which led me for about an hour along beside the Po, still hardly touched by autumn. I am now the most grateful man in the world – autumnally minded in every good sense of the word; it is my great *harvest time*. Everything comes to me easily, everything succeeds, although it is unlikely that anyone has ever had such great things on his hands. That the first book of the transvaluation of all values is finished, ready for *press*, I announce to to you with a feeling for which I have no words.[10] There will be *four* books; they will appear singly. This time – as an old artilleryman – I bring out my heavy guns; I am

---

10 Reference to *The Anti-Christ*.

afraid that I am shooting the history of mankind into two halves. With that work which I gave you an inkling of in my last letter, we shall soon be ready; it has, in order to save as much as possible of my now invaluable time, been printed with excellent precision.[11] Your quotation from *Human, All Too Human* came just at the right time to be included.[12] This work amounts to a hundred declarations of war, with distant thunder in the mountains; in the foreground, much jollity, of my *relative* sort[13] . . . This work makes it amazingly easy for anyone to gauge my degree of heterodoxy, which really leaves nothing at all intact. I attack the Germans along the whole front – you will have no complaints to make about "ambiguity." This irresponsible race, which has all the great misfortunes of culture on its conscience and at all *decisive* moments in history, was thinking of "something else" (the Reformation at the time of the Renaissance; Kantian philosophy just when a scientific mode of thought had been reached by England and France; "wars of liberation" when Napoleon appeared, the only man hitherto strong enough to make Europe into a political and *economic unity*), is thinking today of the *Reich*, this recrudescence of the world of the petty kingdoms and of culture atomism, at a moment when the great question of value is being asked for the first time. There was never a more important moment in history – *but who knows a thing about it?* The disproportion here is altogether necessary; at a time when an undreamed-of loftiness and freedom of intellectual passion is laying hold of the *highest* problem of humanity and is calling for a decision as to human destiny, the general pettiness and obtuseness *must* become all the more sharply distinct from it. There is no "hostility" to me whatever – people are simply deaf to anything I say; *consequently* there is neither a *for* nor an *against* . . .

To Jacob Burckhardt

On January 6, 1889
[Postmarked Turin, January 5, 1889]

Dear Professor:

Actually I would much rather be a Basel professor than God; but I have not ventured to carry my private egoism so far as to omit creating the world on his account. You see, one must make sacrifices, however and wherever one may be living. Yet I have kept a small student room for myself, which is situated opposite the Palazzo Carignano (in which I was born as Vittorio Emanuele)[14] and which moreover allows me to hear from its desk the splendid music below me in the Galleria Subalpina. I pay twenty-five francs, with service, make my own tea, and do my own shopping, suffer from torn boots, and thank heaven every moment for the *old* world, for which human beings have not been simple and quiet enough. Since I am condemned to entertain the next eternity with bad jokes, I have a writing business here which really leaves nothing to

11   Reference to *Twilight of the Idols*.
12   Another reference to *The Anti-Christ*: Nietzsche had added a reference to *Human, All Too Human* in *AC* 55.
13   Nietzsche's note: "With the immense tension of this period, a duel with Wagner was for me a perfect *relaxation*; also it was necessary, now that I am entering the lists in open warfare, to prove once and for all *publicly* that I have 'my hand free' . . ." The last expression indicates that he is "sparring for a fight."
14   Vittorio Emanuele II (1820–78), king of Italy.

be desired – very nice and not in the least strenuous. The post office is five paces away; I post my letters there myself, to play the part of the great *feuilletonist* of the *grande monde*.[15] Naturally I am in close contact with the *Figaro*, and so that you may have some idea of how harmless I can be, listen to my first two bad jokes:

Do not take the Prado case seriously. I am Prado, I am also Prado's father, I venture to say that I am also Lesseps.[16] . . . I wanted to give my Parisians, whom I love, a new idea – that of a decent criminal. I am also Chambige – also a decent criminal.

Second joke. I greet the immortals. M. Daudet is one of the *quarante*.[17]

Astu[18]

The unpleasant thing, and one that nags my modesty, is that at root every name in history is I; also as regards the children I have brought into the world, it is a case of my considering with some distrust whether all of those who enter the "Kingdom of God" do not also come *out of* God. This autumn, as lightly clad as possible, I twice attended my funeral, first as Count Robilant (no, he is my son, insofar as I am Carlo Alberto, my nature below), but I was Antonelli myself.[19] Dear professor, you should see this construction; since I have no experience of the things I create, you may be as critical as you wish; I shall be grateful, without promising I shall make any use of it. We artists are unteachable. Today I saw an operetta – Moorish, of genius[20] – and on this occasion have observed to my pleasure that Moscow nowadays and Rome also are grandiose matters. Look, for landscape too my talent is not denied. Think it over, we shall have a pleasant, pleasant talk together, Turin is not far, we have no very serious professional duties, a glass of Veltliner could be come by. Informal dress the rule of propriety.

With fond love   Your   Nietzsche

I go everywhere in my student overcoat; slap someone or other on the shoulder and say: *Siamo contenti? Son dio, ho fatto questa caricatura*[21] . . .

Tomorrow my son Umberto is coming with the charming Margherita whom I receive, however, here too in my shirt sleeves.

---

15   French: writer of features on high society (e.g. for the Parisian paper *Le Figaro*).

16   Prado and Chambige were criminals whose trials had recently been in the news; Ferdinand de Lesseps (1805–94) was the French engineer responsible for building the Suez Canal (1859–69) and starting to build the Panama Canal (1879).

17   French: forty. Alphonse Daudet (1840–97), French novelist, whose most recent work was *L'Immortel* (*The Immortal*, 1888).

18   Greek: city. Also a punning allusion to the hero of Daudet's *L'Immortel*, Léonard Astier.

19   Politician Count Robilant (1826–88) had recently died; he was reputed to be the illegitimate son of Carlo Alberto, king of Sardinia (1798–1849), whose legitimate son was Vittorio Emanuele II (see note 14 above). Nietzsche's apartment in Turin overlooked the Piazza Carlo Alberto, in which the infamous incident with the carthorse took place. Alessandro Antonelli (1798–1888) – architect of the Mole Antonelliana, Turin's highest point and most striking feature – had also recently died.

20   Nietzsche had developed a taste for French operetta by the later 1880s, and had been bowled over by the Spanish zarzuela opera *La gran via* when he heard it in mid-December 1888.

21   Italian: "Are we happy? I am God, I made this caricature."

The *rest* is for Frau Cosima . . . Ariadne[22] . . . From time to time we practice magic
. . .

I have had Caiaphas put in chains;[23] I too was crucified at great length last year by the German doctors. Wilhelm Bismarck and all anti-Semites done away with.[24]

You can make any use of this letter which does not make the people of Basel think less highly of me.

22   Both refer to Wagner's widow Cosima (1837–1930), to whom Nietzsche (in the guise of Dionysus) wrote on January 3, 1889 as "Princess Ariadne, my beloved."

23   Caiaphas was the Jerusalem high priest who found Jesus guilty of blasphemy and sent him to Pilate for sentencing (Matthew 26: 57ff.; John 18: 13ff.).

24   That is, the German emperor Wilhelm II (1859–1941) and Chancellor Otto von Bismarck (1815–98).

A Guide to Further Reading

Primary Works

1 Nietzsche in German

Briefwechsel: Kritische Gesamtausgabe, ed. Giorgio Colli, Mazzino Montinari, Norbert Miller and
Annemarie Pieper, ca. 20 vols (Berlin and New York: de Gruyter, 1975–).
Frühe Schriften, ed. Hans Joachim Mette, Karl Schlechta and Carl Koch, 2nd edn, 5 vols (Munich:
Beck, 1994).
Sämtliche Briefe: Kritische Studienausgabe, ed. Giorgio Colli and Mazzino Montinari, 8 vols (Berlin
and New York: de Gruyter; Munich: dtv, 1986).
Sämtliche Werke: Kritische Studienausgabe, ed. Giorgio Colli and Mazzino Montinari, 2nd edn,
15 vols (Berlin and New York: de Gruyter; Munich: dtv, 1988; CD-ROM 1995).
Werke: Kritische Gesamtausgabe, ed. Giorgio Colli, Mazzino Montinari, Wolfgang Müller-
Lauter, and Karl Pestalozzi, ca. 40 vols (Berlin and New York: de Gruyter, 1967–).

2 Nietzsche in English

2.1 Collections

Basic Writings of Nietzsche, ed. and trans. Walter Kaufmann (New York: Modern Library, 1968).
The Complete Works of Friedrich Nietzsche, ed. Oscar Levy, 18 vols (Edinburgh and London:
Foulis, 1909–13).
The Complete Works of Friedrich Nietzsche, ed. Ernst Behler and Bernd Magnus, 20 vols
(Stanford, CA: Stanford University Press, 1995–).
The Portable Nietzsche, ed. and trans. Walter Kaufmann (New York: Viking, 1954).

2.2 Individual Published Works

The Anti-Christ, Ecce Homo, Twilight of the Idols and Other Writings, ed. Aaron Ridley, trans.
Judith Norman (Cambridge and New York: Cambridge University Press, 2005).
Beyond Good and Evil, trans. Walter Kaufmann (New York: Vintage Books, 1966).
Beyond Good and Evil, trans. R. J. Hollingdale (Harmondsworth: Penguin, 1973).
Beyond Good and Evil, trans. Marion Faber (Oxford and New York: Oxford University Press,
1998).
Beyond Good and Evil, ed. Rolf-Peter Horstmann and Judith Norman, trans. Judith Norman
(Cambridge and New York: Cambridge University Press, 2001).
The Birth of Tragedy and The Case of Wagner, trans. Walter Kaufmann (New York: Vintage
Books, 1967).
The Birth of Tragedy, trans. Shaun Whiteside (Harmondsworth and New York: Penguin, 1993).
The Birth of Tragedy and Other Writings, ed. Raymond Geuss and Ronald Speirs, trans. Ronald
Speirs (Cambridge and New York: Cambridge University Press, 1999).
The Birth of Tragedy, trans. Douglas Smith (Oxford and New York: Oxford University Press,
2000).
Daybreak, trans. R. J. Hollingdale (Cambridge and New York: Cambridge University Press, 1982).
Dithyrambs of Dionysus, trans. R. J. Hollingdale (Redding Ridge, CT: Black Swan Books, 1984;
repr. London: Anvil Press, 2001).
Ecce Homo, trans. R. J. Hollingdale, 2nd edn (Harmondsworth and New York: Penguin, 1992).
Ecce Homo, trans. Duncan Large (Oxford and New York: Oxford University Press, 2006).
The Gay Science, trans. Walter Kaufmann (New York: Vintage Books, 1974).
The Gay Science, ed. Bernard Williams, trans. Josefine Nauckhoff and Adrian Del Caro
(Cambridge and New York: Cambridge University Press, 2001).

Human, All Too Human, trans. Marion Faber with Stephen Lehmann (Lincoln: University of Nebraska Press, 1984).

Human, All Too Human, trans. R. J. Hollingdale (Cambridge and New York: Cambridge University Press, 1986).

On the Advantage and Disadvantage of History for Life, trans. Peter Preuss (Indianapolis: Hackett, 1980).

On the Genealogy of Morality, ed. Keith Ansell Pearson, trans. Carol Diethe (Cambridge and New York: Cambridge University Press, 1994; 2nd rev. edn 2006).

On the Genealogy of Morals, trans. Douglas Smith (Oxford and New York: Oxford University Press, 1996).

On the Genealogy of Morality, trans. Maudemarie Clark and Alan J. Swensen (Indianapolis: Hackett, 1998).

Thus Spoke Zarathustra, trans. R. J. Hollingdale (Harmondsworth and Baltimore: Penguin, 1961).

Twilight of the Idols and The Anti-Christ, trans. R. J. Hollingdale (Harmondsworth and Baltimore: Penguin, 1968).

Twilight of the Idols, trans. Richard Polt (Indianapolis: Hackett, 1997).

Twilight of the Idols, trans. Duncan Large (Oxford and New York: Oxford University Press, 1998).

Unmodern Observations, trans. William Arrowsmith (New Haven, CT and London: Yale University Press, 1990).

Untimely Meditations, trans. R. J. Hollingdale (Cambridge and New York: Cambridge University Press, 1983).

2.3 Individual Unpublished Works and Notes (= *Nachlass*)

The Birth of Tragedy and Other Writings, ed. Raymond Geuss and Ronald Speirs, trans. Ronald Speirs (Cambridge and New York: Cambridge University Press, 1999).

Friedrich Nietzsche on Rhetoric and Language, ed. and trans. Sander L. Gilman, Carole Blair, and David J. Parent (New York and Oxford: Oxford University Press, 1989).

Philosophy in the Tragic Age of the Greeks, trans. Marianne Cowan (Chicago: Regnery, 1962).

Philosophy and Truth: Selections from Nietzsche's Notebooks of the Early 1870s, ed. and trans. Daniel Breazeale (Atlantic Highlands, NJ: Humanities Press, 1979).

The Pre-Platonic Philosophers, trans. Greg Whitlock (Urbana and Chicago: University of Illinois Press, 2001).

The Will to Power, ed. Walter Kaufmann, trans. Walter Kaufmann and R. J. Hollingdale (New York: Random House, 1967).

Writings from the Late Notebooks, ed. Rüdiger Bittner, trans. Kate Sturge (Cambridge and New York: Cambridge University Press, 2003).

2.4 Correspondence

Selected Letters of Friedrich Nietzsche, ed. and trans. Christopher Middleton (Chicago and London: University of Chicago Press, 1969; repr. Indianapolis: Hackett, 1996).

Secondary Works on Nietzsche in English (and English Translation)

The following is a list of selected secondary works on Nietzsche in English. In addition, two academic journals are exclusively devoted to publishing articles on Nietzsche in English: *The Journal of Nietzsche Studies*, published by the Pennsylvania State University Press on behalf of the Friedrich Nietzsche Society (UK), and *New Nietzsche Studies*, published by the Nietzsche Society (USA). Each year the Fall issue of *International Studies in Philosophy* (Binghamton University, NY) contains a selection of papers delivered to the North American Nietzsche Society, and the yearbook *Nietzsche-Studien* (Berlin and New York: de Gruyter) contains articles in English as well as German, French, and Italian.

1 Bibliographies

Hilliard, B. Bryan (ed.), *Nietzsche Scholarship in English: A Bibliography 1968–1992* (Urbana, IL: North American Nietzsche Society, 1992).
—— and Earl Nitschke (eds), *Nietzsche Scholarship in English: A Bibliography 1968–1992. Supplement* (Urbana, IL: North American Nietzsche Society, 1993).
Reichert, Herbert W. and Karl Schlechta (eds), *International Nietzsche Bibliography*, 2nd edn (Chapel Hill: University of North Carolina Press, 1968).
Schaberg, William H., *The Nietzsche Canon: A Publication History and Bibliography* (Chicago and London: University of Chicago Press, 1995).
Stiftung Weimarer Klassik and Herzogin Anna Amalia Bibliothek (eds), *Weimarer Nietzsche-Bibliographie*, 5 vols (Stuttgart: Metzler, 2000–2).

2 Biographies

Bergmann, Peter, *Nietzsche: "The Last Antipolitical German"* (Bloomington and Indianapolis: Indiana University Press, 1987).
Cate, Curtis, *Friedrich Nietzsche* (London: Hutchinson, 2002).
Chamberlain, Lesley, *Nietzsche in Turin: The End of the Future* (London: Quartet, 1996); *Nietzsche in Turin: An Intimate Biography* (New York: Picador, 1998).
Diethe, Carol, *Nietzsche's Women: Beyond the Whip* (Berlin and New York: de Gruyter, 1996).
—— *Nietzsche's Sister and the Will to Power: A Biography of Elisabeth Förster-Nietzsche* (Urbana and Chicago: University of Illinois Press, 2003).
Gilman, Sander L. (ed.), *Conversations with Nietzsche: A Life in the Words of his Contemporaries*, trans. David J. Parent (New York and Oxford: Oxford University Press, 1987).
Hayden, Deborah, "Friedrich Nietzsche, 1844–1900," in *Pox: Genius, Madness, and the Mysteries of Syphilis* (New York: Basic Books, 2003), pp. 172–99.
Hayman, Ronald, *Nietzsche: A Critical Life* (London: Weidenfeld & Nicolson; New York: Oxford University Press, 1980).
Hollingdale, R. J., *Nietzsche: The Man and his Philosophy*, 2nd edn (Cambridge and New York: Cambridge University Press, 1999).
Köhler, Joachim, *Zarathustra's Secret: The Interior Life of Friedrich Nietzsche*, trans. Ronald Taylor (New Haven, CT and London: Yale University Press, 2002).
Peters, H. F., *Zarathustra's Sister: The Case of Elisabeth and Friedrich Nietzsche* (New York: Crown, 1977).
Pletsch, Carl, *Young Nietzsche: Becoming a Genius* (New York: Free Press, 1991).
Safranski, Rüdiger, *Nietzsche: A Philosophical Biography*, trans. Shelley Frisch (New York: Norton; London: Granta, 2002).

Schain, Richard, *The Legend of Nietzsche's Syphilis* (Westport, CT and London: Greenwood Press, 2001).

Small, Robin, *Nietzsche and Rée: A Star Friendship* (Oxford: Clarendon Press; New York: Oxford University Press, 2005).

3 Introductions

Brandes, Georg, *Friedrich Nietzsche* (Ludlow: Living Time Press, 2002).

Danto, Arthur C., *Nietzsche as Philosopher*, 2nd edn (New York: Columbia University Press, 2005).

Emmanuel, Steven M. (ed.), *The Blackwell Guide to the Modern Philosophers: From Descartes to Nietzsche* (Malden, MA and Oxford: Blackwell, 2000).

Fink, Eugen, *Nietzsche's Philosophy*, trans. Goetz Richter (London and New York: Continuum, 2003).

Gilman, Sander L., *Nietzschean Parody: An Introduction to Reading Nietzsche* (Bonn: Bouvier Verlag Herbert Grundmann, 1976).

Holub, Robert C., *Friedrich Nietzsche* (New York: Twayne; London: Prentice Hall International, 1995).

Jaspers, Karl, *Nietzsche: An Introduction to the Understanding of his Philosophical Activity*, trans. Charles F. Wallraff and Frederick J. Schmitz (Chicago: Regnery; Tucson: University of Arizona Press, 1965; repr. Baltimore and London: Johns Hopkins University Press, 1997).

Kaufmann, Walter, *Nietzsche: Philosopher, Psychologist, Anti-Christ*, 4th edn (Princeton, NJ and London: Princeton University Press, 1974).

Krell, David Farrell and Donald L. Bates, *The Good European: Nietzsche's Work Sites in Word and Image* (Chicago and London: University of Chicago Press, 1997).

Salomé, Lou, *Nietzsche*, trans. Siegfried Mandel (Redding Ridge, CT: Black Swan Books, 1988; repr. Urbana and Chicago: University of Illinois Press, 2001).

Solomon, Robert C. and Kathleen M. Higgins, *What Nietzsche Really Said* (New York: Schocken Books, 2000).

—— (eds), *Reading Nietzsche* (New York and Oxford: Oxford University Press, 1988).

Spinks, Lee, *Friedrich Nietzsche* (London and New York: Routledge, 2003).

Stern, J. P., *A Study of Nietzsche* (Cambridge and New York: Cambridge University Press, 1979).

Tanner, Michael, *Nietzsche* (Oxford and New York: Oxford University Press, 1994).

van Tongeren, Paul J. M., *Reinterpreting Modern Culture: An Introduction to Friedrich Nietzsche's Philosophy* (West Lafayette, IN: Purdue University Press, 2000).

Vattimo, Gianni, *Nietzsche: An Introduction*, trans. Nicholas Martin (London: Continuum; Stanford, CA: Stanford University Press, 2002).

Welshon, Rex, *The Philosophy of Nietzsche* (Chesham: Acumen, 2004).

4 Critical Studies

4.1 General Studies

4.1.1 Edited Collections

Allison, David B. (ed.), *The New Nietzsche: Contemporary Styles of Interpretation*, 2nd edn (Cambridge, MA and London: MIT Press, 1985).

Bloom, Harold (ed.), *Friedrich Nietzsche* (New York, New Haven, CT, and Philadelphia: Chelsea House, 1987).

Conway, Daniel W., with Peter S. Groff (eds), *Nietzsche: Critical Assessments*, 4 vols (London and New York: Routledge, 1998).

Gillespie, Michael Allen and Tracy B. Strong (eds), *Nietzsche's New Seas: Explorations in Philosophy, Aesthetics, and Politics* (Chicago and London: University of Chicago Press, 1988).

Harrison, Thomas (ed.), *Nietzsche in Italy* (Saratoga, CA: Anma Libri, 1988).

Kemal, Salim, Ivan Gaskell, and Daniel W. Conway (eds), *Nietzsche, Philosophy and the Arts* (Cambridge and New York: Cambridge University Press, 1998).

Koelb, Clayton (ed.), *Nietzsche as Postmodernist: Essays Pro and Contra* (Albany: State University of New York Press, 1990).

Krell, David Farrell and David Wood (eds), *Exceedingly Nietzsche: Aspects of Contemporary Nietzsche-Interpretation* (London and New York: Routledge, 1988).

Lippitt, John (ed.), *Nietzsche's Futures* (Basingstoke and London: Macmillan; New York: St. Martin's Press, 1999).

Magnus, Bernd and Kathleen M. Higgins (eds), *The Cambridge Companion to Nietzsche* (Cambridge and New York: Cambridge University Press, 1996).

O'Hara, Daniel T. (ed.), *Why Nietzsche Now?* (Bloomington and Indianapolis: Indiana University Press, 1985).

Richardson, John and Brian Leiter (eds), *Nietzsche* (Oxford and New York: Oxford University Press, 2001).

Rickels, Laurence A. (ed.), *Looking After Nietzsche* (Albany: State University of New York Press, 1990).

Schrift, Alan D. (ed.), *Why Nietzsche Still? Reflections on Drama, Culture, and Politics* (Berkeley, Los Angeles, and London: University of California Press, 2000).

Sedgwick, Peter R. (ed.), *Nietzsche: A Critical Reader* (Oxford: Blackwell, 1995).

Solomon, Robert C. (ed.), *Nietzsche: A Collection of Critical Essays* (Garden City, NY: Anchor Books, 1973).

White, Richard (ed.), *Nietzsche* (Aldershot and Burlington, VT: Ashgate, 2002).

Yovel, Yirmiyahu (ed.), *Nietzsche as Affirmative Thinker: Papers Presented at the Fifth Jerusalem Philosophical Encounter, April 1983* (Dordrecht and Boston: Martinus Nijhoff, 1986).

4.1.2 Monographs and Single-Authored Collections

Ackermann, Robert John, *Nietzsche: A Frenzied Look* (Amherst and London: University of Massachusetts Press, 1990).

Alderman, Harold, *Nietzsche's Gift* (Athens: Ohio University Press, 1977).

Bataille, Georges, *On Nietzsche*, trans. Bruce Boone (London: Athlone Press; New York: Paragon House, 1992).

Conway, Daniel W., *Nietzsche's Dangerous Game: Philosophy in the Twilight of the Idols* (Cambridge and New York: Cambridge University Press, 1997).

Cox, Christoph, *Nietzsche: Naturalism and Interpretation* (Berkeley, Los Angeles and London: University of California Press, 1999).

Del Caro, Adrian, *Nietzsche contra Nietzsche: Creativity and the Anti-Romantic* (Baton Rouge and London: Louisiana State University Press, 1989).

Deleuze, Gilles, *Nietzsche and Philosophy*, trans. Hugh Tomlinson (London: Athlone Press; New York: Columbia University Press, 1983).

—— *Difference and Repetition*, trans. Paul Patton (London: Athlone Press; New York: Columbia University Press, 1994).

Habermas, Jürgen, *The Philosophical Discourse of Modernity: Twelve Lectures*, trans. Frederick Lawrence (Cambridge, MA: MIT Press; Cambridge: Polity, 1987).

Heidegger, Martin, *Nietzsche*, ed. David Farrell Krell, trans. David Farrell Krell et al., 4 vols (San Francisco and London: Harper & Row, 1979–87).

Heller, Erich, *The Importance of Nietzsche: Ten Essays* (Chicago and London: University of Chicago Press, 1988).

Heller, Peter, *Studies on Nietzsche* (Bonn: Bouvier, 1980).

Klein, Wayne, *Nietzsche and the Promise of Philosophy* (Albany: State University of New York Press, 1997).

Krell, David Farrell, *Infectious Nietzsche* (Bloomington and Indianapolis: Indiana University Press, 1996).

Lacoue-Labarthe, Philippe, *The Subject of Philosophy*, ed. Thomas Trezise, trans. Thomas Trezise et al. (Minneapolis and London: University of Minnesota Press, 1993), pp. 14–98 (chs 2–4 on Nietzsche).

Lea, F. A., *The Tragic Philosopher: A Study of Friedrich Nietzsche* (London: Methuen; New York: Philosophical Library, 1957; repr. London and Atlantic Highlands, NJ: Athlone Press, 1993).

Lukács, Georg, *The Destruction of Reason*, trans. Peter Palmer (London: Merlin; Atlantic Highlands, NJ: Humanities Press, 1980).

Magnus, Bernd, *Nietzsche's Existential Imperative* (Bloomington and London: Indiana University Press, 1978).

Marsden, Jill, *After Nietzsche: Notes Towards a Philosophy of Ecstasy* (Basingstoke and New York: Palgrave Macmillan, 2002).

Montinari, Mazzino, *Reading Nietzsche*, trans. Greg Whitlock (Urbana and Chicago: University of Illinois Press, 2003).

Müller-Lauter, Wolfgang, *Nietzsche: His Philosophy of Contradictions and the Contradictions of his Philosophy*, trans. David J. Parent (Urbana and Chicago: University of Illinois Press, 1999).

Richardson, John, *Nietzsche's System* (New York and Oxford: Oxford University Press, 1996).

Rosset, Clément, "Notes on Nietzsche," in *Joyful Cruelty: Toward a Philosophy of the Real*, trans. David F. Bell (New York and Oxford: Oxford University Press, 1993), pp. 22–69.

Schacht, Richard, *Nietzsche* (London and Boston: Routledge & Kegan Paul, 1983).

—— *Making Sense of Nietzsche: Reflections Timely and Untimely* (Urbana and Chicago: University of Illinois Press, 1995).

Schutte, Ofelia, *Beyond Nihilism: Nietzsche without Masks* (Chicago and London: University of Chicago Press, 1984).

Sloterdijk, Peter, *Thinker on Stage: Nietzsche's Materialism*, trans. Jamie Owen Daniel (Minneapolis: University of Minnesota Press, 1989).

Small, Robin, *Nietzsche in Context* (Aldershot and Burlington, VT: Ashgate, 2001).

Stambaugh, Joan, *The Problem of Time in Nietzsche*, trans. John Fred Humphrey (Lewisburg, PA: Bucknell University Press; London and Cranbury, NJ: Associated University Presses, 1987).

—— *The Other Nietzsche* (Albany: State University of New York Press, 1994).

Staten, Henry, *Nietzsche's Voice* (Ithaca, NY and London: Cornell University Press, 1990).

Taylor, Quentin P., *The Republic of Genius: A Reconstruction of Nietzsche's Early Thought* (Rochester, NY and Woodbridge: University of Rochester Press, 1998).

Waite, Geoff, *Nietzsche's Corps/e: Aesthetics, Politics, Prophecy, or, The Spectacular Technoculture of Everyday Life* (Durham, NC and London: Duke University Press, 1996).

White, Alan, *Within Nietzsche's Labyrinth* (New York and London: Routledge, 1990).

4.2 Specific Studies

4.2.1 Texts

Thus Spoke Zarathustra

Allison, David B., *Reading the New Nietzsche: "The Birth of Tragedy," "The Gay Science," "Thus Spoke Zarathustra," and "On the Genealogy of Morals"* (Lanham, MD and Oxford: Rowman & Littlefield, 2001), pp. 111–79 (ch. 3 on *Zarathustra*).

Goicoechea, David (ed.), *The Great Year of Zarathustra (1881–1981)* (Lanham, MD: University Press of America, 1983).

—— and Marco Zlomislić (eds), *Joyful Wisdom: Zarathustra's Joyful Annunciations Of . . .* (Port Colborne, Ontario: Thought House, 1996).

Gooding-Williams, Robert, *Zarathustra's Dionysian Modernism* (Stanford, CA: Stanford University Press, 2001).

Higgins, Kathleen Marie, *Nietzsche's "Zarathustra"* (Philadelphia: Temple University Press, 1987).

Jung, C. G., *Jung's Seminar on Nietzsche's "Zarathustra,"* ed. James L. Jarrett (Princeton, NJ: Princeton University Press, 1997).

Lampert, Laurence, *Nietzsche's Teaching: An Interpretation of "Thus Spoke Zarathustra"* (New Haven, CT and London: Yale University Press, 1986).

Rosen, Stanley, *The Mask of Enlightenment: Nietzsche's "Zarathustra"* (Cambridge and New York: Cambridge University Press, 1995).

Santaniello, Weaver, *Zarathustra's Last Supper: Nietzsche's Eight Higher Men* (Aldershot and Burlington, VT: Ashgate, 2005).

Shapiro, Gary, *Alcyone: Nietzsche on Gifts, Noise, and Women* (Albany: State University of New York Press, 1991).

Whitlock, Greg, *Returning to Sils-Maria: A Commentary to Nietzsche's "Also sprach Zarathustra"* (New York: Lang, 1990).

On the Genealogy of Morality

Allison, David B., *Reading the New Nietzsche: "The Birth of Tragedy," "The Gay Science," "Thus Spoke Zarathustra," and "On the Genealogy of Morals"* (Lanham, MD and Oxford: Rowman & Littlefield, 2001), pp. 181–247 (ch. 4 on the *Genealogy*).

Havas, Randall, *Nietzsche's Genealogy: Nihilism and the Will to Knowledge* (Ithaca, NY and London: Cornell University Press, 1995).

Leiter, Brian, *Nietzsche on Morality* (London and New York: Routledge, 2002).

Ridley, Aaron, *Nietzsche's Conscience: Six Character Studies from the "Genealogy"* (Ithaca, NY and London: Cornell University Press, 1998).

Schacht, Richard (ed.), *Nietzsche, Genealogy, Morality: Essays on Nietzsche's "Genealogy of Morals"* (Berkeley, Los Angeles and London: University of California Press, 1994).

Other Texts

Abbey, Ruth, *Nietzsche's Middle Period* (Oxford and New York: Oxford University Press, 2000).

Allison, David B., *Reading the New Nietzsche: "The Birth of Tragedy," "The Gay Science," "Thus Spoke Zarathustra," and "On the Genealogy of Morals"* (Lanham, MD and Oxford: Rowman & Littlefield, 2001).

Grundlehner, Philip, *The Poetry of Friedrich Nietzsche* (New York and Oxford: Oxford University Press, 1986).

Higgins, Kathleen Marie, *Comic Relief: Nietzsche's "Gay Science"* (New York and Oxford: Oxford University Press, 2000).

Lampert, Laurence, *Nietzsche's Task: An Interpretation of "Beyond Good and Evil"* (New Haven, CT and London: Yale University Press, 2001).

Porter, James I., *The Invention of Dionysus: An Essay on "The Birth of Tragedy"* (Stanford, CA: Stanford University Press, 2000).

Shapiro, Gary, *Nietzschean Narratives* (Bloomington and Indianapolis: Indiana University Press, 1989).

Silk, M. S. and J. P. Stern, *Nietzsche on Tragedy* (Cambridge and New York: Cambridge University Press, 1981).

Solomon, Robert C. and Kathleen M. Higgins (eds), *Reading Nietzsche* (New York and Oxford: Oxford University Press, 1988).

Steinbuch, Thomas, *A Commentary on Nietzsche's "Ecce Homo"* (Lanham, MD and London: University Press of America, 1994).

4.2.2 Subject Areas

Art/Aesthetics

Del Caro, Adrian, *Dionysian Aesthetics: The Role of Destruction in Creation as Reflected in the Life and Works of Friedrich Nietzsche* (Frankfurt am Main: Lang, 1981).

Gillespie, Michael Allen and Tracy B. Strong (eds), *Nietzsche's New Seas: Explorations in Philosophy, Aesthetics, and Politics* (Chicago and London: University of Chicago Press, 1988).

Kemal, Salim, Ivan Gaskell, and Daniel W. Conway (eds), *Nietzsche, Philosophy and the Arts* (Cambridge and New York: Cambridge University Press, 1998).

Martin, Nicholas, *Nietzsche and Schiller: Untimely Aesthetics* (Oxford: Clarendon Press; New York: Oxford University Press, 1996).

Megill, Allan, "Friedrich Nietzsche as Aestheticist," in *Prophets of Extremity: Nietzsche, Heidegger, Foucault, Derrida* (Berkeley, Los Angeles, and London: University of California Press, 1985), pp. 27–102.

Pothen, Philip, *Nietzsche and the Fate of Art* (Aldershot and Burlington, VT: Ashgate, 2002).

Rampley, Matthew, *Nietzsche, Aesthetics and Modernity* (Cambridge and New York: Cambridge University Press, 2000).

Shapiro, Gary, *Archaeologies of Vision: Foucault and Nietzsche on Seeing and Saying* (Chicago and London: University of Chicago Press, 2003).

Waite, Geoff, *Nietzsche's Corps/e: Aesthetics, Politics, Prophecy, or, The Spectacular Technoculture of Everyday Life* (Durham, NC and London: Duke University Press, 1996).

Winchester, James J., *Nietzsche's Aesthetic Turn: Reading Nietzsche after Heidegger, Deleuze, and Derrida* (Albany: State University of New York Press, 1994).

Young, Julian, *Nietzsche's Philosophy of Art* (Cambridge and New York: Cambridge University Press, 1992).

See also **Music** *below*

Classical Antiquity

Bishop, Paul (ed.), *Nietzsche and Antiquity: His Reaction and Response to the Classical Tradition* (Rochester, NY and Woodbridge: Camden House, 2004).

Dannhauser, Werner J., *Nietzsche's View of Socrates* (Ithaca, NY and London: Cornell University Press, 1974).

New Nietzsche Studies, 4/1–2 (Summer–Fall 2000): "Nietzsche, Philology, and Ancient Greece: 1872–2000."

O'Flaherty, James C., Timothy F. Sellner, and Robert M. Helm (eds), *Studies in Nietzsche and the Classical Tradition* (Chapel Hill: University of North Carolina Press, 1976).

Tejera, V[ictorino], *Nietzsche and Greek Thought* (Dordrecht: Nijhoff, 1987).

See also **4.2.3 Themes: Tragedy** *below*

Education

Cooper, David E., *Authenticity and Learning: Nietzsche's Educational Philosophy* (London and Boston: Routledge & Kegan Paul, 1983).

Derrida, Jacques, "Otobiographies: The Teaching of Nietzsche and the Politics of the Proper Name," trans. Avital Ronell, in Derrida, *The Ear of the Other: Otobiography, Transference, Translation*, ed. Christie McDonald (New York: Schocken Books, 1985), pp. 1–38.

Peters, Michael, James Marshall, and Paul Smeyers (eds), *Nietzsche's Legacy for Education: Past and Present Values* (Westport, CT: Bergin & Garvey, 2001).

Epistemology/Knowledge and Truth

Clark, Maudemarie, *Nietzsche on Truth and Philosophy* (Cambridge and New York: Cambridge University Press, 1990).

Grimm, Rüdiger H., *Nietzsche's Theory of Knowledge* (Berlin and New York: de Gruyter, 1977).

Havas, Randall, *Nietzsche's Genealogy: Nihilism and the Will to Knowledge* (Ithaca, NY and London: Cornell University Press, 1995).

May, Keith M., *Nietzsche on the Struggle between Knowledge and Wisdom* (Basingstoke: Macmillan; New York: St. Martin's Press, 1993).

Poellner, Peter, *Nietzsche and Metaphysics* (Oxford: Clarendon Press; New York: Oxford University Press, 1995).

Sadler, Ted, *Nietzsche: Truth and Redemption. Critique of the Postmodernist Nietzsche* (London and Atlantic Highlands, NJ: Athlone Press, 1995).

Wilcox, John T., *Truth and Value in Nietzsche: A Study of his Metaethics and Epistemology* (Ann Arbor: University of Michigan Press, 1974).

See also **4.2.3 Themes: Perspectivism** *below*

Ethics/Morality

Berkowitz, Peter, *Nietzsche: The Ethics of an Immoralist* (Cambridge, MA and London: Harvard University Press, 1995).

Bernstein, John Andrew, *Nietzsche's Moral Philosophy* (Rutherford, NJ: Fairleigh Dickinson University Press; London: Associated University Presses, 1987).

Brobjer, Thomas H., *Nietzsche's Ethics of Character: A Study of Nietzsche's Ethics and its Place in the History of Moral Thinking* (Uppsala: Uppsala University Department of History of Science and Ideas, 1995).

Hunt, Lester H., *Nietzsche and the Origin of Virtue* (London and New York: Routledge, 1991).

Leiter, Brian, *Nietzsche on Morality* (London and New York: Routledge, 2002).

May, Simon, *Nietzsche's Ethics and his War on "Morality"* (Oxford: Clarendon Press; New York: Oxford University Press, 1999).

Murray, Peter Durno, *Nietzsche's Affirmative Morality: A Revaluation Based in the Dionysian World-View* (Berlin and New York: de Gruyter, 1999).

Schacht, Richard (ed.), *Nietzsche's Postmoralism: Essays on Nietzsche's Prelude to Philosophy's Future* (Cambridge and New York: Cambridge University Press, 2001).

Scott, Charles E., *The Question of Ethics: Nietzsche, Foucault, Heidegger* (Bloomington: Indiana University Press, 1990).

Solomon, Robert C., *Living with Nietzsche: What the Great "Immoralist" Has To Teach Us* (New York and Oxford: Oxford University Press, 2003).

White, Richard J., *Nietzsche and the Problem of Sovereignty* (Urbana and Chicago: University of Illinois Press, 1997).

Wilcox, John T., *Truth and Value in Nietzsche: A Study of his Metaethics and Epistemology* (Ann Arbor: University of Michigan Press, 1974).

See also **4.2.1 Texts: *On the Genealogy of Morality*** *above*

Language/Philology

Blondel, Eric, *Nietzsche: The Body and Culture: Philosophy as a Philological Genealogy*, trans. Seán Hand (London: Athlone Press; Stanford, CA: Stanford University Press, 1991).

Crawford, Claudia, *The Beginnings of Nietzsche's Theory of Language* (Berlin and New York: de Gruyter, 1988).

Graybeal, Jean, *Language and "the Feminine" in Nietzsche and Heidegger* (Bloomington and Indianapolis: Indiana University Press, 1990).

Journal of Nietzsche Studies, 22 (Autumn 2001): "Nietzsche's Language and Use of Language," ed. Herman Siemens.

New Nietzsche Studies, 4/1–2 (Summer–Fall 2000): "Nietzsche, Philology, and Ancient Greece: 1872–2000."

Porter, James I., *Nietzsche and the Philology of the Future* (Stanford, CA: Stanford University Press, 2000).

See also **Rhetoric/Style** *below*

Literature

Bishop, Paul and R. H. Stephenson, *Friedrich Nietzsche and Weimar Classicism* (Rochester, NY and Woodbridge: Camden House, 2004).

Dürr, Volker, Reinhold Grimm, and Kathy Harms (eds), *Nietzsche: Literature and Values* (Madison and London: University of Wisconsin Press, 1988).

Journal of Nietzsche Studies, 13 (Spring 1997): "Nietzsche and German Literature," ed. Duncan Large.

Magnus, Bernd, Stanley Stewart and Jean-Pierre Mileur, *Nietzsche's Case: Philosophy as/and Literature* (New York and London: Routledge, 1993).

Martin, Nicholas, *Nietzsche and Schiller: Untimely Aesthetics* (Oxford: Clarendon Press; New York: Oxford University Press, 1996).

—— (ed.), *Nietzsche and the German Tradition* (Oxford and Berne: Lang, 2003).

Nehamas, Alexander, *Nietzsche: Life as Literature* (Cambridge, MA and London: Harvard University Press, 1985).

Schrift, Alan D. (ed.), *Why Nietzsche Still? Reflections on Drama, Culture, and Politics* (Berkeley, Los Angeles, and London: University of California Press, 2000).

Williams, W. D., *Nietzsche and the French: A Study of the Influence of Nietzsche's French Reading on his Thought and Writing* (Oxford: Blackwell, 1952).

Medicine/Physiology

Ahern, Daniel R., *Nietzsche as Cultural Physician* (University Park: Pennsylvania State University Press, 1995).

Blondel, Eric, *Nietzsche: The Body and Culture. Philosophy as a Philological Genealogy*, trans. Seán Hand (London: Athlone Press; Stanford, CA: Stanford University Press, 1991).

Metaphysics

Haar, Michel, *Nietzsche and Metaphysics*, trans. Michael Gendre (Albany: State University of New York Press, 1996).

Houlgate, Stephen, *Hegel, Nietzsche and the Criticism of Metaphysics* (Cambridge and New York: Cambridge University Press, 1986).

Poellner, Peter, *Nietzsche and Metaphysics* (Oxford: Clarendon Press; New York: Oxford University Press, 1995).

Music

Fischer-Dieskau, Dietrich, *Wagner and Nietzsche*, trans. Joachim Neugroschel (New York: Seabury Press; London: Sidgwick & Jackson, 1976).

Hollinrake, Roger, *Nietzsche, Wagner and the Philosophy of Pessimism* (London and Boston: Allen & Unwin, 1982).

Köhler, Joachim, *Nietzsche and Wagner: A Lesson in Subjugation*, trans. Ronald Taylor (New Haven, CT and London: Yale University Press, 1998).

Liébert, Georges, *Nietzsche and Music*, trans. David Pellauer and Graham Parkes (Chicago and London: University of Chicago Press, 2003).

Love, Frederick R., *Young Nietzsche and the Wagnerian Experience* (Chapel Hill: University of North Carolina Press, 1963).

New Nietzsche Studies, 1/1–2 (Fall–Winter 1996): "Nietzsche and Music," pp. 1–78.

Nature/Human Nature

Acampora, Christa Davis and Ralph R. (eds), *A Nietzschean Bestiary: Becoming Animal Beyond Docile and Brutal* (Lanham, MD and Oxford: Rowman & Littlefield, 2004).

Del Caro, Adrian, *Grounding the Nietzsche Rhetoric of Earth* (Berlin and New York: de Gruyter, 2004).

Miller, Elaine P., *The Vegetative Soul: From Philosophy of Nature to Subjectivity in the Feminine* (Albany: State University of New York Press, 2002), ch. 6 on Nietzsche.

Moles, Alistair, *Nietzsche's Philosophy of Nature and Cosmology* (New York: Lang, 1990).

New Nietzsche Studies, 5/1–2 (Spring–Summer 2002): "Nietzsche's Ecology," pp. 1–94.

New Nietzsche Studies, 5/3–4 and 6/1–2 (Winter 2003 and Spring 2004): "Ecology, Dynamics, Chaos, Nature."

See also **4.2.3 Themes: Will to Power** *below*

Philosophical Precursors

Donnellan, Brendan, *Nietzsche and the French Moralists* (Bonn: Bouvier, 1982).

Dudley, Will, *Hegel, Nietzsche, and Philosophy: Thinking Freedom* (Cambridge and New York: Cambridge University Press, 2002).

Foucault, Michel, "Nietzsche, Freud, Marx," trans. Alan D. Schrift, in Gayle L. Ormiston and Alan D. Schrift (eds), *Transforming the Hermeneutic Context: From Nietzsche to Nancy* (Albany: State University of New York Press, 1990), pp. 59–68.

Green, Michael Steven, *Nietzsche and the Transcendental Tradition* (Urbana and Chicago: University of Illinois Press, 2002).

Hill, R. Kevin, *Nietzsche's Critiques: The Kantian Foundations of his Thought* (Oxford: Clarendon Press; New York: Oxford University Press, 2003).

Houlgate, Stephen, *Hegel, Nietzsche and the Criticism of Metaphysics* (Cambridge and New York: Cambridge University Press, 1986).

Janaway, Christopher (ed.), *Willing and Nothingness: Schopenhauer as Nietzsche's Educator* (Oxford: Clarendon Press; New York: Oxford University Press, 1988).

Jurist, Elliot L., *Beyond Hegel and Nietzsche: Philosophy, Culture, and Agency* (Cambridge, MA and London: MIT Press, 2000).

Kellenberger, J[ames], *Kierkegaard and Nietzsche: Faith and Eternal Acceptance* (Basingstoke: Macmillan; New York: St. Martin's Press, 1997).

Lampert, Laurence, *Nietzsche and Modern Times: A Study of Bacon, Descartes, and Nietzsche* (New Haven, CT and London: Yale University Press, 1993).

Love, Nancy S., *Marx, Nietzsche, and Modernity* (New York and Guildford: Columbia University Press, 1986).

Löwith, Karl, *From Hegel to Nietzsche: The Revolution in Nineteenth-Century Thought*, trans. David E. Green (New York: Holt, Rinehart & Winston, 1964).

Martin, Nicholas (ed.), *Nietzsche and the German Tradition* (Oxford and Berne: Lang, 2003).

Parkes, Graham (ed.), *Nietzsche and Asian Thought* (Chicago and London: University of Chicago Press, 1991).

Simmel, Georg, *Schopenhauer and Nietzsche*, trans. Helmut Loiskandl, Deena Weinstein, and Michael Weinstein (Amherst: University of Massachusetts Press, 1986; repr. Urbana and Chicago: University of Illinois Press, 1991).

Stack, George J., *Lange and Nietzsche* (Berlin and New York: de Gruyter, 1983).

—— *Nietzsche and Emerson: An Elective Affinity* (Athens: Ohio University Press, 1992).

Williams, W. D., *Nietzsche and the French: A Study of the Influence of Nietzsche's French Reading on his Thought and Writing* (Oxford: Blackwell, 1952).

See also **Classical Antiquity** *above*

Politics

Appel, Fredrick, *Nietzsche contra Democracy* (Ithaca, NY and London: Cornell University Press, 1999).

Bergmann, Peter, *Nietzsche: "The Last Antipolitical German"* (Bloomington and Indianapolis: Indiana University Press, 1987).

Conway, Daniel W., *Nietzsche and the Political* (London and New York: Routledge, 1997).

Derrida, Jacques, "Otobiographies: The Teaching of Nietzsche and the Politics of the Proper Name," trans. Avital Ronell, in Derrida, *The Ear of the Other: Otobiography, Transference, Translation*, ed. Christie McDonald (New York: Schocken Books, 1985), pp. 1–38.

Detwiler, Bruce, *Nietzsche and the Politics of Aristocratic Radicalism* (Chicago and London: University of Chicago Press, 1990).

Dombowsky, Don, *Nietzsche's Machiavellian Politics: The Outlaw Prince* (Basingstoke: Palgrave Macmillan, 2004).

Gillespie, Michael Allen and Tracy B. Strong (eds), *Nietzsche's New Seas: Explorations in Philosophy, Aesthetics, and Politics* (Chicago and London: University of Chicago Press, 1988).

Golomb, Jacob and Robert S. Wistrich (eds), *Nietzsche, Godfather of Fascism? On the Uses and Abuses of a Philosophy* (Princeton, NJ and Oxford: Princeton University Press, 2002).

Hatab, Lawrence J., *A Nietzschean Defense of Democracy: An Experiment in Postmodern Politics* (Chicago and La Salle, IL: Open Court, 1995).

McIntyre, Alex, *The Sovereignty of Joy: Nietzsche's Vision of Grand Politics* (Toronto and London: University of Toronto Press, 1997).

New Nietzsche Studies, 2/1–2 (1997): "Nietzsche and the Political."

Owen, David, *Nietzsche, Politics and Modernity: A Critique of Liberal Reason* (London, Thousand Oaks, CA and New Delhi: Sage, 1995).

Patton, Paul (ed.), *Nietzsche, Feminism and Political Theory* (London and New York: Routledge, 1993).

Schrift, Alan D. (ed.), *Why Nietzsche Still? Reflections on Drama, Culture, and Politics* (Berkeley, Los Angeles and London: University of California Press, 2000).

Strong, Tracy B., *Friedrich Nietzsche and the Politics of Transfiguration*, 3rd edn (Urbana and Chicago: University of Illinois Press, 2000).

Thiele, Leslie Paul, *Friedrich Nietzsche and the Politics of the Soul: A Study of Heroic Individualism* (Princeton, NJ and London: Princeton University Press, 1990).

Waite, Geoff, *Nietzsche's Corps/e: Aesthetics, Politics, Prophecy, or, The Spectacular Technoculture of Everyday Life* (Durham, NC and London: Duke University Press, 1996).

Warren, Mark, *Nietzsche and Political Thought* (Cambridge, MA and London: MIT Press, 1988).

Psychology/Psychoanalysis

Assoun, Paul-Laurent, *Freud and Nietzsche*, trans. Richard L. Collier, Jr. (London and New Brunswick, NJ: Athlone Press, 2000).

Bishop, Paul, *The Dionysian Self: C. G. Jung's Reception of Friedrich Nietzsche* (Berlin and New York: de Gruyter, 1995).

Dixon, Patricia, *Nietzsche and Jung: Sailing a Deeper Night* (New York: Lang, 1999).

Foucault, Michel, "Nietzsche, Freud, Marx," trans. Alan D. Schrift, in *Transforming the Hermeneutic Context: From Nietzsche to Nancy*, ed. Gayle L. Ormiston and Alan D. Schrift (Albany: State University of New York Press, 1990), pp. 59–68.

Golomb, Jacob, *Nietzsche's Enticing Psychology of Power* (Ames: Iowa State University Press; Jerusalem: Magnes Press, 1989).

—— Weaver Santaniello, and Ronald L. Lehrer (eds), *Nietzsche and Depth Psychology* (Albany: State University of New York Press, 1999).

Huskinson, Lucy, *Nietzsche and Jung: The Whole Self in the Union of Opposites* (Hove and New York: Brunner-Routledge, 2004).

Lehrer, Ronald, *Nietzsche's Presence in Freud's Life and Thought: On the Origins of a Psychology of Dynamic Unconscious Mental Functioning* (Albany: State University of New York Press, 1995).

Parkes, Graham, *Composing the Soul: Reaches of Nietzsche's Psychology* (Chicago and London: University of Chicago Press, 1994).

Zupancic, Alenka, *The Shortest Shadow: Nietzsche's Philosophy of the Two* (Cambridge, MA and London: MIT Press, 2003).

Religion

Fraser, Giles, *Redeeming Nietzsche: On the Piety of Unbelief* (London and New York: Routledge, 2002).

Geffré, Claude, Jean Pierre Jossua, and Marcus Lefébure (eds), *Nietzsche and Christianity* (Edinburgh: Clark; New York: Seabury Press, 1981).

Golomb, Jacob (ed.), *Nietzsche and Jewish Culture* (London and New York: Routledge, 1997).

Heidegger, Martin, "The Word of Nietzsche: 'God is Dead'," in Heidegger, *The Question Concerning Technology and Other Essays*, trans. William Lovitt (New York: Harper & Row, 1977), pp. 53–115.

Jaspers, Karl, *Nietzsche and Christianity* (Chicago: Regnery, 1961).

Journal of Nietzsche Studies, 19 (Spring 2000): "Nietzsche and Religion."

Kellenberger, J[ames], *Kierkegaard and Nietzsche: Faith and Eternal Acceptance* (Basingstoke: Macmillan; New York: St. Martin's Press, 1997).

Lippitt, John and Jim Urpeth (eds), *Nietzsche and the Divine* (Manchester: Clinamen, 2000).

Love, Frederick R., *Nietzsche's Saint Peter: Genesis and Cultivation of an Illusion* (Berlin and New York: de Gruyter, 1981).

Mandel, Siegfried, *Nietzsche and the Jews: Exaltation and Denigration* (Amherst, NY: Prometheus Books, 1998).

Mistry, Freny, *Nietzsche and Buddhism: Prolegomenon to a Comparative Study* (Berlin and New York: de Gruyter, 1981).

Morrison, Robert G., *Nietzsche and Buddhism: A Study in Nihilism and Ironic Affinities* (Oxford and New York: Oxford University Press, 1997).

Murphy, Tim, *Nietzsche, Metaphor, Religion* (Albany: State University of New York Press, 2001).

Natoli, Charles M., *Nietzsche and Pascal on Christianity* (New York: Lang, 1985).

New Nietzsche Studies, 4/3–4 (2000–1): "Nietzsche and the Death of God(s)."

O'Flaherty, James C., Timothy F. Sellner, and Robert M. Helm (eds), *Studies in Nietzsche and the Judaeo-Christian Tradition* (Chapel Hill: University of North Carolina Press, 1985).

Roberts, Tyler T., *Contesting Spirit: Nietzsche, Affirmation, Religion* (Princeton, NJ and Chichester: Princeton University Press, 1998).

Santaniello, Weaver, *Nietzsche, God, and the Jews: His Critique of Judeo-Christianity in Relation to the Nazi Myth* (Albany: State University of New York Press, 1994).

—— (ed.), *Nietzsche and the Gods* (Albany: State University of New York Press, 2001).

Yovel, Yirmiyahu, *Dark Riddle: Hegel, Nietzsche, and the Jews* (Oxford: Polity; University Park: Pennsylvania State University Press, 1998).

Rhetoric/Style

Blanchot, Maurice, "Nietzsche and Fragmentary Writing," in Blanchot, *The Infinite Conversation*, trans. Susan Hanson (Minneapolis: University of Minnesota Press, 1993), pp. 151–70.

Darby, Tom, Béla Egyed, and Ben Jones (eds), *Nietzsche and the Rhetoric of Nihilism: Essays on Interpretation, Language and Politics* (Ottawa: Carleton University Press, 1989).

de Man, Paul, *Allegories of Reading: Figural Language in Rousseau, Nietzsche, Rilke, and Proust* (New Haven, CT and London: Yale University Press, 1979), pp. 79–131 (chs 4–6 on Nietzsche).

Derrida, Jacques, *Spurs: Nietzsche's Styles / Éperons: Les Styles de Nietzsche*, trans. Barbara Harlow (Chicago and London: University of Chicago Press, 1979).

Gilman, Sander L., *Nietzschean Parody: An Introduction to Reading Nietzsche* (Bonn: Bouvier Verlag Herbert Grundmann, 1976).

Kofman, Sarah, *Nietzsche and Metaphor*, trans. Duncan Large (London: Athlone Press; Stanford, CA: Stanford University Press, 1993).

Moore, Gregory, *Nietzsche, Biology and Metaphor* (Cambridge and New York: Cambridge University Press, 2002).

Murphy, Tim, *Nietzsche, Metaphor, Religion* (Albany: State University of New York Press, 2001).

Pasley, Malcolm (ed.), *Nietzsche: Imagery and Thought. A Collection of Essays* (London: Methuen; Berkeley and Los Angeles: University of California Press, 1978).

Pettey, John Carson, *Nietzsche's Philosophical and Narrative Styles* (New York: Lang, 1992).

Thomas, Douglas, *Reading Nietzsche Rhetorically* (New York and London: Guilford Press, 1999).

See also **Language/Philology** *above*

Science

Babich, Babette E., *Nietzsche's Philosophy of Science: Reflecting Science on the Ground of Art and Life* (Albany: State University of New York Press, 1994).

—— and Robert S. Cohen (eds), *Nietzsche and the Sciences*, 2 vols (Dordrecht, Boston, and London: Kluwer, 1999).

Moore, Gregory, *Nietzsche, Biology and Metaphor* (Cambridge and New York: Cambridge University Press, 2002).

—— and Thomas H. Brobjer (eds), *Nietzsche and Science* (Aldershot and Burlington, VT: Ashgate, 2004).

Richardson, John, *Nietzsche's New Darwinism* (New York and Oxford: Oxford University Press, 2004).

See also **Medicine/Physiology**; **Psychology/Psychoanalysis** *above*

Women

Burgard, Peter J. (ed.), *Nietzsche and the Feminine* (Charlottesville and London: University Press of Virginia, 1994).

Crawford, Claudia, *To Nietzsche: Dionysus, I Love You! Ariadne* (Albany: State University of New York Press, 1995).

Derrida, Jacques, *Spurs: Nietzsche's Styles / Éperons: Les Styles de Nietzsche*, trans. Barbara Harlow (Chicago and London: University of Chicago Press, 1979).

Graybeal, Jean, *Language and "the Feminine" in Nietzsche and Heidegger* (Bloomington and Indianapolis: Indiana University Press, 1990).

Irigaray, Luce, *Marine Lover of Friedrich Nietzsche*, trans. Gillian C. Gill (New York: Columbia University Press, 1991).

Journal of Nietzsche Studies, 12 (Autumn 1996): "Nietzsche and Women," ed. Carol Diethe.

Krell, David Farrell, *Postponements: Woman, Sensuality, and Death in Nietzsche* (Bloomington and Indianapolis: Indiana University Press, 1986).

Oliver, Kelly, *Womanizing Nietzsche: Philosophy's Relation to the "Feminine"* (New York and London: Routledge, 1995).

—— and Marilyn Pearsall (eds), *Feminist Interpretations of Friedrich Nietzsche* (University Park: Pennsylvania State University Press, 1998).

Patton, Paul (ed.), *Nietzsche, Feminism and Political Theory* (London and New York: Routledge, 1993).

Picart, Caroline Joan S., *Resentment and the "Feminine" in Nietzsche's Politico-Aesthetics* (University Park: Pennsylvania State University Press, 1999).

Shapiro, Gary, *Alcyone: Nietzsche on Gifts, Noise, and Women* (Albany: State University of New York Press, 1991).

4.2.3 Themes

Eternal Recurrence

Hatab, Lawrence J., *Nietzsche and Eternal Recurrence: The Redemption of Time and Becoming* (Washington, DC: University Press of America, 1978).

—— *Nietzsche's Life Sentence: Coming to Terms with Eternal Recurrence* (New York and London: Routledge, 2004).

Journal of Nietzsche Studies, 14 (Autumn 1997): "Eternal Recurrence."

Klossowski, Pierre, *Nietzsche and the Vicious Circle*, trans. Daniel W. Smith (London: Athlone Press; Chicago: University of Chicago Press, 1997).

Löwith, Karl, *Nietzsche's Philosophy of the Eternal Recurrence of the Same*, trans. J. Harvey Lomax (Berkeley, Los Angeles and London: University of California Press, 1997).

Stambaugh, Joan, *Nietzsche's Thought of Eternal Return* (Baltimore and London: Johns Hopkins University Press, 1972).

Genealogy

Blondel, Eric, *Nietzsche: The Body and Culture. Philosophy as a Philological Genealogy*, trans. Seán Hand (London: Athlone Press; Stanford, CA: Stanford University Press, 1991).

Foucault, Michel, "Nietzsche, Genealogy, History," trans. Donald F. Bouchard and Sherry Simon, in *The Foucault Reader*, ed. Paul Rabinow (New York: Pantheon Books, 1984; Harmondsworth: Penguin, 1986), pp. 76–100.

See also **4.2.1 Texts: *On the Genealogy of Morality*** *above*

Nihilism

Darby, Tom, Béla Egyed, and Ben Jones (eds), *Nietzsche and the Rhetoric of Nihilism: Essays on Interpretation, Language and Politics* (Ottawa: Carleton University Press, 1989).

Havas, Randall, *Nietzsche's Genealogy: Nihilism and the Will to Knowledge* (Ithaca, NY and London: Cornell University Press, 1995).

Morrison, Robert G., *Nietzsche and Buddhism: A Study in Nihilism and Ironic Affinities* (Oxford and New York: Oxford University Press, 1997).

Schutte, Ofelia, *Beyond Nihilism: Nietzsche without Masks* (Chicago and London: University of Chicago Press, 1984).

Perspectivism

Cox, Christoph, *Nietzsche: Naturalism and Interpretation* (Berkeley, Los Angeles, and London: University of California Press, 1999).

Hales, Steven D. and Rex Welshon, *Nietzsche's Perspectivism* (Urbana and Chicago: University of Illinois Press, 2000).

Tragedy

May, Keith M., *Nietzsche and the Spirit of Tragedy* (Basingstoke: Macmillan; New York: St. Martin's Press, 1990).

Porter, James I., *The Invention of Dionysus: An Essay on "The Birth of Tragedy"* (Stanford, CA: Stanford University Press, 2000).

Sallis, John, *Crossings: Nietzsche and the Space of Tragedy* (Chicago and London: University of Chicago Press, 1991).

Silk, M. S. and J. P. Stern, *Nietzsche on Tragedy* (Cambridge and New York: Cambridge University Press, 1981).

Will to Power

Golomb, Jacob, *Nietzsche's Enticing Psychology of Power* (Ames: Iowa State University Press; Jerusalem: Magnes Press, 1989).

New Nietzsche Studies, 1/1–2 (Fall–Winter 1996): "The Will to Power: Current Debates," pp. 79–153.

Williams, Linda L., *Nietzsche's Mirror: The World as Will to Power* (Lanham, MD and Oxford: Rowman & Littlefield, 2000).

5 Reception

5.1 Comparative

Behler, Ernst, *Confrontations: Derrida/Heidegger/Nietzsche*, trans. Steven Taubeneck (Stanford, CA: Stanford University Press, 1991).

Diethe, Carol, *Historical Dictionary of Nietzscheanism* (Lanham, MD and London: Scarecrow Press, 1999).

Foster, John Burt, Jr., *Heirs to Dionysus: A Nietzschean Current in Literary Modernism* (Princeton, NJ and Guildford: Princeton University Press, 1981).

Golomb, Jacob and Robert S. Wistrich (eds), *Nietzsche, Godfather of Fascism? On the Uses and Abuses of a Philosophy* (Princeton, NJ and Oxford: Princeton University Press, 2002).

Görner, Rüdiger and Duncan Large (eds), *Ecce Opus. Nietzsche-Revisionen im 20. Jahrhundert* (Göttingen: Vandenhoeck & Ruprecht, 2003).

May, Keith M., *Nietzsche and Modern Literature: Themes in Yeats, Rilke, Mann and Lawrence* (Basingstoke: Macmillan; New York: St. Martin's Press, 1988).

Owen, David, *Maturity and Modernity: Nietzsche, Weber, Foucault and the Ambivalence of Reason* (London and New York: Routledge, 1994).

Schrift, Alan D., *Nietzsche and the Question of Interpretation: Between Hermeneutics and Deconstruction* (New York and London: Routledge, 1990).

Winchester, James J., *Nietzsche's Aesthetic Turn: Reading Nietzsche after Heidegger, Deleuze, and Derrida* (Albany: State University of New York Press, 1994).

5.2 Britain and America

Bohlmann, Otto, *Yeats and Nietzsche: An Exploration of Major Nietzschean Echoes in the Writings of William Butler Yeats* (Basingstoke: Macmillan; Totowa, NJ: Barnes & Noble, 1982).

Bridgwater, Patrick, *Nietzsche in Anglosaxony: A Study of Nietzsche's Impact on English and American Literature* (Leicester: Leicester University Press, 1972).

Donadio, Stephen, *Nietzsche, Henry James, and the Artistic Will* (New York and Oxford: Oxford University Press, 1978).

Journal of Nietzsche Studies, 9/10 (Spring–Autumn 1995): "American Nietzsches," ed. Daniel W. Conway.

Pütz, Manfred (ed.), *Nietzsche in American Literature and Thought* (Columbia, SC: Camden House, 1995).

Stavrou, C. N., *Whitman and Nietzsche: A Comparative Study of their Thought* (Chapel Hill: University of North Carolina Press, 1964).

Stone, Dan, *Breeding Superman: Nietzsche, Race and Eugenics in Edwardian and Interwar Britain* (Liverpool: Liverpool University Press, 2002).

Thatcher, David S., *Nietzsche in England, 1890–1914: The Growth of a Reputation* (Toronto: University of Toronto Press, 1970).

5.3 France

Forth, Christopher E., *Zarathustra in Paris: The Nietzsche Vogue in France, 1891–1918* (DeKalb: Northern Illinois University Press, 2001).

Journal of Nietzsche Studies, 7 (Spring 1994): interviews by Richard Beardsworth with Jacques Derrida ("Nietzsche and the Machine," pp. 7–66) and Jean-François Lyotard ("Nietzsche and the Inhuman," pp. 67–129), both trans. Richard Beardsworth.

Large, Duncan, *Nietzsche and Proust: A Comparative Study* (Oxford: Clarendon Press; New York: Oxford University Press, 2001).

Mahon, Michael, *Foucault's Nietzschean Genealogy: Truth, Power, and the Subject* (Albany: State University of New York Press, 1992).

Schrift, Alan D., *Nietzsche's French Legacy: A Genealogy of Poststructuralism* (New York and London: Routledge, 1995).

Smith, Douglas, *Transvaluations: Nietzsche in France 1872–1972* (Oxford: Clarendon Press; New York: Oxford University Press, 1996).

5.4 The German-Speaking World

Aschheim, Steven E., *The Nietzsche Legacy in Germany, 1890–1990* (Berkeley, Los Angeles, and London: University of California Press, 1992).

Bauer, Karin, *Adorno's Nietzschean Narratives: Critiques of Ideology, Readings of Wagner* (Albany: State University of New York Press, 1999).

Furness, Raymond, *Zarathustra's Children: A Study of a Lost Generation of German Writers* (Rochester, NY and Woodbridge: Camden House, 2000).

Journal of Nietzsche Studies, 3 (Spring 1992): "Nietzsche/Heidegger."

Journal of Nietzsche Studies, 13 (Spring 1997): "Nietzsche and German Literature," ed. Duncan Large.

Reichert, Herbert W., *Friedrich Nietzsche's Impact on Modern German Literature: Five Essays* (Chapel Hill: University of North Carolina Press, 1975).

Taylor, Seth, *Left-Wing Nietzscheans: The Politics of German Expressionism, 1910–1920* (Berlin and New York: de Gruyter, 1990).

Thomas, R. Hinton, *Nietzsche in German Politics and Society, 1890–1918* (Manchester and Dover, NH: Manchester University Press, 1983).

5.5 Russia and Eastern Europe

Clowes, Edith W., *The Revolution of Moral Consciousness: Nietzsche in Russian Literature, 1890–1914* (DeKalb: Northern Illinois University Press, 1988).

Freifeld, Alice, Peter Bergmann, and Bernice Glatzer Rosenthal (eds), *East Europe Reads Nietzsche* (Boulder, CO: East European Monographs; New York: Columbia University Press, 1998).

Rosenthal, Bernice Glatzer (ed.), *Nietzsche in Russia* (Princeton, NJ and Guildford: Princeton University Press, 1986).

—— (ed.), *Nietzsche and Soviet Culture: Ally and Adversary* (Cambridge and New York: Cambridge University Press, 1994).

5.6 Other

Borland, Harold H., *Nietzsche's Influence on Swedish Literature: With Special Reference to Strindberg, Ola Hansson, Heidenstam and Fröding* (Göteborg: Elanders boktr., 1956).

Ilie, Paul, "Nietzsche in Spain: 1890–1910," *PMLA* 79/1 (March 1964), pp. 80–96.

McDonough, B. T., *Nietzsche and Kazantzakis* (Washington, DC: University Press of America, 1978).

Shao, Lixin, *Nietzsche in China* (New York: Lang, 1999).

Index